Ethical Economy. Studies in Economic Ethics and Philosophy

For further volumes:
http://www.springer.com/series/2881

Alexander Brink

Editor

Corporate Governance and Business Ethics

 Springer

Editor
Prof. Alexander Brink
University of Bayreuth
Institute for Philosophy
95440 Bayreuth
Germany
alexander.brink@uni-bayreuth.de

ISSN 2211-2707   e-ISSN 2211-2723
ISBN 978-94-007-1587-5   e-ISBN 978-94-007-1588-2
DOI 10.1007/978-94-007-1588-2
Springer Dordrecht Heidelberg London New York

Library of Congress Control Number: 2011933587

Printed on acid-free paper

Springer is part of Springer Science+Business Media (www.springer.com)

Preface

Despite being right at the beginning of this volume, these lines are the last ones written. With them, I have finalized a book project which has taken more than three years.

This volume picks up a discussion which has become more than just that of current interest since the financial crisis. We are living in turbulent times and the tension between economic imperatives and social demands has never been more dramatic than nowadays. The question guiding this volume is how to find a real reconciliation, a new balance between these both positions in a globalized world.

Therefore, the volume comprises some selected papers from our very successful conference on "Corporate Governance and Business Ethics" which took place at the Private University of Witten/Herdecke in June 2008. In addition to these articles, I have asked some friends and colleagues from all over the world for their assessments. The authors joining our project are all without exception well known scientists of various disciplines, mainly business ethicists, but also economists, psychologists, management scientists and philosophers, who present their very own perspectives on corporate governance and business ethics, knowing clearly that a balance could only be worked out in a collaborative discourse beyond the disciplines.

To publish such a volume is a great pleasure, but it is also hard work. I was given considerable help by many people in finishing this volume. In particular, I would like to thank Sebastian Becker. Only due to his tireless effort and precise editorial work for several months was this volume realized. I have been equally lucky in the support I have received from Adrian Wenke, who time-consumingly and accurately checked all the references in the volume. My special thanks goes to Catherine Irvine, who did the final proof. I would further like to thank the referees for their instructive and helpful comments on the submitted papers which were invaluable in helping me to revise and clarify some parts of the book.

From the Private University of Witten/Herdecke, I would like to thank Birger P. Priddat, my PhD supervisor, mentor and colleague, as well as Maxim Nohroudi, who both supported my idea of releasing this conference within the First Corporate Governance Congress from the very beginning.

Furthermore, thanks to Springer Verlag for the smooth wrap up of this volume. My gratitude to Peter Koslowski, the editor of the Studies of Economic Ethics and

Philosophy (SEEP) series, as well as to the SEEP Referee Board for giving me the opportunity to publish such a volume within this excellent series. And finally, I thank the authors for their great and valuable papers, their patience and their overall engagement.

Whoever approaches such an extensive project can satisfactorily look back for a moment on the past work. But finally, it is up to you, the readership, to evaluate the authors' ideas. I wish you great pleasure while reading the book.

Witten/Bayreuth, Germany   Alexander Brink
1st August 2011

Corporate Governance and Ethics: An Introduction

Alexander Brink

Contents

Introduction

Corporate governance has enjoyed a long tradition in the English-speaking world of management sciences since the 1990s. Following its traditional understanding, corporate governance is defined as leadership and control of a firm with the aim of securing the long-term survival and viability of that firm (cf. Shleifer and Vishny 1986, p. 462). But recent business scandals and financial crises continue to provide ample cause for concern and have all fuelled interest in the ethical aspects. Since then, corporate governance has been criticized by many social groups. Some critics have demanded extensive management responsibility that would consider all stakeholder interests. In contrast, others appear to see the solution as a return to the economic core of corporate governance.

Despite innumerable written contributions on this issue, economic sciences have failed to provide a clear definition of the corporate governance concept or even to sufficiently demarcate the underlying context of consideration. However, given a tight economic interpretation of corporate governance, one could see it as regulation within the framework of the principal-agent relationship. But this is nothing but a shortened perspective. Corporate governance is much more complex and far from trivial. It picks up the traditional question regarding the primary goal of a corporation and discusses the strategic legitimation of stakeholders.

Complexity increases if we embed the economic approach of corporate governance in a philosophical context. Then, of course, the normative legitimation of corporate governance is complementary to its pure strategic implementation. And on the horizon arises a business ethics perspective on corporate governance which combines economics and philosophy. From such a standpoint corporate governance is more than transparency and accountability, more than legal and compliance aspects, and more than risk management. It refers to relationships, trust, values, culture, and norms (cf. Arjoon 2005). It is the aim of this volume to explore corporate governance first from a traditional economic standpoint, second from a philosophical standpoint, and third from an integrated business ethics perspective.

Traditional Foundations of Corporate Governance

The Economic Bases

In classical economic theory – which was shaped by Adam Smith (among others) – corporations do not play a significant role. However, the Scottish economist and philosopher did see such institutions as the law and norms as important components for the functionality of markets. Following the classical liberal thesis, from an economic perspective the wealth of nations is increased through the pursuit of one's own interests within the limits of existing regulations and through the invisible hand of the market in an open and functioning competition. Quite early on, thus long before Ronald Coase, Smith had referred to the development of institutions in his first book of *Wealth of Nations*:

> As soon as stock has accumulated in the hands of particular persons, some of them will naturally employ it in setting to work industrious people, whom they will supply with materials and subsistence, in order to make a profit by the sale of their work, or by what their labour adds to the value of the materials. (1776/1999a, p. 151)

Smith already recognized a general tendency concerning the division of labor and motivation, namely that managerial inefficiency was caused by a deficient motivational structure. In his first and fifth book he even refers to principal-agent as a problem, which later in the management sciences was called moral hazard and shirking[1]:

> The directors of such companies, however, being the managers rather of other people's money than of their own, it cannot well be expected, that they should watch over it with the same anxious vigilance with which the partners in a private copartnery frequently watch over their own. Like the stewards of a rich man, they are apt to consider attention to small matters as not for their master's honour, and very easily give themselves a dispensation

---

[1] Later, this idea would be adopted and solidified by Berle and Means (1932) in regard to stock companies.

from having it. Negligence and profusion, therefore, must always prevail, more or less, in the management of the affairs of such a company. (Smith 1776/1999b, pp. 330f.)

However, neoclassical economics, which developed out of classical economic theory, neglected the meso-level of corporations.[2] Generally speaking, neoclassical theory is based upon a wealth of other presuppositions, such as the homogeneity of goods and services, a completely informed market (perfect market transparency), complete contracts (with total specifications, no fraud, and no uncertainty), and an absence of transaction costs, etc. The neoclassical premises were criticized as being severely reductionistic. Translated to corporations, neoclassical economics assumes that those contracts signed with contract partners are complete: there are no implicit contracts. As such, neoclassical economics did not recognize institutions in a way corporate governance does.

The concept of *economic man*, described by Anglo-Saxon economists, was first introduced in a systematic way at the end of the nineteenth century by Vilfredo Pareto (who used the Latin expression *homo economicus*) (cf. Manstetten 2002, p. 48, note 9). In so-called methodological individualism, the homo economicus is the basic idea of neoclassical theory (cf. Katterle 1991). It became known as an idealized model of the human being and has been utilized primarily by economists for reconstructing and modeling particular constellations of economic problems and decision-making processes (cf. Eurich and Brink 2006). Despite its astounding pervasiveness, the homo economicus has experienced exceptionally strong criticism.[3]

Fundamental criticism of neoclassical economics was the birthplace of *new institutional economics*, which understands itself as a development of neoclassical doctrine (cf. Furubotn and Richter 2005). Economic transaction continues to occur in markets, however in carrying out their transactions, market actors now take advantage of institutions. According to Furubotn and Richter (2005), "[a]n institution is understood (...) as a set of formal or informal rules, including their enforcement arrangements (the 'rules of the game'), whose objective it is to steer individual behavior in a particular direction" (p. 560). Three research areas of new institutional economics can be identified: *transaction cost theory* (cf. Coase 1960; Williamson 1979, 1985), *property rights theory* (cf. Coase 1960; Grossman and Hart 1986; Hart 1995; Hart and Moore 1990), and *principal-agent theory* (cf. Ross 1987; Jensen and Meckling 1976).

Ronald H. Coase, the founder of transaction cost theory, can also be considered the father of the new institutional economics of corporations due to his work on *The Nature of the Firm* (cf. Coase 1937). Coase examines a foundational question of corporate governance: Why do corporations emerge if markets are the most efficient

---

[2] In economics, the term *neoclassicism* goes back to Thorstein Veblen, who used it to describe Alfred Marshall's economic theory. Others who promoted neoclassical economics included Léon Walras and Vilfredo Pareto. See here especially Aspromourgos (1996).

[3] In the meantime an excessive amount of literature has been produced on the *homo economicus*. For an overview, see Kirchgässner (1991).

form of trade activity and economic transaction? Coase argues that corporations emerge in order to reduce transaction costs (of which he lists information, search and bargaining costs, as well as the costs of contract enforcement; cf. Coase 1937, pp. 390f.).[4]

According to *property rights theory*, the owner of an *asset* can determine its use and is also to receive the fruits of that use. Furthermore he has the right to change its form, substance, or location. On this point, Grossman and Hart (1986) write, "[T]he owner of an asset has the residual right of control of that asset, that is, the right to control all aspects of the asset that have not been explicitly given away by contract" (p. 695). At this stage, it remains unclear who, from all possible stakeholders, would then possess property rights in this sense (cf. Jansson 2005, p. 2). In contrast to the textbook opinion, some scientists have been promoting the opinion that it is not merely the shareholder (as owner) who possesses property rights within a corporation (cf. Kay 1996; Blair 1995, 1998; as well as Blair and Stout 1999).

Out of the three directions taken by new institutional economics, I would like to examine *agency theory* and the *principal-agent problem* in the following section in particular.

Agency Theory and Principal-Agent Problem

Agency theory dominates research in corporate governance. In contrast to the origins of new institutional economics (as an economic theory), we encounter here an application in *management*. At one point, Jensen (1983) notes, "The foundations are being put into place for a revolution in the science of organizations" (p. 319). A few years later, Ross (1987) emphasizes again that agency theory is the central theory for the explanation of managerial behavior. Within the bounds of economic imperialism, agency theory has gained a foothold in other social sciences, such as sociology and the political sciences (cf. Eisenhardt 1989).

The principal-agent theory distinguishes between two differing theoretical branches: a normative and a positive principal-agent approach (cf. Jensen 1983, pp. 334ff.; Furubotn and Richter 2005).[5] It deals with the problematic relationship between principals and agents which has arisen with the separation of ownership and

---

[4] The concept of transaction costs can be traced back to Commons (1931), who used it to refer to property rights as the fundamental, underlying concept of economic analysis. Furubotn and Richter (2005) see the idea of new institutional economics as follows: "central to the New Institutional Economics is the solution of the coordination problem of economic transactions between individuals by mutual agreement under the assumption of transaction costs" (p. 291).

[5] The normative principal-agent approach (cf. Hart 1989, pp. 1758ff.; Bamberg and Spremann 1987; Stiglitz 1989) is a mathematical continuation on the basis of the neoclassical apparatus yet with a new actor's model. The positive principal-agent approach is neither mathematical nor empirical. The reader should note that the normative dimension of the principal-agent theory has nothing to do with norms and values in the philosophical sense, but rather with calculable entities (along the lines of those familiar to us from the field of mathematics).

control (cf. Fama and Jensen 1983b). To take a broad definition, one could describe the relationship as follows:

> Whenever one individual depends on the action of another, an agency relationship arises. The individual taking the action is called the agent. The affected party is the principal. (Pratt and Zeckhauser 1985, p. 2)

If one adds here the perspective from contract theory, then the corresponding definition by Jensen and Meckling (1976) seems most appropriate.

According to this definition, one can reconstruct the agency relationship as a "contract under which one or more persons (the principal[s]) engage another person (the agent) to perform some service on their behalf which involves delegating some decision-making authority to the agent" (p. 308).

While it is true that owners (i.e., shareholders in our case) do have decision rights, in the sense that they vote in general meetings on issues such as mergers and acquisitions or dividends, the majority of the decision-making is delegated to management (cf. Jansson 2005, pp. 1f.). The shareholder (principal) employs the manager (agent) to act in his or her interests, namely so that the capital invested by the principal might bear as much interest as possible. Thus, according to capital market theory, neoclassical economics, and the shareholder value concept, management is faced with the task of directing the entire corporate strategy toward the benefit of shareholders and their interests. The shareholder bears the residual financial risk since it is broadly assumed that the manager will act rationally and attempt to increase his or her own advantage by taking benefit of the lead in information. Normally, this advantage is incompatible with the interests of shareholders. Ghoshal (2005) writes:

> In courses on corporate governance grounded in agency theory (...) we have taught our students that managers cannot be trusted to do their jobs – which, of course, is to maximize shareholder value – and that to overcome 'agency problems', managers' interests and incentives must be aligned with those of the shareholders by, for example, making stock options a significant part of their pay. (p. 75)

As such, agency theory distinguishes between two resulting agency problems. The first and well-known problem is called *moral hazard*, i.e., the agent's opportunistic behavior *after* signing a contract. Here, either the agent receives new information which was not perceived by the principal (hidden information) or the agent's activities cannot be observed or controlled without high costs (hidden action). One special type of moral hazard is *shirking:* the agent invests too little time and work into the delegated task, takes too many risks (or too few), wastes resources, and generally enjoys his or her advantages. This is evident in so-called *consumption on the job,* where the employer's resources are used by employees for private purposes (e.g., private use of the internet). A further form of moral hazard is *hold-up*: this occurs due to the factor specificity of transactions. Williamson (1989/1996) understood specificity to be a characteristic of transactions, namely a determinant of economic dependency.

> Asset specificity has reference to the degree to which an asset can be redeployed to alternative uses and by alternative users without sacrifice of productive value. This has a relation to the notion of sunk cost. (p. 59)

To fight this problem, the principal establishes monitoring systems in order to control management. In Germany, the *Aufsichtsrat* (or supervisory board) has been created precisely to assume this function. In addition to the *ex post* information asymmetries mentioned above, there are also, secondly, the so-called *ex ante* information asymmetries, i.e., a principal-agent problem that occurs *before* closing a contract. This is also called *hidden characteristics* or *adverse selection* and, according to Akerlof, negative selection in the used car market provides a prominent example (cf. Akerlof 1970).

The agency problems noted above can be reduced especially by reducing information asymmetries in two ways: in *screening*, the principal investigates the corporation, e.g., by running controls; in *signaling*, the agent gives signals to the principal, either in accordance with the law (e.g., through reporting), voluntarily (e.g., through codes of ethics) or in a mixed form (e.g., through a code of corporate governance). Other control and monitoring systems include control of shareholders' voting rights, control through capital and product markets, control through employment and manager markets, or control through liability. Normally, the principal must invest money into such monitoring which then reduces his or her return – and according to the theory, it is only the principal who is entitled to residuals. Thus, corporate governance is a form of leadership and control of a corporation in the interests of its shareholders. Next to monitoring, a second option might be the unification of principal and agent interests in advanced wage and incentive systems, which were typical in the 1990s when wages were often paid in shares or stock options (cf. Kürsten 2002). Finally, management can build up reputation capital.

Central to the principal-agent theory are so-called *agency costs*. Jensen and Meckling have provided some initial orientation in this respect (cf. Jensen and Meckling 1976, pp. 308ff.; Fama and Jensen 1983a, p. 327): *Monitoring costs* are borne by the principal to control and direct the agent (e.g., the costs of closing contracts and monitoring the execution of that contract). *Bonding costs* are borne by the agent to ensure his or her performance (e.g., rendering of accounts, reporting) and the *residual loss* is borne by the principal due to the failure of agents to achieve the first-best solution. This residual loss represents a risk for the principal and forms the central basis of legitimation for the principal's interests.

Main Structure and Contributions to This Volume

This volume is divided in three divisions: The first part, *Economic Foundations of Corporate Governance,* comprises an economic perspective on our topic (6 articles), the second part, *Philosophical Foundations of Corporate Governance,* represents a philosophical perspective of corporate governance (3 articles), and finally the third part, *Corporate Governance and Business Ethics,* integrates both disciplines (9 articles).

Economic Foundations of Corporate Governance

Thomas Clarke challenges in his article *The Globalisation of Corporate Governance? Irresistible Markets Meet Immovable Institutions* whether a universal corporate governance system is practical, necessary, or desirable. The increasingly recognized premium for governance is considered in the context of a globalizing economy. Based on the inevitable contest between the more insider, relationship based, stakeholder oriented corporate governance system and the more outsider, market based, shareholder value oriented system, implications of the deregulation of finance and the globalization of capital markets are examined. Clarke focuses on the growth of equity markets and the dominant position of the Anglo-American stock exchange (comparing to European and Asia-Pacific models). He debates the convergence thesis, examining different theoretical arguments for and against the inevitability of convergence of corporate governance systems. Finally, the future direction of corporate governance trends is questioned, with the likelihood of greater complexity rather than uniformity emerging from current developments. While capital markets have acquired an apparently irresistible force in the world economy, it still appears that institutional complementarities at the national and regional level represent immovable governance objects. Clarke's article gives an excellent introductory overview and deep insights in future challenges.

The following contribution *Regulation Complexity and the Costs of Governance* written by *Steen Thomsen* is motivated by the Sarbanes-Oxley Act and similar legislation in Europe. Thomsen examines psychological origins and costs of regulation complexity. After briefly reviewing economic theories of information costs and bounded rationality, he focuses on psychological determinants of regulation costs including perception bias, memory loss, cognitive bias, superstitious learning, learned helplessness, rejection, denial, groupthink, and herding effects. In combination, these factors suggest high costs of complexity. Besides the direct costs of compliance, non-compliance, and enforcement, there are potentially more important opportunity costs of distorted decisions, risk aversion, opportunism, and creativity loss. Companies and individuals attempt to mitigate complexity costs by alternative strategies including non-compliance, trial and error, imitation, and professional advisors. When the costs of complexity become prohibitively high, decision makers will cease to use existing markets. Thomsen hypothesizes that a wave of delistings from major stock exchanges may have been caused at least partly by costs of complexity. Thomsen's contribution gives a helpful understanding of the complexity of corporate governance from an economic and psychological standpoint.

During the international financial crisis in 2008, the effectiveness of existing corporate governance institutions has been questioned, both in the scientific community and in the media. Based on this idea, *Margit Osterloh, Bruno S. Frey,* and *Hossam Zeitoun* publish their considerations in an article entitled *Corporate Governance as an Institution to Overcome Social Dilemmas*. A special focus of this contribution lies in the containment of opportunistic behavior. In the corporate governance literature, the dominant approaches axiomatically assume individuals with self-interest or opportunistic behavior. The modern research stream of psychological economics, however, has shown that prosocial preferences exist and do matter. When the determinants of prosocial behavior are considered, the implications for the design of corporate governance institutions may clash with conventional wisdom. The authors suggest that the following measures help to overcome social dilemmas at the firm level: board representation of knowledge workers who invest in firm-specific human capital; attenuation of variable pay-for-performance; selection of directors and managers with prosocial preferences; and employee participation in decision-making and control. With their approach, Margit Osterloh, Bruno S. Frey, and Hossam Zeitoun make a rare attempt to apply psychological economics to a complex institution, namely corporate governance.

Kai Kühne and *Dieter Sadowski* compare in their article *Scandalous Co-determination* the academic evaluation of supervisory board co-determination in Germany with its portrayal in the mass media. According to empirical research, co-determination does not have a detrimental effect on firm performance and can thus be regarded as simply an element of corporate governance within Germany. However, a content analysis capturing characterisations of co-determination in German newspapers between 1998 and 2007 shows that this institution is depicted more and more critically in the press. There is thus a noticeable discrepancy between empirical evidence and the interpretative schemata of mass media. In their paper, the authors investigate the reasons for this divergence as well as its consequences. Whereas economists increasingly exclude detrimental effects of co-determination on corporate productivity and profitability, journalists increasingly emphasize these detrimental effects. Unlike scientific findings, which are hardly mentioned at all, scandals involving labour representatives play a significant role in press editorials. In this way, the arguments of the opponents of co-determination receive publicity that sharply contrasts with the doubtful empirical validity of their position. It is the achievement of this paper, that – while findings of empirical economic research are obviously ignored for the most part – scandals involving labour representatives play a considerable role in the public discourse on co-determination.

Till Talaulicar focuses in his contribution *Corporate Codes of Ethics: Can Punishments Enhance Their Effectiveness?* on written statements about moral norms which are issued by a company to obligate corporate actions. In essence, these documents shall promote ethical behavior within the company and make corporate misbehavior less likely. In his article, Talaulicar argues that codes can be helpful for improving the ethicality of corporate actions. However, merely developing and establishing codes is not enough because the code by itself cannot guarantee that its addressees act in accordance with its norms. Rather, the company has to carry out serious attempts to implement its code of ethics. In this context, Talaulicar finds out that properly designed and executed punishments can be viewed as a promising, and even indispensable, measure for enhancing code effectiveness. Based on theories of sanctions, the proper design and execution of punishments has to consider output and process determinants of sanctions. Output determinants sanction severity, certainty, and celerity. In contrast to deterrence theories, it is not proposed that punishments necessarily promise to be the more effective, the more severe, certain, and celeritous they are. Rather, considerations of justice and process determinants suggest a more deliberate specification of the outcome values. Process determinants demand that (potential) code offenders are treated with respect to offer them the opportunity to explain their case and to make sanction decisions unbiased as well as transparent. With codes of ethics, Talaulicar refers to a proper instrument to apply corporate governance to economic reality.

The Chinese stock market is the focus of the last contribution of the first chapter, *Corporate Governance at the Chinese Stock Market: How It Evolved,* written by *Junhua Tang* and *Dirk Linowski*. Listed firms at the Chinese stock market are typically former state-owned enterprises (SOEs), nowadays characterized by a concentrated ownership structure with the state, represented by its agencies at central and local levels, acting as the controlling shareholder. Over the past 30 years of China's economic transition, three stages of SOE reforms have exerted great influence on the formation of the current corporate governance model at the Chinese stock market. This contribution reviews the status and changes of the governance practices at each of the three stages in China's SOE reforms. It further explains how these changes took place by examining the most influential factors in the evolution of governance practices. The authors argue that a path dependence exists, mainly driven by a learning process, in China's corporate governance evolution. Tang and Linowski give detailed insights and an extensive overview into the Chinese corporate governance system.

Philosophical Foundations of Corporate Governance

Steve Letza, *Clive Smallman*, *Xiuping Sun*, and *James Kirkbride* refer in their article *Philosophical Underpinnings to Corporate Governance: A Collibrational Approach* to a pure philosophical position. The current debate on corporate governance can be characterised as a search for the perfect model. The academic discourse is polarised either on the shareholder paradigm, where the primary focus is on maximisation of shareholder wealth, or on the stakeholder paradigm, where a broader set of issues are presented as pertinent to best practice corporate governance. In the practitioner discourse, the debate is fundamentally focused on practical mechanisms to discipline directors and other actors where the emphasis is on developing regulation either in the form of law or codes. The authors argue that both discourses rely on a homeostatic view of the corporation and its governance structures. Further, they argue that both discourses pay inadequate attention to the underlying philosophical presuppositions resulting in a static approach to the understanding of corporate governance. Letza and his colleagues present an alternative, a processual approach, as a means of avoiding the traditional trap in corporate governance theorising. Using this approach, the authors argue that a collibrated mechanism is more likely to emerge and consequently a better understanding of the heterogeneity of corporate governance practice will follow, providing deeper insight into the fluxing nature of corporate bodies and their governance structures.

The starting point of the contribution *Aristotelian Corporate Governance,* written by *Alejo José G. Sison,* is the fact that neoclassical doctrines assume human beings as economic agents, independent of all social bonds. Reading economics in a contractual way, the key to corporate governance lies in the alignment of the shareholders' interests. But economic theory does not give reasons why efficiency should be measured in terms of shareholder value maximization, nor for the underlying social web that makes contractual agreements possible. Sison would like to take a different focus. His paper intends to have a more constructive outlook. It explains how Aristotelian corporate governance founded on the corporate common good might be conceived, taught, and practiced. Aristotelian corporate governance requires a radical change of tack from neoclassical theory or from new institutional economics. Sison develops his idea in three major stages. He argues for an Aristotelian theory of the firm, fully aware that Aristotle himself did not deal with such an institution in his writings. The proper locus and purpose of the firm is within the overall context of society. He offers, through an analogy with the common good of the *polis* or the state, an account of the common good of the firm. Sison proposes ways in which this particular common good of the firm could be integrated or subordinated to the wider common good of the political community. Finally, he explains the theory and practice behind what could stand as Aristotelian corporate governance, one that seeks to achieve the corporate common good. Sison aims at an important philosophical aspect of corporate governance which is in this form unique.

In their article *Deliberative Democracy and Corporate Governance, Bert van de Veen* and *Wim Dubbink* take a philosophical and political stand on corporate social responsibility (CSR) as a special form of corporate governance appearance. Since the 1990s there has been a movement within the field of business ethics to develop a political conception of CSR. This is accompanied by the attribution of new moral duties to corporations, especially in the global context. Relatively new concepts like corporate citizenship and stakeholder democracy have been introduced to develop a new conceptual language for discussing the responsibilities of corporations. In their paper, the authors explore the implications of this politicization of the corporation at the level of corporate governance. Normatively speaking, Jürgen Habermas' theory of deliberative democracy is taken as given. The authors work out its implications for stakeholder democracy. Van de Veen und Dubbink reject Peter Ulrich's radical view on the matter and opt for a more moderate model of "stakeholder capitalism". They also assess from the sociological point of view the constraints put on the application of the new concepts and discuss whether current views on the future of capitalism leave room for the possibility of stakeholder influence and co-determination. On the basis of comparative research into capitalist economies, they argue that the extent and institutionalization of stakeholder democracy within a capitalist economy is largely dependent on the institutional history, or path, taken within a national business system as well as on the adaptive strategies of the economic actors. On the basis of the authors' argument they question the value of producing blueprints that fix the ways in which stakeholder democracy must be materialized at the level of corporate governance in particular situations.

The authors therefore formulate four principles that should be made relevant in particular historical circumstances, both at the national and the international level.

Corporate Governance and Business Ethics

Josef Wieland aims in his article *The Firm as a Nexus of Stakeholders: Stakeholder Management and Theory of the Firm* to develop a pure economic concept of stakeholder management. The theoretical underpinning for this endeavor is the economics of governance, which is defined as the science of the governance, management, and control of cooperative relations through adaptively efficient governance structures. According to this perspective, companies are not just one form of governance of stakeholder relations; they should rather be understood as a nexus of stakeholder relations in a constitutive sense. The governance of this network is defined as a two-step process of identifying and prioritizing a team's relevant stakeholders, which in turn are defined as resource owners who together constitute and operatively reproduce a company. From an economics of governance point of view, a firm is thus defined as a contractual nexus of stakeholder resources and stakeholder interests, whose function is the governance, i.e., the management and control of the resource owners with the aim of creating economic added value and distributing cooperative rent. It is through this theoretical lens that this article discusses the conventional theories of stakeholder management. The focus here is primarily on the widely acknowledged weaknesses of the stakeholder theory – such as the fact that it does not offer a generally recognized definition of what a stakeholder is, but also and above all on the major theoretical shortcomings with regard to identifying and prioritizing the stakeholders. Finally, Wieland outlines an allocation mechanism for distributing the team's cooperative rent.

Aloy Soppe picks up another interesting point in his article *Corporate Governance, Ethics and Sustainable Development*. In English and American finance literature, the "good governance" question basically comes down to the discipline of "market of corporate control" (external control). In that perspective, it is the threat of international market competition and takeovers (whether hostile or friendly) that primarily disciplines the management of a company. The European approach clearly has a more institutional character. In that model, which can be classified as a network model, the historical and sociological ownership structure dominates the empirical landscape. Germany, France, Italy, and the Netherlands, for example, clearly have specific corporate governance structures where internal control is more important than external control. Corporate democracy and stakeholder values are key paradigms in these corporate structures. The problem, however, is that the stakeholder society is hindered by three key problems: a dearth of pledgeable income, deadlocks in decision-making, and lack of clear mission for management. Departing from the need for governance and sustainability and stewardship-based economics, Soppe elaborates on corporate governance as a key element in corporate democracy, stakeholder politics, and sustainable development. Sustainable development in governance aims to redress the balance in the relationship between individual interests and collective or community interests through leadership.

Alexei M. Marcoux writes a very interesting article on the *Triadic Stakeholder Theory Revisited.* The author follows the idea of Donaldson and Preston, which asserts the existence of an omnibus stakeholder theory, consisting of mutually supporting normative, instrumental, and descriptive theses, with the first as the theory's core. Marcoux argues that: (i) Donaldson and Preston's three theses, though perhaps mutually supporting, are not distinctly and genuinely normative, instrumental, and descriptive; (ii) their normative thesis is neither morally substantial nor their omnibus theory's center; (iii) although one can construct distinctly and genuinely normative, instrumental, and descriptive theses, these reconstructed theses are neither mutually supportive of nor grounded in the normative; and (iv) Donaldson's attempt to establish relations of mutual support between the normative and instrumental theses fails. Therefore, there is no omnibus theory and each kind of stakeholder thinking must stand or fall on its own merits. If correct, this conclusion's importance extends beyond the merits of Donaldson and Preston's paper. It has significant implications for the *corporate governance debate* in business ethics. Marcoux suggests a meaningful normative corporate governance debate in business ethics.

Andrew J. Felo points out in his article *Corporate Governance and Business Ethics* that corporate governance can be an important defense against unethical corporate behavior. For example, a firm's board of directors is responsible for overseeing firm management. If the board does not adequately perform this oversight, then – following the author – it may be easier for managers to behave unethically. In fact, Hoffman and Rowe report that various investigations found that poor oversight of management by boards was an important factor in various corporate scandals. Two additional issues dealing with unethical corporate behavior that firms should consider when structuring their corporate governance are potential conflicts of interest between the firm and its shareholders and transparency concerning corporate activities. Possible conflicts of interest in corporate governance include whether the CEO is also the chairman of the board (often referred to as CEO duality), the independence of board members, executive compensation (including backdating of stock options), and director elections. Since all of these situations could result in directors or managers placing their interest ahead of shareholder interests, they are all ethical issues. Transparency is an ethical issue because "insiders", such as managers and directors, essentially control the information that "outsiders", such as shareholders and regulators, receive. As a result, "insiders" can prevent "outsiders" from learning about sub-optimal behavior (such as conflicts of interest) through less transparency.

Chris Low examines in his paper *When Good Turns to Bad: An Examination of Governance Failure in a Not-for-Profit Enterprise* the assumption that is present in society (if not in law) that not-for-profits are unlikely to exhibit unethical behaviour in their governance function. It explores this issue by examining a recent case of governance failure within a not-for-profit social enterprise that had unethical behaviour at its root. This failure ultimately led to the organisation going bankrupt. A parallel is drawn with governance failures within the private sector which also resulted in bankruptcy. The author draws on theories of governance and stakeholder management in order to reflect on whether unethical governance behaviour is a continuing threat to all sectors. In doing so, he concludes that there is merit in challenging the assumption that values-based organisations are immune to such a threat to their organisational existence. Chris Low gives a very interesting example of corporate governance in the not-for-profit sector.

Scott Lichtenstein, Les Higgins, and *Pat Dade* start their contribution *Integrity in the Boardroom: A Case for Further Research* with the argument that directors believe integrity is vital to the board. Yet, no shared opinion exists about what integrity means. This is because its meaning is dependent on one's personal values. This paper builds on research into integrity and top teams by investigating how integrity varies according to the individual's personal values. It will explore how an individual's definition of integrity is based on his or her values, beliefs, and underlying needs and call for further research into boards' values. Data from British society was collected from 500 British adults, aged 18 and over. Data from European managers was collected in separate studies of 163 and 73 owner, senior and middle managers. Results of the research found that definitions of integrity vary based on one's value system. Future research on directors' values should explore how integrity differs from other directors and employees with different values. Recommendations for further research also include analysing the board agenda to determine whether it resonates with directors' personal values to create board engagement. A passionate board requires integrity plus action; action without integrity equals indifference.

G.J. (Deon) Rossouw analyses in his article *The Ethics of Corporate Governance in Global Perspective* the connection between ethics and corporate governance from a global perspective. Although corporate governance has become a familiar term in all regions of the world, substantial regional variations with regard to basic assumptions, terminology, and conceptual distinctions have been identified in comparative corporate governance studies. Such regional variations are particularly evident in the case of the ethical dimension of corporate governance. All corporate governance regimes are premised upon ethical assumptions about the role and responsibilities of corporations in society. In some corporate governance regimes these ethical premises are explicitly articulated, whilst in others the ethical premises are only implicit, but not less real. A number of conceptual distinctions related to the ethics of corporate governance will first be introduced, that will then be used to identify and articulate the ethical dimension of corporate governance regimes in Africa, Asia-Pacific, Europe, Latin America, and North America. After the ethical dimensions peculiar to each of these regional corporate governance regimes have been identified, a discussion of the main factors that can explain differences in the ethics of corporate governance within and across the above-mentioned regions will follow.

In his paper *Do Stakeholder Interests Imply Control Rights in a Firm?* the author *Ronald Jeurissen* examines the question of to what extent the legitimate interests of stakeholders towards a firm also imply the need, or even the right, to exercise control over that firm's decisions. The thesis that stakeholders should have control rights over a firm is advanced by several authors. Jeurissen refers to the so-called "stakeholder capitalism", which is based on the fundamental assumption that a company is not anyone's specific business and that its achievements are rather the result of the joint effort and mutual trust of many parties. Jeurissen explores whether and how the notion of stakeholder capitalism involves the extension of decision rights in a company to other stakeholders than the shareholders only. He firstly makes a distinction between economic and social stakeholders, and argues that control rights are most plausible for the economic stakeholders of a firm, less so for social stakeholders. Next, he puts this conclusion into perspective by pointing to the increased prominence and prevalence of the open-systems and values-chain approaches to stakeholder management, which tend to decentralize the role of the firm in relation to its stakeholders. The resource-based view of the firm helps understand why the question of which stakeholder controls the firm is increasingly superseded by the question of which stakeholder owns which resource that is critical to the achievement of the common goals of the networked partners in the values chain.

John R. Boatright focuses in his article *The Implications of the New Governance for Corporate Governance* on the implications of the new governance for corporate governance. In the development called "the new governance", corporations, especially multinational or transnational corporations, have become politically engaged and have assumed new functions that have traditionally belonged to governments alone. One question that arises about the concept of new governance or, alternatively, corporate citizenship or republican ethics is its bearing on corporate governance. The aim of this contribution is to examine the question of what implications, if any, the new governance has for corporate governance and, by extension, the theory of the firm. Is the new governance compatible with traditional systems of corporate governance, which are based on the standard economic theory of the firm, or are some changes required? If some changes are required, what are these changes and, more importantly, why are they required? The main conclusion of this examination is that the new governance has some implications for corporate governance and the theory of the firm. However, these implications are due primarily to broader changes in the competitive environment of present-day corporations of which the features cited in the new governance literature are only a relatively small part. One value of Boatright's contribution, aside from addressing the question of the implication for corporate governance, is to place the new governance in a larger context and identify some additional forces at work in its development.

References

Akerlof, G.A. 1970. The market for 'Lemons': Quality uncertainty and the market mechanism. *Quarterly Journal of Economics* 84: 488–500.

Arjoon, S. 2005. Corporate governance: An ethical perspective. *Journal of Business Ethics* 61: 343–352.

Aspromourgos, A. 1996. *On the origins of classical economics: Distribution and value form William Petty to Adam Smith*. London: Routledge.

Bamberg, G., and K. Spremann. 1987. *Agency theory, information, and incentives*. Berlin: Springer.

Berle, A.A., and G.C. Means. 1932. *The modern corporation and private property.* New York, NY: Macmillan.

Blair, M.M. 1995. *Ownership and control: Rethinking corporate governance for the twenty-first century.* Washington, DC: The Brookings Institution.

Blair, M.M. 1998. For whom should corporations be run? An economic rationale for stakeholder management. *Long Range Planning* 31: 195–200.

Blair, M.M., and L. Stout. 1999. A team production theory of corporate law. *Virginia Law Review* 85: 247–328.

Coase, R.H. 1937. The nature of the firm. *Economica* 4: 386–405.

Coase, R.H. 1960. The problem of social cost. *The Journal of Law and Economics* 3: 1–44.

Commons, J.R. 1931. Institutional economics. *The American Economic Review* 21: 648–657.

Eisenhardt, K.M. 1989. Agency theory: An assessment and review. *Academy of Management Review* 14: 57–74.

Eurich, J., and A. Brink. 2006. Vom Eigennutz zur Sinnsuche. Anmerkungen zum Modell des homo oeconomicus und Aspekte seiner Weiterentwicklung. *Glaube und Lernen* 21: 58–71.

Fama, E.F., and M.C. Jensen. 1983a. Agency problems and residual claims. *Journal of Law and Economics* 26: 327–349.

Fama, E.F., and M.C. Jensen. 1983b. Separation of ownership and control. *Journal of Law and Economics* 26: 301–325.

Furubotn, E.G., and R. Richter. 2005: *Institutions & economic theory. The contribution of the new institutional economics,* 2nd ed. Ann Arbor, MI: The University of Michigan Press.

Ghoshal, S. 2005. Bad management theories are destroying good management practices. *Academy of Management Learning & Education* 4: 75–91.

Grossman, S., and O. Hart. 1986. The costs and benefits of ownership: A theory of vertical and lateral integration. *Journal of Political Economy* 94: 691–719.

Hart, O. 1989: An economist's perspective on the theory of the firm. *Columbia Law Review* 89: 1757–1774.

Hart, O. 1995. *Firms, contracts, and financial structure.* Oxford: Oxford University Press.

Hart, O., and J. Moore. 1990. Property rights and the nature of the firm. *Journal of Political Economy* 98: 1119–1158.

Jansson, E. 2005. The stakeholder model: The influence of the ownership and governance structures. *Journal of Business Ethics* 56: 1–13.

Jensen, M. 1983. Organization theory and methodology. *Accounting Review* 58: 319–339.

Jensen, M.C., and W.H. Meckling. 1976. Theory of the firm: Managerial behavior, agency costs and ownership structure. *Journal of Financial Economics* 3: 305–360.

Katterle, S. 1991. Methodologischer individualismus and beyond. In *Das Menschenbild der ökonomischen Theorie. Zur Natur des Menschen,* eds. B. Bievert and M. Held, 132–152. Frankfurt: Campus.

Kay, J. 1996. *The business of economics.* Oxford et al.: Oxford University Press.

Kirchgässner, G. 1991. *Homo Oeconomicus. Das ökonomische Modell individuellen Verhaltens und seine Anwendung in den Wirtschafts- und Sozialwissenschaften.* Tübingen: Mohr.

Kürsten, W. 2002. Managerentlohnung, Risikopolitik und Stakeholder-Interessen – Eine theoretische Analyse der Konsequenzen von Aktienoptionsplänen. In *Corporate governance. Herausforderungen und Lösungsansätze,* eds. M. Nippa, K. Petzold and W. Kürsten, 175–190. Heidelberg: Physica.

Manstetten, R. 2002. *Das Menschenbild der Ökonomie. Der homo oeconomicus und die Anthropologie von Adam Smith.* Freiburg: Alber.

Pratt, J.W., and R.J. Zeckhauser. 1985. Principals and agents: An overview. In *Principals and agents: The structure of business,* eds. J. Pratt and R. Zeckhauser, 1–35. Boston, MA: Harvard Business School Press.

Ross, S.A. 1987. The interrelations of finance and economics: Theoretical perspectives. *American Economic Review* 77: 29–34.

Shleifer, A., and R. Vishny. 1986. Large shareholders and corporate control. *Journal of Political Economy* 94: 461–488.

Smith, A. 1776/1999a. *The wealth of nations: Books I-III* (edited with an introduction and notes by Andrew Skinner). London: Penguin.

Smith, A. 1776/1999b. *The wealth of nations: Books IV-V* (edited with an introduction and notes by Andrew Skinner). London: Penguin.

Stiglitz, J. 1989. Principal and agent. In *The new Palgrave. Allocation, information and markets,* eds. J. Eatwell, M. Murray and P. Newman, 241–253. London: Macmillan.

Williamson, O.E. 1979. Transaction cost economics: The governance of contractual relations. *Journal of Law and Economics* 22: 233–261.

Williamson, O.E. 1985. *The economic institutions of capitalism: Firms, markets, relational contracting.* New York, NY: Free Press.

Williamson, O.E. 1989/1996. Transaction cost economics. In *The mechanisms of governance,* ed. O.E. Williamson, 54–87. New York, NY: Oxford University Press.

Contents

Part III   Corporate Governance and Business Ethics

Contributors

John R. Boatright Raymond C. Baumhart, S.J., Professor of Business Ethics, Professor of Management, Graduate School of Business, Loyola University of Chicago, Chicago, IL, USA, JBOATRI@luc.edu

Alexander Brink Professor of Business Ethics, University of Bayreuth, Germany, and permanent Visiting Professor for Corporate Governance & Philosophy, Witten/Herdecke University, Germany, alexander.brink@uni-bayreuth.de

Thomas Clarke Professor of Management, Director, UTS Research Centre for Corporate Governance, Sydney, NSW, Australia, Thomas.Clarke@uts.edu.au

Pat Dade Founding Director, Cultural Dynamics Strategy and Marketing Ltd, London, UK, thegurupat@cultdyn.co.uk

Wim Dubbink Associate Professor of Business Ethics, Department of Philosophy, Tilburg University, Tilburg, The Netherlands, W.Dubbink@uvt.nl

Andrew J. Felo Associate Professor of Accounting, School of Graduate Professional Studies at Great Valley, Pennsylvania State University, University Park, PA, USA, ajf14@gv.psu.edu

Bruno S. Frey Professor of Behavioural Science, Warwick Business School, University of Warwick, United Kingdom; Professor of Economics, University of Zurich, Zurich, Switzerland, bsfrey@iew.uzh.ch

Les Higgins Founding Director, Cultural Dynamics Strategy and Marketing Ltd, London, UK, leshiggins@cultdyn.co.uk

Ronald Jeurissen Professor of Business Ethics, Director, European Institute for Business Ethics, Nyenrode Business University, Breukelen, The Netherlands, R.Jeurissen@nyenrode.nl

James Kirkbride Professor of International Business Law, Vice-Rector, London School of Business and Finance, London, UK, jkirkbride@lsbf.co.uk

Kai Kühne Research Associate, Institute for Labour Law and Industrial Relations in the European Community, University of Trier, Trier, Germany, kuehne@iaaeg.de

Steve Letza Professor of Corporate Governance, Director, European Centre for Corporate Governance, Liverpool John Moores University, Liverpool, UK, S.Letza@ljmu.ac.uk

Scott Lichtenstein Senior Lecturer, St James Business School, London, UK, scottl@evsconsulting.co.uk

Dirk Linowski Director, Institute for International Business Relations, Steinbeis University Berlin, Berlin, Germany, linowski@stw.de

Chris Low Head of the Division of Health and Wellbeing, Department of Health Sciences, University of Huddersfield, Huddersfield, UK, C.Low@hud.ac.uk

Alexei M. Marcoux Associate Professor of Business Ethics, School of Business Administration, Loyola University Chicago, Chicago, IL, USA, alexei.marcoux@gmail.com

Margit Osterloh Professor of Management Science, Warwick Business School, University of Warwick, Coventry, United Kingdom; Professor of Management, University of Zurich, Zurich, Switzerland, osterloh@iou.uzh.ch

G.J. (Deon) Rossouw Extraordinary Professor in Philosophy, University of Pretoria, Pretoria, South Africa; CEO, Ethics Institute of South Africa, Pretoria, South Africa, deon.rossouw@ethicsa.org

Dieter Sadowski Professor of Business Administration, Director, Institute for Labour Law and Industrial Relations in the European Community, University of Trier, Trier, Germany, sadowski@uni-trier.de

Alejo José G. Sison Professor of Philosophy, University of Navarre, Pamplona, Spain, ajsison@unav.es

Clive Smallman Professor of Management and Head of School, School of Management, University of Western Sydney, Sydney, NSW, Australia, HoS.MGT@uws.edu.au

Aloy Soppe Associate Professor of Financial Ethics, Erasmus School of Law, Erasmus University Rotterdam, Rotterdam, Netherlands, soppe@frg.eur.nl

Xiuping Sun Lecturer, Leeds Business School, Leeds Metropolitan University, Leeds, UK, x.sun@leedsmet.ac.uk

Till Talaulicar Professor of Corporate Governance and Board Dynamics, Witten/Herdecke University, Witten, Germany, Till.Talaulicar@uni-wh.de

Junhua Tang Research Associate, Chair of Microeconomics, University of Rostock, Rostock, Germany, junhua.tang@uni-rostock.de

Steen Thomsen Professor, Department of International Economics and Management, Copenhagen Business School, Copenhagen, Denmark; Director, Center for Corporate Governance, Copenhagen Business School, Copenhagen, Denmark, st.int@cbs.dk

Bert van de Ven Assistant Professor, Department of Philosophy, Tilburg University, Tilburg, The Netherlands, B.W.vdVen@uvt.nl

Josef Wieland Professor of Business Administration & Economics with emphasis on Business Ethics, Director, Konstanz Institute for Intercultural Management, Values and Communication, University of Applied Sciences Konstanz, Konstanz, Germany, wieland@htwg-konstanz.de

Hossam Zeitoun Doctoral Student and Assistant, Department of Business Administration, University of Zurich, Zurich, Switzerland, hossam.zeitoun@iou.uzh.ch

Part I
Economic Foundations
of Corporate Governance

Chapter 1
The Globalisation of Corporate Governance? Irresistible Markets Meet Immovable Institutions

Thomas Clarke

Contents

A Universal Corporate Governance System?

In the contest between three resolutely different approaches to corporate governance in the Anglo-American, European and Asia-Pacific models, the question arises: is one system more robust than the others and will this system prevail and become universal? The answer to this question appeared straightforward in the 1990s. The US economy was ascendant, and the American market-based approach appeared the most dynamic and successful. Functional convergence towards the market based system seemed to be occurring inexorably driven by forces such as:

- increasingly massive international financial flows which offered deep, liquid capital markets to countries and companies that could meet certain minimum international corporate governance standards;

T. Clarke (✉)
Professor of Management, Director, UTS Research Centre for Corporate Governance, Sydney, NSW, Australia
e-mail: Thomas.Clarke@uts.edu.au

A. Brink (ed.), *Corporate Governance and Business Ethics*, Ethical Economy. Studies in Economic Ethics and Philosophy 39, DOI 10.1007/978-94-007-1588-2_1, © Springer Science+Business Media B.V. 2011

- growing influence of the great regional stock exchanges, including the NYSE and Nasdaq, London Stock Exchange, and Euronext – where the largest corporations in the world were listed regardless of their home country;
- developing activity of ever-expanding Anglo-American based institutional investors, advancing policies to balance their portfolios with increasing international investments if risk could be mitigated;
- expanding revenues and market capitalization of multinational enterprises (predominantly Anglo-American corporations, invariably listed on the New York Stock Exchange even if European based) combined with a sustained wave of international mergers and acquisitions from which increasingly global companies were emerging;
- accelerating convergence towards international accounting standards; and a worldwide governance movement towards more independent auditing standards and rigorous corporate governance practices.

Together these forces have provoked one of the liveliest debates of the last decade concerning the globalization and convergence of corporate governance (cf. Hansmann and Kraakman 2001; Branson 2001; McDonnell 2002; McCahery et al. 2002; Hamilton and Quinlan 2005). How high the stakes are in this debate is revealed by Gordon and Roe (2004):

> Globalization affects the corporate governance reform agenda in two ways. First, it heightens anxiety over whether particular corporate governance systems confer competitive economic advantage. As trade barriers erode, the locally protected product marketplace disappears. A country's firms' performance is more easily measured against global standards. Poor performance shows up more quickly when a competitor takes away market share, or innovates quickly. National decision makers must consider whether to protect locally favored corporate governance regimes if they regard the local regime as weakening local firms in product markets or capital markets. Concern about comparative economic performance induces concern about corporate governance. Globalization's second effect comes from capital markets' pressure on corporate governance. First, firms have new reasons to turn to public capital markets. High tech firms following the US model want the ready availability of an initial public offering for the venture capitalist to exit and for the firm to raise funds. Firms expanding into global markets often prefer to use stock, rather than cash, as acquisition currency. If they want American investors to buy and hold that stock, they are pressed to adopt corporate governance measures that those investors feel comfortable with. Despite a continuing bias in favor of home-country investing, the internationalization of capital markets has led to more cross-border investing. New stockholders enter, and they aren't always part of any local corporate governance consensus. They prefer a corporate governance regime they understand and often believe that reform will increase the value of their stock. Similarly, even local investors may make demands that upset a prior local consensus. The internationalization of capital markets means that investment flows may move against firms perceived to have suboptimal governance and thus to the disadvantage of the countries in which those firms are based. (p. 2)

In the inevitable contest between the insider, relationship based, stakeholder oriented corporate governance system and the outsider, market-based, shareholder value oriented system, it is often implied that the optimal model is the dispersed ownership with shareholder foci for achieving competitiveness and enhancing any economy in a globalised world. The OECD, World Bank, IMF, Asian Development Bank and other international agencies, while they have recognized the existence of different governance systems and suggested they would not wish to adopt a one-size-fits-all approach, have nonetheless consistently associated the *rules-based* outsider mode of corporate governance with greater efficiency and capacity to attract investment capital, and relegated the relationship based insider mode to second best, often with the implication that these systems may be irreparably flawed. The drive towards functional convergence was supported by the development of international codes and standards of corporate governance.

The vast weight of scholarship, led by the financial economists, has reinforced these ideas to the point where they appeared unassailable at the height of the new economy boom in the US in the 1990s (which coincided with a long recession for both the leading exponents of the relationships based system, Japan and Germany), supporting the view that an inevitable convergence towards the superior Anglo-American model of corporate governance was occurring. This all appeared an integral part of the irresistible rise of globalisation that was advancing through the regions of the world in the late 1990s and early 2000s, with apparently unstoppable force. Economies, cultures, and peoples increasingly were becoming integrated into global markets, media networks, and foreign ideologies in a way never before experienced. It seemed as if distinctive and valued regional patterns of corporative governance would be absorbed just as completely as other cultural institutions in the integrative and homogenising processes of globalisation. The increasing power of global capital markets, stock exchanges, institutional investors, and international regulation would overwhelm cultural and institutional differences in the approach to corporate governance.

Yet there is a developing literature comparing different models of capitalism from alternative analytical frameworks highlighting the nature and extent of diverse forms of capitalism, their relative strengths and weaknesses, and the prospects for institutional diversity when confronted with growing pressures for international economic integration (cf. Deeg and Jackson 2006). The varieties of capitalism thesis elaborated by Hall and Soskice (2001) adopts a firm centred approach focusing on the incentives for coordination; a wider typology of governance mechanisms in terms of social systems of production is offered by Hollingsworth and Boyer (1997); and a national business systems approach of Whitley (1999) examines the internal capacities of business firms.

Just as there are many countries that continue to value greatly the distinctions of their culture and institutions, they would not wish to lose to any globalised world, people also believe there are unique attributes to the different corporate governance systems they have developed over time, and are not convinced these should be sacrificed to some unquestioning acceptance that a universal system will inevitably be better. The field of comparative corporate governance has continued to develop however, and a different and more complex picture of governance systems is now emerging. The objectives of corporate governance are more closely questioned; the qualities of the variety and relationships of different institutional structures are becoming more apparent; the capability and performance of the different systems more closely examined; and different potential outcomes of any convergence of governance systems realized. While capital markets have acquired an apparently irresistible force in the world economy, it still appears that institutional complementarities at the national and regional level represent immovable objects.

Globalisation of Capital Markets

A major driver of the globalisation phenomenon has proved the massive development of finance markets, and their increasing influence upon every other aspect of
the economy:

> Financial globalisation, i.e., the integration of more and more countries into the interna-
> tional financial system and the expansion of international markets for money, capital and
> foreign exchange, took off in the 1970s. From the 1980s on, the increase in cross-border
> holdings of assets outpaced the increase in international trade, and financial integration
> accelerated once more in the 1990s. In EMU, monetary integration boosted the integration
> of financial markets, which had begun under the single market programme, even further.
> The internationalisation of finance was driven by technical advances, above all the decrease
> in the cost of communication and information processing as well as policy changes, in
> particular the spreading liberalisation of cross-border financial flows (...). Plainly, trade
> integration (which is beneficial in itself) and financial integration reinforce each other in
> various ways. The past decade has also seen widespread improvements in macroeconomic
> and structural policies that may to some extent be linked to a disciplining effect of financial
> integration. Moreover, there is evidence that financial linkages have strengthened the trans-
> mission of cyclical impulses and shocks among industrial countries. Financial globalisation
> is also likely to have helped financing the build-up of significant global current account
> imbalances. Finally, a great deal of the public and academic discussion has focussed on the
> series of financial crises in the 1990s, which has highlighted the potential effects of capital
> account liberalisation on the volatility of growth and consumption. (European Commission
> 2005, p. 19)

The complex explanation for this massive *financialisation* of the world economy is
pieced together by Ronald Dore thus:

- Financial services take up an ever larger share of advertising, economic activity
  and highly skilled manpower.
- Banks respond to the decline in loan business with a shift to earning fees for
  financial and investment services and own account trading.
- Shareholder value is preached as the sole legitimate objective and aspiration of
  corporations and executives.
- Insistent and demanding calls for "level playing fields" from the World Trade
  Organisation and Bank of International Settlements (BIS), with pressures for the
  further liberalisation of financial markets, and greater international competition
  forcing international financial institutions and other corporations to work within
  the same parameters (cf. Dore 2000, pp. 4ff.).

What is resulting from this insistent impulse of the increasingly dominant financial
institutions are economies (and corporations) increasingly dependent upon financial
markets:

> Global integration and economic performance has been fostered by a new dynamic in finan-
> cial markets, which both mirrors and amplifies the effects of foreign direct investment
> and trade driven integration. The economic performance of countries across the world is
> increasingly supported by – and dependent on – international capital flows, which have
> built on a process of progressive liberalisation and advances in technology since the 1980s.
> (European Commission 2005, p. 8)

The Growth of Equity Markets

A vital dimension of the increasing financialisation of the world economy is the growth of capital markets, and especially the vast growth of equity markets, where volatility has been experienced at its furthest extremities. The American zone equity markets (entirely dominated by the NYSE and Nasdaq) were propelled from a total market capitalization of $4,000 billion in 1990 to $24,320 billion in 2007. This onward progress was violently punctuated by the market collapse of 2001/2002, with a fall from $16,450 billion in 2000 to $11,931 in 2002 (Fig. 1.1).

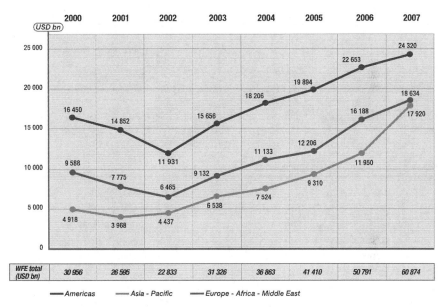

Fig. 1.1   Recent evolution of domestic equity market capitalization
Source: World Federation of Exchanges (2007, p. 37)

The European zone markets grew from just over $2,000 billion in 1990 to $18,634 in 2007, experiencing a similar shock with the fall from $9,588 billion in 2000 to $6,465 billion in 2002. Finally market capitalization in the Asia Pacific zone grew slowly from just under $4,000 billion in 1990 to $4,918 billion in 2000, and after the 2001 fall exploded to $17,920 billion dollars in 2007 (World Federation of Exchanges 2007, p. 37).

Traditionally the Anglo-American world has revealed a greater enthusiasm for share trading, but in recent years this enthusiasm has been taken up in both European and Asian markets. In the Americas share trading reached a peak of $34,070 billion in 2000, collapsing to $17,899 billion in 2003, before recovering and once again taking off to $48,363 billion in 2007 (Fig. 1.2).

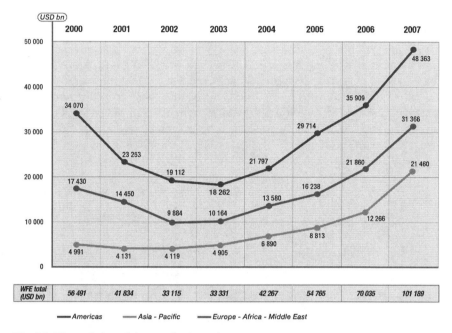

Fig. 1.2 The evolution of share trading by region
Source: World Federation of Exchanges (2007, p. 39)

In the European zone, trading reached a peak of $17,430 billion in 2000, collapsed to $9,884 billion in 2002, and quickly trebled to $31,366 billion in 2007. In the Asia-Pacific, trading was more modest until 2003 when it quadrupled to $21,460 by 2007 (cf. World Federation of Exchanges 2005, p. 56). Because they have adopted regional time zones which fit their trading patterns over the 24 h of each day opening with the Asia Pacific markets, followed by the European, and closing with the US markets, the World Federation of Exchanges has to an extent concealed the enormous concentration of equity markets by including South America in with the United States, Africa and the Middle East in with Europe, and South Asia in with Southeast Asia, Japan, and Australia. A more accurate picture of the paucity of equity markets in the developing world is highlighted for example by the 2002 inflows of total portfolio investment into low income countries which amounted to 0.009% of the world total, and into middle income countries (excluding China) that amounted to 4.2% of the world total, while the high income countries claimed almost 90% of the total inflows of portfolio investment (cf. Gunter and van der Hoeven 2004).

In the past, the supremacy of the NYSE was unchallenged. The Anglo-American exchanges, comprising the NYSE, Nasdaq, London, Toronto, and Sydney stock exchanges, have played a dominant role in equity markets, but more recently Euronext and the Deutsche Börse have become significant players. More startlingly, there are now five Asian stock exchanges in the largest 12 including Tokyo, Shanghai, Hong Kong, Bombay, and the National Stock Exchange of India. In recent years, the substantial growth of the regional stock exchanges in Europe and Asia has threatened the dominant position of the NYSE, and this explains the interest of the NYSE in the merger with Euronext which was completed in 2007.

This concentration of equity market activity is more apparent in share trading (Tables 1.1 and 1.2), with the NYSE, Nasdaq, and London having a combined total of share trading of $55,563 billion in 2007 (World Federation of Exchanges 2007, p. 39) (perhaps further compounded by the NYSE merger with Euronext, and LSE merger with Borsa Italiana). However, share trading has increased significantly in European markets, and dramatically in the Shanghai, Shenzhen, and Hong Kong exchanges. There remains a predominance of Anglo-American institutions and activity in world equity markets, though not as great as in the past, and to an extent these markets continue to reflect Anglo-American investment interests. Yet much of the rest of the world is adopting a greater use of equity markets rather than more traditional sources of finance. However this increasing global pre-eminence of equity markets is a very recent phenomenon.

Table 1.1 Largest stock exchanges in market capitalization year-end 2007

Exchange	USD bn end-2007	USD bn end-2006	% Change in USD	% Change in local currency
1. NYSE Group	15,651	15,421	1.5	1.5
2. Tokyo Stock Exchange Group	4,331	4,614	−6.1	−12.0
3. Euronext	4,223	3,713	13.7	2.6
4. Nasdaq Stock Market	4,014	3,865	3.8	3.8
5. London Stock Exchange	3,852	3,794	1.5	−0.2
6. Shanghai Stock Exchange	3,694	918	302.7	276.8
7. Hong Kong Exchanges	2,654	1,715	54.8	55.2
8. TSX Group	2,187	1,701	28.6	9.0
9. Deutsche Börse	2,105	1,638	28.6	15.9
10. Bombay Stock Exchange	1,819	819	122.1	97.8
11. BME Spanish Exchanges	1,799	1,323	36.1	22.7
12. National Stock Exchange on India	1,660	774	114.5	91.0

Source: World Federation of Exchanges (2007, p. 37)

Historically, the primary way most businesses throughout the world (including in the Anglo-American region) have financed the growth of their companies is internally through retained earnings. In most parts of the world until recently, this was a far more dependable source of finance rather then relying on equity markets. Equity finance has proved useful at the time of public listing when entrepreneurs and venture capitalists cash in their original investment, as a means of acquiring other companies or providing rewards for executives through stock options. Equity finance is used much less frequently during restructuring or to finance new product or project development (cf. Lazonick 1992, p. 457). In Europe and the Asia-Pacific however, this finance was in the past provided by majority shareholders, banks, or other related companies (to the extent it was needed by companies committed to organic

Table 1.2 Largest exchanges in share trading value 2007

Exchange	USD bn 2007	USD bn 2006	% Change in USD	% Change in local currency
1. NYSE Group	29,910	21,789	37.3	37.3
2. Nasdaq Stock Market	15,320	11,807	29.7	29.7
3. London Stock Exchange	10,333	7,571	36.5	26.1
4. Tokyo Stock Exchange Group	6,476	5,823	11.2	12.2
5. Euronext	5,640	3,853	46.4	34.5
6. Deutsche Börse	4,325	2,737	58.0	45.2
7. Shanghai Stock Exchange	4,070	736	452.7	426.6
8. BME Spanish Exchanges	2,970	1,934	53.6	41.1
9. Borsa Italiana	2,312	1,591	45.3	33.6
10. Hong Kong Exchanges	2,137	832	156.7	157.8
11. Shenzhen Stock Exchange	2,103	423	397.6	374.1
12. Korea Exchange	2,006	1,342	49.5	46.0

Source: World Federation of Exchanges (2007, p. 39)

growth rather than through acquisition, and where executives traditionally were content with more modest personal material rewards than their American counterparts).

The euphoria of the US equity markets did reach across the Atlantic with a flurry of new listings, which formed part of a sustained growth in the market capitalisation of European stock exchanges as a percentage of GDP. This substantial development of the equity markets of France, the Netherlands, Germany, Spain, Belgium, and other countries began to influence the corporate landscape of Europe, and was further propelled by the formation of Euronext. Indeed, as the regulatory implications of Sarbanes Oxley emerged in the United States from 2003 onwards, the market for initial public offerings (IPOs) moved emphatically towards London, Hong Kong, and other exchanges (Fig. 1.3). Concerned about the impact of Sarbanes Oxley on the US economy, a group of authorities formed the Committee on Capital Markets Regulation (CCMR) and highlighted the damage being caused to what for many years was recognised as "the largest, most liquid, and most competitive public equity capital markets in the world" (CCMR 2006, p. ix). However, after the 2001/2002 Nasdaq fall, this picture began to change with Europe and then the Asia Pacific raising more new equity capital than Nasdaq and the NYSE (Fig. 1.3).

Though the US total share of global stock market activity remained at 50% in 2005, as Figure 1.4 demonstrates, the IPO activity had collapsed:

A better measure of competitiveness is where new equity capital is being raised – that is, in which markets initial public offerings ('IPOs') are being done. These companies do have a choice of where to trade. In the late 1990s, the U.S. exchange listed capital markets were attracting 48% of all global IPOs. Since then, the United States has seen its market share of all global IPOs drop to 6% in 2005 and is estimated, year to date, to be only 8% in 2006. This loss of market share exists in both the high-tech and non-high tech sectors and is not restricted to firms from China or Russia, whose companies have been a major source of IPOs in recent years. The headline numbers most often quoted are that last year, 24 of the 25 largest IPOs were done in markets outside the United States and 9 of the 10 largest IPOs in 2006 to date took place outside the United States. (CCMR 2006, p. 2)

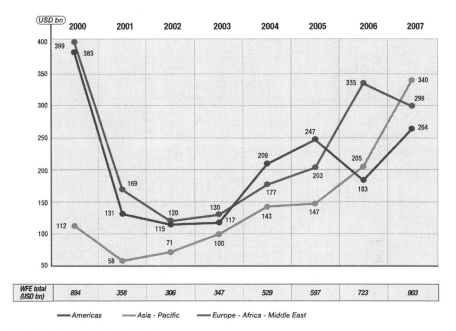

Fig. 1.3 New capital raised by shares
Source: World Federation of Exchanges (2007, p. 44)

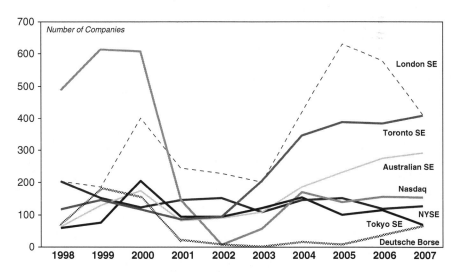

Fig. 1.4 New listings in major markets 1998–2007
Source: WFE's respective annual reports

This greater vibrancy in European markets partly explains the NYSE's interest in merging with Euronext and the Nasdaq's courtship with the LSE. It is likely any such mergers will represent a further US bridgehead into the equity markets of Europe, rather than the converse. Along with the growth in market capitalisation in European exchanges occurred a gradual increase also in trading value. It appears that contemporary equity markets inevitably will be associated with high levels of trading activity.

The important role of equity markets in fostering further international financial integration is recognised by the European Commission (2005):

> Globally, portfolio investment is the largest asset category held cross-border; global portfolios (equity and debt securities) amounted to 19 trillion US dollars at the end of 2003 (IMF CPIS, preliminary data). Turnover in international financial centres is very substantial. At the London Stock Exchange, 7.6 bn euro worth of foreign equity was traded on a daily basis in May 2005. That represents 45% of the total London trading volume. The part of turnover of foreign equity in the New York and Frankfurt stock exchanges stands at 8% and 7%, respectively. Currently, 235 EU firms are listed in US stock exchanges and 140 US firms in London, Frankfurt or at Euronext. Moreover, an agreement on equivalence of accounting standards has been reached, in April 2005, between the US Securities and Exchange Commission and the European Commission. (p. 29)

As equity markets come to play a more powerful role in corporate life in Europe, Japan, and other parts of the world, a set of assumptions and practices are also disseminated which may confront long standing values and ideals in the economies and societies concerned. Specifically, the ascendancy of shareholder value as the single legitimate objective of corporations and their executives usually accompanies increasing dependence upon equity markets. Dore cites a Goldman Sachs study of manufacturing value added in the United States, Germany, and Europe in general, which concluded that

> [t]he share of gross value added going to wages and salaries has declined on trend in the US since the early 1980s. In fact, for the US, this appears to be an extension of a trend that has been in place since the early 1970s (. . .). We believe that the pressures of competition for the returns on capital available in the emerging economies have forced US industry to produce higher returns on equity capital and that their response to this has been to reserve an increasingly large share of output for the owners of capital. (Young 1997, p. 42)

This insistent pressure to drive increases in capital's returns at the expense of labour inherent in Anglo-American conceptions of the nature of equity finance is roundly condemned by Dore (2000) as the negation of essential values previously considered central to economic good in both Europe and Japan:

> Multiple voices are urging Japanese managers to go in the same direction. The transformation on the agenda may be variously described – from employee sovereignty to shareholder sovereignty: from the employee-favouring firm to the shareholder-favouring firm; from pseudo-capitalism to genuine capitalism. They all mean the same thing: the transformation of firms run primarily for the benefits of their employees into firms run primarily, even exclusively, for the benefit of their shareholders (. . .). It means an economy centred on the stock market as the measure of corporate success and on the stock market index as a measure of national well-being, as opposed to an economy which has other, better, more pluralistic criteria of human welfare for measuring progress towards the good society. (pp. 9–10)

The euphoric enthusiasm for the power of equity markets was severely dented by the Enron/WorldCom series of corporate collapses in the US (and the reverberations in the Ahold, Parmalat, and other failures in Europe) (cf. Clarke 2007). With about seven trillion dollars wiped off the NYSE in 2001/2002, and the executives of many leading corporations facing criminal prosecution, the recovery in equity markets came sooner and more robustly than expected. However, part of the price of restoring confidence to the markets was the hasty passage of the Sarbanes Oxley legislation and increased regulation of corporate governance. One reaction to these developments was increased interest in the investment potential or largely unregulated hedge funds that quickly grew from assets of $50 billion in 1993 to $1.18 trillion in 2006. Hedge funds presented the opportunity to acquire corporate assets quickly (and often very briefly) in stealthy interventions, without the usual standards of disclosure and transparency. More recently, private equity has grown in significance from $100 billion in assets in 1993 to $900 billion by 2005, on the way morphing from venture capital and MBOs to highly leveraged, debt fuelled takeovers.

These activist interventions into equity markets proved even more short-lived than the junk-bond takeover era of the 1980s; however, they do indicate the impatience of capital with any regulation or limitation of its powers and the resentment attached to the continuous disclosure regime now introduced in equity markets and corporate governance in many parts of the world. The subprime mortgage crisis, and the elaborate financial instruments developed to pass on risk by investment banks, that has caused a prolonged implosion of financial institutions in 2007/2008 is an indication of the dangers presented by the increasing financialisation of economic activity, and the hazardous context for corporate governance in market oriented economies. Nonetheless, the strength and vigour of capital markets seems destined to continue to advance globally without adequate regulation or oversight.

Convergence of Corporate Governance

Underlying the energy of advancing equity markets and the apparent variety of the corporate governance guidelines and policy documents appearing in such profusion over the last decade is an implicit but confident sense that an optimal corporate governance model is indeed emerging, i.e.,

> [a]n optimal model with dispersed ownership and shareholder foci (…). The OECD and World Bank promote corporate governance reform (…) [i]nfluenced by financial economists and are generally promoting market capitalism with a *law matters* approach, although for political reasons, they do not advocate too strongly market capitalism and allow for other corporate governance systems (i.e. concentrated ownership). (Pinto 2005, pp. 26–27)

Other authorities are less diplomatic in announcing the superiority of the Anglo-American approach that other systems must inevitably converge towards. In an article prophetically entitled *The End of History for Corporate Law*, two eminent

US law school professors, Hansmann and Kraakman (2001), lead the charge of the convergence determinists:

> Despite very real differences in the corporate systems, the deeper tendency is towards convergence, as it has been since the nineteenth century (...). The core legal features of the corporate form were already well established in advanced jurisdictions 100 years ago, at the turn of the twentieth century. Although there remained considerable room for variation in governance practices and in the fine structure of corporate law through-out the twentieth century, the pressures for further convergence are now rapidly growing. Chief among these pressures is the recent dominance of a shareholder-centred ideology of corporate law among the business, government and legal entities in key commercial jurisdictions. There is no longer any serious competitor to the view that corporate law should principally strive to increase long-term shareholder value. This emergent consensus has already profoundly affected corporate governance practices throughout the world. It is only a matter of time before its influence is felt in the reform of corporate law as well. (p. 439)

The irony of this profoundly ideological claim (the most recent in a long histori-cal lineage of similar appeals) is that it attempts to enforce the consensus it claims exists, by crowding out any possibility of alternatives. This is not an isolated exam-ple, but the dominant approach of much legal and financial discussion in the United States, whereas McDonnell (2002) insists the prevailing view is:

> The American system works better and that the other countries are in the process of con-verging to the American system. Though there is some dissent from this position, the main debate has been over why countries outside the United States have persisted for so long in their benighted systems and what form their convergence to the American way will take. The scholarly discussion has converged too quickly on the convergence answer. (p. 342)

It is worth asking by what standards or criteria a system of corporate governance may be defined as "optimal". Most economic analyses simply substitute "efficient" for optimal, but McDonnell offers three relevant values:

- efficiency,
- equity,
- participation.

In considering efficiency there is the question of how well the governance system solves agency problems; how well the system facilitates large scale coordination problems; how well the systems encourage long-term innovation; and how they impose different levels of risk on the participants. Distributional equity is another important value, but again is difficult to measure. For many, distributional equity suggests an increased equality of income and wealth, but others find this less com-pelling. In some instances equity may conflict with efficiency: it could be argued the US system is more efficient, but inevitably results in greater inequality. Finally there is the value of participation, both in terms of any contribution this may make to the success of the enterprise, and as an end in itself in enhancing the ability and self-esteem of people. Corporate governance systems affect the level of participation in decision-making very directly, whether encouraging or disallow-ing active participation in enterprise decision-making (cf. ibid., p. 344). Arguably each of these values is of great importance, and the precise balance between them is part of the choice of what kind of corporate governance system is adopted. Yet there appears increasingly less opportunity to exercise this choice:

> The universe of theoretical possibilities is much richer than a dominant strand of the literature suggests, and we are currently far short of the sort of empirical evidence that might help us sort out these possibilities. Most commentators have focused on efficiency to the exclusion of other values. Moreover, even if convergence occurs, there is a possibility that we will not converge on the best system. Even if we converge to the current best system, convergence still may not be desirable. (ibid., p. 342)

History and Politics

In the past these critical political choices on which system of governance provides the most value in terms of efficiency, equity, and participation have been made and defended. Mark Roe's (1994, 2003) path dependence thesis rests on how political forces in America, anxious about the influence of concentrated financial or industrial monopolies, resisted any effort at concentration of ownership or at ownership through financial institutions, resulting in dispersed ownership. In contrast European social democracy has tended to favour other stakeholder interests, particularly labour, as a system that promotes welfare among all citizens and attempts to prevent wide disparities. In turn this can be viewed as a reaction to the historical rise of fascism and communism (cf. Pinto 2005, p. 494). Fligstein and Freeland (1995) adopt a similar historical view that the form of governance is a result of wider political and institutional developments:

- the timing of entry into industrialisation and the institutionalisation of that process;
- the role of states in regulating property rights and the rules of competition between firms; and
- the social organisation of national elites (cf. ibid., p. 21).

In this way, characteristic institutions of the US economy can be traced back to distinctive political and regulatory intervention, resulting for example in weak banks, diversified companies, and the dominance of the diversified (M-form) corporations. In contrast in Europe and Japan the regulatory environment encouraged a very different approach:

> Regulatory policy in the United States had the unintended consequence of pushing U.S. companies in the direction of unrelated diversification, whereas in Germany and Japan it continued on a pre-war trajectory of discouraging mergers in favour of cartels and of promoting corporate growth through internal expansion rather than acquisitions. In other words, modern regulatory policy in the U.S. produced corporations who relied on markets to acquire ideas and talent, whereas in Germany and Japan it produced corporations whose primary emphasis was on production and on the internal generation of ideas through development of human capital and organizational learning. The implications for corporate governance are straightforward: corporations favour shareholders in the U.S. so as to obtain capital for diversification and acquisitions; they favour managers and employees in the Germany and Japan so as to create internal organizational competencies. (Jacoby 2001, p. 8)

A very different reading of these events is offered by Rajan and Zingales (2003), who argue that widely dispersed shareholdership is related to the development of liquid securities markets and the openness to outside investments, while it was not social democracy but protectionism that kept European and Japanese markets closed from competition with concentrated ownership. As financial economists they favour the globalisation route to open market based competition, which they see as the way to unsettling local elites, achieving dispersed ownership, raising capital, and improving corporate governance.

Law and Regulation

Following a different line of analysis the substantial empirical evidence of La Porta, Lopez-de-Silanes, Shleifer, and Vishny (1998, 1999, 2000, 2002) concerning countries with dispersed and concentrated ownership, which demonstrates differences in the legal protection of shareholders, was very influential. In many countries without adequate laws guaranteeing dispersed shareholder rights, the only alternative appeared to maintain control through concentrated ownership. This led to the conclusion the law determined the ownership structure and system of corporate finance and governance. Jurisdictions where the law was more protective encouraged the emergence of more dispersed ownership (cf. Pinto 2005, p. 492). Coffee (2001) extends La Porta et al.'s acceptance that in the common law system there was greater flexibility of response to new developments offering better protection to shareholders to the argument that the critical role of the decentralised character of common law institutions was to facilitate the rise of both private and semi-private self-regulatory bodies in the US and UK. In contrast in civil law systems the state maintained a restrictive monopoly over law-making institutions (for example in the early intrusion of the French government into the affairs of the Paris Bourse involving the Ministry of Finance approving all new listings). Coffee (2001) concludes that it was market institutions that demanded legal protection rather than the other way around:

> The cause and effect sequence posited by the La Porta et al. thesis may in effect read history backwards. They argue that strong markets require strong mandatory rules as a precondition. Although there is little evidence that strong legal rules encouraged the development of either the New York or London Stock Exchanges (and there is at least some evidence that strong legal rules hindered the growth of the Paris Bourse), the reverse does seem to be true: strong markets do create a demand for stronger legal rules. Both in the U.S. and the U.K., as liquid securities markets developed and dispersed ownership became prevalent, a new political constituency developed that desired legal rules capable of filling in the inevitable enforcement gaps that self-regulation left. Both the federal securities laws passed in the 1930's in the U.S. and the Company Act amendments adopted in the late 1940's in the U.K. were a response to this demand (and both were passed by essentially "social democratic" administrations seeking to protect public securities markets). Eventually, as markets have matured across Europe, similar forces have led to the similar creation of European parallels to the SEC. In each case, law appears to be responding to changes in the market, not consciously leading it. (p. 6)

Culture – Deep Causation

In the search for explanations some have attempted a philosophical approach including Fukuyama (1996) who conceives of business organisations as the product of trust, and the different governance systems as built of different forms of trust relations. Regarding the social foundations and development of ownership structures and the law, other writers have examined the correlations between law and culture. Licht (2001) examines the relevance of national culture to corporate governance and securities regulation, and explores the relationship between different cultural types and the law:

> A nation's culture can be perceived as the mother of all path dependencies. Figuratively, it means that a nation's culture might be more persistent than other factors believed to induce path dependence. Substantively, a nation's unique set of cultural values might indeed affect – in a chain of causality – the development of that nation's laws in general and its corporate governance system in particular. (p. 149)

In working towards a cross-cultural theory of corporate governance systems, Licht, Goldschmidt, and Schwartz (2001) demonstrate that corporate governance laws exhibit systematic cultural characteristics:

> A comparison between a taxonomy of corporate governance regimes according to legal families ("the legal approach") and a classification of countries according to their shared cultural values demonstrates that the legal approach provides only a partial, if not misleading, depiction of the universe of corporate governance regimes. Dividing shareholder protection regimes according to groups of culturally similar nations is informative. The evidence corroborates the uniqueness of common law origin regimes in better protecting minority shareholders. However, statutes in the English Speaking cultural region offer levels of protection to creditors similar to the laws in the Western European or Latin American regions. Our findings cast doubt on the alleged supremacy of common law regimes in protecting creditors and, therefore, investors in general. Finally, we find that analyses of corporate governance laws in Far Eastern countries, a distinct cultural region, would benefit from combining an approach that draws on cultural value dimensions and one that draws on legal families. (p. 40)

Licht et al. conclude that corporations are embedded within larger socio-cultural settings in which they are incorporated and operate. Cultural values are influential in determining the types of legal regimes perceived and accepted as legitimate in any country, and serve as a guide to legislators. Hence cultural values may impede legal reforms that conflict with them, and the naivete underlying quick-fix suggestions for corporate law reform (cf. ibid., pp. 33–34). Culture also influences what are perceived as the maximands of corporate governance – for example in the debate over stockholders versus stakeholders interests as the ultimate objective of the corporation:

> The corporate governance problem therefore is not one of maximising over a single factor (the maximand). Rather, it calls for optimizing over several factors simultaneously. (Licht 2003, p. 5)

Berglöf and Thadden (1999) suggest the economic approach to corporate governance should be generalised to a model of multilateral interactions among a number of different stakeholders. They argue that though protection of shareholder interests may be important, it may not be sufficient for sustainable development, particularly in transitional economies. Licht (2003) concludes:

> Every theory of corporate governance is at heart a theory of power. In this view, the corporation is a nexus of power relationships more than a nexus of contracts. The corporate setting is rife with agency relationships in which certain parties have the ability (power) unilaterally to affect the interests of other parties notwithstanding preexisting contractual arrangements. In the present context, corporate fiduciaries are entrusted with the power to weigh and prefer the interests of certain constituencies to the interests of others (beyond their own self-interest). Given the current limitations of economic theory, progress in the analysis of the maximands of corporate governance may be achieved by drawing on additional sources of knowledge. (p. 6)

Institutional Complementarities

A further development of the path dependence thesis is the emphasis on the interdependence of economic and social institutions:

> Corporate governance consists not simply of *elements* but of *systems* (...). Transplanting some of the formal elements without regard for the institutional complements may lead to serious problems later, and these problems may impede, or reverse, convergence. (Gordon and Roe 2004, p. 6)

Optimal corporate governance mechanisms are contextual and may vary by industries and activities. Identifying what constitutes good corporate governance practice is complex, and cannot be templated into a single form. One needs to identify the strengths and weaknesses in the system but also the underlying conditions which the system is dependent upon (cf. Pinto 2005, p. 26; Maher and Andersson 2000). The institutions that compose the system of corporate governance and complement each other consist not just of the law, finance, and ownership structure.

Complementarities may extend to such things as labour relations and managerial incentive systems. In Germany and Japan the corporation's long term relations with banks, customers, and suppliers facilitates long term commitments to employees. The commitment to permanency promotes extensive firm-specific training, which contributes to flexible specialisation in the production of high quality goods. In contrast in the United States employer training investments are lower than in Japan and Germany, employees are more mobile, and there is less firm-specific skill development. Similarly in the US, fluid managerial labour markets make it easier for ousted managers to find new jobs after a hostile takeover. In contrast in Japan management talent is carefully evaluated over a long period of time through career employment and managerial promotion system. Jacoby (2001) contends:

> It is difficult to disentangle the exogenous initial conditions that established a path from the *ex post* adaptations (...). What's most likely to be the case is that capital markets, labour markets, legal regulations, and corporate norms co-evolved from a set of initial conditions. (p. 17)

He continues with a warning to those who might wish to randomly transplant particular institutional practices into other countries:

> Given institutional complementarities and path dependence, it's difficult for one country to borrow a particular practice and expect it to perform similarly when transplanted to a different context. Two examples: First, despite numerous calls for the Japanese to do more in the way of venture capital, the fact is that Japan lacks the fluid labor markets, legal expertise, and equity-related compensation schemes that are the underpinnings of the U.S. venture-capital approach. The Japanese nevertheless do have high rates of innovation, but they achieve it via corporate spin-offs and big-company funding rather than venture capital. Second, were the Japanese or Germans to adopt a U.S.-style corporate governance approach that relies on takeovers to mitigate agency problems, it would prove highly disruptive of managerial incentive and selection systems presently in place. Hostile takeovers also would be disruptive of relations with suppliers and key customers, a substantial portion of which exist on a long term basis. In Germany and, especially, in Japan, there is less vertical integration of industrial companies than in the United States or the United Kingdom. Rather than rely primarily on arms-length contracts to protect suppliers and purchasers from opportunism, there is heavy use of relational contracting based on personal ties, trust, and reputation. Personal ties are supported by lifetime employment; the business relations are buttressed by cross-share holding. In short, imitation across path-dependent systems is inhibited by the cost of having to change a host of complementary practices that make an institution effective in a particular national system. (ibid., p. 18)

Another way of understanding this, Jacoby suggests, is through the concept of multiple equilibria, which leads to the conclusion there is no best way of designing institutions to support stability and growth in advanced industrial countries:

> Multiple equilibria can arise and persist due to path dependence, institutional complementarities, bounded rationality, and comparative advantage. Sometimes multiple equilibria involve functionally similar but operationally distinctive institutions, such as the use of big firms as incubators in Japan versus the U.S. approach of incubation via start-ups and venture capital. Other times different institutions create qualitatively different outcomes. That is, a set of institutions, including those of corporate governance, may be better at facilitating certain kinds of business strategies and not others. Companies – and the countries in which they are embedded – can then secure international markets by specializing in those advantageous business strategies because foreign competitors will have difficulty imitating them. For example, the emphasis on specific human capital in German and Japan is supportive of production based technological learning, incremental innovation, and high quality production, all areas in which those economies have specialized. By contrast, the U.S. emphasis on resource mobility and on high short-term rewards directs resources to big-bang technological breakthroughs. In short, there are substantial gains to be reaped from sustaining institutional diversity and competing internationally on that basis. (ibid., p. 25)

The discussion of corporate governance is often framed in static efficiency terms, Jacoby contends, as if it was possible to measure the comparative performance of national governance institutions in a static framework. This is inadequate for understanding the dynamic properties of governance systems, especially concerning innovation and long-term growth.

> When there are multiple equilibria and bounded rationality regarding what constitutes an institutional optimum, we are operating in the world of the second best. In that world, there is no reason to believe that revamping a governance system will necessarily move an

economy closer to an economic optimum. The economic case for the superiority of Anglo-American governance – and of the Anglo-American version of "free markets" as we know them, as opposed to a theoretical ideal – is actually rather weak. (ibid., p. 27)

For Hansmann and Kraakman (2001) convergence of corporate governance systems towards the shareholder-oriented model is not only desirable and inevitable, it has already happened. They boldly confirm:

The triumph of the shareholder-oriented model of the corporation over its principal competitors is now assured, even if it was problematic as recently as 25 years ago. Logic alone did not establish the superiority of this standard model or of the prescriptive rules that it implies, which establish a strong corporate management with duties to serve the interests of shareholders alone, as well as strong minority shareholder protections. Rather, the standard model earned its position as the dominant model of the large corporation the hard way, by out-competing during the post-World War II period the three alternative models of corporate governance: the managerialist model, the labour-oriented model, and the state-oriented model. (p. 468)

For Hansmann and Kraakerman alternative systems are not viable competitively, only the lack of product market competition has kept them alive, and as global competitive pressures increase any continuing viability of alternative models will be eliminated, encouraging the ideological and political consensus in favour of the shareholder model.

Hansmann and Kraakerman dismiss the three rivals they set up for the victorious shareholder model. The managerialist model is associated with the US in the 1950s and 1960s, when it was thought professional managers could serve as disinterested technocratic fiduciaries who would guide the business corporation in the interests of the general public. According to Hansmann and Kraakerman this model of social benevolence collapsed into self-serving managerialism, with significant resource misallocation, imperilling the competitiveness of the model and accounting for its replacement by the shareholder driven model in the US (cf. Gordon and Roe 2004).

The labour-oriented model exemplified by German co-determination, but manifest in many other countries, possesses governance structures amplifying the representation of labour, which Hansmann and Kraakerman claim are inefficient because of the heterogeneity of interests among employees themselves, and between employees and shareholders. Firms with this inherent competition of interests would inevitably lose out in product market competition. Finally the state-oriented model associated with France or Germany entails a large state role in corporate affairs through ownership or state bureaucratic engagement with firm managers, allowing elite guidance of private enterprise in the public interest. Hansmann and Kraakerman argue this corporatist model has been discredited because of the poor performance of socialist economies (cf. ibid.).

At the height of the NASDAQ boom when Hansmann and Kraakerman wrote their visionary article it might have appeared that the shareholder model in its US manifestation was certainly globally hegemonic in all of its manifestations. However the post-Enron world is less easily convinced of the inevitable and universal superiority of the US model of governance, and Hansmann and Kraakerman may have written off the prospects of Japan and Europe a little too presumptuously. To take some examples, firstly as Toyota has consolidated its grasp of the global car market with technological supremacy (leaders in fuel-cell and hybrid engineering), and by 2005 Toyota at $134 billion had a larger market capitalisation than General Motors ($16 billion), Ford ($19 billion), and Daimler-Chrysler ($45 billion) combined. Meanwhile GM and Ford were engaged in large scale restructuring and downsizing (GM announcing 113,000 redundancies in March 2006, the largest number ever by any corporation), and it was feared both companies were not far from facing Chapter 11 bankruptcy due to their legacy costs in pensions and health care from another more profitable and less responsible era.

Secondly, the Toulouse based Airbus, founded as a state sponsored consortium of aerospace companies drawn from several European countries and leading with a strong customer focus and innovative designs, went from being a newcomer in the global civilian aerospace market in the 1970s to becoming the leader by 2005. With a string of technological "firsts" including the first twin-aisle, twin-engine commercial jet, the first "fly-by-wire" commercial aircraft, and A380, the first double-decker aircraft with 550 passengers, Airbus has captured the imagination of the industry. In contrast the long established former world leader Boeing, though it was responsible for many of the early innovations in civilian aircraft and consolidated its position of dominance with a string of acquisitions of other aerospace manufacturers in the last 10 years, has struggled to sustain its technological edge. Both companies have faced corporate governance scandals in recent years, Boeing has recovered earlier from its reversals, and is again forging ahead with aggressive marketing of its new planes. Whether Airbus can recapture the dynamism of its development, and finally deliver sufficient numbers of the prestigious A380 to restore its fortunes remains to be seen.

Finally after some time in the doldrums, the industrial powerhouse of Germany is regaining its ascendancy, becoming the world's leading exporter in 2005 with $970.7 billion, followed by the United States with $904.3 billion, China with $762 billion and Japan with $595.8 billion. This industrial renaissance was led by the *Mittelstand*, the small and medium sized family companies that composed the majority of German industry, with a focus on exports leading to strong growth. Eberhard Veit, chief executive of Festo, a leader in automation technology, explained the decision to invest for the long term in this bionic products business meant growth of 5–10% per annum.

> We have growth every year, which is better than having peaks and troughs, because it motivates workers. We have brought 100 new products to the Hanover Messe (the largest industrial trade fare in the world), and that certainly would not be done at a listed group. (Financial Times, 25 April 2006)

None of these graphic illustrations offers much support for Hansmann and Kraakman's messianic vision of the innate advantages of the shareholder value approach in international competition. The best that could be salvaged from their over-confident thesis is that the different corporate governance systems may be better at doing different things.

As Douglas Branson (2001) concludes regarding the globalisation and convergence debate:

[S]eldom will one see scholarship and advocacy that is as culturally and economically insensitive, and condescending, as is the global convergence advocacy scholarship that the elites in United States academy have been throwing over the transom. Those elites have oversold an idea that has little grounding in true global reality. (p. 356)

Bebchuck and Roe's (1999) view still holds that neither shareholder primacy nor dispersed ownership will easily converge. Path dependence has evolved established structures not easily transformed, and complimentary institutions make it more difficult to do so.

Thus keeping existing systems may in fact be an efficient result. This lack of convergence allows for diversity and suggests that globalisation will not easily change the models. (Pinto 2005, p. 501)

Diversity in Corporate Governance

A more realistic global perspective than the convergence thesis is that there will continue to be considerable diversity both in the forms of corporate governance around the world. Different traditions, values, and objectives will undoubtedly continue to produce different outcomes in governance, which will relate closely to the choices and preferences people exercise in engaging in business activity. If there is convergence of corporate governance, it could be to a variety of different forms, and it is likely there will be divergence away from the shareholder oriented Anglo-American model, as there will be convergence towards it.

A surprising claim of Thomsen (2003) is that as US and UK board structures adopt more actively a committee structure with subcommittees of independent outsiders for the key committees of remuneration, auditing, and nomination, which the SEC and NYSE insist upon in the US and which is a central part of the Combined Code in the UK, there are elements of a two tier system of control, which is also implicit in the full separation of the CEO's and chairman's role. Certainly boards of directors in the US and UK in recent years have felt a more immediate responsibility to recognise a wider range of relevant constituencies as stakeholder perspectives have once again become a more prominent part of corporate life. In US firms the spread of equity based compensation, recognition of the growing importance of intellectual capital, and the adoption of high performance work practices have all reemphasised the importance of human capital in a context where previously labour was marginalised in the interests of a single minded shareholder ethos (cf. Jacoby 2001, p. 26). It is ironic that as European and Japanese listed corporations are being forced to recognise the importance of shareholder value Anglo-American corporations are being sharply reminded of their social responsibilities (Fig. 1.5).

Thomsen, citing Gerald Davies, illustrates the transition from a shareholder to a stakeholder view with the symbolic change in rhetoric of the Coca-Cola company. In an earlier mission statement, Coca-Cola declares:

At the Coca-Cola Company our publicly stated mission is to create value over time for the owners of our business. In fact, in our society, that is the mission of any business: to create value for its owners. (quoted after Thomsen 2004, p. 313)

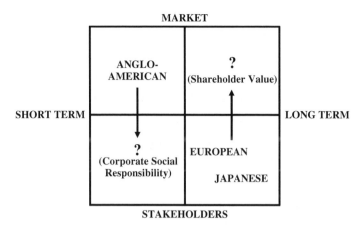

Fig. 1.5 Corporate Governance Objectives
Source: Own figure

On the other hand, in a more recent statement its president announces:

> Fundamentally, the Coca-Cola company, is built on a deep and abiding relationship of trust
> between it and all its constituents: bottlers (. . .), customers (. . .), consumers (. . .), share-
> owners (. . .), employees (. . .), suppliers (. . .), and the very communities of which successful
> companies are an integral part. That trust must be nurtured and maintained on a daily basis.
> (quoted after Thomsen 2004, p. 313)

The widespread adoption among leading Anglo-American corporations of triple
bottom line reporting, publishing social and environmental reports alongside their
financial reports, and actively demonstrating their corporate social responsibility in other more practical ways suggests this is more than simply a rhetorical
change. The formal adoption of *enlightened* shareholder value in the UK Companies
Act indicates a significant move forwards from the more naked pursuit of shareholder value. Further unlikely, but nonetheless real, evidence that the United
States system could in some important ways converging towards the European
model is unearthed by Thomsen (2003). Firstly an unanticipated consequence
of the increasing use of executive stock options in the US has caused a degree
of reintegration of ownership and control. Holderness, Kroszner, and Sheehan
(1999) compared a comprehensive cross-section of 1,500 publicly traded US
firms in 1935 with a modern benchmark of more than 4,200 exchange listed
firms for 1995. They discovered that the percentage of common stock held by
a firm's officers and directors as a group rose from 13% in 1935 to 21% in
1995 (cf. ibid., pp. 435f.). This is partly attributable to the entry into the market of new firms with high ownership concentration (for example in high tech
start ups), and the exit of old economy firms with dispersed ownership due
to merger and acquisitions. Denis and Sarin (1999) find average CEO ownership of 7.2% for a random sample of listed firms. Mehran (1995) examined the

ownership of outside blockholders in the US, which he classified as individuals or entities owning at least 5% of total stock (as this triggers a mandatory SEC filing). He discovered that 56% of randomly selected manufacturing firms had outside blockholders (23% were individuals, 23% other corporations, and 54% institutions).

This pattern of insider ownership and extensive blockholding in the US does not demarcate the American system as sharply from the European as is often suggested. And the trend may be in this direction as apparently the stock market in Anglo-American systems responds positively to higher ownership by financial institutions (one reason for this may be the perception of better monitoring) (cf. Thomsen 2004, p. 310). The increasing importance of institutional investors in the US, and in every other market, means that ownership relations are once again becoming more concentrated (even if the ultimate beneficiaries are highly diffuse). This institutional ownership has begun to create forms of relational investing, which could over time lead to more exercise of voice and less of exit by US shareholders (cf. Jacoby 2001, p. 26). Finally the return of block holding in the US may be enabled by US banking deregulation and the abolition of the Glass Steagal Act and Bank Holding Company Act, which over the longer term could enable US banks to play a more active role in investment banking and corporate governance as in the European system. As US banks grow larger they would be able to take positions in individual firms without incurring excessive risk (cf. Thomsen 2003). Much attention has been focussed upon the pressures driving large listed German corporations to focus more directly on the creation of shareholder value, and upon the insistent pressures for Japanese corporations to demonstrate more transparency and disclosure. Less attention has been paid to the developing pressures upon Anglo-American corporations to exercise greater accountability towards institutional investors and more responsibility in relation to their stakeholder communities (Fig. 1.6).

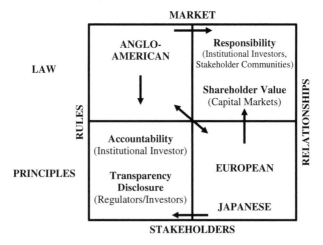

Fig. 1.6 Multiple convergence of governance institutions and relationships
Source: Own figure

With multiple institutions exerting interdependent effects on firm level outcomes (cf. Aguilera and Jackson 2003, p. 448), and with different values informing the objectives for the enterprise in different cultures (cf. Hofstede 2004), the scenario for convergence and diversity of corporate governance models is more complex and unpredictable than many commentators have suggested. A pioneer of corporate governance possessed a more compelling grasp of the possibilities that convergence and divergence may occur *simultaneously*: that is an insistent increase in diversity within an overall trend towards convergence.

> Looking ahead towards the next decade it is possible to foresee a duality in the developing scenarios. On the one hand, we might expect further diversity – new patterns of ownership, new forms of group structure, new types of strategic alliance, leading to yet more alternative approaches to corporate governance. More flexible and adaptive organisational arrangements, entities created for specific projects, business ventures and task forces are likely to compound the diversity. Sharper differentiation of the various corporate governance types and the different bases for governance power will be necessary to increase the effectiveness of governance and enable the regulatory processes to respond to reality (...). But on the other hand, we might expect a convergence of governance processes as large corporations operating globally, their shares traded through global financial markets, are faced with increasing regulatory convergence in company law, disclosure requirements and international accounting standards, insider trading and securities trading rules, and the exchange of information between the major regulatory bodies around the world. (Tricker 1994, p. 520)

In this analysis the strength of diversity rather than uniformity becomes apparent:

> There is then value in maintaining international diversity in corporate governance systems, so that we do not foreclose future alternatives and evolutionary possibilities. The argument resembles the argument for biodiversity in species. (McDonnell 2002, p. 358)

The importance of diversity for the exercise of choice and creativity is paramount, and reveals the dangers involved in national and international policymaking vigorously advocating a one-size-fits-all prescription for corporate governance (cf. ibid., p. 359). Indeed this essential dynamism of corporate governance was fully recognised in the OECD Business Advisory Group's report:

> Entrepreneurs, investors and corporations need the flexibility to craft governance arrangements that are responsive to unique business contexts so that corporations can respond to incessant changes in technologies, competition, optimal firm organization and vertical networking patterns. A market for governance arrangements should be permitted so that these arrangements that can attract investors and other resource contributors – and support competitive corporations – flourish (...). To obtain governance diversity, economic regulations, stock exchange rules and corporate law should support a range of ownership and governance forms. Over time, availability of "off-the-shelf" solutions will offer benefits of market familiarity and learning, judicial enforceability and predictability. (OECD 1998, p. 34)

Future Trends

Contemplating the future of corporate governance systems is a hazardous business. Each of the systems is facing pressures to change. The long term stakeholder orientation of the German and Japanese governance systems is under insistent pressure to deliver shareholder value, particularly from overseas investment institutions. However the market oriented short termism of the Anglo-American approach is itself being challenged by international, national, and community agencies to recognize wider social and environmental responsibilities. The German and Japanese systems are faced with demands for increased transparency and disclosure from both regulators and investors, while Anglo-American corporations are faced with repeated calls for greater accountability from institutional investors and other stakeholder communities.

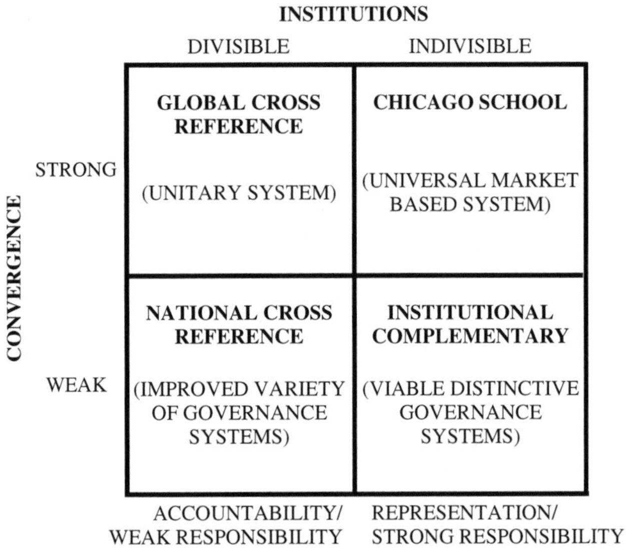

INSTITUTIONS

	DIVISIBLE	INDIVISIBLE
STRONG	**GLOBAL CROSS REFERENCE** (UNITARY SYSTEM)	**CHICAGO SCHOOL** (UNIVERSAL MARKET BASED SYSTEM)
WEAK	**NATIONAL CROSS REFERENCE** (IMPROVED VARIETY OF GOVERNANCE SYSTEMS)	**INSTITUTIONAL COMPLEMENTARY** (VIABLE DISTINCTIVE GOVERNANCE SYSTEMS)
	ACCOUNTABILITY/ WEAK RESPONSIBILITY	REPRESENTATION/ STRONG RESPONSIBILITY

(CONVERGENCE — vertical axis label)

Fig. 1.7 Corporate governance convergence: Alternative directions
Source: Bratton and McCahery (1999, p. 242)

Bratton and McCahery (1999, p. 242) recognized four possible outcomes from the present pressures to converge, and the resilient institutional resistance encountered:

1. a *unitary system* as there is strong convergence towards a global system which assembles the best elements of both major governance systems and combines them together (the least likely alternative);
2. a *universal market based system* as anticipated by the Chicago School of financial economists, representing the triumph of the rules based outsider system;
3. an *improved variety of governance systems* in which there is weak convergence, but some learning from each other between the different national systems;
4. a set of *viable distinctive governance systems,* based on distinctive institutional complementarity each having a unique identity and capability.

Contrary to all of the predictions of an early and complete convergence of corporate governance systems, the final two alternatives are the closest to the present state of play, and are likely to be for some time to come, as this differentiated system has a proven robustness and usefulness (Fig. 1.7).

It is likely the campaign to raise standards of corporate governance will continue for some time in all jurisdictions of the world. There will be a strenuous effort to secure commitment to the essential basis of trust identified by the OECD as fairness, transparency, accountability, and responsibility. However this will occur in countries with different cultures, legal systems, and economic priorities. To assume that all countries will adapt to the same corporate governance structures is unrealistic. It is likely that fundamental features of the European and Asian approaches to corporate governance will be maintained, even where the apparatus of market-based corporate governance are formally adopted. Often these differences will be perceived as part of the cultural integrity and economic dynamism of the economy in question. At the same time countries will adopt the important universal principles such as international accounting standards, but within a culturally diverse set of corporate structures. This is part of the evolving and dynamic complexity of corporate life, in which both convergence and divergence can occur simultaneously. As pressures to conform to international standards and expectations increase, the resilience of historical and cultural differences will continue. The business case for diversity is, if anything, even more compelling. There will be a continual need to innovate around new technologies, processes and markets. This will stimulate new organisational and corporate forms, the shape and objectives of which will be hard to predetermine.

References

Aguilera, R., and G. Jackson. 2003. The cross-national diversity of corporate governance: Dimensions and determinants. *Academy of Management Review* 28: 447–465.

Bebchuck, L.A., and M.J. Roe. 1999. A theory of path dependence in corporate ownership and governance. *Stanford Law Review* 52: 127–170.

Berglöf, E., and E.-L. von Thadden. 1999. The changing corporate governance paradigm: Implications for transitions and developing countries. Working Paper 263, William Davidson Institute, University of Michigan.

Branson, D. 2001. The very uncertain prospects of "global" convergence in corporate governance. *Cornell International Law Journal* 34: 321–362.

Bratton, W., and J. McCahery. 1999. Comparative corporate governance and the theory of the firm: The case against global cross references. *Columbia Journal of Transnational Law* 38: 213–297.

Clarke, T. 2007. *International corporate governance: A comparative approach*. London: Routledge.

Coffee, J. 2001. The rise of dispersed ownership: The roles of law and the state in the separation of ownership and control. *Yale Law Journal* 111: 1–82.

Committee on Capital Markets Regulation (CCMR). 2006. *Interim report of the committee on capital markets regulation*, US Committee on Capital Markets Regulation.

Deeg, R., and G. Jackson. 2006. Towards a more dynamic theory of capitalist variety. Research Paper No. 40, Department of Management, King's College London.

Denis, D., and A. Sarin. 1999. Ownership and board structures in publicly traded corporations. *Journal of Financial Economics* 52: 187–223.

Dore, R. 2000. *Stock market capitalism: Welfare capitalism: Japan and Germany versus the Anglo-Saxons*. New York, NY: Oxford University Press.

European Commission. 2005. *The EU economy: 2005 review: Rising international economic integration. Opportunities and challenges*. Brussels: European Commission.

Fligstein, N., and R. Freeland. 1995. Theoretical and comparative perspectives on corporate organization. *Annual Review of Sociology* 21: 21–43.

Fukuyama, F. 1996. *Trust*. New York, NY: Free Press.

Gordon, J.N., and M.J. Roe. 2004. *Convergence and persistence in corporate governance*. Cambridge: Cambridge University Press.

Gunter, B.G., and R. van der Hoeven. 2004. The social dimension of globalization: A review of the literature. Working Paper No. 24, World Commission on the Social Dimension of Globalization, Geneva: International Labour Office.

Hall, P.A., and D. Soskice. 2001. An introduction to varieties of capitalism. In *Varieties of capitalism: The institutional foundations of comparative advantage*, ed. P.A. Hall and D. Soskice, 1–70. New York, NY: Oxford University Press.

Hamilton, D.S., and J.P. Quinlan. 2005. *Deep integration: How transatlantic markets are leading globalization*. Brussels: Centre for European Policy Studies.

Hansmann, H., and R. Kraakman. 2001. The end of history for corporate law. *Georgetown Law Journal* 89: 439–468.

Hofstede, G. 2004. Business goals and corporate governance. *Asian Pacific Business Review* 10: 292–301.

Holderness, C., R. Kroszner, and D.P. Sheehan. 1999. Were the good old days that good? Changes in managerial stock ownership since the great depression. *Journal of Finance* 54: 435–469.

Hollingsworth, J.R., and R. Boyer. 1997. *Contemporary capitalism: The embeddedness of institutions*. Cambridge, NY: Cambridge University Press.

Jacoby, S. 2001. Corporate governance in comparative perspective: Prospects for convergence. *Comparative Labor Law and Policy Journal* 22: 5–28.

La Porta, R., F. Lopez-de-Silanes, A. Shleifer, and R. Vishny. 1998. Law and finance. *Journal of Political Economy* 106: 1113–1155.

La Porta, R., F. Lopez-de-Silanes, and A. Shleifer. 1999. Corporate ownership around the world. *Journal of Finance* 54: 471–517.

La Porta, R., F. Lopez-de-Silanes, A. Shleifer, and R. Vishny. 2000. Investor protection and corporate governance. *Journal of Financial Economics* 58: 3–27.

La Porta, R., F. Lopez-de-Silanes, A. Shleifer, and R. Vishny. 2002. Investor protection and corporate valuation. *Journal of Finance* 57: 1147–1170.

Lazonick, W. 1992. Controlling the market for corporate control: The historical significance of managerial capitalism. *Industrial and Corporate Change* 1: 445–488.

Licht, A.N. 2001. The mother of all path dependencies: Toward a cross-cultural theory of corporate governance systems. *Delaware Journal of Corporate Law* 26: 147–205.

Licht, A.N. 2003. The maximands of corporate governance: A theory of values and cognitive style. Law Working Paper No. 16, European Corporate Governance Institute (ECGI).

Licht, A.N., C. Goldschmidt, and S.H. Schwartz. 2001. Culture, law, and finance: Cultural dimensions of corporate governance laws. Working Paper, Law and Economics Workshop, University of California, Berkeley.

Maher, M., and T. Andersson. 2000. Corporate governance: Effects on firm performance and economic growth. In *Convergence and diversity of corporate governance regimes and capital markets*, ed. L. Renneboog, J. McCahery, P. Moerland, and T. Raaijmakers, 386–418. Oxford: Oxford University Press.

McCahery, J.A., P. Moerland, T. Raaijmakers, and L. Renneboog. 2002. *Corporate governance regimes: Convergence and diversity*. Oxford: Oxford University Press.

McDonnell, B.H. 2002. Convergence in corporate governance – Possible, but not desirable. *Villanova Law Review* 47: 341–386.

Mehran, H. 1995. Executive compensation structure, ownership and firm performance. *Journal of Financial Economics* 38: 163–184.

OECD. 1998. *Corporate governance: Improving competitiveness and access to capital in global markets*. Paris: OECD.

Pinto, A.R. 2005. Globalization and the study of comparative corporate governance. *Wisconsin International Law Journal* 23: 477–504.

Rajan, R., and L. Zingales. 2003. The great reversals: The politics of financial development in the twentieth century. *Journal of Financial Economics* 69: 5–50.

Roe, M. 1994. *Stong managers, weak owners: The political roots of American corporate finance*. Princeton, NJ: Princeton University Press.

Roe, M. 2003. *Political determinants of corporate governance*. New York, NY: Oxford University Press.

Thomsen, S. 2003. The convergence of corporate governance systems to European and Anglo-American standards. *European Business Organization Law Review* 4: 31–50.

Thomsen, S. 2004. Convergence of corporate governance during the stock market bubble: Towards Anglo-American or European standards? In *Corporate governance and firm organization: Microfoundations and structural forms*, ed. A. Grandori, 297–317. Oxford: Oxford University Press.

Tricker, R.I. 1994. *International corporate governance*. Singapore: Prentice Hall.

Whitley, R. 1999. *Divergent capitalisms: The social structuring and change of business systems*. New York, NY: Oxford University Press.

World Federation of Exchanges. 2005. Annual Report and Statistics 2005, WFE.

World Federation of Exchanges. 2007. Annual Report and Statistics 2007, WFE.

Young, R. 1997. Restructuring Europe: An investor's view. In *Corporate restructuring in Britain and Germany*, ed. G. Owen and A. Richter, 41–57, London: Anglo-German Foundation Report.

Chapter 2
Regulation Complexity and the Costs of Governance

Steen Thomsen

Contents

S. Thomsen (✉)
Professor, Department of International Economics and Management, Copenhagen Business
School, Copenhagen, Denmark; Director, Center for Corporate Governance, Copenhagen Business
School, Copenhagen, Denmark
e-mail: st.int@cbs.dk

A. Brink (ed.), *Corporate Governance and Business Ethics*, Ethical Economy.
Studies in Economic Ethics and Philosophy 39, DOI 10.1007/978-94-007-1588-2_2,
© Springer Science+Business Media B.V. 2011

Complex Regulation

Regulation may be more or less complex.[1] Intuitively complexity is costly, but the costs of complexity are difficult to understand using standard economic theory which assumes rational agents and zero information costs. Recognizing the existence of information costs seems to be a step ahead, but is not very helpful unless we can understand what information costs are and what determines them.

Unfortunately, mathematical information theory does not seem very useful in this respect. A logical theorem may be very simple to a computer, but complicated to human beings. A detailed piece of legislation may contain many pages, but be very easy to deal with because it specifies exactly what you have to do. Nor do information costs appear to capture all costs of complexity. It may be relatively easy to read and understand a piece of legislation, but difficult to implement the rules if they are to be applied to many different activities in different ways. The costs of enforcement, decision making, implementation and monitoring could all increase with complexity. Moreover, information problems can interact with incentive problems, for example if many different parties have to cooperate to comply with a piece of legislation.

Some of this is captured by transaction costs economics (cf. Williamson 2005), which has however tended to focus on analysing other issues related to dependence (asset specificity) in recent years. The concept of "bounded rationality" (cf. Simon 1955), which transaction cost theory has adopted, appears to be closely related to complexity. But even bounded rationality is not very helpful if we do not understand *how* rationality is bounded. To do so we probably have to draw on psychology which is exactly what is attempted in behavioural economics (cf. Kahneman 2003).

In this paper I therefore examine the psychological origins of regulation complexity. As a test case – to avoid blackboard or armchair economics – I use the regulation of corporate governance which – I argue – has become highly complex in recent years with the Sarbanes Oxley Act, corporate governance codes, self reporting and other regulation. The US Committee on Capital Markets Regulation has recently concluded that regulation has seriously damaged the competitiveness of US capital markets (cf. Committee on Capital Markets Regulation 2006).

I go on to examine the economics and psychology of complexity. Reviewing relevant research in psychology I find that complexity introduces error in perception, memory, cognition and learning depending on personality, emotional and social context. I identify alternative strategies to deal with complex regulation including non-compliance and avoidance, but find that they are all costly.

There are many straightforward implications. Laws should be simple and intuitive. They should rely on an underlying logic (principles) which people can understand. Self regulation (e.g., codes of best practice) is less costly than top-down legislation. Complex regulations should preferably be handled by professionals (lawyers, auditors, tax advisors, companies and organizations) rather than ordinary citizens.

---

[1] This paper has benefited from comments by Igor Filatotchev, Gunnar Eliasson and participants at a workshop on "The Economics of the Modern Firm", Jönköping September 2007.

The Sarbanes-Oxley Act as an Example

On 30 July 2002 the Sarbanes-Oxley Act (Public Company Accounting Reform and Investor Protection Act of 2002 abbreviated as SOX) was approved by the US Congress by a vote of 423-3 and by the Senate 99-0. In signing it into law President George W. Bush stated that it included "the most far-reaching reforms of American business practices since the time of Franklin D. Roosevelt" (Bumiller 2002). The act contains 11 sections including provision on the following issues:

- disclosure of mandatory "control of controls systems" related to financial reporting, which must be attested by independent auditors (section 404);
- financial reports to be signed by chief executive officers and chief financial officers (section 302);
- rules on auditor independence (term limits for leading auditor, prohibition against combining consulting and auditing etc);
- creation of a Public Company Accounting Oversight Board (PCAOB), a semi-private institution, which is to supervise the auditing profession;
- mandatory independent audit committees to oversee the relationship between the company and its auditor;
- ban on personal loans to any executive officer or director;
- accelerated reporting of insider trading;
- prohibition on insider trades during pension fund blackout periods;
- significantly increased criminal and civil penalties for violations of securities law;
- protection of whistleblowers who leak information to the public.

The direct costs are considerable. A survey of the 224 largest public firms in the USA by Financial Executives International with regard to the direct costs of complying with Section 404 of the Sarbanes-Oxley Act estimates that the average first-year cost is almost $3 million for 26,000 h of internal work and 5,000 h of external work, plus additional audit fees of $823,200, or an increase of 53% (cf. Zhang 2005). Although the direct cost tend to decrease over time, compliance costs still average $3 million per company and amount to 2–3% of revenues for small companies (cf. The Economist, 21 May 2005). 2–3% is comparable to profit rates in many companies.

These direct cost estimates do not include opportunity costs of time or behavioural effects, for example the uncertain effects of having managers sign off on their responsibilities down the organization or the opportunity costs of top management time spent on auditing and control issues. At the same time other regulatory changes – like corporate governance codes from both NYSE and NASDQ – have contributed with more regulation. Some commentators argue that the administrative costs of these initiatives have spurred delistings from American exchanges (cf. Block 2004; Engel et al. 2005; Marosi and Massoud 2007; Kamar et al. 2006; Leuz et al. 2008) and have led international companies to list elsewhere, e.g., in London. The report issued 30 November 2006 by the Committee on Capital Markets Regulation concluded that US capital markets are loosing competitiveness and that regulation costs play a leading role in this shift (cf. Hubbard 2007; Hubbard and

Thornton 2006a, 2006b; Committee on Capital Markets Regulation 2006). The complexity of regulation is no doubt further increased by the new US enforcement regime, which delegates extensive power to the Securities and Exchange Commission (SEC) and the PCAOB to engage in a specific dialogue with companies which – in the eyes of the regulator – do not to comply with the law.

In sum, Sarbanes-Oxley is a complex contribution to a field of practice which is already extensively regulated by company law and best practice codes.

Although Europe has not been subject to the rigors of Sarbanes-Oxley, she has also had her fill of regulation. There are new EU directives on transparency (2004), prospectuses (2003), transparency, market abuse (2003), takeovers (2004), financial instruments (2004). Moreover, all European countries have now adopted corporate governance codes on a comply or explain basis.

Much of the new corporate governance regulation can be regarded as "second generation" in the sense that it deals not just with control of executives (1st generation regulation) but with control of control (which I will here define as 2nd generation): Auditors are to control internal control procedures which are designed to control the executives. The PCAOB – and audit committees – are to control the auditors who exercise control over the executive through the annual report. Boards who control the executives are to be more accountable to shareholders. Strangely, the same institutions which are believed to have failed in a number of instances – auditors, boards, shareholders – now assume an even greater role in corporate governance. When the control did not work – or rather were claimed not to work – the response was to control the controls – and perhaps third generation controls are not a long way off. It seems inevitable, however, that such elaborate control systems will be more complex and that this will be costly.

As a result corporate decision makers are faced with the complexity of thousands of lines of interrelated codes applied to many different actors and enforced by several different government agencies. Moreover, it is highly likely that the intensity of regulation has increased over the past decade. This motivates the following discussion of regulation costs from the viewpoint of economics and psychology.

Following Adam Smith (writing on taxes), I identify the costs of regulation complexity with "vexation costs", a subspecies of transaction costs:

> [B]y subjecting the people to the frequent visits and the odious examination of the tax-gatherers, it may expose them to much unnecessary trouble, vexation, and oppression; (...) and though vexation is not, strictly speaking, expense, it is certainly equivalent to the expense at which every man would be willing to redeem himself from it. (Smith 1776/1981, Book Five, Chapter II, Part II, Section IV)

The Economics of Regulation Complexity

Following Louis Kaplow (1995) the complexity of regulation is defined by the number and difficulty of the distinctions which the rules make. Difficulty is the effort required to understand the rules. Difficulty is magnified by generality of application, ambiguities and inconsistencies. A complex law regulates many different activities in several different ways based on several different criteria. The volume of code may be an indicator, but not necessarily so, since very detailed provisions may actually make it easier for individual decision makers to find out how they are affected (cf. Ehrlich and Posner 1974).

The costs of complexity consist of

- legislation costs: resources spent on making law (including influence costs);
- information acquisition costs: time spent on verification and interpretation of the rule (including expenditure on advisors);
- decision costs: resources spent on analysis of the consequences;
- private compliance costs (implementation costs);
- public compliance costs: costs of enforcement by government agencies and courts.

In standard neoclassical economics the costs of complexity are simply ignored. Infinitely rational decision makers instantly understand new regulation and adapt efficiently to it. The implicit assumption seems to be that complexity costs are small compared to production costs. This would be the case if the CEO of a large firm had to read a piece of paper and then make marginal adjustments in company operations. Whether it takes 2 or 4 h to read might not be very important compared to the magnitude of the necessary changes (e.g., closing a factory).

At the other extreme, in evolutionary economics (cf. Nelson and Winter 1982), complexity costs are implicitly assumed to be so high that economic agents do not make decisions, but adapt to new rules by trial, error and imitation until new, viable routines are found. We can imagine the regulator or the competition closing down firms which do not comply with the new rules, or alternatively that firms randomly suggest changes in behaviour, until the regulator approves. Here the adaptation is very costly for complex regulation, because it takes time, and because many errors are necessary to ensure compliance. At the extreme a large number of firms which do not comply will have to go out of business.

An intermediate position is found in transaction cost economics which assumes that human actors are boundedly rational (cf. Williamson 2005). Decision making capacity is therefore a scarce resource. It will take time to comply with complex, new legislation. Organizational change will not happen because the CEO writes a memo, it will involve lots of delegation, information loss and incentive problems (cf. Williamson 1985). In earlier versions of transaction costs economics (cf. Williamson 1975) complexity along with uncertainty was considered a key determinant of transaction costs. To the extent that complexity makes agents uncertain about relevant decision parameters the two concepts coincide.

Barzel (1982) draws attention to another source of transaction costs: measurement costs, which he attributes primarily to physical product characteristics (for example it is difficult to verify how an orange tastes until after you have peeled it). Verifiability is a parallel in financial contracting (cf. Hart 2001). Measurement costs will increase in the variability of product characteristics. In this language, regulation complexity might be captured by the variability of economic consequences for the individual firms as well as ambiguity with regard to interpretation and enforcement.

Following this approach, one would imagine that the complexity of regulation would be a function of complexity of goals. For example, legislation based on compromise between several political parties might be more complex or even inconsistent. The same will be the case if there are many bureaucratic offices involved in the genesis and enforcement of a law (for example federal and state organizations as well as judges who may disagree about interpretation). Regulation complexity may also be enhanced by rent seeking (cf. Schuck 1992). Politicians, bureaucrats, lawyers and auditors will often benefit from more detailed regulation which can increase their revenue and social importance.

The Psychology of Regulation Complexity

Introspection and Common Sense

Intuitively – starting with introspection in the spirit of James (1890)[2] – an increase in complexity increases the costs of individual decision makers. First, a complex problem takes more time to solve. Secondly, there is a psychic disutility to complexity – a feeling of stress, powerlessness and anxiety, which will be known to people who try to fill in their tax forms or get computer software to work.

To be sure, there are counterexamples. Some people appear to enjoy working on complex problems in mathematics, Soduku, crosswords or even computer programming. Scientific problems appear to be more attractive to scientists, the more complex they are. In general, however, society would tend to look at complexity lovers as a special kind whose preferences are not widely shared. Furthermore, what is regarded as complex would typically depend on your abilities and what you know. A lawyer would find it impossibly complex to solve an equation while a mathematician might find it difficult to understand tax law.

A similar hypothesis is that complexity is related to learning. A new problem area will seem more complex. What is complex to 6th graders might not be complex to 7th graders. Again, however, people seem to be different. Some appear to like to learn, they are curious and delight in variety and new things to learn. Personality could be a very important determinant of the costs of complexity.

There are several additional elements to the computer and tax frustrations described above.

- The problems are not voluntary, they are obstacles, which block other more desired activities – like going to football match that Sunday afternoon or getting on with your job. Clearly motivation is very important.
- Moreover, there is a time pressure. It's late. You become tired and your frustrations increase. You are alone at the office and have no one to ask for help.

---

[2] "Introspective observation is what we have to rely on first and foremost and always" (James 1890, p. 185).

- Third, there is a feeling that the problems are arbitrary and trivial. They could easily have been avoided if the programming had been a little better, or if the explanation in the manual had been a little better. Compare this to a scientific problem, the solution to which could bring you everlasting glory and the joy of understanding something fundamental.

- In addition, some people get angry at being subjected to authority. This feeling may be worse when filling out your tax forms than in computer frustrations, where you have the feeling that you might choose not to work with this software. This implies that the costs of complexity are higher if you have less control of the situation.

- The frustration is compounded by your suspicion that learning to solve this problem may not be very useful in the future. The next version of the software or the new tax rules will most likely annihilate the value of your time investment. The costs of complexity are easier to bear if they are believed to be transitory.

- You feel that you should have been able to solve the problem easily, and the longer you work with it, the more frustrated you get at not be able to find the solution. You are reminded of your own lack of success with similar problems in the past, and your self-confidence drops ("this is typical"). You start to make and recall attributions (I am no good with computers), which makes your feel even worse. Your self-efficacy beliefs suffer.

- You are bothered by guilt that you did not prepare well enough. Why does it always have to be the last Sunday before the deadline? Why did I not get my papers ready in time? Why did I not read the manual? Irrational behaviour of this kind is an example of time inconsistent preferences (cf. Rabin 1998, p. 39), which make us postpone unpleasant tasks.

- Many people just give up. After repeated bad experiences and frustrations of not being able to understand, they do not do their tax forms. They are in a condition of learned helplessness which occurs in learning experiments where you punish dogs with random electro shocks. After a while, they give up, loose initiative and become completely passive.

- Since these problems appear to be generic, one may wonder whether they are completely unintentional. Passivity may be in the interest of tax authorities which then effectively get to fill in the tax forms and get fewer complaints. The status of bureaucrats and computer assistants are heightened by the feeling of inferiority and guilt and the corresponding gratitude at getting help. This seems to fit with sociological theories of bureaucracy (cf. Crozier 1964).

- Your irritation will probably be greater if you do not sympathize with the perceived cause of your trouble. For example, you may be extra annoyed at Microsoft if you have leftist sympathies and extra annoyed at your tax accounting if you are conservative and believe that taxes should be cut.

- Finally, and perhaps most importantly, you make mistakes. You press the wrong button and delete files, you do not get the deductions you are entitled to, or you get fined. These mistakes are costly.

In the following I examine the foundations for these conjectures in psychological science.

Perception and Complexity

As emphasized by Kahneman (2003) the borderline between perception and cognition is fuzzy. A substantial body of theory and evidence indicates that people tend to perceive patterns (cf. Bruner and Postman 1949; Gregory 1974; Gibson 1950). Moreover, there is a tendency to prefer certain patterns over others. Gestalt theories (cf. Ehrenfels 1890/1988) came to argue that people prefer relatively simple and symmetrical figures (good gestalts) to more messy and complicated ones. Some of this – like the perception of distance, speed and colour – appears to genetically hard-wired into human nature. If rules and regulation are not simple, logical and internally consistent, it will be more costly to perceive them correctly. To a very large extent we tend to use cues and distinctive features to fit sense impressions into templates and it may be difficult to perceive impressions which do not match the template (for example to find spelling mistakes in your own manuscripts). It will be more costly for us to correctly perceive information which is not stored in templates – for example it difficult to comprehend a random table of allowable tax deductions for depreciation of assets, but it may be easier to perceive a simple rule or formula.

Memory and Complexity

Memory research also stresses the importance of simplicity, coherence and consistency. It is much easier to remember stories or pictures than isolated pieces of information. Isolated bits of information are known to be subject to significant memory loss (cf. Ebbinghaus 1885/1913), while stories and pictures loose details and may be distorted and there is a tendency to fit them into preconceived schemas (cf. Bartlett 1932). As a result, complex regulation runs a greater risk of distortion of meaning and focus, while aspects of it which are difficult to understand will tend to be forgotten.

Cognition and Complexity

Cognitive psychology indicates that complex information will typically be more time consuming and costly to process. Kahneman (2003) describes reason as slow and effortful compared to intuition which is fast and effortless. Moreover, complex information is more likely to give cognitive biases in interpretation (cf., e.g., Kahneman and Tversky 1979; Rabin 1998). For example, Tversky and Kahneman (1986) document systematic mistakes for a complex decision problem. Cognitive bias includes the tendency to seek confirmation for preconceived ideas, to base interpretation on more or less irrelevant contextual benchmarks (anchoring, framing) and to place too much emphasis on particular cases. For example, the status quo bias would imply that new regulation will be evaluated relative to the present situation, and that any losses will seem large relative to advantages (cf. Kahneman and Tversky 1979).

One reason is that people tend to rely on heuristics as a means to reduce complexity when they are faced with complex problems. While heuristics can be useful they tend to lead to "severe and systematic errors" (Kahneman 2003, p. 1460). Recent research on this question suggests that people tend to focus on a salient attribute of the specific problem and then to substitute that attribute with a heuristic attribute – a prototype, which comes readily to mind (cf. Kahneman 2003; Kahneman and Frederick 2002). If nothing else, the heuristic can be affective, so that for example the evaluation of costs is decided intuitively on the basis of like or dislike. Reason may interfere and correct gut feeling, but the cognitive effort commonly spent on ex post rationalization will obviously not improve decision making. Nor is it true that the decision quality will necessarily improve when decisions have significant economic consequences (cf. Camerer and Hogarth 1999).

Finally, decision quality – and the cost of complexity – will be lower under time pressure and when people are involved in other cognitive tasks (cf. Kahneman and Frederick 2002). This may also apply when business companies in intense competition are subjected to complex regulatory shocks.

Personality and Complexity

The definition of complexity will depend on personality. Gardner (1983) proposed that there are multiple types of intelligence. Depending on the type of regulation in question the level of complexity can seem greater to less linguistically or mathematically intelligent people, although they may be intelligent in other ways (interpersonal or emotional intelligence). There is a fit here with Carl Jung's theory of rational versus emotional personalities. Related research would tend to indicate that the costs of handling complexity are higher among authoritarian personalities (cf. Adorno et al. 1950) and stressed people (cf. Friedman and Rosenman 1959).

This suggests the possibility of a division of labour in which complexity seekers (or alternatively people less adverse to complexity) offer their services to the rest of the population as specialists (tax consultants, computer assistants, lawyers, accountants and mathematicians). However, if the decision problems are complex (and predictability is low), even highly educated experts will continue to make mistakes and may even make more mistakes because of overconfidence (cf. Rabin 1998, p. 31). Nevertheless, people's approach to complexity is probably to some extent changeable. For example, the original definition of intelligence was to regard intelligence as sensitive to schooling (cf. Binet and Simon 1904). Moreover, the capacity to handle complex problem will to some extent depend on other personality factors like self confidence (self efficacy beliefs) which can be influenced by social learning (cf. Bandura 1977). The ability to learn indicates that the costs of complexity would be higher in the short run than in the long run (see below), but as it turns out, effective learning is less likely if the decision problem is highly complex.

Emotions and Complexity

Emotions probably matter a great deal to the psychic costs of complexity, which can give rise to stress, anger and anxiety. The costs of voluntary complexity – as in chess games played voluntarily – are far lower than costs of complexity imposed from the outside. In work situations people with an internal locus of control (who feel that they are in control of the situation) are less likely to become stressed (cf. Rotter 1966). The reaction to complexity also appears to be sensitive to attributions, i.e., how people assign causality to the difficulties encountered (cf. Abramson et al. 1978). If they believe that the situation is permanent and attributable to their own incapacity, they will become more stressed, than if the problems are seen as transitory. It is also possible that complexity can trigger more irrational reactions like denial (cf. Freud 1937).

Motivation and Complexity

Unsurprisingly, motivated individuals appear to handle complexity better (cf. Bandura 1977). If the problems become too complex and if the sanctions are very severe so that that people perceive them as random, they may learn passivity (learned helplessness) like dogs when subjected to random electroshocks (cf. Seligman and Maier 1967) or college students who were "taught" to be less good puzzles solvers if asked to solve unsolvable puzzles. Subsequent research indicates that this de-motivation effect is highly contingent on attributions (cf. Abramson et al. 1978). People with high self-efficacy beliefs tend to have higher ambition levels, to be more persistent in problem solving, to feel more in control and to be less stressed by complex decision problems.

Social Effects and Complexity

More generally, the psychic costs of complexity will be sensitive to social interpretation effects (cf. Moscovici 1984). If a new piece of legislation is regarded as having a good purpose and is well received by opinion leaders or peer groups, individuals may react less negatively to it. This may for example be the case if new environmental standards are believed to have a positive effect on the environment. But herd behaviour may also lead to inadequate or dysfunctional responses to new challenges (cf. Trotter 1919).

Festinger (1957) argues that people prefer to have similar attitudes to a subject and to reduce the cognitive dissonance of unbalanced attitudes. In more extreme instances business elites can become subject to groupthink, where information from the outside world is systematically discarded (cf. Janis 1972). This is a big risk for regulation which aims to change decision processes, but may be received cynically and adopted as a legal formality only.

Learning to Deal with Complexity

It seems plausible that that complexity costs can be reduced over time by learning. However, learning complex behaviour by positive reinforcement (cf. Watson 1903; Skinner 1938) will take more time. The seemingly uncertain rewards involved will create anxiety, and negative rewards (punishment) work badly because the behaviour desired by regulators comes to be associated with negative emotions. Moreover, learning tends to be more effective if you are interested in learning (getting to know your computer) than if you are only interested in performance (cf. Ames 1992), which is unfortunately more realistic for coping with complex legislation. And what you learn is influenced by social mechanisms for example by imitation of role models (cf. Bandura and Walters 1963), which may or may not be in accordance with the intentions of the regulators. Moreover, as people who experience the same frustrations at filling out the tax forms year after year will testify, some people never learn. Psychological research indicates that people continue to make mistakes, and for very complex problems experts may learn slower because they are overly self confident (cf. Rabin 1998, p. 31). In fact, when people are misled by stochastic feedback, misunderstandings and spurious correlations may reinforce superstition rather than learning so that "superstitious learning" takes place (cf. Skinner 1938). Levinthal and March (1993) emphasize some limitations of organizational learning.

Combining Economics and Psychology

In summary, complexity is costly. For most people most of the time there is a direct psychic cost of dealing rationally with complexity. Secondly, it takes longer time to adapt to complex rules. Third, complexity increases the probability of costly mistakes to a near certainty. However, boundedly rational human actors can economize on these costs in numerous ways, and corporations, which have more resources at their disposal, have an even wider choice of strategic options at their disposal.

Non-compliance

Companies can ignore the complexity and continue as they used to. If enforcement and penalties (direct and indirect) are weak, this will often be a cost efficient response for the regulated. For more serious offences this will often be too costly, but despite of this a non-trivial share of the population will usually decide not to comply. Non-compliance may be naïve, but it may also be disguised by deliberate camouflage. For example, top managers may make a formal decision to comply without providing the resources necessary to comply down in the organization and then letting middle managers or other scapegoats take the blame. From the viewpoint of the regulator, this is obviously costly because camouflage is a waste of resources, because more resources will have to be invested in enforcement and because alternative, less complex regulation would perhaps be more cost-effective.

Nevertheless it would probably be an exaggeration to assume that non-compliance is generally the result of a cost-benefit analysis. Non-compliance may equally well be the result of psychological pathologies like denial or learned helplessness.

Rule Adoption

If companies decide to go by the book, this will be costly, because complex learning takes time and effort. They may reduce these costs by *imitation* of routines adopted by other companies, which will save on development costs, but involves a risk that the borrowed routine will not be a good fit with the company. Alternatively, they may outsource problem solving to *advisors* – auditors, lawyers etc. who specialize in dealing with regulation complexity. Professional advisors can play an important role in the diffusion of legitimate, standardised solutions to complex problems.

Again, rule adoption may represent other forces than cost-benefit analysis. Herding – in the sense that all firms adopt the same standards – involves some insurance since it does not affect the competitive situation, if companies are similar. The costs of rule adoption include both disutility, advisor fees, opportunity costs of time and effort and the costs of imposing uniform, one-size-fits-all standards on company behaviour (e.g., board work). In the case of corporate governance regulation there are many examples of firms which adopt rules and standards that are not fitted to their situations. Family firms – for example – often adopt board structures (e.g., independent boards and audit committees), which are intended as a solution to the separation of ownership and control (which is less relevant in family businesses).

Exit and Relocation

Sometimes it is possible to escape regulation by relocation or exit. Plants subject to complex environmental regulation may be closed down or moved to other countries. The same kind of regulation arbitrage may be possible, if there are different regulation regimes within countries, for example listed companies may decide to go private. Obviously, these strategies are also costly. For example, there are private and social costs of closing down production, and firms going private miss the benefits of risk diversification. Exit and relocation strategies have been widely used in the US following Sarbanes-Oxley. Many listed firms have chosen to go private, and fewer foreign firms have their shares listed in the US (cf. Hubbard 2007). Schuck (1992) points to examples where the concerned parties choose to contract around legal complexity, for example when farmers in Shasta County California choose to resolve their disputes outside the law (cf. Ellickson 1991). Private equity funds financed by institutional investors outside the stock exchanges appear to be doing the same.

Strategizing

To some extent firms can influence regulation complexity by rent seeking. While regulators (politicians and bureaucrats) may benefit from complexity for example to extract favours, companies as a group should have a clear direct interest in lower complexity and deregulation. However, it is not self- evident that rent seekers will always lobby for low complexity. Since companies differ in terms of their ability to handle administrative complexity (for example large firms have more resources than small firms), it seems possible that some large firms can benefit relatively speaking from more complex regulation. This applies particularly to rules and regulations which are already in effect. Moreover, advisors will generally have a vested interest in more complex regulation which means more business for them. While lobbying for greater regulation complexity may be privately optimal, it is clearly very costly to society.

In summary, there are large costs of regulation complexity. Firms may react to these costs in various ways, but none of these are free. In addition to the (costly) obedient compliance presumably desired by regulators, firms can adopt a range of other (undesired) strategies like exit and relocation, rent seeking and non-compliance.

What Is Wrong with Sarbanes-Oxley?

We can now return to SOX to re-examine the costs of this particular piece of legislation.

- Complexity of content: First of all, SOX is by any standards a complex piece of legislation. It covers many different aspects of company behaviour from auditing to analysis to internal bookkeeping to insider trading rules to board structure. It is unquestionable that bundling so many initiatives in one law made it a very complex piece of legislation. Arguably, learning makes it possible to adjust efficiently to partial legal changes, but implementing a set of changes enacted as the same time will be much more costly.
- Complexity of enforcement: The creation of a new enforcement agency – the PCAOB – with a strange semi-private status and an unclear division of labour with the Securities and Exchange Commission increased the ambiguity. The

PACOB is entitled to pursue any functions which it deems necessary to promote high professional standards.

- External Control: SOX was enacted top down contrary to the US common law tradition and despite protests from business leaders. It was enacted under perceived time pressure (stock prices were falling). A series of laws with time for discussion would no doubt have given business more time to adjust and met with less resistance. It is interesting to compare this with UK corporate governance, which has to a large extent relied on marginal changes in the best practice corporate governance codes, which are written by businessmen and adopted on a more voluntary comply-or-explain basis. After the Maxwell or the BCCI scandal which prompted UK corporate governance codes, there have been remarkably few financial scandals in British business.
- Unclear legitimacy: The rationale was unclear and disputed from day 1. More than anything else falling stock prices were the aftermath of the internet bubble. Symbolically the law was very much directed at Enron and Arthur, which had already been severely punished by bankruptcy. Despite a relatively simple – easily communicable – storyline in the Enron Anderson story, the law went well beyond prohibiting Enron-type practices by introducing sections 302 and 404, which address problems related to the internal consistency of accounting which has very little to do with the top-level fraud in Enron. The easiest solution to avoiding collusion between companies and their auditors – requiring companies to change their auditing firm at regular intervals – was avoided, perhaps due to lobbying from the auditing profession.
- Non-experts: SOX involved many different people so that implementation could not be left to complexity-loving experts. For example section 302 had branch managers all the way down testify that their accounting was correct accordingly to certain vaguely defined and imperfectly understood standards. US managers responded to section 302 by requiring their lower level managers to sign off all the way down the organization, and this may have been as an unintended response to the law.
- High penalties: The penalties for non-compliance were severe – up to 10 years in prison, which is more severe than sentences for manslaughter. Moreover, the law was religiously enforced. Understandably, this combination of ambiguity and severity created widespread anxiety.

Policy Recommendations

It is relatively easy to provide naïve policy implications. Less regulation is less costly. Whatever regulation there is should be simple. It should be intuitive so that the regulated can understand it. There should be a well-defined rationale which is communicated to the public and helps create legitimacy for the law. Transparency is preferable, but information overload may reduce transparency. Complexity will be less costly when directed at an audience which can handle it – e.g., the auditing profession (cf. Schuck 1992). All else equal, top-down regulation in the civil law tradition is more costly than bottom up approaches based on self regulation, best practice codes and common law.

Since the costs of complexity are large, it will often be optimal for society to make laws less complex even when there are potential benefits of more detailed rules. Obviously, trade offs can arise when (if) there are significant benefits of complex regulation. But there is almost no chance of optimal regulation if the costs of complexity are ignored.

References

Abramson, L.Y., M.E. Seligman, and J.D. Teasdale. 1978. Learned helplessness in humans: Critique and reformulation. *Journal of Abnormal Psychology* 87: 49–74.

Adorno, T.W., E. Frenkel-Brunswik, D.J. Levinson, and R.N. Sanford. 1950. *The authoritarian personality*. New York, NY: Harper and Row.

Ames, C. 1992. Classrooms: Goals, structures, and student motivation. *Journal of Educational Psychology* 84: 261–271.

Bandura, A. 1977. *Social learning theory*. New York, NY: General Learning Press.

Bandura, A., and R.H. Walters. 1963. *Social learning and personality development*. New York, NY: Holt, Rinehart & Winston.

Bartlett, F.C. 1932. *Remembering: A study in experimental and social psychology*. Cambridge: Cambridge University Press.

Barzel, Y. 1982. Measurement cost and the organization of markets. *Journal of Law and Economics* 25: 27–48.

Binet, A., and T.A. Simon. 1904. Méthodes nouvelles pour le diagnostic du niveau intellectuel des anormaux. *L'Année Psychologique* 11: 191–244.

Block, S. 2004. The latest movement to going private: An empirical study. *Journal of Applied Finance* 14: 36–44.

Bruner, J.S., and L. Postman. 1949. On the perception of incongruity: A paradigm. *Journal of Personality* 18: 206–223.

Bumiller, E. 2002. Bush signs bill aimed at fraud in corporations. *The New York Times*, 31 July 2002: A1.

Camerer, C.F., and R.M. Hogarth. 1999. The effects of financial incentives in experiments: A review and capital-labor-production framework. *Journal of Risk and Uncertainty* 19: 7–42.

Committee on Capital Markets Regulation: Interim Report, November 2006, http://www.capmktsreg.org/pdfs/11.30Committee_Interim_ReportREV2.pdf

Crozier, M. 1964. *The bureaucratic phenomenon*. London: Tavistock.

Ebbinghaus, H. 1913. *Memory. A contribution to experimental psychology*. New York, NY: Teachers College, Columbia University. (Original: 1885. *Über das Gedächtnis. Untersuchungen zur experimentellen Psychologie*. Leipzig: Duncker & Humblot.)

Ehrenfels, C. von. 1988. On "Gestalt Qualities". In *Foundations of gestalt theory*, ed. B. Smith, 82–117. Munich, Vienna: Philosophia. (Original: 1890. Über "Gestaltqualitäten". *Vierteljahrsschrift für wissenschaftliche Philosophie* 14: 242–292.)

Ehrlich, I., and R. Posner. 1974. An economic analysis of legal rulemaking. *Journal of Legal Studies* 3: 257–286.

Ellickson, R.C. 1991. *Order without law: How neighbors settle disputes*. Cambridge, MA: Harvard University Press.

Engel, E., R. Hayes, and X. Wang. 2005. The Sarbanes-Oxley Act and Firms' Going-Private Decisions, Working paper, University of Chicago.

Festinger, L. 1957. *A theory of cognitive dissonance*. Evanston, IL: Row & Perterson.

Freud, A. 1937. *The ego and the mechanisms of defence*. London: Hogarth Press. (= The International Psycho-Analytical Library, No. 30).

Friedman, M., and R.H. Rosenman. 1959. Association of specific overt behavior pattern with blood and cardiovascular findings. *Journal of the American Medical Association* 169: 1286–1296.

Gardner, H. 1983. *Frames of mind: The theory of multiple intelligences*. New York, NY: Basic.

Gibson, J.J. 1950. *The perception of the visual world*. Boston, MA: Houghton Mifflin.

Gregory, R.L. 1974. *Concepts and mechanisms of perception*. London: Duckworth.

Hart, O. 2001. Financial contracting. *Journal of Economic Literature* 34: 1079–1100.

Hubbard, R.G. 2007. An action plan for US capital markets. *International Finance* 10: 91–99.

Hubbard, R.G., and J.L. Thornton. 2006a. Is the U.S. losing ground? *Wall Street Journal – Eastern Edition*, 30 October 2006: A12.

Hubbard, R.G., and J.L. Thornton. 2006b. Action plan for capital markets. *Wall Street Journal – Eastern Edition*, 30 November 2006: A16.

James, W. 1890. *The principles of psychology*. New York, NY: Holt.

Janis, I.L. 1972. *Victims of groupthink*. Boston, MA: Houghton Mifflin.

Kahneman, D. 2003. Maps of bounded rationality: Psychology for behavioral economics. *American Economic Review* 93: 1449–1475.

Kahneman, D., and S. Frederick. 2002. Representativeness revisited: Attribute substitution in intuitive judgment. In *Heuristics and biases: The psychology of intuitive judgment*, ed. T. Gilovich, D. Griffin, and D. Kahneman, 49–81. New York, NY: Cambridge University Press.

Kahneman, D., and A. Tversky. 1979. Prospect theory: An analysis of decision under risk. *Econometrica* 47: 263–292.

Kamar, E., P. Karaca-Mandic, and E. Talley. 2006. Going-private decisions and the Sarbanes-Oxley Act of 2002: A cross-country analysis. Economics and Organization Research Paper No. C06-05, Center in Law, University of Southern California.

Kaplow, L. 1995. A model of the optimal complexity of legal rules. *Journal of Law, Economics, and Organization* 11: 150–163.

Leuz, C., A. Triantis, and T. Wang. 2008. Why do firms go dark? Causes and economic consequences of voluntary SEC deregistrations. *Journal of Accounting and Economics* 45: 181–208.

Levinthal, D.A., and J.G. March. 1993. The myopia of learning. *Strategic Management Journal* 14: 95–112.

Marosi, A., and N. Massoud. 2007. Why do firms go dark? *Journal of Financial and Quantitative Analysis* 42: 421–442.

Moscovici, S. 1984. The phenomenon of social representations. In *Social representations*, ed. R. Farr and S. Moscovici, 3–69. Cambridge, Paris: Cambridge University Press, Editions de la Maison des Sciences de l'Homme.

Nelson, R.R., and S.G. Winter. 1982. *An evolutionary theory of economic change*. Cambridge, MA: Harvard University Press.

Rabin, M. 1998. Psychology and economics. *Journal of Economic Literature* 36: 11–46.

Rotter, J.B. 1966. Generalized expectancies for internal versus external control of reinforcement. *Psychological Monographs* 80: 1–28.

Schuck, P.H. 1992. Legal complexity: Some causes, consequences, and cures. *Duke Law Journal* 42: 1–52.

Seligman, M.E.P., and S.F. Maier. 1967. Failure to escape traumatic shock. *Journal of Experimental Psychology* 74: 1–9.

Simon, H.A. 1955. A behavioral model of rational choice. *Quarterly Journal of Economics* 69: 99–118.

Skinner, B.F. 1938. *The behavior of organisms: An experimental analysis*. New York, NY: Appleton-Century-Crofts.

Smith, A. 1981[1776]. *An inquiry into the nature and causes of the wealth of nations*. Indianapolis, IN: Liberty Classics.

The Economist 2005. Price Worth Paying? Special Report Auditing Sarbanes-Oxley. *The Economist*, 21 May 2005: 71.

Trotter, W. 1919. *Instincts of the herd in peace and war*, 4th impression, with postscript, New York, NY: Macmillan.

Tversky, A., and D. Kahneman. 1986. Rational choice and the framing of decisions. *Journal of Business* 59: S251–S278.

Watson, J.B. 1903. Animal education: An experimental study on the psychical development of the white rat, correlated with the growth of its nervous system. *The University of Chicago Contributions to Philosophy Studies from the Psychological Laboratory* 6: 1–125.

Williamson, O.E. 1975. *Markets and hierarchies: Analysis and antitrust implications. A study in the economics of internal organization*. New York, NY: Free Press.

Williamson, O.E. 1985. *The economic institutions of capitalism: Firms, markets, relational contracting*. New York, NY: Free Press.

Williamson, O.E. 2005. The economics of governance. *American Economic Review* 95: 1–18.

Zhang, I.X. 2005. Economic consequences of the Sarbanes-Oxley Act of 2002, Working Paper, William E. Simon Graduate School of Business Administration, University of Rochester.

Chapter 3
Corporate Governance as an Institution to Overcome Social Dilemmas

Margit Osterloh, Bruno S. Frey, and Hossam Zeitoun

Contents

Introduction

While many governments and companies struggle with the aftermaths of the current financial crisis, commentators in the media and in the academic community are trying to understand how the distortions in the financial system could have gone so far. Based on allocated housing loans, financial experts designed complicated financial instruments that were sold to investors. These financial instruments were often repackaged several times, which made it difficult for investors to estimate the actual value of their investments. A considerable information asymmetry developed between the designers of financial instruments and the ultimate investors. The dangers of this information asymmetry were hardly noticeable as long as the market

M. Osterloh (✉)
Professor of Management Science, Warwick Business School, University of Warwick,
Coventry, United Kingdom; Professor of Management, University of Zurich, Zurich, Switzerland
e-mail: osterloh@iou.uzh.ch

A. Brink (ed.), *Corporate Governance and Business Ethics*, Ethical Economy.
Studies in Economic Ethics and Philosophy 39, DOI 10.1007/978-94-007-1588-2_3,
© Springer Science+Business Media B.V. 2011

for these financial instruments was very liquid due to a long period of rising housing prices. This changed dramatically in summer 2007. A combination of rising interest rates and falling housing prices made the market for these financial instruments collapse. A number of banks saw themselves forced to keep large amounts of these assets in their books although they had intended to resell them. Moreover, a vast number of investors noticed that they had invested in "toxic" assets with very uncertain value. It became clear that part of these financial instruments were based on mortgage loans that had been offered to people with very low or no income. Once the housing prices began falling, many of these mortgage loans became distressed.

A number of observers are wondering why banks with solid reputations allocated hazardous housing loans to people with very low creditworthiness. It is widely believed that some bankers abused their informational advantage in order to make short-term gains. In more general terms, the current financial crisis is partly attributed to opportunistic behavior, a culture of "greed", and failures in corporate governance. These attributions are quite surprising since the major focus of recent corporate governance regulations was actually the containment of greed and opportunistic behavior. In the wake of the Enron scandal, legislators all over the world debated on measures to reduce managerial opportunism and to align the interests of managers and shareholders.

Why did the widespread adoption of the dominant corporate governance paradigm fail to reach its primary objective, namely the containment of opportunism? We argue that the dominant paradigm has an important shortcoming: it assumes managerial self-interest and potential opportunism as an axiom. However, the new and fast-growing field of psychological economics has offered much evidence that self-interest and opportunistic behavior are not given characteristics of people. Individuals vary systematically in their inclination toward self-interested behavior. To a great degree, self-interested behavior can be influenced by institutions.

In this chapter, we apply insights from psychological economics to corporate governance. In our analysis, we present different perspectives on corporate governance and their shortcomings. Then we suggest our view that corporate governance can be seen as an institution to overcome the possibilities of free riding or, in other words, social dilemmas. In today's companies, which are characterized by more and more knowledge work, the traditional mechanisms of behavior and outcome control (cf. Ouchi 1978) become less and less effective (cf. Osterloh 2006). Therefore, social dilemmas need to be overcome by means of voluntary self-control. Taking account of psychological economic insights, we suggest that voluntary self-control is not just wishful thinking but indeed possible. The key to voluntary self-control are institutions fostering prosocial preferences. When viewing corporate governance as an institution that fosters prosocial preferences, our analysis leads to suggestions that clash with conventional wisdom. We suggest that the following measures help to overcome social dilemmas: board representation of knowledge workers who invest in firm-specific human capital, attenuation of variable pay-for-performance, selection of directors and managers with prosocial preferences, and employee participation in decision-making and control.

This article proceeds as follows. In the section "Corporate Governance Based on Self-Interest as an Axiom", we present the dominant agency paradigm in the corporate governance literature and the theory of incomplete contracts, which are both based on self-interest as an axiom. While both theories have their shortcomings, the theory of incomplete contracts serves as a basis for newer corporate governance approaches based on psychological economics. In the section "The Financial Crisis and Corporate Governance", a brief analysis of the current financial crisis is provided, followed by important implications concerning the theory of corporate governance. In the section "Corporate Governance Based on Psychological Economics", we first explain the team production theory of corporate governance as an alternative to the dominant paradigm. Then, we contrast this team production perspective with our own approach of corporate governance as an institution to overcome social dilemmas. Both approaches are partly based on the same psychological foundations, however, there are important differences as well. Based on empirical findings in the field of psychological economics, we explain our recommendations concerning the design of corporate governance institutions. In the last section, we conclude.

Corporate Governance Based on Self-Interest as an Axiom

Corporate governance can be defined as "the determination of the broad uses to which organizational resources will be deployed and the resolution of conflicts among the myriad participants in organizations" (Daily et al. 2003, p. 371). This definition raises two major questions (cf., e.g., Steinmann 1969; Steinmann and Gerum 1992). *First*, whose interests should guide the companies' strategies and policies (question of legitimacy)? *Second*, how should formal decision-making procedures be designed in order to serve these interests (question of organization)?

The dominant paradigm in the corporate governance literature is based on institutional economics, in particular property rights and agency theory (cf., e.g., Jensen and Meckling 1976). This paradigm considers the first question as resolved. Companies are viewed as a "nexus of contracts" between different resource owners who cooperate in order to generate quasi-rents. Quasi-rents are the difference between the value of a resource used in combination with other resources and its value in a market transaction (cf., e.g., Zingales 1998). Except for shareholders, all other parties are assumed to protect their claims ex ante by means of clearly defined contracts. Shareholders, however, are considered as residual claimants. They specialize in monitoring the other cooperation partners (cf. Alchian and Demsetz 1972) and in diversifying their risks (cf. Jensen and Meckling 1976). In return, they receive a claim on the residual surplus of the company after all contractual obligations with other stakeholders have been fulfilled. Since all contracts are clear and complete, there are no conflicts of interest between shareholders and other stakeholders. The only conflicts of interest remain between shareholders and self-interested managers. These conflicts of interest become particularly salient when ownership is separated from control (cf. Berle and Means 1932) in companies with widely dispersed share ownership. In this perspective, the legitimate guiding interest of a company's strategy and policies is shareholder value. The question is merely how to incentivize a company's management to focus on the maximization of shareholder wealth.

The question of organization arises from the principal-agent-relationship between shareholders and managers. While shareholders are the principals, managers fill the role of agents who have no or little residual claims. Because of information asymmetries, managers have the possibility to expropriate outside investors. Therefore, corporate governance institutions need to be designed in a way that protects outside investors against expropriation.

Based on the assumption of self-interest as an axiom, a number of disciplining institutions are suggested to protect shareholders against expropriation. These institutions are both inside and outside the firm, such as the board of directors, the market for corporate control, the market for managers, and the audit firm (cf., e.g., Kräkel 1999; Witt 2003). The board of directors is proposed to represent the interests of shareholders, thereby reducing the problem of rational apathy by minority shareholders (cf. Berle and Means 1932) who have an incentive to free-ride rather than control the management's activities. The control of management is considered to be particularly effective if the directors on the board are independent of management. Both the pay of board members and the pay of managers are suggested to be tied to the company's performance in order to ensure an alignment of their interests and the interests of shareholders.

These suggestions have largely been followed in practice. The Sarbanes-Oxley Act, for example, is founded on the ideas of agency theory. It reinforces monitoring and sanctioning of management and can be described as "corporate governance for crooks" (Osterloh and Frey 2004). Agency theory has had a particularly strong influence on management compensation. Two decades ago, the high proportion of fixed compensation for managers, which resembled the salaries of bureaucrats (cf. Jensen and Murphy 1990), was deplored. Only a few years later, the fixed compensation for US managers amounted to just 25% of their total income (cf. Murphy 1999), largely due to stock options. At the same time, the difference between the average incomes of employees and top managers in S&P 500 companies has risen sharply (cf. Klinger et al. 2002). However, these developments did not lead to a strong relationship between managerial pay and companies' performance (cf., e.g., Barkema and Gomez-Mejia 1998; Bebchuk and Fried 2004) that can be attributed to above-average managerial performance (cf. Hall and Murphy 2003). Less than 5% of managerial income can be explained by performance factors (cf. Tosi et al. 2000). Not only is the impact of variable managerial pay on companies' performance ambiguous, but variable pay may also cause distortions. Among the companies that were convicted for fraud by the Security and Exchange Commission (SEC), the median value of variable income related to shares and stock options was twice as high as in non-fraud companies (cf. Johnson et al. 2009). Moreover, the number of restatements of US corporations is highly correlated with the proportion of stock options relative to the total income of top managers.

Many empirical studies have illustrated that top managers are able to manipulate the performance criteria according to which they are measured (cf. Bebchuk et al. 2001; Becht et al. 2002). An example for these manipulations is "earnings management", that is, influencing the company's profits by means of accrual and amortization (cf. Healy and Wahlen 1999) or manipulating reference groups that are chosen to compare managerial income (cf. Benz et al. 2002; Bertrand and Mullainathan 2001). These developments were reinforced by the use of compensation consultants and the disclosure of top management's income that was required by the SEC (cf. Bizjak et al. 2008; Schiltknecht 2004). Even in agency theory, it has been acknowledged that variable pay has led to considerable abuse (cf., e.g., Bebchuk and Fried 2004; Fuller and Jensen 2002; Hall and Murphy 2003; Hall 2003; Schiltknecht 2004). However, it is believed that the system of variable managerial pay can be improved to eliminate negative side-effects.

There are also other suggestions derived from the principal-agent approach that do not find convincing empirical corroboration. Ambiguous relationships have been found between stock-based compensation of board members and companies' performance (cf. Dalton et al. 2003) and between the proportion of independent board members and companies' performance (cf. Dalton et al. 1998; Hermalin and Weisbach 2003). Other studies have examined the market for corporate control. Management is assumed to be controlled efficiently if there are no obstacles to takeovers. Protections against takeovers, such as poison pills or staggered boards, are seen as detrimental since they allow inefficient management teams to stay in office. However, it has been shown in the US that poison pills did not systematically deter takeovers or cause a demise of the market for corporate control (cf. Comment and Schwert 1995). In sum, while the principal-agent approach is very popular in theoretical debate and in practical application, it has not been an empirical success story (cf. Daily et al. 2003). Therefore, it makes sense to consider alternative theoretical perspectives.

Many alternative theoretical perspectives question the assumption that, except for shareholders, all other stakeholders are able to protect their claims ex ante. A particularly influential alternative perspective is the theory of incomplete contracts. The theory of incomplete contracts (cf., e.g., Tirole 2001; Zingales 1998) submits that not all future circumstances can be specified in contracts. Some stakeholders, in particular employees, carry out firm-specific investments in human capital that generate quasi-rents. These quasi-rents are lost when the cooperative relationship with other stakeholders is terminated. As a consequence of their firm-specific investments, the employees' outside opportunities are worsened (cf. Zingales 1998). Unless they are offered control rights after the conclusion of the contract, they are in a weak bargaining position and may face the risk of hold up. Employees anticipate this risk and therefore prefer to invest in general rather than firm-specific human capital. A lack of investment in firm-specific human capital has negative consequences for the company. As the knowledge-based theory of the firm emphasizes, one of the most relevant assets for a company's sustained competitive advantage is firm-specific human capital, which needs to be generated, accumulated, transferred, and protected (cf., e.g., Penrose 1959; Rumelt 1984; Mahoney and Pandian 1992; Grant 1996; Kogut and Zander 1996; Spender 1996; Teece et al. 1997; Foss and Foss 2000; Grandori and Kogut 2002).

The theory of incomplete contracts does not offer a universal suggestion concerning the distribution of control rights. While offering control rights to stakeholders induces their firm-specific investments, it may also raise coordination costs due to the heterogeneous interests of different stakeholders (cf. Hansmann 1996; Tirole 2001). Corporate governance is proposed to be designed in a way that maximizes quasi-rents while minimizing the costs of inefficient ex post bargaining (cf. Frick et al. 1999). Under certain circumstances, it might still be most efficient to offer the right of controlling a company to one single stakeholder group, such as shareholders. Although multiple stakeholders may have legitimate interests in guiding a company's strategy and policies, this does not necessarily mean that these stakeholders should be involved in formal decision-making procedures.

While the theory of incomplete contracts has generated valuable insights, it still shares the axiomatic assumptions of the dominant paradigm concerning the self-interest of directors, managers, and employees. We suggest that a theory of corporate governance needs to be based on more refined motivational foundations. The new and fast-growing field of psychological economics (cf., e.g., Fehr and Falk 2002; Frey and Benz 2004; Rabin 1998) is able to provide corporate governance theory with empirically founded psychological insights. Moreover, it contributes to bridging the gap between institutional economics and research on organizational behavior.

It may be argued that the simplistic institutional economic model of human psychology can still generate robust predictions and be scientifically valid (cf. Friedman 1953). While this argument has been criticized at the epistemological level (cf., e.g., Donaldson 1990), a brief analysis of the current financial crisis illustrates that a too simplistic model of human psychology carries the risk of suggesting control measures that produce self-interest as a self-fulfilling prophecy (cf. Frey and Osterloh 2002; Ghoshal and Moran 1996).

The Financial Crisis and Corporate Governance

We refer again to the financial crisis, this time with a specific focus on the implications for corporate governance. Hertig (2009) provides a recent analysis of corporate governance deficiencies preceding the current financial crisis, with a particular emphasis on the failures in risk management. Many firms were not prepared to handle the shocks arising from the financial crisis, in part due to overly simplistic or optimistic scenarios in their "stress testing". This negligence has become particularly visible in the financial sector. However, numerous firms in non-financial sectors were concerned as well. Several factors had caused this negligence in risk management. *First*, the board of directors was under pressure to adopt ill-fated strategies that were favored by investors or executives with short-term preferences. These pressures were enhanced by top management compensation that was often oriented toward short-term performance and, hence, led to excessive risk-taking. *Second*, it was often difficult for sensitive information to reach the board of directors. In many firms, the directors were neither aware of the increase in credit risks nor did they understand the consequences of these risks for the management of the firm's liquidity. *Third*, as Hertig (2009) posits, the focus of corporate governance reforms was not on improving the board's effectiveness, but rather on reducing the board's discretion by means of disclosure and other requirements.[1] *Fourth*, whistle-blowing was not effective. On the one hand, employees had few incentives to blow the whistle because they were often fired, quit under pressure or shifted their duties (cf. Dyck et al. 2007). On the other hand, it was easier to blow the whistle on obvious offences, such as corporate fraud, than on deficiencies in risk management. However, sustainable monitoring by a controlling constituency, such as a strong shareholder, depends on a loyal relationship with managers and employees (cf. Hirschman 1970), which also entails whistle-blowing.

These deficiencies, which preceded the financial crisis, lead to several important conclusions for our subsequent analysis. *First*, series of corporate governance reforms that were inspired by the economic model of self-interested individuals were not able to constrain opportunism. They may even have fostered opportunistic tendencies as a self-fulfilling prophecy. *Second*, incentives do not suffice to align the interests of shareholders, directors, managers, and employees. Rather, corporate governance needs to create the preconditions for a loyal relationship between these constituencies. *Third*, it is important that employees who have informational advantages over directors are willing to contribute to collective goods, such as the firm's reputation and survival. Therefore, a new theory of corporate governance need not be confined to the board of directors as a benevolent ruling body, but rather address cooperative behavior at all levels of the hierarchy.

Corporate Governance Based on Psychological Economics

One of the most salient features of the standard principal-agent approach is that it axiomatically assumes individuals to be self-interested. This assumption is criticized in psychological economics. The field of psychological economics[2] has emerged from criticism at the assumptions of homo economicus, the standard economic model of human behavior.[3] Psychological economics investigates deviations from homo economicus in three main directions (cf., e.g., Frey and Benz 2004). *First*, individuals are boundedly rational. Due to cognitive and emotional constraints, people are often not able to maximize their expected utility rationally. *Second*, individuals are boundedly self-interested. Depending on the circumstances, many persons are not only driven by their own utility but also by prosocial preferences.

---

[1] Hertig's (2009) proposal calls for an outsider representing the equity-oriented interests of managers and employees who collectively hold more than five percent of their firm's equity.

[2] Psychological economics is often referred to as behavioral economics. However, behavioral economics may be mistaken for the behaviorist approach in psychology, which only investigates observable stimulus-response relationships (cf. Watson 1913; Skinner 1965) and neglects psychological cognitive and motivational processes.

[3] See Rabin (1998) and Camerer et al. (2004) for reviews.

These preferences play an important role in overcoming social dilemmas when markets fail. *Third*, the utility concept of homo economicus is bounded. Psychological economics investigates happiness or subjective well-being as a measure for utility that goes beyond financial income. In our analysis, we focus on the aspect of bounded self-interest, since this is arguably the most contested aspect of the agency paradigm in corporate governance.

Psychological economics has rarely made its way into corporate governance theory. A prominent approach to corporate governance, which incorporates some insights from psychological economics, is the team production theory of corporate governance (Blair and Stout 1999, 2001; Stout 2003a). We present this theoretical approach and its shortcomings. Then we contrast it with our own approach of viewing corporate governance as an institution to overcome social dilemmas.

Team Production Theory of Corporate Governance

The team production theory of corporate governance can be seen as a further development of the theory of incomplete contracts described above. It is based on the assumption that multiple stakeholders are not able to protect their firm-specific investments ex ante because of the incompleteness of contracts. In order to induce firm-specific investments by these stakeholders, there is a need for corporate governance mechanisms that protect the interests of these stakeholders. The various stakeholders who provide firm-specific investments can include shareholders, employees, suppliers, customers, and even the local community. They are characterized as members of a "corporate team".

The view of team members forming a corporation is based on the institutional economic team production theory (cf. Alchian and Demsetz 1972). In this theory, team production is defined as the joint production of several actors, in which the output exceeds the sum of the individual contributions and cannot be attributed to individual team members. In other words, the team produces quasi-rents (cf. Klein et al. 1978) or synergies (cf. Foss and Iversen 1997). Since the success of a team production is not attributable to individual team members, there exist incentives to free-ride within the team. The suggested solution is that one team member is appointed as a principal with the task to monitor, pay and direct the other team members. In turn, the principal receives a claim on the residual surplus. All other team members, however, have their claims specified ex ante in their contracts. This solution requires that there are no information asymmetries between the principal and the team members. Therefore, the principal needs to be able to observe and attribute all individual contributions. The team members are assumed to provide undifferentiated inputs that can be traded in atomized markets. Therefore, differential power of the contracting parties is not an issue. The team production is not based on co-specialized inputs or long-term team-specific investments. In assuming that team members are interchangeable and undertake no firm-specific investments, the classical team production theory reformulates the team production problem as a vertical principal-agent problem (cf. Blair and Stout 1999).

The assumed absence of team-specific investments is debatable. Team-specific investments are among the most important sources of quasi-rents, which represent the actual reason for the existence of firms (cf., e.g., Zingales 1998). These investments also make team members interdependent and less interchangeable. Team members are only able to materialize their team-specific investments when the production output has been marketed. Therefore, in addition to shareholders, also other resource providers are exposed to the residual risk arising from firm-specific investments. This is particularly the case for employees (cf. Blair 1995, 1998). Empirical evidence (cf. Topel 1991) has shown that employees who lose their jobs without their fault lose around 15% of their income in their new job. For employees with a firm tenure of more than 21 years, this loss amounts to 44%. This example indicates that employees carry a substantial residual risk. Unless their interests are protected, they will be unwilling to undertake investments in firm-specific human capital. In this perspective, there are several claimants on the residual surplus of the firm. The company is not considered to be a nexus of individual contracts, but rather a nexus of firm-specific investments with various conflicting residual claimants.

The acknowledgement of several residual claimants leads to conflicts of interest. These conflicts are accentuated because the bargaining power of a team member is weakened after carrying out firm-specific investments. Based on refined models of team production (cf. Holmstrom 1982; Rajan and Zingales 1998), the solution for these conflicts is suggested to be a neutral third party that mediates between different conflicting interests (cf. Blair and Stout 1999). This third party, called the "mediating hierarch", undertakes no firm-specific investments and has no residual claim. Team members are argued to submit to this hierarchy for their own benefit. In handing over control rights to the mediating hierarch, team members are assumed to save themselves from their own opportunistic instincts that would prevent team-specific investments. The mediating hierarch controls the team members' firm-specific inputs and the distribution of the output. Its primary function is to maximize the joint welfare of the team as a whole. In corporations, this mediating hierarch is proposed to be the board of directors, since this body has authority over the use of corporate assets and enjoys an independence from individual team members that is protected by law (cf. ibid.).

The mediating hierarchy model is suggested to be supported by the design of American corporate law, which requires an independent board of directors for public corporations (cf. ibid.). Furthermore, some empirical evidence is argued to strengthen the mediating hierarchy model. In the 1970s and 1980s for example, the threat of hostile tender offers induced corporate boards to establish poison pills, staggered boards, and other protective devices without being impeded by judges and corporate regulators (cf. Stout 2003a). More recently, a study comparing IPO firms (initial public offerings) with and without takeover defenses illustrates that the performance of firms with takeover defenses tends to be better in the first 3 years following the IPO (cf. Field and Karpoff 2002). According to the mediating hierarchy model, these findings can be explained by the benefits that shareholders reap if they tie their own hands and ensure a neutral board of directors.

To strengthen the neutrality of the board, the board members are suggested to refrain from undertaking firm-specific investments and receiving stock-based compensation (cf. Stout 2003b). Rather, they need to receive a fixed compensation like judges and referees. Similar to CEOs of a nonprofit organization, they need to submit to a "non-distribution constraint" (cf. Hansmann 1980). The willingness to donate would dry up if the management of a nonprofit organization became profit-maximizing. Similarly, the willingness of team members to carry out team-specific investments would fade if they suspected the board's neutrality to be hampered by its compensation structure. Therefore, the board members' incentives need to be primarily non-monetary. Their motivation is proposed to be based on their reputation and their fulfillment of an obligation. In the mediating hierarchy model, board members do not correspond to the view of rational, self-interested individuals, which is usually assumed in institutional economics.

The demanded neutrality of the board does not mean that all stakeholders need to have the right to elect board members (cf. Blair and Stout 1999). Rather, it is argued that the mediating hierarchy model is compatible with shareholder voting rights for the following reasons. *First*, if voting rights were distributed among stakeholders with heterogeneous interests, voting pathologies may arise (cf. Hansmann 1996). *Second*, the objective of shareholders to maximize the value of a firm's stock can sometimes be an indicator of the total value of rents that are beneficial to other stakeholders as well. *Third*, shareholders are particularly vulnerable since they are not involved in the company's day-to-day activities and therefore rarely have the opportunity to access information and to negotiate directly with the firm's management. *Fourth*, due to their large number and relatively small stakes in widely held firms, shareholders face substantial obstacles to coordinate among themselves. Although shareholders ultimately elect the board members, it is suggested that the board of directors can fulfill its mediating function without submitting to shareholders due to practical and legal protections.

The mediating hierarchy model leaves two issues unanswered. *First*, tensions may arise between the board's mediating function and the functions of monitoring and advice. If the board is supposed to monitor and advise efficiently, board members need to invest in firm-specific human capital to reduce their information asymmetries compared to the company's management. However, they would lose their neutrality (cf. Rajan and Zingales 1998). A loss of neutrality is not necessarily a disadvantage. A meta-analysis has shown no relationship between the number of independent board members and the financial performance of US corporations (cf. Dalton et al. 1998). The mediating hierarchy model therefore underestimates the board's function as a provider of resources, such as knowledge and network resources (cf. Hillman and Dalziel 2003). *Second*, the non-distribution constraint is only claimed for the board of directors as the mediating hierarch of a "corporate team", but the problem of underinvestment in team-specific resources also exists at lower levels of the hierarchy. Modern organizations are characterized by a wealth of teams with possibilities to free-ride. Team leaders are often not able to attribute contributions to individual team members and therefore rely on their voluntary investments in team-specific resources. This problem is particularly pronounced in companies that produce knowledge-intensive products and services (cf. Osterloh and Frost 2002). According to the knowledge-based theory of the firm, firm-specific knowledge is among the most important sources of a sustained competitive advantage (cf., e.g., Grant 1996; Kogut and Zander 1996; Spender 1996). However, knowledge work largely depends on voluntary contributions of team members that cannot be observed and attributed individually (cf. Osterloh and Frey 2000).

Corporate Governance as an Institution to Overcome Social Dilemmas

Our view of corporate governance combines the institutional economic approach with the psychological economic theory of human behavior. In accordance with the team production theory of corporate governance, we consider the firm as a nexus of firm-specific investments rather than a nexus of contracts. Therefore, our approach takes account of stakeholders who undertake firm-specific investments that cannot be protected ex ante through contractual agreements. However, our approach departs from the team production theory of corporate governance in several respects. *First*, we suggest that the board of directors should not only be elected by shareholders but also by knowledge workers (employees) who carry out investments in firm-specific human capital. The representation of shareholders and knowledge workers should be proportional to the investments in financial capital and firm-specific human capital.[4] *Second*, we propose that the board should not only fulfill a mediating function but also the functions of monitoring and advice. Therefore, board members need to undertake investments in firm-specific human capital. Since these investments attenuate their neutrality, there is a need for board members with high integrity and loyalty. *Third*, we consider the mediating and advice function not as a singular feature of the board but rather as a feature of team leaders at all levels of the hierarchy. *Fourth*, we argue that the design of corporate governance institutions has a substantial impact on the extent to which the model of a self-interested homo economicus is fostered or hampered within the firm.

Our approach rests upon the understanding that firms are distinguished from markets in that they incorporate highly interdependent activities (cf. Thompson 1967; Grandori 2001; Frese 2000; Langlois 2002). While highly interdependent activities make it difficult to measure separate contributions of individuals, they are the sources of synergies that make it advantageous to organize employees instead of relying on market transactions (cf. Simon 1991). The difficulty of observing and measuring contributions opens up possibilities of free-riding, both concerning the joint production and the investment in firm-specific resources.

The possibilities to free-ride cause a social dilemma. Social dilemmas arise when rational, self-interested behavior does not lead to collectively desirable results (cf., e.g., Dawes 1980). Therefore, markets that are constituted on the behavior of homo

---

[4] See Osterloh and Frey (2006) for a detailed explanation of this arrangement.

economicus are not systematically suited to solve social dilemmas. At the societal level, it has been argued that state power can solve social dilemmas (cf., e.g., Hardin 1968). At the firm level, hierarchical authority is commonly proposed as a solution (cf. Alchian and Demsetz 1972; Vining 2003). However, firms have a much more comprehensive repertoire of mechanisms to solve social dilemmas (cf. Frost 2003).

Social dilemmas manifest themselves in firms at two levels. The *first* level concerns the contributions of individuals to firm-specific collective goods, such as the contribution to firm-specific knowledge. Even employees who do not contribute to firm-specific knowledge benefit from it. This kind of social dilemma is addressed by team production theory and leads to the suggestion that the interests of knowledge workers need to be protected by a mediating board. The *second* level concerns the maintenance of rules of cooperation. This kind of social dilemma is not addressed by team production theory. Because of information asymmetries, these rules of cooperation cannot be monitored sufficiently by regulators, boards or supervisors. Rather, they depend on the voluntary commitment of employees. Many scandals in recent years have illustrated that employees were aware of fraud even at the lowest levels of hierarchy (cf., e.g., Spector 2003). However, only a few whistleblowers were willing to draw attention to the deficiencies. The reason is that whistle-blowing not only causes psychological costs but also may lead to dismissal. The detection of deficiencies represents a second order public good that is beneficial also to those individuals who do not contribute to it. While punishment is costly to the punisher, the benefits from punishment are diffusely distributed over all employees (cf. Elster 1989).

To solve social dilemmas, hierarchical authority becomes ineffective when knowledge asymmetries between supervisors and employees are substantial. This is particularly the case when knowledge work is important and when companies are divisionalized and distributed geographically (cf. Child and Rodrigues 2003). In these cases, both hierarchical control and output control fail (cf. Ouchi 1978), no matter whether the supervisor is the board of directors or a team leader. Hierarchical control needs to be substituted by voluntary self-control.

The effectiveness of voluntary self-control has been demonstrated in numerous empirical studies (cf., e.g., Ostrom 1999; Weibel 2004). These empirical findings are commonly founded on the following reasoning: Social dilemmas, such as the prisoners' dilemma (cf., e.g., Kollock 1998), need to be transformed into coordination games, in which free-riding is no more the only equilibrium (cf. Sen 1974). This transformation is based on the precondition that prosocial needs are embedded in the individuals' preferences (cf. Weibel 2004).

As we will show below, firms can create the institutional conditions for the selection of individuals with prosocial preferences and for the reinforcement of these preferences (or the prevention of their crowding-out). Corporate governance is an essential part of these institutional mechanisms.

Psychological Foundations of Both Approaches

Both the team production theory of corporate governance and our approach are based on psychological foundations that differ from the view of homo economicus, which is commonly used in institutional economics. In this section, we detail these psychological foundations in order to substantiate the suggested institutions of our approach.

In the mediating hierarchy model, the board of directors has the function to maximize the joint welfare of the team as a whole (cf. Blair and Stout 1999). The board receives control rights from various stakeholders in order to protect them against their own opportunistic instincts. These stakeholders are assumed to be potentially shirking and rent-seeking. Therefore, "they realize that it is in their own self-interest to create a higher authority – a hierarch – that can limit shirking and deter rent-seeking behavior among team members" (ibid., p. 274). In other words, with respect to stakeholders, the mediating hierarchy model sticks to the institutional economic notion of rational, self-interested human behavior. However, the directors of the board are assumed to act in the interest of the "corporate team" as a whole.

How do these diverging assumptions about human behavior fit into the same model? Three main reasons are put forward (cf. ibid.). *First*, directors are compensated for their work and may be interested in keeping their position and serving on additional boards. Therefore, they may benefit from preventing a breakup of the "corporate team" and from establishing a reputation as good directors. This argument is completely rational and does not depend on insights from psychological economics. *Second*, US corporate law severely limits self-dealing by the board of directors. This "non-distribution constraint" (cf. Hansmann 1980) may induce trust by stakeholders who undertake firm-specific investments, because these stakeholders need not fear that the directors will expropriate them for their own monetary benefit. However, this constraint does not explain why directors should be benevolent and act in the interest of all stakeholders. Therefore, there is a *third* argument. Directors may serve their "corporate team" due to corporate cultural norms of fairness and trust. These social norms are proposed to reinforce reputational considerations of directors. However, the directors' desire to protect their reputations is not based on rational self-interest, because they are suggested to be trustworthy even when the costs of being honest and fair outweigh the benefits. The key to such behavior is the "careful selection of trustworthy individuals who are supported by appropriate social norms" (Blair and Stout 1999, p. 319). Similar to nonprofit organizations (cf. Hansmann 1980), the position as a director is expected to attract people who value their reputation and aim at behaving in a way that is viewed as socially appropriate.

In our approach, we share the view that board members need to be selected carefully and supported by appropriate social norms. In particular, we emphasize that they need to have prosocial preferences in order to transform social dilemmas into coordination games. However, rather than confining these features to the directors of the board, we suggest that corporate governance institutions can foster prosocial preferences among all team leaders within the firm. Before the eruption of the current financial crisis, many potentially disastrous decisions were not taken at the board level but rather at lower levels of the hierarchy. In banks, for example, there existed substantial knowledge asymmetries between the board of directors and individual managers. Many arguably trustworthy directors were not able to perceive the dangers that were building up and threatening their company.

To avoid these kinds of dangers, we argue that the view of a self-interested, utility maximizing homo economicus should be revised not only for the board of directors but also for managers and employees. Hence, the question is how to design institutions that foster prosocial preferences at all levels of the hierarchy. Since there are no direct findings on the impact of corporate governance institutions on prosocial preferences, we present empirical findings from other fields that can be applied to corporate governance.

Institutions that Foster Prosocial Preferences

Prosocial preferences form a part of intrinsic motivation. Intrinsic motivation is directed toward activities that are done for their own sake (cf. Deci and Ryan 1985; Frey 1997; Frey and Meier 2004; Osterloh and Frey 1997; Osterloh and Frey 2000; Lindenberg 2001). In contrast, extrinsic motivation is instrumentally directed toward activities that are done for an expected reward. Intrinsic motivation can be divided into hedonic preferences, which serve the individuals' own enjoyment, and prosocial preferences, which serve social norms for their own sake. To overcome social dilemmas in boards and teams, prosocial preferences are essential. The mentioned types of motivation overlap in reality and may be seen as parts of a continuum (cf., e.g., Deci and Ryan 2000). However, institutional economic approaches, such as the principal-agent approach, only consider extrinsic motivation.

The existence of intrinsic motivation has been corroborated in many laboratory and field experiments (cf., e.g., Frey and Jegen 2001; Ledyard 1995; Ostrom 1998; Rabin 1998; Sally 1995). These experiments show that a large percentage of individuals are willing to contribute to collective goods voluntarily and to punish people who diverge from social norms. They also illustrate that this percentage is influenced by economic and social factors (cf., e.g., Bowles 1998; Frey 1997; Henrich et al. 2001). For theoretical analysis, the relationship between extrinsic and intrinsic motivation has primarily been analyzed within the theory of self-determination.[5] Based on this theory, the extent to which intrinsic motivation is reinforced or crowded out especially depends on three factors: autonomy, experience of competence, and social relatedness. The empirical findings shall be structured according to these criteria.

---

[5] See Deci and Ryan (2000) for a review.

Autonomy

Perceived autonomy is an essential precondition for intrinsic motivation. Autonomy is reduced when a voluntary activity is rewarded or punished. The individual no more attributes the activity to herself. In other words, her perceived locus of causality shifts from internal to external. Moreover, her attention shifts from the activity itself to the expected reward or punishment. While the activity loses importance, the person's intrinsic motivation is crowded out. However, this *crowding-out effect* only occurs if a prior intrinsic motivation existed. If there was no intrinsic motivation in the first place, external rewards and sanctions enhance the person's motivation. This effect is shown in an empirical study on the performance of employees who install windshields. In the context of this simple other-directed task, the introduction of a piece rate system enhances worker productivity by 20–36% (cf. Lazear 1999). However, if a task is partly perceived as an exchange of voluntary contributions or a "gift exchange" (cf. Akerlof 1982), variable pay reduces employee motivation. Conversely, autonomy and voluntariness lead to a *crowding-in effect*. A couple of examples shall illustrate these relationships.

Variable pay: A laboratory experiment has shown that voluntariness is important even in gainful employment (cf. Irlenbusch and Sliwka 2005). In a first setting, principals were asked to offer a fixed salary and agents were able to choose their work effort. In a second setting, principals could choose between offering a fixed salary and a piece rate. Agents chose a higher work effort when they were offered a fixed salary. Moreover, they referred less to the welfare of the principal in this situation. The social norm of reciprocity is crowded out in the piece rate situation. In the fixed salary situation, however, it is crowded in.[6]

Punishment: Punishments can cause a crowding-out effect. This effect is shown in a field experiment in a kindergarten (cf. Gneezy and Rustichini 2000). Parents who picked up their children too late at the kindergarten received a fine. This fine caused a substantially reduced punctuality, since the parents conceived that they were paying for their delay. After the fine was abolished, the punctuality did not improve. Apparently the social norm of being considerate was undermined by the fine. Laboratory experiments show, however, that punishments can cause differential effects depending on the perception of the punishers as being self-interested or prosocially motivated (cf. Fehr and Rockenbach 2003). This finding needs to be considered when designing institutions that create sanctions to overcome second order social dilemmas, such as whistle-blowing.

Volunteering: Volunteer work for charity is primarily exercised when there is little external pressure (cf. Frey and Goette 1999; Stukas et al. 1999). In a field experiment, the behavior of children who collected money for charity was analyzed. While one group received no monetary compensation, a control group received a bonus of 1% of the collected sum. This control group collected 36% less money than the first group. When the bonus of the control group was raised to 10%, the children collected substantially more money, however, their performance remained below the performance of the first group.

---

[6] See also Fehr and Gächter (2002).

Competence

Perceived competence arises when individuals understand what they are doing, when they receive positive feedback, and when they feel responsible for the result of their work (cf. Hackman and Oldham 1976). While feedback is important for any type of motivation, intrinsic motivation is only activated when the person's self-determination is not constrained (cf. Deci and Ryan 2000). Therefore, it is important that feedback is perceived as supportive rather than controlling. Supportive feedback and perceived competence enhance the individual's perceived self-efficacy. Empirical findings illustrate that self-efficacy has a positive impact on the contribution to collective goods (cf. Kollock 1998). Hence, rewards that are perceived as a supportive feedback actually crowd-in intrinsic motivation and prosocial behavior. This mechanism explains why unexpected, symbolic rewards can enhance intrinsic motivation (cf. Heckhausen 1989) and why very little proportions of variable pay may enhance performance, while high proportions of variable pay do not cause an additional increase in work performance (cf. Bucklin and Dickinson 2001). Moreover, supportive feedback can crowd in intrinsic motivation when it does not just address the achieved output but also contributes to understanding the processes that have led to the output. This effect has been shown in a comparative study in the airline industry (cf. Gittell 2001). Pure output controls with little communication lead to the result that each team member is anxious to deny any responsibility for mistakes. However, competent process-accompanying feedback and supportive relationships cause individuals to assume responsibility for the output of the team as a whole (cf. Weibel 2004).

Social Relatedness

Social relatedness enhances identification with the group and the willingness to contribute to collective goods (cf. Kollock 1998). The following measures shall illustrate how social relatedness and prosocial preferences can be strengthened.

Instructions about socially appropriate behavior: People contribute more to collective goods when they are instructed about the kinds of behavior that are socially appropriate (cf. Sally 1995). In a laboratory experiment, individuals contributed much more to a collective good when the experiment was labeled as "community game" rather than "wallstreet game" (cf. Liberman et al. 2004). Such differential instructions about socially expected behavior can also result from fines that signal a "new game". This effect has been shown in the kindergarten experiment described above (cf. Gneezy and Rustichini 2000). Such a signaling effect is also evident in another laboratory experiment (cf. Tenbrunsel and Messick 1999). It shows that a threat of punishment for environmental torts changes the way a situation is perceived. This threat makes a majority of individuals believe that their decision is not about a contribution to the collective good of a clean environment. Rather, they conceive their decision as a commercial one.

Procedural fairness: Various empirical studies (cf. Tyler and Blader 2000; Tyler and Lind 1992) have illustrated the importance of perceived procedural fairness.[7] Procedural fairness can lead to the acceptance of decisions, even if they involve negative consequences for the individual. Therefore, procedural fairness is particularly important in situations of conflict, such as restructurings (cf. Cascio 2005). The perceived procedural fairness depends on the possibility to participate in decisions, the neutrality of decision-makers in judging conflicts, and a respectful treatment of the individuals. For the purpose of neutrality, politicians, judges, and bureaucrats receive fixed salaries. Those individuals who determine the rules of the game should have no incentive to bias these rules for their own benefit (cf. Benz and Frey 2007). The fixed salaries also help to prevent self-serving biases. Empirical evidence has demonstrated that even honest people are unconsciously prone to self-serving biases. Their judgment is biased for their own benefit, especially in highly ambiguous situations. In contrast to corruption, such unconscious biases cannot be reduced through punishments (cf. Babcock and Loewenstein 1997; Bazerman et al. 2002). These biases can only be attenuated if the incentives to focus on one's own interests are reduced. With respect to directors and managers, however, the opposite is happening. The creation of variable incentives runs the risk of enhancing self-serving biases and even deliberate manipulations of the performance criteria. Under such circumstances, no neutrality can be expected. If employees do not consider directors and managers to be neutral, they will perceive less procedural fairness and will lose willingness to contribute to collective goods.

Conditional cooperation: Individuals generally contribute more to a collective good if they expect others to contribute as well (cf. Fehr and Fischbacher 2003; Fischbacher et al. 2001; Levi 1988; Ostrom 2000). Conversely, if too many people free-ride, the inclination to behave prosocially is reduced. The honesty of employees deteriorates when they recognize that their supervisors enrich themselves in unjustified ways. They are no longer willing to contribute to collective goods or to criticize colleagues who behave illegally. In Enron, for example, the management team was aware of illegal activities. Moreover, large parts of the workforce were informed as well (cf. Salter 2003). Finally, an empirical study has shown that criminal offenses are substantially lower in companies with a general profit-sharing scheme than in companies with a profit-sharing scheme that is confined to top managers (cf. Schnatterly 2003).

Personal contacts: Measures that reduce social distance enhance contributions to collective goods (cf. Dawes et al. 1988; Ledyard 1995; Frey and Bohnet 1995). Experiments have shown that a few minutes of conversation raise the mutual commitment to contribute to common collective goods (cf. Fischbacher et al. 2001; Frey and Meier 2004). Furthermore, communication offers the opportunity to ask other individuals for their contribution to collective goods. A personal contact increases the willingness to volunteer substantially. These effects have led to an increasing importance of "communities of practice" (cf. Orr 1996; Lave and Wenger 1991).

---

[7] See Frey et al. (2004) for an overview.

These communities not only enhance creativity but also the identification with the group.

These findings show that numerous crowding-in and crowding-out effects can be influenced by institutions. We propose that corporate governance institutions are particularly important in influencing intrinsic motivation and prosocial preferences.

Design of Corporate Governance Institutions

Viewing corporate governance as an institution to overcome social dilemmas has far-reaching implications for the design of the relationships between shareholders, directors, managers, and the workforce. In light of the previous reasoning about firm-specific human capital and prosocial preferences, we suggest that the following institutions are beneficial to a company as a whole.

Voluntary Representation of Knowledge Workers at the Board Level

Our proposal implies that companies should introduce employee representation at the board level voluntarily. Therefore, our approach does not equate to co-determination laws as they exist in many European countries. Empirical studies on the impact of co-determination on performance have shown mixed results (cf., e.g., Addison et al. 2004). The fact that most companies do not introduce co-determination rules voluntarily does not mean that such rules are inefficient, since the market for property rights is far from being efficient (e.g., because of external effects, differential bargaining power, and information asymmetries). Therefore, it has been argued that state intervention may be necessary to avoid a prisoners' dilemma (cf. Freeman and Lazear 1995; Frick et al. 1999; Sadowski 2002).

In our view, companies should introduce employee representation voluntarily for efficiency purposes. Shareholders should approve this proposal in their own long-term interest. Practitioners have readily accepted the notion of "core competencies", however, it should be noted that core competencies and sustained competitive advantages primarily rely on investments in firm-specific human capital. Therefore, corporate governance arrangements should provide sufficient incentives for employees to invest in firm-specific human capital.

Attenuation of Variable Pay-for-Performance

We propose that fixed salaries that are able to compete with market wages offer a number of substantial advantages (cf. Frey and Osterloh 2005). *First*, the directors and members of the management team receive a signal that their behavior is expected to address the collective interests of the company. Moreover, competitive wages make it clear that a strong overall performance is expected. In contrast, variable pay-for-performance signals that an exceptional performance is only considered socially appropriate if it is compensated financially. Variable pay signals a "wallstreet game" rather than a "community game" and causes a self-fulfilling prophecy. *Second*, intrinsic motivation and in particular prosocial preferences are not crowded out. It is of utmost importance that directors and managers have proso-cial preferences in order to induce employees to invest in firm-specific human capital. *Third*, the incentive to manipulate performance criteria is reduced. "Earning management" becomes less attractive. *Fourth*, the non-distribution constraint is upheld. Such a self-restriction of directors and managers is essential to encour-age voluntary, non-observable contributions to collective goods. *Fifth*, unconscious self-serving biases are constrained. These biases are particularly important in the relationship between managers and directors. Members of the board of directors should not be compensated according to the same criteria like managers, since self-serving biases cause the danger of suppressing incentives to monitor the managerial team effectively. *Sixth*, fixed salaries cause a self-selection effect. As a conse-quence, more intrinsically motivated individuals are attracted by the company as an employer.

Selection of Directors and Managers with Prosocial Preferences

To foster conditional cooperation among employees, the behavior of directors and managers needs to make clear that also the individuals at the highest levels of the hierarchy contribute to collective goods. Therefore, prosocial preferences need to complement functional competence as selection criteria. The psychological reper-toire for diagnostic analysis (cf., e.g., Funke and Schuler 2002) offers a variety of instruments that help to select suitable directors and managers with prosocial preferences.

Employee Participation in Decision-Making and Control

Participation in decision-making and control is a central precondition for perceived procedural fairness and social relatedness. Participation strengthens the willingness to behave prosocially in two ways. On the one hand, team members raise their con-tributions of non-observable team-specific investments. On the other hand, they are more willing to identify and reprimand free-riders that can only be detected within the team. Although sanctions generally run the risk of crowding-out intrinsic moti-vation, these rebukes do not crowd-out intrinsic motivation because the punisher is perceived to be prosocially motivated. Mutual control among team members is the more important the more a company relies on decentralized knowledge work.

Conclusions

The question concerning the legitimate interests that should guide a company's strategies and policies can be answered in different ways, depending on the adopted theoretical perspective. The dominant paradigm in corporate governance focuses on the interests of shareholders as the only residual claimants. However, the theory of incomplete contracts, the team production theory of corporate governance, and our approach of corporate governance as an institution to overcome social dilemmas lead to the conclusion that also other stakeholders' interests need to be considered. All these approaches are based on efficiency considerations. In other words, the importance of different stakeholders is not derived from a normative social responsibility of the corporation, but rather from the insight that their firm-specific investments are crucial for the company's sustained competitive advantage.

Even though all these approaches take account of stakeholders' interests, they vary considerably with respect to their psychological assumptions about these stakeholders. The theory of incomplete contracts sticks to the view of self-interested, utility-maximizing individuals. The team production theory of corporate governance partially applies insights from psychological economics. However, these insights are only applied to the board of directors as the mediating hierarch. This approach neglects the need to foster prosocial preferences at lower levels of the hierarchy. Considering the corporate governance failures that preceded the current financial crisis, we suggest that findings from psychological economics can help to design institutions that foster prosocial preferences at all levels of the hierarchy. With this aim, we have developed our own approach of corporate governance as an institution to overcome social dilemmas. We have used insights from institutional economics, psychological economics, and the knowledge-based theory of the firm in order to suggest four measures that help to overcome social dilemmas at the firm level: board representation of knowledge workers who invest in firm-specific human capital, attenuation of variable pay-for-performance, selection of directors and managers with prosocial preferences, and employee participation in decision-making and control.

In sum, the consideration of psychological economics leads to recommendations that clash with conventional wisdom based on the institutional economic approach. At the same time, this synthesis of different theoretical perspectives intensifies the dialogue between institutional economics and research on organizational behavior.

References

Addison, J.T., C. Schnabel, and J. Wagner. 2004. The course of research into the economic consequences of german works councils. *British Journal of Industrial Relations* 42: 255–281.

Akerlof, G.A. 1982. Labor contracts as partial gift exchange. *Quarterly Journal of Economics* 97: 543–569.

Alchian, A.A., and H. Demsetz. 1972. Production, information costs, and economic organization. *American Economic Review* 62: 777–795.

Babcock, L., and G. Loewenstein. 1997. Explaining bargaining impasse: The role of self-serving biases. *Journal of Economic Perspectives* 11: 109–126.

Barkema, H.G., and L.R. Gomez-Mejia. 1998. Managerial compensation and firm performance: A general research framework. *Academy of Management Journal* 41: 135–145.

Bazerman, M.H., G. Loewenstein, and D.A. Moore. 2002. Why good accountants do bad audits. *Harvard Business Review*, November 97: 96–103.

Bebchuk, L.A., and J. Fried. 2004. *Pay without performance. The unfulfilled promise of executive compensation.* Cambridge, MA: Harvard University Press.

Bebchuk, L.A., J.M. Fried, and D.I. Walker. 2001. Executive compensation in America: Optimal contracting or extraction of rents? Discussion Paper No. 3112, Centre for Economic Policy Research, available at SSRN: http://ssrn.com/abstract=297005

Becht, M., P. Bolton, and A.A Röell. 2002. Corporate governance and control. Finance Working Paper No. 02/2002, European Corporate Governance Institute, available at SSRN: http://ssrn.com/abstract=343461

Benz, M., and B.S. Frey. 2007. Corporate governance: What can we learn from public governance? *Academy of Management Review* 32: 92–104.

Benz, M., M. Kucher, and A. Stutzer. 2002. Stock options for top managers – The possibilities and limitations of a motivational tool. In *Successful management by motivation*, eds. B.S. Frey, M. Osterloh, 89–118. Wiesbaden: Springer.

Berle, A.A., and G.C. Means. 1932. *The modern corporation and private property*. New York, NY: Macmillan.

Bertrand, M., and S. Mullainathan. 2001. Are CEOs rewarded for luck? The ones without principals are. *Quarterly Journal of Economics* 116: 901–932.

Bizjak, J.M., M.L. Lemmon, and L. Naveen. 2008. Does the use of peer groups contribute to higher pay and less efficient compensation? *Journal of Financial Economics* 90: 152–168.

Blair, M.M. 1995. *Ownership and control. Rethinking corporate governance for the twenty-first century*. Washington, DC: Brookings Institution.

Blair, M.M. 1998. For whom should corporations be run? An economic rationale for stakeholder management. *Long Range Planning* 31: 195–200.

Blair, M.M., and L.A. Stout. 1999. A team production theory of corporate law. *Virginia Law Review* 85: 247–328.

Blair, M.M., and L.A. Stout. 2001. Director accountability and the mediating role of the Corporate Board. *Washington University Law Quarterly* 79: 403–449.

Bowles, S. 1998. Endogenous preferences: The cultural consequences of markets and other economic institutions. *Journal of Economic Literature* 36: 75–111.

Bucklin, B.R., and A.M. Dickinson. 2001. Individual monetary incentives: A review of different types of arrangements between performance and pay. *Journal of Organizational Behavior Management* 21: 45–137.

Camerer, C.F., G. Loewenstein, and M. Rabin. 2004. *Advances in behavioral economics*. Princeton, Woodstock: Princeton University Press.

Cascio, W.F. 2005. Strategies for responsible restructuring. *Academy of Management Executive* 19: 39–50.

Child, J., and S.B. Rodrigues. 2003. Corporate governance and new organizational forms: Issues of double and multiple agency. *Journal of Management and Governance* 7: 337–360.

Comment, R., and G.W. Schwert. 1995. Poison or placebo – Evidence on the deterrence and wealth effects of modern antitakeover measures. *Journal of Financial Economics* 39: 3–43.

Daily, C.M., D.R. Dalton, and A.A. Cannella. 2003. Corporate governance: Decades of dialogue and data. *Academy of Management Review* 28: 371–382.

Dalton, D.R., C.M. Daily, S.T. Certo, and R. Roengpitya. 2003. Meta-analyses of financial performance and equity: Fusion or confusion? *Academy of Management Journal* 46: 13–26.

Dalton, D.R., C.M. Daily, A.E. Ellstrand, and J.L. Johnson. 1998. Meta-analytic reviews of board composition, leadership structure, and financial performance. *Strategic Management Journal* 19: 269–290.

Dawes, R.M. 1980. Social dilemmas. *Annual Review of Psychology* 31: 169–193.

Dawes, R.M., A.J.C. Vandekragt, and J.M. Orbell. 1988. Not me or thee but we – The importance of group identity in eliciting cooperation in dilemma situations – Experimental manipulations. *Acta Psychologica* 68: 83–97.

Deci, E.L., and R.M. Ryan. 1985. *Intrinsic motivation and self-determination in human behavior*. New York, NY: Plenum Press.

Deci, E.L., and R.M. Ryan 2000. The "what" and "why" of goal pursuits: Human needs and the self-determination of behavior. *Psychological Inquiry* 11: 227–268.

Donaldson, L. 1990. The ethereal hand – Organizational economics and management theory. *Academy of Management Review* 15: 369–381.

Dyck, I.J.A., A. Morse, and L. Zingales. 2007. Who blows the whistle on corporate fraud?, Finance Working Paper No. 156/2007, European Corporate Governance Institute, available at SSRN: http://ssrn.com/abstract=891482

Elster, J. 1989. *The cement of society: A study of social order.* Cambridge, MA: Cambridge University Press.

Fehr, E., and A. Falk. 2002. Psychological foundations of incentives. *European Economic Review* 46: 687–724.

Fehr, E., and U. Fischbacher. 2003. The nature of human altruism. *Nature* 425: 785–791.

Fehr, E., and S. Gächter. 2002. Do incentive contracts undermine voluntary cooperation?, Working Paper No. 34, Institue for Emprical Research in Economics, University of Zurich, available at SSRN: http://ssrn.com/abstract=313028

Fehr, E., and B. Rockenbach. 2003. Detrimental effects of sanctions on human altruism. *Nature* 422: 137–140.

Field, L.C., and J.M. Karpoff. 2002. Takeover defenses of IPO firms. *Journal of Finance* 57: 1857–1889.

Fischbacher, U., S. Gachter, and E. Fehr. 2001. Are people conditionally cooperative? Evidence from a public goods experiment. *Economics Letters* 71: 397–404.

Foss, K., and N.J. Foss. 2000. Competence and governance perspective: How much do they differ? And how does it matter? In *Competence, governance, and entrepreneurship*, eds. N.J. Foss and V. Mahnke, 55–79. Oxford: Oxford University Press.

Foss, N.J., and M. Iversen. 1997. Promoting synergies in multiproduct firms: Toward a resource-based view, Working Paper No. 97–12, Department of Industrial Economics and Strategy, Copenhagen Business School.

Freeman, R.B., and E.P. Lazear. 1995. An economic analysis of works councils. In *Works councils: Consultation, representation, and cooperation in industrial relations*, eds. J. Rogers and W. Streeck, 27–52. Chicago, IL: University of Chicago Press.

Frese, E. 2000. *Grundlagen der Organisation: Konzept – Prinzipien – Strukturen.* Wiesbaden: Gabler.

Frey, B.S. 1997. *Not just for the money: An economic theory of personal motivation.* Brookfield: Edward Elgar.

Frey, B.S., and M. Benz. 2004. From imperialism to inspiration: A survey of economics and psychology. In *The Elgar companion of economics and philosophy*, eds. J. Davis, A. Marciano, and J. Runde, 61–83. Aldershot: Edward Elgar.

Frey, B.S., and I. Bohnet. 1995. Institutions affect fairness – Experimental investigations. *Journal of Institutional and Theoretical Economics* 151: 286–303.

Frey, B.S., and L. Goette. 1999. Does pay motivate volunteers?, Working Paper No. 7, Institue for Emprical Research in Economics, University of Zurich.

Frey, B.S., and R. Jegen. 2001. Motivation crowding theory. *Journal of Economic Surveys* 15: 589–611.

Frey, B.S., and S. Meier. 2004. Pro-social behavior in a natural setting. *Journal of Economic Behavior and Organization* 54: 65–88.

Frey, B.S., and M. Osterloh. 2002. Motivation – A dual-edged factor of production. In *Successful management by motivation*, eds. B.S. Frey and M. Osterloh, 3–26. Wiesbaden: Springer.

Frey, B.S., and M. Osterloh. 2005. Yes, managers should be paid like bureaucrats. *Journal of Management Inquiry* 14: 96–111.

Frey, B.S., M. Benz, and A. Stutzer. 2004. Introducing procedural utility: Not only what, but also how matters. *Journal of Institutional and Theoretical Economics* 160: 377–401.

Frick, B., G. Speckbacher, and P. Wentges. 1999. Arbeitnehmermitbestimmung und moderne Theorie der Unternehmung. *Zeitschrift für Betriebswirtschaft* 69: 745–764.

Friedman, M. 1953. The methodology of positive economics. In *Essays in positive economics*, ed. M. Friedman, 23–47. Chicago, IL: University of Chicago Press.

Frost, J. 2003. *Wieviel Markt verträgt das Unternehmen? Theorien der Firma und organisatorische Steuerung.* Habilitation: University of Zurich.

Fuller, J., and M.C. Jensen. 2002. Just say no to wall street. *Journal of Applied Corporate Finance* 14: 41–46.

Funke, U., and H. Schuler. 2002. *Eignungsdiagnostik in Forschung und Praxis*. Bonn: Hogrefe.

Ghoshal, S., and P. Moran. 1996. Bad for practice: A critique of the transaction cost theory. *Academy of Management Review* 21: 13–47.

Gittell, J.H. 2001. Supervisory span, relational coordination, and flight departure performance: A reassessment of postbureaucracy theory. *Organization Science* 12: 468–483.

Gneezy, U., and A. Rustichini. 2000. A fine is a price. *Journal of Legal Studies* 29: 1–17.

Grandori, A. 2001. *Organization and economic behaviour*. London: Routledge.

Grandori, A., and B. Kogut. 2002. Dialogue on organization and knowledge. *Organization Science* 13: 224–231.

Grant, R.M. 1996. Towards a knowledge-based theory of the firm. *Strategic Management Journal* 17: 109–122.

Hackman, J.R., and G.R. Oldham. 1976. Motivation through design of work – Test of a theory. *Organizational Behavior and Human Performance* 16: 250–279.

Hall, B.J. 2003. Six challenges in designing equity-based pay. *Journal of Applied Corporate Finance* 15: 21–33.

Hall, B.J., and K.J. Murphy. 2003. The trouble with stock options. *Journal of Economic Perspectives* 17: 49–70.

Hansmann, H.B. 1980. The role of nonprofit enterprise. *Yale Law Journal* 89: 835–901.

Hansmann, H.B. 1996. *The ownership of enterprise*. Cambridge, MA: Harvard University Press.

Hardin, G. 1968. The tragedy of the commons. *Science* 162: 1243–1248.

Healy, P.M., and J.M. Wahlen. 1999. A review of the earnings management literature and its implications for standard setting. *Accounting Horizons* 13: 365–383.

Heckhausen, H. 1989. *Motivation und Handeln*. Berlin, Heidelberg, New York, NY: Springer.

Henrich, J., R. Boyd, S. Bowles, C. Camerer, E. Fehr, H. Gintis, and R. McElreath. 2001. In search of homo economicus: Behavioral experiments in 15 small-scale societies. *American Economic Review* 91: 73–78.

Hermalin, B.E., and M.S. Weisbach. 2003. Boards of directors as an endogenously determined institution: A survey of the economic literature. *Economic Policy Review* 9: 7–26.

Hertig, G. 2009. Employee activism and corporate governance, Working Paper, ETH Zurich.

Hillman, A.J., and T. Dalziel. 2003. Boards of directors and firm performance: Integrating agency and resource dependence perspectives. *Academy of Management Review* 28: 383–396.

Hirschman, A.O. 1970. *Exit, voice, and loyalty: Responses to decline in firms, organizations, and states*. Cambridge, MA: Harvard University Press.

Holmstrom, B. 1982. Moral hazard in teams. *Bell Journal of Economics* 13: 324–340.

Irlenbusch, B., and D. Sliwka. 2005. Incentives, decision frames, and motivation crowding out – An experimental investigation, Discussion Paper No. 1758, Institute for the Study of Labor, available at SSRN: http://ssrn.com/abstract=822866

Jensen, M.C., and W.H. Meckling. 1976. Theory of the firm: Managerial behavior, agency costs and ownership structure. *Journal of Financial Economics* 3: 305–360.

Jensen, M.C. and K.J. Murphy. 1990. CEO incentives – It's not how much you pay, but how. *Harvard Business Review*, May–June 68: 138–153.

Johnson, S.A., H.E. Ryan, and Y.S. Tian. 2009. Managerial incentives and corporate fraud: The sources of incentives matter. *Review of Finance* 13: 115–145.

Klein, B., R.G. Crawford, and A.A. Alchian. 1978. Vertical integration, appropriable rents, and the competitive contracting process. *Journal of Law and Economics* 21: 297–326.

Klinger, S., C. Hartman, S. Anderson, J. Cavanagh, and H. Sklar. 2002. *Executive Excess 2002*, Institute for Policy Studies and United for a Fair Economy, http://www.faireconomy.org/files/Executive_Excess_2002.pdf

Kogut, B., and U. Zander. 1996. What firms do? Coordination, identity, and learning. *Organization Science* 7: 502–518.

Kollock, P. 1998. Social dilemmas: The anatomy of cooperation. *Annual Review of Sociology* 24: 183–214.

Kräkel, M. 1999. *Organisation und Management*. Tübingen: Mohr Siebeck.

Langlois, R.N. 2002. Modularity in technology and organization. *Journal of Economic Behavior and Organization* 49: 19–37.

Lave, J., and E. Wenger. 1991. *Situated learning: Legitimate peripheral participation*. Cambridge: Cambridge University Press.

Lazear, E.P. 1999. Personnel economics: Past lessons and future directions. *Journal of Labor Economics* 17: 199–236.

Ledyard, J.O. 1995. Public goods: A survey of experimental research. In *Handbook of experimental economics*, eds. J. Kagel and A.E. Roth, 111–194. Princeton, NJ: Princeton University Press.

Levi, M. 1988. *Of rule and revenue*. Berkeley, CA: University of California Press.

Liberman, V., S.M. Samuels, and L. Ross. 2004. The name of the game: Predictive power of reputations versus situational labels in determining prisoner's dilemma game moves. *Personality and Social Psychology Bulletin* 30: 1175–1185.

Lindenberg, S. 2001. Intrinsic motivation in a new light. *Kyklos* 54: 317–342.

Mahoney, J.T., and J.R. Pandian. 1992. The resource-based view within the conversation of strategic management. *Strategic Management Journal* 13: 363–380.

Murphy, K.J. 1999. Executive compensation. In *Handbook of labor economics*, eds. O. Ashenfelter and D. Card, 2485–2563. Amsterdam: North-Holland.

Orr, J.E. 1996. *Talking about machines: An ethnography of a modern job*. Ithaca, NY: Cornell University Press.

Osterloh, M. 2006. Human resources management and knowledge creation. In *Knowledge creation and management: New challenges for managers*, eds. I. Nonaka and I. Kazuo, 158–175. Oxford: Oxford University Press.

Osterloh, M., and B.S. Frey. 1997. Sanktionen oder Seelenmassage? Motivationale Grundlagen der Unternehmensführung. *Die Betriebswirtschaft* 57: 307–321.

Osterloh, M., and B.S. Frey. 2000. Motivation, knowledge transfer, and organizational forms. *Organization Science* 11: 538–550.

Osterloh, M., and B.S. Frey. 2004. Corporate governance for crooks. The case for corporate virtue. In *Corporate governance and firm organization*, ed. A. Grandori, 191–211. Oxford: Oxford University Press.

Osterloh, M., and B.S. Frey. 2006. Shareholders should welcome knowledge workers as directors. *Journal of Management and Governance* 10: 325–345.

Osterloh, M., and J. Frost. 2002. Motivation and knowledge as strategic resources. In *Successful management by motivation*, eds. B.S. Frey and M. Osterloh, 27–52. Wiesbaden: Springer.

Ostrom, E. 1998. A behavioral approach to the rational choice theory of collective action. *American Political Science Review* 92: 1–22.

Ostrom, E. 1999. *Die Verfassung der Allmende: Jenseits von Staat und Markt*. Tübingen: Mohr Siebeck.

Ostrom, E. 2000. Crowding out citizenship. *Scandinavian Political Studies* 23: 3–16.

Ouchi, W.G. 1978. Transmission of control through organizational hierarchy. *Academy of Management Journal* 21: 173–192.

Penrose, E.T. 1959. *The theory of the growth of the firm*. Oxford: Oxford University Press.

Rabin, M. 1998. Psychology and economics. *Journal of Economic Literature* 36: 11–46.

Rajan, R.G., and L. Zingales. 1998. Power in a theory of the firm. *Quarterly Journal of Economics* 113: 387–432.

Rumelt, R. 1984. Towards a strategic theory of the firm. In *Competitive strategic management*, ed. R. Lamb, 556–570. Englewood Cliffs, NJ: Prentice Hall.

Sadowski, D. 2002. *Personalökonomie und Arbeitspolitik*. Stuttgart: Schäffer-Poeschel.

Sally, D. 1995. Conversation and cooperation in social dilemmas – A meta-analysis of experiments from 1958 to 1992. *Rationality and Society* 7: 58–92.

Salter, M. 2003. Innovation corrupted: The rise and fall of enron, Harvard Business School, HBR Case No. 903–032.

Schiltknecht, K. 2004. *Corporate Governance: Das subtile Spiel um Geld und Macht*. Zürich: Neue Zürcher Zeitung.

Schnatterly, K. 2003. Increasing firm value through detection and prevention of white-collar crime. *Strategic Management Journal* 24: 587–614.

Sen, A.K. 1974. Choice, orderings and morality. In *Practical reason – Papers and discussions*, ed. S. Körner, 54–67. Oxford: Basil Blackwell.

Simon, H.A. 1991. Organizations and markets. *Journal of Economic Perspectives* 5: 25–44.

Skinner, B.F. 1965. *Science and human behavior*. New York, NY: Free Press.

Spector, B. 2003. HRM at Enron: The unindicted co-conspirator. *Organizational Dynamics* 32: 207–220.

Spender, J.C. 1996. Making knowledge the basis of a dynamic theory of the firm. *Strategic Management Journal* 17: 45–62.

Steinmann, H. 1969. *Das Großunternehmen im Interessenkonflikt: Ein wirtschaftswissenschaftlicher Diskussionsbeitrag zu Grundfragen einer Reform der Unternehmensordnung in hochentwickelten Industriegesellschaften*. Stuttgart: Poeschel.

Steinmann, H., and E. Gerum. 1992. Unternehmensordnung. In *Allgemeine Betriebswirtschaftslehre*, eds. F.X. Bea, E. Dichtl, and M. Schweizer, 216–307. Stuttgart: Lucius & Lucius.

Stout, L.A. 2003a. The shareholder as Ulysses: Some empirical evidence on why investors in public corporations tolerate board governance. *University of Pennsylvania Law Review* 152: 667–712.

Stout, L.A. 2003b On the proper motives of corporate directors (or, why you don't want to invite homo economicus to join your board). *Delaware Journal of Corporate Law* 28: 1–26.

Stukas, A.A., M. Snyder, and E.G. Clary. 1999. The effects of "mandatory volunteerism" on intentions to volunteer. *Psychological Science* 10: 59–64.

Teece, D.G., G. Pisano, and A. Shuen. 1997. Dynamic capabilities and strategic management. *Strategic Management Journal* 18: 509–533.

Tenbrunsel, A.E., and D.M. Messick. 1999. Sanctioning systems, decision frames, and cooperation. *Administrative Science Quarterly* 44: 684–707.

Thompson, J.D. 1967. *Organizations in action*. New York, NY: Transaction Publishers.

Tirole, J. 2001. Corporate governance. *Econometrica* 69: 1–35.

Topel, R. 1991. Specific capital, mobility, and wages – Wages rise with job seniority. *Journal of Political Economy* 99: 145–176.

Tosi, H.L., S. Werner, J.P. Katz, and L.R. Gomez-Mejia. 2000. How much does performance matter? A meta-analysis of ceo pay studies. *Journal of Management* 26: 301–339.

Tyler, T.R., and S.L. Blader. 2000. *Cooperation in groups: Procedural justice, social identity, and behavioral engagement*. Philadelphia, PA: Psychology Press.

Tyler, T.R., and E.A. Lind. 1992. A relational model of authority in groups. In *Advances in experimental social psychology*, ed. M.P. Zanna, 115–192, vol. 25. San Diego, CA, London: Academic.

Vining, A.R. 2003. Internal market failure: A framework for diagnosing firm inefficiency. *Journal of Management Studies* 40: 431–457.

Watson, J.B. 1913. Psychology as the behaviorist views it. *Psychological Review* 20: 158–177.

Weibel, A. 2004. *Kooperation in strategischen Wissensnetzwerken: Vertrauen und Kontrolle zur Lösung des sozialen Dilemmas*. Wiesbaden: DUV.

Witt, P. 2003. *Corporate Governance-Systeme im Wettbewerb*. Wiesbaden: DUV.

Zingales, L. 1998. Corporate governance. In *The new Palgrave dictionary of economics and the law*, ed. P. Newman, 497–503. London: Macmillan.

Chapter 4
Scandalous Co-determination

Kai Kühne and Dieter Sadowski

Contents

Empirical Research on Co-determination

Economic consequences of labour law are a well-established topic of economic research in Germany (cf., e.g., Albach et al. 1985; Weiber and Stockert 1987). Likewise, the consequences of the 1976 Co-determination Act, which gives employees of larger corporations a quasi-parity in supervisory boards, have been closely investigated from the very beginning (cf. Küpper 1992, pp. 1414f.). While some empirical studies examining the impact of co-determination on the profitability and productivity of companies show ambiguous results, the vast majority cannot detect any negative effects (cf. Renaud 2007, pp. 693ff.). This finding is a particular feature of studies that apply advanced econometric methods.

Kraft and Ugarkovic (2006), for instance, analyse the impact of increased employee representation in supervisory boards on return on equity by comparing co-determined and non co-determined companies before and after the introduction of the Co-determination Act. They find no empirical support for the hypothesis that the

K. Kühne (✉)

Research Associate, Institute for Labour Law and Industrial Relations in the European Community, University of Trier, Trier, Germany

e-mail: kuehne@iaaeg.de

A. Brink (ed.), *Corporate Governance and Business Ethics*, Ethical Economy.
Studies in Economic Ethics and Philosophy 39, DOI 10.1007/978-94-007-1588-2_4,
© Springer Science+Business Media B.V. 2011

extension of co-determination has decreased return on equity. Using similar research methods, Renaud (2007) even concludes that the enforced quasi-parity in German supervisory boards has increased corporate returns in the long run.

Fauver and Fuerst (2006) study to what extent the degree of employee representation in supervisory boards affects the stock market performance of German firms. They find that the degree of co-determination has a positive effect on both the firm value and the size of dividends: particularly in sectors with complex products, the firm value can be increased by quasi-parity.

From the perspective of empirical economic research, co-determination can thus be seen as a specific, but economically "innocent" element of corporate governance. Until recently, even leading employer representatives subscribed to that view (cf. Bertelsmann Stiftung and Hans-Böckler-Stiftung 1998). Today, however, this has changed dramatically. In 2004, the main employer associations advocated a restriction of co-determination rights (cf. BDA and BDI 2004), and, in 2006, the Biedenkopf Commission found that the different positions of employee and employer representatives were irreconcilable (cf. Kommission zur Modernisierung der deutschen Unternehmensmitbestimmung 2006, p. 7). Members of parliament also raised their voices: deputies of the FDP (a German party which aimed for the abolishment of quasi-parity co-determination already in its manifesto for the federal elections in 2005; cf. Freie Demokratische Partei 2005, p. 14) clearly supported the employers' position (cf. FAZ, 21 December 2006a, p. 11).

Irrespective of empirical evidence, co-determination is thus perceived as a problem by several actors. This ultimately raises the following question: which views make it into public opinion, which into politics – and how?

The Mass Media Discourse on Co-determination

Public and Published Opinion

That politicians should consider public opinion was a prominent idea already in the Renaissance (cf. Machiavelli 1532/1986, pp. 141ff.). Thinkers of the Enlightenment then declared publicity a constitutive element of reasonable ruling (cf. Kant 1795/1923, pp. 468f.). The extent to which its presence conforms to the enlightened ideal of the public sphere may be uncertain (cf. Habermas 1990, pp. 225ff.), but the relevance of public opinion for the political system is uncontroversial; "public opinion is uniformly recognized as a powerful force in democratic politics" (Johnson-Cartee 2005, p. 45). Citizens, or collective forces that mobilise the general public, have political leverage in an electoral system because ignoring public opinion would result in a loss of power for political decision-makers in democracies (cf. Gerhards 1992, p. 314). It is debatable, however, to what extent citizens are able to mobilise the general public or whether they are rather "victims" of a public opinion that today is principally constituted by the mass media (cf. Habermas 1990, pp. 275ff.).

The mass media are certainly not neutral agents of information distribution, but play a highly active role by selecting and interpreting information (cf. McQuail 2005, pp. 523f.). They do not mirror social reality. Instead, they contribute to the societal construction of reality (cf. Luhmann 2004, p. 183). The reality that political decision-making is based upon is essentially the reality of the mass media. They affect the perception of social phenomena by employing specific interpretative frames (cf. Entman 1993, p. 52). Facts covered by the media do not have an intrinsic meaning but are rendered meaningful primarily by these schemata (cf. Gamson 1989, pp. 157f.). In this respect, the mass media affect the audience's perception of reality and hence the perception of political problems (cf. Scheufele 1999, p. 105). Consequently, they must be seen as crucial determinants of political decision-making in modern democracies (cf. Entman 1993, p. 55).

The Portrayal of Co-determination in Press Editorials

We have tried to reconstruct the public debate about co-determination in Germany by analysing three national newspapers: the *Frankfurter Allgemeine Zeitung* (FAZ), the *Süddeutsche Zeitung* (SZ), and the *tageszeitung* (taz) for the period between 1998 and 2007. Among all German national quality newspapers, these papers are most frequently used as sources of information by journalists and hence perform an opinion-leading function for the mass media (cf. Weischenberg et al. 1994, p. 163). They cover a wide range of the political spectrum: on a political continuum ranging from 1 to 3 (where 1 is left and 3 is right), the taz is located at the left pole (1.6), the SZ takes a rather centrist position (1.8), and the FAZ is located at the right (2.3) (cf. Eilders 2002, p. 37).

In the press, opinions are most explicitly expressed in opinion-forming formats such as editorials which are unaffected by journalistic norms of neutrality. The essential function of these formats is to interpret and evaluate current events, actions, and positions of persons and institutions (cf. Pürer 2003, p. 191). Accordingly, these texts are ideal for extracting interpretative frames (cf. Gamson and Modigliani 1989, p. 17).

We have limited our analysis to the editorials of the FAZ, the SZ, and the taz that address the topic of supervisory board co-determination during the period selected. The LexisNexis and F.A.Z.-BiblioNet databases were used to identify those texts published between 1 January 1998 and 31 December 2007 which are explicitly labelled as opinion-forming formats and contain one of the search terms *"paritätische Mitbestimmung"* (parity co-determination), *"Mitbestimmung AND Aufsichtsrat"*, or *"Unternehmensmitbestimmung"* (supervisory board co-determination). The search identified 77 articles.

We then performed a content analysis to capture the interpretative schemata concerning supervisory board co-determination in these texts. All information units that characterise co-determination from the editorial staff's perspective, i.e., all attributes and all propositions whose object is co-determination and whose initiator is the journalistic author, were identified. These information units were classified into four categories (Table 4.1).

The unit of analysis was the paragraph – the smallest unit of meaning in journalistic texts (cf. Jasperson et al. 1998, p. 211). Each paragraph containing at least one characterisation of supervisory board co-determination was included in the content analysis by testing the presence of each of the four categories. Consequently, there are four observations for each coded paragraph.

Table 4.1 Categories of the content analysis

Illegitimacy	Supervisory board co-determination is a violation of shareholders' property rights; it is unfair with regard to foreign corporate colleagues.
Inefficiency	Supervisory board co-determination is bureaucratic and facilitates "wheeling and dealing"; it leads to biased and inappropriate corporate decisions; it creates disadvantages for German companies in business competition.
Contingency	Supervisory board co-determination is a national singularity; it is a historically contingent phenomenon of the German economic system.
Social peace	Supervisory board co-determination is a trade union achievement that contributes to securing social peace; it enables employees to act at eye level with management.

From the 77 articles that conform to the search algorithm, 91 paragraphs contain at least one characterisation of supervisory board co-determination. These 91 paragraphs were coded: 60 from the FAZ, 24 from the SZ, and 7 from the taz. The fact that almost two-thirds of the coded units stem from the FAZ might be due to the reporting focus of this newspaper, which covers economic themes in a particularly extensive manner (cf. Dohrendorf 1990, p. 12). The taz, on the other hand, is generally less comprehensive than the other papers.

Given their political positions, it is hardly surprising that the observed interpretative frames differ between the newspapers (Table 4.2). The observation that the FAZ hardly mentions the contribution of co-determination to social peace can be easily attributed to its conservative ideology. The SZ and the taz, on the other hand, frequently emphasise this aspect, the taz alluding to it the most. This can be put down to the fact that this paper tends to represent left-wing ideologies.

Table 4.2 Categories per newspaper

		Presence of categories[a]			
	Coded paragraphs	Illegitimacy	Inefficiency	Contingency	Social peace
FAZ	$n = 60$	0.30 ($n = 18$)	0.65 ($n = 39$)	0.28 ($n = 17$)	0.03 ($n = 2$)
SZ	$n = 24$	0.13 ($n = 3$)	0.63 ($n = 15$)	0.17 ($n = 4$)	0.33 ($n = 8$)
taz	$n = 7$	0.14 ($n = 1$)	0.43 ($n = 3$)	0.29 ($n = 2$)	0.43 ($n = 3$)
Chi^2 (2)		3.2686	1.3136	1.2791	17.6556***

*** Level of significance: 1%

[a] Share of accordingly coded paragraphs

The results are more instructive, however, with respect to the temporal dimension. Comparing the interpretative frame concerning co-determination during the first 5 years of the period under examination with the one of the last 5 years shows that the share of paragraphs in which co-determination is characterised as inefficient has risen significantly from 45 to 68%, while, in contrast, the presence of the contingency category has declined significantly from 45 to 20% (Table 4.3).

Table 4.3 Categories per period

	Coded paragraphs	Presence of categories[a]			
		Illegitimacy	Inefficiency	Contingency	Social peace
1998–2002	$n = 20$	0.25 ($n = 5$)	0.45 ($n = 9$)	0.45 ($n = 9$)	0.10 ($n = 2$)
2003–2007	$n = 71$	0.24 ($n = 17$)	0.68 ($n = 48$)	0.20 ($n = 14$)	0.15 ($n = 11$)
Chi^2 (1)		0.0095	3.4073*	5.2809**	0.3845

* Level of significance: 10%; ** Level of significance: 5%
[a] Share of accordingly coded paragraphs

The decreased share of textual units that address co-determination in terms of contingency aspects can be regarded as a sign of an increasingly polarised debate: suggesting that co-determination is a specific characteristic of the German economic system is a rather detached, non-judgemental statement and does not imply any compelling need for political action. The decreasing presence of this characterisation in press texts thus indicates a growing controversy. The inefficiency of the German rules, in turn, is mentioned more and more frequently in the press discourse, plainly contradicting simultaneously published results of empirical economic research.

Hence, scientific reasoning and findings apparently do not play a major role in determining the interpretative framework of the mass media; not even business editors seem to take notice of the results of empirical economic research. Indeed, empirical studies are mentioned in only three out of 77 editorials. This raises the question of which other factors might have shaped the discourse about co-determination.

In this context, a look at the chronology of news with reference to supervisory board co-determination is instructive. First of all, it is noticeable that the number of textual units captured by the content analysis varies considerably over time (Fig. 4.1). Whereas, in 2004, 18 editorials with reference to supervisory board co-determination were published altogether, there was not a single editorial in 1999.

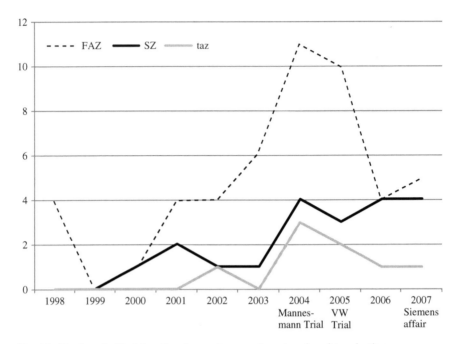

Fig. 4.1 Number of editorials with reference to supervisory board co-determination
Source: Own figure

This variation is apparently related to diversity in news flow. The maximum in 2004 coincides with the Mannesmann trial. In this trial, allegedly excessive bonuses paid to the former chief executive of Mannesmann, after its sale to Vodafone in 2000, were examined by the Düsseldorf District Court. Among the impeached members of the Mannesmann supervisory board that had approved these payments was the former president of the IG Metall, the dominant metalworkers' union in Germany.

In 2005, when the second-largest relevant text quantum was published, systematic misuse of company funds for corrupting labour representatives at Volkswagen was disclosed. Allegations included, among other things, the procurement of prostitutes for employees who were members of the VW supervisory board.

A considerable number of the texts selected for the content analysis refer to one of these events; in 20 out of 77 editorials, either the Mannesmann trial or the VW corruption case is mentioned. Thus, these events, unlike the findings of empirical research, seem to play a considerable role in the press discourse about supervisory board co-determination.

Admittedly, neither the Mannesmann trial nor the VW corruption case pertains exclusively, or even primarily, to problems of supervisory board co-determination. But, as employee representatives were involved in both cases, they generally induced discussions about co-determination. Furthermore, both events share features that differentiate them from other news references to co-determination (such as commission reports or results of empirical studies) and render them especially attractive for mass media coverage: they can be regarded as scandalous events.

The Role of Scandals

Scandals refer to "actions or events involving certain kinds of transgressions which become known to others and are sufficiently serious to elicit public response" (Thompson 2000, p. 13). By disclosing a moral order that is temporarily disrupted, scandals ritually afford the opportunity to validate or modify norms (cf. Jacobsson and Löfmarck 2008, pp. 204f.); they induce public negotiation of a society's moral preferences on the basis of concrete cases (cf. Burkhardt 2006, p. 158). Scandals are inherently relevant for the mass media: massive public attention provoked by transgressions against the moral order is both a constituent element of scandals and the ultimate purpose of mass media organisations. The prevalence of scandals in contemporary mass media thus can be seen as a consequence of the logic of commercial news production (cf. Lull and Hinerman 1997, p. 1).

Both the Mannesmann trial and the VW corruption case are obviously scandalous events. Not only moral norms were transgressed, but even legal norms were allegedly violated in each case. More precisely, the members of the Mannesmann supervisory board were charged with embezzlement (§§ 263 and 266 StGB – Strafgesetzbuch, German Criminal Code) (cf. Neue Juristische Wochenschrift, 1 November 2004, p. 3275); the perpetrators of the VW affair were, among other things, convicted of embezzlement (§§ 263 and 266 StGB) and awarding preferential treatment to works council members (§ 119 para. 1 subpara. 3 BetrVG – Betriebsverfassungsgesetz, Works Constitution Act) (cf. Zwiehoff 2009). Public response, on the other hand, is reflected in the considerable share of editorials referring to the Mannesmann trial or the VW affair.

One of the apparent reasons for this public response (i.e., one of the features that render both incidents particularly scandalous) relates to the identities of the transgressors involved. The size of scandals is "an increasing function of the social stature of those who are compromised" (Adut 2005, p. 220). Among those who were compromised by the Mannesmann trial and the VW affair were persons of unquestionably high social status: the chief executive of Germany's biggest commercial bank and the president of the largest German blue-collar union were in the dock of the Mannesmann trial. The VW affair, on the other hand, involved, among others, the company's personnel director, who was the architect of the red-green government's labour-market reforms, and VW's works council chief. VW itself is not only Europe's biggest carmaker, but is also reckoned to be a "symbol of Germany's traditional consensual model of business" (The Economist, 9 July 2005, p. 52). Hence, those involved in the Mannesmann trial and the VW affair can be regarded as representatives of particularly prominent institutions of the German economy and, for this reason, their transgressions are especially prone to scandal coverage.

Another feature that renders these incidents potentially scandalous is related to the discrepancy between moral standards and factual action.

Transgressions are magnified to the extent that they reveal hypocrisy; there will naturally be
a greater chance of interest from the public if the transgression undermines the high moral
claims of the offender. (Adut 2004, p. 534)

Individuals with exposed organisational positions are again especially at risk,
because, by virtue of their position, they are thought to represent their organisations' values and beliefs, i.e., their behaviour is assessed in terms of these ideals
(cf. Thompson 2000, p. 16). With regard to the incidents at Mannesmann and VW,
it goes without saying that the behaviour of the labour representatives involved conflicts with the ideals that these persons are thought to stand for. Collusion between
labour representatives and management, as it was practiced at the VW boardroom,
is definitely not compatible with the principle of solidarity among workers, which is
traditionally regarded as a crucial value of the labour movement (cf. Lassalle 1919,
p. 239). Giving a single manager DM 59 million, on the other hand, might conflict with conceptions of social justice in general and with critical positions towards
inflated manager remuneration (which are regularly taken by trade unions officials;
cf., e.g., DGB 2009) in particular. Hence, given the values and beliefs of the labour
movement, the behaviour of the labour representatives involved in the Mannesmann
trial and the VW corruption case is particularly scandalous.

Because of the massive public attention and the strong feelings they are apt
to mobilise, scandals do not only serve the commercial interests of mass media
organisations, but are also regularly exploited for political purposes. Indeed, the
construction of political relevance can be regarded as an essential feature of modern media scandals (cf. Burkhardt 2006, pp. 338ff.); "the use of scandal by political
actors is routine, almost banal" (Adut 2004, p. 532). First and foremost, scandals are
inherently useful for discrediting individual politicians. By undermining reputation,
scandals can deprive politicians of their symbolic capital, on which the exercise of
political power in modern democracies depends to a large degree (cf. Thompson
2000, pp. 96ff.). For this reason, the personal use of bonus air miles, statements
about German history, or words of honour can have serious occupational consequences for politicians. Beyond these effects on individuals, however, scandals are
also able to affect institutions (cf. Lull and Hinerman 1997, p. 9). Although the logic
of moral responsibility that underlies scandals ultimately requires culpable individuals, these individuals' actions regularly have supra-individual consequences. The
scale of these consequences is, again, dependent on the social status of the transgressors, because elites represent groups in a "synecdochic way" (Adut 2004, p. 534).
Scandalous behaviour of single politicians can discredit entire governments, parties,
or even the political class in general (cf. Jacobsson and Löfmarck 2008, p. 212).
Consequently, scandals are an approved strategy, not only for damaging individual political careers, but also for attacking groups and institutions through their
representative members (cf. Adut 2004, p. 535).

Indeed, discoursive strategies were applied accordingly to both the Mannesmann
trial and the VW affair. Politicians tried to use these incidents to challenge the
established German system of co-determination. In 2004, for example, in a guest
article, a member of the FDP cited the Mannesmann case as a typical example for

wheeling and dealing in German supervisory boards, and concluded that returning to one-third co-determination (i.e., abolishing quasi-parity co-determination) in corporations with more than 2,000 employees was required (cf. Brüderle 2004, p. 12). Thus, the alleged misbehaviour of one particularly exposed employee representative was used to discredit employee representation in general. Eight months later, the same politician, in another guest article in the same newspaper, alluded to the VW affair to advocate the restriction of co-determination rights (cf. Brüderle 2005, p. 16). Even the Siemens affair in 2007 was interpreted analogously by this politician. The fact that managers had illegally financed a pseudo-employee organisation to weaken trade union influence was, according to him, further evidence of the detrimental impact of quasi-parity co-determination, because it showed that the existing legal regulations encouraged bribery. Therefore, they should be disposed (cf. FAZ, 31 March 2007, p. 14). Hence, the political implications that are derived by some politicans from scandals involving labour representatives seem to be independent of the particular nature of their involvement. While the Mannesmann trial and the VW corruption case involved transgressions by labour representatives, the Siemens affair pertained to transgressions by managers who aimed at undermining labour representation. Nevertheless, from the point of view of certain discourse participants, both scandals apparently implied the same conclusion, namely the need for abolishing quasi-parity co-determination. Thus, the violation of labour rights by Siemens managers was seen as arguing the case for the abolishment of these rights.

The evaluation of scandals and the deduction of potential consequences are rarely uncontroversial, but basically indeterminate; media scandals can be regarded as symbolic civil wars, with adverse discourse coalitions struggling for the power of interpretation (cf. Burkhardt 2006, pp. 383f.). The interpretative schemata mentioned above did not remain uncontested either, but were expressly challenged in the press. In one editorial, for instance, exploiting the VW affair to discard the Co-determination Act is rejected as crude populism and the German system of corporate governance is defended (cf. taz, 4 July 2005, p. 11). Several other editorials, however, conduct a line of argument that runs parallel to the conclusions of the cited politician, in that they refer to the scandals at VW or Mannesmann in the context of critical evaluations of co-determination. According to these texts, the Mannesmann trial proves that co-determination leads to insufficient control of management (cf. Piper 2004, p. 4) and that trade union officials in supervisory boards are unable to prevent wrong decisions (cf. FAZ, 23 October 2004, p. 9); consequently, reforming (cf. SZ, 19 February 2003, p. 4), or abolishing (cf. FAZ, 23 October 2004, p. 9), the obsolescent German model of co-determination should be considered; altogether, the Mannesmann judgement can be regarded as a disastrous verdict on the failure of the German system of co-determination (cf. Dunsch 2004, p. 11). Similarly, the VW affair is cited as an example for labour representatives and management colluding to the detriment of German companies (cf. SZ, 31 August 2006, p. 4); it shows what misconceived companionship in co-determined supervisory boards can lead to and it would have been avoided under a system of one-third co-determination (cf. Steltzner 2005, p. 11); in that respect, the VW affair is a strong attack against parity co-determination (cf. FAZ, 16 November 2006b, p. 1).

In fact, in the editorials considered in the content analysis, legitimising critical attitudes towards co-determination seems to be a crucial reason for referring to scandals. The proportion of paragraphs stressing the inefficiency of co-determination is significantly higher in those editorials that refer to either the Mannesmann or the VW scandal; it is 73 instead of 56% (Table 4.4). Seen the other way round, 47% of those paragraphs in which co-determination is characterised as inefficient are associated with scandals, compared with 29% of all other paragraphs. Thus, nearly half of all the statements pertaining to the inefficiency of co-determination refer somehow to scandalous events. Clearly, these events have played a considerable role in the press debate about co-determination during the last years.

Table 4.4 Categories and scandals

Reference to scandals[b]	Coded paragraphs	Presence of categories[a]			
		Illegitimacy	Inefficiency	Contingency	Social peace
no	$n = 54$	0.22 ($n = 12$)	0.56 ($n = 30$)	0.35 ($n = 19$)	0.15 ($n = 8$)
yes	$n = 37$	0.27 ($n = 10$)	0.73 ($n = 27$)	0.11 ($n = 4$)	0.14 ($n = 5$)
Chi^2 (1)		0.2765	2.8461*	6.9066**	0.0304

* Level of significance: 10%; ** Level of significance: 5%
[a] Share of accordingly coded paragraphs
[b] Mannesmann trial or VW affair is mentioned in the editorial

In this respect, we can conclude that the scandals at VW and Mannesmann were not conducive for the appreciation of supervisory board co-determination in the mass media discourse. Admittedly, whether the occurrence of scandals ultimately affected the interpretative schemata in editorials, or whether the increasingly frequent quotation of scandals was caused by the increasingly negative attitude towards co-determination, can not be definitely derived from the data. As general changes in the political climate before 2007 certainly did not foster appreciation of government intervention in labour markets and business decision-making, the increasingly frequent reference to scandals might primarily reflect this development. But even if this were the case, the scandals can at least be seen as welcome inducements for the expression of anti-co-determination attitudes, insofar as they obviously served the interests of those discourse participants who possess such attitudes.

Conclusion

There is a considerable discrepancy in the perception and the assessment of co-determination between the discourse of the mass media and empirical economic research. Whereas economists increasingly exclude detrimental effects of co-determination on corporate productivity and profitability, journalists increasingly emphasise these detrimental effects. Unlike scientific findings, which are hardly mentioned at all, scandals involving labour representatives play a significant role in press editorials. In this way, the arguments of the opponents of co-determination receive publicity that sharply contrasts with the doubtful empirical validity of their position. Whether this position will ultimately have an impact on political decision-making certainly also depends on factors that exceed the interpretative schemata in the German press – the informal pressure of interest groups, for instance (cf. Mitchell 1997, pp. 61ff.), or developments at European or international level (cf. Windolf 2007, pp. 68ff.). Furthermore, the mass media discourse has apparently not captured public opinion yet. Opinion polls show that 83% of Germans want to maintain the established model of supervisory board co-determination, while 77% consider supervisory board co-determination as an advantage for German companies (cf. Böckler Impuls 2006, p. 4). Hence, public opinion is obviously more consistent with the findings of empirical economic research than with the interpretative schemata of the mass media. Whereas scientific results seem to have no impact on the press discourse about co-determination, the press discourse seems to have no impact on public opinion. Nevertheless, the importance of interpretive dominance in the mass media discourse should not be underestimated. It can be shown, for instance, that scandalous behaviour of individual politicians actually weakens public regard for political institutions (cf. Bowler and Karp 2004). Accordingly, we cannot exclude that repeated reference to scandals like the Mannesmann trial or the VW corruption case might, in the long run, damage the appreciation of co-determination in general. In addition, the mass media's preference for assumptions contradicting empirical economic research is accompanied by analogous tendencies in jurisprudential discourse: empirical results concerning economic consequences of labour law seem to have either no, or at best an ambivalent, impact on the opinion of German lawyers (cf. Zachert 2007, p. 422). The prevalent interpretative schemata concerning supervisory board co-determination therefore require vigilance. On the other hand, economists should maybe ask themselves why their findings are ignored by the public in spite of their public relevance.

References

Adut, A. 2004. Scandal as norm entrepreneurship strategy: Corruption and the French investigating magistrates. *Theory and Society* 33: 529–578.

Adut, A. 2005. A theory of scandal: Victorians, homosexuality, and the fall of Oscar Wilde. *American Journal of Sociology* 111: 213–248.

Albach, H., R. Clemens, and C. Friede. 1985. *Kosten der Arbeit: Einflußfaktoren der Personalaufwendungen in Abhängigkeit von der Unternehmensgröße.* Stuttgart: Poeschel.

Bertelsmann Stiftung, and Hans-Böckler-Stiftung, eds. 1998. *Mitbestimmung und neue Unternehmenskulturen – Bilanz und Perspektiven: Bericht der Kommission Mitbestimmung.* Gütersloh: Verlag Bertelsmann Stiftung.

Brüderle, R. 2004. Mitbestimmung ist Teil einer Illusion. Standpunkte. *Frankfurter Allgemeine Zeitung*, 3 November 2004: 12.

Brüderle, R. 2005. Veraltete Mitbestimmung. Standpunkte. *Frankfurter Allgemeine Zeitung*, 12 July 2005: 16.

Bundesvereinigung der Deutschen Arbeitgeberverbände (BDA), and Bundesverband der Deutschen Industrie (BDI), eds. 2004. *Mitbestimmung modernisieren – Bericht der Kommission Mitbestimmung.* Berlin: BDA.

Bowler, S., and J.A. Karp. 2004. Politicians, scandals, and trust in government. *Political Behavior* 26: 271–287.

Böckler Impuls. 2006. Zustimmung zum deutschen Modell stabil. 13/2006: 4–5.

Burkhardt, S. 2006. *Medienskandale: Zur moralischen Sprengkraft öffentlicher Diskurse*. Cologne: Halem.

Deutscher Gewerkschaftsbund (DGB). 2009. *Stellungnahme des DGB zum Entwurf eines Gesetzes zur Angemessenheit der Vorstandsvergütung (VorstAG)*, DGB 2009, http://www.dgb.de/themen/++co++article-mediapool-15070ec1b2cace8ad8e01b6f8728f1c9?k:list= Mitbestimmung&k:list=Corporate%20Governance&k:list=Einkommen

Dohrendorf, R. 1990. *Zum publizistischen Profil der "Frankfurter Allgemeinen Zeitung"*. Frankfurt a. M.: Lang.

Dunsch, J. 2004. Zwischen Maßlosigkeit und Kontrollwahn. *Frankfurter Allgemeine Zeitung*, 1 April 2004: 11.

Eilders, C. 2002. Conflict and consonance in media opinion: Political positions of five German quality newspapers. *European Journal of Communication* 17: 25–63.

Entman, R.M. 1993. Framing: Toward clarification of a fractured paradigm. *Journal of Communication* 43: 51–58.

Fauver, L., and M.E. Fuerst. 2006. Does good corporate governance include employee representation? Evidence from German corporate boards. *Journal of Financial Economics* 82: 673–710.

Frankfurter Allgemeine Zeitung (FAZ). 2004. "Prämien an Manager sind kein Fall für den Staatsanwalt". *FAZ*, 23 October 2004: 9.

Frankfurter Allgemeine Zeitung (FAZ). 2006a. Kommission will Mitbestimmung kaum ändern. *FAZ*, 21 December 2006: 11.

Frankfurter Allgemeine Zeitung (FAZ). 2006b. Systemfehler. *FAZ*, 16 November 2006: 1.

Frankfurter Allgemeine Zeitung (FAZ). 2007. "Hier ist eine ganze Organisation gekauft worden". *FAZ*, 31 March 2007: 14.

Freie Demokratische Partei. 2005. *Arbeit hat Vorfahrt. Deutschlandprogramm 2005*, FDP 2005, http://files.liberale.de/fdp-wahlprogramm.pdf. Accessed on 18 Jul 2011.

Gamson, W.A. 1989. News as framing: Comments on Graber. *American Behavioral Scientist* 33: 157–161.

Gamson, W.A., and A. Modigliani. 1989. Media discourse and public opinion on nuclear power: A constructionist approach. *American Journal of Sociology* 95: 1–37.

Gerhards, J. 1992. Dimensionen und Strategien öffentlicher Diskurse. *Journal für Sozialforschung* 32: 307–318.

Habermas, J. 1990. *Strukturwandel der Öffentlichkeit*. Frankfurt a. M.: Suhrkamp.

Jacobsson, K., and E. Löfmarck. 2008. A sociology of scandal and moral transgression. *Acta Sociologica* 51: 203–216.

Jasperson, A.E., D.V. Shah, M. Watts, R.J. Faber, and D.P. Fan. 1998. Framing and the public agenda: Media effects on the importance of the federal budget deficit. *Political Communication* 15: 205–224.

Johnson-Cartee, K.S. 2005. *News narratives and framing: Constructing political reality*. Lanham, MD: Rowman and Littlefield.

Kant, I. 1795/1923. *Zum ewigen Frieden*. In *Schriften von 1790–1796. Immanuel Kants Werke, Band VI*, ed. A. Buchenau, E. Cassirer, and B. Kellermann, 425–476. Berlin: Bruno Cassirer.

Kommission zur Modernisierung der deutschen Unternehmensmitbestimmung, ed. 2006. *Bericht der wissenschaftlichen Mitglieder der Kommission*, Kommission zur Modernisierung der deutschen Unternehmensmitbestimmung 2006, http://www.bundesregierung.de/Content/DE/Archiv16/Artikel/2006/12/Anlagen/2006-12-20-mitbestimmungskommission,property= publicationFile.pdf. Accessed on 18 Jul 2011.

Kraft, K., and M. Ugarkovic. 2006. Gesetzliche Mitbestimmung und Kapitalrendite. *Jahrbücher für Nationalökonomie und Statistik* 226: 588–604.

Küpper, H.-U. 1992. Mitbestimmung. In *Handwörterbuch des Personalwesens*, ed. E. Gaugler, and W. Weber, 1408–1419, 2nd ed. Stuttgart: Schäffer-Poeschel.

Lassalle, F. 1919. Die Wissenschaft und die Arbeiter. In *Ferdinand Lassalle – Gesammelte Reden und Schriften: Zweiter Band*, ed. E. Bernstein, 203–284. Berlin: Paul Cassirer.

Luhmann, N. 2004. *Die Realität der Massenmedien*, 3rd ed. Wiesbaden: VS Verlag.

Lull, J., and S. Hinerman. 1997. The search for scandal. In *Media scandals*, ed. J. Lull and S. Hinerman, 1–34. Cambridge: Polity Press.

Machiavelli, N. 1532/1986. *Il Principe – Der Fürst*. Stuttgart: Reclam.

McQuail, D. 2005. *Mass communication theory*, 5th ed. London: Sage.

Mitchell, N.J. 1997. *The conspicuous corporation: Business, public policy, and representative democracy*. Ann Arbor, MI: University of Michigan Press.

Neue Juristische Wochenschrift. 2004. Verletzung aktienrechtlicher Pflichten und Untreue. *NJW* 57: 3275–3286.

Piper, N. 2004. Szenen einer Ehe. *Süddeutsche Zeitung*, 3 March 2004: 4.

Pürer, H. 2003. *Publizistik- und Kommunikationswissenschaft*. Konstanz: UVK.

Renaud, S. 2007. Dynamic efficiency of supervisory board co-determination in Germany. *Labour* 21: 689–712.

Scheufele, D.A. 1999. Framing as a theory of media effects. *Journal of Communication* 49: 103–122.

Steltzner, H. 2005. Transparente Unternehmen. *Frankfurter Allgemeine Zeitung*, 8 July 2005: 11.

Süddeutsche Zeitung (SZ). 2003. Im Reich der Märchen. *SZ*, 19 February 2003: 4.

Süddeutsche Zeitung (SZ). 2006. Ein Symbol wird 30. *SZ*, 31 August 2006: 4.

The Economist. 2005. An icon under fire. *The Economist*, 9 July 2005: 52.

Thompson, J.B. 2000. *Political scandal: Power and visibility in the media age*. Cambridge: Polity Press.

Weiber, R., and A. Stockert. 1987. *Rechtseinflüsse auf Personalentscheidungen: Eine konfirmatorische Analyse*. Stuttgart: Poeschel.

Weischenberg, S., M. Löffelholz, and A. Scholl. 1994. Merkmale und Einstellungen von Journalisten in Deutschland. *Media Perspektiven* 25: 154–167.

Windolf, P. 2007. Mitbestimmung im Institutionen-Wettbewerb. In *Perspektiven der Corporate Governance*, eds U. Jürgens, D. Sadowski, G.F. Schuppert, and M. Weiss, 55–75. Baden-Baden: Nomos.

Zachert, U. 2007. Der Arbeitsrechtsdiskurs und die Rechtsempirie: Ein schwieriges Verhältnis. *WSI Mitteilungen* 60: 421–426.

Zwiehoff, G. 2009. Betriebsratsbegünstigung als strafbare Untreue? – Die VW-Affäre. *Juris Praxisreport Arbeitsrecht* 2, note 6.

Chapter 5
Corporate Codes of Ethics: Can Punishments Enhance Their Effectiveness?

Till Talaulicar

Contents

Introduction

Corporate codes of ethics are written statements about moral norms which are issued by the respective company and which shall obligate corporate actions. In essence, these documents shall promote ethical behavior within the company and make corporate misbehavior to occur less likely. Although codes are widely distributed in many different countries (cf., e.g., Kaptein 2004), their effectiveness is still open to debate. Whereas some studies conclude that codes can be a valid means for enhancing the ethicality of corporate actions (cf., e.g., Trevino and Weaver 2001), other studies found no significant effects (cf., e.g., Cleek and Leonard 1998). In this article, I argue that codes can be helpful for improving the ethicality of corporate actions. However, merely developing and establishing codes is not enough

T. Talaulicar (✉)
Professor of Corporate Governance and Board Dynamics, Witten/Herdecke University,
Witten, Germany
e-mail: Till.Talaulicar@uni-wh.de

A. Brink (ed.), *Corporate Governance and Business Ethics*, Ethical Economy.
Studies in Economic Ethics and Philosophy 39, DOI 10.1007/978-94-007-1588-2_5,
© Springer Science+Business Media B.V. 2011

because the code itself cannot guarantee that its addressees act in accordance with its norms. Rather, the company has to carry out serious attempts to implement its code of ethics. Although this view may be widely shared, wisdom about appropriate code implementation is still fragile.

Implementation measures intend to make it more likely that the code norms are obeyed by the code addressees. In this respect, implementation measures are not restricted to the enactment of the code after the document had been developed. Rather, implementation measures refer to all efforts of the company which shall enhance adherence to the code norms. Therefore, implementation measures are only and always necessary under those conditions that the code norms are not observed anyway. In other words, codes that go beyond codifying common practices need implementation measures in order to become effective.

In principle, code implementation can either be preference- or constraints-based (cf. Talaulicar 2006). Preference-based measures intend to shape the attitudes, motives and beliefs of code addressees. Eventually, actors shall be convinced that the code norms are appropriate and that they deserve to be adhered to due to their deference. Hence, actors shall primarily be intrinsically motivated to act in accordance with the code because they prefer to do so. In contrast, constraints-based measures of code implementation do not intend to influence the actors' preferences. Rather, these measures modify conditions of the situation actors face, in a way that shall make code adherence to be evaluated more favorably by code addressees. As a consequence, the addressees are – primarily – extrinsically motivated to act in accordance with the code because conformity is rewarded and deviance is punished by the company.

Many business ethicists have articulated skepticism that constraints-based implementation efforts can succeed. I agree that preference-based implementation efforts are important. At the same time, however, I argue that constraints-based implementation measures, namely punishments, neither can nor should be discarded. More specifically, I show that properly designed and executed punishments can be viewed as a promising, and even indispensable, measure for enhancing code effectiveness. In the following, I first review the literature on constraints-based measures for code implementation. In doing so, I show that these measures are a common part of ethics programs in practice, although empirical evidence on their effectiveness is far from unanimity. I argue that this ambiguity can, at least partly, be traced back to the different designs of constraints-based measures, which is highly ignored in the empirical studies available. Therefore, the subsequent section outlines recommendations on the proper design of constraints-based measures for code implementation. These recommendations are derived from sanction theories which have a long tradition in legal philosophy and became subject of many empirical analyses, too. On this base, I differentiate outcome and process determinants of constraints-based implementation measures and discuss their characteristics in more detail.

Literature Review

Rewards and Punishments

In essence, constraints can be distinguished with regard to their valence. Rewards set positive incentives in order to make code compliance more attractive for the code addressees. On the contrary, punishments are disciplinary measures which make code deviance more costly and hence less attractive for employees. Many business ethicists state that code conformity can be improved neither by rewards nor by punishments.

Rewards which are not supplementary but intend to be an all-embracing measure for code implementation are indeed inappropriate because codes contain norms, the obedience to which is mandatory rather than voluntary within the company. Obeying the code norms for doing the right thing is one of the duties an employee assumes when entering the respective company. However, people are not used to getting or receiving rewards for doing what is right and for fulfilling one's duties (cf. Trevino 1990; Trevino and Youngblood 1990; Weaver and Trevino 2001). Based on interviews with (57) employees, managers and ethics officers in Canada, Schwartz (2004) confirms this view because most of his respondents "believed that compliance or doing the right thing is already part of your job for which you are being compensated, and therefore need not be explicitly rewarded in any sense" (p. 337).

Therefore, rewarding code conformance could lead astray to the awkward impression that code deviance is left to the actor's discretion because lack of compliance seems to be compensated by waiving of the rewards which are announced otherwise. Rewards generally imply that norm obedience is optional rather than obligatory (cf. Schwartz and Orleans 1967, p. 281). As Kaptein (1998) puts it:

> If a corporation rewards moral conduct too much, it may create the impression that morally responsible conduct is not mandatory. A reward is given for extra performance, which implies that such extra performance is not mandatory. (p. 177)

Thus, the bindingness of the code norms becomes relative to the rewards announced for code compliance. Therefore, code norms tend to be violated if deviance cannot be observed and hence cannot jeopardize the compensation.

Against this background, constraints-based measures for code implementation have to rely predominantly on punishments, i.e., negative sanctions in reaction on code violations. However, many criticisms were raised against this kind of code enforcement as well (cf., e.g., Berenbeim 1987; Brien 1996; Appelbaum et al. 1998). Essentially, these critics complain that punishments set a negative tone and lead to the fact that code addressees do not strive to obey the code norms because it is the right thing to do but to avoid punishment. Accordingly, code observance becomes less likely under those conditions when code violations can hardly be detected and verified. As a consequence, critics fear a circulus vitiosus because the company will be inclined to establish additional rules for guiding its employees and to carry out additional controls in order to observe whether rules are followed. However, employees will not appreciate being patronized and will be inclined to fill out unavoidably remaining gaps in discordance with the spirit of the code. The aspirational and motivational force a code can exert is crowded out due to this kind of code implementation.

Basically, these criticisms borrow arguments which are very well-known in organization theory because they were originally put forward against bureaucratic forms of organization (cf., e.g., Crozier 1964). This analogy comes as little surprise because codes are formal measures of organizations for coordinating the actions of their members. Whereas these critics show important perils codes can invoke, they are far from being universally valid. These risks do not necessarily become real if the design of the punishments meets standards to be outlined below. The relativity of these criticisms is worth mentioning because otherwise companies would face a dilemma insofar as many constituencies expect them to establish, and execute, negative sanctions against code offenders.

Indispensability of Punishments

General criticisms against code punishments are at odds with the prevailing demand that corporate codes of ethics should include sanctions because they would otherwise be perceived within and outside the company as mere window dressing. Negative sanctions are expected in order to symbolize and substantiate the binding character of the norms put forward by the code. The waiving of these enforcements feeds the impression that code obedience is up to the addressees' discretion and not mandatory within the company. As a consequence, codes without sanctions are easily discredited as being ineffective. As Badaracco and Webb (1995) put it: "[W]hen violations go unpunished, codes become simply another wall decoration or file-drawer filler" (p. 24). The lack of an appropriate enforcement system diminishes the credibility attached to codes. Kaptein (1998) explains that norms "whose violations are not sanctioned lose their credibility" (p. 176).

In particular, external stakeholders will evaluate the existence of sanctions and use them as a lackmus test for verifying the seriousness of the company to implement the code norms even in those situations where being ethical and obeying the code norms appear (at least in the short run) to cost money and impair profits. Carroll (1978) has already pointed out that,

> [o]ne of the reasons the public – and indeed employees in many organizations – have questioned businesses' sincerity in desiring a more ethical environment has been businesses' unwillingness to discipline violators. (p. 9)

Thus, there is a wide consensus that codes need to be backed by sanctions in order to be perceived as normative guides, rather than as a merely voluntary navigator, through ethically demanding situations within the company. Many authors deem sanctions therefore as indispensable. Post (2000), for instance, emphasizes that a

[c]ode without teeth is not worth the commitment. Enforcement is essential for an effective code of conduct. (p. 111)

This view is shared by practitioners, too, who frequently level the comment "they aren't worth the paper that they are printed on" at codes when meaningful sanctions are missing (cf. Murphy 1995, p. 731).

Introducing a system of negative sanctions is furthermore advisable because some advantages of codes cannot be realized otherwise. For instance, the existence of a code can limit the liability or culpability of the company if corporate actors do wrong and break the law. Most prominently, the Federal Sentencing Commission Guidelines offer incentives to establish an ethics and compliance program which contains standards and procedures (i.e., norms) to prevent and detect criminal conduct because such a program can reduce the culpability score and eventually the fine imposed by the court in order to penalize corporate wrongdoings. However, the Federal Sentencing Guidelines are not content with the existence of standards and procedures to prevent and detect criminal conduct. Rather, a compliance and ethics program must also feature means of ensuring the observance of these standards in order to be distinguished as an effective program. Doubtlessly, providing objective evidence that the company has an appropriate enforcement system in place will be much simpler if negative sanctions are established for deterring code violations.

Empirical Evidence

Against this background, the frequency of code sanctions in practice comes as little surprise, notwithstanding the prevalent criticisms against code sanctions to which reference has been made before. The vast majority of corporate codes mention explicitly enforcement or compliance procedures (cf., e.g., Ferrell et al. 1998, p. 508; Murphy 2000, p. 303; Carasco and Singh 2003, p. 86). This share apparently increased over time and tends to be higher among US companies than in other countries – a development which is related to different regulatory and legal environments and their changes (cf. Talaulicar 2006). In addition, codes which do not make reference to sanctions can nonetheless be associated with a system of punishments because sanctions can also be communicated through different means (e.g., the organization handbook, the employment contract or other organizational instructions by the employer). In sum, empirical evidence indicates that code sanctions are widely spread and commonly established in firms with codes of ethics.

By contrast, the empirical evidence with regard to the effectiveness of code sanctions is less univocal. In the meantime, several studies have addressed this topic. In concordance with the empirical findings about the effectiveness of codes in general, the results of these studies remain inconsistent, too. Whereas some studies showed that code enforcement is related to higher degrees of ethicality (cf., e.g., Weaver and Ferrell 1977; Trevino and Weaver 2001; Vitell et al. 2003), other studies did not reveal statistically significant associations between code sanctions and their effectiveness (cf., e.g., Weaver 1995; Brief et al. 1996). At large, the need for sanctions seems to outweigh possible objections. For instance, Laczniak and Inderrieden (1987) conclude, "[W]hen sanctions are attached to (. . .) codes, behavior becomes more ethical in nature" (p. 304). However, the generality of this relation is hardly tenable. Obviously, sanctions are not either beneficial or harmful. Rather, the benefits of sanctions will depend on the kind of sanctions the company has established and practiced. Yet very little is known about how to design a sanction system which promises effectiveness.

Design of Proper Punishments

Theories of Punishment: Prevention and Retribution

Insights into how to design code sanctions can rely on theories of punishment which have a long tradition in legal philosophy. Basically, these theories develop reasons for justifying punishments, i.e., why and under which conditions should it be deemed appropriate that a sanctioning entity (i.e., the sanction subject) imposes a disadvantage (or punishment, respectively) on an actor (i.e., the sanction object). Albeit many different (and more or less elaborated) theories and approaches have been developed, the two most influential theories justify punishments with regard to their effects of either deterrence or retribution. Theories of deterrence (prospectively) justify punishments if they deter actors from norm violations. These (consequentialist) theories suggest that actors are the more deterred from breaking the code, the more severe, the more certain, and the more celeritous code offenders are punished (cf., e.g., Geerken and Gove 1975; Gibbs 1975; Beyleveld 1979). On the contrary, retributivist theories are retrospective. They justify punishments because the preceding norm violation deserves punishment in order to restore corrective (or retributive, respectively) justice. Theories of retribution therefore suggest that punishments have to be strictly conditional on a preceding wrongdoing and proportional to this wrongdoing (cf., e.g., Walker 1991; Hirsch 1992; Kershnar 2001).

In their pure forms, both groups of theories are apparently inappropriate. Deterrence theories contradict basic standards of justice because they cannot consistently prohibit punishing innocents if such sanctions promise better deterrence and, as a consequence, better code obtainment (cf., e.g., Bradley 2003; Huigens 2003; Lacey 2003). Retributivist theories are afflicted with their retrospectiveness. They are anti-consequentialist and as such doomed to fail (cf. Rawls 1999) because no deontological reason can be strong enough to be adhered irrespective of any consequences. To design a proper code sanction strategy, companies have thus to integrate elements of both theories, deterrence and retribution. This integration cannot only be additive, because simple additions would also add the disadvantages of the pure theories, but needs to be dialectical. I suggest a principle-based integration which weights the principles of deterrence and retribution against the aims of promoting the code norms in a just manner (cf. Talaulicar 2006). Accordingly, deterrence is important because companies cannot wait for code violations to occur before they initiate their implementation efforts. At the same time, considerations of justice are important because code addressees as well as corporate constituencies will evaluate the appropriateness of the pursued strategy of code sanctions. In this regard, punishments as just deserts mirror the intuitions of many people about how sanctions should look alike (cf. Sunstein 2003).

To sum up, code sanction strategies have to contain elements of both deterrence and retribution. The integration of these elements should be carried out principle-based and weigh up which of the partly competing sanction purposes takes priority under specific conditions. Whereas the principle-based appreciation of competing norms and values is necessarily contextualized, some general remarks can offer at least preliminary guidance about how to design proper punishments, as will be shown in the remainder of this article. These recommendations take into consideration the empirical evidence about sanction consequences which previous research in the fields of sanction and justice theories has revealed. In this regard, two important distinctions have to be made. First, sanction effects do not only affect the (specific) addressee of the sanction (i.e., the sanction object). Rather, these sanctions are also observed by other addressees of the code norms and the corporate constituencies at large. Therefore, specific and general effects of sanctions have to be distinguished. Obviously, sanctions can be evaluated differently and have different consequences from the perspective of the specific actor to be punished, on the one hand, and from the view of more or less uninvolved observers, on the other hand. For instance, reactance can be a common attitude which sanctions invoke at the specific addressee who has to suffer from the punishment (cf. Braithwaite 1997). In contrast, the same sanction can be deemed as appropriate by uninvolved observers who endorse that the norm offender deserves to be punished accordingly. General sanction effects, i.e., their indirect effects on observers' attitudes and behaviors, tend to be more important than their specific (or direct) effects on violators because they influence a greater number of people (cf. Trevino 1992, p. 669). However, the company must not ignore the direct effects of punishments and their respective justification because norm offenders must not be instrumentalized in order to promote the underlying code norms. Justice considerations prohibit using punishments as an example and scapegoating violators. These considerations are widely shared and will therefore thwart such sanction efforts.

Sanctions tend to be evaluated more negatively by convicted offenders than by observers. However, reactance and hostility are no inevitable consequences of sanctions (as the proponents of a circulus vitiosus may suggest). Rather, psychological research has shown that these downsides of disciplinary actions can be avoided if the punishment process is designed properly. The second important distinction, therefore, refers to the outcome vis-à-vis the process of punishments. The effectiveness of sanctions depends on both output and process determinants. The outcome dimension indicates what kind of sanctions are eventually imposed on the violator as a reaction on a specific norm violation. In accordance with deterrence theory, outcome measures are the severity, certainty, and celerity of punishments. Whereas these variables are borrowed from deterrence theory, assessing their proper values must go beyond deterrence theory and take into account justice considerations as well. The process dimension reflects how sanction decisions are made, i.e., how the (potential) offender is treated by the company when the norm violation and the appropriate sanction is determined. Whereas there is wide agreement that the fairness of procedures is important, disagreements remain which variables can indicate whether procedures are fair or not. I suggest a quite small number of four variables in order to measure the fairness of punishment procedures. These variables are respect, voice, neutrality, and transparency.

Output Determinants

Sanction Severity

With regard to the severity of punishments, code norms tend to be the more obeyed, the stronger the sanctions of code violations are. Severe sanctions symbolize the bindingness of the underlying code norms. They can communicate censure and call on the offender to recognize that they have done wrong (cf. Duff 2001, p. 82). This signal is also perceived by observers whereas weak punishments like verbal reprimands can hardly be recognized outside of the dyad between the superior (as the sanction subject) and the offender (i.e., the sanction object).

However, threatening strong sanctions is not sufficient for guaranteeing code compliance because even draconic punishments can eventually be meaningless if they are not applied (i.e., the sanction certainty is minimal) or if they are imposed in the infinite future (i.e., the sanction celerity is minimal). Notwithstanding the multiplicative combination of sanction severity, certainty, and celerity in models of deterrence (cf., e.g., Becker 1968; Nagin 1998; Mendes 2004), the behavioral impact depends on the perceived specification of the sanction strategy (not on its real features). Accordingly, sanction strategies can turn out to be effective although they only threaten but hardly impose strong punishments. This effect is particularly likely if the (risk averse) actor perceives the penalty as prohibitively high, if he can easily comply with the code, and if he refrains from a detailed cost-benefit-analysis. Under these conditions, minimal amounts of threat believability may be sufficient in order to make the code addressees to obey the code norms (cf. Luckenbill 1982).

One has to take into account, though, that code addressees do not only calculate (more or less rationally) the costs and benefits of norm compliance. Rather, their assessments are also influenced by normative considerations and particularly evaluations whether or not the pursued sanction strategy meets common standards of justice. Obviously, intentionally draconic punishments which definitely lack standards of proportionality contradict common perceptions of justice shared by the majority of organizational members and stakeholders. In addition, code sanctions have to meet ethical standards and must not humble the offender. Otherwise, these illegitimate sanctions can also diminish the legitimacy of the corresponding code norms and lead to denial that the company is sincerely promoting the code. Thus, the validity of the code norms themselves comes into question. I therefore suggest:

Proposition 1: Code sanctions tend to be the more effective, the more proportional punishment severity is to the corresponding code violation. Code sanctions tend to be ineffective if punishments are viewed as either negligible or draconic.

Sanction Certainty

The certainty of sanctions indicates how likely it is that code violations entail punishment. Accordingly, this variable refers to (at least) two discrete occurrences, i.e., the detection of code violations and the imposition of the corresponding sanction. The higher the detection certainty is, the fewer code violations remain undetected. The higher the imposition certainty is, the fewer detected code violations remain with impunity. Abandoning punishments after code violations were detected with sufficient rigor can hardly be imagined as appropriate regarding both their deterrence and retribution effects. If the preceding detection of code violations has been carried out with diligence, leniency will undermine the mandatory nature of the code norms. Abandoning punishments (like dismissing the offender) due to the alleged importance of the (possibly high-ranking) actor, who cannot be replaced adequately, gives the impression that the code does not obligate all members of the organization equally but that some (high-ranking) members are eventually allowed to ignore the code. Such an impression will hardly add to the legitimacy of the code, but can aid and abet that employees view the code as means of constraining their discretion rather than as a true commitment to enhance the ethicality of the company.

Proposition 2: Code sanctions tend to be the more effective, the more certainly the corresponding punishments are imposed.

Deterrence theory suggests a high detection certainty in order to tap the full threatening potential of punishments. The detection certainty tends to be higher if code obtainment is closely monitored and if potential code violations are scrutinized in detail. Thus, the detection certainty also includes the subsumption of a sanction norm, i.e., to determine whether its preconditions are given in a specific constellation or relevant exculpations apply. Against this background, justice considerations, at first glance, converge with deterrence theory because punishments are not perceived as just if they affect only a few offenders while many similar code violations remain undetected (and, as a consequence, unpunished).

Pure theories of deterrence assume that the degrees of punishment certainty and severity are substitutable (cf., e.g., Tullock 1974, p. 107). Accordingly, prevention losses due to a lower detection certainty can be compensated by threatening more severe punishments. However, the rate of substitution can vary. Theoretical considerations easily demonstrate that the rate of substitution depends on the risk attitude of the actors (cf. Becker 1968, p. 178). In addition, empirical evidence took the assumption of constant substitution rates into question because the marginal deterrence effect of sanction certainty turned out to be higher than the corresponding effect of sanction severity (cf. Doob and Webster 2003). Irrespective the empirical effectiveness of compensating detection gaps with more severe punishments, this substitution is normatively inappropriate because such a sanction strategy would instrumentalize the (severe) punishment of the few detected offenders.

Maximizing the detection certainty does not appear to be promising, though, because (too) high rates of detection certainty are costly and can have dysfunctional side-effects. Overly intense controls can lead to the impression that all employees are suspects and distrusted to obey the code norms. Therefore, controls do not only tie up important management resources but also cause (a culture of) mistrust which is likely to compromise the course of business. To be sure, controls do not necessarily convey mistrust. Rather, they can also signal the relative importance of tasks at work in general and code obtainment in particular (cf. Larson and Callahan 1990; Niehoff and Moorman 1993). Negative side-effects are avoidable if the code addressees appreciate the legitimacy of the code norms and the necessity of their enforcement. Achieving this appreciation depends on characteristics of the punishment process (see below). The optimal rate of detection certainty is reached if the marginal costs and the marginal benefits of the corresponding control measures are equal. In general, intensifying detection activities is worthless if these efforts neither reveal additional code violations nor enhance deterrence because the actors were sufficiently deterred before.

Proposition 3: There is an inverse u-shaped relationship between code sanction effectiveness and the certainty that code violations are detected.

Sanction Celerity

Sanction celerity measures the time between the violation of a norm and the sanction of this violation. The more expeditiously norm violations are detected (detection celerity) and – according to the sanction norms – punished (imposition celerity), the higher is the sanction celerity. Deterrence theory generally assumes a positive effect of sanction celerity on deterrence and hence sanction effectiveness. However, theoretical attempts to justify this relation are not necessarily convincing. If celerity is modeled as an independent predictor of deterrence effects, theoretical reasonings generally rely on conditional psychology and argue that celeritous punishments are necessary because the sanction objects could otherwise fail to relate the punishment to the preceding deviance they had been engaged in (cf., e.g., Singer 1970). On the one hand, this line of argumentation is convincing insofar as the sanction objects have indeed to understand their norm violation as the (just) cause of their punishment. On the other hand, however, human adults (in contrast to animals and young children) are obviously able to relate their experiences over long periods. They have the cognitive capacity in order to connect acts with temporally remote causes and consequences. Against this background, the importance of celeritous punishments becomes thus debatable (cf., e.g., Gibbs 1975; Howe and Brandau 1988; Nagin and Pogarsky 2001).

Nonetheless, there are good reasons for celeritous punishments. But these reasons are related to the determinants of punishment severity and certainty. First, economic calculations suggest that delayed punishments need to be discounted and imply hence a lower cost than an immediate sanction (cf., e.g., Eide 1994). Whereas this reasoning appears to be plausible, it is not necessarily empirically valid. Its validity depends on the presence- or future-orientation of individuals, i.e., their balancing between present and future events or returns, respectively. Nagin and Pogarsky (2001) found that people can even have negative discount rates, i.e., they give more weight to events in the future than in the present. Accordingly, these people will be the more deterred, the more delayed the punishment is imposed.

Yet, celeritous punishments appear to be expedient in order to limit the benefits associated with the norm violation. The higher the sanction celerity, the less time remains for the offender to benefit from his illicit act. Punishment celerity also counters the emergence of the impression that norms may be violated without any consequences. Finally, attempts to accelerate the process of punishment may be necessary in order to realize a sufficiently high rate of detection. Detecting code violations may become much more difficult if there is too much time-lag between the occurrence of potential deviance and the efforts to verify wrongdoing.

Notwithstanding these positive effects of celeritous punishments, detection celerity should – in accordance with the detection certainty – not be maximized. Again, the costs (for accelerating punishments) have to be balanced against the associated benefits of more celeritous punishments. In addition, sanction celerity has to be limited due to process considerations because a fair sanction process involves offering potential offenders the opportunity to present their view of the facts and to make, on behalf of the company, well-founded sanction decisions. Ad hoc punishments accelerate sanction celerity, but fall below standards of procedural fairness. However, when the appropriateness of a specific sanction has been determined with sufficient rigor, imposing the corresponding sanction should not be delayed in order to avert the impression that just punishments are not executed (for the sake of other goals of the company).

Proposition 4: There is an inverse u-shaped relationship between code sanction effectiveness and the detection celerity.

Proposition 5: Code sanctions tend to be the more effective, the more celeritous the corresponding punishments are imposed.

Process Determinants

Respect

Many codes of ethics explicitly state that all people have to be treated with fairness, trust, and respect. Regarding the process determinants of sanction strategies, there is wide consensus that potential norm violators have to be treated ethically, i.e., by respecting their rights and dignity (cf. Newton 1999; Valentine and Fleischmann 2002; Reynolds and Bowie 2004). This respect prohibits to design the sanction process instrumentally and to impose punishments for the sake of other purposes that may appear to be economically desirable but are not ethically justified. Furthermore, the principle of respect dictates that gathering information about potential norm violators and methods of observation must neither involve deception nor invade privacy (cf. Leventhal 1980). In this regard, legal stipulations may make the principle of respect mandatory at least to some degree although labor laws and the protection of privacy are codified differently from country to country.

Treating potential violators with respect is not only justified for ethical (or legal) reasons. Rather, this treatment avoids alienating parts of the workforce and is thus a precondition for averting negative side-effects of sanctions because "undignified, disrespectful, or impolite treatment by an authority carries the implication that one is not a full member of the group" (Tyler and Lind 2001, p. 76). When sanctions are imposed in such a manner as to insult the dignity of persons, they can increase rather than reduce future norm violations since offenders are more likely to feel personal admonishment and to become angry and defiant (cf. Paternoster et al. 1997).

Averting this alienation tendency of sanctions is also particularly essential with regard to the general effects of the corresponding sanction strategies. Other members of the organization will carefully observe how actors are treated who have been suspected of having broken the code. There is some empirical evidence that these appraisals about the appropriateness of sanctions are biased by the past performance of the potential violator. More specifically, Niehoff et al. (1998) found that when violators performed poorly in the past, they will be judged by observers as more deserving of punishment than violators with good performance records. In any case, however, dignified and respectful treatment will be appreciated because it conforms with observers' sense of justice and can be interpreted as a cue how observers expect to be treated in a comparable situation.

> Proposition 6: Code sanctions tend to be more effective, if the company treats (potential) code offenders with dignity and respect.

Voice

Fair procedures demand that potential offenders receive the opportunity to state one's case and to explain one's point of view. Establishing these voice procedures is advisable because the company would otherwise be at risk of making important decisions like the imposition of sanctions on an ill-founded information base. In this regard, Folger et al. (1979) have shown that

> voice may be preferable to mute procedures because the latter are based on incomplete information. A mute procedure may not take into account the claims of disputants and hence may entail an inferior, or at least suspect, decision. (p. 2259)

A sound preparation of the sanction decision thus requires including the (partly privileged) information of the employees.

Of course, offenders appreciate receiving the opportunity to state their case because this hearing allows them to reveal mitigating facts and to influence the reasons considered in the subsequent judgment about the (appropriate) sanction. This instrumental or self-interested justification of voice procedures and their positive effects is sometimes characterized as the "instrumental view" (Tyler 1990, p. 6) or as a "self-interest model" (Lind and Tyler 1988, p. 222). Besides this instrumental view of the voice effect, empirical studies of procedural justice have shown that voice procedures are also viewed as an end in itself (and appreciated accordingly). These procedures are viewed as just and desirable, regardless of their influence on the eventual sanction decision (cf. Folger and Greenberg 1985). Lind, Kanfer, and Earley (1990) found that "fairness judgments are enhanced by the opportunity to voice opinions even when there is no chance of influencing the decision" (p. 957). Thus, the opportunity to speak out one's own point of view is appreciated because it demonstrates the employees' input is of value (cf. Niehoff and Moorman 1993). Paternoster et al. (1997) therefore explain that "the opportunity to state one's case is valued not because it is linked to favorable outcomes but because of its 'value expressive' function" (p. 167). Therefore, this line of justification is sometimes characterized as the "group value model" (Lind and Tyler 1988, p. 230).

Hence, favorable reactions to voice procedures do not only stem from instrumental reasons and the corresponding opportunity to influence the sanction decisions but reflect an assessment of this procedure as an end-in-itself (cf. Folger and Greenberg 1985). Paternoster et al. (1997, p. 166) add that the opportunity to put forward one's case before the sanction authority makes its decision enhances the legitimacy of this authority and fosters compliance. Even if the outcome is not influenced by the statements of the offenders, the voice procedure can enhance the perceived fairness of the sanction procedure. This fairness effect only demands the perception that stated opinions have a fair chance to influence the decision and that the decision-making process does not systematically ignore the arguments put forward by the offenders. This leads to the third process determinant, i.e., the neutrality of the sanction process.

> Proposition 7: Code sanctions tend to be more effective, if the company offers (potential) code offenders the opportunity to explain their point of view.

Neutrality

The neutrality of the sanction process calls for an unbiased and impartial preparation of the sanction decision. In this regard, accurate information has to be gathered and evaluated without biases. According to Niehoff and Moorman (1993) the "gathering of accurate and unbiased information is one of the basic components of procedural fairness" (p. 528). Decisions have to be made on a level playing field in which every argument has a fair chance to influence the outcome of the decision preparation (cf. Tyler and Lind 2001). Hence, predetermined outcomes or decisions based on prejudices strictly contradict the principle of neutrality.

Again, psychological research revealed that people appreciate unbiased and impartial procedures, regardless of the favorableness of the decision outcome. Paternoster et al. (1997) explain that

> [i]ndependent of the favorableness of the outcome, persons are more likely to impute fairness and legitimacy to authorities and behave in accordance with rules when they perceive that authorities have acted in an impartial and unbiased manner. (p. 168)

Even more, the apparent absence of a sufficient degree of neutrality can abolish the positive voice effects mentioned before. Under such circumstances, the effectiveness of voice procedures could even backfire (cf. Folger and Greenberg 1985) because code addressees will react negatively if they perceive to be deceived and to be treated unfair. Of course, distress and reactance tend to be the more likely the more unfavorable the outcome of the process is (cf. Conlon 1993).

Proposition 8: Code sanctions tend to be the more effective, the less biased sanction decisions are made.

Proposition 9: Code sanctions tend to be less effective, if the company offers (potential) code offenders the opportunity to explain their point of view but systematically ignores these comments when preparing sanction decisions.

Transparency

Finally, realizing the intended effects of punishments demands that offenders and observers comprehend the sanction system and its justification. Thus, the appropriateness of the sanction system in general and the reasons for specific sanctions have to be sufficiently transparent in order to be comprehensible. Obviously, appreciating the justification of sanctions calls for appreciating the appropriateness of the enforced code norms. Compared with the remaining three process determinants as well as the outcome determinants of sanctions, transparency bears a particular meaning because the intended consequences of the remaining determinants can only be accomplished if the sanction characteristics are perceived by the code addressees. In this regard, transparency creates the necessary visibility of the sanction strategy and makes its foundation more comprehensible.

Offenders will react favorably to the provision of adequate causal accounts (cf. Ball et al. 1992). In general, justifications and explanations can add legitimacy to decisions. In contrast, lack of transparency is always susceptible and feeds the fear that the company intends to conceal important information. Transparency can only be achieved by providing adequate and authentic information (not by attempts to manipulate or bias the perceptions and evaluations of employees and other stakeholders). If misinformation is once detected, clashes of trust can hardly be remedied. The necessary degree of transparency varies and depends on the information base and demand of the addressees. While more transparency is generally seen as beneficial, the principle of respect limits the scope of data allowed to be released. Of course, the reasons for specific sanctions have to be made transparent towards the specific sanction object. But this information must not be exposed congruently to other actors as well in order to protect the identity of the offender.

Proposition 10: Code sanctions tend to be the more effective, the more transparent the sanction system is.

Implications and Conclusion

Companies are well advised to back their codes of ethics with sanctions. Codes without sanctions cast doubt on the sincerity of the code establishment and lead to question whether the company truly strives for code effectiveness. Such doubts impede that the code of ethics is considered in mitigation if the company faces legal proceedings after corporate misbehavior occurred and can generally diminish esteem which the code, and the overall ethical engagement of the company, can gain among external constituencies. Even worse, and even more important, codes without sanctions can lead employees to perceive the code norms as voluntary suggestions rather than as mandatory obligations. Of course, the effectiveness of codes of ethics tends to be limited if their addressees are not sufficiently aware of their bindingness.

Code sanctions are therefore deemed to be indispensable. However, code sanctions cannot guarantee code observance, but can even have dysfunctional effects. For tapping the potential of codes and their sanctions, the proper design and execution of punishments becomes essential. This article has developed propositions about the adequate design of such punishments. Based on theories of sanctions, the proper design and execution of punishments has to consider output and process determinants. Output determinants are sanction severity, certainty, and celerity. In contrast to deterrence theories, I do not propose that punishments necessarily promise to be the more effective, the more severe, certain, and celeritous they are. Rather, considerations of justice and process determinants suggest a more deliberate specification of the outcome values. Process determinants demand to treat (potential) code offenders with respect, to offer them the opportunity to explain their case, and to make sanction decisions unbiased as well as transparent.

I am aware that establishing and implementing a suggested system of punishments is costly. Furthermore, I am aware that enforcements of codes of ethics in practice do not fully comply with the considerations developed above. In this regard, my recommendations also aim at (further) improving code implementation in practice. Bearing the efforts associated with a proper code implementation also symbolizes that the company takes its ethics program seriously. Future research should study whether the proposed relations can be empirically corroborated. Such studies have to reflect the intentions of the company authorities who establish and execute the sanctions, as well as how employees and other corporate constituencies perceive the sanction system and its execution. Eventually, these perceptions will determine whether or not the code implementation will succeed. However, it can be expected that aiming at code success premises sincere intentions on behalf of the company and its officials.

References

Appelbaum, S.H., M. Bregman, and P. Moroz. 1998. Fear as a strategy: Effects and impact within the organization. *Journal of European Industrial Training* 22: 113–127.
Badaracco, J.L. Jr., and A.P. Webb. 1995. Business ethics: A view from the trenches. *California Management Review* 37: 8–28.

Ball, G.A., L.K. Trevino, and H.P. Sims. 1992. Understanding subordinate reactions to punishment incidents: Perspectives from justice and social affect. *Leadership Quarterly* 3: 307–333.

Becker, G.S. 1968. Crime and punishment: An economic approach. *Journal of Political Economy* 76: 169–217.

Berenbeim, R.E. 1987. *Corporate ethics*. New York (Report No. 900 from The Conference Board).

Beyleveld, D. 1979. Identifying, explaining and predicting deterrence. *British Journal of Criminology* 19: 205–224.

Bradley, G.V. 2003. Retribution: The central aim of punishment. *Harvard Journal of Law & Public Policy* 27: 19–31.

Braithwaite, J. 1997. On speaking softly and carrying big sticks: Neglected dimensions of a republican separation of powers. *University of Toronto Law Journal* 47: 305–361.

Brief, A.P., J.M. Dukerich, P.R. Brown, and J.F. Brett. 1996. What's wrong with the treadway commission report? Experimental analyses of the effects of personal values and codes of conduct on fraudulent financial reporting. *Journal of Business Ethics* 15: 183–198.

Brien, A. 1996. Regulating virtue: Formulating, engendering and enforcing corporate ethical codes. *Business & Professional Ethics Journal* 15: 21–52.

Carasco, E.F., and J.B. Singh. 2003. The content and focus of the codes of ethics of the world's largest transnational corporations. *Business and Society Review* 108: 71–94.

Carroll, A.B. 1978. Linking business ethics to behavior in organizations. *S.A.M. Advanced Management Journal* 43: 4–11.

Cleek, M.A., and S.L. Leonard. 1998. Can corporate codes of ethics influence behavior? *Journal of Business Ethics* 17: 619–630.

Conlon, D.E. 1993. Some tests of the self-interest and group-value models of procedural justice: Evidence from an organizational appeal procedure. *Academy of Management Journal* 36: 1109–1124.

Crozier, M. 1964. *The bureaucratic phenomenon*. Chicago, IL: University of Chicago Press.

Doob, A.N., and C.M. Webster. 2003. Sentence severity and crime: Accepting the null hypothesis. *Crime and Justice: A Review of Research* 30: 143–195.

Duff, R.A. 2001. *Punishment, communication, and community*. Oxford: Oxford University Press.

Eide, E. 1994. *Economics of crime: Deterrence and the rational offender*. Amsterdam: North-Holland.

Ferrell, O.C., M.D. Hartline, and S.W. McDaniel. 1998. Codes of ethics among corporate research departments, marketing research firms, and data subcontractors: An examination of a three-communities metaphor. *Journal of Business Ethics* 17: 503–516.

Folger, R., and J. Greenberg. 1985. Procedural justice: An interpretive analysis of personnel systems. *Research in Personnel and Human Resources Management* 3: 141–183.

Folger, R., D. Rosenfield, J. Grove, and L. Corkran. 1979. Effects of "voice" and peer opinions on responses to inequity. *Journal of Personality and Social Psychology* 37: 2253–2261.

Geerken, M.R., and W.R. Gove. 1975. Deterrence: Some theoretical considerations. *Law and Society* 9: 497–513.

Gibbs, J.P. 1975. *Crime, punishment, and deterrence*. New York, NY: Elsevier.

Hirsch, A. von. 1992. Proportionality in the philosophy of punishment. *Crime and Justice: A Review of Research* 16: 55–98.

Howe, E.S., and C.J. Brandau. 1988. Additive effects of certainty, severity, and celerity of punishment on judgments of crime deterrence scale value. *Journal of Applied Social Psychology* 18: 796–812.

Huigens, K. 2003. Dignity and desert in punishment theory. *Harvard Journal of Law & Public Policy* 27: 33–49.

Kaptein, M. 1998. *Ethics management: Auditing and developing the ethical content of organizations*. Dordrecht: Kluwer.

Kaptein, M. 2004. Business codes of multinational firms: What do they say? *Journal of Business Ethics* 50: 13–31.

Kershnar, S. 2001. *Desert, retribution, and torture*. Lanham, MD: University Press of America.

Lacey, N. 2003. Penal theory and penal practice: A communitarian approach. In *The use of punishment*, ed. S. McConville, 175–198. Cullompton: Willan.

Laczniak, G.R., and E.J. Inderrieden. 1987. The influence of stated organizational concern upon ethical decision making. *Journal of Business Ethics* 6: 297–307.

Larson, J.R. Jr., and C. Callahan. 1990. Performance monitoring: How it affects productivity. *Journal of Applied Psychology* 75: 530–538.

Leventhal, G.S. 1980. What should be done with equity theory? New approaches to the study of fairness in social relationships. In *Social exchange advances in theory and research*, ed. K.J. Gergen, M.S. Greenberg, and R.H. Willis, 27–55. New York, NY: Plenum.

Lind, E.A., and T.R. Tyler. 1988. *The social psychology of procedural justice*. New York: Plenum.

Lind, E.A., R. Kanfer, and P.C. Earley. 1990. Voice, control, and procedural justice: Instrumental and noninstrumental concerns in fairness judgments. *Journal of Personality and Social Psychology* 59: 952–959.

Luckenbill, D.F. 1982. Compliance under threat of severe punishment. *Social Forces* 61: 811–825.

Mendes, S.M. 2004. Certainty, severity, and their relative deterrent effects: Questioning the implications of the role of risk in criminal deterrence policy. *Policy Studies Journal* 32: 59–72.

Murphy, P.E. 1995. Corporate ethics statements: Current status and future perspectives. *Journal of Business Ethics* 14: 727–740.

Murphy, P.E. 2000. Corporate ethics statements: An update. In *Global codes of conduct: An idea whose time has come*, ed. O.F. Williams, 295–304. Notre Dame, IN: University of Notre Dame Press.

Nagin, D.S. 1998. Criminal deterrence research at the outset of the twenty-first century. *Crime and Justice: A Review of Research* 23: 1–42.

Nagin, D.S., and G. Pogarsky. 2001. Integrating celerity, impulsivity, and extralegal sanction threats into a model of general deterrence: Theory and evidence. *Criminology* 39: 865–891.

Neue Juristische Wochenschrift. 2004. Verletzung aktienrechtlicher Pflichten und Untreue. *NJW* 57: 3275–3286.

Newton, L. 1999. The many faces of the corporate code. In *Ethical issues in business: A philosophical approach*, ed. T. Donaldson and P.H. Werhane, 519–526. Upper Saddle River, NJ: Prentice Hall.

Niehoff, B.P., and R.H. Moorman. 1993. Justice as a mediator of the relationship between methods of monitoring and organizational citizenship behavior. *Academy of Management Journal* 36: 527–556.

Niehoff, B.P., R.J. Paul, and J.F.S. Bunch. 1998. The social effects of punishment events: The influence of violator past performance on observers' justice perceptions and attitudes. *Journal of Organizational Behavior* 19: 589–602.

Paternoster, R., R. Brame, R. Bachman, and L.W. Sherman. 1997. Do fair procedures matter? The effect of procedural justice on spouse assault. *Law and Society Review* 31: 163–204.

Piper, N. 2004. Szenen einer Ehe. *Süddeutsche Zeitung*, 3 March 2004: 4.

Post, J.E. 2000. Global codes of conduct: Activists, lawyers, and managers in search of a solution. In *Global codes of conduct: An idea whose time has come*, ed. O.F. Williams, 103–116. Notre Dame, IN: University of Notre Dame Press.

Rawls, J. 1999. *A theory of justice*, revised edition. Cambridge, MA: Harvard University Press.

Reynolds, S.J., and N.E. Bowie. 2004. A Kantian perspective on the characteristics of ethics programs. *Business Ethics Quarterly* 14: 275–292.

Schwartz, M.S. 2004. Effective corporate codes of ethics: Perceptions of code users. *Journal of Business Ethics* 55: 321–341.

Schwartz, R.D., and S. Orleans. 1967. On legal sanctions. *University of Chicago Law Review* 34: 274–300.

Singer, B.P. 1970. Psychological studies of punishment. *California Law Review* 58: 405–443.

Sunstein, C.R. 2003. On the psychology of punishment. *Supreme Court Economic Review* 11: 171–188.

Talaulicar, T. 2006. *Unternehmenskodizes: Typen und Normierungsstrategien zur Implementierung einer Unternehmensethik*. Wiesbaden: Gabler/DUV.

The Economist. 2005. An icon under fire. *The Economist*, 9 July 2005: 52.

Trevino, L.K. 1990. A cultural perspective on changing and developing organizational ethics. *Research in Organizational Change and Development* 4: 195–230.

Trevino, L.K. 1992. The social effects of punishment in organizations: A justice perspective. *Academy of Management Review* 17: 647–676.

Trevino, L.K., and G.R. Weaver. 2001. Organizational justice and ethics program "follow-through": Influences on employees' harmful and helpful behavior. *Business Ethics Quarterly* 11: 651–671.

Trevino, L.K., and S.A. Youngblood. 1990. Bad apples in bad barrels: A causal analysis of ethical decision-making behavior. *Journal of Applied Psychology* 75: 378–385.

Tullock, G. 1974. Does punishment deter crime? *The Public Interest* 36: 103–111.

Tyler, T.R. 1990. *Why people obey the law*. New Haven, NJ: Yale University Press.

Tyler, T.R., and E.A. Lind. 2001. Procedural justice. In *Handbook of justice research in law*, ed. J. Sanders and V.L. Hamilton, 65–92. New York, NY: Kluwer/Plenum.

Valentine, S., and G. Fleischmann. 2002. Ethics codes and professionals' tolerance of societal diversity. *Journal of Business Ethics* 40: 301–312.

Vitell, S.J., J.G.P. Paolillo, and J.L. Thomas. 2003. The perceived role of ethics and social responsibility: A study of marketing professionals. *Business Ethics Quarterly* 13: 63–86.

Walker, N. 1991. *Why punish?* Oxford: Oxford University Press.

Weaver, G.R. 1995. Does ethics codes design matter? Effects of ethics code rationales and sanctions on recipients' justice perceptions and content recall. *Journal of Business Ethics* 14: 367–385.

Weaver, G.R., and L.K. Trevino. 2001. The role of human resources in ethics/compliance management. A fairness perspective. *Human Resource Management Review* 11: 113–134.

Weaver, K.M., and O.C. Ferrell. 1977. The impact of corporate policy on reported ethical beliefs and behavior of marketing practitioners. In *Contemporary marketing thought 1977 educators proceedings*, ed. B.A. Greenberg and D.N. Bellenger, 477–481. Chicago, IL: American Marketing Association.

Chapter 6
Corporate Governance at the Chinese Stock Market: How It Evolved

Junhua Tang and Dirk Linowski

Contents

D. Linowski (✉)
Director, Institute for International Business Relations, Steinbeis University Berlin,
Berlin, Germany
e-mail: linowski@stw.de

A. Brink (ed.), *Corporate Governance and Business Ethics*, Ethical Economy.
Studies in Economic Ethics and Philosophy 39, DOI 10.1007/978-94-007-1588-2_6,
© Springer Science+Business Media B.V. 2011

Abbreviations

ABC	Agricultural Bank of China
bn.	billion
BOC	Bank of China
CBRC	China Banking Regulatory Commission
CCB	China Construction Bank
CEO	Chief executive officer
CFFEX	China Financial Futures Exchange
CNPC	China National Petroleum Corporation
CPC	Communist Party of China
CSRC	China Securities Regulatory Commission
FDI	foreign direct investment
GDP	gross domestic product
GEM	Growth Enterprises Market
GLF	Great Leap Forward
HKD	Hong Kong Dollar
ICBC	Industrial and Commercial Bank of China
IMD	International Institute for Management Development
IPO	initial public offering
LLDPE	linear low-density polyethylene
LLSV	La Porta, Lopez-de-Silanes, Shleifer, and Vishny
m.	million
NPC	National People's Congress
NPL	non-performing loan
NYSE	New York Stock Exchange
OTC	over-the-counter
PBOC	People's Bank of China
PRC	People's Republic of China
PTA	purified terephthalic acid
QDII	Qualified Domestic Institutional Investor
QFII	Qualified Foreign Institutional Investor
RMB	Renminbi (Chinese currency)
SEZ	Special Economic Zone
SHFE	Shanghai Futures Exchange
SINOPEC	China Petroleum & Chemical Corporation
SME	small and medium-sized enterprises
SOE	state-owned enterprise
SSE	Shanghai Stock Exchange
SZSE	Shenzhen Stock Exchange
T-bond	treasury bond
TVE	Township and Village Enterprise
USD	US Dollar
WEF	World Economic Forum
WTO	World Trade Organization
YGX	Yinguangxia (a listed firm's name)

Introduction

Shortly after the foundation of the People's Republic of China (PRC) in October 1949, the Chinese government socialized the country's total economy.[1] By doing so, a planned system in reference to the former Soviet Union was built up and directed the Chinese economy for almost three decades. Upon the end of the Cultural Revolution (1966–1976), China began to reform and open up its economy to the outside world in 1978 under the leadership of Deng Xiaoping (1904–1997), who has been widely regarded as designer of China's economic reform and opening-up era since 1978.

Initial reform efforts in China were to combine plan and market together. The central government introduced incentives for agricultural productions and to the state sector, aligned prices to the underlying supply and demand, and opened the economy up to the outside world (cf. Qian 1999a, p. 3). The most important reform policy was the dual-track price system, introduced in the mid-1980s. Under this system, any commodity carried a planned price for the production quota set by the state and a market price set by the market supply and demand. Until early 1990s, most commodities were priced by the market, while the planned price track largely phased out (cf. Qian and Wu 2000, p. 7). In 1992, the central government altered its course from "combining plan and market together" to a "socialist market economy" with "Chinese characteristics", i.e., a competitive market system in which public ownership predominates. While the adjective "socialist" characterizes the political system in China, the term "market economy" clearly points to China's overall reform goal.

China had faced in the pre-reform era a number of problems such as enormous population pressure, severe shortages of human capital and natural resources, very poor industrial and infrastructure bases, and the difficulty of maintaining financial stability (cf. Qian 1999b, p. 2). In 1978, as the reform era began, 250 million Chinese were still living in absolute poverty (cf. GRRB 2008, p. 3). Since the reform and opening-up policies were adopted, the number of Chinese living in absolute poverty has been substantially cut down and came to merely 14.8 million by the end of 2007 (cf. ibid., p. 3). Meanwhile, China's national nominal GDP has achieved nearly a 10% average growth rate and proliferated from 364.5 billion RMB in 1978 to 30,067.0 billion RMB in 2008 (cf. NBSC 2007a, b, 2008b). Starting from almost nil (0.167 billion USD in 1978), its foreign exchange reserves now rank the first in the world (1,946.0 billion USD by the end of 2008).[2] In 2008, China ranked 17th in the World Competitiveness Yearbook of the International Institute for Management Development (cf. IMD 2008) and 30th in the Global Competitiveness Report of the World Economic Forum (cf. WEF 2009), respectively, and thus stood out among all the transition economies and developing countries.

A few remarkable features characterize China's economic transition over the past three decades. Firstly, China has been following a gradual transition path. Many

---

[1] The authors cordially thank Mr. André Poddubny for his valuable comments and careful revision of the text.

[2] See SAFE 2010 for the data of the respective years.

reforms had been initially carried out on an experimental basis and in some local-ities, before successful experiences were extended into a wider or even national scale by policies. Almost all important reform policies in China were based on for-mer steps on lower and local levels. Secondly, China's transition succeeded without complete market liberalization. Though the state sector has been shrinking in its weight in the national economy, the state[3] still holds a big stake in several key indus-tries (transportation, telecom, banking, oil, steel, etc.) and controls their operations. Thirdly, privatization and private property rights were not essential components of China's first three decades of transition. It was not until middle 1990s that the central government allowed privatization of small- and middle-sized SOEs. As recently as in March 2007, private property rights became de jure recognized by the Real Rights Law.[4] Last but not least, China's transition has been progressing without democrati-zation. The Communist Party of China dominates in governing the country, and this one-party system is supposed to further exist for a long time.[5]

China's economic success as well as the Chinese characteristics makes its tran-sition path an attractive object for economical researches. One of the most popular research areas is the booming Chinese stock market. Early literature in this area tends to prefer initial public offerings and stock pricings. Recently, more and more researchers have become interested in the corporate governance issues at the Chinese stock market. In this paper, we conduct a study on the evolution of the corporate governance model at the Chinese stock market.

The structure of this paper is organized as follows: the section "Backgrounds of the Financial System in China" briefly describes China's financial system, includ-ing its current structure, the development of the banking system, and the capital markets. It provides important background information for a better understand-ing of the succeeding parts of this paper. The section "Corporate Governance in China" outlines the major corporate governance issues in China, sketches the cor-porate governance model at the Chinese stock market, and compares it with classical corporate governance models. It raises some important research questions to be answered in the subsequent sections. The section "Governance Practices in Chinese SOEs: Content of Change" refers to how governance practices changed at different stages along China's economic transition. The section "Driving Forces in China's Corporate Governance Evolution: Process of Change" deals with the deep roots of

---

[3] The term "state" is to some extent a vague term. In our paper, it refers to the central gov-ernment on behalf of all the Chinese people or local governments on provincial and municipal levels, as the case may be. After a wave of administrative decentralization in 1970, most large-size SOEs were delegated to local governments, while the central government supervised less than 150 SOEs. In this context, "the state" rather refers to local governments in the context of managing and monitoring SOEs.

[4] Article 4 of the Real Rights Law states: "The real right of the state, collective, individual or any other right holder shall be protected by law, and may not be damaged by any entity or individual."

[5] Very recently, Wu Bangguo, chairman of the Standing Committee of the National People's Congress (NPC), proclaimed during NPC's annual meeting in 2009 that China will never become a Western-style democracy in terms of a multiple party system and a separation of legislative, executive, and judicial powers (cf. Zhu 2009).

the whole process of the changes in Chinese governance practices. In the summary, we summarize our major views of the corporate governance evolvement in China.

Backgrounds of the Financial System in China

Financial System Structure

We describe the Chinese financial system in a simplified sense, namely one that barely consists of the banking system, the stock market, and the bond market. For each component, we utilize banking assets, the stock market capitalization, and the bond depository balance, respectively, to measure their slices in the entire financial industry pie (see Fig. 6.1). In 2008, banking assets amounted to 69% of the entire financial system's assets. Bonds ranked a distant second with a proportion of 17%. Stocks stood closely behind bonds with a share of 14%. China's banking system is more than twice as big as its bond and stock markets together.

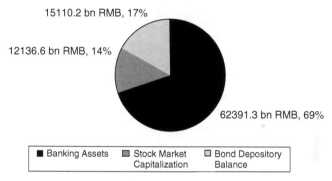

15110.2 bn RMB, 17%

12136.6 bn RMB, 14%

62391.3 bn RMB, 69%

■ Banking Assets   ▨ Stock Market   ☐ Bond Depository
Capitalization   Balance

Fig. 6.1 China's financial system structure, 2008
Source: http://www.pbc.gov.cn, http://www.chinabond.com.cn, http://www.cbrc.gov.cn

Figures 6.2 and 6.3 demonstrate the banking assets structure[6] and the bond structure, respectively. In 2008, half of the banking assets (51%) were owned by the four state-owned commercial banks, namely the Bank of China (BOC), the China Construction Bank (CCB), the Agricultural Bank of China (ABC), and the Industrial and Commercial Bank of China (ICBC). At present, 12 joint-stock commercial banks[7] are performing in China. They held 14% of the entire banking assets in

---

[6] The banking institutions include policy banks, state-owned commercial banks (SOCBs), joint stock commercial banks (JSCBs), city commercial banks, rural commercial banks, urban credit cooperatives (UCCs), rural credit cooperatives (RCCs), postal savings, foreign banks, and non-bank financial institutions (NBFIs).

[7] Bank of Communication, China Citic Bank, China Everbright Bank, Hua Xia Bank, Guangdong Development Bank, Shenzhen Development Bank, China Merchants Bank, Shanghai Pudong Development Bank, Industrial Bank, China Minsheng Banking Corp., Evergrowing Bank, China Zheshang Bank.

2008. Municipal commercial banks, operating in regional areas, had a share of 7% in the banking assets in 2008. Other institutions include policy banks, rural commercial banks, rural and urban credit cooperatives, foreign financial institutions, company finance houses, trust and investment corporations, financial leasing companies, automobile finance companies, currency brokers, post-office saving banks, etc. They took the remaining proportion of 28%.

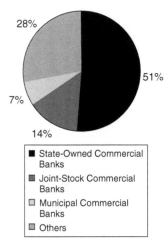

Fig. 6.2 Banking assets structure, 2008
Source: http://www.cbrc.gov.cn

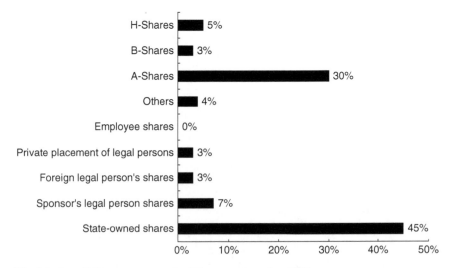

Fig. 6.3 Overall Share structure at the Chinese stock market, 2005
Source: CSRC (2006), http://www.wind.com.cn/

Within the bonds structure, government bonds, central bank bonds, and financial bonds (mostly policy bank bonds) are the three dominating segments. They added up to over 90% of the total bond depository balance in 2008 (see Fig. 6.4). By contrast, corporate bonds had a small quotient of 5%.

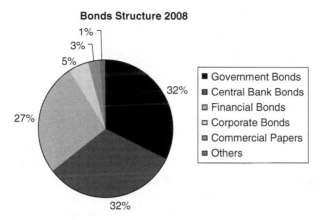

Fig. 6.4 Bonds structure, 2008
Source: http://www.chinabond.com.cn

It can be stated that China's financial system is a banking-centric one. China's banking system dominates by far in the financial system structure. Among all the Chinese banks, the four state-owned commercial banks possess the largest stake of all banking assets. China's stock market and bond market are, compared with the size of China's banking system, underdeveloped. Both of them are dominated by the state. By 2005, the state prevailed with a proportion of nearly 50% in the overall shareholding structure.[8] The bond market is mostly used to issue government and central bank bonds, while corporate bonds are not a common financing tool in China.

Chinese Banking System

Prior to the reform era, China had been following a Soviet-style banking system.[9] The People's Bank of China (PBOC), founded in 1948 under the Ministry of

---

[8] Before 2005, state-owned shares belonged to the non-tradable share types. With the 2005 non-tradable share reform launched, most of state-owned shares have become tradable ordinary A-shares and are not reflected in the official market statistics any longer. But the state maintains its control, as long as the shares are not sold (cf. the sections "Chinese Capital Markets" and "Corporate Goverance in China" below).

[9] Though foreign banks have been operating for some time in China, their market share is, compared with domestic banks, still small. Thus, we focus in our brief description on the Chinese banks.

Finance, had been the only bank in China and combined the roles of central and commercial banking. By 1978, it controlled about 93% of the total financial assets in China and settled almost all financial transactions (cf. Allen et al. 2009, p. 5).

With the reforms launched, the PBOC became a separate entity by 1979. From 1978 to 1984, its commercial banking businesses were taken over by four large state-owned commercial banks (BOC, CCB, ABC, ICBC), known as the *Big Four.* The Big Four were initially designated a different sector of the economy (foreign trade and exchange, construction, agriculture, industrial and commercial lending) which they were allowed to serve only. Since 1985, the Big Four have been competing in all sectors. During the 1980s, regional banks, in which local governments typically had a big stake, were established in the so-called Special Economic Zones (SEZs) in the coastal areas. Meanwhile, a net of credit cooperatives was implemented in both rural and urban areas.

The asset quality of the four state-owned banks worsened substantially during the 1990s, as their policy-lendings for SOEs were typically not repaid. As a solution to this problem, the central government founded three policy banks in 1994 to undertake the policy-lending activities instead of the Big Four, while the Minister of Finance issued 270 billion RMB government special bonds to recapitalize the four banks in 1998. In 1999, four state-owned asset management companies[10] bought the non-performing loans (NPL) at the face value of 1.4 trillion RMB.

Two important bank laws were issued in 1995. The 1995 *Central Bank Law* of China confirmed the PBOC as the central bank and significantly reduced the influence of local governments on credit allocation decisions. The 1995 *Commercial Bank Law* officially termed the four state-owned banks as commercial banks, directing them more towards commercial business based on market principles instead of policy-lending (cf. Berger et al. 2009, p. 117). New joint-stock banks, some of which privately owned, also entered the market in the mid-1990s. At the same time, foreign investors were allowed to hold minority stakes in regional Chinese banks under regulatory permission.

Significant reforms of the Chinese banking system took place after China joined the World Trade Organization (WTO) in 2001. The 1995 Central Bank Law and Commercial Bank Law were revised to be compliant with the WTO agreement. China Banking Regulatory Commission (CBRC) was established in 2003 to oversee reforms and regulations. CBRC took two strategies to improve Chinese banks' management and efficiency. In 2003, it allowed foreign investors to own up to 25% of any domestic bank, whereas the ownership from any one investor had to be between 5% and 20%, subject to regulatory approval. Introduction of foreign investors firstly occurred at Chinese joint-stock commercial banks,[11] and then spread to three of

---

[10] China Great Wall Asset Management Corporation, China Cinda Asset Management Corporation, China Orient Asset Management Corporation, China Huarong Asset Management Corporation.

[11] In 2003, Shanghai Pudong Development Bank sold 5% stake to Citigroup, while Industrial Bank sold 24.98% stake to a consortium made up by Hang Seng Bank Ltd. and others. In 2004, Shenzhen Development sold about 18% stake to Newbridge Capital Ltd., while Bank of Communications sold 19.9% stake to HSBC.

the Big Four.[12] Another strategy was to encourage the Chinese banks to issue shares[13] so as to set up external monitoring. Since 2005, some joint-stock commercial banks as well as CCB, BOC, ICBC have gone public in Hong Kong and Shanghai.

Chinese Capital Markets

Under the Chinese planned system before 1978, funds had been allocated to enterprises by the central and local governments. There had been no need for capital markets for enterprises to raise money. After 1978, relaxation policies over the business conduct generated capital demand from economic entities. In this context, bonds, stocks, and future contracts came into being in China. With the two stock exchanges established in Shanghai and in Shenzhen, respectively, the Chinese capital markets were established. The foundation of the Securities Committee and the China Securities Regulatory Commission (CSRC) brought the capital markets under a nationwide regulatory system.

Analogously to other reforms in China's transition process, the development of the Chinese capital markets has been mainly driven by the central government. New market segments and products were typically launched on an experimental basis, before expanding across the country. In some cases, the development progresses were ceased and corrected by the regulators and then relaunched.

The development of the capital markets was strongly backed by Deng Xiaoping. On his southern tour to promote the reform and opening-up policies in early 1992, he stated,

> Are securities and the stock market good or bad? Do they entail any dangers? Are they peculiar to capitalism? Can socialism make use of them? We allow people to reserve their judgement, but we must try these things out. If, after one or two years of experimentation, they prove feasible, we can expand them. Otherwise, we can put a stop to them and be done with it. We can stop them all at once or gradually, totally or partially. What is there to be afraid of? So long as we keep this attitude, everything will be all right, and we shall not make any major mistakes. (Deng Xiaoping 1992/1994, p. 361)

Stock Market

Emergence

The emergence of stocks can be traced back to the shareholding reforms that were initiated in rural areas in China. During the late 1970s, the earliest joint-stock

---

[12] The CCB sold 9% stake to the Bank of America, 5.1% stake to Temasek in 2005. The BOC sold 20% stake to Royal Bank of Scotland and Temasek in 2005. ICBC sold 10% stake to Goldman Sachs Group Inc., Allianz AG, and American Express Co. in 2006.

[13] Funds raised at stock exchanges outside mainland China are not subject to the 25% restriction on foreign ownership.

township enterprises were built up by farmers. In the mid-1980s, shareholding reforms spread to the urban areas. A few large and medium-sized enterprises were permitted to conduct a shareholding experiment and to issue shares. In doing so, the primary stock market emerged. Most of those issued shares were offered to employees of the enterprises and local residents, without participation of underwriters. They were similar to bonds, as they guaranteed fix dividends, were sold at par, and redeemed on maturity. In 1986, over-the-counter (OTC) transactions appeared for stocks.

In 1990, the central government approved of establishing two stock exchanges in Shanghai and Shenzhen, respectively, aiming at broadening external financing channels and improving the operating performance for former SOEs.[14] From the beginning, short sale of shares was not allowed in the exchange trading. Both exchanges launched their respective composite indices in 1991.[15] By the end of 1991, eight stocks were listed on the Shanghai Stock Exchange (SSE), while the Shenzhen Stock Exchange (SZSE) had six listings. Later, RMB-denominated ordinary shares for domestic residents and institutions to invest in were called A-shares for short. In 1991, China also undertook a pilot scheme to issue shares, known as B-shares, to foreign investors. B-shares are domestically listed, denominated in RMB, but subscribed to and traded in USD or HKD by overseas investors.[16]

Market Growth

Since 1992, the Chinese stock market has boomed and become one of the worldwide largest in a relatively short lapse of time. Starting from 53 in 1992, the number of firms listed on SSE and SZSE increased about 30 times to 1,594 in 2008 (see Fig. 6.5). More than 2,230 billion RMB and 5.09 billion USD were raised through A-share and B-share offerings, respectively, while the market capitalization totaled over 10 trillion RMB since 2007. More than 40 million investment accounts were opened (see Table 6.1). After the rally in 2007, the Chinese stock market reached a market capitalization of over 30 trillion RMB. This volume overstepped not only China's nominal GDP for the first time (see Fig. 6.6), but, as exhibited in Table 6.2,

---

[14] For example, CSRC issued in December 1996 the *Notice of Several Regulations on Share Issuance*, which required local authorities to "give preference to the 1,000 key enterprises determined by the state, especially 300 of them, as well as to the 100 enterprises and 56 enterprise groups in experiment with the modern enterprise system" (own translation). The key enterprises were mostly SOEs.

[15] The Shenzhen Composite Index was launched on April 4, 1991, taking the previous days as the base of 100 points. SSE took December 19, 1990 as its base of 100 points for the Shanghai Composite Index and launched it on 15 July 1991.

[16] Since 2001, domestic residents can trade in B-shares as well.

most of the developed stock markets and ranked No. 2 behind the New York Stock Exchange (NYSE).[17]

In the first decades of China's stock market, regulators and exchanges preferred listing of big SOEs in several industries. From 2001 on, the SZSE began to explore the possibility of building up a Growth Enterprises Market (GEM). As the first step, the SZSE set up the Small and Medium-sized Enterprises (SME) Board in May 2004. By the end of 2008, there were 273 firms listed on the SME Board in Shenzhen, having raised over 120 billion RMB through IPOs and refinancing (see Table 6.3).

Opening-up

To attract foreign investment, China's opening-up policies covered the stock market as well. The introduction of B-shares in 1991 was the first step to open up China's stock market to the outside world. Soon thereafter, domestic firms were allowed in 1993 to go public on overseas stock exchanges. The Chinese stocks listed and traded in Hong Kong, New York, London, and Singapore are, in reference to A- and B-shares, also called H-shares, N-shares, L-shares, and S-shares. From 1993 to 2007, Chinese firms raised more than 100 billions USD through overseas listings (see Fig. 6.7). Since overseas listings connected domestic firms to international capital market more closely, the B-share market became less important in fund raising (see Table 6.1).

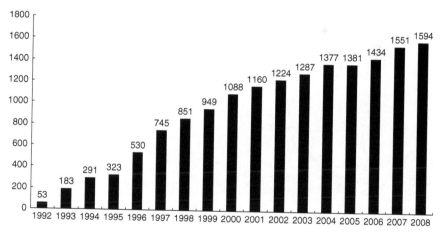

Fig. 6.5 Number of listed firms, 1992–2008
*The number includes listed firms which have only issued A-shares or B-shares, or both types
Source: CSRC (2006)

---

[17] Although SSE alone ranks just six in the annual report and statistics (2007) of the World Federation of Exchanges, we come to this result by adding up the market capitalization of SZSE to it and comparing the total value with the data of other exchanges.

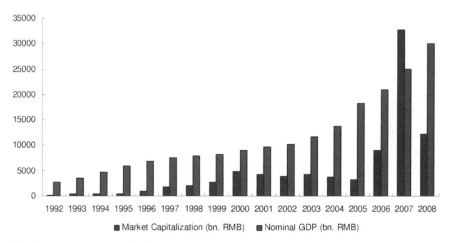

Fig. 6.6 Stock market capitalization versus nominal GDP in China, 1992–2008
Source: SSE (2006), CSRC (2008), NBSC (2009), CSDCC (2009)

Table 6.1 Total funds raised, number of investment accounts, 1992–2008

Year	Total funds raised through A-shares (bn. RMB)	Total funds raised through B-shares (bn. USD)	Number of investor accounts (stock + fund) (m.)	Total market capitalization of A- and B-shares (bn. RMB)
1992	5.00	0.80	2.7	104.8
1993	27.64	0.70	8.4	354.2
1994	9.98	0.40	11.1	369.1
1995	8.55	0.40	12.9	347.4
1996	29.43	0.60	24.2	984.2
1997	82.59	1.30	34.8	1,752.9
1998	77.80	0.30	42.6	1,952.2
1999	89.40	0.05	48.1	2,647.1
2000	152.70	0.20	61.5	4,809.1
2001	118.20	0	69.7	4,352.2
2002	78.00	0	72	3,832.9
2003	82.00	0.04	73.4	4,245.8
2004	83.60	0.30	75.9	3,705.6
2005	33.80	0	77.1	3,243.0
2006	246.40	0	82.5	8,940.4
2007	772.80	0	138.8 (118.8)[a]	32,714.1
2008	339.60	0	152 (132.8)[a]	12,136.7
Total	2,237.50	5.09		

[a]Number of the active investment accounts
Source: CSRC (2006), NBSC (2008a), NBSC (2008b), SSE (2008a), SZSE (2008), CSDCC (2008)

Table 6.2 Market capitalization of leading stock exchanges, 2006–2007

Stock exchanges	end 2007 (bn. USD)	end 2006 (bn. USD)	Change (in USD)	Change (in local currency)
01. NYSE Group	15,651	15,421	1.50%	1.50%
02. Tokyo Stock Exchange Group	4,331	4,614	−6.10%	−12.00%
03. Euronext	4,233	3,713	13.70%	2.60%
04. Nasdaq Stock Market	4,014	3,865	3.80%	3.80%
05. London Stock Exchange	3,852	3,794	1.50%	−0.20%
06. Shanghai Stock Exchange	3,694	918	302.70%	276.80%
07. Hong Kong Exchanges	2,654	1,715	54.80%	55.20%
08. TSX Group	2,187	1,701	28.60%	9.00%
09. Deutsche Börse	2,105	1,638	28.60%	15.90%
10. Bombay Stock Exchange	1,819	819	122.10%	97.80%
11. BME Spanish Exchanges	1,799	1,323	36.10%	22.70%
12. National Stock Exchange India	1,660	774	114.50%	91.00%
SSE+SZSE	4,479	1,145	291.20%	265.90%

Source: WFE (2007), SZSE (2006, 2007)

Table 6.3 Total funds raised on the SME Board, 2004–2009

	2004	2005	2006	2007	2008	Total
New listings	38	12	52	100	71	273
Total raised funds (bn. RMB)	9.11	2.91	17.93	48.95	41.01	119.91

Source: finance.sina.com.cn/stock/

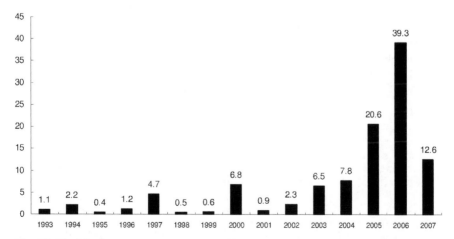

Fig. 6.7 Total funds raised through overseas listings, 1993–2008
Source: CSRC (2008)

On its WTO accession, China made a few commitments concerning the securities industry. First, foreign securities firms could directly trade in B-shares. Second, representative offices of foreign securities firms in China could apply for special membership at all domestic exchanges. Third, foreign service providers could set up joint ventures for securities trading and fund management, with initial shareholdings capped at 33% and 49% within three years after the WTO accession. Fourth, within three years of the WTO accession, foreign securities firms could set up joint ventures with shareholding not exceeding 33%, and the joint ventures could, without the need to enlist the service of an Chinese intermediary, underwrite A-shares, underwrite and trade B-/H-shares and government/corporate bonds, as well as launch funds (cf. CSRC 2008, p. 184).

By the end of 2006, Beijing had complied rather fully with China's 2001 securities industry WTO commitments, both in formal (legislative and regulatory) terms and in implementation of the WTO mandated regime (cf. Howson 2007, p. 153). The authorities also adopted some additional policies in opening up the stock market. For example, in November 2002, foreign companies were allowed to purchase state-owned shares and legal person shares of Chinese listed firms.[18] In February 2006, foreign investors were allowed to make strategic investments in the A-share of listed companies.[19]

In December 2002, the CSRC launched the Qualified Foreign Institutional Investor (QFII) program, which licenses foreign institutional investors to trade A-shares on the secondary market. By the end of 2007, 52 foreign institutional investors had been granted the QFII status, 49 of which had been allocated quota of totally 10 billion USD, while five foreign banks had been permitted to provide QFIIs custodian services (cf. CSRC 2008, p. 32).

By the end of 2007, there were seven Sino-foreign securities firms and 28 Sino-foreign fund management companies operating in China, of which 19 firms had a foreign shareholding of above 40% (cf. ibid., p. 31). Four representative offices of foreign securities firms became special members of the Shanghai and Shenzhen Stock Exchanges; 39 and 19 foreign securities firms were trading B-shares on Shanghai and Shenzhen Stock Exchanges, respectively (cf. ibid., p. 31).

Meanwhile, the authorities further promoted connections to overseas capital markets. In May 2006, the Qualified Domestic Institutional Investor (QDII) program was launched, allowing licensed domestic institutional investors to invest in

---

[18] According to the *Notice Regarding Transfer to Foreign Investors of State-Owned Shares and Legal Person Shares of Listed Companies* (CSRC 2002), only those industries that are opened to foreign investors can conduct such a share transfer, while the Chinese controlling shareholder should maintain his (relative) controlling status after the transfer.

[19] According to the *Measures for Strategic Investments by Foreign Investors upon Listed Companies* (MCPRC 2005), foreign investors may acquire A-shares of the Chinese listed firms having finished the reform of non-tradable shares by means of long- and mid-term strategic investment. They may acquire A-shares by means of contract transfer or share offering, while the proportion of obtained shares should be no less than 10% after the first investment and should not be transferred within three years.

overseas markets. By the end of 2007, 15 fund management firms and five securities firms had been granted QDII status with an aggregate investment quota of 24.5 billion USD (cf. ibid., p. 32).

Bond Market

From 1954 on, the central government issued its first treasury bonds (T-bonds), so-called Economic Construction Bonds, for five years in succession. In 1959, the issuance of T-bonds was stopped. In 1981, the central government relaunched T-bonds. T-bonds in the early 1980s typically had a long maturity (10 years) and were non-transferable. From 1982 on, a few enterprises took the initiative to issue enterprise bonds. In 1987, the State Council stipulated that further enterprise bond issuances were subject to approval by the PBOC, and that PBOC, the State Planning Commission, and the Ministry of Finance would set a cap on the total amount of enterprises bonds to be issued annually. A third type of bonds, so-called financial bonds, appeared in 1984. They were issued by banks to support the completion of construction projects that ran short of funds. Since then, they have served as a regular financing tool for Chinese banks.

In April 1988, experiments with OTC trading of T-bonds by individual investors were made in a few big cities. Two months later, the permission for individual transactions expanded to 28 provinces and municipalities, and 54 large and medium-sized cities (cf. CSRC 2008, p. 6). By the end of 1988, trading of T-bonds had spread across the country. The secondary bond market emerged. In December 1990, trading of T-bonds was introduced by SSE. In 1995, all OTC bond markets were closed by the central government, because the once uncontrolled business caused high risks. In consequence, SSE and SZSE became the only legal bond markets. In 1996, a big amount of book-entry T-bonds began to be issued and repurchased on SSE and SZSE, which marked the formation of bond market on exchanges.

In 1997, Chinese commercial banks withdrew from bond business at exchanges.[20] In the same year, the PBOC established the inter-bank bond market on the basis of China Foreign Exchange Trading System. Besides commercial banks, other financial institutions such as insurance companies, credit cooperatives, securities firms, securities investment funds, finance houses, foreign institutional investors, non-financial institutions, and pension annuities gained access to the inter-bank bond market in the following years. International institutions were permitted to issue bonds denominated in RMB, known as Panda bonds. The types of bonds issued by financial institutions included short-term, ordinary, foreign currency, subordinated, hybrid and asset-backed bonds, bond forwards, and enterprise bonds.

Since 2002, commercial banks have offered, as an extension of the inter-bank bond market, counter services for individual investors and SMEs to trade in T-bonds. In January 2009, commercial banks listed on Chinese exchanges were experimentally allowed to return to the bond market at exchanges.

---

[20] As a big amount of bank deposits flew into the stock market through bond repurchase business early this year, PBOC ceased bond repurchase and dealing by commercial banks.

Futures Market

As early as in October 1990, Zhengzhou Grain Wholesale Market was opened, and forward contracts were introduced there. In October 1992, Shenzhen Nonferrous Metals Futures Exchange made the first standard futures contract in China. In 1993, the commodity futures market flourished. There were over 50 commodity futures exchanges and more than 300 futures brokerage companies across the country. Meanwhile, T-bond futures came into existence. In December of 1992, SSE introduced the first T-bond futures. In early 1995, the number of exchanges dealing in T-bond futures increased to 14.

However, the futures market was fraught with speculations and manipulations due to insufficient regulation (cf. CSRC 2008, p. 19). In 1993, the State Council emphasized that its Securities Committee and the CSRC were the regulators of the Chinese futures market and began to clear it. Futures brokers which were either unqualified or acting illegally were closed or suspended. Dealing of a number of commodities, including steel, sugar, coal, rice, and rap oil, was suspended. In May 1995, trading of T-bond futures was suspended as well. In 1998, the existing 14 futures exchanges were consolidated into three (Shanghai, Dalian, Zhengzhou).

From 1999 to 2002, the State Council and the CSRC promulgated the first regulations on futures trading, exchanges, and brokerage firms at the futures market, starting to establish a legal and regulatory framework. From 2004 on, new commodity futures contracts were introduced, including cotton, fuel oil, corns, soybean, sugar, soybean oil, purified terephthalic acid (PTA), zinc, rapeseed oil, linear low-density polyethylene (LLDPE), and palm oil. The three commodity futures exchanges have been gradually unifying their trading rules and expanding the use of a common trading portal. In May 2006, the first Sino-foreign futures joint venture[21] was established, marking the start of foreign participants in China's futures market. In September 2006, the China Financial Futures Exchange (CFFEX) was set up in Shanghai. The preparation on introduction of stock index futures is still ongoing. Up to now, *Trading Rules of China Financial Futures Exchange* has been promulgated; and nearly 80 members have been licensed for transactions (cf. CFFEX 2008). Mock trading of stock index futures has been ongoing for testing purposes since October 2006, but there is still no fixed plan or schedule to launch the stock index futures.[22] In January 2008, the Shanghai Futures Exchange (SHFE) introduced the first futures contract on gold.

---

[21] The futures brokerage was established by China Galaxy Securities Co. and ABN AMRO Asia Futures Limited with 60% and 40% stake, respectively.

[22] The CFFEX General Manager, Zhu Yuchen, stated during an interview on 9 March 2009 that the financial crisis hindered the introduction of stock index futures and there was no schedule of launching them (cf. Hu 2009).

Corporate Governance in China

How Did Corporate Governance Become Popular?

While China's stock market has been expanding impressively, it is meanwhile conspicuous that this development has so far been inconsistent with China's economic success measured by its nominal GDP (see Fig. 6.6). As the national economy recorded a yearly GDP growth of at least 8% since the 1990s, the stock market capitalization, in spite of increasing listings, fluctuated heavily over the same time period. Especially from 2000 to 2005, albeit the number of listed firms blew up by about one-third and the issued shares doubled, the market capitalization shrank apparently due to collapsing stock prices. In identifying the causes for this conjuncture, the attention of the market regulators and participants was soon directed to the deficiencies of the corporate governance practices in China.

More precisely, it was several unveiled Enron-alike scandals as well as capital tunneling by controlling shareholders that struck the overall investors' confidence at the Chinese stock market. Two cases illustrate these problems.[23] One involved the one-time top performer, North China-based firm *Yinguangxia* (YGX), whose stock price leaped by about 440% in 2000. Barely one year later, two journalists called YGX's brilliant achievements into question and disclosed that YGX had been forging documents and misrepresenting information. The official investigation by the CSRC in 2002 fixed a total fraudulent profit of 770 million RMB by YGX from 1998 to 2001 (cf. Guo 2007). The other example relates to Sanjiu Pharma who inadequately disclosed transactions with related parties, including the controlling shareholder and other subsidiaries of it, and created fictitious transactions in order to raise cash from banks (cf. Chen et al. 2005). The CSRC investigation revealed that Sanjiu Pharma had extracted as much as 2.5 billion RMB, about 96% of the firm's equity, through related transactions (cf. CSRC 2001).

Although the conception of corporate governance had been introduced to China as early as in the mid-1990s,[24] it did not arouse much interest until during the long lasting bear market from 2000 to 2005. Both the Chinese government and the stock market regulators are now aware of the importance of good corporate governance practices.

Why Is Corporate Governance Important?

Social Stability

The young stock market in China has brought forth a tremendous number of shareholders from individuals over institutional investors to state agencies. According to China Securities Depository and Clearing Corporation, more than 140 million

---

[23] For more information on the two cases see Chen et al. (2005).

[24] For example, Masahiko Aoki and Hyung-Ki Kim published in 1995 the book "Corporate Governance in Transition Economies" (cf. Aoki/Kim 1995).

investment accounts (stocks and investment funds totally), overwhelmingly held by small individual investors, had been opened until the end of 2007 (cf. CSDCC 2008, pp. 14f.). If every account was indeed owned by one person,[25] it would correspond to one tenth of China's whole population or one fourth of its urban population directly engaging in the stock transactions. As for institutional investors who manage the wealth of individuals, there are more than 350 mutual funds, over 50 QFIIs, several large domestic insurers as well as the National Social Security Fund trading actively on the market. Moreover, an unknown, but large amount of banks loans have been flowing into the stock market through gray or illegal channels (cf. Liu 2006, p. 416). Notably, the central and local governments who are managing state assets on behalf of Chinese people still maintain the lion's share in many listed firms through their asset management administrations. The number of directly and indirectly involved small shareholders is so large that a thorough breakdown of the stock market would very likely rock the boat. Therefore, it is not difficult to understand that the central government as well as other state agencies and exchanges warned loudly of an overheated market several times as the stock prices were skyrocketing in 2007.[26] A failed stock market may cause social uncertainty that remains one of the government's primary concerns.[27]

Capital Competition

The more integrated China becomes in the world economy, the more affected will it be by international rules and conventions which have mainly been set down by developed countries. Hoping international investors to buy and hold their shares, Chinese listed firms have to adjust themselves to those corporate governance practices preferred by global investors. The internationalization of the capital markets is nevertheless a two-edged sword for all developing economies: capital can as easily flow out from a market with weak investor protection as into it. The East Asian financial crisis in late 1990s demonstrates that opened capital markets without well-developed corporate governance mechanisms can be easily abandoned by capital flows. Even though China's extraordinary achievements in the last three decades and the internationally broadly recognized prospect for the near future may keep the interest of foreign investors high – the list of QFIIs is constantly getting longer – and in this way compensate for the negative impacts of its weak corporate governance practices, this is not expected to work in the long run. It is thus in China's interest to make its corporate governance practices attractive for foreign investors.

---

[25] It appears that in reality a number of these accounts are old, inactive, fake, or controlled by some institutions. Nonetheless, the number of small Chinese shareholders is immense.

[26] For example, the "Guidelines of Shanghai Stock Exchange on Individual Investors' Behavior" (SSE 2008b), which were issued in July 2007, insisted on the principle of caveat emptor.

[27] For example, Deng noted in 1989: "In China the overriding need is for stability. Without a stable environment, we can accomplish nothing and may even lose what we have gained" (Deng Xiaoping 1989/1994).

Further Transition

China's economic transition toward a Chinese "socialist market economy" is still ongoing and the current, in 1990s launched round of SOE reforms has not finished yet (see the section "Governance Practices in Chinese SOEs: Content of Change" for more details). Only some of the former SOEs are listed in Shanghai and Shenzhen. The remaining ones are waiting for an initial public offering as a vital channel for their future fund-raising. Hence, the central and local governments who mostly hold claims on SOEs have sufficient incentives to maintain the stock market as a well-functioning platform for financing SOEs. It should also be mentioned that the establishment of a stock market is the first step towards completing the capital markets in China, whereas the stock market itself still needs to complete its functions as well as to diversify its investment product line. The success of the following steps, say, derivative products including stock index futures and a corporate bond market, will depend on the success of the stock market. They could not be executed if the firstly built stock market had already collapsed. China's further transition and capital markets development cannot afford a failed stock market.

What Has Been Done to Improve Corporate Governance?

In dealing with the deficiencies at the stock market, the Chinese government began to improve its corporate governance framework by enacting and revising a series of governance-related guidelines and laws. After the first corporate governance code for listed companies had been issued by the CSRC in 2002, both the *Company Law* and the *Securities Law* were revised by the National People's Congress (NPC) in 2005. The new regulations address some problems at the stock market, including the independence of the boards of directors, firms' information disclosure, and expropriation of small shareholders.

With respect to investigation of illegal activities at the capital market, the CSRC did not set up a law enforcement bureau (Bureau I) until 1995. It further established subordinate local enforcement bureaus in several big cities. In 2002, the CSRC instituted another law enforcement bureau (Bureau II) for investigation of market manipulation and insider trading, while Bureau I took the responsibility for investigating fraud in securities issuances, dishonesty in statements, and other offences. In 2003, the Ministry of Public Security established the Securities Crime Investigation Bureau to cooperate with the CSRC for investigation of offences at the securities market. In 2007, the CSRC instituted the Sanction Committee, Chief Enforcement Officer, and the Law Enforcement Task Force in its headquarters to lead the enforcement system. Meanwhile, local enforcement bureaus were reinforced with a larger work force. From 2003 to 2007, the CSRC investigated 736 cases, forwarded 104 of them for criminal charges, imposed sanctions on 212 cases involving 180 entities and 987 individuals, and banned the entry of 165 professionals and executives into the securities market for extended periods (cf. CSRC 2008, p. 22).

At present, all of the public firms have, in accordance with the CSRC, introduced independent directors as an internal monitoring mechanism into the board, as required by the CSRC. More chairmen are now separated from the CEO function. Listed firms are obliged to make clear statements on their efforts in improving governance structure and revealing information on compensations for the board members and executives. The relations of the board members to the controlling shareholder are defined in annual closures. The regulators and exchanges are making efforts in oversight of affiliated transactions between listed firms and their controlling shareholders among which tunneling of assets had usually taken place. These alterations in corporate governance have let the public firms become more transparent for investors as previously.

How Different Is the Chinese Model?

Classical Models

Corporate governance models vary across countries. Yet researchers tend to identify two prevailing corporate governance models: the Anglo-American market-based shareholder model and the insider models of, say, Germany and Japan (cf. Shleifer and Vishny 1997; La Porta et al. 1998, 1999; Bebchuck and Roe 1999). The preference for one of the two types of models is mainly attributable to each country's economic success in 1980s and 1990s, respectively (cf. Becht et al. 2002, p. 32).

In the Anglo-American model, public equity is widely dispersed, while directors make all the decisions or have exclusive power to initiate them (cf. Enriques and Volpin 2007, p. 127). In spite of several accounting scandals unveiled at the turn of the century in the USA, the listed firms in this model still face strictest legal restrictions and enforcement in respect of minority shareholder protection,[28] and there is a highly competitive product market to boost the firms' performance. Whilst the external mechanisms for investor protection are strong in this model, the internal governance structure is no more than a principal-agent relation set between shareholders and the board of directors through the general meeting. Both the management and monitoring functions at the corporate level are combined in the board of directors. By contrast, the equity of public firms in the German and Japanese models is more concentrated. Although the market mechanisms are less strong than in the US model,[29] the German and Japanese models have evolved into a more

---

[28] See for example Roe (2003) for more details of US securities regulation.

[29] For example, La Porta et al. (1998) found that "common law countries generally have the strongest, and French civil law countries the weakest, legal protections of investors, with German and Scandinavian civil law countries located in the middle" (p. 1113). Yet Shleifer/Vishny (1997) concluded that "the differences between them [USA, Germany, Japan] are probably small relative to their differences from other countries" (pp. 737–738). In the last two decades, Germany has made a lot of efforts in empowering shareholders, enhancing disclosure and strengthening public enforcement. Thus, its external mechanisms are moving towards the market-based model.

sophisticated internal governance structure that takes in other stakeholders such as labor unions, banks, and employees as co-principals of the firms.

Chinese Model in Comparison

Figure 6.8 illustrates in a simplified sense the corporate governance models in the USA, Germany, and China. The dot-dash frame symbolizes the external governance-related environments at the national level. A bolder frame indicates that an economy is by and large equipped with more developed capital markets, a stronger legal system with more effective enforcement, and a more competitive product market, whereas a more thinly lined frame matches a weaker governance environment. Compared with the USA and the German models, the Chinese corporate governance model has a weak external environment with regard to market and legal mechanisms. This fact is not surprising in consideration of China's ongoing process of transition to a market economy and corresponding constructing of its rule of law.

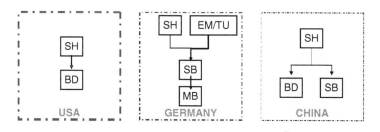

⌐ ⌐ Product Market Competitiveness, Capital Market, Legal System
       and Enforcement

SH = Shareholders, BD = Board of Directors, EM = Employees,
TU = Trade Union, SB = Supervisory Board, MB = Management Board

Fig. 6.8 Corporate governance models in the USA, Germany, and China
Source: Own figure

External Aspects

Product Market

Product market competition drives producers and service suppliers to improve their performance. However, the Chinese product market lacks of competition in some industries: The central government considers industries such as utilities, transportation, telecommunication, banking, oil, and steel to be of strategic importance and keeps the entry of other suppliers under strict control. Therefore, it is big SOEs who dominate in these industries. Another cause of weak competition is local protectionism for the sake of regional economic development. In their procurement process, provincial and municipal governments usually favor local products and encourage local enterprises to purchase locally manufactured materials and products. This is becoming more obvious in dealing with the current world financial crisis since 2007: while planning a huge amount of spending in order to guarantee economic growth, ten provincial governments have issued documents on purchasing local products including electrical appliances, vehicles, and steels (cf. 21CBH 2009).

Capital Market

The Chinese stock market is dynamic in terms of a rapidly increasing number of investors and market capitalization. Yet it is so far underdeveloped in other more important aspects. First, the entire financial system in China is dominated by a large, state-controlled bank system, implying that the financing through the Chinese stock market is limited. The limits usually result from the government's tight control in the number and size of public issuances and in the choice of firms to be listed: the authorities prefer the state sector. Second, the Chinese stock market lacks alternative investment products. Third, the stock market is rather a domestic one than an international one. By now, it is to a limited extent opened to a small number of foreign institutional investors. Similarly, domestic investors barely have any access to overseas stock markets except for a few products of QDIIs. Listings of foreign-invested firms have been announced[30] to accelerate the market internationalization. However, no rules or schedule have been made yet.

Legal Institutions

The legal institutions in China provide an interesting picture. On the one hand, the Chinese legal system represents sufficient shareholder protection. Using the measures of La Porta, Lopez-de-Silanes, Shleifer, and Vishny (LLSV) (1998) on legal provisions for publicly traded firms, Allen, Qian, and Qian (2005) compared the shareholder protection in China with that in LLSV countries. They found out that China reaches the average level of all LLSV countries. China's score falls in between the English-origin countries that have the highest measures of protection and German-origin countries that have the poorest protection. With measures drawn from independent international rating agencies, they further compared the law enforcement in China with that in LLSV countries. This time, they came to a very different result: China's law enforcement is significantly below the average level of all LLSV countries. The inconsistent results suggest that China's shareholder protection is relatively strong on paper, but weak in practice. The reasons that the laws are not effectively being enforced in China are (1) lack of

---

[30] After the third round of China-U.S. Strategic Economic Dialogue in December 2007, both sides promised to further open up its financial markets to the other. China agreed to allow, in accordance with relevant prudential regulations, qualified foreign-invested companies, including banks, to issue RMB-denominated stocks; qualified listed companies to issue RMB denominated corporate bonds; and qualified incorporated foreign banks to issue RMB denominated financial bonds. See U.S. Department of The Treasury (2007).

qualified legal professionals, and (2) conflict of interest between fair play in practicing law and the monopoly power of the single ruling party (cf. Allen et al. 2005, p. 11).

Internal Aspects

Governance Structure

As to the internal governance structure, the Chinese model looks, at first appearance, quite similar to the two-tier board system of the German model. In Germany, the public firm is governed by a management board (*Vorstand*) and a supervisory board (*Aufsichtsrat*). The managing board is in charge of the daily operations of the firm, while the supervisory board is responsible for appointing, supervising, and advising the management board and directly involved in developing strategies of the firm (cf. Mallin 2007). In the Chinese model, management and monitoring tasks are delegated to the board of directors and the board of supervisors, respectively. The Chinese board of supervisors also takes in employee representatives, which makes it more like the German way of co-determination (*Mitbestimmung*). However, there is no such hierarchical relationship between the board of directors and the board of supervisors as in the German model. While the German supervisory board has the authority to appoint and, if necessary, even dismiss the members of the management board, the two boards in the Chinese model are run on the same level, and the directors and supervisors are all appointed or dismissed by shareholder action. In view of this structural arrangement, it is doubtful whether the board of supervisors have enough power to conduct the supervising work effectively.

Overall Ownership Structure

The ownership structure at the Chinese stock market is deeply characterized by the state's design. Typically, former SOEs were approved to go public, and the share distribution was regulated by the central government. A large proportion of the shares were prevented from being transacted at the exchanges. Until 2005, Chinese shares were divided into two types: non-tradable shares that were not allowed to be publicly traded, and tradable shares that were entitled to transactions at the exchanges. Each type was further divided into different classes, depending on their shareholder or listing location.

Non-tradable shares mainly comprised state-owned shares and legal person shares. State-owned shares were in the possession of the central and local governments through their underlying asset management agencies, while legal person shares are those owned by entities with a legal person status. The legal persons referred to domestic sponsors, foreign companies, and other legal entities who had taken part in a non-public offering of the relevant firms.[31] Other untradeable shares were in the hands of employees or private individuals.

---

[31] By 1994, many Chinese joint-stock companies had been founded through non-public offering by 1994. Yet this is not allowed since the Company Law was brought into effect in July 1994.

Table 6.4 Ownership structure of Chinese public firms 2005

Year 2005		Shares (bn.)	% of total
Non-tradable	State-owned shares	343.3	44.82
	Sponsor's legal person shares	55.2	7.21
	Foreign legal person's shares	22.6	2.95
	Private placement of legal person's shares	24.3	3.17
	Employee shares	0.4	0.05
	Others	28.7	3.75
Tradable	A-shares	228.1	29.78
	B-Shares	21.8	2.84
	H-Shares	41.6	5.43

Data Source: CSRC (2006), http://www.wind.com.cn/

Table 6.4 provides a snapshot of Chinese public firms' overall share structure in 2005. At the year end, about two-thirds of the shares at the Chinese stock market were non-tradable. Among them, state-owned shares have the dominant proportion of approximately 45%. Since domestic sponsors of public firms are usually former SOEs under control of the state's agencies, the state indeed controlled more than half of all shares of the listed firms. By contrast, tradable A- and B-shares which were dispersed among private and institutional investors summed up to slightly over 30%. Therefore, the Chinese stock market is state-dominated.

Before 2005, the only legal channel of transacting non-tradable shares was equity transfer between enterprises, provided that the agreement had been approved by relevant authorities and regulators. In 2005, the regulators launched a reform of non-tradable shares in order to make them tradable. Against compensation in cash or stocks, shareholders of the one-time non-tradable shares have gained the right to sell them after certain lockup periods (12–24 months) have expired.

Although the 2005 non-tradable shares reform has enhanced the equity liquidity of the listed firms in China, it has not significantly changed the market's ownership structure and the state's dominance. Even though the state's directly and indirectly controlled shares are now entitled to market transfer, the state and its agencies need not do so. Consequently, the state's role in the governance structure has not changed.

Why and How Do We Survey the Causality in the Formation of the Chinese Model?

Shleifer and Vishny (1997) argued that the Anglo-American and the German/Japanese corporate governance models are efficient, because they have a good complementarity between the level of legal protection and ownership concentration. Countries with poor investor protection typically exhibit more concentrated control of firms than countries with good investor protection (cf. La Porta et al. 1998, 1999; Claessens et al. 2000).

In reference to these theoretical and empirical works, one may argue that China's weak legal protection for shareholders has given rise to a concentrated ownership structure. However, this logic does not really match the situation in China. The main reason is that in China, the state has been playing a decisive role in both the formation of the legislation, including legal protection for investors, and the establishment of a corporate governance structure that emerged in the 1990s. Hence, both the general legal protection for investors and the ownership structure at the Chinese stock market rather reflect the will of the central government than build up certain causalities by themselves.

In summary, three features make the corporate governance model at the Chinese stock market different from the classical models: (1) a weak external environment that does not exert sufficient market and legal constraints on listed firms; (2) a simple internal governance structure without a strong supervisory function available; and (3) dominance of the state in the ownership structure. Nevertheless, the causality in the formation of the Chinese model is still unclear, if legal protection for investors is not a drive. How did the Chinese model evolve over the past decades? What backed every big change in its evolution? These questions are crucial for a good understanding of the corporate governance model in China.

Since most listed firms at the Chinese stock market have SOE backgrounds, it makes sense to look back at Chinese SOEs' development process, and to trace the roots of the Chinese corporate governance model. In doing so, we utilize the distinction between the content of change and process of change in the organizational change studies (cf. van de Ven 2009), and principal-agent relationships as the overall framework of this survey.

Governance Practices in Chinese SOEs: Content of Change

In the planned economy before 1978, state ownership was considered the sole legal form of enterprises.[32] This concept provided justification for state planners to mobilize human and financial resources and allowed them to assess production and distribution demands. The state did not only own the property rights of, but operated the SOEs through its officials who were executing the managerial powers. This model served as an organizer of economic resources and activities as well as a tool binding the state, SOEs, and employees to each other (cf. Shipani and Liu 2002, p. 8). That is to say, SOEs were operating on the state's coffers as the sole financial input, while employees were living on salaries earned at the SOEs. Therefore, SOEs had some social security functions other than just production units. A job at a certain SOE was once called an "iron rice bowl" that symbolized a secured life with salary, housing, medical treatment, and pension offered by the SOE.

---

[32] Article 15 of the Chinese Constitution of 1982 declared, "The state practices economic planning on the basis of socialist public ownership".

Having learned a bitter lesson from abolishing the development of the national economy during the ten year long Cultural Revolution and seen the economic success in the developed countries, the central government intended to increase productivity and raise living standards in 1978 by reforming its economic model systematically into a more competitive one. On the Third Plenum of the Eleventh Chinese Communist Party Congress at the end of 1978, the Party out set to shift its focus from class struggles to economic development (cf. CPC 1978). Following this ideological turning, the Chinese reform era began.

Depending on the central government's major policies for reforming SOEs and their management, we identify three governance stages of Chinese SOEs since 1978: (1) the incentive stage from 1978 to 1983, (2) the contracting model from 1984 to 1992 and (3) the corporatization model since 1993. As summarized in Fig. 6.9, governance practices at the three stages differ in their features with regard to the goal of relevant policies and the roles of the state as well as SOEs and their executives (managers) as participants.

The Incentive Stage (1978–1983)

The experiment of SOE reform had started even shortly before the Third Plenum of the Eleventh Chinese Communist Party Congress was held. In autumn 1978, six SOEs in the Sichuan Province were selected by the local government to be the first ones to undertake an experiment along the lines of "expanding enterprise autonomy and introducing profit retention" (Qian 1999a, p. 8). In 1979, the number of experimenting SOEs in Sichuan was increased to about 100. The selected SOEs were given more autonomy in a way that they could produce and sell goods to the external free market[33] and retain some profits in case they had fulfilled the plan quotas. They were also authorized to promote some middle-level managers, who still had to be approved by the government.

In summer 1979, the central government issued *Some Provisions on Enlarging Industrial SOEs' Autonomy* (cf. CPC 2008) and other four documents to extend the SOE reform experiments to other provinces. By 1980, more than half of Chinese SOEs (in terms of output value) were involved in the experiments and obtained some limited autonomy in production planning, material purchasing, employment, sales, and use of retained profits.[34] These incentives had an active effect on SOEs' performance of that time. Compared with 1978, the delivered profits of all SOEs to

---

[33] The external free market was established as the government allowed peasants to sell their surplus products.

[34] The central government required SOEs to split their retained profits into funds for housing, bonuses for employees and funds for production development, while the government would not interfere with the use of these funds.

the state grew in 1979 by 10.1%. The government deficit of 1 billion RMB in 1978 was replaced by a surplus of 13.5 billion RMB in 1979. The income from SOEs rose by 7.5% as against the previous year (cf. Wang 2006, p. 10).

However, these practices were de facto no change of the dominating planned system, but a cautious testing of a profit-orientation of the SOEs. Planned production quotas still took priority on SOEs' task lists. Only those who were able to complete their production plans and to mobilize surplus human and financial resources could enjoy the profit retention. Although the state shared some decision-making rights with SOEs, it remained pervasive in SOEs' operations. It owned all the enterprises on behalf of the Chinese people and delegated officials to manage SOEs' operations. At the same time, it assessed production and distribution demands, formed production schemes for SOEs, and monitored the realization of these schemes. Apart from material resources, the state furthermore supplied funds to finance SOEs' operations. In fact, the state provided all SOEs with the input resources and distributed their output according to its plans. In this context, SOEs were rather "production units" or factories, as they were often called in Chinese, than real business enterprises with an orientation to increase returns and profits for their investors via active management. SOEs were not regarded as independent legal persons. Unsurprisingly, the term legal person never existed in the central-planning period. In nature, the governance practices in SOEs had not changed much in comparison with those in the planned system.

The Contracting Stage (1984–1992)

Dual-Track System

It was not until 1984, as the government issued *On Regulations of Further Expanding Autonomy of SOEs* and officially permitted a market track alongside with the planned track for industrial goods, that the SOE reform in China got a new push. Under the dual-track system, which was officially activated in early 1985 for all economic agents, SOEs were to sell industrial goods up to an appointed quota quantity to the state at a planned price, while any surplus products were allowed to be sold at the market and priced freely. Consequently, any kind of good was priced twofold with a planned price and an unregulated one. Chinese SOEs were now for the first time linked with the market. Due to decreasing market prices mainly caused by tight monetary policy in 1990, the price difference between the planned and the market track became insignificant. By the mid-1990s, most provinces had undertaken liberalization in prices and the planned-price track had almost ended for most industrial goods.

	Stage 1 (1978–1983)	Stage 2 (1984–1992)	Stage 3 (1993-)
	Planning + Incentives	Contracting	Corporatization
Goal	• Testing via Greater Autonomy	• Separation of Government from Management	• Modern Company System
		• Making SOEs Responsible for Their Own Gains and Losses in the Market	• State Sector Restructuring
State	• Owner & Manager	• Owner	• Shareholder
	• Planner & Supervisor	• Supervisor (Localized)	• Supervisor
	• Finance Provider	• Finance Provider (per Banks)	
SOEs	• Production Unit "Factory"	• Legal Person	• Transformed into Different Business Corporations
		• Some Decision Rights in Operation	• New Corporate Governing Bodies: Shareholders, Boards
		• Holding Enterprises/Groups	• New Corporate Positions: Chair, CEO
Executives	• Government Officials	• Selected Managers with Overall Responsibilities	• Relative Professional Managers
	• Fulfilling Production Plans		

Fig. 6.9 Three Governance stages of Chinese SOEs Since 1978
Source: Own figure

Contracting for SOEs

More importantly in this phase, the central government launched the *Contract Responsibility System* at the beginning of 1987, trying to separate the state from the management of SOEs and to encourage the latter to expand production and earn profits. Under this system, the director of a SOE signed a contract, which governed the relationship between the SOE and its factory director, with the local government for a period of time of at least three years,[35] so that he or she would be fully responsible for the SOE's operation and gained consequently more control rights over the enterprise's operation than before. The focus of such a contract rested mainly with the profit sharing between the government and the SOE: The SOE as an entity should contribute a fixed proportion or a minimum amount of profit to the government, while the total income of managers and employees were dependent on the operational performance – the rest of the profit after tax. The contract responsibility system had a political advantage because the government, managers, and workers could all derive a benefit, if the SOE performed well.[36] Hence, the incentive effect was high for all these parties. By 1989, almost all SOEs were subject to a responsibility contract. In 1992, this practice was promoted through the issue of *Regulations on Transforming the Management Mechanism of State-Owned*

---

[35] The proportion of profit retention was to be bargained yearly in the incentive model.

[36] However, in case the SOEs had not achieved a satisfying profit, they were still liable for paying the fixed amount to the state.

Industrial Enterprises that granted SOE managers more control rights in areas of foreign trade, investment, employment, wages, etc.

Roles of the State

At this contracting stage, the state began to loosen its control over SOEs and cut its roles in the SOEs' governance from owner, manager, planner, supervisor, and finance provider down to three: owner, supervisor, and finance provider. The "State-owned Industrial Enterprises Law of China" (SOEs law) prescribed that the local organization of the Chinese Communist Party should guarantee and supervise the implementation of the Party's and the state's guiding principles and policies, so that the SOEs' supervision by the state became actually localized. This was particularly important with regard to the state's new financial policies referring to SOEs.

The new financial policies, which intended to strengthen constraints for SOEs, stepwise introduced a tax system to replace the former way of profit retention. As mentioned, in the incentive stage SOEs had gained full freedom in using their retained profits. However, the proportion or sum of retained profits remained dependent on the quota and therefore arbitrary. Addressing this problem, the State Council approved in 1983 *On Methods of Promoting SOE Taxation instead of Profit Retention*, according to which large- and medium-sized SOEs should be taxed by 55% upon their incomes, while small-sized SOEs were subject to a progressive tax rate from 7% to 55%. In the light of differences in industries, the second step tax reform was carried out after the *Provisional Regulations of the People's Republic of China on Enterprises Income Tax* had been issued in late 1984. New tax items, such as tax on industrial products, sales tax, value added tax, city planning tax, real estate tax, and resource tax, were introduced. As a result, the state made an advance in governing SOEs, for it tried to replace an arbitrary administrative control (setting the retained profits) with clear law provisions (tax rates).

In addition, the way SOEs obtained financing changed along with the fiscal reform of banks. As early as in 1970, local governments were made responsible for material allocation and fixed investment. With the fiscal decentralization in 1980, provincial governments could not only share their budgetary income revenue, but had the authority to determine the structure of their expenditures including the financing of SOEs. In 1983, the state strengthened the financial constraints for SOEs by introducing bank loans instead of appropriations for SOEs' circulating capital. Now, alongside the contractual system in force, local governments gained great influence over credit decisions of the regional branches of the central bank and state specialized banks for SOEs and even had the authority to determine whether a loan should be paid back by the relevant SOEs.

Roles of SOEs

At this stage, the Chinese government set up big enterprise groups which should link SOEs vertically and horizontally. This policy aimed at promoting a more rational production structure, technological development, and intra-group cross-financing as well as creating large conglomerates. Accordingly, a new level in the governance structure between the state/government and a number of SOEs came into existence. As stated in a Party's document from 1984,[37] SOEs themselves were to be transformed into legal entities whose management should enjoy full management authority and full responsibilities for their own profits and losses. With the SOEs Law that was adopted in 1988, a legal person status was granted to SOEs by law.

The factory director acted now as the legal representative and exercised leadership in the operation of the enterprise. For the first time in Chinese SOE history, the factory director occupied the central position in the enterprise operation. According to the SOEs Law, the director should be selected through a "competitive process". Although no details were issued on how to fulfill this requirement, it provided incentives to select a higher qualified director for the enterprise. Besides, some measures were introduced to facilitate SOEs' management. For example, SOEs were allowed, through the employees' congress and other forms, to practice "democratic management", while employees might take part in the management and its supervision. The SOEs Law also required the establishment of a management committee or a similar consulting body to assist the director with decision-making on important issues.

The Corporatization Stage (since 1993)

Unsuccessful Contracting

Despite the major reform efforts made for the state sector since 1978, it still proved to be uncompetitive in contrast to the private sector that expanded impressively in the first 15 years of China's reform and opening-up policies. There was steady increase in SOE losses since the managements obtained more decision-making power (cf. Sachs and Woo 1997, p. 24). Even though no SOE had ever been closed down, the state sector was no longer the main strength of the national economy by the end of 1993. The share of the state sector in the industrial output descended from 78% in 1978 to 43% in 1993 (cf. Qian 1999a, p. 15). Even its share in total non-farm employment was down from 60% to about 30% in the same time period (cf. ibid., p. 15).

The contracting system did not help SOEs to expand and function well due to some deficiencies in its design. As far as profit retention is concerned, it was difficult to fix a reasonable minimum profit for the SOEs to pay to the state. The responsibility system was itself experimental, which means there was no ready-made standard for setting the minimum proportion or sum of profits. In addition, the contracting system said nothing about what to do when SOEs could not make a desired profit or suffered a loss. Nonetheless, the profit paid to the state was obligatory. With regard to the entire reform policies, the state leadership had not planned to establish a rule-based market through their first reform attempts. For this

---

[37] See the the Central Committee of the Chinese Communist Party's "Decision on Reform of the Economic Structure" (CPC 1984).

reason, the contracting system rather aimed at stimulating improving efforts from inside SOEs than to generate incentives and to enhance constraints through outside forces like more competitive environment and stricter legislation. Besides, neither the ownership nor the property rights issues were included in the contracting system. Logically, the state would undertake all the losses of its SOEs in the end to avoid SOEs' bankruptcy, which actually reduced the incentives for SOEs' efforts to make more profits. As a result, some incentives for the SOEs per se were either short-term or got reduced in view of the state's soft budget constraints. To solve these problems, SOE reform entered a new corporatization phase compatible with the establishment of a market economy by the government.

SOE Corporatization and Restructuring

In 1993, the Third Plenum of the Fourteenth Party Congress adopted the "Decision on Issues Concerning the Establishment of a Socialist Market Economic Structure". The Decision formulated clear goals in the areas of the reform strategy (coherent package and appropriate sequencing of reforms), a rule-based system (unified foreign exchange rate and tax rates and accounting rules for all enterprises regardless of ownership), market-supporting institutions (formal fiscal federalism, centralized monetary system, social safety net), and property rights and ownership (transforming SOEs), respectively (cf. Qian 1999b, pp. 23f.).

Unlike at the incentive and contracting stages, which centered on the extension of SOEs' autonomy and profit sharing, the *Decision* addressed SOE reforms in terms of property and ownership rights in several ways. First, it intended to transform SOEs into modern enterprises with "clear property rights, clarified rights and responsibilities, separation of enterprises from the government, and scientific management" (CPC 1993).[38] Second, the Decision implied the privatization of small SOEs:

> With regard to small SOEs, the management of some can be contracted out or leased; others can be shifted to the partnership system in the form of stock sharing or sold to collectives and individuals. (ibid.)

Third, the Decision supported the development of a financial market, advocating "[s]tandardizing issuances and listings of shares, and gradually enlarging the scale" (ibid.). Through this policy, the Chinese stock market was combined with SOE reforms.

In 1993, the "Company Law" was enacted to facilitate the new policies in SOE reform. In 1995, the new SOE reform guidelines were brought into action. After

---

[38] Shareholders of modern SOEs are entitled to enjoy their shareholders' rights in proportion to their shares and are obligated to transfer ownership of their investment to the corporation. Rights, obligations, and liabilities between and among the corporation, shareholders, employees, creditors, consumers, and other stakeholders should be delineated clearly. The government should separate itself from SOEs' operation. SOEs should avoid random decision-making, relaxed management, undisciplined job performances, and low-level managerial abilities and implement democratic decision-making processes, efficient execution, and strong supervision over decision-making.

local governments in Shandong, Guangdong, and Sichuan had conducted first experiments, small SOEs were privatized and employees laid off nationwide on a large
scale. The central government promoted the restructuring of the state sector with the
slogan "grasping the large and letting go the small".[39] "Small" SOEs had played a
very important role in China's planned economy, for the Chinese state sector was
made up dominantly by small- and medium-sized enterprises. In 1993, they still
accounted for 95% in number, 57% in employment and 43% in output of the state
industrial sector (cf. Cao et al. 1999, p. 109). By the end of 1996, some 70% of small
SOEs had been privatized in several pioneering provinces and about half were privatized in many other provinces. From 1996 to 1997, over 20 million SOE employees
were laid off throughout China. Until 2005, another 20 million SOE employees
were laid off. After reaching a peak of 112.6 million in 1995, the total state sector
employment shrank to 64.3 million in 2006 (cf. NBSC 1996, 2007a). Even though
no large SOE was privatized, the share of state industry was reduced by almost half
through releasing the small- and medium-sized SOEs (cf. Qian and Wu 2000, p. 39).

"Grasping the large" referred to keeping a number of backbone large and
medium-sized SOEs, particularly those in some strategic industries such as transportation, telecom, banking, oil, steel, etc. Based on the provisions in the Company
Law, "to be grasped" large and medium-sized traditional SOEs were "corporatized"
instead of following a privatization process, that is, converted into different western-
type corporate entities predominantly in the form of limited liability companies
and joint-stock companies,[40] while the state still maintained its control. The new
corporation forms of SOEs vary from their predecessors in their better-defined ownership structure, shareholder rights, and management accountability. With corporate
entities officially coming into being in People's Republic of China, the term "corporate governance" is since then relevant for the governance issues of Chinese firms.
Before, there had been no "corporate" governance, but governance issues or practices of SOEs. However, to the government's disappointment, SOEs' performance
continued to decline in the 1990s (cf. Qian 1999b, p. 30).

The Fourth Plenum of the Fifteenth Party Central Committee in 1999 adopted
more aggressive policies for the SOE reform. One of them was the "readjustment
of the layout of the state economy" (CPC 1999, section III) in the sense to narrow
the state sector. Specifically, the state decided to concentrate its control over four

---

[39] The slogan emerged in the central government's work report at the Ninth NPC. Yet the practices
had been ongoing for a period of time. At the last few Plenums of the Eighth, the concept had
already been implicitly expressed in the central government's work reports.

[40] These corporate entities include wholly state-owned corporations, closely held corporations,
and publicly held corporations. According to the Company Law of 1993, a wholly state-owned
corporation is a limited liability corporation invested and established solely by the state-authorized
investment institutions or government agencies. A closely held corporation is a small company
with few shareholders and of small capital size. A publicly held corporation, also called a joint
stock limited company, is a corporation whose total capital is divided into equal shares, and is
owned by shareholders who assume liability towards the company to the extent of their respective
shareholdings.

main types of industries – industries related to national security, natural monopolies, industries providing important public goods and services, pillar industries as well as backbone enterprises in high and new technology industries, while withdrawing from other areas. Committing the government to withdrawing from most industrial and services sectors was a significant and encouraging step forward in transforming the state sector in the economy. Obviously, these types were vaguely defined. That being the case, obstacles to privatization in areas other than the core industries could arise, say, due to local governments' interest there. Nonetheless, this deficiency might slow down but not prevent the privatization process of small SOEs, compared to its potential speed.

Another policy adopted at the Fourth Plenum of the Fifteenth Party Central Committee was the diversification of ownership structure for those enterprises still under state control. Except for a few enterprises solely funded by the state, all other enterprises should become joint stock companies with multiple owners involving private investors or foreign investors. This policy accelerated listings of SOEs both inland and abroad. China Telecom, China National Petroleum Corporation (CNPC), China Petrochemical Corporation (SINOPEC), and the Legend Group are some examples. Another new policy concerned the establishment of a corporate governance system. The term "corporate governance" appeared in a Party document for the very first time.

Roles of the State and SOEs

At the current corporatization stage, the state has changed its role from the only owner of SOEs to the shareholder possessing property rights over the state-owned part of a corporatized SOE's assets. The state continually acts as the supervisor of SOEs, but the way it finances them has changed a lot, and it has relegated the job to the capital markets. SOEs have changed into different types of companies and introduced, indispensably according to the Company Law, three corporate governing bodies: shareholders, the board of directors, and the board of supervisors.[41] Some new functions such as the chair of the board of directors and the chief manager in the sense of a Chief Executive Officer (CEO) have been introduced as well. The Chinese corporate governance model has been built up.

Today, registered SOEs accounted for about 5% of all industrial companies and about 15% of the total output value.[42] Large scale SOEs still constitute the backbone of the economy. The state sector continues to place a disproportionally large claim on economic resources, for instance, bank lending.

---

[41] In case of small firms with few shareholders, the boards are not indispensable, but a CEO is required.

[42] Calculated with data of NBSC (2007a).

Driving Forces in China's Corporate Governance Evolution: Process of Change

While the most advanced economies – Western Europe, the United States, and Japan – have converged in economies, business practices, and living standards over the last few decades, their corporate ownership and governance remained different, and different degrees of ownership concentration and labor influence have persisted. In identifying the rationale behind the different corporate ownership and governance patterns, Bebchuk and Roe developed in 1999 a theory of the path dependence of corporate structure. They argued that

> a country's pattern of ownership structures at any point in time depends partly on the patterns it had earlier. Consequently, when countries had different ownership structures at earlier points in time – because of their different circumstances at the time, or even because of historical accidents – these differences might persist at later points in time even if their economies have otherwise become quite similar. (Bebchuck and Roe 1999, p. 127)

Although Bebchuck and Roe have the most developed countries in their sights, in our opinion, the consistency of the state's dominance in Chinese SOEs' ownership structure demonstrates a clear path-dependent process as well. That is, how the Chinese SOEs were owned at the starting point affected much the way they would be owned later. Every important change which happened in Chinese SOEs' corporate governance was carried out on the basis of the existing ownership structure and did not mean to replace it with a different model, for example, a dispersed or a bank-based ownership.

It is worth noting that Bebchuck and Roe (1999) argued in their path-dependence theory that a structure- and a rule-driven path dependence exists. In this article, however, we mainly take the structure-driven path, i.e., how the governance structure of SOEs has evolved, into account, as official rules (laws, regulations) on SOE reforms have typically been brought into effect to support those structural changes. For example, the Company Law was enacted after the central government decided to transform traditional SOEs into modern enterprises. Therefore, the rule-driven path dependence in SOE reforms is de facto in keeping with the structure-driven one.

One may argue that the SOE ownership is self-evident, for the term of state-ownership already literally describes the ownership structure. This view is correct as far as the owner or blockholder of SOEs is concerned. However, the term of state ownership alone conceals any significant information on the structural changes in Chinese SOEs' governance. Neither does it reflect what differences occurred in SOEs' ownership structure and control along the reform path, as described in the section "Governance Practices in Chinese SOEs: Content of Change", nor does it imply the driving forces behind such changes. In the following, we highlight several historical and environmental factors during China's transition to a market economy, which have had significant impacts on the evolvement of the SOE reforms.

Two Radical Campaigns

Two radical campaigns that had hit China's economy very hard took place in the first three decades of the People's Republic of China. The first one happened shortly after China's planned economy had been established by 1957. The initial planned system followed the former Soviet model that featured concentration of authority in the central government. Yet Mao Zedong was doubtful of the validity of the Soviet style (cf. Qian 1999a, p. 24). Under his leadership, China began to restructure the Soviet planning model only one year after its establishment. In 1958, the Great Leap Forward (GLF), as the radical reform was called, was initiated to realize an accelerated and infeasible industrialization.[43] However, the unrealistic economic expansion and continuously unfavorable weather conditions led to a disastrous famine, causing millions of deaths[44] in rural areas during 1959–1961. At the same time, China's light industry output and national income declined annually by 2% and 3.1%, respectively (cf. Qian 1999a, p. 25) due to overemphasis of heavy industry, especially steel output (cf. Luo 2004, pp. 25f.).

The second big-bang campaign began as Mao initiated the Cultural Revolution in 1966, aiming at "a further revolution under proletarian dictatorship".[45] Although the national economy still grew moderately during the 10 years (1966–1976) of this mass movement, the growth was slower than in the 14 years before and the six years after it (cf. Chen 2008), implying that the radical movement suppressed the potential of China's economy. Big problems during the Cultural Revolution included serious imbalance of the proportions among the sectors of the national economy and of the proportions between reserves and expenses, greatly lowered economic performance, and appearance of government deficit. Also the central government admitted later that the national economy suffered huge losses during these 10 years (cf. CPC 1981).

The Great Leap Forward and the Cultural Revolution were accompanied by two waves of administrative decentralizations, which have taken great influences on China's transition path. Both of the two decentralization waves took place under Mao's leadership. For Mao, centralization would offer few incentives for people's initiatives,[46] and he preferred decentralization of government authority to local levels (cf. Qian 1999a, p. 24). Mao's preference was not purely personal, but backed by the communists' long-time experience in time of war (cf. CPC 1981). In those days, the revolutionary bases of the communists had been run in separate rural areas,

---

[43] The plan of this mass movement was that the industrial output of China should surpass that of Great Britain and the United States within 15 years. See Luo (2004, pp. 25f.).

[44] Surveys of Chinese scholars assess the number to be in the range of 17 and 40 millions. See Li (2006).

[45] So was it explained in the "Resolution on Certain Questions in the History of Our Party Since the Founding of the People's Republic of China" (CPC 1981).

[46] As summarized in "Resolution on Certain Issues in the History of Our Party Since the Founding of the People's Republic of China" (CPC 1981), one of Mao's core thoughts was following the mass line (zou qun zhong lu xian).

and mobilization of local incentives for production in each base had been the main concerns of communists (cf. ibid.).

The first wave of decentralization occurred alongside the Great Leap Forward. Two institutional changes were made with regard to restructuring the planning system. On the one hand, the central government deputed the control over most SOEs as well as the planning authority to local governments (cf. Qian 1999a, p. 25). While there had been 9,300 SOEs subordinated to the central government in 1957, there were only 1,200 in 1958 (cf. ibid., p. 24). The local government gained the authority to make most decisions on regional fixed investments, material allocation, and expenditures. On the other hand, China established numerous People's Communes, which served as local authorities and were responsible for agricultural production, commerce, bank affairs, education, and public health in the rural areas. Within a few months after the movement initiation, 99% of the peasants were organized in about 24,000 People's Communes, with an average size of 5,000 households (cf. ibid., p. 25). With the communes established, a large number of so-called commune and brigade enterprises were founded to expand non-agricultural activities.

The disaster caused by the Great Leap Forward forced the central government to correct its 1958 policy. In the urban areas, recentralization of the planning system began. From 1961 on, all large and medium-sized industrial enterprises were again subordinated to the central government (cf. ibid., p. 26). Between 1959 and 1965, SOEs under the control of the central government increased from 2,400 to 10,533 (cf. ibid., p. 26). In rural areas, the central government carried out a more liberal policy: communes were sustained, but became a less powerful institution; production teams consisting of 40–50 households became the basic production units; peasants were allowed to cultivate small private plots, run sideline productions, and open rural free markets (cf. ibid., p. 25).

During the Cultural Revolution, a second wave of administrative decentralization began in China due to a goal of high growth in the Fourth Five Year Plan (1971–1975)[47] and the preparation for war.[48] From 1970 on, the economic planning was mainly conducted on regional levels. The 1970 wave of decentralization was similar to the 1958 one, but went much further. The control over most large SOEs as well as some planning authority in material allocation and fixed investment was again delegated to the local governments. After the decentralization, the central government supervised barely 142 SOEs, down from 10,533 in 1965. The types of material allocated through the central government were reduced from 579 in 1966 to 217 in 1971. The share of within-budget fixed investment by local governments rose from 14%

---

[47] For example, steel production was required to double within five years (cf. Qian 1999a, p. 27). To achieve the goal of high growth, the central government believed that local initiative must be mobilized through decentralization.

[48] Mao assessed that a Soviet invasion and the beginning of World War III was nearing. In consequence, the government proposed dividing the country into 10 cooperative regions, each of which should be a relatively complete and self sufficient industrial system to deal with the war (cf. Qian 1999a, p. 27).

in 1969 to 27% in 1971 (cf. ibid., p. 27). For a second time, however, the administrative decentralization caused disarray and some recentralization measures were taken by the central government in 1973 under the name of consolidation (cf. Qian 1999b, pp. 25f.). Yet in comparison with 1958, the extent of 1970 decentralization was greater, whereas the recentralization afterwards was much weaker (cf. Qian 1999a, p. 26).

Incremental Reforms in the Non-State Sector

After the Cultural Revolution came to an end, the reformers, who could be divided into moderate and radical groups (cf. Guo 2004, p. 396), took control of the central government. Moderate and radical reformers all agreed on the necessity of economic reforms,[49] but disagreed on the content, scope, and pace or extent of reforms (cf. ibid., p. 396). Moderate reformers insisted on maintaining basic socialist principles (such as planned economy, public ownership, and distribution according to labor). They were cautious and skeptical about dramatic departures from the planned economy and looked on the market as a supplementary mechanism for the allocation of resources and determination of prices to help establish a planned commodity economy (cf. ibid., p. 396). They favored a slow, gradual, and experimental approach to reforms, through which imbalances generated by reforms could be repaired during readjustment periods (cf. ibid., p. 396f.).

In contrast, radical reformers favored a much less restrictive definition of socialist principles that should exclude the planned economy and remold the principle of public ownership more flexibly, so as to promote a diversified ownership structure while maintaining the dominant position of public ownership (cf. Harding 1987, pp. 78–83). They wished to launch a market economy and favored a rapid and comprehensive structural reform to quickly remove the inefficiencies and rigidities of the traditional planned economy (cf. Guo 2004, p. 396).

After three decades of economic transition, most of those reform ideas from radical reformers have been realized in today's China. Interestingly, the path of China's transition has been one that was suggested by moderate reformers. In late 1970s, the central government under Deng Xiaoping at last chose to go down a gradual reform path and to change the national economy slowly in stages. Under the dual-track system, the market track facilitated several reforms in form of regional experimentations, including agricultural contracting, establishment of non-state enterprises, and special economic zones (SEZs). Without touching the existing ownership structure under tight governmental control, these reforms were incremental to the planning system.

---

[49] The "Communiqué of the Third Plenary Session of the 11th CPC Central Committee" (CPC 1978) stated, "The Plenum decided that (...) from 1979 on, the work of the CPC should focus on the socialist modernizations."

Agricultural Household Contract Responsibility System

Before the dual-track system covered SOEs in 1984 (see the section "Dual-Track System" above), it had started in rural areas, with rapid and comprehensive liberalization of the agricultural sector. In 1978, as the rest of the Chinese rural areas were still operating under the collective farming system, several households in the Fengyang County of the Anhui Province began to contract with the local government for delivering a fixed quota of grain in exchange for farming on a household basis. This practice was soon imitated by other counties in the province and promoted by the provincial government. In 1980, the experimentation in Anhui was promoted by the central government through the official introduction of the Agricultural Household Contracting Responsible System (cf. CPC 1980) to replace the commune-bridge system of collective farming.

Under the Agricultural Household Contracting Responsible System, individual peasant households were allowed to lease the former commune land by signing a contract. With the contract signed, the peasant households would take the full responsibility for the piece of land allocated for their use.[50] Although these households remained obliged to fulfill the grain quota as set by the state, they obtained residual claims and control rights over the production on their land, say, cultivating more valuable crops and selling the surplus goods on the free market. By 1984, almost all peasant households across China had adopted the contracting method.

This contracting reform in the rural areas turned out to be a huge success. During the period of 1978–1994, growth in agriculture provided the major impetus to the Chinese economy (cf. Sachs and Woo 1997, p. 10). Shortly after the launch of the reform, the national grain production grew by 8.7% in 1982 and by 9.2% in 1983 (cf. NBSC 1982, 1983). From 1978 to 1984, the per capita real income in the rural areas increased by more than 50% (cf. Qian 1999a, p. 9). In the same period, the per capita consumption doubled in real terms (cf. Sachs and Woo 1997, p. 30).

However, this growth turned out to be rather temporary. From 1985 onward, the growth in the rural areas stagnated due to (1) farmers' uncertainty about future land use rights, (2) state procurement prices not being raised in line with the increases in input prices, and (3) large reductions in state investment in agricultural infrastructure (cf. ibid., pp. 31f.).

Rural Enterprises

Under the dual-track system in the 1980s, a few important relaxation policies in favor of free markets and the non-state sector were adopted. For example, all the previous black markets were now legal. Regulations on the registration and supervision of non-state enterprises were less strict than before. Private enterprises were

---

[50] In China, land in rural areas is collectively owned, while land in urban areas is state-owned. Before the reform era, pieces of land were allotted by administrative authorities for agricultural and industrial use. Since the 1980s, local governments in urban areas transfer rights of land's use for a determined period against compensation.

allowed to employ more than eight people, which was illegal before 1984. The governments in rural areas encouraged collectives and peasants to invest in or to pool their funds to jointly set up various kinds of enterprises. Fiscal decentralization in this period, which primarily aimed at the state sector, also provided incentives for local governments to develop non-state enterprises, since the local governments did not have to share taxes generated through the non-state sector within the planning system (cf. Qian 1999a, p. 11). These measures were greatly conductive to the emergence and growth of the rural enterprises. Between 1983 and 1988, total rural enterprise output increased by more than fivefold (cf. Qian 1999a, p. 12).

In non-agricultural areas, most of the impetus has been coming from so-called township and village enterprises (TVEs). From 1983 to 1984, the former People's Communes were changed into townships, and the erstwhile commune and brigade enterprises were renamed as TVEs. They were mostly owned directly by township and village governments and collectively by members of a village, and in some cases by private persons. Local governments enthusiastically supported TVEs, because (1) previous administrative restrictions against rural enterprise entry and expansion were removed from almost all industries due to liberalization policies on rural industrialization, and (2) they themselves relied heavily on the development of rural industry as the way to generate their revenue (cf. Qian 1999a, p. 12). Since their emergence, TVEs have been expanding at a remarkable rate and dominating in the non-agricultural growth. Their share in total employment in China increased from 7% in 1978, to 11% in 1984, and further to 21% in 1995 (cf. Sachs and Woo 1997, p. 33). In 1987, TVEs were allowed to take part in foreign trade. Since then, TVE exports have experienced a dramatic growth, with a share of overall exports rising from 9.2% in 1986 to more than 40% in 1996 (cf. ibid., p. 33).

The governance features of TVEs are quite different from those of SOEs. For example, TVEs' ownership and property rights are clearly defined as held by the local governments or individuals (cf. Lin 2001, p. 11). Another feature of TVEs is that they face hard budget constraints. In the late 1980s and early 1990s, the total size of the SOE industrial output was about twice that of TVEs, while loans to SOEs and TVEs accounted for about 86% and 8%, respectively (cf. Qian 1999b, p. 16). In case of a deficit, the local government cannot finance it without the approval of the central government. Since local governments are in deed involved in TVEs as owners, they logically have incentives to ensure TVEs' efficiency and profitability by improving management (cf. Lin 2001, p. 11).

Opening-Up

The dual-track approach was also adopted to gradually open up China to the outside world and to attract foreign investment. In 1980, the central government chose four cities in the coastal areas in South China (Shenzhen, Zhuhai, Shantou, and Xiamen) to be the first four special economic zones (SEZs). The SEZs were export-oriented and had a special institutional environment. The local governments were granted the authority over their own economic development. They were allowed to approve foreign investment projects up to 30 million USD and to retain 70% of the increased foreign exchanges from exports. Foreign enterprises were subject to lower taxes than elsewhere in China. The SEZs were also allowed to become market economies dominated by private ownership, while the rest of China was still under strict central planning and public ownership.

In 1984, the central government declared another fourteen coastal cities[51] as "coastal open cities", which began to enjoy authority similar to that of the first SEZs. Each of these cities gained broader authorities in approving foreign investment projects and setting up development zones, where they could implement more liberal tax and foreign exchange policies for attracting foreign capital and technology. In 1988, Hainan became a separate province and was added as the largest SEZ. In 1992, five additional cities[52] along the Yangtze River, thirteen border cities and towns,[53] and eleven provincial capitals[54] were granted special privileges as coastal cities.

As shown by statistical data (cf. NBSC 1991, 1992, 1993), China's extensive opening-up policies in early 1990s immediately boosted foreign investment and exports: Foreign direct investment (FDI) increased by 160% to 11.1 billion USD in 1992, and further by 130% to 25.8 billion USD in 1993. Registered enterprises with foreign investment expanded from 37 thousand in 1991 to 84 thousand in 1992, and further to 167.5 thousand in 1993. The value of exports in 1992 was 85.0 billion USD, up 18.2%, and that in 1993 was 91.8 billion USD, up 8%. In contrast, China's exports in 1980, as the first SEZs were established, merely reached 27.2 billion RMB (1 USD equalized 1.5 RMB in 1980 and 8.7 RMB in 1993). More notably, enterprises with foreign investment raised their share in exports from 16.8% in 1991 to 20.4% in 1992 and further to 27.5% in 1993.

Overall Performance of the Non-State Sector

Under the dual-track system, the total non-state sector, including household agriculture, rural industries, private enterprises, urban collective, and joint ventures, had been outperforming the state sector and changed the economy structure in China. Accordingly, the share of SOE production fell from 78% in 1978 to 69% in 1984, and further to 43% in 1993; while SOEs' share in commerce was down from 55% in 1978 to 40% by 1993 (cf. Sachs and Woo 1997, p. 10; Qian and Wu 2000, p. 5). As no SOE had been privatized by 1993, the changes of the relative weight of the state sector were solely caused by the rapid growth of the non-state sector.

Learning Process in SOE Reforms

Figure 6.10 demonstrates the connections between the SOE reforms and the historical and environmental factors, i.e., the knowledge and experiences that the Chinese

---

[51] Tianjin, Shanghai, Dalian, Qinhuangdao, Yantai, Qingdao, Lianyungang, Nantong, Ningbo, Wenzhou, Fuzhou, Guangzhou, Zhanjiang, and Beihai.

[52] Wuhu, Jiujiang, Yueyang, Wuhan, and Chongqing.

[53] Heihe, Suifenhe, Huichun, Manzhouli, Pingxiang, Dongxing, Hekou, Wanding, Ruili, Yining, Tacheng, Bole, and Erlianhaote.

[54] Taiyuan, Hefei, Nanchang, Zhengzhou, Changsha, Chengdu, Guiyang, Xi'an, Lanzhou, Xining, and Yinchuan.

government gained before and during the transition has mainly backed its choice of the reform path for SOEs. The boxes marked with PRC (for the People's Republic of China) over the time axis symbolize the path dependence of China's SOE reforms at different stages since 1949 (see the section "Governance Practices in Chinese SOEs: Content of Change"). Being dominated by the state ownership, changes on this path are accompanied and affected by factors described in the sections "The Radical Campaigns" and "Incremental Reforms in the Non-State Sector" above, shown in the boxes under the time axis. In the following, we discuss how these factors affected the starting point of SOEs' ownership structure and its later changes.

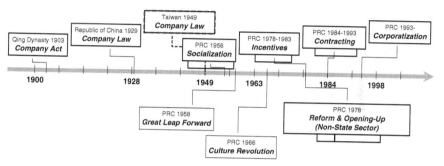

Fig. 6.10 Path dependence in China's SOE reforms
Source: Own figure

Lessons from the Mistakes

As we have described, the central government firstly chose not to touch the existing planned system in urban districts at the beginning of the transition. This choice can be attributed to the central government's concerns about the potential losses due to radical reforms. At that moment, it must have been be difficult for the central government to answer the question whether replacing the planned system and public ownership structure with a market economy and a diversified ownership structure, as radical reformers put it forward, would largely improve China's economy. After all, there had been no experiences about how a market economy would function in China. Neither were there transition examples for China to learn from at that time.

Interestingly, if we look further back along the time axis in Fig. 6.10, we will find another path dependence of ownership structure in China's history since 1900. Before the foundation of the People's Republic of China, private ownership of enterprises had existed in the Qing Dynasty and been protected by the Dynasty's "Company Act" promulgated in 1903. The Republic of China, followed by the authorities in Taiwan, continued this path. In mainland China, however, this path was discontinued by the socialization process beginning in 1956. Such a break-off was not directly responsible for the later disasters during the Great Leap Forward and the Cultural Revolution, but it had excluded all existing private ownership and facilitated a total deviation from the former economy model to a state ownership model. The risks of such a total deviation were evidenced by the economy development during the Great Leap Forward and the Cultural Revolution, implying that the government should be cautious with radical economic reforms. Under concerns about failures and uncertainty of success, it was rational and low-risk for the central government to start with incremental reforms.

Our analysis echoes Bebchuck and Roe's (1999) path dependence theory, in which the two authors define efficiency as one of the major reasons why prior ownership structures in an economy might affect subsequent structures. In a simplified sense, efficiency concerns the profits and costs of rebuilding the existing ownership structures or enacting a set of legal rules that support different ownership structures. Although a different type of ownership structure could appear more efficient from today's perspective, a total reconstruction of the current system would be, in view of its potential profits, too costly to be realized. In their paper, Bebchuck and Roe give a numerical example of how companies will compare the potential profits and costs and decide not to restructure the existing ownership model into a different one. In contrast, at the beginning of China's reform era, no such calculation was feasible. Thus, lessons learned in the previous radical campaigns might have helped the central government to make its choice of the reform path.

Pre-Reform Institutional Bases

In both of the two waves of decentralization and the recentralization measures afterwards, the changes mainly adjusted the relationship between the central and local governments and not the relationship between the state and SOEs. On the one hand, the de- and recentralizing policies dealt with the issue which governmental level should directly take the leadership in SOE operations. In other words, it was about how to allocate the SOE property rights within the administrative structure of the Chinese government. On the other hand, SOEs had not become autonomous economic entities, but remained subject to production instructions from either the central or the local governments. Consequently, the governmental control over SOEs was tight throughout the first three decades of the People's Republic of China (cf. Qian 1999a, p. 28).

Nonetheless, the two waves of decentralization had exerted a big influence on the structure of China's planning system, making it not as centrally organized as in the Soviet model. Unlike the Soviet model, the Chinese planning system performed not through the central government granting power to subordinate local agencies to carry out its plans, but to a great extent directly on regional levels. Hence, a complete administrative centralization hardly ever existed in the Chinese planning system, except for the very beginning. Local governments and their agencies practically exerted much control, which made it easier to launch reforms on local bases, especially where the bureaucratic interests were weak (cf. ibid., p. 5).

In Bebchuck and Roe's (1999) path dependence theory, another source of power for the persistence of old ownership are rent-seeking activities, practiced by the interest groups who have been enjoying the rents provided by their positions in the actual ownership structure. If a new ownership system pattern, however efficient it is supposed to be for a single firm or the whole economy, noticeably reduces their current rents, those interest groups would have incentives to impede the efforts to introduce such a pattern as well as the supporting legal rules for it.

In a rent-seeking context, the structural character of China's planning system could explain why real reforms did not initially take place in SOEs in urban areas, but in rural areas. Provided that the central government had been thinking about a radical SOE reform (for example, a diversification of the ownership) in the 1970s, there could have been much resistance against it from those agencies and persons who had been controlling SOEs for a long time, because their control would be reduced, and the profits of the reform were not certain. Compared to that in urban areas, governmental control in the rural areas was, on the one hand, less tight after the first wave of decentralization. On the other hand, bureaucratic interests in the agricultural sector were weak, and the vested interests of local officials at the commune and the brigade levels were not well organized (cf. Qian 1999a, p. 6). Wan Li, the former party secretary in the Anhui province, who led the first rural reform in the late 1970s, once confirmed the situation:

> Why did reform make its first breakthrough in the rural area? This is by no means an accident and has historical reasons. This is because peasants suffered the most under the old rigid system and thus had the strongest desire for reform. At the same time, rural areas were the weak sector in the old system, and became the breakthrough point of reform. (ibid., p. 5)

Learning from the Non-State Sector

As we have discussed in the sections "Lessons from the Mistakes" and "Pre-Reform Institutional Bases" above, pre-reform mistakes and existing institutions bases can explain why China's reforms started in areas outside of the planning system. After China's transition began, experimentation with relaxation over the non-state sector has been providing abundant and exemplary experiences with other forms of ownership and governance structure for SOEs to learn from. Such a method has been useful for China's transition, because, as argued by Qian (1999b, p. 8), reform was a highly uncertain event and the government's knowledge about it had been very limited. Considering the high uncertainty, experimentation is a way to minimize costs through structured learning.

Experiences gained with those incremental reforms in the non-state sector have practically backed the SOE reforms. Seeing the impressive agricultural growth in the early 1980s, decision-makers in the central government firstly borrowed the idea of contracting from the agricultural reform to launch a similar system for the state sector. However, the contracting approach did not function well for the state sector, suggesting that the government should not only provide incentives, but also reform the entire state sector.

The rise of the non-state enterprises had helped to establish and to strengthen market forces in China. In the early 1990s, the planned track was largely phased out, and prices were mostly determined by the market rather than the state. SOEs were facing direct competition in a number of industries. This environmental change facilitated not only the launch of a market economy in China, but the corporatization

and the restructuring of the state sector as well. On the one hand, it was more efficient for the state to draw back from where SOEs had been uncompetitive and to
focus on a few industries where the state has been enjoying a monopoly status. On
the other hand, rent-seeking activities by interest groups became much less in those
uncompetitive SOEs. As a result, reforms were much easier due to less resistance.
More importantly, the experiences gained in the non-agricultural sector outside of
the state-sector could further be utilized by SOEs in their reforms. Among the non-
state enterprises, especially the huge success of TVEs impressed the leadership in
Beijing. Deng Xiaoping said on 12 June 1987,

> In the rural reform our greatest success – and it is one we had by no means anticipated – has
> been the emergence of a large number of enterprises run by villages and townships (...).
> Their annual output value has been increasing by more than 20 percent a year for the last
> several years. This increase in TVEs, particularly industrial enterprises, has provided jobs
> for 50 percent of the surplus labor in the countryside. Instead of flocking into the cities,
> the peasants have been building villages and townships of a new type (...). Our success
> in rural reform increased our confidence, and, applying the experience we had gained in
> the countryside, we began a reform of the entire economic structure, focused on the cities.
> (Deng Xiaoping 1987/1994, p. 236)

Deng Xiaoping's statements showed that the central government had been thinking
about transplanting the experiences in the non-state sector to SOEs. In fact, the
SOE reforms at the corporatization stage since 1993 have absorbed a few important
elements of TVE's governance. Both ownership/property rights and hard budget
constraints have been taken in by the SOE corporatization policies to enhance SOEs'
efficiency.

With respect to China's opening-up practices, we believe that they have not only
exceedingly contributed to the growth of FDI and exports, but also to the changes
of SOE governance. For one thing, the boost of foreign enterprises and joint ventures are themselves vivid examples of how modern enterprises look and how to
manage them efficiently. For another, China's increasing exchanges with developed
countries have helped the Chinese to master know-how in management as well as
modern firm theories. Slogans like "separation of enterprises from the government"
and "scientific management" demonstrated that the SOE corporatization process has
been learning from the opened environment.

Summary

In the early 1990s, China's stock market was established to broaden the external
financing channels for SOEs. Ever since, it has been booming in respect of listings, market capitalization, and investors. Lately, the long lasting bear market from
2000 to 2005 and a few scandals of Chinese listed firms drew the public's and the
government's attention to corporate governance issues.

The corporate governance model at the Chinese stock market has weak external
mechanisms. The product market and the capital markets are still underdeveloped
and therefore prove insufficient market forces to improve listed firms' performance.

The shareholder protection in China is strong on paper, but weak in practice, as far as law enforcement is concerned. The internal governance of Chinese-listed firms has a two-tier board structure: the board of directors is responsible for the management, while the board of supervisors conducts the monitoring. Considering the parallel structure of the internal governance, it is doubtful whether the supervisors can efficiently monitor the directors. In common with the entire financial system, the ownership structure of the Chinese stock market is dominated by the state which owns a big stake in the listed firms through its central and local asset management agencies or holding SOEs/SOE Groups.

Corporate governance practices at the Chinese stock market evolved with the SOE reforms, which have undergone three stages since 1978: the incentive stage (1978–1983), the contracting stage (1984–1992), and the corporatization stage (since 1993). We consider this evolvement as a path-dependent process which is characterized by the state's dominance. The main changes happened in governance practices of Chinese SOEs have not changed the state's dominance in the ownership structure. At the very beginning of China's reform era, this dominance equalized the state's full control over all SOE assets and operations through various levels of its agencies though. At the incentive and contracting stages of SOE reforms, the state's dominance or full control remained unchanged in a way that the central government made efforts to enhance management incentives instead of clarifying SOEs' ownership structure. It was not until the corporatization stage that the central government began to deal with the ownership issues. At this current stage, the state's dominance in SOEs lessened, since (1) countless small SOEs were privatized during the restructuring of the state sector, and (2) non-state shareholders have been introduced into the ownership structure of SOEs after their corporatization. New governance bodies such as the board of directors and the board of supervisors were introduced. Nonetheless, the state, owing to its blockholding of shares, still dominates in the operation of those corporatized, big-sized SOEs, which further features the Chinese stock market.

The state's dominance in the SOE governance was determined at the beginning of the reform era, as the Chinese government chose to start with incremental reforms in the non-state sector instead of restructuring the state sector. Two radical campaigns, the Great Leap Forward and the Cultural Revolution, had significantly affected this choice. On the one hand, the disasters caused by the two movements taught the Chinese government a bitter lesson that they must be cautious with radical reforms. On the other hand, two waves of decentralization during the two campaigns facilitated local reforms on experimental basis rather than radical reforms of the entire planned economy. Further SOE reforms at contracting and corporatization stages, which led to changes in SOE governance, were largely backed by a learning process during the transition. Experiences gained in successful reforms of the non-state sector, including agriculture, rural industries, and foreign investment, were utilized in the SOE reforms by the government.

The authors believe that the state will still keep its dominant role in the governance of the large SOEs for a long while, but will adopt more and more best practices into its corporate governance model.

References

21 Century Business Herald (21CBH). 2009. Delegates on the two conferences criticized regional protectionism (Chinese), 21CBH 2009, http://www.21cbh.com/HTML/2009-3-12/HTML_X156J121PPJ0.html

Allen, F., J. Qian, and M. Qian. 2005. Law, finance, and economic growth in China. *Journal of Financial Economics* 77: 57–116.

Allen, F., J. Qian, M. Qian, and M. Zhao. 2009. A review of China's financial system and initiatives for the future. In *China's Emerging Financial Markets: Challenges and Opportunities*, ed. J.R. Barth, and J.A.Tatom, G. Yago', 3–72. New York, NY: Springer. (= The Milken Institute Series on Financial Innovation and Economic Growth, Vol. 8).

Aoki, M., and H.-K. Kim. 1995. *Corporate governance in transition economies*. Washington, DC: World Bank.

Bebchuck, L.A., and M.J. Roe. 1999. A theory of path dependence in corporate ownership and governance. *Stanford Law Review* 52: 127–170.

Becht, M., P. Bolton, and A.A. Röell. 2002. Corporate governance and control. Finance Working Paper No. 02/2002, European Corporate Governance Institute, available at SSRN: http://papers.ssrn.com/sol3/papers.cfm?abstract_id=343461

Berger, A.N., I. Hasan, and M. Zhou. 2009. Bank ownership and efficiency in China: What will happen in the world's largest nation?. *Journal of Banking and Finance* 33: 113–130.

Cao, Y., Y. Qian, and B.R. Weingast. 1999. From federalism, Chinese style to privatization, Chinese Style. *Economics of Transition* 7: 103–131.

CFFEX (China Financial Future Exchange). 2008. Trading rules of china financial futures exchange (Chinese), CFFEX, http://www.csrc.gov.cn/pub/newsite/flb/fgwj/zyzlgz/200803/t20080314_61809.htm

Chen, D. 2008. Review of the national economy during the cultural revolution (Chinese). *Contemporary China History Studies* 15: 63–72.

Chen, G., M. Firth, D.N. Gao, and O.M. Rui. 2005. Is China's securities regulatory agency a toothless tiger? Evidence from enforcement actions. *Journal of Accounting and Public Policy* 24: 451–488.

Claessens, S., S. Djankov, and L.H.P. Lang. 2000. The separation of ownership and control in East Asian corporations. *Journal of Financial Economics* 58: 81–112.

CPC (Chinese Communist Party). 2008. Communiqué of the Third Plenary Session of the 11th CPC Central Committee, adopted on 22 December 1978, http://www.bjreview.com.cn/special/third_plenum_17thcpc/txt/2008-10/10/content_156226.htm

CPC. 2008. Some provisions on enlarging industrial SOEs' autonomy (Chinese), adopted by the State Council on 12 July 1979, http://law.lawtime.cn/d552312557406.html

CPC. 1981. Resolution on certain questions in the history of our party since the founding of the people's republic of china, adopted by the Sixth Plenary Session of the 11th CPC Central Committee on 27 June 1981, in: CPC: *Resolution on CPC History (1949–1981)*, 1–86. Beijing: Foreign Languages Press.

CPC. 1984. Decision on reform of the economic structure, adopted by the Third Plenary Session of the 12th CPC Central Committee on 20 October 1984, *China Daily*, 22 October 1984.

CPC. 1993. Decision on some issues concerning the establishment of a socialist market economic structure (Chinese), adopted by the Third Plenary Session of the 14th CPC Central Committee on 14 November 1993, http://www.china.com.cn/chinese/archive/131747.htm.

CPC. 1999. Decision of the central committee of CPC on major issues concerning the reform and development of state-owned enterprises, adopted by the Fourth Plenary Session of the 15th CPC Central Committee on 22 September 1999, http://english.mofcom.gov.cn/aarticle/lawsdata/chineselaw/200211/20021100053897.html.

CSDCC (China Securities Depository and Clearing Corporation). 2008. China securities registration and settlement: Statistical yearbook 2008, CSDCC 2008, http://www.chinaclear.cn/main/03/0305/1245741212038.pdf

CSDCC. 2009. China securities registration and settlement: Statistical yearbook 2009, CSDCC 2009, http://www.chinaclear.cn/main/03/0305/1277889134195.pdf.

CSRC (China Securities Regulatory Commission). 1996. Notice of several regulations on share issuance, CSRC, English version available at http://www.lawinfochina.com/law/display.asp?id=3147

CSRC. 2001. Announcement of reprimanding Sanjiu Pharma and concerned individuals (Chinese), http://www.csrc.gov.cn/pub/zjhpublic/G00306212/200804/t20080418_14340.htm

CSRC. 2002. Notice regarding transfer to foreign investors of state-owned shares and legal person shares of listed companies, CSRC, English translation available at: http://www.paulweiss.com/files/Publication/2ee7962c-7e85-430a-8e79-1f33dca92091/Presentation/PublicationAttachment/ac31168e-8016-4cbc-82bf-931ddbe65b11/China.pdf.

CSRC. 2006. *China securities and futures statistical yearbook 2006*. Shanghai: Xuelin Publishing House.

CSRC. 2008. *China capital markets development report*. Beijing: China Financial Publishing House.

Deng Xiaoping. 1987/1994. We shall speed up reform. In *Selected Works of Deng Xiaoping, Volume III (1982–1992)*, ed. Deng Xiaoping. Beijing: Foreign Languages Press.

Deng Xiaoping. 1989/1994. The overriding need is for stability. In *Selected Works of Deng Xiaoping, Volume III (1982–1992)*, ed. Deng Xiaoping. Beijing: Foreign Languages Press.

Deng Xiaoping. 1992/1994. Excerpts from talks given in Wuchang, Shenzhen, Zhuhai and Shanghai. In *Selected Works of Deng Xiaoping, Volume III (1982–1992)*, ed. Deng Xiaoping. Beijing (Foreign Languages Press).

Enriques, L., and P.F. Volpin. 2007. Corporate governance reforms in Continental Europe. *Journal of Economic Perspectives* 21: 117–140.

Gong Ren Ri Bao – Worker Daily (GRRB). 2008. 30 years reforms and opening-up: Population in absolute poverty down from 250 to 14.79 million (Chinese), http://www.cpad.gov.cn

Guo, H. 2007. Xinguangxia in 2001 (Chinese), http://www.eeo.com.cn

Guo, S. 2004. Economic transition in China and Vietnam: A comparative perspective. *Asian Profile* 32: 393–411.

Harding, H. 1987. *China's second revolution: reform after Mao*. Washington, DC: Brookings Institution Press.

Howson, N.C. 2007. China and WTO liberalization of the securities industry: Le Choc des mondes or L'Empire immobile? *Asia Policy* 3: 151–185.

Hu, Y. 2009. No timetable for stock index futures. China Daily, 9 March 2009, http://www.chinadaily.com.cn/bizchina/2009npc/2009-03/09/content_7555640.htm

IMD (International Institute for Management Development) 2008. World competitiveness yearbook. Lausanne: IMD.

La Porta, R., F. Lopez-de-Silanes, A. Shleifer, and R. Vishny. 1998. Law and finance. *Journal of Political Economy* 106: 1113–1155.

La Porta, R., F. Lopez-de-Silanes, and A. Shleifer. 1999. Corporate ownership around the world. *Journal of Finance* 54: 471–517.

Li, Q. 2006. Review of several issues in researches on the great leap forward over the past 10 years (Chinese). *Contemporary China History Studies* 13: 53–65.

Lin, C. 2001. Corporatisation and corporate governance in China's economic transition. *Economics of Planning* 34: 5–35.

Liu, Q. 2006. Corporate governance in China: Current practices, economic effects and institutional determinants. *CESifo Economic Studies* 52: 415–453.

Luo, H. 2004. The second session of the Eighth Party Congress and the launch of the Great Leap Forward (Chinese). *GEMS of Culture and History* 2004: 23–31.

Mallin, C.A. 2007. *Corporate governance*, 2nd ed. Oxford: Oxford University Press.

MCPRC (Ministry of Commerce of the People's Republic of China). 2005. Measures for strategic investments by foreign investors upon listed companies, MCPRC Decree No. 28, http://english.mofcom.gov.cn/aarticle/policyrelease/announcement/200804/20080405507111.html

NBSC (National Bureau of Statistics of China). 1982. *Statistical Communiqué 1982*. Beijing: China Statistics Press.

NBSC. 1983. *Statistical Communiqué 1993*. Beijing: China Statistics Press.

NBSC. 1991. *Statistical Communiqué 1991*. Beijing: China Statistics Press.

NBSC. 1992. *Statistical Communiqué 1992*. Beijing: China Statistics Press.

NBSC. 1993. *Statistical Communiqué 1993*. Beijing: China Statistics Press.

NBSC. 1996. *China Statistical Yearbook 1996*. Beijing: China Statistics Press.

NBSC 2007a. *China Statistical Yearbook 2007*. Beijing: China Statistics Press.

NBSC 2007b. *Statistical Communiqué 2007*. Beijing: China Statistics Press.

NBSC 2008a. *China Statistical Yearbook 2008*. Beijing: China Statistics Press.

NBSC 2008b. *Statistical Communiqué 2008*. Beijing: China Statistics Press.

NBSC 2009. *China Statistical Yearbook 2009*. Beijing: China Statistics Press.

Qian, Y. 1999a. The Process of China's market transition (1978–98): The evolutionary, historical, and comparative perspectives, Paper prepared for the Journal of Institutional and Theoretical Economics symposium on "Big-Bang Transformation of Economic Systems as a Challenge to New Institutional Economics", Wallerfangen/Saar, Germany, 9–11 June 1999, http://web.rollins.edu/~tlairson/easia/chinareforms.pdf

Qian, Y. 1999b. The institutional foundations of China's market transition, Conference Paper, Annual Bank Conference on Development Economics, Washington, DC, April 1999, available at SSRN: http://ssrn.com/abstract=187568

Qian, Y., and J. Wu. 1999. China's transition to a market economy – How far across the river? Conference Paper on Policy Reform in China, Center for Research on Economic Development and Policy Reform (CEDPR), Stanford University, 18–20 November 1999, revised in May 2000, http://elsa.berkeley.edu/~yqian/how%20far%20across%20the%20river.pdf

Roe, M.J. 2003. Delaware's competition. *Harvard Law Review* 117: 588–646.

Sachs, J.D., and W.T. Woo. 1997. Understanding China's economic performance, Working Paper No. 5935, National Bureau of Economic Research 1997, http://www.nber.org/papers/w5935.pdf?new_window=1

SAFE (State Administration of Foreign Exchange). 2010. Data and statistics, http://www.safe.gov.cn/model_safe_en/tjsj_en/tjsj_list_en.jsp?id=4

Shipani, C.A., and J. Liu. 2002. Corporate governance in China: then and now. *Columbia Business Law Review* 2002: 1–69.

Shleifer, A., and R.W. Vishny. 1997. A survey of corporate governance. *Journal of Finance* 52: 737–783.

SSE (Shanghai Stock Exchange). 2006. *China corporate governance report 2006 – the corporate governance of state holding listed companies*. Shanghai: Fudan University Press.

SSE. 2007. Monthly report, December 2007, http://www.sse.com.cn/sseportal/ps/zhs/yjcb/ybtj/sse_stat_monthly_200712.pdf

SSE. 2008a. Monthly report, December 2008, http://www.sse.com.cn/sseportal/ps/zhs/yjcb/ybtj/sse_stat_monthly_200812.pdf

SSE. 2008b. Guidelines of Shanghai Stock Exchange on individual investors' behavior (Chinese), http://static.sse.com.cn/ps/zhs/fwzc/flfgk_szsywgz.shtml.

SZSE (Shenzhen Stock Exchange). 2006/2007. Monthly statistics (Chinese) 2006, 2007, http://www.szse.cn/main/marketdata/tjyb_front/

SZSE (Shenzhen Stock Exchange). 2008. Fact book, 2008, http://www.szse.cn/main/files/2009/05/07/760410685444.pdf

U.S. Department of the Treasury. 2007. The third U.S.-China strategic economic dialogue: Joint fact sheet. Beijing, 12–13 December 2007, http://www.treasury.gov/press-center/press-releases/Pages/hp732.aspx

Van de Ven, A.H. 2009. Organizational change. In *The Blackwell Encyclopedia of Management*, ed. C.L. Cooper, Blackwell: Blackwell Publishing, Reference Online.

Wang, K. 2006. *Corporate governance and agency cost under large shareholder control*. Beijing: Encyclopedia of China Publishing House.

WEF (World Economic Forum). 2009. The global competitiveness report 2008–2009, https://members.weforum.org/pdf/GCR08/GCR08.pdf

World Feder ation of Echanges (WFE). 2007. Annual report and statistics 2007, http://www.world-exchanges.org/statistics/annual/2007

Zhu, Z. 2009. Wu: We should not copy western system. *China Daily*, 10 March 2009, http://www.chinadaily.com.cn/china/2009-03/10/content_7557637.htm

Part II
Philosophical Foundations
of Corporate Governance

Chapter 7
Philosophical Underpinnings to Corporate Governance: A Collibrational Approach

Steve Letza, Clive Smallman, Xiuping Sun, and James Kirkbride

Contents

Introduction

High profile corporate fraud and failure is a depressingly familiar litany. Action has certainly been taken both by the courts and the legislature in response to great public concern. Yet, what knowledge is this action based upon? One of the legislative strategies emphasizes the need for a singular governance structure for all

This paper extends work previously presented at the Academy of Management 2006 and 2007 conferences.

S. Letza (✉)
Professor of Corporate Governance, Director, European Centre for Corporate Governance,
Liverpool John Moores University, Liverpool, UK
e-mail: S.Letza@ljmu.ac.uk

A. Brink (ed.), *Corporate Governance and Business Ethics*, Ethical Economy.
Studies in Economic Ethics and Philosophy 39, DOI 10.1007/978-94-007-1588-2_7,
© Springer Science+Business Media B.V. 2011

corporations. However, research shows that no single model or structure of corporate governance can work at all times; there is no one-size-fits-all approach.

Moreover, the dialectic theoretical orthodoxy is at best questionable. Recognition of these issues alongside the changing nature of economy and society suggests that we need to rethink corporate governance theory. Hence, if we want to push the bounds of our current theories and research, we must move beyond the conventional static and poorly contextualized models that have dominated to date, enabling the development of evidence-based and actionable knowledge, grounded in studies of process and focused upon improving practice.

Corporate Governance Models, Assumptions and Problems

There are four main perspectives in the corporate governance literature: the principal-agent or finance model, the myopic market model, the abuse of executive power model and the stakeholder model (cf. Blair 1995; Keasey et al. 1997).

The Principal-Agent or Finance Model

The principal-agent or finance model is the dominant theory of corporate governance. The model assumes that the only purpose of corporations is the maximisation of shareholders' wealth, whilst acknowledging that shareholders do not have enough control and influence over managerial action due to their distance from the day-to-day operations. Therefore, it argues regulation enhances the power and control of shareholders.

As the cornerstone of agency theory, the principal-agent relationship exists in any co-operative situation and thus at all levels of a corporation in which the principal delegates work to an agent who performs that work on behalf of the principal. Based on the assumption of self-interested human behaviour, agency theory asserts that managers as agents may pursue their own interests at the expense of the shareholders, hence the so-called "agency problem" (cf. Jensen and Meckling 1976). For agency theorists, to solve the agency problem is to determine the most efficient contract that governs the principal-agent relationship.

Agency theory assumes that all social relations in economic interaction can be reduced to a set of contracts (specifying duties, rewards and the rights of the principal to monitor corporate performance) between principals and agents, where the role of contracts serves as a vehicle for voluntary exchange by actors (cf. Alchian and Demsetz 1972). Thus, the firm is best described as a "nexus of contracts" with the behaviour of the firm simulating the behaviour of a market, i.e., "the outcome of a complex equilibrium process" (cf. Jensen and Meckling 1976).

The main goal of agency theory is to determine the most efficient or optimal contract governing the principal-agent relationship. The question is especially related to whether behaviour-oriented governance (e.g., salaries, hierarchical governance) is more efficient than outcome-oriented contractual governance (e.g., commissions, stock options) (cf. Eisenhardt 1989). For agency theorists, market-oriented governance structures best discipline managers' behaviour. Financial theorists, however, claim that since managerial behaviour could be constrained by the pressures of capital markets, factor markets and the market for corporate control can best address the issue of management underperformance (cf. Manne 1965). The advocates of this model insist that current corporate governance mechanisms should be allowed to operate freely and that any interference with the market governance mechanisms is irrational and distorts them (cf. Hart 1995).

The Myopic Market Model

The myopic market model shares with principal-agent theory the position that the purpose of corporations is to maximise shareholders' wealth. However, it argues that the maximisation of shareholders' well-being is not synonymous with share price maximisation because the market systematically undervalues long-term capital investment. It also argues that the Anglo-American style of corporate governance is flawed by an over concern with short-term return on investment, short-term corporate profits, short-term management performance, short-term stock market prices and short-term expenditures (cf. Charkham 1994; Hayes and Abernathy 1980; Moerland 1995; Sykes 1994). Furthermore, the theory posits that the threat of hostile takeover produces an effect of distortion and distraction from true value creation. For example, otherwise loyal and diligent managers could be forced to take measures against hostile takeover rather than to enhance longer-term performance.

The myopic market model suggests that corporate governance reform should provide an environment in which shareholders and managers are encouraged to share long-term performance horizons. It is thus necessary to increase shareholders' loyalty and voice while reducing the possibility of shareholders' exit to encourage "relationship investing" to lock financial institutions into long-term positions, to restrict the takeover process and restrain voting rights for short-term shareholders and to empower other groups such as employees and suppliers who have long-term relationships with the corporation (cf. Keasey et al. 1997).

The Abuse of Executive Power Model

This model believes that Anglo-American companies suffer from a widespread abuse of executive power. The current corporate governance arrangements leave excessive power in the hands of management, who may abuse it to serve their own interest at the expense of shareholders and society as a whole (cf. Hutton 1995). Supporters of such a view argue that the current institutional constraints on managerial behaviour, such as shareholder involvement in major decisions, disclosed information, non-executive directors, the audit process or the threat of takeover, are inadequate to prevent corporate power from being abused because shareholders that are protected by liquid assets markets are simply uninterested in most abuses of corporate power (cf. Keasey et al. 1997).

It is arguable that the principal-agent analysis is not a realistic description of the current corporate governance structure and process since such a relationship may actually work in the reverse (cf. Kay and Silberston 1995). This assumes that managers are trustees of the corporation as a whole rather than agents of shareholders. Therefore, a new proposal for corporate governance reform is advocated, in which the statutory duties of directors should be to promote the business of the company as a whole and to balance it with shareholders' claims, more power should be given to the independent directors for nominating and selecting senior managers and the appointment of a CEO should be for a fixed four-year term with only one renewal of contract.

The Stakeholder Model

The stakeholder model in corporate governance has been regarded as the most fundamental challenge to the principal-agent model. The central proposition of this model is that the objective and purpose of the corporation should be defined more widely than the maximisation of shareholder wealth alone. The corporation should recognise the well-being of other groups such as employees, suppliers, customers and managers who have a long-term association with the firm and thus some "stakes" in its long-term success. A wider objective function of the corporation is not only economic equitability, but also social accountability and efficiency (cf. Keasey et al. 1997).

Instrumental stakeholder theory sets up a framework for examining the connections between the practice of stakeholder management and the achievement of corporate performance goals (cf. Freeman 1984). The assumption is that if corporations practice stakeholder management, their performance, such as profitability, stability and growth, will be relatively successful. Thus, stakeholder management becomes a significant strategy for managers who would be sensitive to future change. However, there is no clear guideline in the stakeholder model to ensure managers perform stakeholders' benefits and social obligation. Some suggestions for stakeholder management include trust relationships and long-term contractual associations, interlocking shareholdings and inter-firm co-operations, ethical behaviour, employees' participation in decision-making and ownership-sharing scheme.

Common Assumptions

Despite their competing and conflicting diagnoses of and solutions to corporate governance ills, these perspectives share some common assumptions in terms of the nature of corporation, the governance structures and the reason for governance. It is these assumptions and their underlying presuppositions that suggest some fundamental and irresolvable problems with current governance theory.

The current debate on corporate governance is traceable to a nineteenth century argument on the nature of the corporation in corporate law theory, between the "aggregate theory" and the "nature-entity theory". The aggregate theory claims that the corporation as a legal person is not a real person, but an artificial person created by law or the state as a matter of convenience. The corporation is only a collective name for its members and the aggregate rights of its members. By contrast, the nature-entity theory argues that the reality of the corporation is a real person with its own enduring personality, distinctive mind and will and a capacity to act through its organs. The corporate personality is rightly recognised, and not simply created, through the process of incorporation (cf. Arthur 1987; Barker 1950; Mayson et al. 1994). The aggregate-entity debate eventually suggests an "individualistic" view versus a "holistic" view of the nature of the corporation, which largely influences the current debate in corporate governance between shareholder and stakeholder perspectives. Generally, economists are interested in the organisation of economic actors regardless of their legal form (cf. Loasby 1998). In this context, a firm is no more than a "nexus of contracts" joining inputs to produce outputs among actors and between principals and agents in order to maximise behaviour of all individuals. Whilst shareholder perspectives share the individualistic view of the corporation, stakeholder perspectives tend to view the corporation more or less as a broader collective unity, as an enduring entity and more than just the totality of the shareholdings. Both perspectives attempt to claim a solid, clear-cut, self-contained, enduring and describable characteristic of either an individual atomic entity as the foundation of the corporation or corporate-as-a-whole entity beyond individuals. Those entities are regarded as neutral objects waiting for our discovery and analysis and seem to be pre-given and already existent "out there" independently of our minds. In either case, these entities are extant, socially and legally constructed systems, which we as individuals discover and analyse and to which we add our own constructs and interpretations. Furthermore, the corporation as a social system either bound by contracts or by laws is normally rational with maximum goals, reasonable actions and optimal solutions for the sake of economic efficiency. In both shareholder and stakeholder perspectives, the corporation is viewed as a social tool for the purpose of governance and control in order to maximise the economic interests of shareholders or certain stakeholders.

Following these assumptions, both perspectives try to discover an optimal governance structure that can effectively solve the agency problem or the problem of abuse of executive power. Thus, the market governance mechanisms advocated by the principal-agent model and the hierarchical forms of governance by the other three models are regarded as competing alternatives for rational selection and appropriate design. Both sides of the debate assert that only one optimal and universal governance structure is effective in disciplining management performance, which could be repetitively tested and objectively chosen. The criterion of selecting the optimal governance structure for all the perspectives accords to the principle of economic efficiency since, it is argued, institutional change has its root cause in efficiency. There exists a rational process of ensuring that more efficient economic forms and governance structures prevail over less efficient ones (cf. Williamson 1975). Economic rationality or efficiency is seen as a common reason for both shareholder perspectives and stakeholder perspectives to search for an elegance, purity, certainty and universality of governance form – "the ultimate demonstration of rationality at its best" (Solomon and Higgins 1997, p. 29). In agency theory, rationality is embodied in the optimisation of contracts. The myopic market model suggests curbing irrational short-termism by forcing actors to take a more considered (rational) long-term view. The abuse of executive power model seeks a similar route to rationality, insisting that irrational (in the eyes of the corporate whole) directors' powers be curtailed, with independent scrutineers seeking the optimum path. Stakeholder theory seeks a collective rationality, in which the demands of one group cannot disproportionately outweigh the requirements of others.

Issues with Current Corporate Governance Analysis

While the above models have significantly developed our understanding of corporate bodies and provide valuable perspectives on corporate governance, emerging evidence from the news media and public inquiries into major corporate failure, as well as the authors' experience as practitioners, demonstrates that the claim of universal principles and optimal governance structures explicitly made by the four models is at best only partially supported in corporate governance practice. This raises the question of whether there is any solid and objective foundation such as individual entity or corporate entity for building an optimal and universal structure. As all of the four models suggest that the validity of the competing analyses on corporate governance relies on supporting empirical evidence (cf. Keasey et al. 1997), therefore, either market governance or hierarchical governance, as alternative solutions, should be demonstrated in practice to be optimal or superior. However, this is not the case as the evidence available does not simply support any single governance structure claimed to be most effective. Counter-evidence from all quarters of the corporate governance debate denies both market governance to be optimal and hierarchical governance effectiveness. Indeed, corporate governance has experienced perhaps too much of both "hierarchical dysfunction" and "market failure" in Anglo-American business history. Whilst hierarchical governance failure is largely due to reluctant shareholders and defective boards of directors (cf. Bishop 1994; Hart 1995; Hawley and Williams 1996; Jensen 1993; Latham 1999; Sternberg 1998), market governance failure is primarily due to short-termism and unreliable market forces (cf. Bishop 1994; Hart 1995; Herman and Lowenstein 1988; Parkinson 1995; Pound 1993). For example, the designed function of hierarchical governance relies on shareholders' effective monitoring such as vote, voice and proxy fight. However, since the increasing separation of ownership from control in the early twentieth century (cf. Berle and Means 1932), individual shareholders are less inclined and have less incentive to participate in the monitoring system due to the free-rider problem, lack of information, useless proposals, managers' manipulation and legal restrictions. It is arguable that this incentive problem might be offset by the gravitas of large institutional directors, and there are signs that pension funds and their "city"-based managers are not atomised, but aggregated in global "investment villages". Further, there is some evidence that major fund holders are using their "muscle" to leverage the behaviour of boards in search of improvements in effectiveness (cf. Bhojraj and Sengupta 2003), but this same evidence also suggests problems with other performance measures. Chief amongst several issues, institutional shareholders suffer from a corporate form of disassociated multiple personality disorder, since their small shareholders require them to monitor corporates on their behalf, whilst at the same time they must act as investors whose duty is to maximise the returns for their beneficiaries. Whilst they may be able to strike a balance, conflict and dissociation will occur where they take a long-term view of their positions and incur expense in intervening in management under-performance, whereas simultaneously as investors enjoying the freedom to incur the least expense in intervening in management to secure the best return for their beneficiaries. These roles are not easily reconcilable and fail by dint of a compound agency problem (cf. Short and Keasey 1997). Thus, shareholders in practice fail to monitor both directors and managers who should act on behalf of shareholders under the current governance arrangements.

As an alternative to hierarchical governance, market discipline is highly valued by the principal-agent theorists. The hostile takeover movement, the so called market for corporate control, reached a peak in the US and the UK in the 1980s, but was quickly ended at the end of the 1980s due to the collapse of the junk bond market, resistance by managers, political pressure and an economic downturn. Market governance has been seriously criticised as less effective and too costly in improving corporate performance and promoting long-run wealth (cf. Bishop 1994; Latham 1999; Parkinson 1995; Pound 1993). Stock market and share price are in fact less unbiased and useful indicators of the "fundamentals" of corporate performance, rather it often reflects shareholders' psychology, guessing, changing moods and prejudices and thus routinely misprice assets (cf. Keynes 1936; Shiller 1989).

Furthermore, the conception of economic rationality and efficiency has been criticised as too narrow and too static. Economic logic is the prevailing core assumption in current corporate governance analysis. The principal-agent or finance model is deeply rooted in market efficiency theory originated in both classical and neo-classical economics. The other three corporate governance models, as described above, challenge the "market-optimum" assumption and propose hierarchical-like governance structures based on various internal monitoring mechanisms. Nevertheless, underpinning all these models is the notion of economic rationality as well. The only difference is that those three models prefer long-term, rather than short-term, corporate performance horizons shared together by shareholders or stakeholders with managers. Although some aspects of the stakeholder theory emphasise corporate ethical behaviour and social responsibility, the main purpose of this model is instrumentalist, based on the principles of economic rationality and efficiency such as managerial strategies and long-term business success.

The main criticism of the economic logic as an explanation of social phenomena is that it presupposes pure economic conditions and a level playing field in considering rational selections in a corporation, under which the selections are simplified and isolated from other social processes such as social (non-economic) relationships, structural power and institutional contexts (cf. Roy 1997). It is also arguable that economic rationality and efficiency is an overly narrow conception which loses insight of the complexity and many sides of rationality as well as inevitable irrationality in human life (cf. Rescher 1988). Further, empirical evidence in corporate governance has shown that there is no rationality of action or some absolute standard of efficiency at all, nor one most efficient mode of organisation and optimal governance structure in the world, nor only one way to pursue organisational goals. The rules by which realities are constructed can be negotiated and changed as the outcome of the social interactions between key players/actors such as managers, their corporations and government agencies (cf. Fligstein 1990).

The essential problem with the dominant economic logic in governance is that "a static conception of governance (...) ignores the continuous and ongoing interaction between choices made, and the context into which choices are embedded" (Mueller 1995, p. 1220). Obviously, the static approach in corporate governance analysis presupposes and inherits *a priori* principles, ready-made concepts and taken-for-granted notions, such as principal-agent relationships, market efficiency and hierarchical structure, and then identifies, classifies and simplifies the complex practices of corporate governance with these conceptual templates for analysis and explanation. In doing so, the dynamic practice and lived experiences of corporate governance are forced to fit theoretical models, which become increasingly abstracted, isolated, fixed, endured and finally static and dogmatic.

This privileging of a homeostatic and entitative conception of reality generates an attitude that assumes the possibility and desirability of symbolically representing the diverse aspects of our phenomenal experiences using an established and atemporal repository of terms and conceptual categories for the purposes of classification and description. For it is only when portions of reality are assumed to be stable and hence fixable in space-time that they can be adequately represented by symbols, words and concepts. A representationalist epistemology thus orients our thinking towards *outcomes* and *end-states* rather than on the processes of change themselves. It is this basic epistemological assumption which provides the inspiration for the scientific obsession with precision, accuracy and parsimony in representing and explaining social and material phenomena, including the practices of corporate governance. These social phenomena are regarded as relatively enduring, concrete and observable entities which can straightforwardly be subjected to factor analysis. The consequences of this on the direction which research and theorising in the field of corporate governance has taken must not be underestimated. Indeed, it has instilled a set of instinctive "readinesses" (cf. Vickers 1984) amongst management academics to construe theories as being straightforwardly "about" an externally existing and pre-ordered reality. This predisposition explains the intellectual orientation of the orthodox approach to analyses of corporate governance. It justifies prevalent notions such as "the marvel of the market", "the finance notion of control", "the principal-agent relationship", "nexus of contracts", "self-regulation" and "internal monitoring" as relatively enduring and universally valid conceptual entities which are taken for granted and seemingly theoretically unproblematic.

With the awareness of the fallacy of representationalism, all the justifications of the theoretical entities about corporate governance, including the preoccupied concepts of market governance and hierarchical governance and their related assumptions, must consequently be questionable. If the corporate governance issues cannot simply be interpreted by an economic logic founded upon a static and entitative conception of reality, then an alternative processual approach can better describe and explain corporate governance practice.

A Process Philosophy Approach to Corporate Governance

A process approach must not be equated with the commonsensical idea of the process that an individual or a system as a separate and solid entity undergoes in transition from one place to another caused linearly by external forces or power. Rather, it is a metaphysical orientation that emphasises an ontological primacy in the "becoming" of things; that sees things as always momentarily stabilised outcomes: "[S]tability (. . .) waves in a sea of process" (Rescher 1996, p. 53). This process ontology promotes a dispersive view of reality as a heterogeneous concatenation of event-occurrences that cannot be comprehensively captured by static symbols and representations. For process philosophers (cf. Bergson 1903; James 1909, 1911; Whitehead 1929/1978, 1933/1961), the principles of process, such as movement, change, indeterminacy and probability, are the fundamental features of reality. Process and modes of change rather than things and fixed stabilities best represent our encounters with and in the natural and social world. The immediate and dynamic intuition of living experience is more faithful to reality than the conceptual work of thought, for thought can only deal with stable things. The symbolic system of representation (e.g., language) is always inadequate in capturing the real world, since much of what we experience remains tacit and unspeakable. Thus, processes cannot be described or explained in terms of non-processual elements. A much clearer understanding of the processual approach can be seen in three dimensions (or principles, sub-approaches) of processes, including interrelatedness, systemic-wholeness and periodic-historicity.

Interrelatedness, interconnection, interdependence or interrelationship is the core principle of process thought: the "principle of relativity". The logic of interrelatedness is that our raw experiences refer to action, activity and acting rather than fixed things and forms; acting is relating in character, relating the whole with the constituents, relating one constituent with all others. By their interrelational acting, all constituents are naturally "bound" or "bonded" together to form a particular whole. Thus, everything is not independent and absolute, but conditional, relative and interdependent: "[A]ll things are by their participation in other things" (Jungerman 2000, p. 6). In the interconnected systemic whole, each event or element as a locus is a creative integration of relations; it embodies aspects of all the others, contains the information of the whole.

The very essence of an ongoing process is not fragmented and unconnected, neither as coincident factors artificially given or analytically put together, but integrated and co-ordinated where a macroprocess organises microprocesses into a *systemic whole* and microprocesses and macroprocesses cannot be split and isolated. A process is not just one event or "occasion of experience", but a series of inter-connected eventual developments, a co-ordinated group of changes and an ordered society of occurrences, which are systematically connected to one another causally or functionally.

Process is essentially related to a time dimension (cf. Rescher 1996). An instant is not a process. The self-identity of a process must be manifested within a period through which a unitary whole is realised. The character, pattern or form of a process only exhibits in a whole period of action. A process by definition cannot be understood merely by a collection of sequential properties as with the conventional mode of thinking, but by a spatiotemporal continuity in which an ongoing process "combines existence in the present with tentacles reaching into the past and the future" (ibid., p. 39), that is, by historical connections. Everything is "becoming" – integrating and incorporating all past events, experiences and possibilities to create something new and become what it is. "Becoming" is one-way direction: any present potentiality and actuality are conditioned, though not completely deterministic, by its history, by its predecessors and by its retrospective necessary connections. Thus, "an entity's relations to its predecessors are essential, constitutive or internal for the entity; but its relations to successors are inessential or external" (Hartshorne 1984, p. 59).

What the processual approach offers is an opportunity to view the corporation in its original sense as a human construction, a social world that is fully constituent of human minds and direct experiences in addition to physical materials, which are fundamentally processual in nature. This worldview has no pre-given, neutral and fixed essence and meaning unless it is individually experienced and understood and collectively perceived and constructed. It has its own logic and intrinsic value embedded in its social processes characterised by interrelatedness, systemic-wholeness and periodic-historicity. What the processual approach offers is the option to turn our attention away from the theoretical abstraction of governance models to the fundamental human experience and practice of governing processes. It affords us the means to develop keen sensitivity and awareness of the subtle and complex governing relationships and forces, the tacit and explicit knowledge generated in direct and indirect experiences, the firm-specific and contextual-dependent governing problems and their pragmatic solutions. It fully accomodates the rational and irrational, conscious and intuitive sides of social attitudes and behaviours, and the ceaseless and endless search for the reflective and renewable understanding of governance practices for continuous improvements.

Corporate Governance as Self-Generating Order

The "true" and "objective" representation of a fixed corporate reality in current corporate governance theory is misleading, since, "truth" and "objectivity" are in and of themselves relative constructs around which scientific and pseudo-scientific debate often turns. This is particularly so in social realities such as corporate governance for even the standing of a "fixed" legal entity may be subject to change as a result of a political process. The distinctiveness of the social reality from the natural world is that it is fully composed of human minds (conscious and unconscious) and ideas (practical and theoretical), which are the most basic elements of the social world and from which our attitudes, behaviours, actions, social relations and social conventions derive and are generated. Since mental activities are always in flux (cf. Rescher 1996, pp. 105–118) and social reality as mind-composed and mind-mediated is, fundamentally, processual rather than substantial, any perceived enduring pattern or social stability in practice are relative in themselves (i.e., temporary in history and during a period) and subject to manipulation and collective maintenance.

Hence, in a truly processual sense, corporate governance is a process of governing which varies continuously and emerges from social interaction. The current crop of governance models are evidently unsupported because they are simplified abstractions filtering out the concrete experiences and complex dynamics of governing practice, based upon historical "snapshots" taken from the continually moving and flowing processes of governance that is moving towards an uncertain future. Rather than searching for general, universal and timeless principles (cf. Porter 1991), corporate governance theorists would do better to become aware of the sensitivity of time, process and history (cf. Tsoukas 2001), that is, the actual workings of reality where ambiguous perceptions, individualistic understandings, local contingencies, pragmatic actions and solutions, rational and irrational behaviours prevail.

The concepts of "spontaneous order" (cf. Hayek 1982) and "emergent pattern" (cf. Morgan 1997) better than any fixed notions describe the fluid character of corporate governance practice. Social systems are intrinsically open to diversities of individual actions, since individual actions depend on individual perceptions and understandings, which are inextricably bounded with individual properties of experiences (cf. Sayer 1984; Tsoukas 1992, 1994) ("subject-referring properties"; cf. Taylor 1985). Individual experiences cannot be exactly repeated over time and across contexts, and individuals are in the process of continuous learning, developing and interacting with others. Hence, self-understandings and self-interpretations as both responses to local contingencies and "enactment" of environments (cf. Weick 1977, 1979) are necessarily implicated in defining individual actions. This eventually means that under close scrutiny, individual actions and behaviours are self-governed patterns that emerge from a combination of their own historical experiences, current understandings, local conditions and multiple possibilities. As human beings, we experience our life-processes in our own activities and in our own acts of free will, rather than as being driven and determined purely by external forces. This means that the emergent patterns of self-governance are not directly imposed from outside such as through hierarchical orders or through predetermined logic (cf. Morgan 1997, p. 266), but through self-determination (cf. Frankl 1959). Thus, power (essentially, governance) is not a possessed, fixed and abstracted thing, a sense of imposed domination and centralisation (cf. Foucault 1979/1988).

Rather, it must be exercised, existent in relationships and expressed in actions. Power as exercised is not simply an obligation or a prohibition on those who "do not have power"; it is manifest in the reaction to and reflection of the given pressure, in their attitudes, willing and intent. The outcome of power and governance is transmitted by them and through them in the process of obeying, disobeying, negotiating, debating and compromising. External forces and pressures are only possibly influential on individual perceptions and reactions, as one of the elements of individual "enactment" in their environments. However, it is important to recognise that when self-governance is defined as spontaneously emergent and individually distinctive, it does not mean that it is isolated from social processes. On the contrary, as social beings, individuals' understandings and interpretations are the results of social interactions through communications, observations, learning and thinking. Hence, self-generating pattern and spontaneous order in a society and in the corporation are largely characterised (or coloured) by collectively constructed pattern and order through more or less shared values, beliefs, cultures, conventions, habits, negotiated meanings, compromised actions, *inter alia* (cf. Berger and Luckmann 1966).

Given the subjectivity of meaning-generations and mind-dependence of social actions, corporate governance should not be understood as pre-defined in the context of pre-designed structures, fixed and unchangeable entities, imposed and externalised order; rather, it should be generated from daily experiences and dynamic practices. Thus, belief in corporate governance frameworks that are prescribed and specified in rules, regulations or agreements such as corporate laws, company articles and private contracts is overly simplistic and unnatural. Governance that relies on maintaining a fixed definition by the provision of rules is impossible to practice and sustain in the long-term. No doubt that governance is often embedded within contextual rules for guiding behaviours and actions. However, in the process of application in practice, the interpretation of governing rules is dependent upon the understandings of the individual actors and complex social interactions, for rules can never "provide for their own interpretation independently of those agencies whose interpretations instantiate, signify or imply them" (Clegg 1989, p. 97). Hence, power or governance is a nexus not of contracts, but of contested meanings and interpretations within multiple possibilities and a socially negotiated order and collectively constructed reality. Governance is not rule-reification and rule-implementation in general, but in the process of rule adapting to local conditions within specific contexts.

Given the emergent and self-generating nature of corporate governance, what theorists and practitioners need to deal with corporate governance issues effectively is not to presuppose a mechanic and machine-like notion of corporate entity that can be governed externally and objectively through the traditionally designed three-tier hierarchical structure of governance or through the market for corporate control. They need to evaluate specific contexts, historical backgrounds, temporary circumstances and contingent factors that condition the process of governing practices and which are sensitive to the processual character of direct experiences, particular interpretations, meaning-generating and sense-making in both collective sense and individual manner. In a processual view, self-governance itself is not a fixed notion either; it is a continuously renewing and innovative pattern. What is needed for theorists and practitioners is not to attempt to stop and freeze or ignore change, but to flow with and facilitate it (cf. Morgan 1997), leaving room for individual interactions, innovations, judgement and adjustment so as to enable effective actions. Looking inward both intuitively and thoughtfully to address the contingencies and temporary issues at hand and generating order out of chaos from "inside" is a more effective route to understanding and facilitating corporate governance.

From Governance to Governing

Currently dominant theories of corporate governance, despite their contrasting and competing perspectives, remain trapped in the same mode of thinking which assumes that the reality of governance practice should be force-fitted to idealised models. However, such an approach is not likely to be applied in practice and would not improve corporate governance if it did, and "the alternative approach – of adapting the model to reality rather than reality to the model – deserves equal consideration" (Kay and Silberston 1995, p. 86).

The fundamental problem with the current analyses of corporate governance is that their perspectives are constructed through a purely homeostatic approach (cf. Kirkbride and Letza 2004) that ignores the continuous interaction between choices made and their specific contexts, and the continuous flow of corporate governance practices including especially issues of precedence, personal incentives, individual perceptions and societal approval. Although the competing models may claim that their perspectives are based on corporate governance practice and drawn from observations and investigations, there is, in fact, little evidence of their theoretical viability. The main reason for this is quite simply that such research and analyses rely upon a static and entitative view of reality which presupposes that situations, definitions and contexts remain stable and are hence not subjected to the necessary vagaries of change and interpretation.

Thus, they tend to deal only with abstract conceptual frameworks and pre-given assumptions as well as *a priori* principles rather than on discrete empirical factuality, continuity and radical experiences. The preoccupation is thus on consistency rather than on relevance. Taking their hypothetical and theoretically established "entities" and "generative mechanisms" as ontologically unproblematic, they justify their theses by insisting that their perspectives are truthful in so far as they accurately represent the "objective" realities of corporate governance practice. By so doing, they commit to "the fallacy of misplaced concreteness": mistaking theories for reality itself (cf. Whitehead 1929/1978, 1933/1961).

We argue that corporate governance cannot be viewed as a pre-designed, universalised and fixed model; rather, it is a process of governing, an emergent pattern continuously generated from complex social interactions in historical and contextual specifications. It is an ongoing reality-constituting and reality-maintaining activity in which all participants both inside and outside corporations actively participate in shaping and reshaping perceptions and priorities. In this sense, principles, assumptions, issues, problems and solutions cannot be interpreted as pre-given, objective and taken-for-granted. They are always in the process of constructing, reconstructing, changing and renewing. We thus suggest that to comprehend corporate governance practice, one should not attempt to subscribe to theoretical linearity, extremity and absoluteness and ignore the dynamics and flexibility of human minds, character, behaviours and social interactions. What is needed is to draw attention to and understand the "rationality of practice", the diverse responses to localised requirements and the continently emerged governing pattern, having its own logic and intrinsic value and being acceptable at a given moment. A significant inspiration for "governors" in practice is an "art of governance" (cf. Foucault 1974), an art "which concerns all and which touches each" and "which presupposes thought" (Burchell et al. 1991, p. x). Human minds, thought and ideas enjoy real power in the construction and change of social reality and governance. An art of governance is, in contrast to the "science" of governance, to work with the invented and changeable ideas, appreciate different viewpoints, respect distinctive ways of doing things, set fluid targets, take flexible measures and solutions, adjust and readjust strategies and techniques. Governance is a non-linear and unstable equilibrium. It is to prepare for change, flow with change and forward to change.

The term "governing" as a descriptive action verb is better than the static noun "governance" as the intended description of governing activities in continuing processes, "here and now", rather than the abstracted description of any end-state and outcome of activities, "there and then". "Governing" directs our attention to what is emerging and happening in practice, what is being done and relating to people involved in specific governing processes, and what people are directly experiencing, ideally perceiving and socially communicating and interacting. It avoids directing interest to abstracted theorising and modelling. Above all else, governance suggests the past, whereas governing is firmly in the "here and now", albeit with one eye on a multiplicity of uncertain futures.

Future Research Directions

Perhaps the major issue in corporate governance research stems from our limited understanding of what really goes on in directors' minds and inside boardrooms – the "fields", "symbolic capital" and "habitus" that comprise the "practice" (cf. Bourdieu 1984) of corporate governance. Current theories focus upon external impacts based around a static view of the corporate entity. Conventional models do not look at the process of governing as the evolving sum of experiences of those who govern. Related to this is a research issue that focuses upon developing a deeper understanding of directors' knowledge, experience and skills and the effects of these upon behavior, particularly in decision making processes. Some of this type of research has occurred (cf. Leblanc and Gillies 2005; McNulty et al. 2005), but its findings, whilst valuable, are often limited by methodology focused on variance analysis and as such are far from definitive or significant. Such research is also important if we are to build a picture of the state and nature of the "talent pool". Also, we must recognise in all of this that governance does not take place in a vacuum; context is critical, and our accounts of governing must in turn account for the influence of politics, polity, culture, economics and the natural environment.

These related issues reflect a renewed interest in the "practice turn" in organisation and management studies (cf. Schatzki et al. 2001), particularly in what key organisation members do to realise strategy. An approach that focuses upon process will allow the research community to fully and properly understand the complexities of governing and to assess the implementation of best practice or deep causation in decision making.

Methodological Issues

At the heart of this research agenda is *process*, which presents to us a methodological issue, since much of extant governance theory is derived from the traditional "variance approach" to social science (cf. Mohr 1982). This approach focuses on studying fixed entities with varying attributes (which have a single meaning over time) and which only "synopsizes" reality (cf. Tsoukas and Chia 2002). Explanations are based upon necessary and sufficient causality and upon efficient causality. The generality of theory derived from this approach depends upon uniformity across contexts. Time ordering among independent variables is not relevant and the emphasis of such work is on immediate causation. This approach to theory development does not accommodate all types of forces that influence the process of governance, and the research strategies used focus upon deterministic causation (cf. van de Ven and Poole 2005). This approach cannot explain phenomena that "encompass continuous and discontinuous causation, critical incidents, contextual effects, and the effects of formative patterns" (Poole et al. 2000, p. 4).

Research in corporate governance requires an approach that will clarify similarities and differences among theories in order to facilitate theoretical integration and to generate a comprehensive understanding of governance. This requires a rigorous epistemological base, built upon an ontology that is more in keeping with understanding governing processes. We argue that the requirement is for an approach that accommodates a "fluxful", changeable and emergent post-modern world, emphasizing reality as inclusively processual. A processual approach acknowledges that corporate governance practice around the world developed and continues to develop in a variety of unique cultural, historical and social circumstances.

In this approach, explanations of events would be based on necessary causality, as well as final (goal), formal (structure) and efficient causality, which means that explanations would be layered and incorporate *both* proximal and distal causation. This is because such explanations recognize that change and interconnectedness are predominant characteristics of nature. Generality depends on versatility across cases and time and time ordering is paramount. What emerges from such an approach is a process study narrating the emergence of the social construction of governance (cf. van de Ven and Poole 2005).

Well specified though they may be, many of the "variance theoretical" papers are based upon an analysis of corporate financial data. Consequently, we need more evidence from acts of governing rather than the output from such acts. If we are to develop a deeper understanding of governance, then we need to understand directors as well as the artifacts that they produce. In other words our research designs must capture data about the process of corporate direction over time (cf. Ancona et al. 2001). Capturing time-oriented action leads to a focus on events, which represent a temporally stable picture of individual and collective actions or experience and which inevitably change the context in which processes occur. Developing process studies of governance requires researchers to intimately observe the actions and interactions of organisation members in the real-time instantiation of governing processes, through deploying ethnographic and participant observer methods in order to access and generate data (cf. Boden 1990). Such methods enable the researcher to identify events; characterize process sequences and their properties over time; test for temporal dependencies in process sequences; evaluate hypotheses of formal and final causality; recognize coherent patterns that integrate narratives; and evaluate development models (cf. Poole et al. 2000, p. 92). However, the data produced by such approaches is more complex than the norm, requiring that we employ different approaches to its analysis if we are to discover patterns in governing processes and to develop grounded explanations of these processes (cf. ibid., p. 5).

Parting Thoughts

Our current *knowledge* of the practice of corporate governance is limited, mainly because of ideological posturing in favour of shareholder or stakeholder primacy that goes back to the 1930s and beyond. As a consequence, evidence-based *action* in pursuit of improved governance in response to public concern is similarly often ideologically limited. Carter and Lorsch (2004) call for a return to the "drawing board" for corporate governance in order that practice reflects the complex world. Reflecting complexity requires that we understand the practice (cf. Leblanc and Gillies 2005) of governance and the processes that comprise this practice. This, in turn, requires that we researchers too should return to the drawing board seeking deeper and more meaningful evidence from which to inform and improve practice.

Acknowledgements The author is grateful for comments made by reviewers and those in attendance at the conferences.

References

Alchian, A.A., and H. Demsetz. 1972. Production, information costs, and economic organization. *American Economic Review* 62: 777–795.
Ancona, D.G., G.A. Okhuysen, and L.A. Perlow. 2001. Taking time to integrate temporal research. *Academy of Management Review* 26: 512–529.
Arthur, E.E. 1987. The ethics of corporate governance. *Journal of Business Ethics* 6: 59–70.
Barker, E. 1950. Introduction. In *Natural law and the theory of society 1500 to 1800*, ed. O.F. von Gierke, ix–xci. Cambridge: Cambridge University Press.

Berger, P.L., and T. Luckmann. 1966. *The social construction of reality: A treatise in the sociology of knowledge*. Garden City, NY: Doubleday.

Bergson, H. 1903. *An introduction to metaphysics*. London: Macmillan.

Berle, A.A., and G.C. Means. 1932. *The modern corporation and private property*. New York, NY: Macmillan.

Bhojraj, S., and P. Sengupta. 2003. Effect of corporate governance on bond ratings and yields: The role of institutional investors and outside directors. *Journal of Business* 76: 455–475.

Bishop, M. 1994. Watching the boss. *The Economist*, 29 January 1994: 3–5.

Blair, M.M. 1995. *Ownership and control: Rethinking corporate governance for the twenty-first century*. Washington, DC: Brookings Institution.

Boden, D. 1990. The world as it happens: Ethnomethodology and conversation analysis. In *Frontiers of social theory: A new synthesis*, ed. G. Ritzer, 185–213. New York: Columbia University Press.

Bourdieu, P. 1984. *Distinction: A social critique of the judgement of taste*. London: Routledge.

Burchell, G., C. Gordon, and P. Miller. 1991. Preface. In *The Foucault effect: Studies in governmentality*, ed. G. Burchell, C. Gordon, and P. Miller, ix–x. Hemel Hempstead: Harvester Wheatsheaf.

Carter, C.B., and J.W. Lorsch. 2004. *Back to the drawing board: Designing corporate boards for a complex world*. Cambridge, MA: Harvard Business School Press.

Charkham, J. 1994. *Keeping good company: A study of corporate governance in five countries*. Oxford: Clarendon.

Clegg, S.R. 1989. Radical revisions: Power, discipline and organizations. *Organization Studies* 10: 97–115.

Eisenhardt, K.M. 1989. Agency theory: An assessment and review. *Academy of Management Review* 14: 57–74.

Fligstein, N. 1990. *The transformation of corporate control*. Cambridge, MA: Harvard University Press.

Foucault, M. 1974. *The order of things*. London: Tavistock.

Foucault, M. 1979/1988. Politics and reason. In *Michel Foucault: Politics, philosophy, culture. interviews and other writings 1977–1984*, ed. L.D. Kritzman, 57–85. London: Routledge.

Frankl, V.E. 1959. *Man's search for meaning*. Boston, MA: Beacon Press.

Freeman, R.E. 1984. *Strategic management: A stakeholder approach*. Boston, MA: Pitman.

Hart, O. 1995. Corporate governance: Some theory and implications. *The Economic Journal* 105: 678–689.

Hartshorne, C. 1984. Whitehead as central but not sole process philosopher. In *Whitehead und der Prozessbegriff (Whitehead and the Idea of Process)*, ed. H. Holz and E. Wolf-Gazo, 34–38. Freiburg, Munich: Verlag Karl Alber.

Hawley, J.P., and A.T. Williams. 1996. Corporate governance in the United States: The rise of fiduciary capitalism – A review of the literature. Working Paper, Saint Mary's College of California, School of Economics and Business Administration.

Hayek, F.A. von. 1982. *Law, legislation and liberty*. London: Routledge & Kegan Paul.

Hayes, R.H., and W.J. Abernathy. 1980. Managing our way to economic decline. *Harvard Business Review*, July–August, 67–77.

Herman, E.S., and L. Lowenstein. 1988. Efficiency effects of hostile takeovers. In *Knights, raiders and targets: The impact of the hostile takeover*, ed. J.C. Coffee, L. Lowenstein, and S. Rose-Ackerman, 211–240. New York, NY: Oxford University Press.

Hutton, W. 1995. *The state we're in*. London: Jonathan Cape.

James, W. 1909. *A pluralistic universe*. Lincoln, NE: University of Nebraska Press.

James, W. 1911. *Some problems of philosophy*. Lincoln, NE: University of Nebraska Press.

Jensen, M.C. 1993. The modern industrial revolution, exit, and the failure of internal control systems. *Journal of Finance* 48: 831–880.

Jensen, M.C., and W.H. Meckling. 1976. Theory of the firm: Managerial behavior, agency costs and ownership structure. *Journal of Financial Economics* 3: 305–360.

Jungerman, J.A. 2000. *World in process: Creativity and interconnection in the new physics*. Albany, NY: State University of New York Press.

Kay, J., and A. Silberston. 1995. Corporate governance. *National Institute Economic Review* 153: 84–107.

Keasey, K., S. Thompson, and M. Wright. 1997. Introduction: The corporate governance problem – Competing diagnoses and solutions. In *Corporate governance: Economic and financial issues*, ed. K. Keasey, S. Thompson, and M. Wright, 1–17. New York: Oxford University Press.

Keynes, J.M. 1936. *The general theory of employment, interest and money*. New York, NY: Harcourt, Brace.

Kirkbride, J., and S. Letza. 2004. Regulation, governance and regulatory collibration: Achieving an "holistic" approach. *Corporate Governance* 12: 85–92.

Latham, M. 1999. The corporate monitoring firm. *Corporate Governance* 7: 12–20.

Leblanc, R., and J. Gillies. 2005. *Inside the boardroom: How boards really work and the coming revolution in corporate governance*. Mississauga, Ontario: John Wiley & Sons Canada, Ltd.

Loasby, B.J. 1998. On the definition and organisation of capabilities. *Revue Internationale de Systémique* 12: 13–26.

Manne, H.G. 1965. Mergers and the market for corporate control. *Journal of Political Economy* 73: 110–120.

Mayson, S.W., D. French, and C.L. Ryan. 1994. *Company law*. London: Blackstone Press.

McNulty, T., J. Roberts, and P. Stiles. 2005. Undertaking governance reform and research: Further reflections on the Higgs review. *British Journal of Management* 16: S99–S107.

Moerland, P.W. 1995. Alternative disciplinary mechanisms in different corporate systems. *Journal of Economic Behavior and Organization* 26: 17–34.

Mohr, L.B. 1982. *Explaining organizational behavior*. San Francisco, CA: Jossey-Bass.

Morgan, G. 1997. *Images of organization*, 2nd ed. Thousand Oaks, CA: Sage.

Mueller, F. 1995. Organizational governance and employee cooperation: Can we learn from economists? *Human Relations* 48: 1217–1235.

Parkinson, J. 1995. The role of "exit" and "voice" in corporate governance. In *Corporate governance and corporate control*, ed. S. Sheikh and W. Rees, 75–110. London: Cavendish.

Poole, M.S., A.H. van de Ven, K. Dooley, and M.E. Holmes. 2000. *Organizational change and innovation processes: Theory and methods for research*. New York: Oxford University Press.

Porter, M.E. 1991. Towards a dynamic theory of strategy. *Strategic Management Journal* 12: 95–117.

Pound, J. 1993. The rise of the political model of corporate governance and corporate control. *New York University Law Review* 68: 1003–1071.

Rescher, N. 1988. *Rationality: A philosophical inquiry into the nature and the rationale of reason*. New York: Oxford University Press.

Rescher, N. 1996. *Process metaphysics: An introduction to process philosophy*. Albany, NY: State University of New York Press.

Roy, W.G. 1997. *Socialising capital: The rise of the large industrial corporation in America*. Princeton, NJ: Princeton University Press.

Sayer, A. 1984. *Method in social science: A realist approach*. London: Hutchinson.

Schatzki, T.R., K. Knorr Cetina, and E. von Savigny. eds. 2001. *The practice turn in contemporary theory*. London: Routledge.

Shiller, R.J. 1989. Do stock prices move too much to be justified by subsequent changes in dividends? In *Market volatility*, ed. R.J. Shiller, 105–130. Cambridge, MA: MIT Press.

Short, H., and K. Keasey. 1997. Institutional shareholders and corporate governance. In *Corporate governance: Responsibilities, risks and remuneration*, ed. K. Keasey and M. Wright, 23–60. Chichester: Wiley.

Solomon, R.C., and K.M. Higgins. 1997. *A passion for wisdom. A very brief history of philosophy*. New York, NY: OUP.

Sternberg, E. 1998. *Corporate governance: Accountability in the marketplace*. London: Institute of Economic Affairs.

Sykes, A. 1994. Proposals for internationally competitive corporate governance in Britain and America. *Corporate Governance* 2: 187–195.

Taylor, C. 1985. *Philosophy and the human sciences*. Cambridge: Cambridge University Press. (= Philosophical Papers, Vol. 2).

Tsoukas, H. 1992. The relativity of organizing: Its knowledge presuppositions and its pedagogical implications for comparative management. *Journal of Management Education* 16: 147–162.

Tsoukas, H. 1994. Socio-economic systems and organizational management: An institutional perspective on the socialist firm. *Organization Studies* 15: 21–45.

Tsoukas, H. 2001. Re-viewing organization. *Human Relations* 54: 7–12.

Tsoukas, H., and R. Chia. 2002. On organizational becoming: Rethinking organizational change. *Organization Science* 13: 567–582.

Van de Ven, A.H., and M.S. Poole. 2005. Alternative approaches for studying organizational change. *Organization Studies* 26: 1377–1404.

Vickers, G. 1984. *The art of judgement*. London: Harper & Row.

Weick, K.E. 1977. Enactment processes in organizations. In *New directions in organizational behaviour*, ed. B.M. Staw and G.R. Salancik, 267–300. Chicago, IL: Saint Clair.

Weick, K.E. 1979. *The social psychology of organizing*, 2nd ed. New York, NY: McGraw-Hill.

Whitehead, A.N. 1929/1978. *Process and reality: An essay in cosmology*. Corrected edition D.R. Griffin and D.W. Sherburne. Cambridge: Cambridge University Press.

Whitehead, A.N. 1933/1961. *Adventures of ideas*. Harmondsworth: Penguin.

Williamson, O.E. 1975. *Markets and hierarchies: Analysis and antitrust implications*. New York, NY: Free Press.

Chapter 8
Aristotelian Corporate Governance

Alejo José G. Sison

Contents

Introduction

Elsewhere (cf. Fontrodona and Sison 2006; Sison 2007, 2008), I had laid out and argued against the different theories that configure today's dominant conception of the firm, its assumptions regarding human beings and their behavior, and the corporate governance model it proposed. According to the neoclassical paradigm (cf. Roberts 2004), further enriched with contributions from transaction cost economics (cf. Coase 1937), shareholder theory (cf. Friedman 1970) and agency theory (cf. Jensen and Meckling 1976), the firm is fundamentally a nexus of contractual relationships between shareholder-principals and manager-agents for the purpose of maximizing the value of the shareholder-principals' investments.

These doctrines imply that human beings are, before anything else, economic agents, fully constituted as individuals, that is, independent of all social bonds. They manifest rationality precisely by choosing, among available options, those which promises the highest returns in terms of utility. Although in the end, utility – money

A.J.G. Sison (✉)
Professor of Philosophy, University of Navarre, Pamplona, Spain
e-mail: ajsison@unav.es

A. Brink (ed.), *Corporate Governance and Business Ethics*, Ethical Economy.
Studies in Economic Ethics and Philosophy 39, DOI 10.1007/978-94-007-1588-2_8,
© Springer Science+Business Media B.V. 2011

or power – requires transformation into pleasure or psychological satisfaction in order to actually benefit human beings, it is nevertheless posited as the supreme good or object of desire. Human actions are to be evaluated solely on the basis of consequences, in particular, their usefulness in bringing about states of satisfaction. Just like any other organization, the business firm functions as the result of more or less coordinated individual actions. The key to corporate governance, therefore, lies in subverting through contracts the utility of other agents (mainly managers) so much so that it becomes aligned with the interests of shareholders.

Very few of the different premises that served to support the neoclassical theory of the firm would be of use in articulating an Aristotelian version of the corporate common good and corporate governance. The main reason is that the kind of activity they describe does not qualify, strictly speaking, as human action (*praxis*). At most, it belongs to the category of artisanal production (*poiesis*, *techne*) in Aristotle's own classification or theory of action. It refers to activities befitting slaves or guest foreign workers – no matter how knowledgeable or expert they may be – but not free men or citizens, in accordance with the characteristics of the social classes in Aristotelian politics. These activities are carried out primarily for the production of an external good, a material object or service (extended to mean utility, profit or shareholder value) and not for the agent himself, his technical, intellectual, cultural or moral growth and improvement (in a word, virtues).

Much has already been said, by way of criticism, of the individualism, utilitarianism, and consequentialist reasoning deeply embedded in the neoclassical economic conception of the firm. Similarly, much has been written with regard to the corollary theories of why production should be carried out in the firm instead of the market, how the relationship between capital providers and manager-employees should be framed, and what the firm's overarching purpose ought to be. Certainly, transaction cost economics could explain the existence of the firm vis-à-vis the market because of greater efficiency, and agency theory could provide an economic and legal template for the contract between workers and capitalists. But in themselves, they do not give reasons why efficiency should be measured in terms of shareholder value maximization, nor for the underlying social web that make contractual agreements possible. Although in the past, I myself have offered my own reading of these issues, this time, I would like to take a different focus. This paper intends to have a more constructive outlook and explain how Aristotelian corporate governance founded on the corporate common good might be conceived, taught and practiced.

In light of the foregoing, Aristotelian corporate governance requires a radical change of tack from conventional theories. I shall attempt to develop this broad theme in three major stages. First, I will render something that could pass for an Aristotelian theory of the firm, fully aware that Aristotle himself did not deal with such an institution in his writings. I will have to provide an account of the proper locus and purpose of the firm within the overall context of society. Secondly, I will offer, through an analogy with the common good of the *polis* or the state, an account of the common good of the firm. I will also propose ways in which the particular common good of the firm could be integrated or subordinated to the wider common good of the political community. Lastly, I will try to explain the theory and practice behind what could stand as Aristotelian corporate governance, one that seeks to achieve the corporate common good.

What Kind of Community Is the Firm?

The Firm as an Artificial and Imperfect Society, the Firm as an Intermediate Body

On account of their end or purpose, states are considered by Aristotle in the *Politics* to be "natural" and "perfect" societies. By contrast, therefore, modern day corporations could be characterized as examples of "artificial" and "imperfect" associations.

The state, like the family and the village, is a "natural" society, because it stems from an innate tendency in human beings (cf. Politics, henceforth Pltcs, p. 1252b). The family, which issues from the union of man and woman as husband and wife, is "natural" because it arises in response to a deeply felt need in human beings to leave behind living images of themselves in and through their children. The village, too, is "natural" because the human instinct for self-preservation requires that one look beyond the daily needs satisfied within the household to the requirements of a longer term of existence. The village – which includes children, grandchildren and other relatives by blood or marriage – is, in this sense, like a prolongation or extension of one's original family. Next down this line of "natural" institutions comes the state, which results from several villages being united in a single, complete community.

From among these three "natural" institutions, however, only the state is "perfect" because it alone is "self-sufficing" for the good life. Not only day to day needs, but also those of a life whole and entire can be expected to be met within the bounds of the state. Only in the state can human beings truly aspire to live a completely good life. The state thus represents the "end" or "final cause", the fully developed stage of human existence (cf. Pltcs, p. 1252b). For this reason, although the state may be considered chronologically posterior to both the family and the village, it is in reality prior to them:

> The proof that the state is a creation of nature and prior to the individual is that the individual, when isolated, is not self-sufficing; and therefore he is like a part in relation to the whole. (Pltcs, p. 1253a)

Individuals, then, just like the families and the villages they form, are like parts with respect to the whole represented by the state. Moreover, although nature has implanted in all human beings a social instinct, only in the state can this innate tendency be fully developed and perfected through the institutions of law and justice. Otherwise, outside of the state, human beings become the most savage and worst of animals (cf. Pltcs, p. 1253a).

Within the context of Aristotle's political architecture, just how does the firm fit? First of all, although Aristotle does not mention business firms and corporations in the *Politics*, we could find allusions to them in the "family connections, brotherhoods, common sacrifices and amusements" (Pltcs, p. 1280b) that draw human beings together. In contrast with the family and the village, and most importantly, with the state, the firm may be considered an "artificial" society because it arises neither directly nor organically from human nature. Rather, the firm is based on voluntary bonds of "friendship" – a foreshadowing of contracts – primarily among citizens of the same state. It is also called an "imperfect" society because it is not self-sufficing for the good life. A business corporation is an example of an "intermediate body or association" situated between individuals and their families, on the one hand, and the state, on the other. As such, it is not meant to substitute for the family in the provision of the daily needs for survival, nor the state as the proper locus of a full and flourishing human life. Rather, like all other intermediate bodies, its purpose is to supply some of the necessary means – in this particular case, goods and services – for the good life in the state (cf. Pltcs, p. 1280b).

The Economic End of the Firm

In the welter of intermediate bodies normally found in a healthy state, a special place is reserved for those that broadly seek economic ends, and it is among these that we include firms and business corporations. A primarily economic focus distinguishes businesses from other possible intermediate groups such as churches, professional colleges, sports associations, neighborhood councils, cultural clubs and the like. It's not that these other intermediate bodies lack any economic dimension or significance; it's just that such an economic dimension or significance is not their main concern, unlike firms and business corporations.

Business firms and corporations, then, are intermediate bodies that pursue economic goals. But what exactly are these goals?

Returning once more to Aristotle's *Politics*, we are told that the economy was born within the family, as "household management" (Pltcs, p. 1253b). His treatment of the economy in its original, etymological meaning of "household management" begins with a survey of the different parts necessary for a complete household and the relationships among them:

> [T]he first and fewest possible parts of a family are master and slave, husband and wife, father and children. We have therefore to consider what each of these three relations is and ought to be: I mean the relation of master and servant, the marriage relation (the conjunction of man and wife has no name of its own), and thirdly, the paternal relation (this also has no proper name). (Pltcs, p. 1253b)

Early in his discussion of the economy as household management, Aristotle distinguishes between the art of household management in itself and the art of getting wealth or chrematistics (cf. Pltcs, p. 1253b). In both arts, however, Aristotle acknowledges the difference between a natural and a non-natural form.

Natural chrematistics pertains to the provision of "such things necessary to life, and useful for the community of the family or state, as can be stored" (Pltcs, p. 1256b), whereas non-natural chrematistics of "riches and property [which] have no limit" (Pltcs, p. 1267a). Natural wealth-getting is based on the premise that true riches, the kind and amount of property needed for a good life, is not without limit. There is a level beyond which the mere accumulation of material things becomes more of a nuisance or a liability to human flourishing than an advantage or help. Nowadays, one could think of having more cars than could fit in the garage, or more foodstuffs than the refrigerator could store, for example.

Non-natural wealth-getting, on the other hand, believes that "more is always better" and that for the good of the economy there should be no stop in piling up possessions. Although the example may be a bit dated, by non-natural wealth-getting Aristotle referred primarily to retail trade and exchange, which allowed one to accumulate riches in the form of money or coin, practically without limit. But,

> coined money is a mere sham, a thing not natural, but conventional only, because, if users substitute another commodity for it, it is worthless, and because it is not useful as a means to any of the necessities of life, and, indeed, he who is rich in coin may often be in want of necessary food. But how can that be wealth of which a man may have great abundance and yet perish with hunger (. . .)? (Pltcs, p. 1257b)

Somehow we can still relate to the situation Aristotle describes if we imagine ourselves in a foreign country without the proper currency or where our credit cards are not honored. Whatever wealth or money we think we have is rendered useless, unable to pay even for a piece of bread.

However, the art of household management or economy properly speaking seems to refer more to the use of property rather than to its acquisition, Aristotle implies. Once again, in the use of property or its corresponding art we ought to differentiate between the natural or proper and the non-natural or improper. Take the case of a shoe: if it is used for wear, one makes a proper use, while if it is used for exchange, one makes an improper use, "for a shoe is not made to be an object of barter" (Pltcs, p. 1257a). The proper use of any material possession acknowledges a limit or a further end that makes the activity honorable, whereas its improper use is void of limit and thus becomes censurable. To illustrate this unnatural and inappropriate use of wealth – once more, within the context of a primitive economy – Aristotle points out to

> usury, which makes a gain out of money itself (. . .). For money was intended to be used in exchange, but not to increase at interest. (Pltcs, p. 1258b)

It is important to realize that, both in the acquisition and the use of wealth, the difference between the natural and the non-natural depends more on the dispositions of human beings than on the material things themselves (cf. Pltcs, pp. 1257b–1258a). Unbridled desires, the want of wealth and pleasure or enjoyment untutored by virtue, lead human beings to non-natural forms of getting and using material possessions. This way, unbeknownst to them, their search for happiness or flourishing becomes self-defeating. Failure then won't be the fault of the material things but of their own vices.

Speaking about the non-natural art of chrematistics or wealth-getting in which business firms and corporations ultimately engage, Aristotle states that in the first community, indeed, which is the family, this art is obviously of no use, but it begins to be useful when the society increases. For the members of the family originally had all things in common. (Pltcs, p. 1257b)

The next stage, characterized by a still natural form of chrematistics, begins when the family grows and becomes big enough to be

divided into parts, the parts shared in many things, and different parts in different things, which they had to give in exchange for what they wanted, a kind of barter (. . .); giving and receiving wine, for example, in exchange for corn, and the like. (Pltcs, p. 1257a)

Finally, non-natural chrematistics inevitably takes place when a society's needs become more complex. Together with it comes the widespread use of money and the establishment of the first businesses or firms. As Aristotle relates,

[W]hen the inhabitants of one country became more dependent on those of another, and they imported what they needed, and exported what they had too much of, money necessarily came into use. (Pltcs, p. 1257a)

These new functions resulting from the development of the economy and society can only be carried out effectively by larger organizations such as corporations or firms, understood as extensions of the family or "economic friendships" (Pltcs, p. 1280b).

Insofar as business firms and corporations play a role in the production of goods and services, they operate within the realm of wealth-getting or chrematistics. And inasmuch as business firms and corporations are artificial societies, they are meant as a help or complement to the material resources that nature, in principle, ought to provide. In other words, the activity of business firms and corporations forms part of the so-called non-natural chrematistics. What is clear by Aristotle's reckoning is that business firms and corporations only fulfil a subordinate or secondary function in the economy, which

attends more to men than to the acquisition of inanimate things, and to human excellence more than to the excellence of property which we call wealth, and to the excellence of freemen more than to the excellence of slaves. (Pltcs, p. 1259b)

That is to say, the main purpose of the economy is to facilitate the development of human excellence or virtue by guaranteeing – to the extent possible – the material conditions for its practice. And virtue, in turn, is sought primarily because it affords us happiness, a good, flourishing life.

Getting back to our initial query of how business firms and corporations fit in the state, we can now say, in accordance with Aristotle's teachings, the following: As a class of artificial intermediate bodies, business firms and corporations belong to the realm of the economy. In particular, their purpose is the non-natural acquisition or provision of material goods beyond the capabilities of the family. Resulting from a variant of the art of wealth-getting or chrematistics, business firms and corporations should be subject to the superior art of the economy itself, which consists in the administration and use of material goods. All economic activity in turn – and the institutions it gives rise to, such as business firms or corporations and the market – should function under the guidance of ethics, which is the "practical science" or art of virtue. The economy has as its mission to facilitate the practice of virtue by establishing favorable material conditions among the citizens of a state. And virtues, in the final analysis, are sought insofar as they help us attain happiness or a flourishing life in the state, under the tutelage of politics.

Only within this hierarchy of disciplines and institutions, each one with its own proper object, can the true role of business firms and corporations within society be ascertained. Because "the end of the state is the good life, and these [i.e., family connections, brotherhoods, common sacrifices, and amusements, and by extension, firms] are the means towards it" (Pltcs, p. 1280b). The economic ends that corporations seek are simply means to the political end that city-states for their part propose. The production of goods and services which is the purpose of business corporations and firms is not at all self-justifying. It is desirable and acquires meaning only insofar as it contributes to a flourishing life in the state. Later on, we shall have the occasion to draw from here implications for the proper governance of business corporations and firms.

The Common Good of the Firm

The Political Common Good and the Corporate Common Good

The notion of the common good was initially formulated by Aristotle with reference to the *polis*. It is none other than *eudaimonia* or the full flourishing of human beings as citizens of the well-ordered *polis*. To the extent that he was Aristotle's follower and commentator, Thomas Aquinas was met with the challenge of making room for the Judeo-Christian God within the general notion of the common good, while keeping intact the aspect of human flourishing. Largely through the use of analogy, he was able to make the connection between God and human fulfilment, conveniently recast as *beatitudo* or blessedness. As heir to Aristotelian and Thomistic teachings on the common good, the Catholic Church's social doctrine develops the concept further by highlighting its historical conditioning or determination. Modern scholars have likewise proposed a hierarchical structure or guide through which the political common good could be attained, under varying socioeconomic and cultural circumstances.

However, the crucial link that renders possible the inception of a common good proper to the firm as an intermediate body and the political common good is the Church's teaching on work. Despite using Aristotelian and Thomistic terminology, the content is radically new yet potent enough to meet all the requirements that have so far been established. This will be the ground of what I hope to explain as an Aristotelian-inspired theory of the firm, and consequently, an Aristotelian-inspired theory of corporate governance as well.

Aristotle and the Common Good of the Polis

What is the "good"? In the opening lines of the Nicomachean Ethics, Aristotle defines the good as "that at which everything aims" (Nicomachean Ethics, henceforth NE, p. 1094a), the end of a given appetite, desire, inclination, or tendency. Basing himself on Aristotle, Aquinas explains that the good perfects being not only by way of knowledge, as with the truth, but also in reality, as the best state of being in itself (cf. De Veritate, q. 21, a. 1, c).[1] Elsewhere he teaches that the good is an aspect of all being, insofar as it is an object of desire, is perfect, and in act (cf. Summa Theologiae, henceforth ST, I, q. 5, a. 1, c).[2] We call something "good", therefore, inasmuch as it is or exists and in the measure that it has reached its end or perfection, being able to transmit this perfection to others.

And what about the "common good"? For Aristotle, the common good has to do with the *polis*:

> [T]he good of the *polis* is apparently a greater and more complete good to acquire and preserve. For while it is satisfactory to acquire and preserve the good even for an individual, it is finer and more divine to preserve it for a people and for *poleis* [the plural form of *polis*]. (NE, p. 1094b)

The common good, the good of the *polis,* is thus explained in contrast to the exclusive good of the individual, which is inferior. Aquinas is even more explicit in his commentary on the Nichomachean Ethics: the common good as a cause is "more divine because it shows greater likeness to God, who is the ultimate cause of all good" (Commentary on the Ethics, henceforth Comm., I, 2, 30).[3]

Apart from the common good and the good exclusive to an individual, we find in the Nicomachean Ethics yet another classification of goods: those pursued in themselves and those pursued because of another. Aristotle indicates that a good pursued in itself is always better because it is complete (cf. NE, p. 1097a). Among the different possible goods pursued in themselves, *eudaimonia* or "happiness", a flourishing human life, stands out as most choiceworthy, complete and self-sufficient (cf. NE, p. 1097b). This self-sufficiency, however, needs clarification:

> not what suffices for a solitary person by himself, living an isolated life, but what suffices also for parents, children, wife and in general for friends and fellow-citizens, since a human being is a naturally political [animal]. (NE, p. 1097b)

Thus, *eudaimonia* consists in a good life in common, shared with one's family, friends and fellow-citizens in the *polis*. Not only is this the supreme human good but it is also the common good.

By and large, Aristotle's Politics is nothing else but a treatise on how full human flourishing can be achieved within the *polis* (cf. Pltcs, p. 1252a). This depends on the manner in which the *polis* is governed. The plurality of political regimes is a function of the number of people who govern and, more importantly, for whose good, advantage or interest they govern. In this respect,

> governments which have a regard to the common interest [*sumpheron koinon*] are constituted in accordance with strict principles of justice, and are therefore true forms; but those which regard only the interest of the rulers are all defective and perverted forms, for they are despotic, whereas a *polis* is a community of freemen. (Pltcs, p. 1279a)

---

[1] "Q. 21" refers to the 21st question of "De Veritate", "a. 1" to the first article of the respective question, and "c" to the *responsio* or body (corpus) of this article.

[2] "I" refers to the first part (*prima pars*) of the Summa Theologiae.

[3] Book I, chapter 2, § 30.

Further specifications are made, such that true forms of government are divided into "monarchies", "aristocracies", and "constitutional rules", when only one, a few, and many rule, respectively (cf. Pltcs, pp. 1279a-b). In a similar way, with the defective forms of government, one can distinguish among "tyrannies", "oligarchies" and "democracies", depending on the number of rulers:

> For tyranny is a kind of monarchy which has in view the interest of the monarch only; oligarchy has in view the interest of the wealthy; and democracy, of the needy: none of them the common good [*agathon koinon*] of all. (Pltcs, p. 1279b)

The regard for the common good, therefore, serves as criterion for determining whether a *polis* is properly governed and achieves its goal of *eudaimonia*.

A few explanations are in order concerning the expression *sumpheron koinon*, "common interest or advantage", which Aristotle prefers, and *agathon koinon*, "common good", which he uses rather sparingly. (Aquinas, for his part, also speaks of *utilitas communis*, "common utility", and *bonum commune*, "common good", quite indistinctly.) Unlike their translations into modern English and most other European languages contaminated by utilitarian thinking, nothing in the original texts deters us from understanding both terms as synonymous. Michael A. Smith, in an excellent monograph, suggests that Aristotle employed *sumpheron koinon*, "common interest or advantage", to distance himself from the Platonic Idea of the Good:

> [T]he good, for Aristotle, is the good of someone or something. The common good is the good of all members of a political community once these members have actualized their disposition to live in common. They organize themselves in view of the good which political life can provide them, they enjoy the advantages of life in common. And these advantages can vary from one period of time to another, and also from one place to another. (Smith 1995, p. 63)

The common good which Aristotle proposes is concrete, contingent in time and place, and specific to a *polis*. That's why he declares, in allusion to Platonic doctrine, that "even if the good predicated in common is some single thing, or something separated, itself in itself, clearly it is not the sort of good a human being can pursue in action or possess" (NE, p. 1096b). Knowing fully well that such notion of the good would have been unconscionable for Plato, nonetheless Aristotle as a philosopher insists that "it presumably seems better, indeed only right, to destroy even what is close to us if that is the way to preserve the truth" (NE, p. 1096a).

How do individuals in the *polis* relate to the common good? They share or take part in the common good through citizenship. In the Politics, Aristotle introduces the institution of citizenship upon observing that the "*polis* is composite, [and] like any other whole [is] made up of many parts – these are the citizens, who compose it" (Pltcs, p. 1274b).

According to Aristotle, "a citizen in the strictest sense" is he who "shares in the administration of justice, and in offices" (Pltcs, p. 1275a). The essential task of the citizen is to participate in deciding what is good and just in the *polis* and in putting this into effect. A citizen is a "juryman and member of the assembly", to whom "is reserved the right of deliberating or judging about some things or about all things" (Pltcs, p. 1275b). Although many people in a *polis* may actually participate in the process of deliberating and deciding on the common good, only citizens do so by right. What characterizes a citizen, therefore, is "the power to take part in the deliberative or judicial administration of any *polis*" (Pltcs, p. 1275b). This does not mean, however, that a citizen always has to hold public office. It suffices that he at least has the power to occupy such a post, for citizenship requires "sharing in governing and being governed" (Pltcs, p. 1283b). The common good is the product of the joint deliberation, decision and action of the citizens of a *polis*.

To the extent that citizens are involved in deciding the common good and in dispensing justice, they are like the soul, the most important element in the *polis*. Aristotle states that

> as the soul may be said to be more truly part of an animal than the body, so the higher parts of the *polis*, that is to say, the warrior class, the class engaged in the administration of justice, and that engaged in deliberation, which is the special business of political understanding – these are more essential to the *polis* than the parts which minister to the necessaries of life. (Pltcs, p. 1291a)

Certainly, citizenship affords one the possibility to participate in the common good, preeminently in government, by deliberating and administering justice; although it does not in fact guarantee an equal share for all.

In summary, for Aristotle, the common good is the good of the *polis* and of each and every citizen. Another name for it is *eudaimonia,* which is also man's highest good because of his social nature. In the study of politics, the common good of the *polis* is the criterion for distinguishing true, just or constitutional regimes from false, perverse or despotic rules. By virtue of their citizenship, human beings are able to participate in the common good, primarily – though not exclusively – by sharing in government or the administration of justice.

Aquinas on God as the Common Good

What modifications does Aquinas introduce to the Aristotelian understanding of the common good? Being a Christian philosopher, Aquinas could no longer accept the earthly *polis* as the highest community to which human beings belong and in which they achieve their ultimate perfection. Because of this, he was somewhat forced to elaborate a richer conception of the common good that could, above all, accommodate God and communion with Him. He was able to do this through the use of analogy, although he himself did not elaborate an analogy of the common good, properly speaking. However, in every one of the terms to which he applies the "common good", its fundamental nature as the good of the whole and of each of its parts remains unchanged (cf. Froelich 1989, p. 42).

In a short theological treatise describing the perfection of the spiritual life, Aquinas writes,

> [I]n this community by which all people agree on happiness as an end, each and every man is considered as a certain part: but the common good of the whole is God himself, in whom consists the happiness of all. (De perfectione vitae spiritualis, c. 13, n. 634)[4]

---

[4] Chapter 13, note 634.

For Aquinas, God is not only the common end or perfection of every human being and of the whole human species, but He is also the ultimate cause of all good. Such an affirmation, of course, concurs with Aquinas' idea of God as the supreme being.

What's the relation between God and other common goods, such as *eudaimonia* in the earthly *polis*? Among the different terms to which the expression "common good" applies in Aquinas, one could establish an analogy of proportionality (cf. Smith 1995, pp. 72ff.). "Common good" refers more properly to a final cause than to a mere logical predicate. There are at least two ways in which the "common good" acts as a final cause or common end of the whole human species and of every human being: first, in the case of God, as an extrinsic, ontological and speculative common good and second, in the case of *eudaimonia* in the earthly *polis*, as an intrinsic, social and practical common good. The first fulfills the nature of the common good better and on it depends the second, as we shall later on see. To the second, *eudaimonia* as the political common good, are subordinated the *bona communia* (cf. Comm., I, 7, 95), the means or instruments for its preservation.

The *bona communia* constitute an "integral whole" which, in turn, could be divided into formal or material parts and, subsequently, into act or potency. For example, water in a public reservoir is an "integral whole" divisible into material parts as a common good in potency. It never really is a good unless it has already been divided and distributed among the many different persons who use it for drinking or washing. Insofar as the quantity of water diminishes as it is divided and distributed, this "integral whole" is composed of material parts. And in the measure that the water one uses for drinking or washing cannot be used by another, this "integral whole" cannot be a common good in act, but only in potency. In this sense, water is one of the *bona communia*, the material and potential common goods that are to be distributed as means or instruments in accordance with distributive justice among the members of the *polis*.

A different "integral whole" is that instantiated by a well-functioning *polis*, characterized by the rule of justice and law, where each citizen is a formal-rational part that cannot be replaced by another (unlike material parts). Inasmuch as each human being already is a substantial unity, together they could only form unities of order as the family or the *polis*. And to the extent that a flourishing life in common or *eudaimonia* is the good sought in the *polis*, it never is simply a potential common good, but always an actual one. Furthermore, due to the uniqueness of every human being, no one could be substituted by another, strictly speaking, in the family, *polis* or any other group.

Notice that *eudaimonia* does not diminish as the number of citizens who participate in it increases; on the contrary, it becomes even greater. In this regard, *eudaimonia* is similar to what has come to be known in modern economic theory as a "public good" or a "collective consumption good", characterized by nonrivalrous and nonexcludable consumption (cf. Samuelson 1954). Unfortunately, precisely because of these traits, these goods encourage free-riding and chronic underinvestment.

Since all intrinsic orders – such as the family, the *polis* or the whole universe, for that matter – necessitate an extrinsic cause, they cannot but point to a separate being as their final cause and ultimate end. This separate being which, in a sense, is its own cause and explains and causes all other intrinsic orders in the universe is God himself; He is their common good, end and perfection. From the viewpoint of human beings as rational creatures, God alone is the extrinsic, ontological and speculative common good: "extrinsic" because he is separate from the whole universe as its primary cause; "ontological" because he is a being unto himself rather than a mere unity of order; and "speculative" because he is not produced by human action but is instead the object of contemplation. For Aquinas, this contemplation of God is the supreme human good, the only true *eudaimonia* and common good *par excellence*.

In Aquinas' teaching, therefore, we find a correspondence between the common good in predication and the common good which refers to a "universal whole", between the common good as an extrinsic cause and God as the common good referred to as a "potential whole", and between the common good as an intrinsic cause and *eudaimonia* as the common good referred to as a "integral whole" in which citizens themselves participate as the formal and actual parts by means of the *bona communia* as the material and potential parts.

The analogy of the common good developed in Aquinas' teaching allows for the usage of the term in other contexts aside from the *polis*. The common good could be employed in reference to God or to the order in the universe, for example. God as the common good becomes the highest object of contemplation not only for a privileged few, as in the Aristotelian *polis*, but for every human being, at least, potentially. The common good could also be used with regard to the family, specifically, to the children as the common good of both spouses (cf. Smith 1995, p. 76; Walshe 2006, p. 242). Husband and wife come together for the purpose of begetting children and educating them. Each child is a good of the father only insofar as it is also a good of the mother, and a child's being a good for each parent is inseparable from its being a good for both spouses. Neither parent can beget a child alone; yet that it has been begotten by both does not diminish each parent's participation in the child's generation: the "mine" and the "yours" of each spouse are inextricably fused into the "ours" of both parents. In the family as in the *polis*, the dynamics of the common good is the same.

After all of these clarifications, we are now in a position to identify the common good of the firm: the production of goods and services in which human beings participate through work. From the Aristotelian viewpoint, this is the good of the firm as an intermediate association and of each of its members; collectively, it is also their highest good. In the measure that the firm achieves this goal, it fulfils its purpose or function: it is a "good firm", well-governed and makes its members good. And in the same way that citizens participate in the common good of the *polis* or state by exercising their citizenship, that is, by engaging in joint political deliberation, decision and action, workers participate in the common good of the firm by carrying out their productive activity in common.

From the Thomistic perspective, this common good of the firm may be described as intrinsic, social and practical. It is "practical" because it refers to productive work, the activity realized by the members of the firm; "social" because it cannot be achieved by any single member but depends on the coordinated effort of a community of persons; and "intrinsic" because it is internal to the firm and cannot exist independently of it. This common good of the firm could also be described as an "integral whole" wherein workers are "formal" and "actual" parts. Workers are "actual" parts because, strictly speaking, they realize the common good of the firm only when they carry out their productive activity on its behalf and not in their other endeavors. And they are "formal" parts because they engage in their work as free, intelligent and unique agents which could never really be replaced or substituted by others. The "material" and "potential" parts of the common good of the firm as an "integral whole" would analogously refer to the sum total of nonpersonal conditions, resources, instruments and means that make work and production possible.

Notice that our definition of the common good of the firm does not relate, at first hand, to the goods and services in themselves, as material, tangible or objective realities. The common good of the firm does not lie primarily in these material things, but in their production, in the joint effort or work of a group of human beings. That production, joint activity or work in common, then, is the reason people come together and constitute the firm as an intermediate community. Certainly their activity does not take place in a void, as if they were pure spirits. Material resources and conditions are needed, but they share more directly in the work that produces the goods and services than in the resulting goods and services as such. For example, maintenance personnel at a university do not deliver lectures, but they participate in the collective effort that allows the university as an institution to teach. In a direct manner, teaching is incumbent only upon professors.

The emphasis on production instead of the goods and services produced is because the common good of the firm is, first and foremost, a network of activities, a host of practices; it is work in common. To be sure, work consists in a purposive and free human act (cf. NE, p. 1111a), although not all purposive and free human acts qualify as work. Rather, work is normally reserved to designate productive actions exclusively (cf. NE, pp. 1139a–b). Productive actions are those which focus on concrete, individual objects, with a view to changing or transforming them. They differ from pure theory or abstract thought, which simply aims at uncovering or reflecting what is universal and necessary in reality.

Work is a form of activity, and activities themselves are ideally of two kinds: making (*poiesis*) or doing (*praxis*) (cf. Pltcs, p. 1254a). In Aristotle's time, productive work was identified with *poiesis* and, as such, it was not the sort of activity in which citizens would engage. Rather, it was reserved for slaves and foreign workers. During Aquinas' time, however, the intellectual activity (study, preaching or lecturing, akin to *praxis*) carried out by the members of the Mendicant Orders came to be recognized as a form of spiritual work (cf. De opere manuali, a. 2; Contra impugnantes Dei religionem et cultum, c. 5). The radical separation between *poiesis* and *praxis*, therefore, started to disappear, and with it came a growing cognizance of the double nature of work. This insight has reached its most advanced stage of development in the Church's Social Doctrine.

Each time a human being acts on previously existing matter, two different results can be expected. The first is an objective result, usually something capable of independent existence from the human agent, or at least, something that manifests itself externally and is observable by others. The second is a subjective result that inheres in the agent himself and is inseparable from him; it need not show itself directly to the outside, although it would have consequences in his actions.

Examples of making (*poiesis*) would be the crafts (*techne*) and the fine arts (cf. NE, p. 1174a). What is important in making is the external object itself, considered as a work of art or craft, with the skill of the artist or artisan taking second place. How does one differentiate between the work of an artisan and that of an artist? Whereas the rule or norm for craftsmanship is external to production itself, in the fine arts, it is internal. In the crafts, the procedure or steps to be taken could, in principle, be externally observed and expressed in instructions or guidelines. In theory, by following an instructions manual for crafts, anyone could obtain guaranteed results. In the fine arts, however, no such set of instructions or guarantee exists. Instead, the rule is heuristic and idiosyncratic to each work of art. That is why objects belonging to the crafts could be mass-produced, while those belonging to the fine arts are unique.

The other kind of activity that focuses on the subjective result is what we normally call doing (*praxis*). As an activity, it is more immanent or reflexive than transient or transitive; it proceeds from the agent and ends in himself, not in an external object. The human being is, at the same time, agent and patient of the production process. In a remarkable sense, we are before a process of "self-production", where man is maker (*homo faber*) of himself. The main result of doing is not an artifact, but an operative moral habit or virtue. Through the acquisition of virtues, the process of "self-production" becomes, at the same time, a process of self-perfection. While making is guided by the skills either of craftsmanship or of a fine art, doing is guided above all by the habit of prudence, practical reasoning or practical wisdom.

Nowadays, we understand that making and doing are two inseparable dimensions present in any form of work or productive human activity. In theory, one could choose to put a greater emphasis on the external result (making or *poiesis*) than on the internal result (doing or *praxis*). As said earlier, for Aristotle, this would be the case with the productive or working class. Not being citizens, they participate very limitedly in the political common good. This alternative, however, would be inconsistent with the principles of the Church's social teaching which, aside from acknowledging the fundamental equality among all human beings, also grants primacy to the internal or subjective dimension of work over its external or objective dimension (cf. Laborem exercens, section 6; Compendium of the Social Doctrine of the Church, henceforth CSDC, pp. 270f.). For Aristotle, this would only be possible for the elite, made up of citizens engaged in leisure, democratic deliberation and contemplation.

We have now come to realize that human beings are always more important than the things they produce. And although in the course of their work they have a chance to develop the skills of craftsmanship and the fine arts, these are secondary in importance to the moral virtues they could acquire. Work is not a mere commodity for economic exchange or a simple factor of productivity.

The common good of the firm is the work in common that allows human beings not only to produce goods and services (the objective dimension), but more importantly to develop technical, artistic and moral virtues (the subjective dimension). Among the latter, entrepreneurial initiative, creativity and cooperation deserve special mention (cf. CSDC, p. 336).

Aside from the productive activity *per se*, working in a firm also serves as an occasion for meaningful exchange, relationship and encounter among human beings. Because of its intrinsic social dimension (cf. CSDC, p. 273), work is, at the same time, the manner in which human beings participate in the firm. Participation through work is simultaneously a duty and a right. It is a duty insofar as every human being is expected to contribute to the development of economic, cultural, political and social life (cf. CSDC, p. 189). And it is a right because work enables human beings to share not only in a firm's profits, but also, to the extent possible, in its management and ownership (cf. CSDC, p. 281).

Participation in the common good of the firm is, therefore, not limited to the shareholders only, as the dominant financial theory of the firm suggests (cf. Friedman 1970), but it is also open to other stakeholders or interest groups (cf. Freeman 1984). Shareholders participate in the measure that the financial resources they contribute represent their accumulated or capitalized work, put at the service of the firm. We could proceed analogously with each and every stakeholder group, tracing their participation through the work they perform: employees, customers, suppliers, competitors and so forth (cf. Sison 2008, pp. 86–93). There is a hierarchy, however, to be observed among them such that persons take precedence over non-persons, such as the environment, and direct stakeholders over indirect stakeholders. Management workers who, at the same time, have equity stakes in the firm are the best positioned to contribute, achieve and benefit from the common good of the firm.

Effective participation in the common good of the firm is never automatic. It requires the virtue of justice, both in its distributive and legal forms. Distributive justice refers to the duties and obligations of the whole – in this case, the firm – to its parts, while legal justice spells out the duties and obligations of the parts – primarily, workers and other stakeholders – to the whole. Distributive justice demands, for instance, paying a just wage, while legal justice requires that workers dedicate their best efforts to the firm and that they take care of its resources. In a relationship, duties and obligations of one party always correspond to the rights of another. So to insist on the fulfilment of duties and obligations necessarily entails the respect and observance of rights, both in the personal as well as in the institutional levels. Yet to conceive the whole gamut of personal and institutional relationships taking place in the firm exclusively in terms of rights and responsibilities would be an impoverished view. For justice and law can only prescribe minimum conditions, not the states of excellence or perfection in virtue, that should be pursued.

Moreover, for a firm to fulfil its common good, it is necessary that the goods and services produced in common be truly useful, that is, that they satisfy the legitimate needs and wants of people in the market. Production or work in common must also seek to make the best use of the limited resources available; in other words, it should strive to be efficient. Only then can businesses be able to comply with their social function of contributing to the wider common good, by observing economic discipline while at the same time upholding superior values (cf. CSDC, p. 338).

The Structure of the Corporate Common Good of the Firm and Subsidiarity

In an insightful commentary Millán-Puelles (1971) speaks of the political common good in the Church's social teaching as a hierarchical structure composed of three levels. These levels are, from the lowest to the highest, material well-being, peace and concord, and cultural values widely construed. Material well-being should not be confused with the material goods necessary for it. Rather, it is the satisfaction that one derives from participating in such goods. Material goods – earlier referred to as *bona communia* – are external means or instruments that lead to a sense of satisfaction or well-being. Surprisingly, satisfaction or well-being in itself is not material. This is, of course, consistent with the view of the human being as a substantial unity composed of body and soul. Material well-being forms part of the common good because it is necessary that each and every member of society has sufficient means for a decent life. It is not simply a matter of meeting the biological requirements for survival, but of making social life and acts of virtue possible (cf. Rerum novarum, section 45).

The next level represented by peace and concord does not depend exclusively on material goods, although it demands a minimum of them. At the same time, there could even be an abundance of material goods without achieving material well-being, due to unjust distribution. A just distribution of material resources among the members of society is a requisite for there to be peace and concord. St. Augustine defines peace as the "tranquillity in order" (De civitate Dei, b. 19, c. 13)[5] experienced not by individuals alone but by the entire political community. Aquinas, for his part, describes concord as the condition when two men freely agree to something that is good for both, resulting in true peace (cf. ST II-II, q. 29, a. 3, ad 1). Concord cannot come about by fear, coercion, or imposition. This is not to say that there is no room for the use of force or violence in a society that adheres to the common good; only that force and violence are the prerogatives solely of the legitimate ruler in his role as guardian of justice (cf. ST II-II, q. 66, a. 8).[6] In the same way that material well-being is a condition for peace and concord, peace and concord are indispensable for human beings to be able to share and participate in superior cultural values.

Cultural values include a broad variety of technical, artistic, intellectual, ethical and spiritual goods. They may not present themselves with the same urgency as the two previous levels, but they are even more important for authentic human

---

[5] Book 19, chapter 13.

[6] "II-II" refers to the second part of the second part (*secunda secundae partis*) of the Summa Theologiae.

flourishing and perfection as they belong to a superior order. The reason we seek peace and concord is that they facilitate participation in these cultural values catering to the higher aspirations of human beings. And this should be the case for all members of society, not only for the elite.

Each of these levels is to be integrated into an organic, living whole, such that if any one were lacking, the other two would be unable to fulfil their function properly. There is a positive feedback loop among all three. Material well-being for all promotes peace and concord, but so do peace and concord promote material well-being for everyone. Peace and concord facilitate the realization of cultural values, but so do cultural values facilitate peace and concord. And the same relationship holds between material well-being and cultural values. Nonetheless, a hierarchical order still ought to be observed, such that the lower level is put at the service of the higher. Peace and concord certainly require the just distribution of material means among the populace. However, this should be done not simply to increase their material well-being but, above all, to further their spiritual and moral perfection.

This same three-level synthesis proposed by Millán-Puelles (1971) regarding the structure of the political common good could be applied to the corporate common good. In the case of the firm, material well-being refers to the factors or conditions that affect its economic viability and sustainability, such as profits. Profits are an indicator of how well the firm is doing, but their generation *per se* cannot be the purpose of the firm nor exhaust its common good (cf. Centesimus annus, section 43). Next, peace and concord would correspond to good governance or management practices, in establishing the right rules, procedures and structures. And finally, cultural values in a broad sense would encompass not only technical know-how but also artistic, ethical and spiritual values, including an openness to God that one can develop through the course of his work. Managers should constantly keep an eye on all three levels, instead of mistakenly thinking that enlightened governance practices would only matter once certain profit levels have been attained or that concerns for the further cultural development of workers must only be taken into account when labor relations are in smooth sailing. Often, solutions to problems in one level are to be found in the superior one, given the positive feedback loop among all three.

Having explained the content and structure of the corporate common good, we could now establish its relation to the political common good. The common good of the firm is a particular good with regard to the common good of the larger society. The appropriate relationship between the state or *polis* and an intermediate group such as the firm is one of "subsidiarity" (cf. CSDC, pp. 186f.). Given that both the state and firms have their own legitimate objectives and spheres of action, they owe each other mutual respect, notwithstanding the proper hierarchy between them which acknowledges the superiority of the state. There is a double dimension to the state's role with regard to business firms as intermediate associations. It is incumbent upon the state as the superior-order society to positively help, support and assist – even to promote and develop – lesser order intermediate bodies. Put negatively, the state should refrain from replacing or absorbing intermediate bodies such as firms and misappropriating their functions.

By encouraging the growth of firms as private initiatives, the state contributes to a healthy pluralism and diversity in society. The state should delegate to these groups tasks that they would carry out better by themselves, being in closer contact with the needs and desires of the people. Furthermore, by fostering the legitimate initiatives of intermediate groups, the state makes a more rational and efficient use of limited resources, focusing instead on matters that are of its exclusive competence, such as defense, foreign relations or the administration of justice. Subsidiarity guards against statism in its many forms, from excessive centralization or the usurpation of decision-making powers, through bureaucratization or the shirking of personal responsibility, to welfarism or paternalism. The principle of subsidiarity provides the most effective protection against a self-serving state, ensuring that the state serve its citizens and the institutions – such as business firms and corporations – they form.

We are confronted, therefore, by two different communities, each with its own common good. Business firms are artificial and imperfect intermediate associations seeking an economic goal, particularly, the non-natural acquisition or provision of material means for human flourishing. They are subordinated to the political community, the natural and perfect society which provides the context wherein human flourishing takes place. The common good of the firm, the production of goods and services in which human beings participate through work, becomes a particular good with respect to the common good of the political community, *eudaimonia* or human flourishing. However, the subordination of the firm to the state ought to be governed by the principle of subsidiarity.

In summary, business firms contribute to the political common good in two ways. One is through the goods and services (the objective dimension of the work in common) that satisfy human needs and wants and the other through the joint production effort itself (the subjective dimension), inasmuch as it provides an opportunity for workers to develop technical, artistic, moral and intellectual virtues. In consonance with the Aristotelian-Thomistic tradition, as well as with the Church's social teachings, the second contribution is superior to the first, although the first is a necessary condition to obtain the second.

Conclusion: Corporate Governance as Praxis and the Common Good

At this stage, one thing we have learned for sure: Corporate governance should not consist in the maximization of shareholder value nor in balancing conflicting stakeholder interests, but in seeking the common good of the firm. By the expression the "common good of the firm" we ought to understand "work carried out in common", insofar as it provides an opportunity for self-perfection through the acquisition of virtues (the subjective or *praxis* dimension) simultaneously with the production of goods and services that society needs (the objective or *poiesis* dimension). A hierarchy must be observed such that the subjective or *praxis* dimension always takes precedence over the objective or *poiesis* dimension of work, notwithstanding the inseparability of the two. Although the objective dimension better reflects the nature of the firm as an economic institution dedicated to the provision of goods and services beyond the capacities of the family, it nevertheless has to be subjected to both ethical (concerning virtue) and political (pertaining to happiness or flourishing) considerations, in line with Aristotelian-Thomistic thinking.

Another way of looking at the common good of the firm, in keeping with the Church's social doctrine, is through a triple-level structure suggested by Millán-Puelles (1971): the material well-being of constituents at the base, followed by good management practices that foster justice and harmony, topped by the nurturing of values and virtues. An important proviso for correctly understanding this structure, however, is that one should not wait until the requirements of each level are fully satisfied before attending to those of the next. Requirements are socially, historically and culturally conditioned and because of this never absolutely satisfied. Furthermore, it is by focusing on the demands of the superior level, often, that one is able to adequately address the needs of the inferior one. The higher level is not only the next destination, but it also acts as a guide for the previous one.

Similarly, the corporate common good should always be viewed with respect to the political common good. Despite its influence and relevance, the firm is but an artificial and imperfect body and in that regard inferior to both families and civil society or the state. Although modern society is largely dependent on firms to supply material or economic needs, firms in themselves cannot provide what human beings ultimately desire, that is, a full, flourishing life. Only wider civil society or the state could furnish that. This does not mean, of course, that the state should supplant firms; rather, it should help and encourage them, in accordance with the principle of subsidiarity.

In an important measure, my proposal on the common good of the firm transcends the original Aristotelian understanding of work as *poiesis,* that is, a purely productive activity not carried out by citizens which results in an external object. To some degree, it also goes beyond the Thomistic conception of work, specifically manual work, the value of which lies in helping us avoid the vice of idleness, in controlling lower bodily instincts, and in obtaining sustenance (cf. De opere manuali, a. 1). Although Aquinas, in his discussion, began to make room for the intellectual work, its value remained very much within the realm of the instrumental. In fact, the emphasis on the subjective or *praxis* dimension of work did not come in full force until several centuries later, with the publication of John Paul II's encyclical in 1981 (cf. Laborem exercens, sections 6–8). But none of this would have been possible without the conceptual ground-breaking accomplished by Aristotle and Aquinas' contributions.

If the common good of the firm consists in pursuing work in its two distinguishable but inseparable dimensions, while respecting the priority of the subjective aspect over the objective aspect, then corporate governance itself must be considered as an activity following the *praxis* model rather than the *poiesis* or technical model.

Corporate governance actually refers to a distinct and special form of politics, writ small, limited to an intermediate association (cf. Sison 2006). It is an instance of action, rather than of mere production. As such, corporate governance should be analyzed and evaluated on the basis of the changes it introduces in the agent himself, rather than in the agent's surroundings or physical environment. This means that in order to govern well, one needs, above all, to cultivate the excellences, character traits, or virtues (*aretai*) proper to a ruler. These are far more important than the rules, principles, or laws that he may later on set down. Not that a good governor could totally dispense with rules, but they are only secondary, to be considered once excellent character traits or virtues are in place. Granted that "rules are meant to be broken", only the ruler's virtue can ensure that the goods rules are supposed to protect are actually kept safe, even when the rules themselves are overrun. Furthermore, rules by themselves are useless or could even be harmful, unless they are properly interpreted and implemented. And the proper interpretation and implementation of rules depend on the moral and intellectual dispositions – ultimately, the virtues – of the governors or the people entrusted with this function.

Most other approaches consider governance as an activity belonging to the category of *poiesis* or production. In consequence, they are more concerned with the formulation of some sort of rule-book as the corresponding external product or object on which the success of the activity rests or should be judged. Their aim seems to be the creation of a fool-proof instructions manual on the task of good governance. There is an undue emphasis on the setting up of structures and the design of processes as if these carried the key. They tend to forget that the outcome of good governance cannot be separated from the internal or personal dispositions – in other words, virtues – of the agent. Firstly, it is impossible to perfectly codify a set of rules or institute infallible structures and processes. But even if that were not the case, their observance alone would not guarantee the desired results.

To perform a *praxis* such as governance well, beyond following the rules, the right intention and moral dispositions aside from the appropriate circumstances also have to be assured. For this, there is nothing better than the holistic education of the ruler in the virtues of mind and character. It is not that Aristotle holds written laws or principles in disdain. They certainly form a necessary bulwark against arbitrariness in the governor and exert a powerful influence in molding habit and custom amongst a people. Yet he still thinks that habit and custom are superior to the law. Except in the case of physical coercion, it is only from habit and custom that the law could draw force and strength. Whereas the excellence of *poiesis* is called technique or art, i.e., the right reason in production, such as the one used in the crafting of governance laws, structures, and procedures, that of *praxis* is called prudence, i.e., the right reason in action, i.e., the paramount virtue of the ruler or governor.

Indeed, prudence or practical wisdom is a character trait acquired through habit, appropriate mentoring, and discipleship, as well as a broad experience. Notwithstanding the doctrine regarding the "unity of the virtues", according to which any particular excellence in character requires all the others for its full development, prudence is said to encompass all the human virtues. Prudence, therefore, includes moderation or temperance, truthfulness, courage, and so forth; character traits indispensable for a good governor. It is demonstrated in the ability of individuals to judge particular situations on their merits and to act accordingly; not to be confused with the mechanical application of impersonal, purportedly general rules (cf. NE, p. 1141b). Such rules or laws would be valid perhaps in the realm of the physical and mathematical sciences, but not in human behavior, which being free is messy and unpredictable. If the good in human action is nevertheless to be sought, it should be done with an eye or certain sensitivity to the particular good of the people involved and to the contingency of circumstances (cf. NE, p. 1143b). None of these could be adequately covered by universal laws.

As Kane and Patapan (2006) have pointed out in their reflections on managerial reform, the development of prudence has been thwarted in most institutions and organizations,

> first, by the imposition of artificial external disciplines on decision making, such as those provided by a market (...); second, by a general technocratic approach to decision making (...); and third, by attempts to approach the problem in a counterproductive, piecemeal fashion. (ibid., p. 712)

Furthermore, they diagnose an even deeper cause for the current flaws in governance that digs its roots in Weber's analysis of bureaucracy: the substitution of prudence by the rational-legal structures of a purely instrumental form of rationality (cf. ibid.). These are defects glaringly present in the majority of corporate governance codes and literature on best practices. Emphasized are techniques, theories *du jour* on human behavior and decision making, and short term, tunnel vision objectives while the virtues are completely ignored.

Good governance should be understood primarily as the proper exercise of power and authority at the topmost level of an organization such as the business firm. It refers not so much to the "how", to the ways and means, the rules, structures and procedures to be implemented when exercising power and authority, as to the "what for", to the purpose or end of whoever exercises them. Such a question warrants a response based on a "good", particularly on the specific contribution to the "common good" of society as a whole that any corporation is meant to deliver. Here we find the ultimate justification for the existence of corporations.

The goods and services produced by the community of persons working in a firm figure in a whole, complex range of material and spiritual goods, internal and external goods, goods in themselves and instrumental goods, the one final good or end and the common good. In order to recognize or "perform" such goods and to assign them their proper place in the hierarchy in cases of conflict, virtue – pre-eminently, prudence – is needed. A merely physical or mechanical recognition and production or performance of these goods is not enough if they are to be articulated and seamlessly woven into the larger fabric of societal common good. That's why certain people, at one point or another, sometimes fail to acknowledge and therefore to heed the "calling" of a good yearning to be realized. More than anything else, it may be due to their lack of virtue. Excellence of character not only enables one to do things properly, technically and ethically speaking. It also allows him to detect the convenience or need for that good, when many other people of inferior virtue would nonchalantly pass it by, oblivious even of that good's existence. Virtue makes one perspicacious of goods to be achieved in any given circumstance.

Because virtue is needed not only to properly interpret and implement the rules of governance, but also to correctly identify and produce the goods involved, it becomes clear that the key to good governance ultimately lies in the education of the governors or rulers. Even the kind of regime dominant in an organization just amounts to a host of formal conditions that best allow for the proper on-going education in the virtues of the governors or rulers. Unless this principle is sufficiently acknowledged, all attempts at corporate governance reform will be, at best, superficial or cosmetic and, at worst, ruefully ineffective, as the already long list of reforms that have preceded it.

The possession of the virtues of mind and character, notably, of prudence, is crucial not only for the proper interpretation and implementation of rules, but also for the correct identification and production or performance of the goods that a corporation and its governors should seek, both personally and as a body. Hence, a true and effective corporate governance reform should start with the proper ethical and political education of a firm's directors or governors. Only when this condition is satisfied could any discussion regarding rules, structures, procedures, best practices and so forth meaningfully proceed.

References

Aristotle. 1985. *Nicomachean ethics* (trans: Irwin, T.). Indianapolis, IN: Hackett Publishing.

Aristotle. 1990. *The politics*. Ed. by S. Everson. Cambridge: Cambridge University Press.

Aquinas, T. 1953. De veritate. In T. Aquinas: *Quaestiones disputatae*, ed. R.M. Spiazzi, Vol. I. Taurini: Marietti.

Aquinas, T. 1954. De perfectione vitae spiritualis. In T. Aquinas: *Opuscula theologica*, ed. R.M. Spiazzi, Vol. II. Taurini: Marietti.

Aquinas, T. 1962. Commentary on the ethics (trans: Litzinger, C.I.). In *Medieval political philosophy*, ed. R. Lerner and M. Mahdi, 272–296. Ithaca, NY: Cornell University Press.

Aquinas, T. 1970. Contra impugnantes Dei religionem et cultum. In *Opuscula polemica pro mendicanti bus*, ed. T. Aquinas, Vol. 41 A. Rome: Ad Sanctae Sabinae, Commissio Leonina.

Aquinas, T. 1996. De opere manuali. In *Quaestiones de quolibet. Quodlibet VII*, ed. T. Aquinas, Vol. 25/2. Rome, Paris: Commissio Leonina-Éditions du Cerf.

Aquinas, T. 2006. In *Summa theologiae*, ed. English Province of the Order of Preachers. Cambridge: Cambridge University Press.

Augustine of Hippo. 1964. *The City of God (De Civitate Dei)* (trans: Walsh, G.G., and Honan, D.J.). Washington, DC: Catholic University of America Press.

Coase, R.H. 1937. The nature of the firm. *Economica* 4: 386–405.

Fontrodona, J., and A.J.G. Sison. 2006. The nature of the firm, agency theory and shareholder theory: A critique from philosophical anthropology. *Journal of Business Ethics* 66: 33–42.

Freeman, R.E. 1984. *Strategic management: A stakeholder approach*. Boston: Pitman.

Friedman, M. 1970. The social responsibility of business is to increase its profits. *The New York Times Magazine* 13 September 1970: 32–34.

Froelich, G. 1989. The equivocal status of bonum commune. *The New Scholasticism* 63: 38–57.

Jensen, M., and W. Meckling. 1976. The theory of the firm: Managerial behavior, agency costs and ownership structure. *Journal of Financial Economics* 3: 305–360.

John Paul II. 1981. Encyclical letter Laborem excercens. Vatican: Libreria Editrice Vaticana, http://www.vatican.va/holy_father/john_paul_ii/encyclicals/documents/hf_jp-ii_enc_14091981_laborem-exercens_en.html.

John Paul II. 1991. Encyclical letter Centessimus annus. Vatican: Libreria Editrice Vaticana, http://www.vatican.va/holy_father/john_paul_ii/encyclicals/documents/hf_jp-ii_enc_01051991_centesimus-annus_en.html.

Kane, J., and H. Patapan. 2006. In seach of prudence: The hidden problem of managerial reform. *Public Administration Review* 66: 711–724.

Leo XIII. 1891. Encyclical letter Rerum novarum. Vatican: Libreria Editrice Vaticana, http://www.vatican.va/holy_father/leo_xiii/encyclicals/documents/hf_l-xiii_enc_15051891_rerum-novarum_en.html.

Millán-Puelles, A. 1971. Bien común. In *Gran Enciclopedia Rialp*, ed. S.V. Villar, Vol. 4, 225–230. Madrid: Ediciones Rialp.

Pontifical Council for Justice and Peace. 2004. *Compendium of the social doctrine of the church*. Rome: Libreria Editrice Vaticana.

Roberts, J. 2004. *The modern firm: Organizational design for performance and growth*. New York: Oxford University Press.

Samuelson, P.A. 1954. The pure theory of public expenditure. *Review of Economics and Statistics* 36: 387–389.

Sison, A.J.G. 2006. Governance and government from an Aristotelian perspective. In *Global perspectives on ethics of corporate governance*, ed. G.J. (Deon) Rossouw and A.J.G. Sison, 77–89. New York, NY: Palgrave Macmillan.

Sison, A.J.G. 2007. Toward a common good theory of the firm: The Tasubinsa case. *Journal of Business Ethics* 74: 471–480.

Sison, A.J.G. 2008. *Corporate governance and ethics: An Aristotelian perspective*. Cheltenham: Edward Elgar.

Smith, M.A. 1995. *Human dignity and the common good in the Aristotelian-Thomistic tradition*. Lewiston, NY: Edwin Mellen.

Walshe, S. 2006. *The primacy of the common good as the root of personal dignity in the doctrine of Saint Thomas Aquinas*. Rome: Pontifical University of St. Thomas.

Chapter 9
Deliberative Democracy and Corporate Governance

Bert van de Ven and Wim Dubbink

Contents

Introduction

Since the 1990s there has been a movement within the field of business ethics to develop a political conception of corporate social responsibility (CSR). Relatively new concepts such as "corporate citizenship" (cf. Matten and Crane 2005a; Moon et al. 2005; Néron and Norman 2008; Wood and Logsdon 2002) and "stakeholder democracy" (cf. Driver and Thompson 2002; Matten and Crane 2005b) have been introduced to explore the new responsibilities of corporations. Even stronger than older concepts such as corporate social responsibility, these new concepts suggest that corporations have responsibilities that go above and beyond the responsibilities that they have towards their direct stakeholders (i.e., the stakeholders with which they have contractual relations.) Terms such as "corporate citizenship" and "stakeholder democracy" turn corporations – in some sense – into real members of their communities, where membership has its privileges, but also comes with responsibilities (cf. Néron and Norman 2008, p. 12). One such civic responsibility is to contribute to the betterment of the community through programs of corporate giving. Another points to the contribution of corporations in solving public problems

B. van de Ven (✉)
Assistant Professor, Department of Philosophy, Tilburg University, Tilburg, The Netherlands
e-mail: B.W.vdVen@uvt.nl

A. Brink (ed.), *Corporate Governance and Business Ethics*, Ethical Economy.
Studies in Economic Ethics and Philosophy 39, DOI 10.1007/978-94-007-1588-2_9,
© Springer Science+Business Media B.V. 2011

such as unemployment among minorities, the protection of the human rights of people in countries with a poor record in this respect, and so on. What interests us here, however, is that these new concepts also explicitly suggest that corporations have a political or procedural role to play. They have procedural duties, for example, in relation to the influence corporations may have on elections.

Focusing on the formal or procedural aspect of corporate citizenship, Néron and Norman maintain that a normative theory of corporate citizenship needs "a framework for deciding what sorts of political activities and relations with government regulators are appropriate or inappropriate, permissible or impermissible, obligatory or forbidden for corporations" (ibid., p. 15). Such a normative theory has been the focal point of German discussion on republican business ethics (cf. Steinmann and Löhr 1994; several contributions in Ulrich et al. 1999) and Scherer and Palazzo build on this earlier work. They contribute a more explicit discussion of the political dimension of corporations from the perspective of political philosophy (cf. Scherer and Palazzo 2007; Scherer et al. 2006). In particular, they use the Habermasian notion of "deliberative democracy" (cf. Habermas 1996, 1998; Dryzek 2000) to ground the politicized account of CSR (cf. Palazzo and Scherer 2006; Scherer and Palazzo 2007).

In this paper, we explore the implications of a political conception of CSR for corporate governance. We define corporate governance as the framework of rules and practices by which a board of directors ensures accountability, fairness, and transparency in the firms' relation with its stakeholders. Our focus is on the procedural aspect, that is, on the way a corporation can and should participate in political processes that relate to its business activities. We take the normative theory of deliberative democracy as a given, and we elaborate on its implications for corporate governance. Peter Ulrich has worked from the same normative starting point and we take his views on the subject as a stepping stone in working out our own position. Ulrich has described the implications of deliberative democracy for corporate governance in terms of a model, or blueprint, of corporate governance that transforms the current corporate governance system. We reject his radical or "strong" interpretation of the consequences of deliberative democracy for corporate governance, both materially and formally. Materially – or substantively – speaking we think that a less radical proposal is more in line with the possibilities of latter-day capitalism as well as with crucial normative aspects of thinking on deliberative democracy. We name this moderate proposal "stakeholder capitalism". This indicates that it does not presuppose a radical transformation of the corporate governance system, at least not in countries which have a coordinated market economy.

Our formal point can best be introduced by first raising and answering a skeptical question: is there practical room at all for corporate governance arrangements imbued by normative theories on deliberative governance? Here we side with Ulrich and others who believe in this possibility. We will substantiate our position with an analysis of recent sociological research in the field of comparative capitalisms. This research has given much attention to the German situation. This is particularly interesting for our purposes since the German model is typically viewed as the archetype of stakeholder capitalism (cf. Morgan et al. 2005) that leaves some room for a political conception of CSR, as compared to the Anglo-American model that leaves very little room or no room at all. We reject the view of authors such as Lane (2005, p. 85) who argue that due to an expected global convergence to the currently dominant Anglo-American model, the days of stakeholder capitalism are over.[1] Other research shows a more differentiated picture which allows for a hybridization of institutions from the stakeholder and stockholder models. However, the fact of hybridization also implies that Ulrich's attempt to define a model is, formally speaking, misplaced. An academic discussion of complex systems should show some pragmatic courtesy. It should not offer a model, but simply work out general principles for the development of a more democratized form of capitalism. We will limit our own contribution in exactly this way.

In the section "Habermas on Discourse Ethics and Deliberative Democracy", discourse ethics and the model of deliberative democracy as understood by Jürgen Habermas will be examined. In the section "Ulrich's Account of the Implications of Discourse Ethics for Corporate Governance", we will discuss Peter Ulrich's rather radical model of stakeholder democracy. In the section "Stakeholder Democracy and Varieties of Capitalism", we will consider the feasibility of (a more moderate model of) stakeholder democracy in the light of existing systems of corporate governance. Finally, in the section "Four Principles of Stakeholder Capitalism", we will spell out the implications of our moderate form of stakeholder capitalism in terms of normative principles of corporate governance.

Habermas on Discourse Ethics and Deliberative Democracy

We will ground our attempt to sort out the implications of political CSR in terms of corporate governance on the Habermasian theory of deliberative democracy. Habermas grounds deliberative democracy itself in discourse ethics. Central to discourse ethics is the idea of a free acceptance or rejection of validity claims raised in moral and ethical discourse (cf. Habermas 1991, pp. 100–118). According to Habermas, moral norms claim universal validity. They are accompanied by the claim that they deserve recognition by all those affected by the application of the moral

---

[1] The global economic crisis has led to a revaluation of the stakeholder model of capitalism, at least among many European politicians. In the current political climate, it is hard to imagine political support for any further convergence to one form of super-capitalism. The shareholder model has lost some of its attractiveness. This is especially the case since the focus on the maximization of shareholder value has been identified as one of the main causes behind the risk seeking attitude of professionals in finance. However, the arguments developed in this paper do not depend on the assumption that such a convergence is actually advancing. We assume that in many cases the national business system is a hybrid of several elements of the two basic models of shareholder and stakeholder capitalism. Maybe the financial crisis will induce new legislation which will hamper the fixation on shareholder value, but this does not mean that the previous liberalization of the financial markets will be undone. So, the world dominance of one supermodel of capitalism is as unlikely as before.

norms (cf. Habermas 1984, pp. 59, 75). Habermas formulates his Universalizability Principle (U-principle) as follows:

> [A] morally valid norm should meet the condition that the foreseeable consequences and side-effects of a general compliance with the norm for the fulfillment of everybody's interests, can be freely accepted by all those involved. (Habermas 1984, p. 75; 1991, p. 12)

According to Habermas, the orientation towards reaching a universal consensus about moral norms is built into the communicative presuppositions of discourse itself.

> The gentle force of unavoidable presuppositions of argumentation requires participants to take on the perspectives and to consider equally the interests of all others. (Habermas 2005, p. 266)

These presuppositions are that participants who are oriented towards reaching mutual understanding allow all relevant arguments to be brought forward. Nobody whose interest is affected by the norms which are being discussed is excluded from the discourse. In addition, all participants have an equal chance to formulate their opinions (cf. Habermas 1984, pp. 177f.).

The communicative model for deliberation about, and justification of, disputed propositions fits well with what Habermas calls a post-traditional idea of justice.

> The more the substance of a prior consensus about values has evaporated, as is the case in modern post-conventional societies, the more the idea of justice itself amalgamates with the idea of an impartial justification (and application) of norms. The more advanced the erosion of innate representations of justice, the more "justice" comes to be articulated as a procedural, but by no means less demanding, concept. (Habermas 2005, pp. 264f.)

Since friction between various cultural forms of life – both inter- and intranational – leads to conflicts that need to be adjudicated without relying on culturally determined conceptions of justice, this procedural approach to questions of justice and morality seems to have an important advantage for the context of (international) business. The U-principle for moral discourse offers us a clear rule which indicates how everybody's interests can be safeguarded in the discourse itself. If a stakeholder dialogue were to be organized in a way that fulfils the condition of this U-principle, the outcome of this debate would have moral validity.

Habermas explains and extrapolates the political implications of discourse ethics in his theory of deliberative democracy. This normative theory of democracy holds that, ideally, normative expectations and claims are formulated in a political public space which allows for spontaneous contributions from civil society. The formation of a political will and opinion, based on a civil society with its own autonomous public spheres, is central to this model of deliberative democracy. It is by participating in this public debate that citizens can influence the institutionalized decision making process in the political realm and exercise a form of self-governance. This enriches the self-governance made possible through elections. Deliberative democracy presupposes that governmental institutions are responsive to the themes, values, and programs which are formulated in the informal public sphere (cf. Habermas 1996). A second central feature of the deliberative model is that it understands the rights and principles of the constitutional state as an answer to the question of how the communicative conditions of democratic procedures can be institutionalized (cf. Habermas 1998).

Is it consistent with the model of deliberative democracy to look for ways by which democratic procedures can be embedded within a society's system of economic organization, including corporate governance? This seems to be compatible with the emphasis on the institutionalization of democratic procedures. In addition, this idea is reinforced by Habermas's stated belief that processes of both informal and institutionalized political deliberation can provide the necessary solidarity within a society that is needed as a counterbalance to the systemic forces of money and political power (cf. ibid., p. 249; Scherer and Palazzo 2007, p. 1108). But, if we also take into account Habermas's theory of society, the table turns. In his theory of society Habermas points out that the communicative power of public opinion cannot rule by itself. It can only guide the use of political power in a certain direction (cf. Habermas 1998, p. 250). The functioning of the economic system can thus only be adjusted to democratically legitimized expectations by transforming the normative messages of deliberative discussions into the specific code of the law (cf. Habermas 1996).

The basis of Habermas's theory of society is the theory of differentiated society. Crucial to this theory is the distinction between the "life world", which is primarily integrated by communicative action on the one hand, and the differentiated political and economic systems on the other hand. These systems are primarily integrated through their specific media: power and money (cf. Habermas 1987). Coordination within the economic system is organized mainly through the medium of money. Actors on the market – i.e., corporations – are primarily concerned with profit seeking, at least as a formal criterion of success in the market (it does not say how profits can be obtained). This all means that we must proceed cautiously in working out the implications of deliberative democracy for corporate governance. Habermas's views of discourse ethics seem to endorse a rather radical democratization of society's system of economic organization. But, looking at the matter from the perspective of his theory of society, it is difficult to see how democratic deliberation could influence corporations directly. Corporations do not have a need to reach agreement or mutual understanding with all stakeholders in order to secure their continued existence. Indulging corporations on this issue may, in fact, endanger their survival.

Ulrich's Account of the Implications of Discourse Ethics for Corporate Governance

Peter Ulrich has developed a model of corporate governance which is based on a framework of discourse ethics and on the related theory of deliberative democracy. In this section we will discuss this model in order to grasp the possibilities and limitations of such an endeavor. Ulrich proposes changing existing corporate governance arrangements to the extent that the stakeholders of a firm are allowed to co-determine the company's policies (cf. Ulrich 1993, pp. 404, 428). This does not mean that all stakeholders will have the same kind of rights of participation. Ulrich's idea of an open corporate governance structure requires that this structure should be determined by a democratically obtained consensus about the specific rights of all affected parties. According to Ulrich, this democratization of corporate governance does not lead to a less efficient use of the assets of the corporation. All stakeholders have a stake in the preservation of the capital of the company which is being held in a foundation. Through this institutional change, Ulrich envisions a neutralization of property rights in the sense that the discretionary power to use the assets of a corporation for certain strategic purposes is no longer simply derived from, or attached to, property rights. Ulrich defends his proposal for institutional change by referring to the idea of an impartial settlement of conflicts of interests. According to Ulrich, the power of corporations is insufficiently controlled from a democratic perspective.

We sympathize with the democratic ideals of Ulrich. But we reject his proposal as a model for describing the implications of deliberative democracy for corporate governance. Consequently, we also reject it as a model for displaying the potential implications of a political conception of CSR at that level. First, Ulrich's theory seems inconsistent. On the one hand, he claims that his proposal will not reduce the efficiency of the modern capitalist economy. But on the other hand, he does chain corporate management decision making to a consensus being reached by all affected parties. We do not think these opposing ideas can be so readily reconciled, especially since it is seen as such a crucial aspect of the free market economy that businesses and other actors within the economy are free to decide for themselves what they will do in order to obtain sustainable profits in the future (cf. Kay 1997; de Beus 1989). We think that Ulrich's proposal would lead to a situation in which political power struggles would pre-dominate within any company. It is likely that every citizen would have his own ideas about how to use the assets of a corporation in a way that would fulfil his interests. These differences and power struggles would completely paralyze any company, in the absence of a clear view of the primary interests that must be served by the firm. Hence, the managers of a corporation would no longer be able to pursue what they believe to be the corporate interest independently from a political consensus on the main objectives and strategy of the corporation and the corresponding system of corporate governance and, consequently, might find itself no longer able to adjust to developments within markets.

This argument can also be put in terms of the theory of differentiation, as explained in the previous section. We contend that if Ulrich does not want to negatively affect the efficiency of the modern economy, he should not tinker with the differentiated nature of the modern economy. This differentiation of the economic and political system in separate subsystems of society is what grants economic actors entrepreneurial freedom and this freedom secures efficiency. From this perspective, it is difficult to see how feasible proposals for direct political influence on corporations can be sustained. In a differentiated environment, corporations do not have a need to reach agreement or mutual understanding with all stakeholders in order to secure their continued existence, nor do they have a legal duty to do so. Therefore, from the perspective of the theory of differentiation, the idea of democratization of corporate governance as proposed by Ulrich amounts to a de-differentiation of the economic and political subsystems. It violates the main assumption of the theory of differentiation with respect to the economic system – that the management of a corporation has the discretionary power to decide on corporate strategy and policies.

This brings us to our second objection. Due to the liberalization of international capital markets, there has been a greater readiness of hitherto "national" capital to seek out the most profitable opportunities for investing capital wherever this may be in the world (cf. Lane 2005, p. 88). As a consequence, where, in the past, German banks used to provide "patient capital" and seek a close monitoring relationship with corporations to reduce risk, the new practice of investment banking is based on risk reduction by gaining distance from clients through diversification in assets, quick entry/exit, and deal-based transactions (cf. Deeg 2005, p. 40). For larger corporations, this means that they are increasingly pressured to be an attractive investment opportunity for foreign investment funds. In the international competitive context where a radical stakeholder democracy would have to compete with shareholder based corporate governance systems, it is hard to see how the former will succeed in the long-run.

Our third and final objection follows from a democratic perspective on how the system of corporate governance can be legitimately changed. If the democratically chosen parties in parliament prefer the shareholder model of corporate governance above the stakeholder model, this choice should be respected as democratically legitimate. Therefore, one cannot argue that the strong interpretation of the stakeholder model with the accompanying change of property rights and of the corporate governance system is universally the best option from a democratic perspective. It is possible that a political community prefers a more effective national business system of corporate governance to a system in which the participation rights of all stakeholders is guaranteed. So even if we agree with Ulrich that the economy should serve the interests of all stakeholders involved, one still might argue that these interests are best served by preserving discretionary power on the part of the management of corporations to develop a corporate strategy independently of the approval of a community of stakeholders.

Based on these arguments, we conclude that stakeholder democracy in relation to the firm cannot have the strong meaning that Ulrich envisions. It is not compatible with the concept of a free market economy (nor with the theory of differentiation) in which (the directors of) corporations are free to develop a corporate strategy in order to sustain the corporation's assets. Next, the actual trends in international finance make it more difficult to sustain a stakeholder democracy. Even the model of co-determination by works councils is under a great deal of pressure nowadays and, in the absence of a political coalition which would endorse the rights of employees to co-determination more strongly, may not survive in the future (cf. Lane 2005). Furthermore, Ulrich's proposal is not necessarily the most democratic. It is also possible that a political community may prefer a corporate governance arrangement that grants the management of corporations the discretionary power to rule the corporation efficiently.

Stakeholder Democracy and Varieties of Capitalism

Our criticism of the feasibility of Ulrich's interpretation of a political conception of CSR raises the issue of whether political CSR is possible at all, given today's circumstances. Are there enough "degrees of freedom" (cf. Hancké and Goyer 2005) anyway? What can democratization and related concepts such as stakeholder democracy possibly mean, given the differentiation of the economic and political systems?

In order to shed light on this issue, we will discuss some findings from the literature of comparative capitalism. In this literature, a conceptual distinction is made between coordinated market economies (CMEs) and liberal market economies (LMEs) (cf. Hall and Soskice 2001). Germany is considered to be the paradigm case of a CME whereas the LME is found in the United Kingdom and the United States. Soskice mentions three important characteristics of a CME: (i) companies securing long-term relations with their owners; (ii) unions and employer associations playing an important role in the regulation of labor markets (in the case of Germany, we need to stress the role of works councils and the supervisory board with employee representatives); (iii) companies being closely integrated into training systems and cooperating with each other through powerful industry associations.

Two aspects of the latter-day discussion on the theory of comparative capitalisms are of particular importance to us. First, it is maintained within the literature that any form of stakeholder democracy is dependent upon a CME framework. The CME framework allows for "stakeholder capitalism" as opposed to the shareholder capitalism of the LME (cf. Soskice 1997, p. 219). Without that, no form of political CSR within companies is likely to prosper. Second, there is discussion on the future prospects of CME. This explains why so much attention is given to the German situation. On the one hand, many notice fundamental changes that are going on in the German system. On the other hand, it is believed that Germany is of fundamental importance for the survival of CME. Lane, for example, is motivated to focus on the German model by the argument that if the very cohesive German system can be shown to be in the process of fundamental change, then the other continental European business systems may be vulnerable, too (cf. Lane 2005, p. 79).

Lane's work forms a good starting point for our discussion. Lane argues that a process of convergence, a one-sided adaptation of the CME model to that of the liberal market economy, is occurring. She bases her case on the force of the cultural and ideological diffusion of shareholder-oriented thinking and the presupposition of an inherent strain for system coherence. In order to build her case, Lane gives a description of the main features of the German financial system and form of corporate governance and contrasts these with the features of the liberal market economy. The German model is conditioned by a high degree of stability within the financial system, and the absence of a market of corporate control is also important. Until the mid 1990s, there was indeed a degree of stability. Due to an underdeveloped stock market, concentrated (family) ownership, and interlocking directorships, hostile takeovers were almost unknown. Banks had a special insider position of control which was based on their ability to cast proxy votes on behalf of the many small investors whose shares they administered (cf. ibid., p. 86). As a consequence, the decision-making in large Germans firms tended to be consensus oriented, with a low constraint to deliver very high returns to shareholders. Instead, the stability of the firm and market growth, together with adequate profits, have been management goals. According to Lane, this picture has changed fundamentally. We have already mentioned above the liberalization of international capital markets. As a consequence of this liberalization, the actions of worldwide operating investment funds have put pressure on listed firms to restructure their operations in line with fund managers' expectations about the improvement of shareholder value. In addition, increased international competition in product markets has made it important to attain sufficient size and market power, and this has exerted pressure for capital concentration through merger and acquisition. On occasion, this in turn has precipitated listing on stock markets (cf. ibid., p. 89). A third source of change, according to Lane, is the increased acceptance and diffusion of shareholder value and associated motivations, cognitions, and scenarios for action. The new generation of German managers, especially, has absorbed these through participation in new programs of management education, particularly the MBA. A further important change in the German financial system is the modernization of the German stock market itself which fuelled the expansion and influence of the stock market on firms. According to Lane, the market

> is shaping many managers' expectations and interests, as external monitoring of listed companies has become prevalent. Even companies not exposed to shareholder pressures have adopted elements of the notion of "shareholder value" to legitimate restructuring and a greater performance orientation. (ibid., p. 91)

But Lane's claim does not go undisputed. Deeg (2005), for example, thinks that the spread of shareholder value is actually limited and that it often only follows "the logic of similarity". Shareholder value-thinking is adopted as a rhetoric that lends legitimacy to other goals being pursued by management. Deeg also refers to the KonTraG, an important piece of legislation on corporate governance in Germany, which "did not alter the internal relations among corporate stakeholders" (ibid., p. 42). It upheld the key normative principles of co-determination and stakeholder capitalism, in part by leaving untouched the fiduciary responsibility of managers to the firm as a whole without giving primacy to any particular constituency. Several other authors support Deeg's position that the changes in the German system of corporate governance do not necessarily lead to a convergence with the shareholder model and that one system can contain elements of both the CME and the LME model (cf. Becker 2001; Deeg 2005; Gourevitch and Shinn 2005). The same is true for key institutions within the model such as the firm-level co-determination scheme found in Germany. Hancké and Goyer, for instance, claim that firm-level co-determination is perfectly compatible with financial transparency under a shareholder value-oriented system (cf. Hancké and Goyer 2005, p. 68). We conclude that, as it stands, in the debate on the convergence of varieties of capitalism to one form of "super-capitalism" (cf. Reich 2007), which would be the Anglo-American shareholder model, the jury is out.

Still, we can draw two important conclusions with respect to the development of a political conception of CSR which is based on deliberative democracy. First, at the level of the firm there are degrees of freedom within a national system of economic organization. Most systems of economic organization in continental Europe are hybrid forms of the ideal types of the CME and LME model. Germany, for instance, has developed a dual system in which the largest banks and listed corporations have adopted substantial elements of the LME model. But German corporate managers can still choose to maintain an insider and stakeholder-oriented approach, as long as the ownership of their firm remains concentrated (cf. Deeg 2005, p. 44). This means that the strategies of actors within an economy also affect the precise shape that their changing institutional environment will take. Hancké and Goyer have shown how actors can use institutional reforms in unforeseeable ways to adapt themselves to perceived challenges. As a consequence, the degree to which a national business system, including its corporate governance arrangement, is open to the interests of stakeholders depends also on the strategies of these stakeholders themselves and on the political institutions in a country (cf. Gourevitch and Shinn 2005). In Germany, the historically-grown practice of worker co-determination has produced works councils which are strong enough to take co-responsibility for the competitiveness of the firms in which they work. This has reduced managerial incentives to act in a unilateral manner. A second important conclusion follows up on the first: any system of economic organization has its own specific history. The specific form that stakeholder involvement will take is the outcome of a historically developed path. The kind of cooperation common in Germany, for example, is dependent on the specific institutional path chosen in that country. Hence, that specific form of cooperation is difficult to copy in different institutional settings. In relation to our purpose of reflecting on the possibilities of a political conception of CSR, this means that there is little sense in designing a theoretical model, regardless of the actual development of a national business system. The purpose and meaning of a political conception of CSR at the level of corporate governance must always be defined relative to the features of a specific national business system. It follows that it seems better to limit any attempt to work out the consequences of a political conception of CSR at the level of corporate governance to describing and advocating the *principles* involved.

Four Principles of Stakeholder Capitalism

In this last section, we will work out our own view on the implications of political CSR at the level of corporate governance. This view is more moderate than Ulrich's view in the sense that our suggestion does not presuppose or implicate a radical transformation of the economic system or current corporate governance arrangements, at least not in countries which have a coordinated market economy. Grafting onto the literature on comparative capitalism, we refer to our proposal as "stakeholder capitalism". We limit our proposal to justifying a number of principles that ought to guide the design of any concrete corporate governance arrangement.

As a preliminary exercise, we briefly return to Habermas's thinking on deliberative democracy and carve out its three core values. On the basis of these core values, we derive four principles that together constitute our account of stakeholder capitalism.

Obviously, *self-determination* is at the heart of deliberative democracy. According to Habermas, this notion of self-determination should be clearly distinguished from the autonomy of the "atomistic" individual in liberal political philosophy.[2] Self-determination is mediated through processes of deliberation with other citizens: one can be influenced by the insights provided by the association with others. *Openness* to cultural differences is another value central to the idea of deliberative democracy. Openness to other cultures makes clear how self-determination in a deliberative democracy differs from an early modern (e.g., Italian city state) republican ideal of citizenship. Habermas believes that in modern societies, there is a plurality of cultural life forms which do not share a common conception of the good life. (This would make the value of openness to other cultures redundant.) That is why an ethical discourse about the right way to live, in most cases, will not generate the consensus needed to coordinate conflicts of interests. A more promising way to deal with cultural heterogeneity is to build compromise and to concentrate on those norms which are in the interest of everybody to accept, even if one has differing world views in a moral discourse (cf. Habermas 1998).

A third value central to the model of deliberative democracy is *solidarity*. Habermas believes that citizens can only develop a mutual understanding of the inescapable differences of opinion through open and non-coerced discourse. In the words of Habermas:

> Certainly the democratic right to self-determination includes the right to preserve one's own political culture, which forms a concrete context for rights of citizenship, but it does not include the right to self-assertion of a privileged cultural form of life. (Habermas 1996, p. 514)

In our view, these three core values prompt four principles relevant to stakeholder capitalism. These principles can be institutionalized in different ways, thus allowing for adaptation to the specific development of institutions within a national business system. The first two principles are directed at the national level. Both are derived from the democratic value of self-determination. The first principle holds that (a) citizens should have a say in those corporate policy areas which have an effect on them. The second principle is (b) that corporations are not allowed to influence the formation of the political will other than by discursive means.

The third and fourth principles are derived from the values of openness and solidarity. They are (c) that a corporation should be responsive to legitimate claims from all those affected by corporate activity and (d) that a corporation should, on balance, make a positive contribution to the society in which it operates.

---

[2] Many proponents of the liberal model of democracy actually do not neglect the influence of discourse and of a shared culture on self-governance. Nevertheless, the liberal model has been criticized for adopting an "atomistic view" on the individual (cf. Taylor 1979).

The first principle is very general and leaves open several possibilities of institutionalizing the influence of citizens on corporate governance. By means of this principle alone we cannot derive what will constitute the best or most democratic form of corporate governance in a particular instance. In a democratic state, citizens and their interest groups can influence legislation on corporate governance and on policy areas. If, for example, the congress of the United States has adopted laws in favor of a shareholder model, this is itself a result of democratic self-regulation. In this respect, we subscribe to the conclusion drawn in a report of the World Bank that "the voluntary CSR practices of private enterprise cannot be an effective substitute for good governance" (Ward 2004, p. 7).[3] Moreover, the effectiveness of "soft" regulation such as codes of conduct depends on a strong and well-functioning public sphere. This also holds true for corporate governance. In some cases, national legislation on corporate governance has restricted the influence of stakeholders; in others it has institutionalized the co-determination of workers.

Principle (b) lays an important restriction on the ways in which the political influence of citizens can legitimately be organized. The self-governance of a people can only be taken seriously if powerful stakeholders such as corporations do not "buy" the support of politicians and their parties by providing them with campaign funding and other types of gifts. In practice, corporations use their Corporate Political Activity (CPA) usually as an instrument to further their corporate strategies and to improve their profitability in circumstances of increased competition (cf. Reich 2007; Schuler et al. 2002). Hillman et al. (2004) state,

> It is indisputable that business firms spend considerable money and are among the most prominent political players not only in Washington, DC but in capitals across the globe. (p. 838)

We agree with Reich who stresses the importance of integrity in a democracy. It is imperative that the legislative process is not corrupted by the competitive struggle of corporations to influence legislation to further their interests (cf. Reich 2007). This does not mean, however, that corporations should refrain from any attempt to influence legislation. It is legitimate to warn about the unwanted side-effects of new legislation or to propose more effective ways of reaching certain policy goals. In a deliberative democracy, there should be room for corporations to participate in pragmatic discourse about the effectiveness of measures. Vogel even suggests that "the most critical dimension of corporate responsibility may well be a company's impact on public policy" (Vogel 2005, p. 171).

Furthermore, in CMEs, corporations and their employer associations can legitimately further their interests by bargaining with unions and other stakeholders, for instance representatives from (environmental) NGOs, and here negotiations on the basis of power will probably be the dominant mode of interaction. However, we also believe that discourses based on the mutual exchange of arguments can play an important role, for instance, in establishing the legitimacy of certain normative claims. There may also be room for collaboration between corporations

---

[3] See also Vogel (2005, pp. 169–173).

and stakeholders in order to come to a shared problem-solving approach (cf. Gray 1989). Some authors take the argument for stakeholder involvement one step further and suggest that the inclusion of stakeholders other than employees could lead to a change in company law which would establish a new form of representative stakeholder democracy. Driver and Thompson, for instance, have proposed the form of a four-tier structure involving the traditional shareholders meeting, the social or works council, the board of directors, and a "corporate senate" which would incorporate stakeholder interests by including persons who championed a particular cause such as "consumer interests" or "environmental interests" and would act as a steward for that interest within the company's governing structure (cf. Driver and Thompson 2002, p. 126). Driver and Thompson are not clear whether the legal status of this corporate senate would be that of a decision-making body or a mere advisory board. If this institution is thought of as a decision-making body, we think that the same objections can be made to this proposal as are made to Ulrich's radical model of stakeholder democracy. Obviously, it is tempting to think in terms of decision-making since the word "democracy" literally refers to the self-government of a people. But we hold that, in a democracy, this aspect is ideally covered by means of legislation and by the continuous influence of public debate on new legislation (see the section "Introduction" above). Using laws relevant to the system of corporate governance, the participation of specific stakeholders in decision-making and self regulatory processes can be extended. In this sense, our weak interpretation of the political account of CSR potentially goes beyond the shareholder model. Furthermore, we take it that managerial freedom to decide on corporate strategy is a necessary condition for the functioning of a free market. Therefore, co-determination of stakeholders should not interfere too much with management's discretion to attempt to further the interest of the firm. This managerial freedom implies responsibility and accountability to several different stakeholders in a firm; and this is where the third principle of deliberative democracy comes in.

The notions of stakeholder collaboration and stakeholder dialogue suggest an openness to the arguments of the stakeholders of a firm and accountability for the way the firm has performed with respect to several legitimate stakeholder claims and the natural environment. Hence, principle (c) states that a corporation should be responsive to legitimate claims from all those affected by corporate activity. In order to appreciate our proposal of stakeholder capitalism, it is important to note that the principle is broader and deeper than the currently predominant stakeholder theories. It is *broader* in the sense that it is more inclusive with respect to the types of stakeholder claims that should be recognized in a stakeholder dialogue. It is *deeper* in the sense that the concept of moral legitimacy is not based on the actual social status of stakeholders, but on a general theory of deliberate democracy and discourse ethics in the post-national area. We will clarify these two points in succession, starting with the ways in which our proposal is broader than the usual one. Our formulation of principle (c) is rather old-fashioned. In our account of what constitutes a stakeholder, we include the interests of *all parties affected* by the behavior of a corporation, whereas in latter day formulations of stakeholder theory, it has become customary to focus on the stakeholders who are strategically relevant (cf. Phillips 2003; Phillips et al. 2003). Persons who do not have a voluntary, mutually bene-ficial relationship with the firm are excluded as stakeholder, or at least excluded as primary stakeholder. According to Phillips, normative stakeholders are "those to whom the organization has a moral obligation, an obligation of stakeholder fairness, over and above that due other social actors simply by virtue of them being human" (Phillips 2003, p. 31). Accordingly, derivative stakeholders "are those groups whose actions and claims must be accounted for by managers, due to their potential effects upon the organization and its normative stakeholders" (ibid., p. 31). An obligation of stakeholder fairness is created when the organization voluntarily accepts the con-tributions of some group or individual. So, if you happen to be so unfortunate as to have no mutually beneficial relationship with a firm, while this firm violates your rights as a human being, you will be considered a non-stakeholder. Phillips et al. (2003) emphasize that this does not mean that a moral judgment based on human rights should be ignored, "but such judgments rely on concepts outside of stake-holder theory as herein delimited" (p. 493). Still, if such a claim may justifiably be omitted from stakeholder analysis, how are you to address a firm that violates your rights under these circumstances? You are not included in any stakeholder dialogue, you are not part of any stakeholder management initiative; you are, most probably, out of sight.[4] This myopia is especially painful in the context of human rights vio-lations by transnational corporations in countries which fail to protect these rights. The possibility that human rights violations will be considered on the basis of a derivative stakeholder relationship makes the acknowledgement of human rights-based claims dependent on the strategic considerations of the management of a firm. This contradicts the role of human rights in the legitimization of claims in what Habermas has called the post-national constellation. In reflecting upon the meaning of democracy beyond the borders of the nation state, Habermas contends that democratic legitimization is no longer primarily based on participation and the formation of the political will, but on the legitimizing force of the discursive quality of the deliberative process itself (cf. Habermas 1998, p. 166). This quality depends upon the fulfillment of human rights with respect to political participation and com-munication. Furthermore, appeals to human rights historically have an energizing and liberating effect in the political domain. This is because an approach based on rights emphasizes that one can justifiably claim something:

> The rhetoric of rights disputes established powers and their categories and seeks to empower the powerless; it is the rhetoric of those who lack power but do not accept the status quo. (O'Neill 1989, p. 201)

The same can be said of the relative success of action groups and non-governmental organizations that focus on the violation of human rights by international business. Obviously, human rights, because of the moral universalism expressed in them, can form a basis for solidarity between citizens all over the world. It would therefore be

---

[4] For a more extensive criticism of stakeholder theory as a normative theory of business ethics see Hendry (2001).

a mistake to exclude these affected parties from stakeholder dialogues, especially in the international context.

Thus, on the basis of these (Habermasian) considerations, we infer that the third principle of stakeholder capitalism must transcend the limits of stakeholder theory as leading theorists nowadays tend to conceive of it. These stakeholder theorists may respond that we will be hindered by the perennial difficulty of delimitating the ring of stakeholders, rendering our proposal unusable for practical purposes. And in any case, this problem was one of the reasons behind their delimitation of possible stakeholders to the strategically relevant ones. We contend, however, that if the purpose of the theory is to provide a general model for the obligations of firms with respect to the influence (or self-governance) of people worldwide, the focus on the strategic success of the firm is no longer the principal perspective to take. If stakeholder theory is limited in the sense that it is primarily a theory of strategic management, it can not serve as an all encompassing model of international business ethics.

In order to show that our formulation of principle (c) is also deeper than currently understood, we recall the influential stakeholder theory of Mitchell et al. (1997). These authors suggest that the salience of particular stakeholders can be determined on the basis of their legitimacy, their urgency, or their power. The problem of their definition of legitimacy, however, is that it is a definition of *social* legitimacy[5] which is based on "[a] generalized perception or assumption that the actions of an entity are desirable, proper, or appropriate within some socially constructed systems of norms, values, beliefs and definitions" (Mitchell et al. 1997, p. 866). This social concept of legitimacy refers to the conditions under which a certain entity gains social acceptance within a given social context. However, principle (c) is based on moral legitimacy. Moral legitimacy is not restricted to social legitimacy and should not be reduced to it. Moral norms claim to have universal validity independent of any particular context. Of course, it is not certain that this claim will be recognized by the actual consent of all the people on earth. But this does not mean that the claim of a moral norm is not itself of a universal nature.

The relevance of the difference between social and moral legitimacy can be explained by way of an example. In the multicultural settings of international business the social concept of legitimacy does not provide us with a criterion for dealing with cultural diversity. If, for instance, human rights such as freedom of expression are violated in China by censoring the internet and if the Chinese government defends such actions by referring to the general interest of the Chinese people in political stability and security, the concept of social legitimacy would focus attention on the cultural authenticity of this claim of the Chinese government (which is also of a doubtful nature). There is no normative basis, however, for going beyond the cultural context and referring to universal norms with respect to freedom of oppression and the like. A shortcoming of the social concept of legitimacy, therefore, is that it cannot deal with actual cultural diversity with respect to moral legitimacy. It

---

[5] This definition is taken from Suchman (1995).

shares the problems of cultural relativism in this respect. Hence, the perspective of deliberative democracy needs to make explicit that principle (c) endorses a moral concept of legitimacy. As such, it offers a normative basis for inclusive stakeholder dialogues.

The fourth and last principle of stakeholder capitalism states that a corporation should on balance make a positive contribution to the society in which it operates. This principle is based on a normative ideal of solidarity between citizens all over the world in respect of their basic right to live a life free from coercion and with sufficient resources to lead a meaningful life. It is well-known that determining what is needed in order to live a meaningful life is a tremendously complicated job and we will not attempt any contribution to this discussion here. Instead, we focus on the legitimization of this principle for the international business system and look at the implications for corporate governance.

In reality, there is of course no such thing as a universal solidarity between people. Generally, the sources of sympathy and compassion are considered to be limited, although occasionally they can be mobilized through media campaigns to help the distant poor or the unfortunate. The normative ideal of universal solidarity is therefore based, not on a solidarity that actually exists, but on the assumption that the way transnational corporations operate is of interest to a growing number of people because of the globalization of the world economy. In some respects, for instance in relation to the problem of global warming, one can hold that mankind has indeed several shared interests with respect to the sustainability of the economic system. We assume, too, that international justice is also an important interest that is shared by all people. Injustice in the form of exploitation of labor, or the pollution of land on which people depend, is increasingly something which can happen to workers and citizens in any country, insofar as governments are pressured to compete with each other in providing the best conditions for transnational corporations by reducing the legal protection of workers and other stakeholders. It is, therefore, in the interests of an increasing number of parties affected by the global economy that corporations (i) adopt the standards of organizations such as the United Nations (Global Compact) and the OECD guidelines and (ii) further justice by contributing to the communities where they do business. This last duty is a general positive duty leaving open the extent to which a corporation invests in projects which do not immediately enhance their reputation or profitability. It is legitimate that corporations will first seek to invest in those projects that improve their competitive environment, as Porter and Kramer (2002, 2006) have suggested. But we do not think that a firm is infringing a fiduciary duty to the shareholders of the firm if they take a broader perspective on how they can relieve the poverty or misery of the communities in which they are active, as long as the sort of help and the resources involved are in balance with the business results generated. It has to work both ways. So, the management of the corporation should still have discretion over the content and resources used in what some theorists call corporate citizenship. It follows from this that the implications for corporate governance of the fourth principle of deliberative democracy coincide with the implications of the third principle. That is, stakeholder dialogues and stakeholder collaboration are the forms in which we expect businesses to be able to discover and develop their responsibilities towards the legitimate claims of the stakeholders of a firm. In some countries, these forms of collaboration might become more institutionalized in future, but whether this will have more far-reaching consequences for corporate governance will depend on other institutions and on their historical development in any given country.

Conclusion and Summary

In this paper, we set out to explore the implications of the political conception of corporate social responsibility for corporate governance. More specifically, we discussed the implications of Habermas's theory of deliberative democracy for this political conception. Peter Ulrich's radical model of stakeholder democracy was discussed and rejected. The model turned out to be incompatible with the differentiation of the economic system. It also seems to ignore the fact that one can democratically opt for a national business system that restricts to a minimum the participation rights of stakeholders in order to preserve the competitiveness of corporations in a globalized economy. Next, the degree of freedom of economic actors within varieties of capitalism was discussed in order to determine whether there is room for stakeholder influence and co-determination. Although the debate about a possible convergence to the shareholder model is still undecided, we argued that there are good reasons to believe that the extent and institutionalization of stakeholder democracy within a capitalist economy is largely dependent on the institutional history or path taken within a national business system, together with the adaptive strategies of economic actors themselves. Finally, we laid out our proposal which we called "stakeholder capitalism". This proposal not only differs from Ulrich's in being more moderate but is also restricted in that it lays out only principles. In this way, our proposal is sensitive to the fact that history specifies the paths that the various varieties of capitalism may take. The four principles that make up our proposal are (a) that citizens should have a say in those corporate policy areas which affect them; (b) that corporations are not allowed to influence the formation of the political will other than by discursive means; (c) that a corporation should be responsive to legitimate claims from all those affected by its corporate activity and (d) that a corporation, on balance, should make a positive contribution to the societies in which it operates.

References

Becker, S. 2001. *Einfluss und Grenzen des Shareholder Value. Strategie- und Strukturwandel deutscher Großunternehmen der chemischen und pharmazeutischen Industrie*. Frankfurt a. M.: Peter Lang.

De Beus, J. 1989. *Markt, democratie en vrijheid. Een politiek-economische studie*. Zwolle: Tjeenk Willink.

Deeg, R. 2005. Path dependency, institutional complementarity, and change in national business systems. In *Changing capitalisms? Internationalization, institutional change, and systems of economic organization*, ed. G. Morgan, R. Whitley, and E. Moen, 21–52. Oxford: Oxford University Press.

Driver, C., and G. Thompson. 2002. Corporate governance and democracy: The stakeholder debate revisited. *Journal of Management and Governance* 6: 111–130.

Dryzek, J. 2000. *Deliberative democracy and beyond: Liberals, critics, contestations*. Oxford: Oxford University Press.

Gourevitch, P., and J. Shinn. 2005. *Political power and corporate control. The new global politics of corporate governance*. Oxford: Princeton University Press.

Gray, B. 1989. *Collaborating: Finding common ground for multiparty problems*. San Francisco, CA: Jossey-Bass.

Habermas, J. 1984. *Vorstudien und Ergänzungen zur Theorie des kommunikativen Handelns*. Frankfurt a. M.: Suhrkamp.

Habermas, J. 1987. *The theory of communicative action. Lifeworld and system*. Cambridge: Polity Press.

Habermas, J. 1991. *Erläuterungen zur Diskursethik*. Frankfurt a. M.: Suhrkamp.

Habermas, J. 1996. *Between facts and norms. Contributions to a discourse theory of law and democracy*. Cambridge, MA: MIT Press.

Habermas, J. 1998. *The inclusion of the other. Studies in political theory*. Cambridge, MA: MIT Press.

Habermas, J. 2005. *Truth and justification*. Cambridge, MA: MIT Press.

Hall, P., and D. Soskice. 2001. *Varieties of capitalism*. Oxford: Oxford University Press.

Hancké, B., and M. Goyer. 2005. Degrees of freedom: rethinking the institutional analysis of economic change. In *Changing capitalisms? Internationalization, institutional change, and systems of economic organization*, ed. G. Morgan, R. Whitley, and E. Moen, 53–77. Oxford: Oxford University Press.

Hendry, J. 2001. Missing the target: Normative stakeholder theory and the corporate governance debate. *Business Ethics Quarterly* 11: 159–176.

Hillman, A., G. Keim, and D. Schuler. 2004. Corporate political activity: A review and research agenda. *Journal of Management* 30: 837–857.

Kay, J. 1997. The stakeholder corporation. In *Stakeholder capitalism*, ed. G. Kelly, D. Kelly, and A. Gamble, 125–141. London: Macmillan Press.

Lane, C. 2005. Institutional transformation and system change: Changes in the corporate governance of German corporations. In *Changing capitalisms? Internationalization, institutional change, and systems of economic organization*, ed. G. Morgan, R. Whitley, and E. Moen, 78–109. Oxford: Oxford University Press.

Matten, D., and A. Crane. 2005a. Corporate citizenship: Toward an extended theoretical conceptualization. *Academy of Management Review* 30: 166–179.

Matten, D., and A. Crane. 2005b. What is stakeholder democracy? Perspectives and issues. *Business Ethics: A European Review* 14: 6–13.

Mitchell, R., B. Agle, and D. Wood. 1997. Toward a theory of stakeholder identification and salience: Defining the principle of who and what really counts. *Academy of Management Review* 22: 853–886.

Moon, J., A. Crane, and D. Matten. 2005. Can corporations be citizens? Corporate citizenship as a metaphor for business participation in society. *Business Ethics Quarterly* 15: 429–453.

Morgan, G., R. Whitley, and E. Moen, ed. 2005. *Changing capitalisms? Internationalization, institutional change, and systems of economic organization*. Oxford: Oxford University Press.

Néron, P.-Y., and W. Norman. 2008. Citizenship, Inc. Do we really want businesses to be good corporate citizens? *Business Ethics Quarterly* 18: 1–26.

O'Neill, O. 1989. *Constructions of reason. Explorations of Kant's practical philosophy*. New York, NY: Cambridge University Press.

Palazzo, G., and A.G. Scherer. 2006. Corporate legitimacy as deliberation: A communicative framework. *Journal of Business Ethics* 66: 71–88.

Phillips, R. 2003. Stakeholder legitimacy. *Business Ethics Quarterly* 13: 25–41.

Phillips, R., R.E. Freeman, and A.C. Wicks. 2003. What stakeholder theory is not. *Business Ethics Quarterly* 13: 479–502.

Porter, M., and M. Kramer. 2002. The competitive advantage of corporate philanthropy. *Harvard Business Review*, December 80: 56–69.

Porter, M., and M. Kramer. 2006. Strategy and society: The link between competitive advantage and corporate social responsibility. *Harvard Business Review*, December 84: 78–93.

Reich, R. 2007. *Supercapitalism. The transformation of business, democracy and everyday life.* New York, NY: Knopf.

Scherer, A.G., and G. Palazzo. 2007. Toward a political conception of corporate social responsibility: Business and society seen from a Habermasian perspective. *Academy of Management Review* 32: 1096–1120.

Scherer, A.G., G. Palazzo, and D. Baumann. 2006. Global rules and private actors: Toward a new role of the transnational corporation in global governance. *Business Ethics Quarterly* 16: 505–532.

Schuler, D., K. Rehbein, and R. Cramer. 2002. Pursuing strategic advantage through political means: A multivariate approach. *Academy of Management Journal* 45: 659–672.

Soskice, D. 1997. Stakeholding yes; the German model no. In *Stakeholder capitalism*, ed. G. Kelly, D. Kelly, and A. Gamble, 219–225. London: Macmillan Press.

Steinmann, H., and A. Löhr. 1994. Unternehmensethik – Ein republikanisches Programm in der Kritik. In *Markt und Moral. Die Diskussion um die Unternehmensethik*, ed. S. Blasche, W.R. Köhler, and P. Rohs, 145–180. Bern: Haupt.

Suchman, M.C. 1995. Managing legitimacy: Strategic and instrumental approaches. *Academy of Management Review* 20: 571–610.

Taylor, C. 1979. Atomism. In *Powers, possessions and freedom*, ed. A. Kontos, 39–61. Toronto, ON: University of Toronto Press.

Ulrich, P. 1993. *Transformation der ökonomischen Vernunft. Fortschrittsperspektiven der modernen Industriegesellschaft.* Bern, Vienna, Stuttgart: Haupt.

Ulrich, P., A. Löhr, and J. Wieland, ed. 1999. *Unternehmerische Freiheit, Selbstbindung und politische Mitverantwortung.* München, Mering: Rainer Hampp Verlag. (= DNWE Schriftenreihe, Vol. 4).

Vogel, D. 2005. *The market for virtue. The potential and limits of corporate social responsibility.* Washington, DC: Brookings Institution Press.

Ward, H.. 2004. Public sector roles in strengthening corporate social responsibility: Taking Stock, The World Bank – International Finance Corporation.

Wood, D., and M. Logsdon. 2002. Business citizenship: From individuals to organizations. *Ruffin Series in Business Ethics* 3: 59–94.

Part III
Corporate Governance
and Business Ethics

Chapter 10
The Firm as a Nexus of Stakeholders: Stakeholder Management and Theory of the Firm

Josef Wieland

Contents

Introduction

In this article, I want to focus on the economic concept of stakeholder management[1] and deal primarily with the company as a form of governance of stakeholder relations. I propose to define the governance of stakeholder relations as a two-step process of first *identifying* and then *prioritizing* the relevant stakeholders of a team, regarding both the team's constitution and the execution of its specific transactions. The *nature* of the company can then be defined as a contractual nexus of stakeholder resources and stakeholder interests, whose *function* is the governance, i.e., leadership, organization and control, of the resource owners with the *aim* of creating economic added value and distributing a cooperation rent. The focus is on the

---

[1] For interesting economic approaches motivating this study, see Blair (1998), Boatright (2002), Hill and Jones (1992), Quinn and Jones (1995), Osterloh and Frey (2005). See also the interesting discussion by Brink (2010).

J. Wieland (✉)
Professor of Business Administration & Economics with emphasis on Business Ethics, Director, Konstanz Institute for Intercultural Management, Values and Communication, University of Applied Sciences Konstanz, Konstanz, Germany
e-mail: wieland@htwg-konstanz.de

A. Brink (ed.), *Corporate Governance and Business Ethics*, Ethical Economy. 225
Studies in Economic Ethics and Philosophy 39, DOI 10.1007/978-94-007-1588-2_10,
© Springer Science+Business Media B.V. 2011

problem and form of cooperation, which is denoted by the phrase "firm as a nexus of stakeholders" (cf. Wieland 2007, pp. 15–37). The following diagram (Fig. 10.1) illustrates these definitions by making clear three separate facts:

1. First, each stakeholder invests his/her specific resources in a collaborative team intended for infinite stability (arrows pointing to the center).
2. Second, each stakeholder, in addition, cooperates not only with the team, but potentially also with all other stakeholders of the team (ruled lines), whether bilaterally or multilaterally.
3. The value of the stakeholder resources is thus defined both by the stakeholder's position in the team and the stakeholder's network.

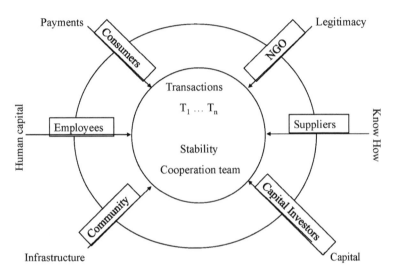

Fig. 10.1 The firm as a nexus of stakeholders
Source: Own figure

Based on these definitions, we can develop suggestions to address the central but not yet satisfactorily resolved problem of identifying and prioritizing stakeholders. I am not interested in a normative approach to this issue, which is logically possible based on both Rawls's theory of fairness (cf. Phillips 2003, chapter 3; Rawls 1971) and contractual ethics (cf. van Oosterhout et al. 2006, pp. 532ff.). My only concern is in reconstructing stakeholder management in the context of an economics of governance theory of the firm. The economics of governance is the theory of the leadership, organization, and control of collaborative relations and adaptively efficient governance structures (cf. Williamson 1996, 2005; Arena and Longhi 1998).

This constitutes a radical change of perspective compared to the relatively widespread notion that the identification and prioritization of stakeholder interests is essentially necessary because of the fact that the companies' decisions have consequences for them as interest groups.[2] According to the concept of stakeholders as interest groups, stakeholders have to be able to proactively bring to bear their interests on the companies, i.e., without having suffered a prior infringement of their interests or rights. Looking at the issue of identifying and prioritizing stakeholder relations in this light, the first problem that arises is, of course, identifying all those who are potentially "involved". However, this is consistently frustrated by the incomplete information we have about both the potential candidates and the future consequences of action. Moreover, it does not yet address at all the problem of prioritizing the interest groups; the prioritization, after all, cannot be inferred from the mere existence of a claim or demand but requires its own decision-making algorithm. Confronted with these difficulties, one can refer to corporate monologues, i.e., to self-exploration and self-questioning characterized by fairness, or to aspects of practicability, which only means, however, that the theoretical problem gets postponed to the next round. Even if one agrees that stakeholders, aside from their passive claims and demands, are also able to actively harm or even benefit companies, the theoretical and operationalizable deficiencies do not go away; rather, one ends up with power-strategic but completely inconsequential considerations about stakeholders' potential to cooperate and to threaten (cf., e.g., Carroll and Bucholtz 2008, pp. 21f., 54ff.; Mitchell et al. 1997). In addition, Jones, Felps, and Bigley (2007) point out correctly that there is a broader and more differentiated range of stakeholder cultures in the management of companies than is suggested by the dichotomy of threat and benefit. But I do not intend to explore these aspects in greater detail. My main contention with this conceptualization of interest groups or power groups is that both versions, in spite of their differences, share the notion that stakeholders have to be understood as entities that are foreign to and not constitutive of the company, towards whom the company therefore has – or fails to have – a moral responsibility or a utilitarian relationship determined by economic or power-strategic considerations.

What if one drops this idea of positive or negative externalities and sees stakeholders as resource owners without whom a company could not be constituted and operationally reproduced? Seeing the company as a nexus of stakeholder resources, the efficient and effective identification, prioritization and governance of these resources and competencies is an essential prerequisite for a company's competitiveness and ability to create added value.[3] Whether and to what extent the cooperation and the generation of a cooperation rent succeed depends on the characteristics of the governance form of this nexus, i.e., on the concrete configuration of the governance structure regarding the selection, hierarchization, and integration of stakeholders. I will come back to this in greater detail at the end of this article. In the following sections, I want to propose several arguments in favor of this

---

[2] See the section "Stakeholder Governance through Identification", in which the definition will be discussed more thoroughly.

[3] In this respect, my interpretation is based on the resource-based view of the firm, see Barney (1991) and Teece et al. (1997).

theoretical concept, hoping to make a contribution to an economics of governance view of the firm. Although this article will deal only cursorily with some ethical and moral aspects of this problem, it outlines the economic context (cf. Wieland 2008, 2009) in which these aspects actually can become effective. Governance ethics and the economics of governance are complementary research strategies, which only in combination help to analyze and shape the phenomena of the governance of modern societies.

Stakeholder Management as a Theory of Added Value

From an economic perspective, stakeholder management is strategic management, based on the central idea that the economic success or failure of a company is determined by those actors that take an interest in the company's success because it simultaneously helps them realize their own interests. Management theories that deal with the function of stakeholders are basically specific value-added theories whose main assumption is that taking into account and integrating the interests of the actors involved in company decisions and transactions creates economic value and new docking points for economic transactions, both for the company and the involved actors. This version of stakeholder theory is not interested in economic democracy, co-determination, corporate social responsibility, etc. (cf. Freeman 2004), but in shaping the conditions for the economic success of a network of economic actors (cf. Freeman et al. 2011). According to Freeman, these conditions are essentially described by three principles, the "principle of stakeholder cooperation", the "principle of stakeholder responsibility", and the "principle of complexity" (ibid., pp. 26ff.).

1. The "cooperation principle" says,

> Value can be created, traded and sustained because stakeholders can jointly satisfy their needs and desires by making voluntary agreements with each other that, for the most part, are kept. (ibid., p. 26)

This is the contractual theory component of the stakeholder theory; it is irrelevant whether the mutual agreements and promises are based on formal or informal contracts.

2. The "responsibility principle" says,

> Value can be created, traded and sustained because parties in agreement are willing to accept responsibility for the consequences of their actions. (ibid., p. 26)

This is the consequentialist component of the stakeholder theory; it plays a role in answering the question of who among the many potential stakeholders will become actual stakeholders of an organization, namely those who are willing to take responsibility for the results of the stakeholder cooperation.

3. The "complexity principle" says,

> Value can be created, traded and sustained because human beings are complex psychological creatures capable of acting according to different values and points of view. (ibid., p. 26)

This is the behavioral theory component of the stakeholder theory; it essentially argues that one-sided concepts such as the maximization of benefit are not sufficient to understand the behavioral dimensions of economic actors; this incomplete understanding can negatively influence an organization's ability to generate added value, because it excludes too many options for action and too narrowly defines the expected range of advantages.

It is not difficult to establish that all three principles are based on an integration of economic and ethical decision-making logic, of economic and moral values as prerequisites for added value and exchange in modern economies. While the "complexity principle" focuses the aspect that actors have – and want to act upon – their moral preferences, the "responsibility principle" comprises the actors' moral responsibility for their actions. The theoretical core of the integration of economic calculation and ethical claims, and thus also of the economics of governance and the ethics of governance, is the "cooperation principle" based on contractual theory because every form of contract always automatically includes moral ideas and responsibilities:

> It should be clear from the start that the notion of contracting is not a morally neutral idea, as it already assumes an adherence to certain values, rights, and background institutions without which no normatively appealing understanding of contractual commitment could exist. (van Oosterhout et al. 2006, p. 525)

Sharing this perspective, the economic as well as the ethical theory of governance emphasize that cooperation is a quality of social life which cannot be further interrogated or reduced (cf. Wieland 2001, 2005). Indeed, cooperation is the ultimate driving force of economic and moral development. It also determines the nature of the stakeholder management. The management of stakeholder relations, which satisfies the three principles mentioned above, refers to three areas that need to be differentiated, i.e., a) the company as an organization, b) its processes and procedures, and c) its specific transactions (cf. Freeman 2004, p. 231). The reference unit is the interests and resources relevant to each area, being components of the added-value process taking place in that area. Here, the management has to take into account that not all stakeholders are able – or willing – to make a positive contribution to the cooperation project. Acknowledging this fact, Freeman et al. (2004, pp. 15ff.) draw a distinction between "definitional" and "instrumental stakeholders". While the former group comprises customers, employees, suppliers, shareholders, and local communities, which play a key role for the growth and survival of the company, the latter group includes competitors, the media, government and administrative bodies, and non-governmental organizations (NGOs), which are able to positively or negatively influence the relationship of the company to its primary stakeholders ("definitional stakeholders") and thus the primary stakeholders' willingness to contribute their interests and resources. Seen from this perspective, governments and state administrative bodies which act in a law-making and law-enforcing capacity cannot be stakeholders of a company because they are as such not voluntary contractual partners (cf. van Oosterhout et al. 2006, p. 532).

To summarize the discussion so far, the stakeholder theory as a theory of added value and of exchange is based on three fundamental assumptions about the nature of the firm and the management of this firm:

1. The nature of the firm is defined as a collaborative process among stakeholders (mostly customers, suppliers, employees, creditors, communities) that aims to deliver success and growth for all stakeholders involved and to create added value.
2. Consequently, the nature of management can only be understood as the strategic management of social relations with the goal of:
3. "Creating values for stakeholders" (Freeman et al. 2011), i.e., a cooperation rent. These two assumptions about the nature of the firm and its management correspond to an integrative methodology, which seeks to define the relationship between corporate and social interests, business and ethics, or strategic management and organizational ethics.[4]

Economics of Governance and Stakeholder Management

The economics of governance shares the stakeholder theory's assumptions about the nature of the firm and the management, but formulates them in the terminology of the new organizational economics (cf. Williamson 1996). Seen from this perspective, companies are a nexus of formal and informal contracts through which owners of resources or competencies form a team. Teams are defined as a *form of governance of specialized resource owners* who combine their respective productivity advantages and thus attain a higher level of gain from cooperation than by deploying their resources individually. Understanding companies as teams or team production means interpreting them as collaborative projects that gain a competitive advantage by pooling resources and competencies in specific ways, which in turn leads to a cooperation rent that can and must be distributed among the team members according to the resource contributions made by each member. This contractual theoretical interpretation includes an organizational-theoretical interpretation of the firm as a team. Essentially, the cooperation between specialized owners of resources and skills goes hand in hand with the interdependence of and the resulting conflicts among these actors. To stabilize the cooperation between the individual resource owners in the long term, it requires appropriate forms and processes of organization. Creating order by means of the legal, economic, and moral responsibility of all involved actors is thus not only a *sine qua non* of every organization, but also of the

---

[4] On this last point, see Phillips (2003).

contractual constellation preceding it. These forms and processes of order symbolize and stabilize the team as a contractually constituted, distinctive collective actor vis-à-vis its stakeholders. According to the economic logic of advantage, only those who can contribute both *organization-specific* and *transaction-related assets* will become team members – or, as I will argue, stakeholders. This is true both from the perspective of the already existing team and from the perspective of the potential new member.

Organization-specific assets are assets that contribute to the durability of the form and processes of organization, to the identification with and commitment to the team, and to the adherence to the legal and moral, internal and external rules of the team – in short, the team member's willingness and ability to exhibit "organizational citizenship behavior".[5] The ultimate aim of a company as an "entity of its own" is to essentially ensure its permanence, i.e., its existence.

Transaction-related assets, on the other hand, are assets that help identify and successfully perform distinctive economic exchanges under competitive conditions – e.g., technical or functional competencies of the team member. These competencies can be general or specific, provided they are related to the transaction.

The reference unit of the economics of governance is, of course, a specific transaction, while the form and process of organization are elements of the governance form for this specific transaction (cf. Williamson 1979). This fundamental theoretical conception can also be applied to the management of stakeholder interests and is reflected in the following definition of the term "stakeholder":

> A stakeholder is a resource owner in a collaborative team that has been constituted through explicit and implicit contracts and whose aim is to generate a cooperation rent by realizing a distinct transaction by means of an appropriate and durable form of governance.

This definition has consequences for the process of identifying and prioritizing stakeholders as a form of governance of stakeholders. Potential stakeholders are stakeholders who have organization-specific or transaction-specific resources but are not members of the team. They become actual stakeholders, i.e., members of the team, through the process of their identification and prioritization. Identification means answering the question of who is a stakeholder and why. Prioritization means asking which stakeholders represent resources and interests that are seen as worthy of preference in the eyes of the team and its members. Freeman's concept answers both questions by drawing a distinction between definitional/instrumental and primary/secondary stakeholders. "Definitional stakeholders" are responsible contract partners in terms of the process of added value, while "instrumental stakeholders" are not contractual partners but are capable of influencing these contractual partners positively or negatively. The question of which interests are worthy of receiving preferential treatment is resolved by the normative principle of "stakeholder fairness".[6] Because firms are the result and means of people's cooperation, the gains from this cooperation, according to Phillips, first and foremost have to be distributed

---

[5] For a survey, see Podsakoff et al. (2000).

[6] For an informative discussion, see Phillips (2003, Chapters 5 and 6).

fairly among the "definitional stakeholders". "Secondary stakeholders" only possess a derivative legitimacy, i.e., a legitimacy derived from the interests of the "primary stakeholders". That means that their interests are only taken into account to the extent that they benefit rather than harm the interests of the "primary stakeholders".

The economics of governance agrees with this distinction between potential and actual stakeholders, but at the same time permits the following specifications:

1. Stakeholders can only be those who have resources that are relevant either for the team's durability or for its distinct transactions.[7] Resources can be quite varied, including material resources (e.g., capital, payments) and immaterial resources (e.g., knowledge, social skills), economic resources (e.g., venture capital, raw materials) and moral resources (e.g., character, virtue).
2. Stakeholders who contribute these resources to a team thus agree to an informal or formal contract that makes them team members. Due to the distinction between formal and informal contracts, both managers and employees (formal contract) and, for example, NGOs or communities (informal contract) can be team members. This is, of course, important for the firm's boundaries, which, however, cannot be discussed here.
3. Through their resources and by accepting the contract, stakeholders have to make a contribution to the sustainable generation of a cooperation rent. This contribution can be pecuniary (e.g., reduction of costs, demand) or non-pecuniary (e.g., reputation, risk perception), functional (e.g., specific information, know-how) or structural (e.g., contributions to the organizational culture, business ethics).

These are the central theoretical requirements for a team's identification and prioritization of stakeholders. It should be added that the stakeholder definition proposed in this article and the criteria to identify and prioritize stakeholders can potentially include all conceivable public interests that may result from the existence and the transactions of a team (e.g., an interest in environmental and social standards). However, this does not mean that actors who formulate and communicate these interests automatically become stakeholders and thus team members. Stakeholders who represent legitimate societal interests but have no resources to realize these interests or who are not willing – or able – to contribute existing resources to the team in order to make a contribution to the team's cooperation rent cannot become team members. I would like to propose to call such stakeholders "societal stakeholders", while team members are "organizational stakeholders". Let me illustrate this with an example: By arguing that companies should assume social responsibility, NGOs, for instance, formulate a legitimate interest. They communicate this interest publicly and thus contribute to identifying and raising awareness of the social risks of globalization. This contribution can be valuable for both society and its companies, influencing the current or future cooperation rent. But this is not enough to make an NGO a stakeholder of a team.

---

[7] This is the argument made by van Oosterhout et al. (2006, p. 532).

NGOs can only be "organizational stakeholders" if they are able and willing both to contribute resources (note the broad definition of resources!) to the solution of the problems they point out and to take responsibility for the consequences of these solutions. According to the definition proposed in this article, it is this willingness for "shared dilemma" that makes an NGO a potential team member.

Whereas the above-mentioned indicators of team membership, i.e., the availability of organization-specific and transaction-related assets, constitute selection criteria both for the existing team and potential stakeholders, the question of identifying and prioritizing stakeholders entails a change of perspective towards the already existing team. The problem of selecting and ranking stakeholders only makes sense from the perspective of an already existing team, i.e., in the context of a management theory. Obviously, the exact opposite is true from the perspective of a political stakeholder theory, where it is the normative criteria of democratic processes that, from the point of view of society, determine who can – or cannot – be considered a legitimate stakeholder. Seen from this perspective, companies become stakeholders of society, rightly so, and have to submit to its criteria for identification and prioritization. However, from a stakeholder management perspective in the context of an economics of governance, social groups must be considered to be potential stakeholders of a production team. In any case, teams will, both in the active and passive version, adhere to the two-step process of stakeholder governance proposed here – step 1: identification; step 2: prioritization – as long as there is a contribution to its cooperation rent. The realm of public – or, more precisely, governmental – regulation lies outside of this criterion and, as I have already mentioned above, cannot be dealt with in the framework of a stakeholder theory for reasons inherent to this theory itself.

Stakeholder Governance Through Identification

In this section, I would like to examine what these definitions mean in terms of the identification and prioritization of stakeholders. The definition of the stakeholder as an owner or possessor of resources or competencies, which he contributes to a team by means of an informal or formal contract, has a number of consequences for the management of this organizational type.

1. In the context of the economics of governance, the definition of the term "stakeholders" as "interest group" is misleading. What the term – and moreover, the German translation, *Anspruchsgruppe*, which means "claimants" – does not take into account is the fact that only those who have previously invested resources in the formation and/or the success of a team can make demands or claims. However, as soon as stakeholders have done so, they are always already members of this team who cannot make demands of this team from the outside. Stakeholders – and this is also true for NGOs – are actors who have a business interest; it would be more accurate to say that they represent specific interests rather than call them "claimants". The idea of stakeholders as claimants probably derives from the generally known definition by Freeman (1984),

according to which a stakeholder is somebody "who can affect or is affected by the achievement of an organization's objectives" (p. 46), with the claimant only reflecting the passive impact ("affected by"), but not the active contribution of resources ("can effect"). In the first case, the status of the claimant derives from a negative external effect of the organization's actions. However, only by incorporating this negative effect into the team, a claimant can become a stakeholder who invests interests and resources in a team. In the second case, on the other hand, the status as stakeholder is constituted by an a priori positive internal organizational effect, which is not identical with a mere claim to or demand on the team. It follows from these reflections that the identification and prioritization of stakeholders do not result from (moral or legal) claims they make of a company, but from the kind and extent of the stakeholders' investment of resources in a team.

2. The investment of resources constitutes the (organizational) stakeholders, but their status is further qualified by the kind of contractual relationship with the team. In terms of contractual theory, every form of economic organization, be it a company or a stakeholder dialogue initiated or supported by this company, is based on an explicit and/or implicit contract (cf. Williamson 1985, pp. 20ff.). Explicit, or formal, contracts are characterized by a codified specification of contributions and their enforcement by third parties such as, for example, the legal system. This category includes labor contracts, supply agreements, purchase contracts, etc. However, every formal contractual relationship of a team always also includes an implicit, or psychological, contract (cf. Schein 1965; Brink 2010), consisting of mutual promises and expectations that are binding to a certain extent, even though they are not explicitly stipulated in the formal contract and thus cannot be enforced legally, or only with difficulty. Labor contracts imply career promises, supply agreements imply integrity agreements, purchase contracts imply guarantees of quality, to name just a few examples. However, NGOs – to use the example already mentioned above – who are members or stakeholders of a team are members or stakeholders on the basis of an implicit social contract, which I will get to shortly. In the transaction cost theory, the distinction between explicit and implicit contracts corresponds to three contract forms that are all possible foundations for the constitution and transactions of a team. These are the classical, neoclassical, and relational contracts (cf. Williamson 1985, pp. 69ff.), which differ as to the kind and extent of their incompleteness and thus the legal ability to enforce explicit and implicit contracts. In classical contracts, legal claims are clearly specified and fully enforceable. The identity of the contract partners does not count. Neoclassical contracts are characterized by long-term contractual relations and thus by interdependencies between the partners. This bilateral dependence circumscribes the legal enforceability of the contractual relation; in case of contract fulfillment problems, the identity of the contract partners counts. Relational contracts are also characterized by mutual dependence and prohibitive enforcement costs; contractual problems have to be solved internally, because they can rarely be documented to and solved by third parties. While the classical contract is a purely explicit contract, the implicit contract is becoming more and more important for

the other two forms of contract. If we use this contract theory distinction for the identification of stakeholders – which is what I want to propose – then it becomes clear that owners, long-term investors, managers, and employees become stakeholders by means of a relational contract, while short-term investors, customers, suppliers, and creditors are bound to the team either by a classical or a neoclassical contract. Given the primacy of the essential permanence of the collective actor as an "entity of its own", the relational, neoclassical, and classical forms of contract suggest one aspect of the prioritization of interests, according to which they are prioritized in this particular order.

3. Communities, governments, and NGOs do not have a classical, neoclassical or relational contractual relationship to a team. However, depending on a specific transaction, they can still be stakeholders of the team, because – and to the extent that – they contribute their resources and competencies to this team. I would now like to propose that this status is based on a social contract. This is supported by the fundamental assumption of the stakeholder theory that firms and teams, as distinctive collective actors, are members of a given society. This is expressed not least and first and foremost by the fact that communities, i.e., the immediate social environment of a company, are, to use Freeman's terminology, "primary stakeholders" or "definitional stakeholders"; "they are vital to the continued growth and survival of any business" (Freeman et al. 2004, p. 15).

4. If we depict this argument in a matrix highlighting the strategic primacy of the "entity of its own", i.e., the durability of contractual relations, we get the following result (Fig. 10.2):

Governance of Cooperation	Stakeholders	Duration of Contract	Resources
Relational Contract	▪ Private Owners ▪ Long-term Investors ▪ Employees ▪ Management ▪ …	▪ Long-term ▪ Long-term ▪ Long-term ▪ Long-term ▪ …	▪ Capital ▪ Commitment ▪ Skills, Character ▪ Loyalty ▪ Coordination ▪ …
Neoclassical Contract	▪ Suppliers ▪ Customers ▪ Private Equity ▪ …	▪ Long-term ▪ Long-term ▪ Long-term ▪ …	▪ Knowledge ▪ Payments ▪ Venture Capital
Classical Contract	▪ Short-term Investors ▪ One-time Buyers ▪ …	▪ Short-term ▪ Short-term ▪ …	▪ Financing ▪ Efficiency ▪ Payments ▪ …
Social Contract	▪ Communities ▪ NGOs ▪ …	▪ Long-term ▪ Short-term ▪ …	▪ Knowledge ▪ Legitimacy ▪ Infrastructure ▪ …

Fig. 10.2 Stakeholder identification 1
Source: Own figure

Of course, individual buyers, suppliers, etc. can be seen as short-term, transaction-specific stakeholders of a team, but they are not constitutional, organizational stakeholders. What short-term investors and some NGOs have in common is the short time span of their involvement in a team. But they differ as to the contractual basis of their involvement. Short-term investors rely on explicit, legally enforceable contracts, while NGOs rely on implicit, politically and morally enforceable social contracts. It follows that short-term oriented investors can be defined as organizational stakeholders, while short-term oriented NGOs are "societal stakeholders". It follows further that the governance of stakeholder relations depends on different mechanisms of enforcement, which are depicted in the next figure (Fig. 10.3):

Governance of Form of Contract	Stakeholders	Specific Forms of Governance
Relational Contract	▪ Private Owners ▪ Long-term Investors ▪ Employees ▪ Management ▪ …	▪ Team Culture ▪ Co-determination ▪ …
Neoclassical Contract	▪ Suppliers ▪ Customers ▪ Private Equity ▪ …	▪ Arbitration Processes ▪ Guarantees ▪ …
Classical Contract	▪ Short-term Investors ▪ One-time Buyers ▪ …	▪ Market ▪ Court-Ruling ▪ …
Social Contract	▪ NGOs ▪ Communities ▪ …	▪ Deliberative Processes ▪ Lobbying ▪ …

Fig. 10.3 Stakeholder identification 2
Source: Own figure

It is within the mechanisms of enforcement of team-contracts that one can find the definitional characteristics of explicit and implicit contracts, be it in a pure or in a mixed form. Duration and the governance form of enforcement are the main indicators of stakeholder identification.

Stakeholder Governance Through Prioritization

As for the prioritization of stakeholder interests, we first have to distinguish whether these interests refer to the durable constitution of the team as a collective actor or to the team's distinct transactions. As for the constitutive aspect, the forms of contract and the desired duration of contract, as illustrated in Fig. 10.1, seem to be an appropriate criterion for prioritization. I would like to call this – the first of the four following criteria – "*contract relevance*".

1. "Contract relevance": Regarding "contract relevance", the interests of long-term investors and employees are preferable to those of short-term investors and NGOs. However, this constitutional perspective has to be supplemented by the requirements of the specific transaction, whose realization requires the resources of stakeholders. Here, the following criteria are likely to be of interest:
2. "Resource relevance": Stakeholders are owners of resources whose specificity can be of varying significance and importance for realizing a certain transaction. Suppliers or employees as stakeholders can, for example, be distinguished by their technical knowledge related to the production of goods or services, while NGOs can contribute societal knowledge and moral legitimacy regarding a company's corporate social responsibility.
3. "Cooperation relevance": Teams are collaborative projects of stakeholders. From this, it follows that the degree of the willingness and ability to cooperate is of major significance for generating a cooperation rent and reciprocal advantages. Predictability, reliability, the ability to handle conflict situations and assume responsibility are indicators that define the collaborative quality of a stakeholder. Potential stakeholders that have few or none of these qualities cannot become actual stakeholders. The same applies to employees, suppliers and NGOs, but not to actors with classical contracts, since they are controlled by the market.
4. "Investment relevance": The willingness to build up team-specific and transaction-related resources and to invest them in the team is an indicator of the quality and durability of a stakeholder relationship and of the willingness to assume responsibility for the team and the consequences that might arise from its transactions.

Stakeholders with non-team-specific resources are able to contribute to the success of a team by means of transaction-related resources, but the costs of changing to another team are low. That does not mean that it disqualifies them for a certain transaction, but it will probably reduce their loyalty to the team. In this case, it is the job of the stakeholder management to create incentives for team-specific *and* transaction-specific investments (i.e., not just transaction-related investments). Their relevance can be high, medium or low, which also determines their initial prioritization. Stakeholders that are rated "high" in all four areas of relevance should be prioritized over stakeholders that are rated "low" for all four relevance criteria. This decision-making algorithm applies to everybody involved in the constitution of a stakeholder prioritization matrix as shown below (Fig. 10.4):

Fig. 10.4 Stakeholder prioritization matrix
Source: Own figure

Relevance	High	Medium	Low
Contract	Employees		NGO
Resources	NGO	Employees	
Cooperation		Employees NGO	
Investment			Employees NGO

NGOs can be characterized by high resource relevance, medium cooperation relevance and low investment and contract relevance; this means that a team should offer incentives to this stakeholder to invest in team- or transaction-specific resources so that the potential team member can become an actual team member. One such incentive can be a value management system (cf. Wieland 2004), which binds an NGO to a firm by an implicit contract or motivates the NGO's "carriers of expertise" to change from an implicit to an explicit and formal contract status. The same is true for employees who have high contract relevance, medium resource and cooperation relevance and low investment relevance. Here, a potential solution can be to increase the investment specificity of the contributed resource. Generally speaking, the process of prioritizing stakeholder relations should not primarily focus on the acceptance, rejection, or ranking of stakeholders, but always also and first and foremost on their qualifications for a long-term team membership. Stakeholders with low contract, resource, cooperation, and investment relevance will leave the team or will not be admitted to the team. In this sense, the identification and prioritization of stakeholders is a two-step process of the governance of stakeholder relations, i.e., the creation of the formal and informal rules that a team should have to ensure its continuity in realizing transactions and generating cooperation rent.

The Governance of Cooperation Rent

It is time to deal with the objection that stakeholder identification and prioritization, in the final analysis, have to fail because of the inability of stakeholder theories to define the trade-offs among the different stakeholder interests.[8] Switching from a maximization of shareholder value to a maximization of stakeholder value, so the argument goes, has to fail because of the increasing complexity generated by the switch itself. In my opinion, this objection does not hold for an economics of governance interpretation of the cooperation rent because this interpretation of the stakeholder value as cooperation rent is part not of the maximizing, but of the economizing paradigm. In this context, it is important to note the point made by

---

[8] For this criticism, see Jensen (2002).

Williamson (2005, 2011) that the governance of a firm aims less at maximizing value but rather at creating *order and conflict solution mechanisms* and realizing mutual advantages. Below I will try to continue this line of argument by trying to delineate the differences between the cooperation rent and individual income.

In neoclassical language, an economic rent is either the difference between the actually realized income of a production factor in relation to the actual costs of its economic use or the income realized in a market in relation to the next-best use. A rent is thus not the same as a profit, which is defined as the residual income from the difference between the turnover and expenses incurred, but the return from an economic resource, which is not based on any additional performances involving costs or expenses. Therefore, the rent constitutes a violation of the neoclassical model of equilibrium. In our context, however, it is more important that the cooperation rent in this sense is, first of all, a performance-free income, i.e., a rent resulting from the cooperative deployment of a resource as compared to an individual deployment of this resource. However, there are some significant differences between the classical and neoclassical economic rent and the cooperation rent:

First: The classical and neoclassical economic rent is the result of the market mechanism and accrues directly to the individual. The cooperation rent is the result of a cooperation context made possible through organization and thus accrues to this organization. How the rent is distributed among the individual stakeholders or team members has to be decided in a second step. This is a consequence of the non-separability of the production functions in the case of team production, as noted by Alchian and Demsetz (1972). In this theoretical scenario, the distribution of the rent from team production is determined by the "residual claimant", who, in conflict with the "shirkers" in his team, tries to solve the metering problem resulting from this non-separability by monitoring the team members. The cooperation rent, thus, is distributed among a) the income of the residual claimant(s), b) the factor income of the team members and c) the expenses to control opportunistic behavior.

Second: Cooperative production, which is based on team-specific stakeholder investments – ideally, all team members make specific investments because this maximizes the cooperation rent and thus the team value – is characterized by potentially multiple residual claimants (cf. Blair and Stout 2006; Blair 1998). The cooperation rent accrues to the cooperation project and can and must be distributed among the contributed resources as factor income. Therefore, one has to distinguish between the rent and the possible factor income.

Third: Market transactions are monolingually coded, i.e., in the language of financial costs; organizational transactions can be coded polylingually, i.e., economically, legally, technologically, aesthetically, morally, politically, etc. Polylinguality, thus, is the basis for both the non-separability and the material heterogeneity of the cooperation rent (cf. Wieland 2005, pp. 57ff.). What this means for the specification of the cooperation rent is that it can accrue both in material (pecuniary) and immaterial (non-pecuniary) form.

Fourth: The distribution of the rent from cooperation and the factor income do not happen via the market, but via the governance form of the organization. The distribution mechanisms can be contracts, negotiations, allocation, good will, etc. and have to fulfill requirements such as incentive sensitivity, transparency, control, and signaling long-term cooperation. The distribution process is controlled by the supervisory and management functions of a company. These can include managing owners, supervisory boards, management boards, employee organizations, special management functions, and other institutional units (cf. Blair 1998; Blair and Stout 2006). In cases where there is only one "residual claimant", e.g., a managing owner, he/she determines the mechanisms and the process to distribute the cooperation rent among all stakeholders. In the case of multiple "residual claimants", the distribution of the cooperation rent is the responsibility of the supervisory board and the management board, which act in a fiduciary capacity for all stakeholders (cf. Blair 1998).

Fifth: The amount of the cooperation rent is an expression of the team's competitiveness in the market. It determines the total value of a company and thus also the kind and amount of the pecuniary and non-pecuniary factor gains that can be achieved from the cooperation rent. This last aspect is illustrated in the following figure of possible factor gains from stakeholder resources,[9] although the list does not claim to be exhaustive (Fig. 10.5):

Stakeholders	Resources	Factor gains
Private Owners	Capital	Profit, Income
Long-term Investors	Commitment	Return on Investment, Acceptance
Employees	Skills, Character, Loyalty	Income, Working Conditions, Career Opportunities
Management	Coordination	Bonuses, Profit-sharing, Power, Status
Suppliers	Knowledge	Payments, Increase in Expertise
Customers	Payments	Value for Money, Status
Private Equity	Venture Capital	Interest, Reliability of Repayments
Short-term Investors	Financing, Efficiency	Return on Investment
One-time Buyers	Payments	Value for Money
Communities	Infrastructure	Taxes, Prosperity
NGOs	Knowledge, Legitimacy	Sponsoring, Power, Reputation
...	...	...

Fig. 10.5 Factor gains from stakeholder resources
Source: Own figure

---

[9] See also the suggestion by Hill and Jones (1992, p. 131).

The cooperation rent is generated – and its amount is determined – by the material and immaterial resources employed in a team *and* by the abilities of the organization, especially its management, to combine these resources as "strategic assets" (cf. Amit and Schoemaker 1993).[10] Producing the complementarity and smooth cooperation of resources is the reason why the cooperation rent accrues to the firm and not the individual resource owners, because "the combined value of the firm's resources and capabilities may be higher than the cost of developing or deploying each asset individually" (ibid., p. 39). In addition to the firm-specificity of the contributed resource, the degree to which it is impossible to imitate the ability of an organization to combine complementary resources therefore determines the cooperation rent that can be achieved. Strictly speaking, it is thus not only the resources that lead to a cooperation rent, but the adaptability of the chosen form of their governance.[11]

Corporate Governance and the Theory of the Firm

We started out by asking about the nature of the firm, and it is now time to try to answer this question based on the arguments developed so far. First of all, it is evident that the firm as a "theoretical link" or "legal fiction" must be seen as non-productive in the context of the firm as a nexus of stakeholders discussed here (cf. Machlup 1967; Jensen and Meckling 1976). The purely economic interpretation of the company as a production aggregate or a mechanism to maximize profits is also deficient because it focuses on only one aspect of economic organization. The two mentioned definitions are necessary but not sufficient characteristics of what constitutes a firm. Ménard (2005) summarizes the well known criticism on these definitions as follows:

> Indeed, firms can better be represented as a complex combination of legal, economic, and social dimensions. As a legal entity, it operates and is liable as one single agent when it comes to the transfer of rights. As an economic device, it relies on a complex set of contractual arrangements coordinated by a hierarchy. And as a social unit, it defines a space in which motivations go far beyond monetary incentives. (Ménard 2005, p. 287)[12]

Let us try an alternative definition: The firm is a project of social cooperation, a nexus of multiple stakeholders with the goal of deploying their resources in the context of market competition. It is a contractual enabling form of organized cooperation.

I would like to explain this definition in greater detail. First, it is based on the assumption that economic cooperation is always also social cooperation, because only then can the resources necessary for the success of a company be mobilized

---

[10] A similar argument is made by Teece et al. (1997).

[11] See also Makadok (2000) and Lado et al. (1997).

[12] For a stimulating discussion on this issue, see also Letza et al. (2004).

and integrated. This view is contrary to a more or less explicit consensus in mainstream economics to conceive of the social order, which constitutes in their language the framework for all business activities, as an exogenous restriction on economic decisions and activities. In such a world, the social responsibility and social role of companies is not necessarily a non-existent event, but an excluded, a "voluntary" event. In my proposed theory, the social character of a firm is made endogenous for economic reasons. This must be distinguished from approaches that emphasize the social character of companies, only to demand that these companies should be subjected to external social control, be it by the state or social discourse mechanisms. My proposed definition does not exclude this perspective; however, it does not systematically include it. Just because discourse ethics agrees with conventional economics as to the exogenous nature of the company's social dimension, both approaches see a company's social nature as a problem of external control. In contrast, my perspective sees stakeholder dialogues, multi-stakeholder forums, deliberative discourses, etc. as possibilities to manage the resources of a team, whose necessity results from a resource's specificity for the execution of a distinct transaction.

Seen from this perspective, corporate governance cannot be limited to a mere monitoring function. Corporate governance is rather the ability to lead, manage, and control the resources of a cooperation project whose aim is to generate factor income and a cooperation rent. According to this definition of corporate governance, stakeholder management is fundamentally a strategic task of corporate governance and not of a company's communications department.

The legitimacy that a company can gain because of its discourse capabilities can manifest itself in "brand building" or a reputation for reliability, quality, and service or integrity. Nee and Swedberg (2005) have called this a "condition of fitness" (p. 802) that can increase the survival and development possibilities of a cooperation team, because and to the extent that it proves successful in the economic and political contexts. This does not yet make the firm a political nor a politicized actor (cf. Crane and Matten 2004; Palazzo and Scherer 2008) – in which case its decisions would have to be able to follow a political codification as leading codification for its decisions – but an economic actor in a political market. The fact that the economic actor is capable of moving successfully in those markets has to do with its nature as a social cooperation project that is capable of organizing the necessary resources (such as the integration of political stakeholder interests) and appropriate forms of governance (stakeholder discourses) for mutual advantage. A team of resource owners, thus, brings the same contribution into political discourses as it does to its economic environment, namely its resources. It is at the core of stakeholder management – which gives concrete form to the social character of the firm as a cooperation project – to identify and prioritize these resources and to create incentives by appropriately assessing the cooperation rent. The question of whether this cooperation project is capable of making a superior or inferior contribution to the solution of social problems or whether this is even desirable or undesirable does not have to be answered here. In both versions, however, the nature of the firm's relationship to society becomes clear. Firms are cooperation projects of society whose members use this organization to invest and to combine their resources to pursue their needs and interests for mutual advantage.

References

Alchian, A.A., and H. Demsetz. 1972. Production, information costs, and economic organization. *American Economic Review* 62: 777–795.

Amit, R., and P.J.H. Schoemaker. 1993. Strategic assets and organizational rent. *Strategic Management Journal* 14: 33–46.

Arena, R., and C. Longhi, eds. 1998. *Markets and organization.* Berlin et al.: Springer.

Barney, J. 1991. Firm resources and sustained competitive advantage. *Journal of Management* 17: 99–120.

Blair, M.M. 1998. For whom should corporations be run? An economic rationale for stakeholder management. *Long Range Planning* 31: 195–200.

Blair, M.M, and L.A. Stout. 2006. Specific investment: Explaining anomalies in corporate law. *The Journal of Corporation Law* 31: 719–744.

Boatright, J.A. 2002. Contractors as stakeholders: Reconciling stakeholder theory with the nexus-of-contracts firm. *Journal of Banking and Finance* 26: 1837–1852.

Brink, A. 2010. Netzwerkgovernance und psychologische Verträge. Making and keeping promises. In *Behavioural business ethics – Psychologie, Neuroökonomik und Governanceethik*, ed. J. Wieland, 167–196. Marburg: Metropolis. (= Series Studies on Governance Ethics, Vol. 8)

Carroll, A.B., and A.K. Buchholtz. 2008. *Business and society. Ethics and stakeholder management*, 7th ed. Mason, OH: South-Western Cengage Learning.

Crane, A., and D. Matten. 2004. *Business ethics.* New York, NY: Oxford University Press.

Freeman, R.E. 1984. *Strategic management: A stakeholder approach.* Boston, MA: Pitman.

Freeman, R.E. 2004. The stakeholder approach revisited. *Zeitschrift für Wirtschafts- und Unternehmensethik* 5: 228–241.

Freeman, R.E., A. Wicks, and B. Parmar. 2011. Stakeholder theory as a basis for capitalism. In *Corporate social responsibility and corporate governance: The contribution of economic theory and related disciplines*, ed. L. Sacconi, M. Blair, E. Freeman, and A. Vercelli, 52–72. Basingstoke: Palgrave Macmillan.

Freeman, R.E., A. Wicks, B. Parmar, and J. McVea. 2004. Stakeholder theory: The state of the art and future perspectives. *Politeia* 20: 9–22.

Hill, C.W.L., and T.M. Jones. 1992. Stakeholder-agency theory. *Journal of Management Studies* 29: 131–154.

Jensen, M.C. 2002. Value maximization, stakeholder theory, and the corporate objective function. *Business Ethics Quarterly* 12: 235–256.

Jensen, M.C., and W.H. Meckling. 1976. Theory of the firm: Managerial behavior, agency costs and ownership structure. *Journal of Financial Economics* 3: 305–360.

Jones, T.M., W. Felps, and G.A. Bigley. 2007. Ethical theory and stakeholder-related decisions: The role of stakeholder culture. *Academy of Management Review* 32: 137–155.

Lado, A.A., N.G. Boyd, and S.C. Hanlon. 1997. Competition, cooperation, and the search for economic rents: A syncretic model. *Academy of Management Review* 22: 110–141.

Letza, S., X. Sun, and J. Kirkbride. 2004. Shareholding vs. stakeholding: A critical review of corporate governance. *Corporate Governance* 12: 242–262.

Machlup, F. 1967. Theories of the firm: Marginalist, behavioral, managerial. *American Economic Review* 57: 1–33.

Makadok, R. 2000. "A general theory of rent creation", Academy of Management Annual Meeting Proceedings, Toronto, ON, A1–A6.

Ménard, C. 2005. A new institutional approach to organization. In *Handbook of new institutional economics*, ed. C. Ménard and M.M. Shirley, 281–318. Berlin: Springer.

Mitchell, R.K., B.R. Agle, and D.J. Wood. 1997. Toward a theory of stakeholder identification and salience: Defining the principle of who and what really counts. *Academy of Management Review* 22: 853–886.

Nee, V., and R. Swedberg. 2005. Economic sociology and new institutional economics. In *Handbook of new institutional economics*, ed. C. Ménard and M.M. Shirley, 789–818. Berlin: Springer.

Osterloh, M., and B.S. Frey. 2005. Corporate governance: Eine Prinzipal-Agenten-Beziehung, Team-Produktion oder ein Soziales Dilemma?. Working Paper, Universität Zürich.

Palazzo, G., and A.G. Scherer. 2008. Corporate social responsibility, democracy, and the politicization of the corporation. *Academy of Management Review* 33: 773–775.

Phillips, R. 2003. *Stakeholder theory and organizational ethics*. San Francisco, CA: Berrett-Koehler.

Podsakoff, P.M., S.B. MacKenzie, J.B. Paine, and D.G. Bachrach. 2000. Organizational citizenship behaviors: A critical review of the theoretical and empirical literature and suggestions for future research. *Journal of Management* 26: 513–563.

Quinn, D.P., and T.M. Jones. 1995. An agent morality view of business policy. *Academy of Management Review* 20: 22–42.

Rawls, J. 1971. *Theory of justice*. Cambridge, MA: Belknap.

Schein, E.H. 1965. *Organizational psychology*. Englewood Cliffs, NJ: Prentice-Hall.

Teece, D.J., G. Pisano, and A. Shuen. 1997. Dynamic capabilities and strategic management. *Strategic Management Journal* 18: 509–533.

Van Oosterhout, J.H., P. Heugens, and M. Kaptein. 2006. The internal morality of contracting: Advancing the contractualist endeavor in business ethics. *Academy of Management Review* 31: 521–539.

Wieland, J. 2001. The ethics of governance. *Business Ethics Quarterly* 11: 73–87.

Wieland, J., ed. 2004. *Handbuch Wertemanagement. Erfolgsstrategien einer modernen Corporate Governance*. Hamburg: Murmann.

Wieland, J., ed. 2005. *Normativität und Governance. Gesellschaftstheoretische und philosophische Reflexionen der Governanceethik*. Marburg: Metropolis. (= Metropolisreihe Studien zur Governanceethik, Vol. 3).

Wieland, J. 2007. Idealistische, ideale und reale Diskurse. Governanceformen des Diskurses. In *Governanceethik und Diskursethik – ein zwangloser Diskurs*, ed. J. Wieland, 13–59. Marburg: Metropolis. (= Metropolisreihe Studien zur Governanceethik, Vol. 5).

Wieland, J. 2008. Governanceökonomik: Die Firma als Nexus von Stakeholdern. In *Die Stakeholder-Gesellschaft und ihre Governance*, ed. J. Wieland, 15–38. Marburg: Metropolis. (= Metropolisreihe Studien zur Governanceethik, Vol. 6).

Wieland, J. 2009. Die Firma als Kooperationsprojekt der Gesellschaft. In *CSR als Netzwerkgovernance – Theoretische Herausforderungen und praktische Antworten. Über das Netzwerk von Wirtschaft, Politik und Zivilgesellschaft*, ed. J. Wieland, 257–288. Marburg: Metropolis. (= Metropolisreihe Studien zur Governanceethik, Vol. 7).

Williamson, O.E. 1979. Transaction-cost economics: The governance of contractual relations. *Journal of Law and Economics* 22: 233–261.

Williamson, O.E. 1985. *The economic institutions of capitalism: Firms, markets, relational contracting*. New York, NY: Free Press.

Williamson, O.E. 1996. *The mechanisms of governance*. Oxford: Oxford University Press.

Williamson, O.E. 2005. The economics of governance. *American Economic Review* 95: 1–18.

Williamson, O.E. 2011. Corporate governance: A contractual and organizational perspective. In *Corporate social responsibility and corporate governance: The contribution of economic theory and related disciplines*, ed. L. Sacconi, M. Blair, E. Freeman and A. Vercelli, 3–32. Basingstoke: Palgrave Macmillan.

Chapter 11
Corporate Governance, Ethics and Sustainable Development

Aloy Soppe

Contents

Introduction

Sustainable development has been a hot item in a large number of economic disciplines for many years now. However, in corporate governance analysis, the sustainability discussion just started. Petschow, Rosenau and Weizsäcker (2005) and Benn and Dunphy (2007) are good examples as they explicitly explore the relationship between governance and sustainability. In Petschow et al. (2005), a range of authors analyse this phenomenon at state, company or civil society level. It is concluded that there is no blueprint to follow with which to reach sustainability in governance. The current road, however, is a sometimes conflict-oriented but always a learning-oriented process. Of course, the future of capitalism is at stake (see the Financial Times, May & June 2009, in which authors like Amartya Sen, Paul Kennedy, Robert Shiller and others shed lights on the current crisis in terms

A. Soppe (✉)
Associate Professor of Financial Ethics, Erasmus School of Law, Erasmus University Rotterdam, Rotterdam, Netherlands
e-mail: soppe@frg.eur.nl

A. Brink (ed.), *Corporate Governance and Business Ethics*, Ethical Economy. Studies in Economic Ethics and Philosophy 39, DOI 10.1007/978-94-007-1588-2_11, © Springer Science+Business Media B.V. 2011

of lessons learnt). In that view, it is primarily the financial and political systems that are to blame, together with the financial sector itself and the lack of cooperation between nations. Corporate governance in the real economic sectors is not yet really an issue, although sustainable development does not use a top-down approach, but requires the inclusion of all players and is thus closely connected to governance structures.

In this article, it is argued that sustainable governance is based on a network approach to social relations of the company, in which normative choices are made by management as derived from rational expectations of future social developments. Boutilier (2009, pp. 2f.) argues that there is a need for a systematic approach in stakeholder politics. Contrary to the leftist/postmodern critique of capitalism, Boutilier argues that stakeholder politics aligns with the global governance perspective that views the private sector's future success as intertwined with the success of the civil and public sectors. In that respect, globalisation has locked the private, the civil and the public sectors into an unprecedented interdependence at all levels of governance. There is a need for a system that converts good intentions into good results. However, no one has yet given managers a systematic framework to help them collaborate with stakeholders towards achieving shared sustainable development goals. Sustainable development may offer a solution between the traditional tense between short term (financial) consequential ethics versus a more virtue ethical approach of leadership. In a post materialist world where governments are losing their control of the social process, we are seeing the ascent of the global civil sector. Benn and Dunphy (2007) describe the limits of the existing models on corporate governance, and attempts are made to redesign governance for sustainability. This article contributes to that discussion.

The next section starts with a short description of the traditional English and American markets of corporate control together with their assumptions and some important results of these theories. In the section "The Shareholder Paradigm and Its Developments", we proceed with the resulting shareholder paradigm and its ethical implications and developments. In the section "Sustainable Corporate Governance", we normatively develop the concept of sustainable governance that is theoretically based on a stakeholder approach to the economic process. The article ends with a conclusion on the relationship between ethics, sustainability and corporate governance.

The "Market of Corporate Control"

In finance, the contractual theory on the nature of the firm (cf. Alchian 1982; Fama and Jensen 1983) had become a widely held one at the end of the last century. In that respect, firms are perceived as a network of contracts, actual and implicit, that specifies the roles of the various participants or stakeholders and defines their rights, obligations and their payoffs under different conditions. Their interest must be harmonized to achieve efficiency and value maximization. Williamson (1988) proposed a combined treatment of corporate finance and corporate governance. Debt and equity were treated not as alternative financial instruments primarily, but rather as alternative governance structures. Williamson analyses extensively the commonalities and the differences between transaction cost analyses and agency relations (cf. Williamson 1988, pp. 569–575). In the transaction cost approach, the transaction is the basic unit of analysis, whereby the most important dimension is asset specificity.

In spite of the broad theoretical scope of the transaction cost approach concerning all possible stakeholders of the company, it is the neoclassical value-maximization of the firm that restricts the conclusions of the models implied. Many stakeholders' transactions are "implicit" transactions and therefore not traded (or inefficiently priced) in markets. This is a severe restriction of the quality of the conclusions of this neoclassical set of models. The microeconomic decision process of firms depends on more factors than those priced in capital markets. Tempelaar (1991) also comes to a similar conclusion in an extensive overview of the theoretical developments in finance. He concludes that as long as the goal of the company is the value maximization of the company in the capital market, its holistic-market oriented concept lacks several elements of the firms' decision-making process. This disturbs the modelling of a firm's microeconomic *decision-making* process (cf. ibid., p. 294).

In security design literature, institutional ownership of financial assets is analysed regarding its consequences for the optimal allocation of securities among investors. All securities are interpreted as claims on the cash flow ensuing from a firm's real assets. Security design literature emphasises the minimisation of the "verification cost" (cf. Townsend 1979). Townsend describes optimal security as being an endogenous asset that minimises the verification cost of the owner of the cash flow. Verification costs are seen as "dead weight loss" reducing the value of the firm. Clientele effects and microstructure analysis enable optimal allocation of heterogeneous risk preferences of investors. The "costly state verification" approach of Diamond (1984) is comparable. In this view, the "insiders" of a company observe the cash flows without costs, while the "outsiders" must pay verification costs.[1]

It is important to note that all the types of costs stated above (verification, costly state) can be seen as a generalisation of the minimisation of agency costs. All assumptions and critical remarks concerning agency theory and ethics apply here (cf., e.g., Bowie and Freeman 1992). It is remarkable that concepts such as fairness and democracy are not at stake when discussing the ownership of the company and its influence on cash flow. In neoclassical theory, it is simply assumed that if there is a distinction between management and ownership, the goals of both groups are not congruent and that "costs" must be made to convince the agent that full cooperation is agreed. This individualised and contractual approach of human (i.e., financial, managerial) behaviour is at odds with modern approaches as illustrated in the following sections. Firstly, we will elaborate on the shareholder paradigm and its theoretical criticism before discussing the core aspect of this contribution: sustainable governance.

---

[1] It is not surprising therefore that in these approaches debt is an optimal security due to its relative low verification cost.

The Shareholder Paradigm and Its Developments

In the previous section, it is the shareholder paradigm that dominates English and American finance literature. In that model, corporate direct investment decisions are separated from the individual stockholders' preferences for consumption, allowing a separation of ownership and management.[2] As a result, shareholders own the corporation and expect the management of the company to maximize their wealth. Theoretically, they can only do this by investing in positive net present value (NPV) projects. The incentive for managers to act in the shareholder's interest is subsequently based on the bonding and monitoring abilities of the shareholder.[3] Moreover, agency theory assumes that a manager will only act according to his own interests; therefore monitoring and bonding costs are effectuated in markets to discipline the manager. The crux of the shareholders wealth paradigm is that shareholders are considered optimally suited to discipline management and therefore to maximise the wealth of society.

Shareholders only differ from other constituencies of the firm in that they are residual risk-bearers and therefore residual claimholders. As such, they face the particular problem of contracting managers, which is best met by having control. Boatright (1999, Chapter 6) elaborates in depth on this approach and shows that the acceptance of shareholders as ultimate claimholders depends on the theory of the firm that underlies the model. He distinguishes three different theories of the firm. Firstly, there is the *property rights model*, in which the stockholder is owner of the firm and who chooses to do business in corporate form. Then there is the *social institution theory*, which maintains that the right to incorporate is a privilege granted by the state and therefore that the "right to incorporate" inherently has a public aspect. Thirdly, there is the *contractual theory*, in which the corporation is sanctioned by the state to serve the general welfare. Boatright (1999) then states that

> in contrast to the property rights theory, the contractual right theory does not hold that the firm is the private property of the shareholders. Rather, shareholders, along with other investors, employees, and the like, each own assets that they make available to the state. Thus, the firm results from property rights and the right of contract of every corporate constituency *and not from the shareholder alone.* (p. 171; italics by AS)

Boatright argues that shareholders can easily diversify their portfolio of stocks to eliminate idiosyncratic downside risk.[4] The highly skilled employee on the other hand, who developed valuable firm-specific human capital, may possibly assume considerable more residual risk. So why is it the shareholder that carries the residual risk? Boatright is not alone in his criticism on shareholder dominance and agency

---

[2] Because the individual consumption preferences can freely be satisfied in the consumption markets (assuming market efficiency).

[3] This is where, theoretically, ethics come in. The negative perception of human nature is the starting point of the entire agency theory.

[4] On the other side of the probability distribution, the stockholder fully earns the upward potential that comes with ownership.

theory (cf., e.g., Bouckaert and Vandenhove 1994; Bowie and Freeman 1992; Stout 2002, 2007 and many others). Within the limits of the financial theory itself, alternative paradigms in finance are also scarce but do exist. In this section, we briefly mention, respectively, 1) finance and fairness, 2) the "postmodern approach" of the firm, 3) the development in CSR and, finally, 4) the stakeholders approach.

Finance and Fairness

Shefrin and Statman introduced the efficiency/fairness frontier in 1993. Starting with a financial case of insider trade, they argue that there is a permanent tug-of-war between fairness and informational efficiency. The policy makers, responsible for the legislative process in a country, operate as if they had utility functions that depend on both efficiency and fairness. Shefrin and Statman (1993) state,

> [P]olicy makers construct an efficiency/fairness framework in much the same way as portfolio managers construct a mean/variance framework. Some combinations of efficiency and fairness dominate other combinations. The efficiency/fairness frontier is composed of combinations that are not dominated (...). Any configuration of regulations can be described as a point in the multidimensional efficiency/fairness space. A regulation is on the frontier unless another regulation improves both fairness and efficiency. (p. 23)

This concept of an efficiency/fairness frontier is a beautiful example of integrating a mere finance concept with the much broader political process of financial legislation. This can also be interpreted as another attack on the one-dimensional shareholder wealth (SHW) paradigm.

Postmodern Approach

The second concept in the series of alternative paradigms could be described as the "postmodern approach" to business and finance. Dobson (1999) brings together two articles as presented in "Business Ethics Quarterly". Firstly, there is John Hasnas's article entitled "The Normative Theories of Business Ethics: A Guide for the Perplexed" (1998), which invokes the stockholder model as a valid normative theory of business ethics.[5] The second article is Thomas W. Dunfee's "The Marketplace of Morality: First Steps Toward a Theory of Moral Choice" (1998). In this article, Dunfee (1998) suggests that "MOM (market place of morality) could provide a unifying framework integrating moral preferences, reasoning, behaviours and organisational context with broader political and economic concepts" (p. 142). Dobson (1999) concludes that both articles imply that the accepted financial-economic view of the firm is a view that can accommodate ethics.[6] He makes a

---

[5] To describe this study at length would be to go beyond the scope of this study, but basically it is based on the arguments as described in previous paragraphs of this section.

[6] Dobson uses the Starkist Tuna case and the Shell Brent Spar case as empirical evidence for his conclusion on the interrelation between financial decisions and business ethics.

distinction between a modernist approach (the stockholder model, the stakeholder model and the social contract theories) and a postmodern approach. The postmodern approach is structured less to achieve a specific end, but more as a type of aesthetic activity, understanding business as an art rather than business as a science. Dobson advocates virtue ethics and its derivatives such as "corporate soulcraft" (cf. Johnson 1997) and "craftsmanship ethics" (cf. Klein 1998).

Corporate Social Responsibility

Literature on CSR and sustainable development is developing rapidly. Crane et al. (2008) provide a very comprehensive overview of the state of the art concerning CSR and discuss whether the theoretical concept of CSR really has contributed to management literature and governance. CSR is more explicitly implemented in the USA than in Europe (cf. Matten and Moon 2008). In 2005, 85% of the executives who participated in an executive poll said that corporate responsibility is essential to their businesses (cf. Dyer et al. 2005), and the majority of the managers believed that businesses should serve as stewards in society and that they have a duty to other stakeholders. A more implicit CSR model has been implemented in Europe. By "implicit CSR", Matten and Moon (2008) refer to a corporation's role within wider formal and informal institutions with regard to society's interests and concerns. Implicit CSR, they argue, normally consists of values, norms and rules that result in requirements (both mandatory and customary) for corporations. In implicit CSR, stakeholder issues are addressed that define the true obligations of corporate players in collective rather than individual terms. National cultures, ethical codes and legislation dominate these types of governance (cf., e.g., Habisch et al. 2005) and are primarily applicable in the European context.[7]

Governance and sustainability also form new challenges for states (cf. Lozano et al. 2008). A major question involves the role of government in general but more specifically the role and the effects of legal regulations in European countries. Two major issues arise:[8] Firstly, there is the question of whether more supervision (either internal or external by independents), or increasing supervision by national law, also indicates more effective supervision. Even the most active and experienced audit committee will have to admit that there are limits to what they can control. In the end, it is always a judgment on the integrity of the relevant stakeholders

---

[7] In addition to the market oriented systems, there are also network oriented corporate governance systems such as the ones existing in, for example, Germany and Japan. These systems can be typified by cross shareholdings in industrial groups such as, for example, the Keiretsu in Japan or the role of the *Aufsichtsrat* (i.e., supervisory board) in Germany. In the latter system there is almost always a representative of a German bank on the board of commissioners of a company. In these countries, the role of the stock market in providing capital is much less dominant than it is in Anglo American markets, as a result of institutional factors in the past.

[8] See Maljers, F.A., opening speech by the Chairman at the symposium: *Corporate Governance & Corporate Finance: A European Perspective*, on 15 March 2007, held at the RSM Erasmus University (for the printed version cf. Maljers 2008).

in, or representatives of, the company. A second fundamental question – the more complicated and crucial one – is whether more and better supervision leads to better company results.

A Stakeholders Approach to Corporate Governance

Inherent to CSR and in contrast to the neoclassical approach in the section "The 'Market of Corporate Control'", Cyert and March (1963), Freeman (1984), Freeman et al. (2004) and many others proposed a more behavioural theory of the firm.[9] In what they refer to as a stakeholders approach to the firm, managers are perceived as human beings that are unable to behave completely rationally and have all sorts of interests and motives aside from their formal organisational ones and their narrow self-interest. They can only achieve the best interest of their stockholders incompletely because they operate from a position of "bounded rationality" (cf. Simon 1982) rather than complete rationality. They also realise that the economic society comprises more stakeholders than simply those who supply capital (i.e., the stockholders). In this perception, sustainable economic growth is only possible if at least the interests of the primary stakeholders such as employees and the environment are taken into account in the policy of the company.

Cornell and Shapiro (1987) were the first to apply the stakeholder approach explicitly to corporate finance and governance. One focus of their paper was the distinction between explicit contractual claims like wage contracts and product warranties on the one hand and implicit claims such as the promise of continuing service to customers and job security of employees on the other. They describe the distinguishing feature of implicit claims as follows:

> [T]hese claims are too nebulous and state contingent to reduce to writing at a reasonable cost (. . .). For this reason, implicit claims have little legal standing. (ibid., p. 6)

They stress that, as long as only explicit claims are considered, stakeholders will not play an important role in the financial policy of the company because their explicit claims are generally senior to those of stockholders and bondholders. As long as the probability of financial distress is small, the explicit claims of stakeholders are essentially risk free and therefore cannot explain variability in the value of the firm. Cornell and Shapiro then develop an "extended balance sheet", in which "net organisational capital" is added on the asset side and "organisational liabilities" on the liability side. Organisational capital (OC) is defined as "the current market value of all future implicit claims the firm expects to sell", and organisational liabilities (OL) equal the "expected costs, from the firms' standpoint of honouring both current and future implicit claims" (ibid., p. 8). It is clearly very difficult to

---

[9] Behavioural theory is used in this context as a collective noun. There are many different models in which human behaviour is explicitly incorporated into the economic and management processes of the firm. For example, Bouckaert and Vandenhove (1994) extensively discuss four different models on social responsibility of the firm.

value both organisational assets and liabilities. The value of the implicit claims is dependent on the character of the company, the product market involved and the nature of its stakeholders.[10] Cornell and Shapiro (1987) predicted "that firms that expect to provide high payoffs on implicit claims will attempt to distinguish themselves *ex ante*" (pp. 9f.). This could be done through an appropriate dividend payout rate or financial structure. The seminal Cornell and Shapiro paper still represents the major challenge in modern finance and governance discussions, in which the normative appeal to ethical leadership and sustainable development becomes increasingly legitimated.

A good example of a new approach to governance is stewardship theory of management (cf., e.g., Donaldson and Davis 1991; Davis et al. 1997). Kao (2007) argues that most economic theories claim an individual has the right to private property ownership but do not consider what stewardship responsibility is. Considering the importance of future generations, Kao argues that individuals are, morally, nothing more than custodians of property.

> They may make proprietary decisions, but they must assume stewardship responsibility. (...) [T]he greed resulting from ownership undermines long term perspectives and stewardship responsibility. (ibid., p. 16)

One way to reduce the negative influence of individual claims to the company is corporate democracy, meaning that collective decisions should be made by those whose interests are at stake. Engelen (2002) argues that corporate democracy basically comes down to a trade-off between effectiveness and inclusiveness. As the number of participants increase, more negotiations result in a "deadlock". In a globalising world, new solutions must be found to cope with the tension of competition and sustainability. Against this background, Soppe (2008) proposes that a sustainable company emits a substantial amount of its equity (at least 51%) to the major stakeholders of that company. The percentage of stocks held by internal stakeholders is called "stakeholders' equity" (SE). This extends the legal claim to the companies' residual profits (including the potential losses) from the capital providers alone to new shareholders who provide capital on the one hand but also have other stakes in the company (e.g., employees, environmental NGOs or suppliers) on the other. The purpose is to strengthen the interests, and the responsibility, of different stakeholders beyond their conventional stakeholder interest. The old shareholders, on the other hand, still get the same reward for investments (although short term expected return – as with highly speculative projects – may diminish). The crucial difference is that capital providers lose ultimate control because ownership is then dispersed among the relevant stakeholders of the company. The stakeholder model does not reject the shareholder model. On the contrary, it builds entirely on shareholders as the ultimate claimants of the company's profits. The crucial difference, however, is with regard to the ownership of the shares.

---

[10] In other words, the value depends on the relevant perception of cultural and ethical values by the society in question.

Sustainable Corporate Governance

To summarise the modern corporate governance literature, there are four different alternative perspectives of corporate governance (cf. Keasey et al. 2005). The first is the traditional principle-agent or finance perspective of Jensen and Meckling (1976). This approach tends to see unrestricted capital and managerial labour markets as an effective check on executive malperformance. Private equity and international hedge funds encourage well-functioning capital markets that will tend to solve both the micro-economic governance problem (see the section "The 'Market of Corporate Control'" on the market of corporate control) and ensure compatibility with the macro-economic level of efficient fund allocation. The opposite stance is taken by those who view the capital market as fundamentally flawed and myopic in its concern for short-term returns (cf. Jensen 1986; Blair 1995). In this second approach, a myopic stock market encourages managers to underinvest in long-term projects, which leads to systematic distortions of investment in the economy to the detriment of long-term growth. The third approach is the stakeholder perspective of Freeman, Wicks and Parmar (2004), Stout (2002) and many others. This approach contends that the shareholder perspective is too narrow to increase societal wealth and should be extended to embrace the interests of other groups associated with the firm, such as employees, creditors and environmentalists. Finally, there is the view that corporate governance reforms should be implemented to restrict, if not prevent, the pathologies that arise from the abuse of executive powers. This more or less institutional approach is suggested by Shleifer and Vishny (1997).

This section argues that sustainable governance contains building blocks as developed in the above mentioned stakeholder and institutional approach. For example, sustainable development today is too urgent a matter to be left to environmental lobbyists or activists protesting against economic globalization. Increasingly, scientific evidence has been gathered that indicates that the earth is warming up and that individual and global measures are needed to change that trend. Welzer (2008) argues that environmental threats even endanger future world peace because of scarce resources like, e.g., water. Additionally, the economic gap between the rich and the poor is widening – not only between countries but also within countries. As Lélé (1991) already noticed, the verbs "to sustain" and "to grow" (or "to develop") are contradictory in themselves, and may therefore need another context than that of the traditional competitive market economy. Fergus and Rowney (2005) argued on a philosophical basis that new insights and perspectives are necessary. Sustainable development in governance aims to redress the balance in the relationship between individual interests and collective or community interests through leadership. The way in which management teams deal with money and finance reflects their deeper interests in sustainable development. For example, macro- and micro-economic savings and direct investment behaviour reveal the controversy regarding present consumption versus the development of the social and physical infrastructure of future generations. At the level of the firm, market competition – between the providers of risky capital, the providers of labour and the general community interest (e.g., protecting the environment) is biased in favour of the providers of capital.

Unbalanced social positions cannot be sustained for a long time. Sustainable development in governance, therefore, must find ways and means with which to restore this unsustainable position.

In an attempt to portray sustainable corporate governance, Fig. 11.1 represents the connection between recent theoretical developments. The radar chart allocates scores for the elements of corporate sustainable governance: ownership concept, mission statement, ethical framework and assumed human nature of the economic subject together with the CSR and SRI concepts for both a traditional and a sustainable company. The six axes of the graph represent the percentage of commitment that a company has to one specific element of sustainability. The ownership concept ranges from the pure shareholder model to the pure stakeholder model,[11] the mission statement depends on the extent to which the three-layered company goal setting is specifically referred to (cf., e.g., Elkington 1997), the ethical framework ranges from strict act-utilitarianism up to an integrity approach, and the assumed human nature of economic players varies from strictly selfish behaviour to optimal stewardship relations. The CSR and SRI concepts are basically derived from similar values. Fig. 11.1 shows a theoretical example of a traditional and a sustainable firm as represented by the chosen points on the six separate axes. The figure depicts a pure company perspective.

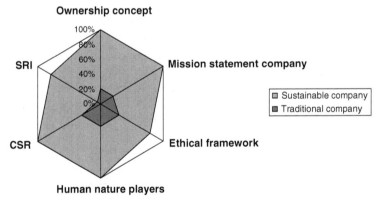

Fig. 11.1 Theoretical elements of the sustainable company
Source: Self designed figure

A CSR company, as generally portrayed in the literature, clearly approaches the market from a stakeholder perspective, which has immediate consequences for managerial policy. The intensity and the number of stakeholders that can be addressed vary between every company and sector. The percentage on the *ownership concept* axis can therefore be positioned anywhere from 0% (pure shareholder model), to

---

[11] See Soppe (2008) for the difference between pure shareholders and dual shareholders. Dual shareholders are defined as stakeholders (employees, NGOs, suppliers) holding shares in a company and who as such acquire a dual interest in the company.

attention for just the environment and customers (e.g., 50%), up to consideration for all relevant stakeholders, including the community (100%). The axis represents a theoretically continuous sustainability score. The *mission statement* of the CSR company is crucial in communicating a sustainable company policy, but is, as such, an insufficient infrastructure with which to measure the company's performance from that perspective. Window dressing is a well-known phenomenon in, for example, environmental management control (cf. Perego 2005) or in general reporting of CSR companies (cf. Idowu and Towler 2004). However, communicating a triple bottom line is an intentional start and a crucial condition for stakeholder awareness and sustainable finance. As far as the *ethical framework* is concerned, the traditional company differs from the CSR company in the sense that the organisation's moral character changes from an amoral institution to a company that pursues organisational integrity as a necessary condition. The strictly utilitarian approach of the traditional company evolves via the more individual responsibility of the virtue-ethical approach to a communitarian approach of the CSR company. The ultimate sustainable company could be based on the integrity approach as proposed in the "balanced company" of Kaptein and Wempe (2002). In that theory of corporate integrity, the company is considered an autonomous moral entity. Then there is the axis of the assumptions on the *human nature of players*. Whereas all finance theory on the traditional firm is based on the assumptions underlying agency theory (the strictly selfish behaviour of rational economic man), the sustainable company relies on a stewardship theory of management (cf. Davis et al. 1997). In stewardship theory, the model of man is based on a steward whose behaviour is arranged in such a way that pro-organisational, collectivistic behaviour has a higher utility than individualistic, self-serving behaviour. This model is the complete opposite of the concept of "rational economic man" as presented in traditional finance literature. The 100% score of the CSR company on this axis is therefore merely a theoretical position assuming cooperative human behaviour of the economic agents involved instead of the selfish human behaviour observed in the traditional company. In summarising the sustainably governed company, we find that this type of company, as distinct from the traditional company, can be explicitly defined in terms of the building blocks of sustainable governance. Sustainable governance is therefore defined as a holistic governance approach in which stakeholders' interests are respected, and corporate democracy and stewardship responsibility are instruments used in corporate competition.

Conclusion

Did we solve the Tirole (2001) problem implying that the stakeholder society is hindered by the dearth of pledgeable income, deadlocks in decision-making and the lack of a clear mission for management? In the civil society, a better economic system starts off with clear intentions in the minds of the responsible managers. The deplorable current state of the art in many industrialised economies following the climate crisis (cf. Stern 2007), the financial crisis of 2008 (see the Financial

Times, May 2009) and moral scandals like Madoff's strongly advocates the need for renewed emphasis on sustainability. Moreover, the national debt positions of the USA and many other nations are burdening future generations on an unprecedented scale. The future of finance and the financial system is at stake and megatrends in globalisation, demographic changes, new market dynamics and a revival of ethics can currently be identified (cf. Bakas and Peverelli 2008). Sustainable corporate governance should therefore start with clear company mission statements, opportunities for new leadership, new management theories and new practical applications.[12] This is what some well-known political figures call change!

References

Alchian, A.A. 1982. Property rights, specialization, and the firm. In *Corporate enterprise in a new environment*, ed. J.F. Weston and M.E. Granfield, 11–36. New York, NY: KCG Productions.

Bakas, A., and R. Peverelli. 2008. *The future of finance*. Schiedam: Scriptum Publishers.

Benn, S., and D. Dunphy. 2007. *Corporate governance and sustainability: Challenges for theory and practice*. New York, NY; London: Routledge.

Blair, M.M. 1995. *Ownership and control: Rethinking corporate governance for the twenty-first century*. Washington, DC: Brookings Institution Press.

Boatright, J.R. 1999. *Ethics in finance*. Malden, MA: Blackwell.

Bouckaert, L., and J. Vandenhove. 1994. *Meer dan strategie? Sociale verantwoordelijkheid als bedrijfsfilosofie*. Leuven: ACCO, Centre for Economics and Ethics.

Boutilier, R. 2009. *Stakeholder politics: Social capital, sustainable development, and the corporation*. Stanford, CA: Stanford University Press.

Bowie, N.E., and R.E. Freeman. 1992. *Ethics and agency theory: An introduction*. Oxford et al.: Oxford University Press.

Cornell, B., and A. Shapiro. 1987. Corporate stakeholders and corporate finance. *Financial Management* 16: 5–14.

Crane, A., A. McWilliams, D. Matten, J. Moon, and D.S. Siegel, eds. 2008. *The Oxford handbook of corporate social responsibility*. Oxford et al.: Oxford University Press.

Cyert, R.M., and J.G. March. 1963. *A behavioral theory of the firm*. Englewoods Cliffs, NJ: Prentice-Hall.

Davis, J.H., F.D. Schoorman, and L. Donaldson. 1997. Toward a stewardship theory of management. *Academy of Management Review* 22: 20–47.

Diamond, D.W. 1984. Financial intermediation and delegated monitoring. *Review of Economic Studies* 51: 393–414.

Dobson, J. 1999. Defending the stockholder model: A comment on Hasnas, and on Dunfee's MOM. *Business Ethics Quarterly* 9: 337–345.

Donaldson, L., and J.H. Davis. 1991. Stewardship theory or agency theory: CEO governance and shareholder returns. *Australian Journal of Management* 16: 49–64.

Dunfee, T.W. 1998. The marketplace of morality: First steps toward a theory of moral choice. *Business Ethics Quarterly* 8: 127–145.

Dyer, B., S. Jordan, S.A. Rochlin, and S. Shah. 2005. State of corporate citizenship in the U.S.: Business perspectives in 2005. Research report, Boston College, Center for corporate citizenship.

Elkington, J. 1997. *Cannibals with forks: The triple bottom line of 21st century business*. Oxford: Capstone.

---

[12] See for example Wirtenberg et al. (2009).

Engelen, E. 2002. Corporate governance, property and democracy: A conceptual critique of shareholder ideology. *Economy and Society* 31: 391–413.

Fama, E.F., and M.C. Jensen. 1983. Agency problems and residual claims. *Journal of Law and Economics* 26: 327–349.

Fergus, A.H.T., and J.I.A. Rowney. 2005. Sustainable development: Epistemological frameworks & an ethic of choice. *Journal of Business Ethics* 57: 197–207.

Freeman, R.E. 1984. *Strategic management: A stakeholder approach*. Boston, MA: Pitman.

Freeman, R.E., A.C. Wicks, and B. Parmar. 2004. Stakeholder theory and 'The corporate objective revisited'. *Organization Science* 15: 364–369.

Habisch, A., J. Jonker, M. Wegner, and R. Schmidpeter, eds. 2005. *Corporate social responsibility across Europe*. Berlin et al.: Springer.

Hasnas, J. 1998. The normative theories of business ethics: A guide for the perplexed. *Business Ethics Quarterly* 8: 19–42.

Idowu, S.O., and B.A. Towler. 2004. A comparative study of the contents of corporate social responsibility reports of UK companies. *Management of Environmental Quality: An International Journal* 15: 420–437.

Jensen, M.C. 1986. Agency costs of free cash flow, corporate finance, and Takeovers, *American Economic Review, Papers and Proceedings of the 98th Annual Meeting of the American Economic Association*, 76, 323–329.

Jensen, M.C., and W.H. Meckling. 1976. Theory of the firm: Managerial behavior, agency costs and ownership structure. *Journal of Financial Economics* 3: 305–360.

Johnson, E.W. 1997. Corporate soulcraft in the age of brutal markets. *Business Ethics Quarterly* 7: 109–124.

Kao, R.W.Y. 2007. *Stewardship-based economics*. Singapore: World Scientific Publishing.

Kaptein, M., and J. Wempe. 2002. *The balanced company: A theory of corporate integrity*. Oxford et al.: Oxford University Press.

Keasey, K., S. Thompson, and M. Wright. eds. 2005. *Corporate governance: Accountability, enterprise and international comparisons*. Chichester: Wiley.

Klein, S. 1998. Don Quixote and the problem of idealism and realism in business ethics. *Business Ethics Quarterly* 8: 43–63.

Lélé, S.M. 1991. Sustainable development: A critical review. *World Development* 19: 607–621.

Lozano, J.M., L. Albareda, and T. Ysa. 2008. *Governments and corporate social responsibility: Public policies beyond regulation and voluntary compliance*. Basingstoke: Palgrave Macmillan.

Maljers, F.A. 2008. Preface by Floris Maljers. In *Corporate governance and corporate finance. A European perspective,* ed. R.A.I. van Frederikslust, J.S. Ang, and P.S. Sudarsanam, xviii-ixx. Abingdon: Routledge.

Matten, D., and J. Moon. 2008. 'Implicit' and 'Explicit' CSR: A conceptual framework for a comparative understanding of corporate social responsibility. *Academy of Management Review* 33: 404–424.

Perego, P.M. 2005. *Environmental management control. An empirical study on the use of environmental performance measures in management control systems*. Dissertation: Radboud University Nijmegen.

Petschow, U., J. Rosenau, and E.U. von Weizsäcker, eds. 2005. *Governance and sustainability: New challenges for states, companies and civil society*. Sheffield: Greenleaf Publishing.

Shefrin, H., and M. Statman. 1993. Ethics, fairness and efficiency in financial markets. *Financial Analysts Journal* 49: 21–29.

Shleifer, A., and R.W. Vishny. 1997. A survey of corporate governance. *Journal of Finance* 52: 737–783.

Simon, H.A. 1982. *Models of bounded rationality, Vol. 1 and 2*. Cambridge, MA: MIT Press.

Soppe, A.B.M. 2008. Sustainable finance and the stakeholder equity model. In *Trends in business and economic ethics,* ed. C.J. Cowton and M. Haase. Berlin, Heidelberg: Springer. (= Studies in economic ethics and philosophy).

Stern, N.H. 2007. *The economics of climate change: The stern review*. Cambridge et al.: Cambridge University Press.

Stout, L.A. 2002. Bad and not-so-bad arguments for shareholder primacy. *Southern California Law Review* 75: 1189–1209.

Stout, L.A. 2007. The mythical benefit of shareholder control. *Virginia Law Review* 93: 789–810.

Tempelaar, F.M. 1991. Theorie van de ondernemingsfinanciering. *Maandblad voor Accountancy en Bedrijfseconomie (MAB)*, June 284–298.

Tirole, J. 2001. Corporate governance. *Econometrica* 69: 1–35.

Townsend, R.M. 1979. Optimal contracts and competitive markets with costly state verification. *Journal of Economic Theory* 21: 265–293.

Welzer, H. 2008. *Klimakriege. Wofür im 21. Jahrhundert getötet wird*. Frankfurt a. M.: S. Fischer.

Williamson, O.E. 1988. Corporate finance and corporate governance. *Journal of Finance* 43: 567–591.

Wirtenberg, J., W.G. Russell, and D. Lipsky, eds. 2009. *The sustainable enterprise fieldbook: When it all comes together*. New York, NY: Greenleaf Publishing.

Chapter 12
Triadic Stakeholder Theory Revisited

Alexei M. Marcoux

Contents

A.M. Marcoux (✉)
Associate Professor of Business Ethics, School of Business Administration,
Loyola University Chicago, Chicago, IL, USA
e-mail: alexei.marcoux@gmail.com

A. Brink (ed.), *Corporate Governance and Business Ethics*, Ethical Economy.
Studies in Economic Ethics and Philosophy 39, DOI 10.1007/978-94-007-1588-2_12,
© Springer Science+Business Media B.V. 2011

Introduction

It is hard to overstate the esteem in which business ethicists hold Tom Donaldson and Lee Preston's "The Stakeholder Theory of the Corporation: Concepts, Evidence, and Implications" (1995).[1] Business ethicists moved by stakeholder theory credit Donaldson and Preston with articulating, better than anyone else has done, their worldview.[2] Perhaps no aspect of their paper commands greater acclaim than the explication of stakeholder theory as a *triad* of theses – one normative, one instrumental, one descriptive[3] – the elements of which are both "interrelated" and "mutually supportive" (Donaldson and Preston 1995, p. 65), with the normative thesis as "the critical underpinning for the theory in all its forms" (ibid., p. 66), and "the core of the theory" (ibid., p. 74). So understood, Donaldson and Preston's stakeholder theory emerges as an *omnibus* theory of the firm, capturing it both as it is (descriptive thesis) and as it ought to be (normative thesis), as well as affording managers useful guidance about how to run it (instrumental thesis). The three theses, corresponding to the three uses, senses, or kinds of stakeholder thinking, are this omnibus theory's main, interlocking components.

Although Donaldson and Preston's contribution meets with overwhelming approval and has become a standard citation in the stakeholder-theoretic business ethics literature, I will argue that their triadic interpretation is conceptually confused and its normative thesis, advertised as the conceptual heart of their omnibus stakeholder theory, is morally trivial. If correct, this conclusion's importance extends beyond the merits of Donaldson and Preston's paper. It has significant implications for the *corporate governance debate* in business ethics.

In the business ethics literature, the corporate governance debate is typically cast as a shareholder-stakeholder debate, i.e., a debate between those who hold that all

---

[1] An earlier and shorter version of this paper was presented at the Society for Business Ethics Annual Meeting, Washington, D.C., 3 August 2001. I thank Robert Audi, John Boatright, Tom Carson, Ian Maitland, Douglas Rasmussen, two anonymous referees, and the editor of this volume for their helpful comments on the original and subsequent drafts of this paper.

[2] Typical of the response are Jones and Wicks who credit Donaldson and Preston with adding "considerable coherence to the stakeholder concept as theory" (Jones and Wicks 1999, p. 206) and endorse Donaldson and Preston's central theme in their own work. Although the approval is considerable, it is not universal – even among stakeholder theorists. In two different papers, R. Edward Freeman lodges two broad criticisms of Donaldson and Preston's triadic interpretation. In his earlier paper, Freeman argues that the triadic interpretation fails to capture the diversity and complexity of both extant and possible stakeholder-theoretic constructions, which constitute "a genre of stories about how we could live" (Freeman 1994, p. 413). In his later paper, Freeman argues that the triadic interpretation rests on a "centuries-old philosophy of science" which, when rejected in favor of what he styles "modern pragmatism", yields a stakeholder theory in which "[t]here is nothing to converge – no separate contributions for philosophers and management theorists. There are just narratives about stakeholders and narratives about narratives – that is, theory" (Freeman 1999, pp. 233f.).

[3] I reverse the order in which Donaldson and Preston advance the theses for reasons of explicatory economy. The argument of the present paper is expressed with greater felicity by considering the theses in reverse order.

firms ought to be managed in the interests of their shareholders and those who hold that all firms ought to be managed in the interests of their stakeholders. This characterization is unfortunate because it fails to capture the diversity of views, both actual (particularly *outside* the business ethics literature) and potential, that can be held on the governance of firms. It also commits contestants on both sides to some unduly stringent views (e.g., that consumer, producer, and worker cooperatives are impermissible). The debate is better characterized as one over *the moral permissibility of the investor-owned firm with fiduciary duties to shareholders alone* – the firm managed with the aim of maximizing its residuum for its equity investors, with that aim secured by imposing fiduciary duties on managers to act on behalf of the equity investors' interest in that residuum. This is so because one may argue for (or against) this firm's moral permissibility on a variety of grounds, not all of which are compatible.[4]

Some proponents of the moral permissibility of the investor-owned firm may argue that this organizational form is necessitated by the peculiar moral status of the shareholder-manager relation (cf., e.g., Marcoux 2003; Goodpaster 1991).[5] Other proponents may argue that there is nothing intrinsically valuable about the shareholder-manager relation, but there are nonetheless strong consequentialist grounds for forming the type of firm in which it features prominently.[6] Still others may argue that any organizational form that results from the free contracting of persons is a permissible form, and the investor-owned firm is one such form (cf., e.g., Macey 1999; Sollars 2002). Similarly, some opponents of the moral permissibility of the investor-owned firm may argue that there exists a particular normative theory of the firm – the stakeholder theory – the correctness of which implies that the investor-owned firm is morally impermissible. Other opponents may argue that the investor-owned firm is morally impermissible not on the basis of a particular theory of the firm (e.g., the stakeholder theory), but instead on the basis of the correctness of a particular moral or normative political theory (cf., e.g., McCall 2001). This or something like it is the preferred tack in the progressive corporate law literature (cf., e.g., several contributions in Mitchell 1995). In short, several positions exist on the moral permissibility of the investor-owned firm, only two of which are represented in the shareholder-stakeholder debate (with one – shareholder theory as it is portrayed by stakeholder theorists – being largely a straw person). Engaging the larger,

---

[4] See Boatright (2002) for a comparatively rare contribution to the business ethics literature that recognizes the terms of the debate and is structured with those terms in mind.

[5] Goodpaster (perhaps owing to his idiosyncratic terminology) is frequently misidentified as a proponent of stakeholder theory despite his explicit endorsement of fiduciary duties to shareholders and his denial that non-shareholding stakeholders are owed fiduciary care. Indeed, Goodpaster's "stakeholder theory" is basically Milton Friedman's theory augmented by additional side constraints (principally against doing harm) on the pursuit of profit maximization. Tom Carson is perhaps alone in the business ethics literature in recognizing explicitly the compatibility of Goodpaster's view with Friedman's shareholder theory (cf. Carson 1993).

[6] See Boatright (1994), who is frequently cited erroneously as a proponent of stakeholder theory and whose paper is with equal frequency cited by a single erroneous title. Cf. citations in Jones and Wicks (1999, pp. 209, 219) and Freeman and Phillips (2002, pp. 333, 347).

richer, more sophisticated debate requires identifying correctly its central point of contention.

Donaldson and Preston's triadic interpretation merits close treatment because the mutual support they claim to find among the theses has important implications. The usual motivation for claiming that multiple theses are interrelated or mutually supporting is to facilitate arguments in which evidence for one thesis is also evidence for another. Indeed, it is hard to imagine why mutual support among multiple theses would be worth arguing for unless it is for that purpose.[7] The triadic interpretation both reflects and informs an argumentative strategy, usually implicit, in the stakeholder-theoretic business ethics literature. This argumentative strategy has two elements, a positive claim and a negative claim, composing the two sides of a single conceptual coin.

The positive claim is this:

> If the practices or policies commended by normative stakeholder theory are shown to have instrumental merits (e.g., they promote profitability, stability, or growth), then this showing bolsters the veracity of both the normative claim and the normative theory generating it.

If the three aspects of Donaldson and Preston's omnibus stakeholder theory are interrelated and mutually supporting, and if the normative aspect undergirds the other two, then this constitutes a strong justification for the positive claim. For if the instrumental thesis depends upon the normative thesis and the instrumental virtues can be demonstrated, then the normative virtues follow: if I depends upon N and I is true, then N must be true also.

The negative claim is this:

> If the practices or policies commended morally under the guise of normative stakeholder theory are shown to have instrumental merits, then this fact undermines the investor-owned firm with fiduciary duties to shareholders alone – the firm whose officers and directors are duty-bound to find and adopt those practices and policies that redound to the benefit of shareholders by promoting profitability, stability, or growth.

This is so, presumably, because extending fiduciary care to shareholders alone entails overlooking, and hence failing to implement, practices or policies redounding to the benefit of shareholders.[8] Call this the *myopia argument*.

The myopia argument expresses the negative corollary of the view that identifying and implementing practices and policies enhancing firm performance is linked inextricably to acting on the prescriptions of a preferred normative ethical theory – normative stakeholder theory. Those who do not heed it are blind

---

[7] Although Donaldson and Preston advance no account of why mutual support among the three theses is an important insight, it is not difficult to determine why it matters to one of the authors. Donaldson elsewhere seeks to "bridge the is-ought gap" (cf. Donaldson and Dunfee 1999). That is just another way of saying that he seeks to lay the groundwork for arguments in which evidence for one kind of thesis (an "is" thesis) is also evidence for another (an "ought" thesis). The attempt to show that the three theses composing Donaldson and Preston's omnibus stakeholder theory are mutually supporting is but another manifestation of that same project.

[8] Although not advanced on behalf of stakeholder theory in particular, this is the upshot of Norman Bowie's paradox-of-hedonism-based arguments (cf. Bowie 1999).

to practices and policies enhancing firm performance, even and especially when enhancing that performance is their explicit aim. Again, if true, the triadic interpretation underwrites this negative claim. For if the instrumental thesis is dependent upon the normative thesis, then the right normative commitments are a necessary prologue to instrumental success: if *I* depends upon *N* and *I* is true, then *N* must be true also.

Consequently, a great deal rides on the triadic interpretation, in general, and on the conceptual primacy of the normative thesis, in particular. In addition to expressing the worldview of many business ethicists identifying with normative stakeholder theory, it underwrites both a normative argumentative strategy and a research program that sees the instrumental merits of practices and policies commended by normative stakeholder theory as evidence of its moral superiority.

Donaldson and Preston: Stakeholder Theory in Triadic Form

Donaldson and Preston aver that the normative, instrumental, and descriptive strands of stakeholder thinking yield the aspectual theses of an omnibus stakeholder theory, at the center of which lies the normative thesis. The theses are interrelated and mutually supporting – meaning, presumably, that there exists some logical relationship among them. Evaluating these claims requires identification and analysis of the three theses. Identification is the task of the present part. Analysis is the task of part III.

Normative Thesis

Donaldson and Preston (1995) claim that the normative thesis is the "fundamental basis" of stakeholder theory and involves acceptance of the following ideas:

> (a) Stakeholders are persons or groups with legitimate interests in procedural and/or substantive aspects of corporate activity. Stakeholders are identified by *their* interests in the corporation, whether the corporation has any corresponding functional interest in *them*.

> (b) The interests of all stakeholders are of *intrinsic value*. That is, each group of stakeholders merits consideration for its own sake and not merely because of its ability to further the interests of some other group, such as the shareowners. (p. 67; emphasis in the original)

Normative stakeholder theory "attempts to interpret the function of, and offer guidance about, the investor-owned corporation on the basis of some underlying moral or philosophical principles" (ibid., p. 72). Normative justifications of stakeholder theory "appeal to underlying concepts such as individual or group 'rights', 'social contract', or utilitarianism" (ibid., p. 74).

The normative thesis finds its practical upshot in *stakeholder management*. Stakeholder management requires, as its key attribute, simultaneous attention to the legitimate interests of all appropriate stakeholders, both in the establishment of organizational structures and general policies and in case-by-case decision making (cf. ibid., p. 67). If true, the normative thesis underwrites morally the practice of stakeholder management.

Instrumental Thesis

Donaldson and Preston's instrumental thesis is the view that stakeholder theory establishes a framework for examining the connections, if any, between the practice of stakeholder management and the achievement of various corporate performance goals. The principal focus of interest here has been the proposition that corporations practicing stakeholder management will, other things being equal, be relatively successful in conventional performance terms (profitability, stability, growth, etc.) (cf. ibid., pp. 66f.).

Instrumental stakeholder theory makes a connection between stakeholder approaches and commonly desired objectives such as profitability. Instrumental uses usually stop short of exploring specific links between cause (i.e., stakeholder management) and effect (i.e., corporate performance) in detail, but such linkage is certainly implicit (cf. ibid., pp. 71f.).

Instrumental justifications of stakeholder theory "point to evidence of the connection between stakeholder management and corporate performance" (ibid., p. 66).

Descriptive Thesis

Donaldson and Preston's descriptive thesis is the view that stakeholder theory presents a model describing what the corporation is. It describes the corporation as a constellation of cooperative and competitive interests possessing intrinsic value (cf. ibid., p. 66).

This descriptive aspect "reflects and explains past, present, and future states of affairs of corporations and their stakeholders" (ibid., p. 71). Descriptive justifications of stakeholder theory "attempt to show that concepts embedded in the theory correspond to observed reality" (ibid., p. 71).

Donaldson and Preston's Triad: Content and Logical Relations

The important questions about Donaldson and Preston's three theses are two:

1. Do the three theses capture conceptually the normative, instrumental, and descriptive strains of stakeholder thinking?
2. Are the three theses mutually supporting in a manner that evidences an omnibus stakeholder theory with normative, instrumental, and descriptive aspects and with the normative aspect at its core?

Trivial Normative Thesis

Donaldson and Preston's normative thesis is peculiar. Indeed, *normative* is something of a misnomer, not because their normative thesis is non-normative, but because it is not *uniquely* normative among the three theses.

To say that *P* is normative is to say that *P* gives *reasons for action* (cf. Raz 1990).[9] Like their "normative" thesis, Donaldson and Preston's instrumental thesis is also normative; it too gives reasons for action. The normative thesis expresses the view that stakeholder-theoretic prescriptions are normative in one way: *morally* normative, giving moral reasons for action. The instrumental thesis expresses the view that stakeholder-theoretic prescriptions are normative in another way: *prudentially* normative, giving prudent reasons for action.[10]

Donaldson and Preston employ the concept of normativity narrowly, denoting moral reasons for action only. For them, normative claims are all and only those expressing the "right (wrong) thing to do" (Donaldson and Preston 1995, p. 72); what philosophers generally call moral claims. This is unproblematic, provided that Donaldson and Preston employ the concept that way consistently. However, no sooner does the reader accommodate herself to this narrow sense of the normative than does she recognize at least one aspect of the normative thesis that is not, in this narrow sense, normative.

Included in Donaldson and Preston's normative thesis is the claim that *stakeholders are identified by their interests* (cf. ibid., p. 67). Whether true or false, this is not, in Donaldson and Preston's sense, a normative claim – a claim about what is the "right (wrong) thing to do". It is instead an *epistemic* claim – a claim about how one knows or recognizes stakeholders. Lest this be thought a mere slip of the pen, Donaldson and Preston later insist that their epistemic claim is a normative proposition. Addressing strategies for grounding or justifying the normative thesis, they write,

> [T]he two normative propositions stated at the beginning of this article – that stakeholders are identified by *their* interests and that the interests of all stakeholders have intrinsic value – can be viewed as axiomatic principles that require no further justification. (ibid., p. 81; emphasis in the original)

Epistemic claims *are* normative in the broadest sense employed by philosophers (cf., e.g., Korsgaard 1996, p. 8). However, so too are prudential (instrumental) claims, to

---

[9] Strictly speaking, this is false. Normative statements include statements of reasons for action, for belief, and for attitudes (cf. Korsgaard 1996, p. 8). However, within the domain of practical reasoning (within which ethics certainly falls), the only forms of normativity that need concern one are those that entail reasons for action.

[10] This, perhaps, is what Donaldson and Preston (1995) advert to when they note that both normative and instrumental stakeholder theory are "prescriptive" (p. 72). But whether prescriptivity captures what is common to their normative and instrumental theses is at least open to doubt. In ethical theory, prescriptivism refers to a particular account of what normativity entails, rather than to normativity generally. It is a view associated with Hare (1952).

which Donaldson and Preston expressly deny the normative mantle. Because the claim *stakeholders are identified by their interests* says nothing about what is the "right (wrong) thing to do", it is not, in their sense, a normative claim.

The more pressing problem attending Donaldson and Preston's normative thesis, however, is that its content is neither unique to nor distinctive of stakeholder theory, even within the limited confines of the corporate governance debate. Their normative thesis advances no proposition or cluster of propositions emblematic of stakeholder theory.

The claim that one ought to afford consideration to the legitimate interests of all stakeholders borders on the tautological. It expresses a moral truism rather than a substantive thesis over which rival theorists contend. Who *denies* that if Q has a legitimate interest, then Q's (legitimate) interest ought to be considered? That an interest is legitimate entails that it ought to be considered.

Moral theorists break ranks and cross swords not over *whether* legitimate interests ought to be considered, but rather (a) over *which* interests are legitimate and (b) over *what kind* of consideration legitimate interests warrant. Within the corporate governance debate, the normative stakeholder theorist's claims are not disputed on the grounds that there is no reason to consider stakeholders' legitimate interests. Instead, they are disputed on the grounds that the interests appealed to are either (a) *not* legitimate or (b) not due the *kind* of consideration for which the normative stakeholder theorist calls. In other words, everyone in the normative corporate governance debate holds that legitimate interests ought to be considered – including those unmoved by stakeholder theory. The *debate* is over which interests are legitimate and what kind of consideration they warrant.

Therefore, if the normative stakeholder theorist has a substantive position, it resides in a *particular account* of legitimacy in interests or in a *particular account* of the kind of consideration legitimate interests warrant. What is stakeholder theory's particular account of legitimacy in interests or of the kind of consideration legitimate interests warrant? For the answer to this question, the careful reader searches Donaldson and Preston's landmark paper in vain.[11]

To express a distinctive and consequential normative position, as many claim that it does,[12] stakeholder theory's normative thesis has to be more substantial than the trivial and virtually universally-held view that *legitimate interests ought to be considered*. Far from standing as its gravitational center, Donaldson and Preston's normative thesis is the omnibus theory's emptiest vessel. It is neither interestingly nor substantively normative.

---

[11] The lack of a substantive, stakeholder-theoretic account of legitimacy in interests, or of the kind of consideration legitimate interests warrant, is not the unique failing of Donaldson and Preston. Freeman and Phillips advance an account of stakeholder theory's normative thesis that rivals Donaldson and Preston's for sparsity of content. In the context of what they aver is a "libertarian defense" of stakeholder theory, they advance as its normative content the view that "managers ought to pay attention to key stakeholder relationships" (Freeman and Phillips 2002, p. 338).

[12] Jones and Wicks (1999) aver both that stakeholder theory is intellectually vibrant and that its normative aspect is its best-developed part.

Parochial Instrumental Thesis

Donaldson and Preston's instrumental thesis avoids the pitfalls of their normative thesis. Whereas their normative thesis commits its adherent to no distinctive normative position, their instrumental thesis is tied to peculiarly stakeholder-theoretic concerns.

For Donaldson and Preston, the instrumental thesis is a predictive claim about the likely consequences of practicing stakeholder management. Because *legitimate* interests are the object of simultaneous managerial attention in stakeholder management (cf. Donaldson and Preston 1995, p. 67), it follows that Donaldson and Preston's stakeholder management is the adoption and practice of what normative stakeholder theory (that branch which concerns itself with moral notions like legitimacy) calls for.[13]

Donaldson and Preston's instrumental thesis is problematic, not because it is non-instrumental,[14] but instead because arbitrarily it confines instrumental stakeholder theory to the generation and testing of hypotheses about the consequences of practicing what normative stakeholder theory commends. There is at least one other project theorists could pursue that is not covered by Donaldson and Preston's instrumental thesis and yet appears to be as much about the instrumental aspects of stakeholder thinking as their preferred project.

Instrumental stakeholder theorists may be interested in exploring the usefulness of *stakeholder analysis* as a discovery procedure for mapping and interpreting a firm's strategic terrain. That is, rather than studying the instrumental merits of a *substantive* view about what managers ought to do (normative stakeholder theory), they may be interested in pursuing the instrumental merits of a stakeholder-oriented *procedure* for managerial decision making (stakeholder analysis). Goodpaster (1991) adverts to this kind of instrumental stakeholder thinking when he writes,

> We can imagine decision-makers doing "stakeholder analysis" for different underlying reasons, not always having to do with ethics. A management team, for example, might be careful to take positive and (especially) negative stakeholder effects into account for no other reason than that the offended stakeholders might resist or retaliate (e.g., through political action or opposition to necessary regulatory clearances). It might not be ethical concern for stakeholders that motivates and guides this analysis, so much as concern about potential impediments to the achievement of strategic objectives. (p. 57)

---

[13] The correctness of this interpretation is made explicit later by Donaldson when he writes that instrumental stakeholder theory "refers to any theory asserting some form of the claim that, all other things being equal, if managers view the interests of stakeholders as having intrinsic worth and pursue the interests of multiple stakeholders, then the corporations they manage will achieve higher traditional performance measures" (Donaldson 1999, p. 238).

[14] Indeed, as Jones and Wicks (1999) observe, instrumental stakeholder theory "posits that certain outcomes will obtain if certain behaviors are adopted. Instrumental theory is contingent theory: the predicted outcomes are contingent on behavior of a certain type" (p. 208). Instrumental theory, they continue, "involves if/then statements" (ibid., p. 213). There can be little doubt that Donaldson and Preston's instrumental thesis entails claims about the outcomes that follow from the adoption of certain actions and that these claims are formulable as if/then statements.

Decision makers can engage in stakeholder analysis without affording priority, or even attention, to the prescriptions of normative stakeholder theory. Indeed, they can engage in stakeholder analysis in complete ignorance of normative stakeholder theory, viewing stakeholder analysis as a useful procedure only. By the same token, an instrumental stakeholder theorist may be interested in the comparative usefulness of this stakeholder-oriented interpretive framework as against alternative ways of conceiving the firm's strategic terrain – again, without reference to normative stakeholder theory or its prescriptions.

It is unreasonable to suppose that this kind of research is insufficiently stakeholder-oriented and therefore rightly excluded from the *very concept* of instrumental stakeholder theory, as Donaldson and Preston's account suggests. Consequently, their instrumental thesis is parochial. It confines arbitrarily the instrumental stakeholder theorist's attention to normatively generated prescriptions.

Conceptually Suspect Descriptive Thesis

Whereas their normative thesis lacks distinctive, substantive content and their instrumental thesis is parochial in outlook, Donaldson and Preston's descriptive thesis fails in other ways.[15] Although they advance a straightforward *statement* of their descriptive thesis, that thesis is not, in fact, descriptive.

Donaldson and Preston's descriptive thesis is the claim that the corporation is "a constellation of co-operative and competitive interests possessing intrinsic value" (Donaldson and Preston 1995, p. 66). This is an aggregation of two more basic claims. The first is descriptive: *the corporation is a constellation of co-operative and competing interests*. The second is normative: the interests adverted to *have intrinsic value*. Establishing the truth of this second claim requires appeal to normative arguments, not to empirical observation. Consequently, the aggregation of the two more basic claims is not (or is not merely) descriptive.[16]

---

[15] Jones and Wicks sidestep descriptive stakeholder theory on the grounds that it seems less promising a mode of inquiry than instrumental stakeholder theory (cf. Jones and Wicks 1999, pp. 207f.). Others may legitimately question the very possibility of descriptive theory (whether stakeholder-oriented or not). What, after all, is a descriptive *theory* over and above a *description*? I will not pursue these issues here.

[16] An anonymous referee commenting on an earlier version of this paper asks whether Donaldson and Preston may defuse this argument by denying a rigid fact/value distinction. They cannot, for Donaldson and Preston's triadic interpretation *itself* depends upon a rigid fact/value distinction. How, except by recognizing significant conceptual cleavage between the descriptive and the normative, may one conclude in a reasoned way that *this* claim is descriptive and *that* is normative? Denying that conceptual cleavage, they would be denying the ground upon which the triadic structure of their theory is built. This is what Freeman adverts to when he criticizes Donaldson and Preston's view for relying on "a centuries-old philosophy of science" (see note 2, above). Freeman believes it best to abandon that philosophy of science and recognizes that the triadic interpretation must be abandoned along with it. I strike from the other side, arguing that even if one accepts that underlying philosophy of science one cannot get where Donaldson and Preston wish to go.

Moreover, Donaldson and Preston's descriptive thesis is at odds with the most intuitive understanding of descriptive stakeholder-theoretic claims. Presumably, descriptive stakeholder theorists may advance and seek to verify a number of descriptive claims. One claim, related to Donaldson and Preston's descriptive thesis but distinct from it, is that *firms are managed as if* (or, *people in firms believe that*) the firm is a constellation of co-operative and competing interests possessing intrinsic value. Another claim, unrelated to Donaldson and Preston's descriptive thesis, is that firms employ stakeholder analysis as part of their managerial decision procedures. Still others could be formulated, all under the rubric of descriptive stakeholder theory. Donaldson and Preston's descriptive thesis is instead a second (and unacknowledged) normative claim.

Mutual Support Among the Theses

Determining whether Donaldson and Preston's normative, instrumental, and descriptive theses are mutually supporting, in the way they understand them to be, is difficult. Although they repeatedly assert that the three theses are mutually supporting, they neither argue for the assertion nor indicate what, exactly, they mean to be asserting. The claim of mutual support among the three theses is most plausibly read as a claim that they are *logically* related. In particular, it is a claim that some theses stand as necessary premises in arguments showing that other theses are true. Because Donaldson and Preston claim that the normative thesis undergirds the other two, they presumably understand it to stand as a necessary premise in arguments showing that the instrumental and descriptive theses are true. That is, they understand the veracity of the instrumental and descriptive theses to *depend* upon the veracity of the normative thesis.

From the foregoing analysis of the three theses, three observations commend themselves readily:

1. The normative thesis is at best trivially normative.
2. The instrumental thesis speaks only to a part of instrumental stakeholder theory – the part seeking to generate and test hypotheses about the probable effects of conformity with the normative thesis's prescriptions.
3. The descriptive thesis is not a descriptive thesis, but instead a second normative thesis.

Consequently, if there are any logical relations at all among Donaldson and Preston's normative, instrumental, and descriptive theses, they are these:

Their normative thesis depends upon their descriptive thesis. If there is a logical relation between the normative and the descriptive theses, the descriptive thesis stands as a premise in an argument intended to show that the normative thesis is true. If "the corporation [i]s a constellation of cooperative and competitive interests possessing intrinsic value" (Donaldson and Preston 1995, p. 66), then the intrinsic value of those interests can be appealed to as a premise in an argument for managing as the normative thesis prescribes.

The converse, however, does not hold. If managers ought morally to manage as the normative thesis prescribes, that does not stand as a premise in an argument designed to show (and hence, some reason for believing) that the corporation is a constellation of cooperative and competitive interests possessing intrinsic value. The normative thesis is equally compatible with the view that the interests referred to in the descriptive thesis are not intrinsically valuable. In fact, Donaldson and Preston imply as much. They argue that normative stakeholder theory is justifiable by reference to *utilitarianism* (cf. ibid., pp. 74, 84), a moral theory holding that interests are valuable only contingently and instrumentally – valuable insofar as they promote aggregate utility (whether construed in terms of happiness or satisfaction of informed preferences) and not valuable otherwise. If the normative thesis is compatible with utilitarianism, then the descriptive thesis (which asserts the intrinsic value stakeholder interests) *cannot* depend upon the normative thesis. Thus, if either thesis depends upon the other at all, the normative thesis depends upon the descriptive thesis. Put differently, if either thesis is "the critical underpinning" of stakeholder theory, it is the descriptive thesis.

Their instrumental thesis is an empirical hypothesis about the probable effects of adopting the prescriptions of the normative thesis, which, in turn, is premised upon their descriptive thesis. The instrumental thesis speaks to the effects of adopting the normative thesis's prescriptions. Consequently, the logical content of the instrumental thesis depends upon the content of the normative thesis. Put differently, the normative thesis expresses some of the necessary content of the instrumental thesis. However, because the descriptive thesis undergirds the normative (if either undergirds the other at all), it follows that "the critical underpinning" of the instrumental thesis is the descriptive thesis. Again, what Donaldson and Preston advertise as a set of interrelated and mutually supporting theses based fundamentally upon the normative thesis is, if the set is interrelated and mutually supporting at all, based fundamentally upon the descriptive thesis.

These logical relations underwrite two significant conclusions:

C1. Donaldson and Preston's normative, instrumental, and descriptive theses advance impoverished conceptions of normative, instrumental, and descriptive stakeholder thinking. In content, their instrumental and descriptive theses are, respectively, a conceptually thin manifestation of and an underlying claim about their conceptually thinner normative thesis.

C2. As their normative thesis may depend upon their descriptive thesis but not the converse, it follows that, contrary to the banner claim of their paper, their normative thesis is not the omnibus theory's center, but instead derivative of and dependent on their descriptive thesis.

Donaldson and Preston neither argue for the existence of an omnibus stakeholder theory, encompassing genuinely normative, instrumental, and descriptive stakeholder theories, nor advance a morally substantial and conceptually central normative thesis. Prospects for establishing the existence of an omnibus stakeholder theory (whether or not grounded in its normative aspect) must lie elsewhere.

Reforming the Triad

Although Donaldson and Preston's three theses do not exhibit mutual support among genuine and distinct normative, instrumental, and descriptive stakeholder theories, perhaps *reformed* versions of the theses – versions better capturing normative, instrumental, and descriptive stakeholder thinking – can be constructed. Perhaps mutual support exists among the reformed theses and, therefore, the reformed theses compose collectively the omnibus theory that Donaldson and Preston seek, but do not provide. In the present part, I construct reformed normative, instrumental, and descriptive theses better capturing these strands of stakeholder thinking.

Reformed Normative Thesis

Donaldson and Preston's normative thesis is troubled for two separate, but related, reasons. First, its content does not separate the normative stakeholder theorist from her opponents by setting out and arguing for a distinctive position. Second, its content, if true, does not imply the moral impermissibility of the investor-owned firm with fiduciary duties to shareholders alone.

These results are peculiar because many stakeholder theorists understand their normative commitments to be incompatible with the investor-owned firm with fiduciary duties to shareholders alone, a firm which Donaldson and Preston (1995) themselves claim is "normatively unacceptable" (p. 82). As they advance no argument for this claim,[17] the most ready explanation is that it is supposed to be, and the reader is supposed to recognize it as, an *implication* of the normative thesis. That is, the normative thesis is *incompatible* with the investor-owned firm with fiduciary duties to shareholders alone. So, if the normative thesis is true, the claim that the investor-owned firm with fiduciary duties to shareholders alone is morally permissible must be false.

But Donaldson and Preston's normative thesis calls only for managers to consider the legitimate interests of all stakeholders. There are many ways to consider stakeholder interests, only some of which are incompatible with extending fiduciary care to shareholders alone. Moreover, there can be rival accounts of which stakeholder interests are legitimate and why, only some of which are incompatible with extending fiduciary care to shareholders alone. Therefore, it does not follow from Donaldson and Preston's normative thesis that the investor-owned firm with fiduciary duties to shareholders alone is morally impermissible. If the normative thesis is to have this upshot, it requires commitment to the claim that (a) the kind of consideration that ought to be given is incompatible with the investor-owned firm with fiduciary duties to shareholders alone – as well as an account of what that kind of

---

[17] They write only that "careful analysis reveals that it is normatively unacceptable" (Donaldson and Preston 1995, p. 82). The careful analysis revealing this is neither conducted nor cited in their article.

consideration is and why it is called for – or (b) the interests that are legitimate are incompatible with the investor-owned firm with fiduciary duties to shareholders alone – as well as an account of what those interests are and why they are legitimate.

Many such accounts could be advanced, but for present purposes let us stipulate only that a reformed normative thesis, in order to advance a non-trivial normative view, includes commitment to (a) a kind of consideration incompatible with extending fiduciary care to shareholders alone or (b) the inclusion of interests the legitimacy of which is incompatible with extending fiduciary care to shareholders alone.

Reformed Instrumental Thesis

In part III, drawing on Goodpaster (1991), I argued that instrumental approaches to stakeholder thinking can facilitate pursuit of questions about the merits of stakeholder analysis as a procedure for mapping and interpreting a firm's strategic terrain. Whereas Donaldson and Preston recognize only research into the effects of practicing normatively-driven stakeholder management, instrumental stakeholder theory can also contemplate hypotheses about the usefulness of stakeholder analysis as a component of decision making, whether or not the prescriptions of normative stakeholder theory are afforded priority or even recognized at all. Jones (1995) contemplates a version of this kind of instrumental stakeholder theory.

A reformed instrumental thesis, capturing adequately the projects, both actual and potential, that can be pursued under its rubric, could be formulated in these terms:

> Instrumental stakeholder theory examines and advances hypotheses about the relationship between various stakeholder-oriented practices and the outcomes of adopting those practices. Among the relationships to be considered and hypothesized about is the relationship between the practices adopted and the outcomes that follow. The instrumental stakeholder theorist maintains that there exist significant relationships between the adoption of stakeholder-oriented practices and the achievement of strategic objectives, whether those practices are advanced under the guise of normative stakeholder theory or merely as a result of stakeholder analysis employed as a decision procedure.

Reformed Descriptive Thesis

Abandoning Donaldson and Preston's statement of the descriptive thesis, one is left with the task of constructing a plausible alternative. Presumably, it will refer to the *behavior* of managers in firms or to the *beliefs and attitudes* informing that behavior. Although Donaldson and Preston's account fails in this regard, the reformed normative and instrumental theses point readily to two commonsense, alternative descriptive theses. Call these the *normative* descriptive thesis and the *instrumental* descriptive thesis.

Normative Descriptive Thesis

The normative descriptive thesis expresses the view that firms are managed in a way that at least attempts to implement what the normative thesis commends. The point is less one about the success or failure of these endeavors than about the *ends* informing managerial deliberation about action. The normative descriptive thesis is just the view that firms, through the actions of their managers, seek to realize the aims that the normative thesis says they ought. Jones and Wicks (1999) contemplate a version of the normative descriptive thesis.

Instrumental Descriptive Thesis

The instrumental descriptive thesis expresses the view that firms adopt stakeholder-oriented practices – whether those commended by normative stakeholder theory or those that merely conceive of the firm's strategic terrain in stakeholder terms – to achieve their objectives. The point is less one about the success or failure of these endeavors than about the *means* by which managers seek to achieve the firm's ends. The instrumental descriptive thesis is just the view that firms, through the actions of their managers, employ the means that the instrumental thesis says they ought to employ. Jones (1994) contemplates a version of the instrumental descriptive thesis.

Rather than select antecedently one version of the descriptive thesis over the other, in part V I will refer to each, as necessary, in order to establish the logical relationship that exists among the three reformed theses. The important differences between Donaldson and Preston's theses and the reformed theses are summarized in Table 12.1.

Table 12.1 Donaldson and Preston (1995) and Reformed theses compared

	Donaldson and Preston (1995)	Reformed
Normative thesis	Legitimate interests of all stakeholders ought to be considered	Legitimate interests of all stakeholders ought to be considered *and either (a) the kind of consideration that ought to be extended or (b) the interests which are legitimate are incompatible with the investor-owned firm with fiduciary duties to shareholders alone*
Instrumental thesis	Stakeholder management (i.e., paying simultaneous attention to the legitimate interests of all stakeholders) secures other valuable, non-moral objectives of the firm	There exist useful relationships between the adoption of stakeholder-oriented practices and the achievement of a variety of objectives Some of these practices may have substance derived from normative stakeholder theory, and others may be merely procedural and bear no connection to normative stakeholder theory
Descriptive thesis	The firm is a constellation of cooperative and competitive interests possessing intrinsic value	Two versions: Normative descriptive: Firms are managed in a way that at least attempts to implement what the normative thesis commends Instrumental descriptive: Firms adopt stakeholder-oriented practices – whether substantive and derived from the normative or procedural and not

Mutual Support Revisited

In the present part, I seek to establish the logical relations, if any, that exist among the three reformed theses. There exists logical support among the three theses if any thesis has as its implication[18] the other two or any two have as their implication the third. As no one thesis will imply the other two if no pair of theses implies the third,[19] the present task is that of determining whether any two theses logically imply the third.

Do the Reformed Normative and Instrumental Theses Imply the Reformed Descriptive Thesis?

The reformed normative thesis is the view that managers ought to afford consideration to the legitimate interests of stakeholders because those interests are intrinsically valuable and that the kind of consideration afforded (or the kind of interests that are legitimate) is incompatible with the investor-owned firm with fiduciary duties to shareholders alone. The reformed instrumental thesis is the view that certain positive effects follow from the adoption of stakeholder-oriented practices, whether substantive or procedural. Assuming that both of these theses are true, it does not follow either that the normative descriptive thesis is true or that the instrumental descriptive thesis is true. From the fact that certain practices are morally best (the reformed normative thesis) and the fact that certain aimed-for consequences follow from the adoption of those practices (the reformed instrumental thesis), it does not follow that people actually adopt those practices, whether for moral reasons (the normative descriptive thesis) or for other reasons (the instrumental descriptive thesis). People remain perfectly capable of being morally obtuse, instrumentally irrational, or both. Therefore, the reformed normative and instrumental theses do not imply the reformed descriptive thesis.

Do the Reformed Normative and Descriptive Theses Imply the Reformed Instrumental Thesis?

Again, the answer is no. From the fact that certain practices are morally best (the reformed normative thesis) and that people engage in them, whether for moral reasons (the normative descriptive thesis) or for other reasons (the instrumental

---

[18] By implication, I mean the conditional expressed in the form "a implies b" or "if a, then b". "a implies b" ("if a, then b") is true in all circumstances except that where a is true and b is false. Thus, if "a implies b" ("if a, then b") is true and a is true, it follows that b is true also. For a good, transparent discussion of the conditional, see Guttenplan (1986, pp. 57ff.).

[19] Let a, b, and c be propositions. Adopt as conventional logical operators "$\rightarrow$" for "implies" (or "if [left side of arrow], then [right side of arrow]") and "&" for "and". If a $\rightarrow$ (b & c), it follows that (a & b) $\rightarrow$ c and that (a & c) $\rightarrow$ b. Consequently, if no two theses imply the third, it cannot be the case any thesis implies the other two.

descriptive thesis), it does not follow that these practices secure other aimed-for ends (the reformed instrumental thesis). It may be the case that the practices' merits are moral alone. Therefore, the reformed normative and descriptive theses do not imply the reformed instrumental thesis.

Do the Reformed Instrumental and Descriptive Theses Imply the Reformed Normative Thesis?

Once more, the answer is no. From the fact that certain practices secure other aimed-for ends (the reformed instrumental thesis) and that people engage in them, whether for moral reasons (the normative descriptive thesis) or for other reasons (the instrumental descriptive thesis), it does not follow that those practices are morally best. It may be the case that the practices' merits are instrumental alone. Therefore, the reformed instrumental and descriptive theses do not imply the reformed normative thesis.

As no pair of reformed theses implies the third, it follows that no logical relations of implication exist among the three reformed theses.

Another Avenue to Mutual Support? Donaldson's "Psychology of the Manager"

In a response to Jones and Wicks (1999), Donaldson (1999) advances an argument he believes demonstrates an important relationship of mutual support between the normative thesis and the instrumental thesis. Donaldson (1999) argues that this relationship resides in what he calls "the psychology of the manager" (p. 239).

Reduced to its essential elements, Donaldson's argument is that, for the manager, belief in stakeholder theory's normative thesis (which he calls *B-Normative*) entails belief in stakeholder theory's instrumental thesis (*B-Instrumental*).[20] This is so because being a manager carries with it a fiduciary duty to maximize returns for

---

[20] Donaldson seeks to run the argument the other way, as well. That is, he argues that holding B-Instrumental entails believing that one ought to act *as if* B-Normative were true. But so what? *Whenever* one acts on the belief that one ought to perform action *A*, one believes that one ought to act as if *every* ought-proposition that entails performing *A* were true – but that does not demonstrate or even provide some reason to believe that any of the ought-propositions that entail performing *A* are true. For example, suppose that I am walking on the south side of the street. I am hungry and I see that my favorite restaurant is on the north side of the street. I form the belief that in order to sate my hunger, I ought to cross to the north side of the street. In so doing, I believe that I ought to act *as if* all of the following (and many more) beliefs are true:

(1) I ought to cross to the north side of the street because north-siders make better lovers.

(2) I ought to cross to the north side of the street because that brings me closer to God.

(3) I ought to cross to the north side of the street because that is the shady side.

shareholders. Thus, if the manager holds B-Normative, the manager must also hold B-Instrumental. Otherwise, the manager's situation is untenable.

> But how is the manager's duty to stakeholders to be reconciled with his or her duty to shareowners? The only comprehensive reconciliation happens in the event that attending to the interests of other stakeholders also happens to serve best the interests of shareowners. If the content of B-Instrumental is true, then reconciliation is possible. If not, the manager's situation becomes conceptually inconsistent. (ibid., p. 240)

According to Donaldson, this is an implication of the principle *ought implies can*: if one ought to do as stakeholder theory's normative thesis demands and one ought to satisfy one's fiduciary duties to shareholders, then it must be the case that one can do both. One can do both only if managerial action satisfying stakeholder theory's normative thesis also is (or does not conflict with) managerial action satisfying fiduciary obligations to shareholders. Therefore, concludes Donaldson, there exists a relationship of mutual support between the normative and instrumental theses where it counts – in the psychology of the manager.

This argument is noteworthy for two, related reasons. First, by asserting the compatibility of managerial action satisfying stakeholder theory's normative thesis with managerial action satisfying fiduciary duties to shareholders, Donaldson asserts the compatibility of stakeholder theory's normative thesis with the investor-owned firm with fiduciary duties to shareholders alone – the firm which Donaldson and Preston (1995) pronounce "normatively unacceptable" (p. 82). As many stakeholder theorists maintain that their theory's normative thesis is incompatible with, and therefore stands athwart, the investor-owned firm with fiduciary duties to shareholders alone, Donaldson's (1999) argument is a retreat from what heretofore has been taken by many of its adherents as an animating commitment of normative stakeholder theory.

Second, though Donaldson's (1999) argument may persuade upon a casual reading, it fails to demonstrate a relationship of mutual support between B-Normative and B-Instrumental. For by situating these beliefs *in the manager's mind*, Donaldson relies implicitly upon at least one *other* belief to make the intended connection. This is the belief that *it is morally permissible for one to be a manager with fiduciary duties to shareholders*. Call this *B-Fiduciary*. In other words, what Donaldson advertises as an implication of the relationship *between* B-Normative and B-Instrumental must be analyzed instead as a relationship *among* B-Normative, B-Instrumental, and B-Fiduciary.

Why is this destructive of his argument? Donaldson's argument is intended to demonstrate the incompatibility of *two* beliefs, such that if the first (B-Normative-true) is true then the second (B-Instrumental-false) must be abandoned in favor of its converse (B-Instrumental-true). Instead, his argument at best demonstrates the incompatibility of *three* beliefs (B-Normative-true, B-Instrumental-false,

---

The truth of the proposition that in order to sate my hunger, I ought to cross to the north side of the street demonstrates *exactly nothing* about the truth of these other propositions (impotence, Satan, and an unrelenting August sun may await me on the north side of the street), even though in crossing the street I will act *as if* they were all true and will *believe* that I ought to act as if they were all true.

B-Fiduciary-true) – but abandoning *any one of those beliefs* cures the incompatibility. Consequently, embracing the normative thesis does not, as Donaldson contends, bring with it embrace of the instrumental thesis.

Consider the following case, Esteban's Dilemma (*ED*):

> ED. Esteban is a manager in an investor-owned firm with fiduciary duties to shareholders alone. He holds B-Normative-true and B-Instrumental-false. Upon reading Donaldson (1999) and recognizing that his situation is untenable, Esteban concludes that some aspect of his belief-structure must be abandoned. But which?

One aspect of Esteban's belief structure that could go is B-Normative-true. If Esteban adopts the converse (B-Normative-false), maintains B-Instrumental-false, and maintains B-Fiduciary-true, he finds himself out of the bind Donaldson identifies. However, suppose that Esteban (like Donaldson) is committed to B-Normative-true. Two other possibilities remain.

The second aspect that could go is B-Instrumental-false. If Esteban maintains B-Normative-true, adopts B-Instrumental-true, and maintains B-Fiduciary-true, he finds himself out of the bind Donaldson identifies. According to Donaldson, this result is *compelled* by the logic of the theses. But because Donaldson does not acknowledge that a third belief is in play, he fails to admit a third possibility (cf. Donaldson 1999, p. 238).

The third aspect that could go is B-Fiduciary-true. If Esteban maintains B-Normative-true, maintains B-Instrumental-false, and, acting upon the normative implications of adopting B-Fiduciary-false, terminates his career as a manager with fiduciary duties to shareholders, he finds himself out of the bind. The normative thesis compels Esteban to manage in a way that, if the instrumental thesis were false, would be incompatible with the aims of the investor-owned firm with fiduciary duties to shareholders alone. Esteban could cure the incompatibility among his three beliefs by abandoning B-Fiduciary-true. Although his belief is inconsistent with remaining a manager in an investor-owned firm with fiduciary duties to shareholders alone, Esteban's belief underwrites being a manager in a firm animated by other aims (e.g., a nonprofit firm, a workers' cooperative), being an anti-corporate activist, or being a perfectly ordinary member of the Society for Business Ethics.

This third conclusion should strike no one strange. It is the conclusion to which more than a few of those impressed by normative stakeholder theory subscribe. They believe that the truth of the normative thesis entails that the investor-owned firm with fiduciary duties to shareholders alone is morally impermissible and, therefore, that managing such a firm toward its animating objectives is morally impermissible, as well. No aspect of their worldview is undermined by the belief that the instrumental thesis is false. Donaldson himself, when writing with Preston, seems to adopt this view when calling for the adoption of a revised, stakeholder-oriented law of corporations (cf. Donaldson and Preston 1995, p. 84).

The important point for present purposes is this: *subscribing to the normative thesis does not compel one to adopt the second alternative*, as Donaldson erroneously maintains. Either the second alternative or the third alternative will cure the incompatibility among the three beliefs, consistent with maintaining B-Normative.[21] Consequently, Donaldson's claimed, necessary relationship in the "psychology of the manager" between belief in the normative thesis and belief in the instrumental thesis is illusory.

Conclusion: Consequences for the Corporate Governance Debate

The late political philosopher Jean Hampton observed that, though they are perhaps reluctant to admit it, philosophers sometimes deal as much in pictures as they do in ideas (cf. Hampton 1993, p. 379). She advanced this claim with respect to social contract theorists, whose theories, she argued, really have little in common other than their appeal to a picture – that of a social contract – to express what they are trying to say. Hobbes, Locke, Rawls, and Gauthier are moral and political philosophers linked neither by their commitments nor (in any deep way) by their methods, but only by appeal to the appealing picture of a social contract.

Hampton's point applies with at least equal force to stakeholder theories. Normative, instrumental, and descriptive stakeholder thinking are linked by nothing deep or symbiotic, as some of stakeholder theory's enthusiasts are eager to claim. Instead, they share only appeal to an appealing picture – that of a stakeholder – to say what turns out to be different and unrelated things. Normative, instrumental, and descriptive stakeholder theories advance independent theses, each of which calls for a different type of evidence or argument to establish its veracity. All may be correct, all may be misguided, or some correct and others misguided (and in different potential combinations), but the connections are thin and few. Donaldson's appeal to the "psychology of the manager" does not overcome the basic problem. This result alters noticeably the terms of the corporate governance debate. Two points are in order.

---

[21] Let Bn = B-Normative, Bi = B-Instrumental, and Bf = B-Fiduciary. Adopt as conventional logical operators "~" for "not", "&" for "and", and "v" for "or". Take as a premise:

(1) ~(Bn & ~Bi & Bf)
which says that Bn, ~Bi, and Bf form an incompatible set. Take also as a premise:
(2) Bn
From (1) and (2) one derives:
(3) ~(~Bi & Bf)
which says that ~Bi and Bf form an incompatible set. Applying DeMorgan's rule, an algorithm for transforming "and" expressions into "or" expressions and *vice versa*, (3) is logically equivalent to:
(4) (Bi v ~Bf)
which says that *at least one of* Bi and ~Bf must be the case – but as there are no further logical deductions that can be made, the truth of Bn carries one no further. Mere commitment to Bn inclines no more in favor of Bi than ~Bi.

First, the moral merit of the investor-owned firm with fiduciary duties to shareholders alone is neither undermined nor weakened by the descriptive accuracy of the descriptive thesis or the veracity of claims advanced under the instrumental thesis's guise. As we see in part IV, there is neither contradiction nor paradox in adopting both the descriptive and instrumental theses and rejecting the normative thesis. This means that the myopia argument is misplaced. That argument finds its mark only if rejection of normative stakeholder theory implies rejection of practices commended by instrumental stakeholder theory – but that implication does not hold, as the argument of part V demonstrates. The important upshot is clear: Only *normative* stakeholder theory can stand athwart the investor-owned firm with fiduciary duties to shareholders alone.[22] Stakeholder theorists cannot by proxy undermine the moral merit of the investor-owned firm with fiduciary duties to shareholders alone, i.e., by appealing to the virtues of descriptive or instrumental stakeholder theory. The moral permissibility of the investor-owned firm with fiduciary duties to shareholders alone stands or falls on the strength of normative arguments alone.

Second, the moral merit of the stakeholder-oriented firm is bolstered by neither the descriptive accuracy of the descriptive thesis nor the prudential merits of the instrumental thesis. As we saw in part V, there is neither contradiction nor paradox in rejecting the descriptive and instrumental theses and adopting the normative thesis. In other words, one cannot establish by proxy the normative thesis's merits, i.e., by appealing to the virtues of the descriptive or instrumental theses. Normative stakeholder theory stands or falls on its merits alone. Its supposed cousins cannot fight its battles.

Normative theories require normative argument. This underscores the need to develop substantive content for normative stakeholder theory and a justificatory apparatus supporting that content. As its proponents seek eagerly to extend an undeveloped normative stakeholder theory, they neglect the more compelling intellectual project found in attending to its insecure foundations.

References

Boatright, J.R. 1994. Fiduciary duties and the shareholder-management relation: Or, what's so special about shareholders? *Business Ethics Quarterly* 4: 393–407.

Boatright, J.R. 2002. Ethics and corporate governance: Justifying the role of the shareholder. In *The blackwell guide to business ethics,* ed. N.E. Bowie, 38–60. Malden, MA: Blackwell.

Bowie, N.E. 1999. *Business ethics: A kantian perspective.* Oxford: Blackwell.

Carson, T.L. 1993. Does the stakeholder theory constitute a new kind of theory of social responsibility? *Business Ethics Quarterly* 3: 171–176.

Donaldson, T. 1999. Making stakeholder theory whole. *Academy of Management Review* 24: 237–241.

Donaldson, T., and T.W. Dunfee. 1999. Social contract approaches to business ethics: Bridging the 'Is-Ought' Gap. In *A companion to business ethics,* ed. R. Frederick, 38–64. Oxford: Blackwell.

---

[22] And then, only insofar as it is supplied with content that has that upshot.

Donaldson, T., and L.E. Preston. 1995. The stakeholder theory of the corporation: Concepts, evidence, and implications. *Academy of Management Review* 20: 65–91.

Freeman, R.E. 1994. The politics of stakeholder theory: Some future directions. *Business Ethics Quarterly* 4: 409–421.

Freeman, R.E. 1999. Divergent stakeholder theory. *Academy of Management Review* 24: 233–236.

Freeman, R.E., and R. Phillips. 2002. Stakeholder theory: A libertarian defense. *Business Ethics Quarterly* 12: 331–349.

Goodpaster, K. 1991. Business ethics and stakeholder analysis. *Business Ethics Quarterly* 1: 53–73.

Guttenplan, S. 1986. *The languages of logic*. Oxford: Blackwell.

Hampton, J. 1993. Contract and consent. In *A companion to contemporary political philosophy,* ed. R. Goodin and P. Pettit, 379–393. Oxford: Blackwell.

Hare, R.M. 1952. *The language of morals*. Oxford: Oxford University Press.

Jones, T. 1994. The Toronto conference: Reflections on stakeholder theory. *Business and Society* 33: 82–83.

Jones, T. 1995. Instrumental stakeholder theory: A synthesis of ethics and economics. *Academy of Management Review* 20: 404–437.

Jones, T., and A. Wicks. 1999. Convergent stakeholder theory. *Academy of Management Review* 24: 206–221.

Korsgaard, C. 1996. *The sources of normativity*. New York, NY: Cambridge University Press.

Macey, J.R. 1999. Fiduciary duties as residual claims: Obligations to nonshareholder constituencies from a theory of the firm perspective. *Cornell Law Review* 84: 1266–1279.

Marcoux, A.M. 2003. A fiduciary argument against stakeholder theory. *Business Ethics Quarterly* 13: 1–24.

McCall, J. 2001. Employee voice in corporate governance: A defense of strong participation rights. *Business Ethics Quarterly* 11: 195–213.

Mitchell, L, ed. 1995. *Progressive corporate law*. Boulder, CO: Westview.

Raz, J. 1990. *Practical reason and norms*, 2nd ed. Princeton, NJ: Princeton University Press.

Sollars, G. 2002. The corporation as actual agreement. *Business Ethics Quarterly* 12: 351–369.

Chapter 13
Corporate Governance and Business Ethics

Andrew J. Felo

Contents

Introduction

Corporate governance can be an important defense against unethical corporate behavior (cf. Carcello 2009). For example, a firm's board of directors is responsible for overseeing firm management. If the board does not adequately perform this

A.J. Felo (✉)

Associate Professor of Accounting, School of Graduate Professional Studies at Great Valley, Pennsylvania State University, University Park, PA, USA
e-mail: ajf14@gv.psu.edu

A. Brink (ed.), *Corporate Governance and Business Ethics*, Ethical Economy.
Studies in Economic Ethics and Philosophy 39, DOI 10.1007/978-94-007-1588-2_13,
© Springer Science+Business Media B.V. 2011

oversight, then it may be easier for managers to behave unethically. In fact, Hoffman and Rowe (2007) report that various investigations found that poor oversight of management by boards was an important factor in various corporate scandals. Two additional issues dealing with unethical corporate behavior that firms should consider when structuring their corporate governance are potential conflicts of interest between the firm and its shareholders and transparency concerning corporate activities. Possible conflicts of interest in corporate governance include whether the CEO is also the chairman of the board (often referred to as CEO duality), the independence of board members, executive compensation (including backdating of stock options), and director elections. Since all of these situations could result in directors or managers placing their interest ahead of shareholder interests, they are all ethical issues. Transparency is an ethical issue because "insiders" such as managers and directors essentially control the information that "outsiders" such as shareholders and regulators receive. As a result, "insiders" can prevent "outsiders" from learning about sub-optimal behavior (such as conflicts of interest) through less transparency.

This essay discusses academic research concerning the impact of corporate governance on business ethics. Corporate governance issues discussed are board involvement in corporate ethics codes, board independence, CEO duality, executive compensation, director elections, and external auditors. The specific business ethics issues discussed are potential conflicts of interest and transparency.

Board Involvement in Corporate Ethics Codes

The first governance topic to be discussed is the board's role in ensuring that firms conduct their activities ethically. Since the board oversees the firm's management, it plays an important role in the "tone at the top" of the firm. The "tone at the top" of a firm helps set expectations for firm conduct.

The Sarbanes-Oxley Act (hereafter referred to as SOX) requires firms to disclose whether they have adopted codes of ethics for their senior financial officers and if not, why they have chosen not to do so (cf. Section 406, Subsection A). SOX defines codes of ethics in terms of promoting "the ethical handling of actual or apparent conflicts of interest between personal and professional relationships" (Section 406, Subsection C, point 1) and "full, fair, accurate, timely, and understandable disclosure in the periodic reports required to be filed by the issuer" (Section 406, Subsection C, point 2). This supports the notion that conflicts of interest and transparency are both ethical issues. In addition, both the NYSE and Nasdaq have implemented rules requiring listed firms to adopt codes of ethics that apply to all employees, executives, and directors. Firms must also disclose amendments to their codes and any time when code provisions are waived for any reason. This is most likely in response to the revelation that Enron waived its code without informing its shareholders on three occasions in order to allow the firm to conduct business with partnerships involving CFO Andrew Fastow.

An implicit assumption underlying these requirements is that an ethics code will help a firm develop a more forthcoming and transparent attitude concerning its disclosures. This view is consistent with the conclusion of the National Commission on Fraudulent Financial Reporting ("Treadway Commission") that firms could enhance the quality of their financial reports by strengthening their internal control environments through formal ethics programs, including ethics codes (cf. National Commission on Fraudulent Financial Reporting 1987, pp. 35f.). Is there empirical evidence to support this expectation? Brief et al. (1996) conduct an experiment concerning the relationship between the adoption of a code and financial reporting quality. Their results imply that simply requiring firms to adopt codes will not improve financial reporting transparency.

Brief et al.'s (1996) results do not support mandatory ethics codes. However, it is possible that simply implementing a code is insufficient to change people's behavior. This could be because a code without sufficient involvement from executives and directors is seen as "window dressing". If this is the case, then it is unlikely that an ethics code will result in greater transparency. This could be what happened at Enron when its board suspended its code as noted above. Possibly in response to this, the Federal Sentencing Guidelines in the United States were revised in 2004 to encourage greater board participation in corporate ethics programs (cf. Hoffman and Rowe 2007). The assumption behind this change is that greater board participation will reduce the likelihood that an ethics program is viewed as simply "window dressing".

What activities can a board perform to demonstrate a greater commitment to a firm's ethics program? Generally speaking, a board can demonstrate its commitment to a firm's ethics program by overseeing the operation of the program. For example, board members may receive reports concerning the status and resolution of calls to the firm's "ethics hotline", review results of "ethics audits", assist in the modification of the firm's ethics code as needed, and review the adequacy of resources allocated for the firm's ethics training sessions. Also, board members can demonstrate the importance of the firm's code by at least partially basing executive compensation on adherence to the firm's code. Johnson & Johnson is an example of a firm that does this. A board can form a standing ethics committee to oversee the program, assign oversight of the firm's ethics program to one of its other standing committees (e.g., the audit or compensation committee), or reserve responsibility for overseeing the program for the board as a whole.

Evidence from Felo (2006) indicates that board oversight has become much more common. In his 1995 sample, approximately 27% of sample boards provided oversight for their ethics programs. By 2001, over 70% of boards provided oversight for their programs. In addition, his results indicate that in 1995 oversight was limited to boards of relatively large firms. In 2001, however, there are no significant differences in firm size between "oversight" and "no oversight" firms.

Is board involvement in ethics programs related to disclosure transparency? Using data predating SOX and the Treadway Commission, Felo (2000) reports that financial analysts find the disclosures made by firms having ethics programs overseen by their boards to be more credible than disclosures made by other firms having ethics programs not overseen by their boards and by firms not having formal ethics programs. These results show the important role board oversight plays in attempts to design regulations to improve disclosure transparency. Using the same measure of disclosure transparency, Felo (2006) reports that firms adding ethics programs overseen by their boards between 1995 and 2001 were more likely to increase their financial disclosure credibility than were other firms. This is important evidence as it demonstrates that board oversight of ethics programs can lead to *improvements* in disclosure transparency. Using a different measure of disclosure transparency, Felo (2007) finds that firms with boards involved in their corporate ethics programs display more transparency than do other firms. For example, they are more likely than other firms to have voluntarily provided information concerning board nominating committees and processes for communicating with directors before this information was mandated by the SEC in 2003. All of these results indicate that going beyond SOX requirements, extending an ethics code throughout an organization, and having the board oversee its development, implementation, and maintenance may result in a more transparent corporate attitude.

As noted above, one dimension of corporate ethics codes according to SOX is the handling of potential conflicts of interest. Consequently, an implicit assumption underlying SOX is that an ethics code will help a firm better manage potential conflicts of interest that may arise in its operations. What is the empirical evidence related to this? Felo (2001) finds that boards actively involved in their ethics program are more independent than are boards at other firms (whether those firms have ethics programs where boards are not involved or whether those firms have no formal ethics program). In addition, compensation committees are more independent at firms where boards are actively involved in ethics programs than at other firms. Since non-independent boards and compensation committees can enrich management at the expense of shareholders, these results indicate that board oversight (and just the existence of an ethics code) can help protect shareholders from being exploited by corporate insiders. Like the results from the disclosure transparency research, these results support the notion that board oversight is an important factor in whether an ethics program is related to fewer conflicts of interest in corporate governance.

In summary, extant research indicates that boards play an important role in determining whether ethics codes reduce the likelihood of unethical corporate behavior. As a result, regulators may want to implement rules mandating board oversight of corporate ethics codes. Absent this mandate, boards may want to voluntarily begin overseeing the development, implementation, and maintenance of their ethics codes.

Director Independence[1]

Carcello (2009) argues that non-independent directors are biased toward management by definition. Similarly, Section 303A.01 of the NYSE listing standards states that,

---

[1] A complete review of empirical research on director independence is beyond the scope of this essay. For a more complete review, the reader is directed to Felo (2009).

[e]ffective boards of directors exercise independent judgment in carrying out their responsibilities. Requiring a majority of independent directors will increase the quality of board
oversight and lessen the possibility of damaging conflicts of interest. (NYSE 2008)

Because lack of proper oversight may allow corporate insiders to enrich themselves
at the expense of shareholders, director independence is an ethical issue.

There is evidence that greater board independence is beneficial to shareholders.
For example, Weisbach (1988) shows that boards of poorly performing firms are
more likely to fire CEOs as director independence increases. In addition, Daily and
Dalton (1994) find that firms filing for bankruptcy have lower percentages of independent directors five years prior to the filing than do similar firms not filing for
bankruptcy. However, Byrd and Hickman (1992) show that director independence
levels above 60% can hurt shareholders. In addition, Bhagat and Black (2002) conclude that increases in board independence may actually hurt shareholders. Both of
these results indicate that boards do more than oversee management. For example,
boards are also charged with providing strategic guidance and advice to company
management. Independent directors may be less able to provide advice to management because they have no ties to the firm other than as directors. As a result, any
attempts to mandate additional independent directors beyond the majority requirement already in place may not be ethical as the potential improvement in oversight
from greater independence may not exceed the reduction in the value of advice and
guidance provided by the board.

CEO Duality

A firm having its CEO also serve as the chairman of its board of directors (commonly referred to as CEO duality) has been identified as a fundamental conflict of
interest by Boyd (1996) and Strier (2005). Despite the seemingly obvious conflict
of interest of having the CEO lead the group that is monitoring his or her performance, there is no mandate from the SEC or the exchanges concerning whether this
is allowed, and no law prohibits firms from having one person perform both duties.
In fact, CEO duality has been quite common in the United States. Even though CEO
duality is still quite common in the US, there is evidence that more firms are splitting the roles (cf. Grinstein and Valles Arellano 2008). One possible reason for the
reduction could be that firms are more sensitive to the potential conflict of interest
this structure presents.

Even though CEO duality seems to be an obvious conflict of interest, the evidence on whether it actually hurts shareholders is mixed. Petra and Dorata (2008)
find that splitting the roles increases the likelihood that CEO compensation will be
kept in check. This supports the view that CEO duality increases the likelihood that
managers (specifically, the CEO) will enrich themselves at the expense of shareholders. On the other hand, Faleye (2007) finds that firms appear to make the decision to
have one person in both roles in a rational way. As a result, CEO duality works well
for some firms but not for others. Specifically, more complex firms tend to benefit
from CEO duality. Although this is not an exhaustive list of empirical studies on the

impact of CEO duality, it is a sampling of the mixed evidence.[2] As a result of the mixed evidence, it does not appear to be in shareholders' best interests for regulators to mandate separating the two roles. However, less complex firms may want to voluntarily split these two roles to eliminate the perception that they are engaged in obvious conflicts of interest with little benefit to shareholders.

Executive Compensation

As executive compensation has increased, shareholders and regulators have looked for ways to provide more insight and transparency into how executive compensation is determined, especially when there are potential conflicts of interest between shareholders and firm insiders. The stock option backdating scandals also increased investors' desire for greater transparency into executive compensation. A recent survey indicates that 75% of directors and 75% of institutional investors believe that the manner in which executive pay is determined in the US is damaging to the image of corporate America (cf. Perkins 2008). Ethical issues related to executive compensation involve both transparency and potential conflicts of interest. Firms can use their corporate governance structures to address the ethical issues related to executive compensation (cf. Adam and Schwartz 2009). This part of the essay discusses research concerning how corporate governance can address ethical issues related to executive compensation.

Say on Pay

One possible conflict of interest related to executive compensation is that shareholders have very little say on how executives are compensated. One possible remedy is to give shareholders the ability to vote on executive compensation plans. Although "say on pay" is not required throughout the US, firms receiving "bailout" funds from the US government are required to allow shareholders to cast advisory votes on executive compensation at their next annual meetings. In addition, a Towers Perrin report by Jim Kroll notes that the number of resolutions to allow shareholders to cast advisory votes on executive compensation has steadily increased over the last few years (cf. Naughton 2009). People who support "say on pay" argue that it provides shareholders, the owners of the company, direct power to influence executive compensation. Although shareholders can show their displeasure with directors and compensation committee members by withholding votes when they come up for election, this power is insignificant, given the way director elections are conducted.[3] Another possible benefit of "say on pay" is that greater transparency will reduce executive compensation. However, "say on pay" has not led to lower executive compensation in the UK (cf. White and Patrick 2007). At the same time, evidence does

---

[2] The reader is directed to Felo (2009) for a more thorough overview of the mixed results.

[3] This issue will be discussed in greater detail below.

indicate that "say on pay" has improved the link between executive compensation and firm performance (cf. Anders 2008). Therefore, "say on pay" does seem to have at least partially alleviated the ethical problem of executive compensation not being linked to firm performance.

Compensation Disclosures

On 26 July 2006, the SEC passed new rules concerning executive compensation and related party disclosures. These new rules are designed "to provide investors with a clearer and more complete picture of compensation to principal executive officers, principal financial officers, the other highest paid executive officers and directors" (SEC 2006, p. 9). The new rules require firms to disclose all components of executive compensation and to provide the information in table form in one area of their proxy statements. In addition, firms must provide a Compensation Discussion and Analysis (CD&A). This must include a discussion and analysis of the factors used in determining the figures presented in the compensation table, including the outcomes the firm is trying to reward. To help investors better understand the new disclosures, they are subject to the SEC's "plain English" requirements. Under these requirements, firms are expected to use short sentences, everyday language, and avoid the use of technical and legal jargon, among other principles.

The main goal of this new information is to make it easier for shareholders to determine whether executives are being paid consistent with shareholder returns. When the SEC issued new compensation disclosure rules in 1992, the link between executive compensation and firm performance improved (cf. Vafeas and Afxentiou 1998). It is too early to determine whether these new rules have improved the pay-performance link. However, there are some initial results. While the SEC says firms are not providing enough information and details to investors, it also has criticized firms for making their CD&As too long and for not conforming to the "plain English" requirements. In a speech, SEC Chairman Christopher Cox reported that an independent analysis showed that the CD&As were as difficult to read as PhD dissertations (cf. Cox 2007). Despite these problems, a survey indicates that 80% of institutional investors and close to 75% of directors believe that the CD&A has improved the transparency of executive compensation practices (cf. Perkins 2008). Since the criticisms of the CD&As are based on the first year that they were required, it is likely that firms will improve these reports. Therefore, it seems fair to conclude that these new rules have improved the transparency of the executive compensation process.

Compensation Committees

Boards of directors typically use compensation committees to determine executive compensation. The NYSE requires that the compensation committees in listed firms consist solely of independent directors. Although Nasdaq does not technically require independent compensation committees, it does require that executive compensation be approved by an independent compensation committee or by a majority of independent directors. The rationale for these requirements is that non-independent directors may be biased toward CEOs, resulting in compensation plans that unfairly enrich managers, typically at the expense of shareholders. What does empirical research tell us about compensation committee independence? First, it does not appear that non-independent compensation committees award more generous compensation packages (cf. Daily et al. 1998; Anderson and Bizjak 2003). However, non-independent committees do tend to weaken the pay-performance link (cf. Vafeas 2003). Since the pay-performance link seems to be a stronger ethical issue than the absolute level of executive compensation, it is reasonable to conclude that independent compensation committees help alleviate ethical issues related to executive compensation.

Compensation Consultants

A recent issue concerning executive compensation is the use of compensation consultants to help compensation committees determine executive compensation packages. According to Cadman, Carter, and Hillegeist (2008), 86% of compensation committees in large firms used consultants to help them develop compensation packages. The ethical issue related to compensation consultants is that there is a potential conflict of interest when the consultant employed by the compensation committee also provides compensation services to the firm's management team. There is a possibility that the consultant will recommend a relatively large compensation package for the CEO as a way to ensure that the CEO will hire the consultant to perform other services for the firm. This is similar to the question of auditors providing non-audit services to their audit clients.

There is little empirical evidence concerning the impact the use of compensation consultants has on executive compensation. Part of the reason for this is probably that there is relatively little disclosure on compensation consultants. That is an ethical problem in itself. One study on this issue shows that while firms using compensation consultants pay their executives more, the pay-performance link at these firms is not weaker (cf. ibid.). In addition, they find that non-independent consultants are not associated with more lucrative pay packages. Based on this limited empirical evidence, it does not appear that the use of compensation consultants enriches executives at the expense of shareholders. However, it is reasonable to expect regulators to require greater disclosure of consultant fees and whether consultants provide other services to the firm in the future, similar to the disclosure of fees paid to external auditors for non-audit services.

Summary

In summary, there are ethical issues related to the transparency of how executive compensation is determined and the potential for conflicts of interest between the firm and its shareholders. Extant research seems to indicate that corporate governance can be used to address these ethical issues. For example, the pay-performance link can be strengthened by giving shareholders the opportunity to cast a vote on executive compensation ("say on pay") and by requiring that compensation committees are fully independent. Although it is too early to determine whether recent disclosures will improve this link, initial results are encouraging. Finally, although there appears to be a conflict of interest when boards use compensation consultants to help determine executive compensation packages, initial evidence seems to indicate that this does not result in managers enriching themselves at the expense of shareholders. However, it is likely that regulators will require additional disclosures surrounding the use of consultants to ensure that using consultants does not hurt shareholders.

Director Elections

Recent corporate scandals have increased attention paid to director elections as a way for shareholders to hold managers and directors accountable for poor firm performance. After all, shareholders are the owners of a corporation. However, shareholder nominees (not supported by the current board) rarely win board seats. For example, Bebchuk (2007) reports that directors at firms with market capitalization greater than $200 million not nominated by the current board won seats only eight times between 1996 and 2005. This indicates that directors are virtually insulated from election challenges once they are initially elected to the board. Therefore, elections are not necessarily effective ways for shareholders to exercise oversight over management, even though shareholders own the firm. This conflict of interest between shareholders and corporate insiders can possibly be addressed through corporate governance. This part of the essay discusses research concerning how corporate governance can address ethical issues related to director elections.

Nominating Committees

Corporations typically delegate responsibility for identifying candidates for director positions to a separate nominating committee. The NYSE and Nasdaq have similar rules for nominating committees as they have for compensation committees. However, this was not always the case. In fact, it was not uncommon for the CEO to be a part of the nominating process in the past. However, this could be a conflict of interest as one of a director's jobs is to oversee management. It is possible that a CEO would only support the nomination of directors who would be willing to "look the other way" when overseeing management. Extant research generally shows that greater CEO influence over the nominating process hurts shareholders. For example, boards are less independent (cf. Shivdasani and Yermack 1999), CEO pay is higher (cf. Core et al. 1999), and the transparency of the executive compensation process decreases (cf. Laksmana 2007) as CEO influence over the nominating process increases. These studies support the notion that lack of independence in the nominating process enriches management at the expense of shareholders. Therefore, it is important from an ethical standpoint that the nominating committee members are independent of firm management.

Director Election Process

A second ethical issue related to director elections involves the rules for nominating directors. Historically, these rules make it very difficult and expensive for shareholders to nominate people for director positions, effectively negating elections as a way to hold directors accountable for failing to properly oversee firm management. Under SEC Rule 14a-8(i)(8), a firm can exclude a shareholder proposal if it "relates to an election for membership on the company's board of directors or analogous governing body" (SEC 2007). The result of this is that incumbent directors rarely face opposition in elections. In fact, Bebchuk (2007) reports that between 1996 and 2005, there were a total of 118 cases where incumbent directors faced opposition in elections. Recently, however, the state of Delaware adopted a law (effective 1 August 2009) permitting companies incorporated in Delaware to amend their bylaws to allow nominees from shareholders to be included in the firm's proxy materials and to make it easier for shareholders making nominations to be reimbursed for expenses incurred to solicit votes for their nominees (cf. Atkins 2009). It is important to note that this law only applies to Delaware corporations (although many firms are Delaware corporations) and that it does not *require* firms to make it easier for shareholders to nominate directors. Therefore, the potential conflict of interest between shareholders and the board with respect to nominating director candidates is an on-going ethical issue that may need to be addressed by regulators.

A related ethical issue involves the way votes are tabulated in director elections. Historically, director elections have been based on the concept of plurality voting. This means that nominees receiving the most votes win the elections even if they do not receive a majority of "yes" votes. While this sounds reasonable, a nominee could win a position even if a majority of shareholders "withheld" their votes from the nominee. That is because in most cases, if nine slots are available, only nine people are nominated because of the difficulty shareholders have in nominating people for director positions. Therefore, plurality voting makes "withheld" votes largely symbolic. This is an ethical problem as directors could be elected even though a majority of shareholders oppose the nominee.

In response to this, "majority voting" has become more common recently. In majority voting, a nominee has to receive a majority of votes cast to be elected. In this case, "withheld" votes actually count against a nominee. A recent study by a Chicago law firm quoted in American Bankers Association (2008) shows that majority voting has become the standard at large companies. According to this survey, 66% of S&P 500 firms and 57% of Fortune 500 firms have adopted some form of majority voting. Therefore, it appears that US firms have voluntarily responded to the potential ethical problem that plurality voting presents. However, it may be necessary for regulators to mandate majority voting as there is still a large percentage of firms that still use plurality voting.

Although the director election process arguably results in ethical problems, do these ethical problems actually harm shareholders? After reviewing empirical research on shareholder power to nominate directors, Stout (2007) concludes that there is little evidence that this actually increases firm value. In addition, Sjostrom and Kim (2007) do not find a statistically significant stock price reaction when firms announce they have adopted or will adopt majority voting, suggesting that the perceived ethical problems with plurality voting do not harm shareholders. These two studies indicate that although the current environment seems to result in an unethical conflict of interest between shareholders and the firm, it appears that this conflict of interest does not impair shareholder welfare.

Summary

In summary, the fact that it is quite rare for incumbent directors to lose their board seats via director elections can be viewed as an ethical problem that can be addressed through corporate governance. Extant research indicates that it is important for firms to maintain independent nominating functions as a check on CEO power. In addition, although the processes used to elect directors (nomination process and plurality voting) appear to result in conflicts of interest between management and shareholders, extant evidence indicates that these apparent conflicts do not negatively impact shareholders.

External Auditors

External auditors are also part of a firm's corporate governance system. Auditors play an important role in ensuring that shareholders and other "outsiders" receive transparent information about firm activities. Improving how audits are conducted is one of the main goals of SOX (cf. Coates 2007). To accomplish this, SOX attempts to reduce the potential for conflicts of interest between auditors and shareholders. As auditors work for shareholders, anything that makes them less likely to look out for shareholders' interests can be viewed as an ethical problem. This part of the essay addresses mandatory partner rotation and the prohibition of non-audit services.

Mandatory Audit Partner Rotation

SOX requires lead and coordinating partners to rotate off engagements every five years. They may return to the engagement after a five-year "cooling off" period. The rationale for partner rotation is that partners may become too "cozy" with their clients or too trusting of their clients if they stay on an engagement too long, creating a potential conflict of interest between the partner and the shareholders of the client firm. If this occurs, then partners may not detect unethical behavior by clients or may actually participate in unethical behavior. However, since it typically takes time for a new partner to get "up to speed" with a new client, mandatory rotation may actually increase the likelihood of unethical behavior as the new partner may miss something that a more experienced partner would catch.

The evidence concerning audit partner tenure and financial reporting quality appears to be mixed. For example, Johnson, Khurana, and Reynolds (2002) find that financial reporting quality is higher when auditors have been on a client between four and eight years then when they have been on a client for only two to three years. In addition, they find no decrease in audit quality when auditor tenure stretches past eight years. However, Carey and Simnett (2006) report evidence that audit quality (measured as the likelihood of issuing a going concern opinion and just missing or beating earnings targets) decreases as audit partner tenure increases. Although not an exhaustive summary of empirical evidence,[4] these two studies demonstrate that existing research concerning whether audit partner rotation reduces the potential for unethical behavior is mixed.

Researchers have also considered the relationship between audit partner rotation and perceived auditor independence. Perceived auditor independence is an important corporate governance issue as investors who perceive that an auditor's independence has been impaired are less likely to trust that there is no conflict of interest between the auditor and investors. Again, the evidence is mixed. For example, Jennings, Pany, and Reckers (2006) show that perceived auditor independence is lower under mandatory partner rotation than under mandatory firm rotation. On the other hand, Kaplan and Mauldin (2008) find that audit firm rotation does not improve perceived auditor independence relative to audit partner rotation.

When SOX was being debated, there was some consideration of requiring firms to change audit firms occasionally. Section 207 of SOX instructs the Comptroller General of the US to conduct a study of the potential impact of mandatory audit firm rotation. The main result of the study is that 79% of respondents believed this would increase the likelihood of unethical behavior as the new firm learned about a client's business (cf. GAO 2003). Not surprisingly, the GAO concluded that mandatory audit firm rotation was not necessary at the time.

Based on all of this evidence, it is not clear that audit partner rotation mandated by SOX is an effective way to improve auditing and financial reporting. In addition, consistent with the GAO report (2003), it does not appear that audit firm rotation would lead to improved financial reporting.

Provision of Non-Audit Services

Academics and practitioners have been arguing for many years that auditors performing non-audit services for their audit clients unacceptably impair auditor independence (cf. Prentice 2006). Opponents argue that auditors may have an incentive to "look the other way" on an audit matter in order to hold on to non-audit work (which is usually more profitable than audit work). Additionally, audit firms could

---

[4] Please see Felo (2009) for a more comprehensive overview of this evidence.

offer to do an audit at a relatively low price (possibly even at a loss) as a way to obtain non-audit work. Even if auditor independence is not actually impaired, opponents argue that the *appearance* of non-independence could result in less faith in the audit process. However, it was not until it was learned that Enron paid Arthur Andersen more for non-audit services than for audit services that this issue became much more important to regulators. To address this, SOX prohibits auditors from performing most non-audit services for their audit clients.

Although the prohibition on non-audit services reduces the likelihood for conflicts of interest between a firm (through its auditor) and shareholders, it is not clear that this is necessarily good for shareholders. In a review of the extensive literature on non-audit services, Francis (2006) concludes that although there is no definitive evidence showing that non-audit services lead to audit failures, significant evidence indicates that investors *perceive* that non-audit services impair independence. Since appearances are important in capital markets, prohibiting non-audit services seems to have been an appropriate ethical response to various corporate scandals.

Summary

Although audit partners working too long on an audit can present ethical problems, it appears that it may be necessary for regulators to re-think the mandatory audit partner rotation mandated by SOX. In addition, although auditor independence may not be impaired by the provision of non-audit services, this seems to cause an ethical problem as investors perceive that independence is impaired. Therefore, the SOX prohibition of most non-audit services appears to be an appropriate response to recent corporate scandals.

Conclusion

Corporate governance is one tool that can help guard against unethical corporate behavior (cf. Carcello 2009). At the same time, certain corporate governance structures can lead to ethical problems such as potential conflicts of interest between shareholders and firm insiders (typically managers and board) and to less than transparent disclosures. This essay discusses empirical research related to corporate governance and corporate ethics.

What has empirical research taught us? First, it is important that a firm's board be actively involved in the development, implementation, and maintenance of the firm's ethics initiatives. Without this oversight, ethics initiatives must be seen as nothing more than "window dressing". Second, although director independence is generally thought of as a "good" thing from a conflict of interest standpoint, it is possible to have "too much" independence on the board of directors. Third, although CEO duality appears to be an obvious conflict of interest, it does not necessarily hurt shareholders. Fourth, mandating "say on pay" may improve the pay-performance link, at least partially alleviating ethical issues related to executive compensation.

In addition, using compensation consultants does not appear to weaken this link. Although the rules used to conduct director elections appear to favor managers and directors over shareholders, evidence reviewed indicates that this does not negatively impact shareholders. Contrary to SOX requirements, it does not appear that audit effectiveness suffers when audit partners have been on an audit for an extended period of time. Finally, the provision of non-audit services seems to be more of an appearance problem with respect to auditor independence than an actual problem. However, the appearance problem can be enough to weaken confidence in audit reports and in firm disclosures. In summary, despite some spectacular corporate failures recently, it appears that current corporate governance guidelines do a reasonably good job of promoting ethical corporate behavior.

References

Adam, A.M., and M.S. Schwartz. 2009. Corporate governance, ethics, and the backdating of stock options. *Journal of Business Ethics* 85: 225–237.

American Bankers Association. 2008. Study shows majority voting for directors more prevalent. *Directors & Trustees Digest* 67: 1–2.

Anders, G. 2008. 'Say on Pay' Gets a push, but will boards listen? *Wall Street Journal*, 27 February: A2.

Anderson, R.C., and J.M. Bizjak. 2003. An empirical examination of the role of the CEO and the compensation committee in structuring executive pay. *Journal of Banking and Finance* 27: 1323–1348.

Atkins, P. 2009. Shareholder proxy access for director elections, The Harvard Law School Forum on Corporate Governance and Financial Regulation. http://blogs.law.harvard.edu/corpgov/2009/04/26/shareholder-proxy-access-for-director-elections

Bebchuk, L.A. 2007. The myth of the shareholder franchise. *Virginia Law Review* 93: 675–732.

Bhagat, S., and B.S. Black. 2002. The non-correlation between board independence and long-term firm performance. *Journal of Corporation Law* 27: 231–273.

Boyd, C. 1996. Ethics and corporate governance: The issues raised by the cadbury report in the United Kingdom. *Journal of Business Ethics* 15: 167–182.

Brief, A.P., J.M. Dukerich, P.R. Brown, and J.F. Brett. 1996. What's wrong with the treadway commission report? Experimental analyses of the effects of personal values and codes of conduct on fraudulent financial reporting. *Journal of Business Ethics* 15: 183–198.

Byrd, J.W., and K.A. Hickman. 1992. Do outside directors monitor managers? Evidence from tender offer bids. *Journal of Financial Economics* 32: 195–221.

Cadman, B., M.E. Carter, and S. Hillegeist. 2008. The role and effect of compensation consultants on CEO pay, Working Paper, University of Pennsylvania, Philadelphia, PA, USA.

Carcello, J.V. 2009. Governance and the common good. *Journal of Business Ethics* 89: 11–18.

Carey, P., and R. Simnett. 2006. Audit partner tenure and audit quality. *The Accounting Review* 81: 653–676.

Coates, J.J. 2007. The goals and promise of the Sarbanes-Oxley Act. *Journal of Economic Perspectives*. 21: 91–116.

Core, J.E., R.W. Holthausen, and D.F. Larcker. 1999. Corporate governance, Chief Executive Officer compensation, and firm performance. *Journal of Financial Economics* 51: 371–406.

Cox, C. 2007. Speech by SEC chairman: Closing remarks to the second annual corporate governance summit, U.S. securities and exchange commission, USC Marshall School of Business, Los Angeles, CA, Mar. 23, 2007. http://www.sec.gov/news/speech/2007/spch032307cc.htm

Daily, C.M., and D.R. Dalton. 1994. Bankruptcy and corporate governance: The impact of board composition and structure. *Academy of Management Journal* 37: 1603–1617.

Daily, C.M., J.L. Johnson, A.E. Ellstrand, and D.R. Dalton. 1998. Compensation committee composition as a determinant of CEO compensation. *Academy of Management Journal* 41: 209–220.

Faleye, O. 2007. Does one hat fit all? The case of corporate leadership structure. *Journal of Management and Governance* 11: 239–259.

Felo, A.J. 2000. Ethics programs, board oversight, and perceived disclosure credibility: Was the treadway commission correct about ethics and financial reporting? *Research on Accounting Ethics* 7: 157–176.

Felo, A.J. 2001. Ethics programs, board involvement, and potential conflicts of interest in corporate governance. *Journal of Business Ethics* 32: 205–218.

Felo, A.J. 2006. Board oversight of corporate ethics programs and changes in financial disclosure credibility. *Journal of Forensic Accounting* 7: 474–494.

Felo, A.J. 2007. Board oversight of corporate ethics programs and disclosure transparency. *Accounting and the Public Interest* 7: 1–25.

Felo, A.J. 2009. Corporate governance practices in the United States. In *Codes of good governance around the world* (Business Issues, Competition and Entrepreneurship Series), ed. F.J. Lopez Iturriaga, 99–132. Hauppauge, NY: Nova Publishers.

Francis, J.R. 2006. Are auditors compromised by nonaudit services? Assessing the evidence. *Contemporary Accounting Review* 23: 747–760.

Grinstein, Y., and Y. Valles Arellano. 2008. Separating the CEO from the chairman position: Determinants and changes after the new corporate governance regulation, Working Paper, Johnson Graduate School of Management, Cornell University, Ithaca, NY, USA.

Hoffman, W.M., and M. Rowe. 2007. The ethics officer as agent of the board: Leveraging ethical governance capability in the post-enron corporation. *Business and Society Review* 112: 553–572.

Jennings, M.M., K.J. Pany, and P.M.J. Reckers. 2006. Strong corporate governance and audit firm rotation: Effects on judges Independence perceptions and litigation judgments. *Accounting Horizons* 20: 253–270.

Johnson, V.E., I.K. Khurana, and J.K. Reynolds. 2002. Audit-firm tenure and the quality of financial reports. *Contemporary Accounting Research* 19: 637–660.

Kaplan, S.E., and E.G. Mauldin. 2008. Auditor rotation and the appearance of independence: Evidence from non-professional investors. *Journal of Accounting and Public Policy* 27: 177–192.

Laksmana, I. 2007. Corporate board governance and voluntary disclosure of executive compensation practices, Working Paper, Kent State University, Kent, OH, USA.

National commission on fraudulent financial reporting. 1987. *Report of the national commission on fraudulent financial reporting*, New York, NY (National Commission on Fraudulent Financial Reporting).

Naughton, J. 2009. Compensation proposals in 2009 proxy season, The Harvard Law School Forum on Corporate Governance and Financial Regulation. http://blogs.law.harvard.edu/corpgov/2009/04/29/compensation-prososals-in-2009-proxy-season/

New York Stock Exchange (NYSE). 2008. *The New York Stock Exchange listed company manual*, New York, NY (New York Stock Exchange). http://www.nyse.com/regulation/listed/1182508124422.html

Perkins, M. 2008. Directors and investors at odds on performance-based compensation. *Directorship* 34: 13.

Petra, S.T., and N.T. Dorata. 2008. Corporate governance and chief executive officer compensation. *Corporate Governance* 8: 141–152.

Prentice, D. 2006. A voice crying in the wilderness for auditor independence: Abe Briloff and section 201 of the Sarbanes-Oxley Act of 2002. *Journal of American Academy of Business* 8: 190–195.

Sarbanes-Oxley Act. 2002. *Public Law 107-204*, 107th United States Congress, 2002.

Securities and Exchange Commission (SEC). 2006, 29 August. *Final rule: Executive compensation and related person disclosure*. Washington, DC: Government Printing Office.

Securities and Exchange Commission (SEC). 2007, 11 December. *Final rule: Shareholder proposals relating to the election of directors*. Washington, DC: Government Printing Office.

Shivdasani, A., and D. Yermack. 1999. CEO involvement in the selection of new board members: An empirical analysis. *The Journal of Finance* 54: 1829–1853.

Sjostrom, W.K., and Y.S. Kim. 2007. Majority voting for the election of directors, Working Paper, Northern Kentucky University, Highland Heights, KY, USA.

Stout, L.A. 2007. The mythical benefits of shareholder control. *Virginia Law Review* 93: 789–809.

Strier, F. 2005. Conflicts of interest in corporate governance. *The Journal of Corporate Citizenship* 19: 79–89.

U.S. General Accounting Office (GAO). 2003. *Public accounting firms: Required study on the potential effects of mandatory audit firm rotation (GAO-04-216)*. Washington, DC: Government Printing Office.

Vafeas, N. 2003. Further evidence on compensation committee composition as a determinant of CEO compensation. *Financial Management* 32: 53–70.

Vafeas, N., and Z. Afxentiou. 1998. The association between the SEC's 1992 compensation disclosure rule and executive compensation policy changes. *Journal of Accounting and Public Policy* 17: 27–54.

Weisbach, M.S. 1988. Outside directors and CEO turnover. *Journal of Financial Economics* 20: 431–460.

White, E., and A.O. Patrick. 2007. Shareholders push for vote on executive pay. *Wall Street Journal*, 26 February B1.

Chapter 14
When Good Turns to Bad: An Examination of Governance Failure in a Not-for-Profit Enterprise

Chris Low

Contents

Introduction

Governance failures in the private sector have received significant attention in recent years. The banking crisis has highlighted the lack of controls on institutional risk-taking which has echoes in earlier cases such as Enron where creditors and shareholders alike were misled (cf. Clarke 2005). Those involved in the governance function in the for-profit sector now effectively find themselves guilty until proven innocent. In contrast, the not-for-profit sector retains a superior reputation despite enduring its own problems with financial mismanagement.[1] This behaviour tends to be analysed as almost accidental rather than wilfully unethical (cf. Dunn and Riley 2004). Therefore, although deficit in board ability does feature in the not-for-profit

---

[1] For an example, see Hayden (2006).

C. Low (✉)
Head of the Division of Health and Wellbeing, Department of Health Sciences, University of Huddersfield, Huddersfield, UK
e-mail: C.Low@hud.ac.uk

A. Brink (ed.), *Corporate Governance and Business Ethics*, Ethical Economy.
Studies in Economic Ethics and Philosophy 39, DOI 10.1007/978-94-007-1588-2_14,
© Springer Science+Business Media B.V. 2011

literature (cf. Abzug and Galaskiewicz 2001; Brown 2002), there is little in the way of a presumption of unethical behaviour being prevalent within the sector.

This divergence in assessing and analysing governance in the for-profit and not-for-profit sectors is echoed in academe. The literature on organisational governance suggests that organisations in each sector exist in parallel worlds. Corporate governance journals tend to have few articles focussing on not-for-profit governance (cf., e.g., Bart and Deal 2006; Turnbull 2007). Most research is published in dedicated not-for-profit journals such as "Nonprofit Management and Leadership". Therefore, as a consequence of this separation, papers seeking to compare governance in these different sectors are "virtually non existent" (cf. Bart and Deal 2006, p. 4).

The analysis of governance in each sector is driven by two distinct theoretical approaches. They can be broadly identified as shareholding and stakeholding (cf. Letza et al. 2004). For-profits tend to receive an analysis that has a shareholding framework at its foundation. This is guided by the assumption that shareholder interest is the primary aim of a firm's existence (cf. Child and Rodrigues 2004). The stakeholder model of governance, by contrast, views the organisation as a means to serve the interests of numerous parties (cf. Iecovich 2005). This in turn requires the board to focus on "co-ordinating with a fairly broad array of constituents" compared to private sector boards which preoccupy themselves with "securing access to capital and enhancing co-ordination" (Miller-Millesen 2003, p. 534). Although some scholars believe that the stakeholder model applies equally to for-profits and not-for-profits (cf. Bouckaert and Vandenhove 1998), it would appear that the continued critique of how for-profits act would raise a question over this (cf. Hutton 1995; Klein 2008). Following these observations, this paper aims to explore the potential for overlaps between governance in the two sectors, guided by the following question:

> Do the for-profit and not-for-profit sectors share governance challenges, including the threat of unethical behaviour?

The paper begins by mapping the principal challenges of governance in each sector. This combination of perspectives is then used to analyse a case study of governance failure within a not-for-profit organisation. The final section discusses the implications of the findings from this study when examining governance within the not-for-profit sector. Conclusions are drawn for further research and theory building.

Governance Challenges within the For-Profit and Not-for-Profit Sectors

Theoretical Underpinnings of the Not-for-Profit Sector

The observation was made above that each sector has its own discrete theoretical underpinning. To reiterate, shareholding is the dominant model within for-profit governance, while the not-for-profit sector has stakeholding as its focus. The shareholding model is preoccupied with the issue of agency and how the board and senior management can be incentivised to act in the interest of shareholders (cf. Letza et al. 2004). This problem emerged from the separation of ownership and control which was brought about by the creation of the limited company form (cf. Berle and Means 1932/1991). The issue rests on why a senior manager, as an agent of the shareholder, will be as careful with shareholder assets as the shareholder would be themselves. Friedman (1970) took great pleasure in emphasising that we are most likely to be irresponsible when spending other people's money. Although other issues feature within this theory of corporate governance, it is still the agency problem that dominates. Monks and Minow (2008) believe that this problem is the "single major challenge" of governance, especially given that shareholders "grant managers enormous discretionary power over the conduct of the business while holding them accountable for the use of that power" (p. 225). This was illustrated by the Enron case where the board was judged to have failed in its fiduciary duties to the large number of small shareholders who ended up losing much of their life savings (cf. Clarke 2005).

Little attention is paid to the agency problem in not-for-profit research. The underpinning assumption appears to be that a not-for-profit organisation which claims to serve its stakeholders will be ethically guided (cf. Mason et al. 2007) and so directors will not act in their own self-interest. This rather optimistic view is quite prevalent within the literature (cf. Hayden 2006). However it is becoming more widely recognised within the literature that not-for-profits are increasingly seeking profit-making opportunities through trading activities and so appear to becoming more like for-profit organisations (cf. Dart 2004). Another reason that agency is not a dominant issue is that both theoretically and legally not-for-profit organisations are owned by the community and as a result they have no shareholders (cf. Pearce 2003). Nobody has a claim on the organisation's assets which are held in trust for the benefit of the community (cf. Dunn and Riley 2004). This means that it is difficult to identify which principal an agent would act on behalf of (cf. Abzug and Galaskiewicz 2001). This does raise questions over transparency (cf. Hayden 2006) and accountability (cf. Dunn and Riley 2004). In contrast to for-profits, this also means that financial demands are not the only ones that stakeholders may demand from an organisation. Managing these demands is the key challenge of governance within the stakeholding model (cf. Letza et al. 2004; Low and Cowton 2004).

Stakeholder Involvement

Researchers make both a moral and an instrumental case for stakeholder involvement in governance (cf. Donaldson and Preston 1995; Abzug and Galaskiewicz 2001). The moral view is that not-for-profits have a democratic ethos that places a duty on them to take into account a broad range of community interests (cf. Iecovich 2005). To facilitate this, the board membership should be diverse and composed in a way that reduces the likelihood of it being dominated by long-serving local elites (cf. Parker 2007). The instrumental case is more pragmatic in that the claim is made that there will be gains in the efficiency and effectiveness of decision-making if stakeholders are involved in governance (cf. Letza et al. 2004). This view has been criticised on the grounds that involving stakeholders is not feasible and nor is it desirable (cf. Sternberg 2000). Even stakeholding advocates accept that there are difficulties in meeting stakeholder needs simultaneously (cf. Goodpaster 1993; Mason et al. 2007). As Abzug and Galaskiewicz (2001) note, "there is no one community interest; there are many" (p. 54).

Diversity of board membership has also become a prominent issue in for-profit studies. The objective of such diversity is different though. It is primarily concerned with how the conduct of boards might be improved by ensuring that there is a reduced likelihood of the "cosy boardroom ties" (Hayden 2006, p. 116) that have been linked to a lack of attention to shareholder interests. There is also an equality dimension to this agenda. As Higgs (2003) noted, questions will be asked of an organisation's commitment to diversity if the board itself appears to be homogenous. Further studies have attempted to evaluate progress on the extent to which board membership has been opened up to broaden the gender and ethnic mix (cf. Ruigrok et al. 2007; Grosvold et al. 2007).

The preceding section has identified two issues to explore within the research context: agency, which is dominant within the shareholding model, and involvement, which is a preoccupation of the stakeholding model. The case study that is examined in the next section offers a not-for-profit research context in which each of these issues is to be examined. A brief description of the methodology employed is followed by the case study. The two issues are then examined and conclusions drawn.

Case Study: ABC

This case study was compiled based on the experiences of a participant within ABC, the focal not-for-profit organisation.[2] It is acknowledged that participant observation may not provide an entirely unbiased perspective on organisational processes and events (cf. Silverman 2000). However, the position taken here is that an insider can help to reveal dynamics that would go undetected by an independent researcher using more objective methods such as surveys (cf. Parker 2007). More specifically, in this instance, board processes and director behaviour were captured and analysed (cf. Samra-Fredericks 2000). The data collection exercise took place over five years and included participant observation alongside the acquisition and consequent analysis of internal documentation such as the organisation's written constitution.

This methodological approach was not the result of a planned and purposive exercise. It was the product of the participant conducting a rigorous retrospective analysis in the light of the organisational failure which resulted in the company's bankruptcy in 2006. No claims are made, therefore, that this case should be viewed as one that is exhaustively validated. It is offered in the spirit of presenting an

---

[2] Thanks go to Chris Chinnock, an MSc student at the University of Huddersfield who conducted the primary data collection.

opportunity to begin a discussion of the possibility of connections being made between governance practices in different sectors.

ABC

ABC was established in Huddersfield, England, in October 2000 as a not-for-profit company limited by guarantee. It lasted six years and was formally wound up in 2006. It was created to provide opportunities for young people to access creative arts activities. The young people it focussed on were those exhibiting anti-social behaviour. Although ABC was constituted as a worker co-operative, it did not have provision to act as a member benefit organisation. It was specifically organised to proscribe members receiving personal rewards, as embodied in the constitution which stated that,

> the surplus of the Co-operative shall be applied as follows, in such proportion and in such a manner as the General meeting shall decide from time to time: to a general reserve for the continuation and development of the Co-operative.

The assets of ABC were similarly locked in to maintain community ownership through a further clause:

> If on the winding up or dissolution of the Co-operative any of its assets remain to be disposed of after its liabilities are satisfied, these assets shall not be distributed among the Members, but shall be transferred instead to some other common ownership enterprise(s), or some other non-profit organisation(s), as may be decided by the members.

Originally the organisation was run by four staff whose positions were supported by funding from the UK government through an employment creation scheme. Young people were referred to ABC by local schools as well as parts of the criminal justice system such as youth offending teams. ABC subscribed to a model of anti-social behaviour that linked it with low educational attainment, unemployment, and crime. They believed that they could reduce the incidence of social exclusion by offering positive alternatives to the usual activities of drug-taking, alcohol, and criminal behaviour. These alternative activities were predominantly workshop-based sessions in music technology, break-dancing, and drama. These sessions were designed to increase confidence and motivation by providing young people with transferable skills.

Initially ABC focussed on Afro-Caribbean young people. There is a sizeable community within the Huddersfield area. Over time the organisation expanded its reach and engaged with white and Asian youths who were also exhibiting anti-social behaviours. Within one year ABC was in a position to establish its own premises within Huddersfield. They acquired space which enabled them to create a number of dedicated facilities including a recording studio, dance studio, training rooms, and office space. Staff was recruited on the basis of their creative talents and their proximity to the organisation. Local artists, musicians, and dancers became mentors who were seen by ABC to be capable of acting as positive role models for the young people on their programmes.

ABC gradually became more established and received recognition for their work. For example they won a regional award in 2004 for being "On the Up". Between 2002 and 2004, annual turnover grew sharply from £38,000 to around £300,000. This was the result of trading, funding awards, and contracting with one government contract alone being worth £150,000. These contracts require an organisation to create formal systems that can deal with monitoring, evaluation, and progression of participants. This meant that a perception grew within ABC that they were meeting the needs of their contractors rather than maximising their effectiveness with regard to users of their service. This formality was making them less flexible and so less responsive to the young people on their programmes. Accountability appeared to be moving away from the community which ABC were set up to serve as they had to meet the increasingly onerous demands of their contractors. After a series of events that shall be described in the following sections, by January 2006 the organisation was in voluntary liquidation. To identify which factors may have contributed to this swift decline, agency and stakeholder involvement from the earlier theoretical discussion will now be explored in the context of the case material.

Agency

A contributory factor to ABC's failure was the agency problem which emerged in the establishment of a subsidiary trading arm focussed on the music industry. This venture aimed to nurture those talented youngsters that had been discovered while attending ABC's creative programmes. These local music artists were given recording opportunities and management support in return for a guaranteed share in future revenues from sales and performance commissions. This artist development programme would therefore be financially supported by commercial trading income. Any profit margin generated could then be invested back into ABC to help subsidise their main social purpose activity. A large amount of working capital was needed to set this programme up and was raised through accessing the company's reserves. After two years, and with the support of two full-time members of staff, it had still failed to generate any income.

Directors failed in their role as agents of both the organisation and the community. It is not uncommon for these types of venture to fail. The music industry is a notoriously difficult one in which to succeed due to its competitive nature. However, the decision-making bears further analysis. Perhaps the venture illustrates the difficulty of balancing the need for not-for-profits to seek financial sustainability against the taking of reasonable risks to secure this sustainability. Another interpretation is to view this venture as the board allowing their own personal interest in the music industry to cloud their judgement. This demoted the social objectives of the company into second place. This behaviour can be defended to some extent and suggest agency failure without questioning the ethics of the board's conduct. However, the evidence from the following section on stakeholder involvement suggests a different conclusion.

Involvement

Stakeholder involvement is enshrined legally in the constitution of a co-operative. In theory at least, it is possible for anyone to become a member. From there, any member is then entitled to put themselves forward for board membership. Therefore, any stakeholder can become involved in the governance function. This is illustrated within ABC's Articles of Association:

> 3. Membership will be open.

The Articles also show their support for the involvement of employees with the clause stating,

> 4. All employees on taking up employment with the Co-operative (. . .) shall be admitted to Membership of the Co-operative, except that the Co-operative in General Meetings may by majority vote decide to exclude from the Membership:
> a. persons under eighteen years of age;
> b. newly appointed employees during such reasonable probationary period as may be specified in their terms and conditions of employment;
> (. . .) provided that any such criteria for exclusion is applied equally to all employees.

These excerpts from the constitution suggest that ABC intended to offer the opportunity to new employees to become members of the organisation and, further, to become involved in governance if they so desired. This opportunity was to be available unless there were exceptional and transparent circumstances which would be determined through a majority vote by the existing membership. However, this clause 4 was used to limit membership and keep it exclusive to the founding members. This was achieved by extending the "reasonable probationary period" detailed in the clause to beyond the length of any existing employee's service. This had the effect of keeping membership perpetually out of reach. The other implication of this was that there was no opportunity for an employee to join the board.

Eventually, the situation did become the subject of a challenge from staff within the organisation as they became more aware of their legal entitlements. Employees began to insist upon the right to membership and hence also pushed for full voting rights at Annual General Meetings. Upon gaining these rights, the membership decided to remove a director from his role against his wishes. His conduct was questionable not least because he had appointed himself both Managing Director and Financial Director. He had also been identified by members as one of the key barriers to any inclusive practices being fully implemented. The other members of the board received more favourable treatment and were granted the right to continue in their roles for another year before being subjected to a membership vote.

Once the inclusive policy was in place, ABC had an open route to membership. This continued for the six months that remained of the organisation's existence. The company continued to struggle in spite of these improvements being made to employee involvement in the governance function. By the autumn of 2005, the organisation was no longer financially viable and was effectively on the verge of collapse. The price was being paid for previous decisions by directors to award themselves hefty pay rises while their new ventures, as with the example above, singularly failed to achieve business success. It fell to the newly elected board members to honour their legal obligation to instigate liquidation proceedings following the holding of an Emergency General Meeting of the membership. This decision was not supported by the original directors who demonstrated little understanding of the legal implications of trading whilst in the full knowledge that the organisation is insolvent. Fortunately, the newly empowered membership was able to impose their will over the old guard and administration and winding-up duly followed.

Discussion

This case analysis has attempted to support the central argument of this paper, namely that for-profit and not-for-profit governance should not always be viewed in isolation of one another. Governance in these two sectors may actually exhibit very similar behaviours in certain circumstances and so there is value in being open to this possibility. However these behaviours will only be identified by researchers if theoretical insights from research in each sector are combined in any framework adopted. Despite a handful of exceptions (cf. Miller-Millesen 2003; Bart and Deal 2006; Parker 2007), there is still a tendency to focus on issues that have been revisited many times in the same sector. The case detailed here has focussed on agency and involvement, two key challenges of governance that are prominent within the for-profit and not-for-profit literatures respectively. By making a link between agency failure and a desire by the board to restrict stakeholder involvement, the case has shown how not-for-profits can be subject to unethical conduct by directors who can undermine governance and so impact negatively on operational decision-making.

Although the agency failure detailed above can be viewed as incompetence, it takes on a more unethical character when taken together with the board's behaviour with regard to involvement and governance. The wilful exclusion of employees took place through undermining the spirit if not the letter of the constitution of the company. Bouckaert and Vandenhove (1998) suggest that an organisation that claims to be socially responsible must "give due regard to the expectations and interests of the various stakeholders in determining and realising the values and mission of the company" (p. 1076). There is little evidence of this "due regard" in the case of ABC. This fact raises doubt around whose interests the board members were serving in their decision-making. Director self-interest may be more common within the for-profit sector but it should not be ruled out in the not-for-profit arena (cf. Hayden 2006).

It is not the intention to suggest that this case indicates a widespread malaise in the not-for-profit sector. It simply highlights that an organisation that is founded on a social principle may still display behaviour that is more usually associated with the for-profit sector. The organisation may still trumpet its values throughout its communications while acting in a way that undermines its claims. Better governance procedures within the not-for-profit sector aim to balance experience with new ideas (cf. Parker 2007). The case of ABC shows how this can be stifled by protecting the cosy arrangements already in place (cf. Hayden 2006). Lack of openness to new board members may pose a threat to the quality of decision-making (cf. Letza et al. 2004) alongside being an issue of ethics. The agency failure of ABC may or may not have been avoided with a more diverse board membership. But at least the adoption of a more pluralistic approach would raise the probability of a more informed approach to the decision-making process. It becomes more likely that the board will be made more sensitive to the demands of stakeholders, including potential consumers and contractors (cf. Abzug and Galaskiewicz 2001).

This field requires conceptual development alongside additional studies examining governance failure within the not-for-profit sector. It is assumed that the current preference will continue amongst governments for the not-for-profit sector to expand in its provision of public services (cf. Parker 2007). Therefore, it is not unreasonable to posit that the incidence of financial collapse will increase, thereby presenting more research opportunities for research. While increased failure is not a desirable scenario, it requires greater scrutiny. Without such scrutiny it is likely that future failures will continue to happen. Greater attention must be paid to the impact of the role played by director conduct and motivation in not-for-profit organisations. The for-profit "scandal" literature does a very good job of analysing this. To help bring this about, more syntheses of the two literatures are needed (cf., e.g., Miller-Millesen 2003). This would then offer the possibility of developing a framework that builds upon the tentative model put forward in this paper.

References

Abzug, R., and J. Galaskiewicz. 2001. Nonprofit boards: Crucibles of expertise of symbols of local identities? *Nonprofit and Voluntary Sector Quarterly* 30: 51–73.

Bart, C., and K. Deal. 2006. The governance role of the board in corporate strategy: A comparison of board practices in 'For Profit' and 'Not For Profit' organisations. *International Journal of Business Governance and Ethics* 2: 2–22.

Berle, A.A., and G.C. Means. 1932/1991. *The modern corporation and private property*. New Brunswick, NJ: Transaction Publishers.

Bouckaert, L., and J. Vandenhove. 1998. Business ethics and the management of non-profit institutions. *Journal of Business Ethics* 17: 1073–1081.

Brown, W.A. 2002. Inclusive governance practices in nonprofit organizations and implications for practice. *Nonprofit Management and Leadership* 12: 369–385.

Child, J., and S.B. Rodrigues. 2004. Repairing the breach of trust in corporate governance. *Corporate Governance* 12: 143–152.

Clarke, T. 2005. Accounting for Enron: Shareholder value and stakeholder interests. *Corporate Governance* 13: 598–612.

Dart, R. 2004. The legitimacy of social enterprise. *Nonprofit Management and Leadership* 14: 411–424.

Donaldson, T., and L.E. Preston. 1995. The stakeholder theory of the corporation: Concepts, evidence, and implications. *Academy of Management Review* 20: 65–91.

Dunn, A., and C.A. Riley. 2004. Supporting the not-for-profit sector: The government's review of charitable and social enterprise. *The Modern Law Review* 67: 632–657.

Friedman, M. 1970. The social responsibility of business is to increase its profits. *The New York Times Magazine*, 13 September 32–34.

Goodpaster, K. 1993. Business ethics and stakeholder analysis. In *Applied ethics: A reader,* ed. E.R. Winkler and J.R. Coombs, 229–248. Oxford: Blackwell.

Grosvold, J., S. Brammer, and B. Rayton. 2007. Board diversity in the United Kingdom and Norway: An exploratory analysis. *Business ethics: A European review* 16: 344–357.

Hayden, E.W. 2006. Governance failures also occur in the non-profit world. *International Journal of Business Governance and Ethics* 2: 116–128.

Higgs, D. 2003. *Review of the role and effectiveness of non-executive directors*. London: Department of Trade and Industry, Her Majesty's Stationery Office.

Hutton, W. 1995. *The state we're in*. London: Jonathan Cape.

Iecovich, E. 2005. The profile of board membership in Israeli voluntary organisations. *Voluntas: International Journal of Voluntary and Nonprofit Organizations* 16: 161–180.

Klein, N. 2008. *The shock doctrine: The rise of disaster capitalism*. New York, NY: Metropolitan Books.

Letza, S., X. Sun, and J. Kirkbride. 2004. Shareholding versus stakeholding: A critical review of corporate governance. *Corporate Governance* 12: 242–262.

Low, C., and C. Cowton. 2004. Beyond stakeholder engagement: The challenges of stakeholder participation in corporate governance. *International Journal of Business Governance and Ethics* 1: 45–55.

Mason, C., J. Kirkbride, and D. Bryde. 2007. From stakeholders to institutions: The changing face of social enterprise governance theory. *Management Decision* 45: 284–301.

Miller-Millesen, J.L. 2003. Understanding the behaviour of nonprofit boards of directors: A theory-based approach. *Nonprofit and Voluntary Sector Quarterly* 32: 521–547.

Monks, R.A.G., and N. Minow. 2008. *Corporate governance*, 4th ed. Oxford: Blackwell.

Parker, L.D. 2007. Internal governance in the nonprofit boardroom: A participant observer study. *Corporate governance* 15: 923–934.

Pearce, J. 2003. *Social enterprise in anytown*. London: Calouste Gulbenkian Foundation.

Ruigrok, W., S. Peck, and S. Tacheva. 2007. Nationality and gender diversity on Swiss corporate boards. *Corporate Governance* 15: 546–557.

Samra-Fredericks, D. 2000. Doing 'Boards-In-Action' research – an ethnographic approach for the capture and analysis of directors' and senior managers' interactive routines. *Corporate Governance* 8: 244–257.

Silverman, D. 2000. *Doing qualitative research: A practical handbook*. London: Sage.

Sternberg, E. 2000. The defects of stakeholder theory. *Corporate Governance* 8: 3–10.

Turnbull, S. 2007. Analysing network governance of public assets. *Corporate Governance* 15: 1079–1089.

Chapter 15
Integrity in the Boardroom: A Case for Further Research

Scott Lichtenstein, Les Higgins, and Pat Dade

Contents

Introduction

Integrity is universally rated by directors as having the greatest impact on successful board performance. Yet, no shared meaning exists about what integrity means. This is because its meaning is dependent on one's personal values. This chapter seeks to understand how the meaning of integrity varies by individuals' different dominant values. By understanding the values and motives of directors, future research can give insight into what integrity *really* means in creating a passionate board: a board agenda ("the talk") that resonates with directors' integrity coupled by action ("the walk").

S. Lichtenstein (✉)
Senior Lecturer, St James Business School, London, UK
e-mail: scottl@evsconsulting.co.uk

A. Brink (ed.), *Corporate Governance and Business Ethics*, Ethical Economy.
Studies in Economic Ethics and Philosophy 39, DOI 10.1007/978-94-007-1588-2_15,
© Springer Science+Business Media B.V. 2011

The objective of this chapter is to investigating the link between values, integrity, and board engagement by:

- examining data on individuals' values and translating them into different interpretations of what integrity means to different value groups;
- proposing the linkage between values and the board agenda and how it can be refocused for optimal decision-making and personal engagement by directors at the level of their values;
- calling for further research into the personal values of the board.

First, a review of integrity's role in the boardroom and leadership is provided. Next, a proposition is developed that is followed by empirical research into the value systems of UK society and its impact on respondents' definition of integrity. Empirical research into European managers' value systems are summarised with implications for future board-level research. Finally, a case for researching integrity, values, and the board agenda is made followed by limitations, future research, and conclusions.

Integrity Is Vital in the Boardroom

The importance of *integrity* in the boardroom is well established (cf. Gay and Dulewicz 1997). Directors are in no doubt of its importance to board performance. In a study by Gay and Dulewicz (1997), *integrity* was consistently rated by directors as the quality/competence that has the greatest impact on successful board performance (please cf. Table 15.1). In a study of 713 directors with at least one year's experience from domestic (546) and international (167) companies, *integrity* was rated out of 38 personal qualities/competences as having (i) the greatest impact on successful board performance for all directors combined (chairmen, chief executive/managing Director (MD), executive directors and non-executive directors), (ii) third highest for the chief executive/MD overall, and (iii) second highest for chief executive/MD of domestic and international companies.

Table 15.1 Ranked personal competences

	Types of company		
	All companies	Domestic	International
All directors	*Integrity*	*Integrity*	*Integrity*
	Change oriented	Change oriented	Critical faculty
	Critical faculty	Critical faculty	Change oriented
	Helicopter	Helicopter	Helicopter
	Judgement	Motivating others	Judgement
The chairman	*Integrity*	*Integrity*	*Integrity*
	Helicopter	Helicopter	Appraising
	Appraising	Appraising	Helicopter
	Critical faculty	Critical faculty	Strategic awareness
	Vision	Vision	Vision

Table 15.1   (continued)

	Types of company		
	All companies	Domestic	International
The chief executive/MD	*Decisiveness*	*Business sense*	*Decisiveness*
	Business sense	Integrity	Integrity
	Integrity	Decisiveness	Business sense
	Motivating others	Motivating others	Motivating others
	Vision	Vision	Vision
The executive director	*Integrity*	*Integrity*	*Integrity*
	Business sense	Motivating others	Business sense
	Motivating others	Change oriented	Achievement
	Change oriented	Business sense	Motivation
	Judgement	Delegating	Judgement
The non-executive director	*Integrity*	*Integrity*	*Integrity*
	Critical faculty	Critical faculty	Critical faculty
	Helicopter	Helicopter	Helicopter
	Change oriented	Change oriented	Change oriented
	Listening	Listening	Listening

Source: Gay and Dulewicz (1997)

These results confirm that integrity has the greatest impact on future personal performance on the board as rated by directors themselves. The results of their research indicate that integrity is vital to boardroom performance. Therefore, integrity is an important area for study because the board believe it is important. This area of study demands greater scrutiny and raises questions such as what role does it play in the boardroom? In the following, we briefly review the role of integrity in leadership and direction.

Business scions such as Warren Buffet claims integrity is the most important out of the three qualities he looks for in any new hires: "If you don't have integrity, then intelligence and high energy don't matter" (as quoted in Gostick and Telford 2003, pp. 3f.). On hiring associates, Dee Hock, ex-CEO of Visa International, clearly positions the importance of integrity relative to other personal qualities:

> Hire and promote first on the basis of integrity; second, motivation; third, capacity; fourth, understanding; fifth, knowledge; and last and least, experience. Without integrity, motivation is dangerous; without motivation, capacity is impotent; without capacity, understanding is limited; without understanding, knowledge is meaningless; without knowledge, experience is blind. Experience is easy to provide and quickly put to good use by people with all the other qualities. (as quoted in Waldrop 1996, p. 84)

The anecdotal evidence of the importance of integrity to leaders and leadership teams is explored in the literature through the scrutiny of two key stakeholder groups, employees and shareholders. MacGregor Burns (1978) and Yukl (1998) argue the willingness of followers to be led is based on the extent to which followers identify personally with the integrity of the leader. Employees continually informally judge the integrity of leaders. Fields (2007) asserts that a lower level of consensus amongst followers about a leader's integrity reduces the leader's influence or "followership". A perceived lack of integrity can create dis-ease amongst followers in the form of resistance to work for a particular boss, and hence, limit the ability of a leader to influence the organisational culture.

Six, de Bakker, and Huberts (2007) highlight the overlooked role of stakeholder groups' who judge the integrity of leader and leadership teams when they break commonly held norms. They found that stakeholder groups scrutinise a leader's integrity at two key junctures: (i) when he/she is first selected and (ii) when allegations are made about misconduct. Using the case of Royal Ahold's executive misconduct, they investigate "disintegrity" that is defined as a judgement of breaking the law and ethical codes of conduct. In the Royal Ahold case, they examined stakeholder groups' judgement of disintegrity and how it ultimately led to the then new CEO Anderes Moberg renouncing his guaranteed bonus of several million euros. Cor Herstroter, CEO of Shell at the time of the Brent Spar affair (1995), declared that companies have to comply with broader notions of stakeholders' values and norms to earn its "license to operate". Other examples of this public outcry, e.g., to US ex-Home Depot CEO Bob Nardelli's $210 million severance pay, re-enforces Six et al.'s (2007) finding that a leader or leadership team's values and integrity may cause discomfort and dis-ease amongst a company's wider stakeholder group if they are sufficiently different from stakeholders' values and norms.

The literature indicates that integrity is vital to board performance, intrinsically linked to leadership in a leaders' ability to attract followership, and, hence, ability to implement the vision of and create value for the organisation as well as central to an organisations' "license to trade". The literature also raises questions, such as, what is meant by integrity? And does it mean the same thing to different people? And if it does, how can we understand it in a practical way to help boards? In the next section, definitions of integrity will be reviewed following an outline of the different elements of integrity with a focus on the link between values and integrity.

The Upper Echelon Theory: An Examination of the Link between Integrity and Values

For the purposes of their study, Gay and Dulewicz (1997) defined someone who has integrity as someone who

> [i]s truthful and trustworthy, can be relied upon to keep his/her word. Does not have double standards and does not compromise on matters of moral principle. (p. ii)

This competency-based definition captures some important aspects of integrity. In a meta-analysis of integrity in the literature, Palanski and Yammarino (2007) summarise five attributes of integrity: (i) wholeness, (ii) authenticity, (iii) words/action consistency, (iv) consistency in adversity, and (v) morality.

Words/action consistency or the importance of leaders' "walking the talk" is a key aspect of integrity that runs through the literature (cf., e.g., Aitken 2007). Simons (2002) stress the importance of "behavioral integrity" – the consistency of words and actions. In this context, "the talk" refers to the personal values of directors and leaders. Badaracco and Ellsworth (1992) describe integrity as consisting of a manager's personal values, daily actions, and basic organisational aims.

A number of authors relate integrity to understanding and owning one's set of values and acting accordingly (cf. Palanski and Yammarino 2007). In this sense, integrity is a director's or managers "authentic talk", not just the espoused values which are uttered to "get along" in the organisation. Simons (2002) actually measures integrity by the consistency of a leader's espoused versus actual values.

Srivastva observes,

> The intriguing fact is that very few of us see ourselves as lacking integrity, yet we can readily point to disintegrity in almost every institution in which we are involved. (Srivastva 1988, p. 18, as quoted in Six et al. 2007)

Srivastva (1988) contends that different actors see things differently due to different "mental maps" and "world views" due to their (our) different values and norms. An actor's or leader's integrity is ultimately determined by other actor's perception that varies by one's values.

This view of values acting as a perpetual filter is supported by the upper echelon theory, which posits that values act as a filter impacting executives' and directors' decisions as seen in Fig. 15.1.

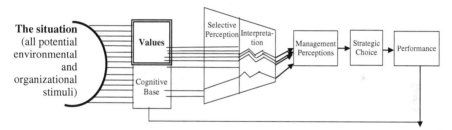

Fig. 15.1 The upper echelon theory
Source: Hambrick and Mason (1984, p. 195)

Extending this to integrity, the literature indicates that actors', i.e., leaders', directors', managers', and employees' perceptions of integrity are filtered by their values. Therefore, the board values dynamic, i.e., the dynamic between the values of the CEO and the rest of the board, influences the varying perceptions of integrity that might exist in the board as well as the board "talk" (the board agenda) and how it behaves (the "walk").

The key element of integrity is words/action consistency that has been briefly reviewed. Key to integrity and words/action constancy is personal values. Values are the authentic "talk" whose consistency with the "walk", i.e., behaviour, is the crux of integrity. The next section will pull the various strands together to make a proposition to be researched.

The following proposition builds on Gay and Dulewicz's (1997) research that integrity is the most important quality to board performance and several authors' (cf., e.g., Badaracco and Ellsworth 1992; Simons 2002) contention that understanding one's dominant values is integral to understanding one's perception of integrity. This is supported by the upper echelon theory that contends that values filter executives' perception of integrity and Srivastva's (1988) view that different actors see things differently due to different "mental maps" and "world views" due to different values and norms that leads us to the following proposition.

Proposition: Integrity varies depending on one's dominant values.

This proposition is examined through exploratory research by empirically analysing and interpreting different value systems of respondents, which is outlined in the next section.

Shortcomings of the Single Values Approach

As long ago as 1961 Gordon Allport suggested that value priorities are the "dominating force" in life as they direct all of an individual's activity towards the achievement of his/her needs. Similarly, Allport (1955) emphasises that individuals' value priorities influence their perception of reality. Therefore, values can be considered to be deep-seated emotional states and beliefs that are oriented towards individuals' underlying needs and motivations. Some characteristics of values are worth highlighting.

Understanding of and previous research into values has suffered from focusing on a single-value approach that (i) results in low reliability, (ii) ignores more equally or more meaningful values, and (iii) ignores that there are trade-offs among competing values. Values form a part of an individual's value system. A value system exists for each person and is more important to understand than a single value (cf. Schwartz 1996; Hambrick and Brandon 1988; Rokeach 1979). Each individual has a hierarchy of values and values are organised in a hierarchical system ordered by relative importance to one another (cf. Schwartz 1992; Rokeach 1979). Although there are universally held values, an individual and groups will hold and espouse a dominant set of values: "At the top of each person's system are a small handful of dominant values of paramount importance" (Hambrick and Brandon 1988, p. 6).

Values theory also suggests that a key characteristic of values is that they are needs-based. Value systems are created by our (changing) underlying needs (cf. Maslow 1970; Allport 1955). Maslow (1970) identified three distinct need types which led to dominance of differing elements in his taxonomy. The basic model of the Hierarchy of Needs provides three levels of needs as shown in Fig. 15.2.

Maslow's Hierarchy of Needs is a model of human psychological development that facilitates understanding of the basis of human values and the way they can change over time from birth to death. Maslow's experience and qualitative research led him to the insight that, as human beings, we are all born with a set of needs that drive our perception of reality and behaviours. These needs are complex and form our "value system". His theory illustrated the nature of the changes in values systems through the life of every person. The changes are hierarchical in nature, i.e.,

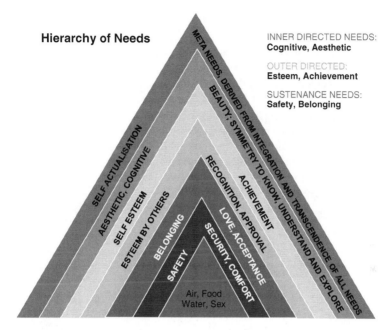

Fig. 15.2 Maslow's hierarchy of needs
Source: Maslow (1970)

some needs need to be met before other needs become important as a determinant of attitudes and behaviours.

The first level is called *Sustenance Driven* needs. At this level the individual is driven by basic physiological needs for air, food, water, sleep, and sex (in post puberty individuals). Once this need is met, the need for safety motivates the person, and eventually the need for belonging kicks in as a motivator of attitude and behaviour. Once this nest of needs is met, and significant proportions of national populations never satisfy these needs, the next level of needs to be met is based on *esteem*, initially the esteem from other and, once that is met, the need for self-esteem drives attitudes and behaviour. These are called *Outer Directed* needs. Once the need for self-esteem is largely met, the values system of the individual changes again. In this third stage of development the needs for a deeper understanding of life, in the understanding of the interdependence among all life, and eventually the transcendence of all needs drives the life of individuals. These are called *Inner Directed* needs. Having briefly introduced a theory-driven approach to values, the next section summarises three value systems in UK Society.

A Summary of the Three Value Systems in UK Society

Abraham Maslow's (1970) Hierarchy of Needs is used as a theoretical framework because most of the values instruments are based on Maslow's theory including Schwartz et al. (2001) Portrait Value System (PVS), that is used in the current research, and because the theory makes a clear link between values, needs, and motivation.

The pre-eminent values instruments are based on Maslow's Hierarchy of Needs (cf. Baker 1996), e.g., Rokeach's Value Survey, Kahle's used in this study, and proprietary instruments of Stanford Research International's Values and Lifestyles (VALS) and Cultural Dynamics Strategy & Marketing Ltd.'s (CDSM) Values Modes (VMs), making Maslow's theory the de facto "industry standard" definition of the structure of values. Moreover, Maslow's theory makes a clear relationship between motivation and values, which makes it amenable to empirical research. As part of his theory on motivation, Maslow defined values as "a gratification of a need". His proposed theory exploring how values are structured is now accepted by a variety of theorists (cf., e.g., Rokeach 1979). Maslovian value groups will be used to categorise respondents in the current research to gain insight into what integrity means for respondents with different value systems.

Research Methodology

The overall research proposition was explored employing a survey of 500 UK adults. The methodology was positivistic, employing quantitative measures of individual's values. The sample for the study was a representative sample using an incentivised internet consumer panel against a quota representative of sex and age of 500 UK adults aged 18+ (see Table 15.2 for sample statistics). Completed responses were accepted until the quotas were fulfilled. The survey was conducted by a market research firm (Global Market Insights Inc.) in January 2007 on behalf of CDSM.

Table 15.2 Descriptive statistics

	Percentage
Inner directed	28
Outer directed	43
Sustenance driven	28
Male	52
Female	48
Age 18–24	11
25–34	17
35–44	20
45–54	17
55–64	15
65+	21

Source: Global Markets Insights Inc.

There is no commonly agreed taxonomy of values. This is reflected in the diversity of values instrumentation. Schwartz et al.'s (2001) 10-value PVS was used because of its proven validity and reliability (cf. Lindeman and Verkasalo 2005) as well as its being amenable to taking a theory-driven approach by categorising values using the Maslovian classification of *Sustenance Driven*, *Outer* and *Inner Directed* value groups. All 10 values surpass Nunnally's (1978) 0.70 value guideline of reliability for the current research. Sub-component values or "portraits" of Schwartz et al.'s (2001) 10 values were analysed to gain finer granularity of the data and used for the purposes of this research. See Table 15.3 for instrument design that summarises the main values of Schwartz et al.'s (2001) 10 values in bold outline and the "portrait" or sub values that make up the value below it. For example, *self direction* is made up of the sub-values of *self choice* and *creativity*.

Table 15.3 Instrument design

Construct	Measure	Source
Personal values	21 items, 10 values portrait value questionnaire	Schwartz et al. (2001)
Values modes	10 question proprietary categorisation method. No reported reliability	CDSM Ltd.
Schwartz et al. (2001) 10 and "Portrait" values	*Measure*	*Current survey Cronbach α*
Self direction	4 item	0.71
Self choice	2 item	0.72
Creativity	2 item	0.55
Power	4 item	0.75
Material wealth	2 item	0.85
Control others	2 item	0.68
Universalism	6 item	0.81
Justice	2 item	0.63
Openness	2 item	0.63
Nature	2 item	0.85
Achievement	4 item	0.80
Visible ability	2 item	0.61
Visible success	2 item	0.65
Security	4 item	0.68
Safety	2 item	0.51
National security	2 item	0.57
Stimulation	4 item	0.83
Novelty	2 item	0.66
Adventure	2 item	0.77
Conformity	4 item	0.74
Rules	2 item	0.57
Propriety	2 item	0.60
Tradition	4 item	0.72
Be satisfied	2 item	0.63
Religion	2 item	0.92
Hedonism	4 item	0.80
Good time	2 item	0.50
Pleasure	2 item	0.74
Benevolence	4 item	0.77
Caring	2 item	0.74
Loyalty	2 item	0.52

Source: Schwartz et al. (2001), CDSM Ltd.

To overcome the limitations of previous values research, a values system approach was used rather than relying on single values. To achieve convergent validity respondents were also categorised into the motivational groups of *Inner Directed*, *Outer Directed* or *Sustenance Driven* using the VM instrument developed by CDSM.

Findings and Interpretation: Value Systems, Integrity, and Some Implications for the Board

The relationship between Maslovian needs and Schwartz's portrait values were investigated using multi-dimensional scaling. See Fig. 15.3 for the values map of the current research. The map reveals that:

1. *Sustenance Driven* respondents espouse the core values of *national security, safety, rules, propriety*, and *be satisfied* in the top right sector,
2. *Outer Directed* respondents espouse the core values of *visible success, visible ability, material wealth, good time*, and *adventure* in the centre left sector, and
3. *Inner Directed* respondents espouse the core values of *creativity, self choice, justice, nature*, and *openness* in the bottom right sector.

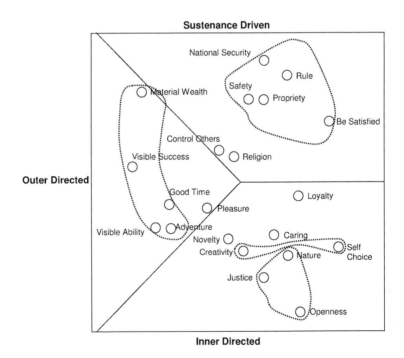

Fig. 15.3 Values map of personal values
Source: Own research

The sheer complexity of modern organisations has favoured the *Inner Directed* value system that is comfortable with and/or actively embracing ambiguity and change. Results from the current research (shown in Fig. 15.4) show rejection of some of the key values in the *Outer Directed* and *Sustenance Driven* value systems, specifically *rules, safety, national security, material wealth,* and *visible success.*

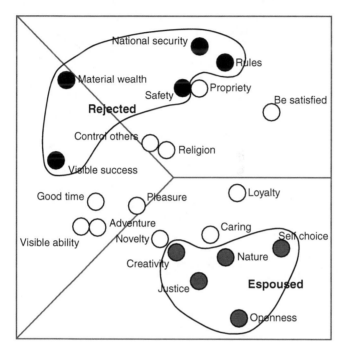

Fig. 15.4 Inner directed values map
Source: Own research

Integrity from this values system is interpreted as "doing better things" (Burgoyne et al. 2005, p. 2) or "stewardship" – that a board's principle job is to make sure that the company continues to benefit future generations. Espousing *self choice*[1] indicates that integrity is closely aligned to "being true to oneself". Espousing the value *nature*[2] points to acting with integrity means creating shareholder value consistent with environmental sustainability.

---

[1] Respondents who strongly agreed that "I like to make my own decisions about what I do, and to be free to plan and choose my own activities" were taken to espouse *self choice*. In the following footnotes, the convictions are spelled out which correspond to the following values.

[2] "I believe that we should care for nature and that it's important to look after the environment."

Concerning the board agenda, espousing the values of *openness*[3] and *justice*[4] translates into the need for greater dialogue, sessions of sitting and actively listening, and knowing that the "top" needs to hear from the "middle" and "bottom". A clear distinction between means and ends and a focus on the latter is important to this value group. Next, the results of the *Outer Directed* value system and its relationship to integrity will be examined.

The next most prevalent value system likely to be found in boards is the *Outer Directed* segment. As new business models and concepts for "survival" and success have appeared, this value system has been highly prized by boards. Results from the research are shown in Fig. 15.5 and include the values of *material wealth, visible ability,* and *visible success*. This includes the rejection of many of the values espoused by the *Inner Directed*.

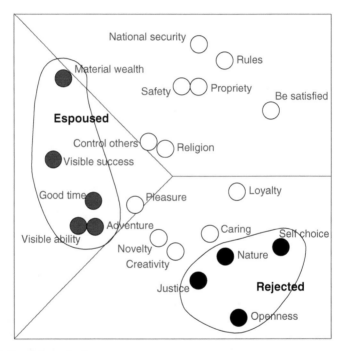

Fig. 15.5 Outer directed values map
Source: Own research

Integrity from this value system is defined as "doing things better", which means whatever it takes to "win" (the ends). Espousing the values of *visible ability*[5] and *visible success,*[6] *visibly* winning is everything. Acting with integrity means increasing "shareholder value" where "value" means "money". If that means taking risks, treading on a few toes, silencing opposition, or polluting a bit of land, air, or water for a generation or two, that's OK in this value system. The ends (winning) justify the means. Finally, results from the *Sustenance Driven* value system and its impact on integrity will be examined.

Boards have given great weight to those who were *Sustenance Driven*: a "safe pair of hands" who "stuck to the knitting". Results from the research are shown in Fig. 15.6 and include the values of *rules*, *propriety*, and *safety*. This includes the rejection of the *Outer* and *Inner Directed* values of *adventure*, *creativity*, and *visible success*.

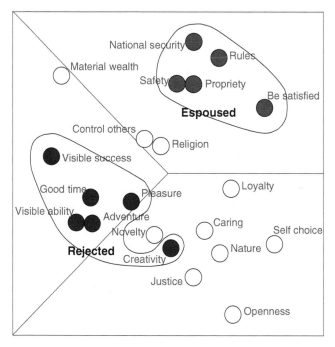

Fig. 15.6 Sustenance driven values map
Source: Own research

Integrity from this values system is defined as doing the "right" thing, which is laid down in the rules, procedures, and expectations of the company and (legal) society.

---

[5] "I need to show my abilities. I want others to admire what I do."

[6] "It's important for me to be very successful and I like to impress others."

Espousing the values of *rules*[7] and *propriety*[8] fiduciary duty will govern all other considerations in the boardroom except for survival, hence their natural inclination to hold the purse strings tight. Valuing *safety*[9] means that "winning" is synonymous with not falling victim to the host of threats "out there". Taking risks in the interests of success is very much a last resort.

Implication for the board agenda is that there will be a preference for keep things "normal and easy to understand" and the complexities of business at bay. Regarding feedback loops, due to belief in hierarchy and the "top down" nature of things, feedback with "subordinates" is pointless: those not on the board cannot know the big picture and, as a result, cannot help the board to make decisions. Having presented the findings of the *Sustenance Driven*, *Outer* and *Inner Directed* value systems and interpreted how they relate to integrity with some implications for the board agenda, the next section will summarise the three value systems of European managers.

A Summary of the Three Value Systems of European Managers

In this section, two values studies are summarised, the first regarding strategic leadership and the next managers. Only the value systems elements of each study will be summarised.

Strategic Leadership Study

As part of strategic leadership research, Lichtenstein (2005) tested the proposition whether executives' values are related to Maslovian needs in the first operationalisation of Maslovian categorisation in a management context.

In a study of 163 owner, senior and middle managers, executives' personal values were measured, and separately executives were categorised in *Sustenance Driven*, *Outer* and *Inner Directed* value groups. The sampling frame of executives was in-work owner/managers (18%), senior managers (48%), and middle managers (34%) from the international business community. In total, 163 responses were received. Respondents were from a broad range of companies and industries from the UK (53%), the rest of Europe (32%), and other countries (15%).

To assess convergent validity, two instruments were used for the categorisation of respondents. Firstly, respondents were categorised into the value groups of *Inner Directed*, *Outer Directed*, or *Sustenance Driven* groups based on Maslow's (1970)

---

[7] "I believe people should do what they are told. I follow rules at all times, even when no-one is watching."

[8] "It's important that I always behave properly and avoid doing anything that others would say is wrong."

[9] "I think it's important to live in secure surroundings. I avoid anything that might endanger my safety."

theory using the Values Modes (VMs) instrument developed by CDSM. The results (Table 15.4) show a small percentage of managers were categorised as *Sustenance Driven*, which supports published reports (cf., e.g., Wilkinson and Howard 1997) on the decline of the working age population in western society who espouse traditional values.

Table 15.4 Values modes

	Frequency	Percent
Sustenance driven	2	1.2
Outer directed	63	38.7
Inner directed	98	60.1
Total	163	100.0

Source: Lichtenstein (2005)

Secondly, Kotey and Meredith's (1997) List of Values (LoV) that shows 28 items on a personal values scale (Cronbach $\alpha = 0.87$) was also used to categorise variables into value groups by subjecting it to principal components analysis. Relying on Maslow's (1970) theory of *Inner Directed, Outer Directed* and *Sustenance Driven* value groups, the a priori criterion (cf. Sharma 1996) was used to derive a three-factor extraction. The rotated solution revealed all three factors showing strong loadings with theoretically predicted results:

1. The *Sustenance Driven* value system espoused the traditional values of *loyalty, trust, compassion*, and *affection* (Cronbach $\alpha = 0.79$),
2. the *Outer Directed* value system espoused the core esteem-seeking values of *power, prestige, ambition*, and *aggression* (Cronbach $\alpha = 0.64$), and
3. the *Inner Directed* value system espoused the entrepreneurial values of *innovation, risk*, and *creativity* (Cronbach $\alpha = 0.72$).

Table 15.5 includes the key values for the Maslovian motivational groups of *Inner* and *Outer Directed* and *Sustenance Driven*.

In a study by Higgs and Lichtenstein (2007) to explore the relationship between personality traits and values, they collected data from 73 in-work MBA students with at least five years' working experience in organisations. Respondents' values were categorised into the value systems of *Sustenance Driven* (*loyalty, trust, compassion*), *Outer Directed* (*power, prestige, ambition*), and *Inner Directed* (*innovation, risk*, and *creativity*) using Kotey and Meredith's (1997) LoV (Cronbach $\alpha = 0.81$ for the current research).

As in previous studies, there were no *Sustenance Driven* managers. Moreover, the proportion of *Outer Directed* (38%) to *Inner Directed* (62%) value systems is approximately the same as in previous studies of executive values (cf. Lichtenstein 2005) indicating a consistent pattern of value groups within the in-work managerial population.

The next section will draw some implications in terms of what we expect to find in board-level research into values.

Table 15.5 Specified
three-factor solution of key
list of values

	Factors		
	1 = Sustenance driven	2 = Outer directed	3 = Inner directed
Trust	0.755		
Compassion	0.723		
Affection	0.669		
Loyalty	0.667		
Nat'l security	0.648		
Prestige		0.637	
Ambition		0.624	
Power		0.614	
Aggressiveness		0.605	
Money		0.537	
Innovation			0.791
Risk			0.691
Creativity			0.685
Competition			0.495
Autonomy			0.460

Source: Lichtenstein (2005)

Implications for Board Research

Based on the previous research and our consulting experience, we would expect
to find (i) very few if any directors with traditional values and (ii) a substantial
proportion of ethically-oriented *Inner Directed* directors. Regarding the paucity of
Sustenance Driven directors, the general shift of boards away from those with this
value system indicates that it is unlikely they exist at board level. Previous samples
of managers (cf. Lichtenstein 2005) have found that out of 267 executives only two
had *Sustenance Driven* needs and values. The *Sustenance Driven* world is context
that business is moving away from, however, due to institutional lag and the need
for survival, the residue of the *Sustenance Driven* value system is still prevalent.

Regarding the prevalence of *Inner Directed* directors, we predict a much higher
proportion of the approximately 2/3–1/3 ratio of *Inner* to *Outer Directed* value
systems pattern revealed in the European management values research. For example, we measured the values of participants (n = 16) attending our track at the
7th Corporate Governance and Board Leadership Conference and all were *Inner
Directed*. We have found in our consulting experience that the higher up in organisations one goes the higher proportion of *Inner Directed* people there are as they
have satisfied their *Sustenance Driven* and *Outer Directed* needs.

This research supports the need for values research to be at the systems level vs.
the individual item level and cries out for testing that must now be taken into the
boardroom if the dynamics of integrity is to be understood and board engagement
to be achieved.

The Case for Researching Values, Integrity, and the Board Agenda

Although this research is exploratory in nature, the results support the proposition that the meaning of integrity varies with one's dominant values. The analysis and interpretation indicate that those with different values will have different interpretations of integrity. This research now needs to be applied to boards and their value systems to truly understand the integrity dynamic in the boardroom in relationship to the board agenda.

It is equally evident that further research must also analyse board agendas to discover whether the board agenda, the "talk", resonates with directors values and is coupled with action to create board engagement. If agendas do not reflect the values of the board, this results in disengagement, dispassionate boards, sub-optimal decisions, and a waste of the board's precious time.

Boards can use values research to re-focus the board agenda on issues that resonant with the values of directors. For example, if further research into director's values confirm that members' operative values are predominantly *Inner Directed*, more time must be devoted to the ethical issues of "doing better things" and less with the *Outer Directed* issues of "doing things better" or compliance issues ("doing the right thing") that resonates with the *Sustenance Driven*. Excessive talk of "shareholder value" – how to make money – which drives the *Outer Directed* is every bit a passion-killer for *Inner Directed* directors if it is not balanced with a discussion of how it is going used for "good works". Taylor's (2003) categorisation of different board styles as shown in Fig. 15.7 reflects a values driven agenda perspective.

Fig. 15.7 Taylor's (2003) Corporate governance systems
Source: Taylor (2003)

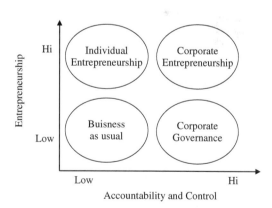

Taylor (2003) argues that most companies operate either "business as usual" or are so obsessed with compliance to Sarbanes Oxley that the board agenda is all about corporate governance control. Whilst this would engage *Sustenance Driven* directors, it disengages *Inner Directed* directors. Individual entrepreneurship is risky, especially if the entrepreneur may not be around forever. Corporate Entrepreneurship is the most engaging role for an *Inner Directed* board to play.

In this system, board leadership is about corporate renewal: inventing tomorrow's company today. Ensuring all board members understand its role and that the board agenda reflects this would help explore underlying assumptions of what directors perceive to be its role and ensure positive emotional engagement. Therefore, board agendas can be rekindled and refocused to ensure positive emotional engagement by taking a values-based approach to scrutinising the values of its directors towards creating passionate boards. A passionate board requires integrity plus action; integrity without action equals indifference.

Research into the values of boards' directors could also be used to gain insight into their board culture, i.e., the dynamic between the personal values of the Chief Executive and those of the other directors. What makes perfect sense to a CEO from his/her values or appear to have "behavioural consistency" from the lens of "shareholder value" will create dis-ease and disengagement amongst directors with different values and vice-versa. Therefore, knowing the values of the board not only facilitates board development in a general sense but also where director's sense of integrity comes together and pulls apart with other directors.

Finally, boards, regardless of directors' personal values, could use values as a tool to discuss issues from different value groups' perspectives that would unearth the key drivers and feelings that underpin board issues. Imagine a board discussing an issue (e.g., whether to take over another company, set up operations in another country, etc.) and discussing it from a particular value groups' perspective, e.g., an *Outer Directed* perspective, by getting into that mental state of mind and, by so doing, thinking and feeling how they perceive it and their likely reactions (and so forth with the *Inner Directed* and *Sustenance Driven* mind sets). This would allow the board to get to the crux of an issue rather than gather opinions from debate and never getting to what's driving those opinions. Moreover, it would allow the board to appreciate issues from different perspectives that are not necessarily represented on the board (e.g., *Sustenance Driven*) and simultaneously getting the perspective of the organisations' different stakeholders' values. It has the added benefit of depersonalising issues as well as challenging and sharpening the director's perspective in a non-threatening and enlightening way.

Limitations, Further Research, and Conclusions

This current study is exploratory and constrained by a number of limitations. The most obvious limitation is the sample, the general population as well as owner, senior, and middle managers, which is the drive for board research in this area. However, the research thus far does have the benefit of providing a culturally and managerially anchored reference point. Although integrity has the greatest impact on board performance, other factors have not been investigated, e.g., competence (cf. Kouzes and Posner 2002).

This research indicates possible future directions. Qualitative research into the personal values of directors and perceptions of integrity could be a useful component to future research. We also suggest further research into the notion of "back up style" (cf. McAlister and Darling 2005) in stressful situations. Board disengagement may be causing sub-optimal decision making, which could make for an interesting area of inquiry. For example, in the case of an *Inner Directed* director not being engaged, e.g., by a conversation about compliance which would be several levels below his/her level of engagement, may lead to him/her falling back to the previous needs level, i.e., *Outer Directed*, resulting in decision making driven by the need for self-esteem. This would cause a sense that his/her own integrity had been compromised. Compound this by a majority of people in the room going through this in their own terms and everyone begins to feel bad about what's happening and, worse, the possibility of sub-optimal decision making. We believe this is a board dynamic worth exploring.

It is clear that research into the personal values of directors is a fruitful area to explore. The tools now exist and the potential applications and benefits are enormous. The question now is, will boards take up the challenge? Will they allow access to do the research? And will funds be made available to make it happen?

References

Aitken, P. 2007. 'Walking the Talk': The nature and role of leadership culture within organisation culture/s. *Journal of General Management* 32: 17–37.

Allport, G.W. 1955. *Becoming: Basic considerations for a psychology of personality*. New Haven, CT: Yale University Press.

Allport, G.W. 1961. *Pattern and growth in personality*. New York: Holt, Rinehart & Winston.

Badaracco, J., and R. Ellsworth. 1992. Leadership, integrity, and conflict. *Management Decision* 30: 29–34.

Baker, S. 1996. Placing values research in a theoretical context. In *Theory building in the business sciences*, ed. T. Elfring, H. Siggaard Jensen, and A. Money, 49–60. Copenhagen: Handelshoyskolens Forlag.

Burgoyne, J., T. Boydell, and M. Pedler. 2005. *Leadership development: Current practice, future perspectives*. Corporate Research Forum, August 2005.

Fields, D.L. 2007. Determinants of follower perceptions of a leader's authenticity and integrity. *European Management Journal* 25: 195–206.

Gay, K., and V. Dulewicz. 1997. An investigation into the personal competences required by board directors of international companies, Working Paper Series, HWP 9701, School of Management, Henley Business School.

Gostick, A., and D. Telford. 2003. *The integrity advantage*. Layton, UT: Gibbs Smith.

Hambrick, D.C., and G.L. Brandon. 1988. Executive values. In *The executive effect: Concepts and methods for studying top managers*, ed. D.C. Hambrick, 3–34. Greenwich, CT: JAI Press. (= Strategic Management Policy and Planning Series, Vol. 2).

Hambrick, D.C., and P.A. Mason. 1984. Upper echelons: The organisation as a reflection of its top managers. *Academy of Management Review* 9: 193–206.

Higgs, M., and S. Lichtenstein. 2007. Lifting the lid on leadership orientation: Is there a relationship between their personality and values?, Conference Paper, Irish Academy of Management Conference, Belfast.

Kotey, B., and G.G. Meredith. 1997. Relationships among owner/manager personal values, business strategies, and enterprise performance. *Journal of Small Business Management* 35: 37–64.

Kouzes, J.M., and B.Z. Posner. 2002. *Leadership challenge*, 3rd ed. San Francisco, CA: Jossey-Bass.

Lichtenstein, S. 2005. Strategy co-alignment: Strategic, executive values and organisational goal orientation and their impact on performance. DBA Thesis, Brunel University, Uxbridge, London, UK.

Lindeman, M., and M. Verkasalo. 2005. Measuring values with the short Schwartz's value survey. *Journal of Personality Assessment* 85: 170–178.

MacGregor Burns, J. 1978. *Leadership*. New York: Haper and Row.

Maslow, A.H. 1970. *Motivation and personality*, 2nd ed. New York: Harper and Row.

McAlister, D.T., and J.R. Darling. 2005. Upward influence in academic organizations: A behavioral style perspective. *Leadership & Organisation Development Journal* 26: 558–573.

Nunnally, J.C. 1978. *Psychometric theory*, 2nd ed. New York: McGraw-Hill.

Palanski, M.E., and F.J. Yammarino. 2007. Integrity and leadership: Clearing the conceptual confusion. *European Management Journal* 25: 171–184.

Rokeach, M. 1979. From individual to institutional values: With special reference to the values of science. In *Understanding human values: Individual and societal*, ed. M. Rokeach, 47–70. New York: Free Press.

Schwartz, S.H. 1992. Universals in the content and structure of values: Theoretical advances and empirical tests in 20 countries. In *Advances in experimental social psychology*, ed. M.P. Zanna, vol. 25, 1–65. San Diego, CA: Academic.

Schwartz, S.H. 1996. Value priorities and behavior: Applying a theory of integrated value systems. In *The psychology of values: The Ontario symposium*, ed. C. Seligman, J.M. Olson and M.P. Zanna, vol. 8, 1–24. Mahwah, NJ: Lawrence Erlbaum.

Schwartz, S.H., G. Melech, A. Lehmann, S. Burgess, M. Harris, and V. Owens. 2001. Extending the cross-cultural validity of the theory of basic human values with a different method of measurement. *Journal of Cross-Cultural Psychology* 32: 519–542.

Sharma, S. 1996. *Applied multivariate techniques*. New York: Wiley.

Simons, T. 2002. Behavioral integrity: The perceived alignment between managers' words and deeds as a research focus. *Organization Science* 13: 18–35.

Six, F.E., F.G.A. de Bakker, and L.W.J.C. Huberts. 2007. Judging a corporate leader's integrity: An illustrated three-component model. *European Management Journal* 25: 185–194.

Srivastva, S. 1988. Introduction: The urgency for executive integrity. In *Executive integrity: The search for high human values in organizational life*, ed. S. Srivastva, 1–28. San Francisco, CA: Jossey-Bass.

Taylor, B. 2003. Board leadership: Balancing entrepreneurship and strategy with accountability and control. *Corporate Governance* 3: 3–5.

Waldrop, M.M. 1996. Dee hock on organizations. *Fast Company* 5: 84.

Wilkinson, H., and M. Howard. 1997. *Tomorrow's women*. London: Demos.

Yukl, G.A. 1998. *Leadership in organizations*, 4th ed. Upper Saddle River, NJ: Prentice Hall.

Chapter 16
The Ethics of Corporate Governance in Global Perspective

G.J. (Deon) Rossouw

Contents

Introduction

The wave of corporate governance reform around the world over the last two decades is often regarded as an attempt to restore trust in business after major corporate scandals had eroded public trust in business.[1] The Cadbury Report, for example, followed in the wake of the Maxwell scandal in the UK, and Sarbanes-Oxley in the USA followed the collapse of Enron (cf. Becht et al. 2002, p. 7). What distinguished these collapses from other corporate collapses and turned them into

---

[1] An earlier version of the chapter has been published in the conference proceedings of the Business Ethics and Corporate Social Responsibility Conference held in Belgaum, India in December 2009 (Kalkundrikar et al. 2010).

G.J. (Deon) Rossouw (✉)
Extraordinary Professor in Philosophy, University of Pretoria, Pretoria, South Africa;
CEO, Ethics Institute of South Africa, Pretoria, South Africa
e-mail: deon.rossouw@ethicsa.org

A. Brink (ed.), *Corporate Governance and Business Ethics*, Ethical Economy. Studies in Economic Ethics and Philosophy 39, DOI 10.1007/978-94-007-1588-2_16, © Springer Science+Business Media B.V. 2011

corporate scandals were the wide-spread and systemic unethical practices in these companies that ultimately resulted in their demise. The corporate governance reform that followed these scandals is perceived as an attempt to ensure that corporations conduct their affairs with integrity and in a fair, transparent, and responsible manner. There is, thus, a link between unethical corporate conduct and corporate scandals, but also a link between corporate governance reform and the hope of reforming corporations to be more ethical and trustworthy. Despite this clear link between corporate governance and ethics, the ethics of corporate governance remains a neglected area in corporate governance research in general, but also specifically in global comparative corporate governance research. This neglect of the ethical dimension in corporate governance research was once more illustrated when ethics and corporate governance was not included as one of the 21 subject matter areas in the Corporate Governance Network that was launched in 2009.

Part of the explanation for this neglect of ethics in corporate governance research can be found in the assumption that corporate governance is a matter of corporate law rather than a matter of corporate ethics. Especially in the US context that still dominates the global corporate governance discourse, corporate governance is regarded as a matter of regulating corporations in order to ensure that managers and directors fulfil their fiduciary duties towards owners of companies. A good case in point is Hansmann and Kraakman's (2001) article that was provocatively titled, "The End of History of Corporate Law", in which they argue that there is global convergence towards a "shareholder-centered ideology of corporate law" (p. 439).

Corporate governance is, however, about more than laws and regulations to control corporations. Although it is not to be denied that corporate governance also deals with the control over how corporations exercise their power, corporate governance encompasses more than legal and regulatory control over business. Control over business is exercised on a variety of levels and by agents other than lawmakers and regulators. This broader notion of corporate governance is well captured in Wieland's (2005) definition of corporate governance as "leadership, management and control of a firm by formal and informal, public and private rules" (p. 76).

The distinction between external and enterprise level corporate governance helps to bring the variety of forms of corporate control in sharper focus (cf. Rossouw et al. 2002). External corporate governance refers to the control over corporations where the locus of control is external to the corporation. Such control can be in the form of control exercised by the state, regulatory bodies, and stock exchanges (cf. Coffee 1998, p. 69; Romano 1998, p. 144). External control, however, can also be exercised in a less formal way through cultural or social norms and expectations that corporations have to heed. A third way of external control over corporations is through the market itself, where mergers and acquisition serve as a mechanism for ensuring that corporations perform according to market expectations (cf. Gedajlovic and Shapiro 1998, pp. 535f.).

Enterprise level corporate governance, in contrast, refers to control of corporations from within corporations. On the enterprise level, the board of directors forms the focal point of control of corporate power. The board takes the responsibility for directing and controlling corporate affairs. In this regard, they carry the responsibility for directing the performance of the company, but also for controlling the company to operate in accordance with legal, regulatory, socio-cultural, and market standards or expectations, as well as in accordance with expectations of stakeholders such as shareholders, managers, employees, and customers.

When corporate governance is understood as more then mere control via corporate law over corporations, it creates the space for the ethical dimension of corporate governance to emerge in corporate governance discourse. In what follows, I will start by introducing the ethical dimension of corporate governance and also by making a number of conceptual and theoretical distinctions that are crucial for making sense of the ethical dimension of corporate governance. These conceptual and theoretical distinctions will then be used to analyse the ethics of corporate governance in five world regions as portrayed in two recent global studies that focused on the ethical dimension of corporate governance. Finally, a discussion of the main factors that can explain differences in the ethics of corporate governance within and across the above-mentioned regions will follow.

Ethics and Corporate Governance

Since corporate governance revolves around the power and control exercised over, but also by corporations, it inevitably entails an ethical dimension. Corporations can be governed, both externally and internally, in ways that impinge on the interests of those who are affected by the corporation in either a beneficial or detrimental manner. Consequently, the governance of corporations can be assessed in ethical evaluative categories such as fair or unfair, responsible or irresponsible, and ethical or unethical. The fact that ethics is not always being dealt with in an explicit manner in corporate law or in corporate governance codes does not in any way diminish the fact that there always is an ethical dimension to corporate governance.

The ethical dimension of corporate governance can be manifested on two levels. The first and primary level that is either implicit or explicit in all corporate governance regimes is the basic ethical orientation of corporate governance regimes. This ethical orientation of corporate governance regimes or codes is called the *ethics of corporate governance* (cf. Rossouw 2005a, p. 37). The other level on which ethics manifests in corporate governance regimes deals with how corporations are required or recommended to manage their own ethical affairs. This dimension will be referred to as the *governance of corporate ethics* (cf. ibid., p. 37). These two manifestations of ethics in corporate governance will be discussed next.

Ethics of Corporate Governance

The ethics of corporate governance refers to the ethical values that underpin and guide a corporate governance regime on the regulatory or the enterprise level. If a value system is understood as a set of convictions about what is important – and thus what should be given priority – then the ethics of governance is an expression of specifically the ethical priorities that inform and guide a corporate governance system. These values that inform and guide a corporate governance system might be articulated openly and explicitly, or they might be invisible and not mentioned at all. Whether the underlying and guiding values are mentioned explicitly or not does not alter in any way the fact that such a value system exists. In the absence of a clear guiding value set, a corporate governance system will be riddled with internal contradictions and confusing clashes.

In cases where the underlying and guiding values of a corporate governance system are not explicitly articulated, it can be uncovered by probing into the interests and objectives that corporate governance is supposed to serve. The regulations or requirements associated with corporate governance convey a perception of what roles, responsibilities, objectives, and obligations corporations have in a given society. By posing questions like, "In whose interests ought corporations to be run?" or "What are the objectives of a corporate governance system?" the underpinning and guiding values of a corporate governance system can be exposed.

Identifying the ethics of a specific corporate governance regime thus boils down to making explicit the ethical responsibilities and obligations of corporations in society as well as the ethical values associated with these responsibilities and obligations. Even in cases where the value system is explicitly articulated, it makes sense to probe whether the professed value system indeed finds expression in the regulations or requirements of the corporate governance system. It is not uncommon to find contradictions between the professed value system and the value system that is lurking implicitly in the regulations or recommendations of a corporate governance system.

Once the value system of a corporate governance regime has been made explicit, the ethical implications of the identified value system can be evaluated. The objectives and interests that are being prioritized by the corporate governance value system can be assessed for how fair, responsible, or socially benevolent they are. It can also be determined how inclusive or exclusive the interests are that are being served by the corporate governance system. Does the corporate governance system, for example, serve the interests of all stakeholders of corporations or only the interests of specific corporate stakeholders? Are all stakeholders being treated equally or are the interests of some stakeholders merely instrumental to the interests of other stakeholders? What objectives are corporations expected to pursue, and how are the various objectives prioritized? What objective(s) trump(s) the others in the case of a trade-off, or are all objectives that corporations are expected to pursue on equal footing? Responses to these kinds of questions provide the ethics of governance profile of a corporate governance system.

Governance of Corporate Ethics

Corporate governance systems impose upon corporations an obligation or expectation to direct and control various aspects of corporate performance like, for example, accounting practices, risk management, and corporate reporting. At least in some corporate governance regimes, there are also requirements or expectations related to the ethical performance of corporations. Such requirements or expectations can originate from both the external and enterprise level of corporate governance.

On the external corporate governance level, there can, for example, be corporate laws that compel companies to have a code of ethics or to manage and report on their corporate social performance. There might also be less formal expectations of companies issuing from the external level of corporate governance in the form of, for example, communities expecting companies to consult with them on new developments or to contribute towards community development.

On the enterprise level, the governance of corporate ethics focuses on how ethical values and standards are institutionalised in companies. It deals with the systems of direction and control that are implemented within a company to ensure that the company identifies and adheres to ethical values, standards, or rules in its interactions with internal and external stakeholders of the company. The governance of ethics on the enterprise level is likely to manifest in an ethics management or corporate responsibility strategy and programme. Corporations might govern their ethics for a variety of reasons: they might, for example, be compelled by law to do so; they might do it to conform to the expectations of a voluntary code of corporate governance; they might want to pre-empt prosecution by being able to demonstrate that they have taken measures to ensure that the corporation is run with integrity and responsibility; they might do it because it is considered to be strategically in the best interest of the company; or they might do it because they are convinced that the company has an intrinsic obligation to ensure high standards of corporate ethics.

Shareholder and Stakeholder Models of Corporate Governance

Corporate governance models can be distinguished in terms of whose interests they prioritize in the exercise of corporate control. In this respect two positions can be discerned, viz., shareholder models and stakeholder models of corporate governance.

Shareholder models of corporate governance are premised upon the assumption that corporations should be governed in the best interests of shareholders. According to this model, shareholders are the rightful owners of corporations and consequently corporations should be run to the benefit of their owners. Managers are regarded as agents of owners and are therefore expected to look after the best interests of their principals (shareholders). From this agency perspective, the central focus of corporate governance is on ensuring that corporate managers do not abuse the power entrusted to them for furthering their own or other non-shareholder interests. Instead, the corporate governance system should ensure that the interests of managers are closely aligned with shareholders' interests. In some jurisdictions boards of directors and managers have a fiduciary duty to act in the best interest of shareholders (cf. Monks and Minow 2004, p. 111). This exclusive orientation of corporate governance towards shareholder interests is evident in Shleifer and Vishny's (1997) definition of corporate governance when they describe it as "the ways in which suppliers of finance to corporations assure themselves of getting a return on their investment" (p. 737).

The shareholder model of corporate governance is clearly reflected in Berle's (1931) classic articulation of this position when he argued that,

> [a]ll powers granted to a corporation or to the management of a corporation, or to any group within the corporation, whether derived from statute or charter or both, are necessarily and at all times exercisable only for the ratable benefit of all the shareholders as their interest appears. (p. 1049)

Equally famous is Milton Friedman's defence of the shareholder model of corporate governance in his 1970 article with the title, "The Social Responsibility of Business Is to Increase Its Profits".

From an ethical perspective, the shareholder model of corporate governance can be assessed in two very different ways. The one ethical assessment is to regard the shareholder model of corporate governance as an ethically constrained model in the sense that it only focuses on the interests of shareholders, while deliberately excluding the interests of other stakeholder groups. This kind of ethical assessment is clearly reflected in Collier and Roberts's (2001) remark with regard to shareholder models of corporate governance when they state that, "the only ethical imperative at work here is a Friedmanesque dictum to pursue profit maximization" (p. 68).

An alternative ethical assessment of the ethics of shareholder models of corporate governance argues that the prioritization of shareholder interests is in the best interest not only of shareholders, but also of other stakeholders. It is argued that focusing on the creation of shareholder value provides a rationale for running corporations in a focussed and efficient manner that benefits all other stakeholders indirectly. Without such a singular focus, managers will be trapped in a wasteland of conflicting stakeholder claims that will ultimately lower corporate efficiency to the detriment of not only shareholders, but also of all other stakeholders of the corporation (cf. Goodpaster 1993). Only corporations, it is argued, that can sustain efficiency over time can keep on creating value for its shareholders and other stakeholders, albeit that at least some stakeholders benefit indirectly from the promotion of the interests of the shareholders.

Stakeholder models of corporate governance are premised upon the assumption that corporate control needs to be exercised in the interest of all legitimate stakeholders. Within stakeholder models companies are not regarded as mere vehicles for creating shareholder value, but as economic institutions that rely on the cooperation and contribution of various stakeholders whose interests should be recognized. The corporation is thus seen a nexus of interconnecting interests that needs to be recognized and reconciled with one another.

In order to make a proper assessment of the ethics of stakeholder models of corporate governance, the distinction drawn by Donaldson and Preston (1995) between descriptive, instrumental, and normative approaches to stakeholder conceptions of corporations need to be kept in mind. According to this distinction, a stakeholder approach does not necessarily constitute an ethical (or normative) commitment to serve the interest of stakeholders. From a descriptive perspective, a stakeholder approach can be a mere description and recognition of the fact that corporations by their very nature require the contribution and collaboration of various stakeholder groups in order to attain their corporate objectives. Exercising corporate control in a manner that will ensure optimum contributions from and collaboration with stakeholders thus does not emanate from ethical considerations, but from the recognition that it is in the best interest of the corporation to consider the interest of stakeholders. An instrumental (or strategic) stakeholder approach implies that stakeholder interests are being respected in pursuit of some corporate objective, for example, the pursuit of shareholder value. Stakeholder interests, consequently, would be given priority only in so far as it contributes to the achievement of corporate objectives. In shareholder approaches to corporate governance, the interests of stakeholders are likely to be treated in such an instrumental manner. A normative (or intrinsic) stakeholder approach is premised on a relationship of ethical obligation between a corporation and its stakeholders. It is based on the assumption that, irrespective of whether it is a factual necessity or a strategic imperative to recognize or respect stakeholder interests, corporations have a moral duty to ensure that interests of stakeholders are considered in the exercise of corporate control.

Ethics and Corporate Governance in Global Perspective

Comparative corporate governance studies have succeeded in identifying a variety of factors that differentiate corporate governance regimes around the world from one another. These factors include initial ownership structures, national or regional corporate laws and rules, cultural values and political ideologies (cf. Bebchuk and Roe 1999, pp. 137, 168, 169). Comparative studies on the ethics of corporate governance regimes on a global scale are, however, much more rare. Two recent studies, however, did focus on the ethics of corporate governance in global perspective. The first study was published in *Business & Society* in 2005 (vol. 44, issues 1 & 2), and a revised version thereof was published under the title "Global Perspectives on Ethics of Corporate Governance" in 2006 (cf. Rossouw and Sison 2006). In this study, a survey was done of the ethical dimension of corporate governance regimes in six world regions. For the purpose of the said study, the world was divided into six regions, viz., Africa, Europe, Japan, Latin America, North America, and the Asia-Pacific region. While the survey was global in its regional coverage, it did not include all countries in each of the six regions. It rather focused on either the most prominent corporate governance developments in each of the regions or on corporate governance regimes that were considered to be typical of a specific region. In total, 45 countries were included in the six regions that were studied.

The second study was published in 2009 in the *International Journal of Law and Management* (vol. 51, issue 1). This study focused on the question whether there is a global convergence or divergence with regard to the ethics of corporate governance. For the purpose of that study, perspectives on the ethics of corporate governance were elicited from four regions of the world, viz., Asia, Continental Europe, North America, and Sub-Saharan Africa (cf. Rossouw 2009a). Once more, not all countries in these four regions were covered in the regional perspectives, but rather the countries that were considered to be typical of the approach to corporate governance in each of the regions.

The perspectives that emerged from the two above mentioned studies will be drawn upon to present a view on the ethics of corporate governance in global perspective. For the purpose of providing such a global perspective, the following regional divisions will be used: Africa, Asia-Pacific, Europe, Latin America, and North America. A brief overview of characteristic features of the ethics of corporate governance in each of these regions follows.

Africa

Based on an analysis of national corporate governance codes issued by ten countries in Sub-Saharan Africa (Ghana, Kenya, Malawi, Mauritius, Nigeria, South Africa, Tanzania, Uganda, Zimbabwe, and Zambia), Rossouw (2005b) concluded that a strong stakeholder orientation prevails in the region. The only country with a corporate governance code that deviated from this stakeholder orientation is Nigeria, which adheres to an explicit shareholder orientation.

The preferred option for a stakeholder orientation in these corporate governance regimes in Sub-Saharan Africa is informed by a number of considerations. These considerations include the influence on the corporate governance dispensation exerted by cultural values that are widely associated with African societies. These African values prioritize human dignity, mutuality, and belonging, captured in terms like "ubuntu". Another consideration that informs the choice for a stakeholder orientation is the prominent role that governments play in the economies in many of these countries through state-owned enterprises. The mere presence of governments as significant participants in the economy implies that political and social objectives are brought into play in the economy, besides mere financial objectives. Furthermore, private corporations are affected by the developmental agenda that is typical of Sub-Saharan economies. Given a range of social infrastructure deficits that characterise this part of the world, private companies often have to look beyond shareholder interests and involve themselves with social and economic development in order to enhance their own sustainability. At least in some countries, like Tanzania, the legacy of post-colonial African socialism also seems to add to the notion that companies have a broader responsibility than creating shareholder value.

Whether this stakeholder orientation that prevails in Sub-Saharan Africa is normative or instrumental is not easy to gauge. There are good grounds for suspecting that the stakeholder orientation is fuelled by both normative and instrumental considerations. The emphasis on African values, the legacy of African socialism, and the participation of governments in the economy all point in the direction of a more normative stakeholder orientation. However, looking after stakeholder interests in an attempt to enhance corporate sustainability brings a distinct instrumental dimension into play. West (2009, p. 14) cautions that beneath the apparent stakeholder orientation of corporate governance regimes in Sub-Saharan Africa there might lurk a deeper underlying shareholder orientation.

The analysis of the above mentioned corporate governance codes in Africa also revealed a rather strong emphasis on the governance of corporate ethics. Various recommendations were found on how companies should manage their corporate ethics. There are at least two explanations for this explicit emphasis on the governance of corporate ethics in Sub-Saharan Africa. The first is that the Sub-Saharan region is characterised by either poorly developed or poorly enforced external corporate governance regimes, which places greater responsibility on corporations to look after their own affairs in the absence of effective external control. The second explanation is to be found in the reality that corporate governance reform in Sub-Saharan Africa is often partly driven by an attempt to curb corruption in the region. Corporations are thus encouraged to improve their ethical performance in an attempt to curb corruption in the region.

Asia-Pacific

From an ethics of corporate governance perspective, the Asia-Pacific region displays considerable variety in the ethical orientation of corporate governance regimes in the region. In the two recent studies that focused on the ethical dimension of corporate governance in the Asia-Pacific region (cf. Kimber and Lipton 2005; Demise 2005; Reddy 2009), five countries in the region were considered to be typical of the variety of corporate governance regimes in the region. The five countries are Australia, China, India, Japan, and Singapore. In terms of their ethical orientation, these countries can be clustered in two groups, namely Australia and Singapore that display a strong shareholder orientation and China, India, and Japan that lean in the direction of a more inclusive stakeholder orientation.

Kimber and Lipton (2005) described the corporate governance regimes of Australia and Singapore as "contractarian" (p. 182), thereby indicating that the corporation is regarded as a nexus of contracts negotiated by self-interested shareholders for the sake of maximising shareholder interests. Although the two countries differ with regard to patterns of corporate ownership, they are rather similar in terms of their primary orientation towards promoting the interests of shareholders. The protection that non-shareholding stakeholders do enjoy emanates from laws that focus on specific stakeholder interests and from stakeholder activism, rather than from the corporate governance regimes of these countries.

China, India, and Japan, by contrast, display a more inclusive stakeholder orientation in their corporate governance regimes. Kimber and Lipton (2005) described the ethical orientation in this region as "communitarian" (p. 183), while Reddy (2009) called it "expansive" (p. 21), thereby indicting that the corporate governance regimes accommodate both shareholder and stakeholder interests. The reasons for this more inclusive accommodation of stakeholder interests, however, vary considerably among the three countries.

In China, it can be ascribed to the prominent role and participation of the state in the economy, which inevitably results in social and political priorities being imposed on the corporate governance regime. In India, the state is also a significant economic player through state-owned enterprises, which also brings social and political issues into play in the realm of corporate governance. In addition, India's tradition of social activism as well as strong cultural values and social norms shapes the corporate governance regime to accommodate the interests of various stakeholder groups, including shareholders, managers, employees, and local communities. In Japan, the corporate governance regime favours the interests of providers of financial and human capital, thus resulting in a dispensation geared towards the interests of banks and institutional investors and towards the interests of employees. There is also evidence of a growing emphasis on corporate social responsibility and of stakeholder engagement and communication in Japan. Across these three countries, the notion prevails that a company director is a virtuous leader and a steward of interests that transcends those of shareholders. Judging from the reasons that inform this broader stakeholder ethic of corporate governance, it is fair to conclude that this ethical orientation is informed by normative considerations and not merely by the instrumental pursuit of shareholder value.

Europe

The majority of corporate governance regimes in Europe lean in the direction of a stakeholder orientation to corporate governance. In his study of corporate governance codes and laws in 22 European countries, Wieland (2005) classified seven countries (Switzerland, Czech Republic, Portugal, Sweden, Finland, Great Britain, and Ireland) as having an overriding emphasis on shareholder interests, while indicating that the other 15 countries (Austria, Belgium, Denmark, France, Germany, Hungary, Italy, Lithuania, Netherlands, Poland, Romania, Russia, Slovakia, Spain, and Turkey) all show a clear stakeholder orientation. Koslowski (2009) concurs with the view that at least Continental Europe displays a stakeholder orientation.

Wieland (2005) uses the way in which the role of the corporation in society is conceptualised as a criterion for determining the ethical orientation of corporate governance regimes in Europe. In this regard, he distinguished between three different conceptualisations of the role of corporations in society. The first way of conceptualising the corporation is to regard it as a vehicle for maximizing shareholder value. This way of understanding the role of corporations inevitably results in the prioritization of shareholder interests, while the interests of all other stakeholders of the corporation are considered from the perspective of how they could serve the objective of shareholder value maximization. A second way of conceptualising the firm is to regard it as a structure created to facilitate economic transactions between various parties in an economically efficient manner. A third way of understanding the role of the corporation is to perceive it as a setting that allows parties with different resources and competencies to cooperate in order to benefit from their respective contributions to the corporation. The latter two ways of conceptualising the role of the corporation give recognition to the intrinsic value of stakeholders of the corporation and do not relegate them to an instrumental status. This does not imply that corporations have a normative obligation to consider the interests of stakeholders. It rather presents a descriptive stakeholder account of the corporation that recognizes that ethical values and behaviour are factors that have a bearing on the ability of corporations to facilitate economic transactions between stakeholders as well as on corporations' ability to serve as settings for fruitful stakeholder cooperation. These conceptualisations of the role of corporations thus legitimize both shareholder and stakeholder interests as well as ethical discourse within and about corporations. This reality is reflected in the corporate laws and codes of corporate governance in Europe as they do emphasize the importance of corporate ethical standards, stakeholder dialogue, and communication as well as corporate social and environmental responsibility (cf. ibid., p. 86). The German two-tier board structure, where employee representatives serve on the supervisory board of companies, can also be regarded as a form of institutional recognition of employees as legitimate stakeholders alongside shareholders (cf. Koslowski 2009, p. 29).

Latin America

In their study of seven Latin American countries (Argentina, Brazil, Chile, Colombia, Mexico, Peru, and Venezuela), Bedicks and Arruda (2005) came to the conclusion that the region can be characterised as being dominated by an almost exclusive shareholder ethic of corporate governance. Within this shareholder ethic of corporate governance, there is a further prioritization of the interests of majority shareholders. Ownership of corporations in Latin American is often concentrated in the hands of the state, powerful elites, or influential families who exercise significant control over corporations. This situation is exacerbated by the fact that corporate law and systems of external control over companies are neither well developed nor effectively executed (cf. Bedicks and Arruda 2005; Ryan 2005, p. 44). As a result, the prevailing corporate governance regimes favour the interests of majority shareholders, but provide little protection for or support to minority shareholders. Corporate law reforms in recent years have secured more protection as well as more voice for institutional investors.

Within these corporate governance regimes that prioritize the interest of majority shareholders, the interests of other stakeholders are either neglected or regarded as instrumental to the promotion of shareholder interests. This reality was confirmed by a 2003 IBGC (Instituto Brasileiro de Governança Corporativa) study, which indicated that boards of directors tend to focus primarily on the interests of shareholders and on matters related to access to capital. Issues related to the interests of other stakeholders tend to receive little attention from boards of directors.

North America

From an ethics of corporate governance perspective, there are some distinct differences between the two neighbouring countries in North America, Canada and the USA. (For the sake of this discussion Mexico was included in Latin America.) In her study of the ethics of corporate governance in North America, Ryan described the Canadian corporate governance regime as a hybrid model that displays both shareholder orientated and stakeholder orientated features, while the USA is characterised by shareholder primacy. Young's (2009) assessment of the ethical orientation of the US corporate governance regime concurs with Ryan's characterisation thereof.

The external control over companies in Canada is decentralised to the respective provinces, which makes for considerable variation in the way in which control over companies are exercised. While some provinces favour control over companies through corporate law, others favour a more principle-based approach that allows for greater corporate discretion and that relies on the integrity of boards of directors and corporate leaders. There is no doubt that the Canadian corporate governance regime protects the interests of especially large shareholders in Canada. Minority shareholders do not enjoy the same level of support or protection. This majority shareholder leaning of the Canadian corporate governance system is, however, checked by forces that ensure that the interests of other stakeholders also enjoy recognition. The tradition of strong social programmes by the Canadian state serves as one countervailing force in support of the protection of non-shareholding stakeholders. Another strong countervailing force is the expectation of the Canadian populace that corporations should shoulder corporate responsibilities that go beyond the maximization of shareholder value. A survey of corporate stakeholders in Canada found that 83% of respondents perceived corporations as having obligation that transcend their conventional economic role (cf. Ryan 2005, p. 66).

In the USA, the role of corporations is perceived much more narrowly. Both corporate law and the population at large perceive corporations as vehicles for maximizing shareholder interests. Directors and executive managers are regarded as having a fiduciary duty to primarily act in the best financial interest of shareholders. The corporate governance regime is geared towards protecting and promoting the interests of majority and minority shareholders. There is wide support for the idea that a system of shareholder primacy is serving the best interest of all corporate stakeholders and of society. The widely dispersed ownership of companies in the USA is seen as implicit support of this idea. The primacy of shareholder interests and the correlating conviction that society as a whole would benefit from it, however, implies that the interests of other stakeholders are only considered in as far as they are relevant to shareholder interests. Corporations, consequently, tend to attend to stakeholder interests only when there is the probability that the latter might affect the maximization of shareholder value either positively or negatively.

Conclusions

The above brief overview of the ethics of corporate governance in different regions is sufficient to demonstrate the diversity in ethical orientations that underpin corporate governance regimes around the world. It is clear that there is no global convergence developing toward either a shareholder or a stakeholder ethic of corporate governance (cf. Rossouw 2009b). It is also clear that shareholder and stakeholder orientations are neither region-specific nor related to developing or developed economies. Both ethical orientations can be found in most world regions and across both developed and developing economies. I will conclude by discussing three factors that do seem to have the biggest impact on the ethical orientation of corporate governance regimes. They are the view that is held of the role of the corporation in society, the socio-cultural context, and some forms of ownership.

All corporate governance regimes are informed by and premised upon a view of the role and responsibilities of the corporation in society. When corporations are seen as vehicles for maximizing the financial interests of those who provide financial capital to the corporation, a shareholder ethic of corporate governance will prevail. A shareholder ethics obviously restricts the moral responsibility of corporations to the legal pursuit of financial returns for shareholders. Although it is often argued that such restriction of corporate moral responsibility is in the best interest of society as a whole (as explained earlier), the credibility of this belief is wearing thin in the light of the series of serious crises (energy crisis, food crisis, financial crisis, climate crisis) to which corporations have all contributed. When corporations are perceived as having roles and responsibilities that go beyond the legal pursuit of financial returns for shareholders, a more inclusive ethic of corporate governance is likely to emerge. Conceptions of the corporation that perceive corporations as having besides fiduciary duties to providers of financial capital also normative obligations towards other stakeholders of the corporation will evidently result in a more inclusive stakeholder ethic of corporate governance. A third way of conceptualising the role of corporations is to view them as institutions that exist for the sake of facilitating mutually beneficial or cost effective exchange between parties involved in business. Although such conceptions of the role of the corporation in society does not prioritize either stakeholder or shareholder interests, it nevertheless is likely to legitimize the role of ethical values and ethical behaviour in creating and maintaining mutually beneficial or cost effective exchange between parties involved in business.

The second factor that has a distinct impact on the ethics of corporate governance is the socio-cultural context within which corporations operate. The ethics of corporate governance is not only determined by formal mechanisms, such as corporate law and corporate governance codes, but also by the social norms, practices, and expectations that prevail in a region. In the above analysis of the ethics of corporate governance in various regions and countries, it became clear that factors such as cultural values, social practices, and societal expectations exert pressure on how corporations conduct their business and also on how they perceive their role and responsibilities in society. It is exactly the lack of recognition of this more subtle and informal form of control over corporations that often blocks out the ethical dimension of corporate governance in the global discourse on corporate governance.

A third factor that shapes the ethics of corporate governance regimes are certain forms of corporate ownership. From the above regional overview, it is clear that whenever the state takes an active ownership role in the economy, it inevitably brings social and political objectives into the corporate domain that have an influence on how the role and responsibilities of corporations are perceived. Also, concentrated family ownership of corporations can and indeed do influence the ethics of corporate governance regimes, although it is more likely to have an effect on the enterprise level than on the external control level of corporate governance. Recognising the impact of state and concentrated family ownership on the ethics of corporate governance does not amount to condoning such influence, but merely recognizes the impact thereof as a factor that co-determines the ethics of corporate governance.

References

Bebchuk, L.A., and M.J. Roe. 1999. A theory of path dependence in corporate ownership and governance. *Stanford Law Review* 52: 127–170.

Becht, M., P. Bolton, and A.A. Röell. 2002. Corporate governance and control, Finance Working Paper No. 02/2002, European Corporate Governance Institute, available at SSRN: http://ssrn.com/abstract=343461

Bedicks, H.B., and M.C. Arruda. 2005. Business ethics and corporate governance in Latin America. *Business and Society* 44: 218–228.

Berle, A.A. 1931. Corporate powers as powers in trust. *Harvard Law Review* 44: 1049–1074.

Coffee, J.C. 1998. Inventing a corporate monitor for transitional economies: The uncertain lessons from the Czech and Polish experiences. In *Comparative corporate governance: The state of the art and emerging research*, ed. K.J. Hopt, H. Kanda, M.J. Roe, E. Wymeersch and S. Prigge, 67–138. New York, NY: Oxford University Press.

Collier, J., and J. Roberts. 2001. Introduction: An ethic for corporate governance? *Business Ethics Quarterly* 11: 67–71.

Demise, N. 2005. Business ethics and corporate governance in Japan. *Business & Society* 44: 211–217.

Donaldson, T., and L.E. Preston. 1995. The stakeholder theory of the corporation: Concepts, evidence, and implications. *Academy of Management Review* 20: 65–91.

Friedman, M. 1970. The social responsibility of business is to increase its profits, *The New York Times Magazine*, 13 September 1970, 32–34.

Gedajlovic, E.R., and D.M. Shapiro. 1998. Management and ownership effects: Evidence from five countries. *Strategic Management Journal* 19: 533–553.

Goodpaster, K.E. 1993. Business ethics and stakeholder analysis. In *Business ethics: A philosophical reader*, ed. T.I. White, 205–220. New York, NY: Macmillan.

Hansmann, H., and R. Kraakman. 2001. The end of history for corporate law. *Georgetown Law Journal* 89: 439–468.

Kalkundrikar, A.B., S.G. Hiremath, and R. Mutkekar, eds. 2010. *Business ethics and corporate social responsibility*. MacMillan: Delhi.

Kimber, D., and Lipton, P. 2005. Corporate governance and business ethics in the Asia-Pacific region. *Business and Society* 44: 178–210.

Koslowski, P. 2009. The ethics of corporate governance: A continental European perspective. *International Journal of Law and Management* 51: 27–34.

Monks, R.A.G., and N. Minow. 2004. *Corporate governance*, 3rd ed. Malden, MA: Blackwell.

Reddy, Y.R.K. 2009. The ethics of corporate governance: An Asian perspective. *International Journal of Law and Management* 51: 17–26.

Romano, R. 1998. Empowering investors: A market approach to securities regulation. In *Comparative corporate governance: The state of the art and emerging research*, ed. K.J. Hopt, H. Kanda, M.J. Roe, E. Wymeersch and S. Prigge, 143–217. New York, NY: Oxford University Press.

Rossouw, G.J. 2005a. Business ethics and corporate governance: A global survey. *Business and Society* 44: 32–39.

Rossouw, G.J. 2005b. Business ethics and corporate governance in Africa. *Business and Society* 44: 94–106.

Rossouw, G.J. 2009a. The ethics of corporate governance: Crucial distinctions for global comparisons. *International Journal of Law and Management* 51: 5–9.

Rossouw, G.J. 2009b. The ethics of corporate governance: Global convergence or divergence? *International Journal of Law and Management* 51: 43–51.

Rossouw, G.J., and A.J.G. Sison, eds. 2006. *Global perspectives on ethics of corporate governance*. New York, NY: Palgrave Macmillan.

Rossouw, G.J., A. van der Watt, and D.P. Malan. 2002. Corporate governance in South Africa. *Journal of Business Ethics* 37: 289–302.

Ryan, L.V. 2005. Corporate governance and business ethics in North America: The state of the art. *Business and Society* 44: 40–73.

Shleifer, A., and R.W. Vishny. 1997. A survey of corporate governance. *The Journal of Finance* 52: 737–783.

West, A. 2009. The ethics of corporate governance: A (South) African perspective. *International Journal of Law and Management* 51: 10–16.

Wieland, J. 2005. Corporate governance, values management, and standards: A European perspective. *Business and Society* 44: 74–93.

Young, S.B. 2009. The ethics of corporate governance: The North American perspective. *International Journal of Law and Management* 51: 35–42.

Chapter 17
Do Stakeholder Interests Imply Control Rights in a Firm?

Ronald Jeurissen

Contents

Introduction

Ethics requires us to take the justified interests of all those into account who can be affected by our actions. We have ethical duties not to harm people, to protect people from harm by others, and even to do good to them (cf. Frankena 1973). Business firms are under this same basic system of ethical duties (cf. Jeurissen 2006, p. 66). Those who can be affected by the actions of a business are called "stakeholders" (cf. Freeman 1984). Businesses are under an ethical obligation to take the justified interests of their stakeholders into account (cf. Freeman et al. 2007). In this paper, I will examine the question of to what extent the legitimate interests of stakeholders towards a firm also imply the need, or even the right, to exercise control over that firm's decisions.

By "control" over a firm, I mean a formalised, statutory right to influence its decisions. Control is a form of influence, but not all influence implies control. Competitors who force each other to sell at the lowest price have each other firmly in their grips and in common parlance could be said to "control" each other's behaviour. In the technical vocabulary of this paper, this would still not be control,

R. Jeurissen (✉)
Professor of Business Ethics, Director, European Institute for Business Ethics, Nyenrode Business University, Breukelen, The Netherlands
e-mail: R.Jeurissen@nyenrode.nl

A. Brink (ed.), *Corporate Governance and Business Ethics*, Ethical Economy. Studies in Economic Ethics and Philosophy 39, DOI 10.1007/978-94-007-1588-2_17, © Springer Science+Business Media B.V. 2011

but influence. Control, as I will use the term here, implies a form of influence that has a formal statutory basis. Control comes mostly in the form of a right that a specific category of stakeholders has: voting rights, the veto right, rights to nominate or appoint, rights to enquire, etc. An important characteristic of the rights that constitute "control" over a firm is their *generalized* nature. Companies conclude many legally binding contracts every day, related to buying and selling for example, and each of these contracts puts the company under the influence of the contracting party. Sellers and buyers can take each other to court over juridical disputes and influence each other's conduct and outcomes that way. Again, this type of contractually related and limited influence is outside the realm of "control" as I will use the term here. Control refers to a role and status of a stakeholder to *permanently* exercise influence over a company's decisions, based on some generalized right to do so.

The thesis that stakeholders should have control rights over a firm is advanced by several authors, whose work can be brought together under the heading of "stakeholder democracy", "stakeholder governance", or "stakeholder capitalism" (cf. Freeman 1996). They develop their point mostly in opposition to the "shareholder" model, where the ultimate control right in a firm is reserved for the shareholders. Robert Freeman is an important spokesperson of stakeholder capitalism. In several papers, he has argued why the primacy of the shareholder is an erroneous and socially disruptive account of how businesses should be governed. It is based on false assumptions of egoistic and competitive human motivation, it crowds out ethical motives from business decisions, it arbitrarily promotes the interests of a dominant group (the shareholders) over others, and it necessitates the development of a big juridical system to protect the society from the consequences of the egoistic and amoral behaviour of the business world (cf. Freeman et al. 2007).

> As businesses change the very composition of human society, its traditional ideology proclaims that it is amoral, that business ethics is an oxymoron, and that business exists only to do what shareholders require. Business, in this view, is to be understood as warfare, and executives are the lonely soldiers on the battlefield of global markets playing 'shoot 'em up' with competitors. This myth of the primacy of the shareholder and its view of business as 'Cowboy Capitalism' leads to a profound public mistrust and misunderstanding of the basic processes that make companies successful. We need a new story – one that elevates business to the higher moral ground that it can occupy (. . .). (Freeman and Liedtka 1997, p. 287)

The new story is called "stakeholder capitalism". It is based on the fundamental assumption that a company is not anyone's specific business and that its achievements are rather the result of the joint effort and mutual trust of many parties. "[S]takeholder capitalism focuses on individuals voluntarily working together to create sustainable relationships in the pursuit of value creation" (Freeman et al. 2007, p. 311). Stakeholder capitalism is "based on freedom, rights, and the creation by consent of positive obligation" (ibid., p. 311).

In this paper, I will explore whether and how the notion of stakeholder capitalism involves the extension of decision rights in a company to other stakeholders than the shareholders only. I will firstly make a distinction between economic and social stakeholders and argue that control rights are most plausible for the economic stakeholders of a firm, less so for social stakeholders. Next, I will put this conclusion into perspective by pointing to the increased prominence and prevalence of the open-systems and values-chain approaches to stakeholder management, which tend to decentralize the role of the firm in relation to its stakeholders. The resource based view of the firm helps understand why the question of which stakeholder *controls* the firm is increasingly superseded by the question of which stakeholder owns which resource that is critical to the achievement of the common goals of the networked partners in the values chain.

Economic and Social Stakeholders

Depending on their relationship to the business, two types of stakeholders can be distinguished: economic and social stakeholders. Economic stakeholders are all those who invest in the economic traffic with the business and who bear part of the risk. Groups that come to mind then are: managers, employees, shareholders, consumers, suppliers, partners in a joint venture, and competitors. What characterises the relationship with economic stakeholders is that there is an economic exchange: labour against wages, capital against dividends, raw materials, supplier services, and consumer products against current prices. It might be surprising that competitors are seen as business stakeholders as well, but businesses do have moral obligations towards competitors. For example, justified competitor interests are at stake when a number of businesses in an industry forms a cartel and thereby puts other competitors at a disadvantage or when a business harms the reputation of the entire industry by behaving irresponsibly.

Corporate moral responsibility does not stop at the circle of economic stakeholders. A business is also responsible for parties in society which may not have any business involvement in the business, but do in some way have an interest in what that business does. Society expects an organisation, business, or industry to recognise obligations with regard to interests, whether they are private or public, that are clearly outside the domain of mutual transactions, but which nevertheless merit being put on the agenda of the board. For example: interests of future generations, the environment, and the underprivileged in society. The list can be made considerably longer and more concrete, so it includes the obligation to be cautious about engaging in genetic experiments or about supplying particular forms of entertainment; the obligation to put political pressure on repressive regimes with which a business, directly or indirectly, has established business relationships; the obligation to make fighting unemployment a separate policy issue, not subject to the business's competitive and financial position; and the obligation to engage in serious dialogue with groups claiming to represent a public interest, but which do not participate in any economic transaction with the firm (cf. van Luijk and Schilder 1997, p. 43). As a result of the increased scale and complexity of businesses, the circle of social stakeholders has expanded considerably. Businesses managing a nuclear power plant are responsible for millions of stakeholders. Companies manufacturing substances that damage the ozone layer can even count humanity as a whole among its stakeholders.

Based on how the scope of a company's ethical responsibilities is defined, a plethora of stakeholders can be considered, and the list of legitimate social stakeholders can be extended indefinitely, it seems. Just consider how far into the future a company's responsibility for future generations should be extended (cf. Jeurissen and Keijzers 2004). I will not go into the details of the question of stakeholder identification here (cf. Mitchell et al. 1997). I will only try to deal with the question of how the influence of social stakeholders should be organized, assuming that such influence is ethically plausible in at least some cases.

Against the Shareholder Control Monopoly

One of the most well-known academic representatives of the idea that control of the business is the shareholders' prerogative is the American economist Michael Jensen. He claims,

> Corporate governance is a concern of great importance to owners of common stocks, because stockholder wealth depends in large part upon the goals of the people who set the strategy of the corporation. Who is the boss, and whose interests come first? The objectives of corporate managers often conflict with those of the shareholders who own their companies. (Jensen and Chew 1995, p. 337)

The idea that corporate governance could also be about interests other than those of the shareholders does not seem to enter the equation in Jensen's view. Jensen bases his idea that control of the business solely belongs to the shareholders on the special interest shareholders have in the business, for they bear the residual risk of the business (the risk connected with the difference between a business's randomised income and expenditure). In other words: it is their money that is on the line. It is fair that they obtain control of the business in exchange (where shareholders can choose to delegate their controlling power to professional management). According to Jensen, it would be unreasonable to consider other interests than those of the shareholders and in doing so limiting shareholder control, since this comes down to playing poker with other people's money (cf. Jensen 1984). Oliver Williamson generalised Jensen's thesis by stating that a party specializing its assets to a particular contract reasonably expects some safeguards. "When there are no safeguards, this party bears the residual risk of the firm and should reasonably expect to 'control' the actions of the firm" (Freeman and Evan 1990, pp. 338f.; cf. Williamson 1984).

According to Williamson, all economic stakeholders, with the exception of shareholders, have bilateral safeguards in their transactions with a business. For example, a supplier has the safeguard that he can file an involuntary bankruptcy against an insolvent business in order to recover at least part of his money. Employees can enforce payment of wages in court, if need be. Shareholders are the only ones who do not have such contractual safeguards – that is part and parcel of their economic role as providers of risk capital. Since shareholders do not have contractual safeguards of their interests, Williamson feels they are entitled to a generalised safeguard in the shape of direct managerial control over the business.

Freeman and Evan (1990) have criticised Williamson's way of thinking. They distinguish the contractual safeguards that Williamson speaks of into two types: *endogenous safeguards*, based on a bilateral agreement between transaction partners, and *exogenous safeguards*, which are supplied by parties other than transaction partners, such as external supervisors and the government. The authors point out that all economic stakeholders, shareholders included, are increasingly protected by exogenous safeguards. The credit crisis of 2008–2009 illustrates this. The economic stakeholders of the banking industry were protected by hundreds of billions of euros in loans and guarantees from governments and central banks. Tens of billions of euros of loans have also been provided to national auto industries. Certain sectors of the economy are just considered "too important to fail" for economic and political reasons, and the political system jumps in to support these sectors. These are exogenous safeguards to businesses and their economic stakeholders on a historically unprecedented scale. In many cases, this financial support of companies was also in support of stockholder equity.

Freeman and Evan's arguments undermine the special status that Williamson and Jensen assign to shareholders on the basis of their unique position with regard to bearing risk. Others have contested the unique position of shareholders as well. Blair (1995) defuses a number of popular arguments in favour of the shareholder monopoly. The argument that shareholders simply happen to be the owners of the firm, and hence "of course" are entitled to control it, is in fact a circular argument. Ownership should be conceptualised as a bundle of rights that can in principle be distributed over many stakeholders in many ways. There is no a priori or natural way in which the bundle of property rights over the company should be broken up in one way or another. Also, the popular idea that the managers of a company, in order to work effectively for the benefit of that company, should be held accountable to a single party, rather than to a diffuse group of stakeholders, does not support the control monopoly of shareholders. It does make clear that procedures of accountability should be carefully drafted, not that the shareholder monopoly is the best governance scheme. Koslowski adds to this that serving the interests of consumers is actually a much more obvious business objective than serving the shareholders. For the overarching goal of company should ideally be able to acquire the consent of all stakeholders. The consumer role is a much more general role in which people relate to the world of business than is the role of the shareholder (cf. Koslowski 2000). Companies often profess that "the customer is king". Why not make that the foundation of their governance as well?

As early as 1927, Dutch economist Cobbenhagen wrote that there is no question of shareholders being the only ones bearing risks in a company. Other parties in the business do so as well. Cobbenhagen wrote in the tradition of the social teaching of the Roman Catholic Church. In this tradition, the involvement of the workers in the governance of the form, and their sharing in the revenues thereof, has always been prominent. Guidance to the Catholic Church's thinking on this issue has been provided by Pope John Paul II in his encyclical Centesimus Annus, where he writes that the Church's social teaching recognizes the legitimacy of workers' efforts to obtain full respect for their dignity and to gain broader areas of participation in the life of industrial enterprises so that, while cooperating with others and under the direction of others, they can in a certain sense 'work for themselves' through the exercise of their intelligence and freedom. (John Paul II 1991, no. 43)

In the German corporate governance model, employee influence has been laid down by law via employee representation in the *Aufsichtsrat* (the German counterpart of the supervisory board). In businesses of over 2,000 employees, the Aufsichtsrat is a paritary committee consisting of members appointed by shareholders and employees respectively (cf. Clark 2006).

Employees have certain vested interests in a business too, such as education fees or costs of moving house in order to be nearer their place of employment. Employees bear risks in a business, e.g., in the shape of loss of jobs, insecurity about their own job, and work-related diseases. These risks may not be capital risks, but there is no reason to assign a priori more importance to capital risks than to other risks. Even when shareholders bear most risks in a business, this does not mean that other stakeholders bearing risk have no right to control the business as well.

Goodijk advocates a tripartite governance model in which governing power over the business is shared by the board of directors, the supervisory board, and the works council:

Officially the Board of Directors has the most important (and final) responsibility for drawing up and executing business policy. The Supervisory Board – as official supervisor – and the (Central) Works Council – as legal organ of employee participation – can more or less actively exert influence on this. Within entrepreneurial dynamics the way in which different parties participate and supervise will be constantly changing. Actual influence will be largely determined by the internal balance of power, quality of input, competence (and competencies), backing (supporters), decisiveness etc. (Goodijk 1998, pp. 56f.)

Putting the exclusive shareholders' right of control into perspective offers openings to more inclusive governance models, such as the model proposed by Goodijk. Apart from shareholders, employees too deserve to have a voice in corporate governance.

Control to the Social Stakeholders?

Shareholders and employees are not the only ones who have major interests in relation to a business and for whom this relationship is a long-term one. Some social stakeholders, too, have a long-term involvement with a business, on the basis of which they can rightly expect their interests to have some form of safeguard. Just consider people living in the area surrounding an international airport who have been battling for years to get the airport to take their interests into account. Is it not high time these stakeholders should have a say in the governance of the airport as well?

According to Swiss business ethicist Peter Ulrich, this step follows logically from the basic ethical principle of a democratic society, i.e., that emancipated citizens try to solve their mutual conflicts of interest and differences in opinion by finding consensus in an open debate in which all stakeholders can participate as equals. This principle is no more than minimal ethics, without which peaceful human co-existence is not possible in the long term. After all, it is not possible to ignore the interests of particular groups for a long time without this having consequences for social peace. According to Ulrich, this basic ethical principle of democratic society should also be applied to corporate governance, for a business and its stakeholders are a miniature society. So, ideally, all conflicts of values and interests in a business should be solved by the participation of all stakeholders in processes of reasonable consensus building.

In stating this, Ulrich advocates an ultimate form of stakeholder governance: a business is governed by all stakeholders. According to Ulrich, this could be laid down by an "open business statute", which would say in what way stakeholders could gain access to a business's decision making process. This can be done, e.g., by legal regulation of stakeholders' rights to consult, oppose, complain, claim damages and participate in decision making (comparable to the way such rights are regulated already for shareholders and employees). The open business statute Ulrich has in mind is a democratically achieved, legally viable, minimal consensus on the insti-tutional organisation of a business and the right of all stakeholders to participate in and oppose the strategic decision making process.

Ulrich is the first to admit his ideas might sound a bit unworldly (cf. Ulrich 1993, p. 429). However, he interprets the open business statute as an ideal to point us in the right direction, an ideal that meets the needs of increasingly emancipated citi-zens to actively participate in the development of society, also in areas where this development is determined by business policies. The growing interest of NGOs in corporate behaviour is indicative of this. They represent the need of large groups of citizens to have greater influence on business policy (especially with regard to social and environmental issues). Businesses, too, are becoming more open to NGO opinions. The relationship between business and NGOs is evolving from a con-flict model into a consensus model, in which NGOs are increasingly turned into consultants and co-owners of a business's social problems. In the long run, there are interesting efficiency advantages to be gained for businesses, Ulrich feels. A business which internalises the dialogue with its stakeholders by involving them in their policy making might incur extra costs in the short term, but in the long term it will reap the benefits of being better informed of what society expects from it. Furthermore, it can save itself money because it avoids future conflicts with pressure groups.

By asking attention for all stakeholders, Ulrich has broadened and sharpened the debate on corporate governance from a business ethics perspective. When it is reasonable for everyone with a legitimate interest to be allowed to influence the way in which that interest is handled and when this is also true for stakeholders, then some form of stakeholder control of business firms is a logical conclusion.

Yet this does not say much about how stakeholder governance should be interpreted exactly. In what way should stakeholder influence be concretely organ-ised? The question is whether this influence should be endogenous, by means of shared governing responsibilities, or whether it could be organised exogenously, by intervention of a democratically elected government. In this context, it is useful to primarily define social stakeholder interest in terms of safeguards, as Williamson suggests. Social stakeholders have the right to expect their interests in a business to be surrounded with adequate safeguards. Freeman and Evan pointed out that these safeguards can take three forms, of which control over the company is only one possibility. Safeguards can be set up by:

1. endogenous, generalised safeguards (social stakeholders participating in controlling the firm, as Ulrich suggest);
2. endogenous, contractual safeguards (e.g., agreements between businesses and NGOs in the form of covenants);
3. exogenous safeguards (provided by the government and other external supervisors).

The question of which of these safeguards offers social stakeholders the best guarantees is an empirical, public administrative question that cannot be answered a priori here. In any case, we can conclude that Ulrich was jumping the gun in concluding that any stakeholder whose legitimate interests are at stake in a company is also entitled to exercise control over that company in some way.

As a rule, however, one could say that the right of a stakeholder to participate in the control of a firm is a function of the importance of the interests of the stakeholder that are at stake and the lock-in of the stakeholder to the firm. People living outside the fence of an international airport bear the brunt of the airport's external costs and their lock-in is high, as they will have to move in order to end their stakeholder status, which is costly. Increased noise from the air traffic may have reduced the value of the real estate in the vicinity of the airport, thus locking in the "fenceholders" even more strongly. A stakeholder in this position would have a strong case for demanding a stake in the control of the airport, including perhaps even a right to a share in the revenues as a proportional compensation for lost property value, harms, and damages.

A Resource Based View on the Influence of Stakeholders

The salience of the problem of the stakeholder control of business firms is put into perspective by acknowledging that influence may matter more to stakeholders than control. Control is just one form of influence, and if exercising control is not achievable, or not feasible, for a certain stakeholder at a specific place and time, some alternative form of influencing the behaviour of the firm might be appropriate and effective as well. The resource based view of the firm has brought to the fore that business firms and their stakeholders are interdependent and that firms are in need of external resources and performances from their environment in order to be able to survive and operate as a social subsystem. In this vein, Pfeffer and Salancik (1978) define an organisation as "a coalition of support" (p. 45). If a resource is important to the firm's operation, then the stakeholder controlling that resource will be able to exercise a strong influence on that company. The impact of this kind of resource based external influence of a stakeholder on a firm may well exceed the influence this stakeholder could ever hope to acquire by any form of control. Resource based influence may also be much more specifically targeted at the specific interest that a stakeholder wants to defend, and applying resource based influence may therefore be much more effective and efficient for stakeholders than exercising control over a company.

Introducing the resource dependence approach in the stakeholder governance debate implies a shift away from the firm as the focal point of attention to the values chain and the network of interacting stakeholders (cf. Rowley 1997).

> The focus shifts from the role of a single organisation towards the roles and responsibilities of different stakeholders such as suppliers, consumers, and governments in the whole production and consumption chain. (Nijhof et al. 2008, p. 161)

Freeman et al. (2007) also identify the increased interdependence of businesses and their stakeholders as one of the hallmarks of "stakeholder capitalism". Rather than argue about whose rights trump whose, they want to acknowledge that a large cast of stakeholders are necessary to sustain value creation.

Stakeholder dialogue and co-operation are important ways for businesses to shape their social responsibility in this situation of interdependence since businesses are often *partially* responsible for causing a social problem. When a business is questioned about its responsibility by its stakeholders, this business in turn can question those stakeholders – just consider issues such as traffic congestion, crime, environmental issues, or the growing problem of obesity. Businesses, the government, and other stakeholders depend on each other here and have a collective responsibility. This requires a social dialogue on issues of public interest, in which all parties involved take part. A term that crops up regularly in this context is "civil society": a society of emancipated citizens and their organisations who collectively take the responsibility, each from their own viewpoint, to actively contribute to the solution of social problems and to steer social developments in the right direction (cf. Scherer and Palazzo 2007).

Different stakeholders can enter into partnerships with each other regarding social issues and in doing so together create the resources that are necessary to realise a solution. An important mechanism within these partnerships is that different parties can mutually influence the conditions of their performance. By taking advantage of this, social parties and groups surrounding an issue can stimulate and support each other to an important extent. An example may clarify this (see Fig. 17.1).

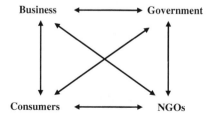

Fig. 17.1 Stakeholder synergy surrounding social issues
Source: Based on Jeurissen (2004)

Suppose a pharmaceutical company wants to reduce animal testing. Consumers can contribute to this by demanding pharmaceutical products that have not been tested on animals. NGOs battling against animal testing can help consumers by setting up websites giving information on animal testing by companies. Pharmaceutical companies can support each other by jointly developing a quality mark which makes it easy for consumers to see whether a particular product has not been tested on animals.

Pharmaceutical companies could even decide to be completely open to NGOs, hoping these NGOs will be less inclined to organise campaigns which can harm the company's image, such as via boycotts. Alternatively, NGOs may find that they can also achieve their goals by consulting companies. As consumers are becoming more aware of the fate of laboratory animals, they will support NGOs which battle against animal testing. This support increases the legitimacy of these NGOs. They can gain power against companies, but they can also put more pressure on the government to develop legislation against animal testing. When more consumers are against animal testing, the government can draw up stricter laws against it. Companies which have already taken steps to reduce animal testing can encourage this legislation, for it gives them a competitive advantage.

A resource based perspective on corporate social responsibility helps us understand that the responsibility for the social effects a business has lies partly outside that business's realm, with stakeholders who can influence that business. When a stakeholder group can influence the conditions under which an ethically better option also offers a straight business advantage, this stakeholder group has a responsibility to do so. Consumers able to positively influence corporate environmental behaviour by buying environmentally friendly products are partly responsible for corporate environmental behaviour.

Secondly, we can see that companies themselves have a responsibility to increase the effect of their efforts, by seeking collaboration with stakeholder groups. An interesting example of this is provided by the Roundtable on Sustainable Palm Oil (RSPO) formed in 2004 with the objective of promoting the growth and use of sustainable oil palm products through credible global sustainability standards developed through involvement of all stakeholders (see the website http://www.rspo.org). The members of this association represents major players along the palm oil supply chain, namely the oil palm grower, palm oil processors and traders, consumer goods manufacturers, retailers, banks and investors, and environmental nature conservation and development NGOs. Together, these 259 (commercial) organizations account for more then 40% of palm oil production and trade worldwide. RSPO has developed a set of standards that define practices for sustainable palm oil production. These standards address the legal, economic, environmental, and social requirements of producing sustainable palm oil. An RSPO Certification system is set up to formally recognise and authenticate growers who are producing palm oil according to the RSPO standards. The certification system can also verify any claims of using or supporting RSPO certified palm oil made by end product manufacturers and processors. With a certificate it is possible for them to claim that "this product contains RSPO certified palm oil", "this product contains x% RSPO certified palm oil", or to claim that "this product supports the trade in sustainable palm oil". One scarce resource in the supply chain of sustainable palm oil turns out to be critical mass. Only when produced on a sufficiently large scale can sustainable palm oil become anywhere near being competitively viable. This situation creates a common interest among a large coalition of stakeholders to jointly make sustainable palm oil a big industry (cf. Zengers 2009).

The transition to a commercially viable sustainable production of palm oil is something that can only be achieved through the concerted effort of many stakeholders in an industry. The question of who controls the decisions of palm oil producers, with a view to turning them towards greater sustainability, is of little relevance in this constellation of industry-wide stakeholder interdependence. It is not the level of control that matters, it is the level of resource dependence. The more stakeholders become perceived by companies as a critical resource to their own goal, the greater this stakeholder's influence will be.

Obliging Dialogues

A warning about stakeholder partnerships is in order, though. This comes in the shape of the old story about four people named Everybody, Somebody, Anybody, and Nobody.

> There was an important job to be done and Everybody was sure that Somebody would do it. Anybody could have done it, but Nobody did it. Somebody got angry because it was Everybody's job. Everybody thought Anybody could do it, but Nobody realised that Everybody wouldn't do it. It ended up that Everybody blamed Somebody when Nobody did what Anybody could have done.

Widen the circle of people involved, and the felt responsibility of each individual party decreases. People start waiting for each other and nobody feels responsible for the whole (cf. Benn 2007). Therefore, there is a need for obliging and result-oriented forms of partnerships among stakeholders. Gray (1989) points out that stakeholder dialogue can serve different purposes: exchanging information, developing a shared vision, reaching consensus, or solving conflicts. Each of these goals requires a different form of organisation. Loosely structured stakeholder dialogues will probably not yield much more than an exchange of information and the promotion of a shared vision. Sometimes that is quite an achievement. In order to get more concrete results, more obliging forms of collaboration are necessary, in which it is not just a matter of consulting each other, but in which parties try to reach consensus on an issue concerning them all. Gray (1989) points out that such a collaboration has five characteristics:

1. stakeholders are interdependent;
2. solutions are found by handling differences constructively;
3. decisions are made on the basis of consensus;
4. joint responsibility for the future;
5. emergence of the process.

A way to ensure all stakeholders can agree to the solution found is to see to it that all parties have realised an improvement in their situation at the end. Handling differences creatively offers possibilities for trade-off and new definitions of the situation. Emerging solutions are often challenging for all stakeholders, and such solutions often have elements nobody had expected since they are the result of interaction and trade-off.

According to Gray (1989), this method of consensus building is, among other things, very appropriate in solving problems with a high NIMBY (not in my backyard) factor, such as the arrival of a new industrial estate or an incinerator. What typifies such problems is that the local community which is saddled with them feels it has to bear disproportionately high costs in favour of many others. From a justice point of view, it is right that this should be compensated. By taking this justified demand as a starting point, creative solutions can be found for almost insolvable problems between businesses and stakeholders. The Canadian province Alberta, for example, succeeded in establishing hazardous waste depots in municipalities which eventually volunteered to have them as a result of an extensive process of information, consultation, and negotiations. Negotiations pertained to tax benefits, economic spin-offs, road improvements, housing construction, and preferential jobs for the local population.

However, differences of opinion between businesses and stakeholders cannot always be solved by looking for a win-win situation. A dispute can also involve more fundamental suppositions and motivations of parties involved. Underlying presuppositions in the debate on biotechnology, for instance, can be that the value of a biotech company in the stock market depends on the expectation that such a company will have a growing control over the food supply in the future, whereas NGOs are worried about the degree of democracy in society. Such differences of opinion do not leave much room for negotiation. In such cases, the dialogue should be raised to the fundamental questions of the social and political role of businesses.

References

Benn, S. 2007. New processes of governance: Cases for deliberative decision-making? *Managerial Law* 49: 196–205.

Blair, M.M. 1995. *Ownership and control: Rethinking corporate governance for the twenty-first century*. Washington, D.C.: Brookings Institution.

Clark, I. 2006. Another third way? VW and the trials of stakeholder capitalism. *Industrial Relations Journal* 37: 593–606.

Cobbenhagen, M. 1927. *De verantwoordelijkheid in de onderneming* [The responsibility within the corporation]. Roermond: Romen & Zn.

Frankena, W.K. 1973. *Ethics*, 2nd ed. Englewood Cliffs, NJ: Prentice Hall.

Freeman, R.E. 1984. *Strategic management: A stakeholder approach*. Boston, MA: Pitman.

Freeman, R.E. 1996. Understanding stakeholder capitalism. *Financial Times*, 19 July 1996, 11.

Freeman, R.E., and W.M. Evan. 1990. Corporate governance: A stakeholder interpretation. *Journal of Behavioral Economics* 19: 337–359.

Freeman, R.E., and J. Liedtka. 1997. Stakeholder capitalism and the value chain. *European Management Journal* 15: 286–296.

Freeman, R.E., K. Martin, and B. Parmar. 2007. Stakeholder capitalism. *Journal of Business Ethics* 74: 303–314.

Goodijk, R. 1998. *Corporate governance en medezeggenschap* [Corporate governance and co-determination]. Assen: Royal Van Gorcum.

Gray, B. 1989. *Collaborating: Finding common ground for multiparty problems*. San Francisco, CA: Jossey-Bass.

Jensen, M.C. 1984. Takeovers: Folklore and science. *Harvard Business Review*, November-December 62: 109–121.

Jensen, M.C., and D.H. Chew. 1995. U.S. Corporate governance: Lessons from the 1980s. In *The portable MBA in finance and accounting*, ed. J.L. Livingstone, 337–404. New York, NY: Wiley.

Jeurissen, R. 2004. Institutional conditions of corporate citizenship. *Journal of Business Ethics* 53: 87–96.

Jeurissen, R. 2006. *Ethics & business*. Assen: Royal Van Gorcum.

Jeurissen, R., and G. Keijzers. 2004. Future generations and business ethics. *Business Ethics Quarterly* 14: 47–69.

John Paul II. 1991. Encyclical letter Centessimus annus. Vatican: Libreria Editrice Vaticana, http://www.vatican.va/holy_father/john_paul_ii/encyclicals/documents/hf_jp-ii_enc_01051991_centesimus-annus_en.html

Koslowski, P. 2000. The limits of shareholder value. *Journal of Business Ethics* 27: 137–148.

Mitchell, R., B. Agle, and D. Wood. 1997. Toward a theory of stakeholder identification and salience: Defining the principle of who and what really counts. *Academy of Management Review* 22: 853–886.

Nijhof, A., T. de Bruijn, and H. Honders. 2008. Partnerships for corporate social responsibility: A review of concepts and strategic options. *Management Decision* 46: 152–167.

Pfeffer, J., and G.R. Salancik. 1978. *The external control of organizations: A resource dependence perspective*. New York, NY: Harper and Row.

Rowley, T.J. 1997. Moving beyond dyadic ties: A network theory of stakeholder influences. *Academy of Management Review* 22: 887–910.

Scherer, A.G., and G. Palazzo. 2007. Toward a political conception of corporate responsibility: Business and society seen from a Habermasian perspective. *Academy of Management Review* 32: 1096–1120.

Ulrich, P. 1993. *Transformation der ökonomischen Vernunft. Fortschrittsperspektiven der modernen Industriegesellschaft*. Bern, Vienna, Stuttgart: Haupt.

Van Luijk, H.J.L., and A. Schilder. 1997. *Patronen van verantwoordelijkheid: Ethiek en corporate governance* [Patterns of responsibility: Ethics and corporate governance]. Schoonhoven: Academic Service.

Williamson, O.E. 1984. Corporate governance. *The Yale Law Journal* 93: 1197–1230.

Zengers, J. 2009. *What's in it for me? Working with competitors in the palm-oil industry to improve environmental sustainability and competitive advantage*, Thesis Master of Science in Management Programme, Nyenrode Business Universiteit, Breukelen.

Chapter 18
The Implications of the New Governance for Corporate Governance

John R. Boatright

Contents

Introduction

In the development called "the new governance", corporations, especially multi-national or transnational corporations, have become politically engaged and have assumed new functions that have traditionally belonged to governments alone.[1] According to Scherer et al. (2006), the task of creating and implementing rules in a globalized world is "no longer a task managed by the state alone" (p. 506). Rather, multinational corporations, along with governments and other civil society groups, participate "in the formulation and implementation of rules in policy areas that were once the sole responsibility of the state" (ibid., p. 506). In addition to this rule-making function, corporations, it is claimed, serve another role traditionally reserved for government, namely as a provider or guarantor of the "triad" of civil, political, and social rights. Because the activities of making rules and administering

---

[1] The original version of the chapter has been published in the conference proceedings of the Corporate Citizenship and New Governance Conference held in Wittenberg, Germany, in November 2009.

J.R. Boatright (✉)
Raymond C. Baumhart, S.J., Professor of Business Ethics, Professor of Management, Graduate School of Business, Loyola University of Chicago, Chicago, IL, USA
e-mail: JBOATRI@luc.edu

A. Brink (ed.), *Corporate Governance and Business Ethics*, Ethical Economy.
Studies in Economic Ethics and Philosophy 39, DOI 10.1007/978-94-007-1588-2_18,
© Springer Science+Business Media B.V. 2011

rights involve close collaboration with many groups in society and also raise issues of legitimacy, Scherer and Palazzo advocate a "communicative framework" for the new governance based on Habermas's idea of deliberative democracy (cf. Palazzo and Scherer 2006; Scherer and Palazzo 2007).

Closely related, if not identical, to this concept of new governance as formulated by Scherer, Palazzo, and Baumann is the thesis of Matten, Crane, and Moon that the corporate role in society can now be characterized as "corporate citizenship" (cf. Moon et al. 2005; Matten and Crane 2005; Matten et al. 2003; Moon 2002), and as the "republican concept" of corporate ethics presented by Steinmann and Löhr (1996). According to Moon et al. (2005), the activities of corporations "can be understood as being in some meaningful way *similar* to that of citizens or citizenship" (p. 432). This citizenship role is filled by corporations by, first, "administering [citizenship] rights *within* the normal operation of a firm", and, second, partnering with governments and non-governmental organizations in "contributing to societal governance *outside* the firm" (Moon et al. 2005, p. 440). For Steinmann and Löhr, a republican conception of the corporation or business ethics is necessary because business organizations have a responsibility not only to engage in economic production but also to help secure peace in society by facilitating processes of conflict resolution. Corporations thus have a "double responsibility" for "both economics *and* ethics" (Steinmann and Löhr 1996, p. 49). In accepting this responsibility, corporations assume a politicized role usually reserved for government. Consequently, they claim,

> [c]orporate *ethics* should be understood as a *discoursive* ethics procedure directed towards a *consensus* about *good reasons* for the *peaceful* resolution of ad-hoc conflicts with the (internal and external) stakeholders of the corporation. (ibid., p. 50)

One question that arises about the concept of new governance or, alternatively, corporate citizenship or republican ethics is its bearing on corporate governance. The *governance* referenced in the phrase "new governance" is not *corporate* governance but the process of decision making in the social and political order, which has traditionally been a function of government and is now performed with the active involvement of private parties, including corporations (cf. Cutler 2003; Hall and Biersteker 2002; Reinicke 1998; Pattberg 2005). *Corporate* governance, by contrast, is the set of legal rules which assigns the decision-making or control rights in business organizations and specifies the processes and procedures for exercising these rights. Assuming that present-day corporations, especially large firms that operate globally, have changed in the ways described by these scholars of the new governance, need the governance systems for corporations that prevail in the world today be altered in any way? In short, does the new governance have any implications for corporate governance?

This question is raised but not answered in one brief passage by Scherer et al. (2006):

> Does the new role of the corporation have consequences for the internal constitution of the corporation and corporate governance? Would it not be appropriate to argue that, given that

corporations act politically, they also have to open up their internal structures and processes for public control, thereby enabling democratic legitimacy? (p. 520)

This suggestion of an affirmative answer is vague, both about the "consequences" that follow from this new role aside from "opening up their internal structures" and enabling more democratic "public control", and about the reasons for these changes that make it "appropriate" to argue for them. Since systems of corporate governance are derived from some theory of the firm, the question of the implications of new governance for corporate governance extends to the need for some change in the theory of the firm, which is a question that is also raised, but not answered, by Scherer et al. (2006, p. 524). None of the other advocates of the new governance or corporate citizenship or republican ethics discusses the possible implications of this development for either corporate governance or the theory of the firm.

The aim of this article is to examine the question of what implications, if any, the new governance has for corporate governance and, by extension, the theory of the firm. Is the new governance compatible with traditional systems of corporate governance, which are based on the standard economic theory of the firm, or are some changes required? And if some changes are required, what are these changes and, more importantly, why are they required? The main conclusion of this examination is that, yes, the new governance has some implications for corporate governance and the theory of the firm. However, these implications are due primarily to broader changes in the competitive environment of present-day corporations of which the features cited in the new governance literature are only a relatively small part. One value of this article, then, aside from addressing the question of the implication for corporate governance, is to place the new governance in a larger context and identify some additional forces at work in its development.

Traditional Corporate Governance

Corporate governance has been understood traditionally as the rules that define the relationship between a firm and its capital providers or financiers. For example, Shleifer and Vishny (1997) write that corporate governance "deals with the ways in which suppliers of finance to corporations assure themselves of getting a return on their investment" (p. 737). This view is based on a theory of the firm in which a corporation is a nexus of contracts in which every group participating in joint production provides some input in return for a claim on revenues. Since the equity capital providers' return is the residual revenues or profits, thereby making them residual risk bearers, they have a special contracting problem that is best addressed by the possession of control rights. Although other groups provide needed inputs, these contributions to production are generally not firm-specific and the return, in any event, can usually be secured by other contractual means. Other groups, thus, have little need of the kind of protections, including control rights, that is possessed by the financiers of the firm, and, consequently, these rights are allocated to the party, namely equity capital providers, to whom they are of the greatest value.

The value of control rights in corporate governance to the financiers of the firm derives from the ability of these rights to solve two key agency problems in joint production. First, the problem of monitoring the contribution of every participant in joint production is solved by assigning residual revenues to the group with control right so as to motivate its members to monitor the activities of other groups (cf. Alchian and Demsetz 1972). Second, and more importantly, corporate governance is designed to address the agency problem inherent in the separation of ownership and control in large publicly held corporations (cf. Fama and Jensen 1983; Jensen and Meckling 1976; Hansmann 1996; Williamson 1985). It is by means of the control rights provided by corporate governance that capital providers can, through the board of directors, ensure that the managers monitor each group's efforts and maximize the residual revenues or profits.

Since the aim of all production decisions is maximal efficiency, the rules of corporate governance that emerge in a market through a process of negotiation between a firm and its equity capital providers, which constitute the rules of corporate governance, also have the aim of efficiency. In general, the forms of corporate governance that emerge when corporate constituencies are able to contract freely in a market will be efficient. Insofar as corporate law is established by government legislation, as opposed to private contracting, one of its aims – some claim its only proper aim – is to codify in law the most efficient relationship between firms and its financiers (cf. Easterbrook and Fischel 1991). Indeed, in the Anglo-American system, much of the law of corporate governance is merely default legislation that provides "off-the-shelf" rules that codify the kinds of contracts that private parties would write themselves. If these rules do not conduce to efficient production, firms are generally free, especially in the Anglo-American system, to contract differently. Any mandatory rules of corporate governance established by government that cannot be contracted around may be assumed to introduce some inefficiency into corporate operations (otherwise they would be adopted voluntarily by private contract). However, they may be enacted into law by government in the pursuit of values other than efficiency, such as fairness or social welfare.

In this traditional account of corporate governance, firms are understood to operate within a market in which private economic actors exercise their property rights through economic exchanges or transactions. The market is thus a sphere of activity in which every party – not only profit-oriented shareholders but other investors, employees, customers, suppliers, and other groups – seek to obtain maximal benefit. The market mechanism is utilized in a capitalist economy, not only to organize production and distribute the wealth thereby created, but also to determine the rules of corporate governance themselves and the assignment of governance rights. The state or government provides the legal structure for market activity – for example, by protecting property rights and enforcing private contracts – along with making rules for other spheres of civic life through the democratic participation of citizens in the rule-making process. In particular, it is the role of the state to provide public goods and protect individuals' civil and political rights.

The Challenge of the New Governance

The world of the new governance, in which corporations participate in rule making and the administration of rights, challenges and is challenged by this traditional account of corporate governance, both from an explanatory and normative perspective. A key feature of the traditional account of corporate governance, which is supported by the underlying economic theory of the firm, is that corporations engage in private, self-interested economic transactions while government attends to its public role of rule making and the administration of rights. Advocates of the new governance, as well of corporate citizenship and republican ethics, assume the effectiveness and legitimacy of the market mechanism, and so there is a need for some explanation of why these new corporate roles should arise in a competitive market – if, indeed, they do.

The only explanation offered by advocates of the new governance is that corporations have taken on the tasks of rule making and administering rights in situations where the government has been ineffective because it lacks either the power or the ability to act effectively. However, the existence of a need does not explain why corporations have moved to fill it. As van Oosterhout observes, new governance scholars offer no plausible reasons why corporations would be efficient rule makers or administrators of right or, more important, why they would take up these responsibilities in the first place (cf. van Oosterhout 2005, p. 678). He writes,

> First, the existence of more powerful and more perfectly functioning mechanisms (. . .) will also punish corporations who engage in activities that these markets are not willing to pay for. But, second, even if corporations could get away with such activities in global competitive markets, why should they assume such extensive responsibilities if there is nothing in it for them? (ibid.)

Missing from the discussion of the new governance, then, is any explanation of how the new roles that corporations have allegedly undertaken could possibly be efficient, so that these responsibilities would be voluntarily undertaken by corporations or imposed on corporations by a state government committed to the pursuit of efficiency or any other values. Beyond this problem, the account of the new governance does not provide any well-articulated theory of the firm that would support these roles for corporations.

Explanation aside, the normative justification for corporations as private actors to undertake these roles is questionable. As a consequence, a problem of legitimacy arises that is examined at length by Palazzo and Scherer (2006). They find a solution for this problem by holding corporations to stricter democratic accountability in a "communication-based approach to political theory" that involves "a continuous process of deliberative discourse" (Palazzo and Scherer 2006, p. 79), following Habermas. However, the very existence of a "problem" with legitimacy indicates that the new roles of corporations cannot be understood within the more conventional framework of corporations as economic actors in competitive markets.

That there should be a problem with legitimacy is itself a problem with the new governance. The standard view of firms as private economic institutions operating in a market is too fundamental to both economics and ethics to give up easily, merely to solve a normative problem about legitimacy, especially when this does nothing to solve the more fundamental problem of explanation.

A Search for New Foundations

Fortunately, it is possible to understand the development of the new governance in a way that explains how the new roles and responsibilities of present-day corporations are an efficient adaptation to a changed competitive environment for business. Such an explanation, furthermore, does not raise any normative problem about legitimacy that would require discarding the fundamental conception of corporations as economic actors. However, this explanation does alter the underlying theory of the firm in ways that lead to significant changes in corporate governance. The main outlines of this explanation are sketched by Luigi Zingales in his article "In Search of New Foundations". The foundations in question are those for corporate finance: needed, in his view, is a new theory of the firm to support the empirical research, practical applications, and policy recommendations of corporate finance. However, the new foundations that he describes can be applied with equal fruitfulness to corporate governance – and the new governance. Many of the features of present-day firms described by Zingales are also present in what Post et al. (2002a, 2002b) call the "extended enterprise", although these writers do not explore its implication for the theory of the firm or corporate governance.

The world has changed dramatically in the past several decades. The changes noted by advocates of the new governance concern primarily what Mathews (1997) calls the rise of "global civil society", in which national governments have lost autonomy and now share power with corporations and nongovernmental organizations (NGOs). In political theory, this change represents the end of the Westphalian system and the beginning of a system of "global governance" (cf. Kobrin 2008; Wolf 2008). By and large, scholars of the new governance have drawn on the immense political theory literature on global civil society and global governance. However, equally significant changes have occurred in business organizations that are not reflected in this literature.

The visible signs of changes in present-day corporations are, first, the breakup of large conglomerates with their standardized forms of organization in favor of smaller, more nimble companies, which have taken a wide variety of original and still-evolving organizational forms. Second, corporations have abandoned their rigid and closed vertically-integrated structure to adopt more flexible, open forms of collaboration in networks. Both of these developments lead to a blurring of organizational boundaries, which are constantly in flux. Third, corporations are ceasing to be hierarchical with extended formal chains of command and are becoming more flattened with multiple, informal reporting relationships. Fourth, corporations are being driven to innovate constantly with new produces and services and improve quality rather than merely reducing costs and expanding output of a standard product line. Innovation and quality improvement have replaced the traditional emphasis on economies of scale and market share as the drivers of corporate strategy.

Behind these visible signs are some less obvious changes with profound implications for corporate finance and government. The optimal strategy for a company in any competitive environment is to identify and exploit opportunities for value creation. In the traditional firm, the key elements have been to employ large fixed tangible assets and realize economies of scale to reduce prices and enlarge market share. In such a firm, control over inputs through vertical integration of natural resources and hierarchical command structures for labor are critical. The most critical input or resource is capital. Because large amounts of capital are needed in a traditional, capital-intensive firm, firms must turn to outside investors who can bear the risk of providing capital through diversification. Since these diversified investors still bear considerable residual risk, it is necessary to offer them strong ownership rights. With outside ownership, however, comes the separation of *de jure* ownership and *de facto* control, which leads to the agency problems that corporate governance is designed largely to solve.

The changed competitive environment of the past several decades has radically altered the strategy that companies must pursue to continue to create value. In his presidential address to the American Finance Association, Michael Jensen (1993) terms the years after 1973 "the modern industrial revolution". In his account, a combination of increasing productivity, technological innovation, declining capital costs, more varied sources of financing, reduced regulation, and the globalization of commerce made the traditional model of growth through expansion and economies of scale counterproductive. Corporations could now create value only by seizing new opportunities that arose mainly from technological innovation and globalization. New and better products were the key to value creation rather than cheaper, more abundant ones.

In this new era, fixed tangible assets are less important than skills and knowledge. Since financial capital is less essential and, in any event, easier to obtain in many different forms, human capital has become more crucial and in demand. At the same time, corporations find that they have less control over employees and other sources of innovation and competitive advantage. Not only can employees easily leave to work for competitors anywhere in the world, but some valuable skills and knowledge are possessed by outsiders in all parts of the globe who cannot be brought inside the firm. As a result, the resources needed for value creation cannot be owned and controlled in a hierarchical organization as in the past, but need to be mobilized in a collaborative network of people and institutions, both inside and outside the organization. Consequently, Post et al. (2002a) observe that "it is *relationships* rather than *transactions* that are the ultimate sources of organizational wealth" (p. 7; original emphasis; citing Leana and Rousseau 2000).

New Foundations and Corporate Governance

This account of changes in the competitive environment of corporations explains developments in the strategies adopted by companies in recent decades as well as in their organization, management, and financing. What are the implications, though, for corporate governance? Can corporate governance still deal only with "the ways in which suppliers of finance to corporations assure themselves of getting a return on their investment" or must it address a broader ranger of groups and their interests? The traditional account holds that only investors are the subject of corporate governance, not because the interests of other groups are not affected or unimportant, but because of three related propositions.

First, only shareholders bear *residual* risk. Other constituencies bear some risk from corporate operations, but given that the returns for their investment in a firm are fixed amounts that can be secured with complete, legally enforceable contracts, they do not bear residual risk – which is the risk that comes from having a return based on residual revenues or profits. Corporate governance, moreover, is a solution for residual risk bearers, so that its protection is appropriate only for investors with residual claims. For other groups with different kinds of risk, different protections are more effective. The crucial point here is that every group should receive an appropriate level of risk protection, but the safeguards for non-residual risk bearers may properly be different from those for residual risk bearers and hence need not be the subject of corporate governance.

Second, only shareholders and not other groups are affected by corporate decision making – as long, of course, as a firm remains solvent. Since all non-shareholder constituencies have fixed claims that are negotiated in the process of forming a firm's nexus of contracts, their return is determined by the prices that their inputs command in the appropriate markets for labor, products, commodities, and so on, which are independent of the performance of a firm. By contrast, the return of equity capital providers, who have claims on the firm's residual revenues or profits, depends directly on the decisions made by management. Management decisions affect the level of profits, but not necessarily the solvency of the firm, which is the major source of firm risk for non-shareholder groups. Only shareholders have an interest that a firm be more than solvent, and corporate governance is the means by which this interest is protected.

Third, only explicit contracts form the basis of each group's claim on corporate revenues. Corporate governance constitutes investors' claims, and the claims of every other group are backed by the agreements that occur in the market transactions for their inputs. However, firms also make implicit contracts that induce input providers to commit firm-specific assets that are not guaranteed by a legally enforceable contract. Zingales observes that a firm with a reputation for fair treatment, for example, may be able to induce employees to make a firm-specific contribution that they would not make in a market. He continues,

> If these investments are indeed valuable and could not have been elicited with an explicit contract, the firm's reputation adds value; it is an organizational asset. (Zingales 2000, p. 1633)

Thus, any theory of the firm that captures all sources of value in a firm must consider implicit as well as explicit contracts. However, the standard economic theory of the firm pays scant attention to these implicit contracts.

It is easy to see that these three propositions, which are central to the traditional account of corporate governance, are called into question by the developments that have taken place in present-day corporations.

First, residual risk is now borne by many groups other than shareholders. With the declining importance of large, tangible assets and economies of scale and the new emphasis on innovation and quality, human capital becomes central to a company's strategy. However, employees can no longer be commanded in a hierarchical structure but must be induced to make firm-specific investments with promises that their contributions will be rewarded and not exploited (cf. Blair 1995). Put differently, the value of human capital in modern production leads to greater quasi-rents due to firm-specific investments, which makes employees vulnerable to exploitation by other groups, specifically shareholders. Moreover, the human capital that is valuable to a firm is held not only by employees *inside* the corporation but also by many groups on the *outside* who are part of a firm's network of resources. These sources of human capital must also be induced to cooperate with promised rewards. Thus, the residual risk of firms is spread further as strategic alliances are formed with partners and suppliers and the organizational boundaries of firms become blurred and porous.

Second, non-shareholder groups are now more affected by corporate decision making than before. The sharp line that once existed between the effects of managerial decisions, which extend only to the level of profits, and those of markets, which determine the prices of inputs, has broken down. As human capital becomes more important, employees are no longer merely sellers of labor, the return for which is determined by the labor market. Management decision making now has a profound impact on the value of the employees' contribution and hence their return. Moreover, as relationships replace transactions, employees operate less in a labor market, merely selling their labor for wages, and more in cooperative enterprises, helping to create value by making firm-specific investments that could not be obtained in a market alone. Similarly, other groups have been drawn into the sphere of corporate activity, not merely as market participants or bystanders, but as resources that constitute part of the value or organizational wealth of a firm. Because they share in the production of wealth and also its distribution, the return to these groups is not determined merely by the market price of their inputs but is directly affected by management decision-making. Again, as firm boundaries become more blurred and porous, the once sharp distinction between being in a relationship with a firm and merely participating in a transaction with one breaks down.

Third, implicit contracts are now as important, if not more important, to business enterprises than explicit contracts. Explicit contracts are central to market transactions but are less crucial to relationships, which are built more on trust and mutual interests and goals. Implicit contracts are also more important in networks, especially with people and organizations outside a firm, than they are in firms with a hierarchical command structure and the vertical integration of resources. The value of relationships and networks to a firm reflects the fact that it is human capital – the utilization of the skills and knowledge of people – and not financial capital – which can be used to secure fixed, tangible assets – that is now they key to wealth creation. And the input of human capital, as opposed to financial capital, is better obtained and employed through implicit rather than explicit contracts.

If traditional corporate governance is built on the three propositions – that only shareholders bear residual risk, that only they are affected by corporate decisions, and that only explicit contracts are at issue – and if these propositions no longer apply, then obviously there is a need to rethink the prevailing allocation of control rights and the processes for their exercise. Zingales (2000) admits, "I am not aware of any formal development of the consequences of this approach [that is, the new foundations] for corporate governance" (p. 1636). It is beyond the scope of this article to attempt any such development, although a few writers have suggested new directions (cf. Bainbridge 2008; Blair 1995; Blair and Stout 1999; Bottomley 2007). What remains to be shown, though, is how this new foundation is related specifically to the main features of the new governance, namely rule making and the administering of rights. More precisely, how can these developments be understood as a part of the changed competitive environment that motivates the search for new foundations?

New Foundations and the New Governance

It has been established so far that the changed competitive environment of present-day corporations has led them to adopt strategies and structures that challenge the traditional foundations of corporate governance and produce a need to search for new foundations. Left unexamined has been the connection, if any, between this changed competitive environment along with its consequences and the developments that constitute the new governance – or corporate citizenship or republican ethics. The development of the new governance is explained by scholars as due primarily to the inability or unwillingness of governments to discharge their traditional roles and responsibility, thus leading corporations to step into the breach. Left unexplained, however, is the problem, raised by van Oosterhout, of why corporations would do this. What's in it for them?

The characteristic features of today's corporate strategies and structures – the breakup of vertically integrated, hierarchical firms that rely on fixed tangible assets, economies of scale, and market share and the substitution of looser forms of collaboration in networks focused on innovation and quality – can also explain the new governance only if there are some links between the new foundations and the new governance. If there are such links, then it can be shown that the new governance is also an efficient adaptation to a changed competitive environment. This outcome would reconcile the new governance with traditional assumptions about the economic nature of corporations, the legitimacy of shareholder primacy, and the profit motive, which are assumptions too fundamental to be discarded lightly.

The new governance has two defining features that, at first glance, appear to be unrelated, namely participation in rule making, or "democratic will formation" in Habermasian terms, and the administration of civil, political, and social rights. The former feature of participation in rule making is alleged to be the result of corporations operating in a global environment, while reasons for the latter feature are largely unexplained in the literature. However, globalization is an incomplete explanation at best because there is no reason why the traditional vertically integrated, asset-intensive firm seeking economies of scale and market share could not operate globally in a traditionally market-based manner. Globalization alone cannot explain why such corporations could not operate efficiently in markets without getting involved in the kind of non-market collaborative decision making and issue management that constitutes the new governance.

To understand the connection between globalization and the new governance, we need to consider what is driving globalization. It is driven, in part, by such standard economic factors as the search for cheaper, more secure resources, such as labor, commodities, and capital, and for larger markets, which fit with the strategy and structure of the traditional firm. However, other drivers of globalization are the same factors that have led to the changed strategies and structures that characterize present-day corporations. Specifically, the need to innovate with its increasing reliance on human capital has led companies to outsource – not merely to use cheaper labor in contract factories, for example, but also to tap creative talent wherever it resides. Furthermore, innovation requires strategic alliances with companies and NGOs that possess different core competencies and capabilities. These alliances take the form of networks of relationships rather than mere market transactions. Innovation also raises social and regulatory issues that would occur even without globalization and inadequate governments and that would attract the concern of other participants in society, including NGOs.

The argument here is that many of the features of today's competitive environment that require corporations to become more political and to engage in public decision making are not distinctive of globalization *per se* but reflect the shift from the traditional vertically integrated, asset-intensive firm to less hierarchical, relationship-based networks. This shift is itself a driver of a globalized economy in which new strategic opportunities are to be found. Thus, globalization and the new governance are both the consequences of a more fundamental and profound change in the competitive environment of business. One does not cause the other, but they are, instead, the consequences of the same deeper, underlying causes.

Moreover, the shift from transactions to relationships, from market-based activity to networks, has the effect of making the returns that people and organizations receive from participating in the "extended enterprise" (to use the phrase of Post, Preston, and Sachs) a matter to be determined not by the market prices of their inputs in explicit contracts but by implicit contracts negotiated in a non-market, public arena. That is, the distribution of the wealth created by joint production in relationship-based networks is no longer simply a matter for the market to determine; rather, this distribution becomes contestable as a matter of public decision making, in which corporations and other constituencies collaborate.

Furthermore, the fact that this return depends on such decision making makes these constituencies residual risk bearers in that the return is not fixed by the market but is variable, depending on firm performance. That is, the people and organizations that participate in a corporation's networks of relationships may receive more or less in return, with the amount to be determined, in part, by the success of the collaboration. This argument contends, then, that in the new competitive environment, other constituencies are residual risk bearers who are affected by corporate decision making and so demand to participate in it. This participation results mainly in implicit, rather than explicit, contracts. Once again, this outcome is not a consequence of globalization but is instead caused by changes in the strategy and structure of present-day corporations that is also itself a driver of globalization.

The same factors that drive both globalization and the increasing politicization of the corporation also explain, to some extent, the new governance role of administering rights. In traditional corporate governance, the distribution of the wealth created by corporations – as well as the costs or burdens – is determined separately by the market, in the form of the price of each group's inputs, and by government. Thus, there are two distribution mechanisms, each with its own separate domain. In consequence, the goods and services that accrue to individuals in society result from their separate roles as economic actors in a market and as citizens of a state. However, in the new competitive environment, the market no longer plays this distributive role to the same extent, and more goods and services become contestable in the public arena. Insofar as these goods and services are viewed as rights, their administration is no longer a matter purely for government but for corporate decision making as well and not merely because of the inability of governments to act but because the decisions necessarily involve corporations. Because non-shareholder corporate constituencies are profoundly affected by these decisions, and also because corporate strategies and forms of organization require wide-based collaboration, the corporation becomes involved in the administration of rights.

These arguments support the conclusion that the main characteristics or defining features of the new governance – namely, participating in rule making and administering rights – are not due to globalization alone but are the consequence of deeper, more fundamental changes in the competitive environment of corporations, which have led to profound changes in corporate strategy and organization and are themselves among the drivers of globalization. Thus, both the new foundations and the new governance are linked as consequences of this changed competitive environment.

Conclusion

The aim of this article is to inquire into whether the new governance has any implications for corporate governance. The answer is, yes, there are some implications that require a rethinking of the traditional account of corporate governance, which is based mainly on an economic theory of the firm. The conclusion that some changes in corporate governance are warranted does not follow directly from the development of the new governance as described by scholars. The activities of rule making and administering rights are fully compatible with the prevailing systems of corporate governance, with their doctrines of shareholder primacy and shareholder wealth maximization. The implications are revealed only by understanding the new governance as itself a consequence of the changes in the strategies and forms of organization that have arisen in response to the changed competitive environment of the past several decades. These changes in strategy and organization call into question three key assumptions of corporate governance: that only shareholders bear residual risk; that only shareholders are affected by corporate decisions; and that only explicit, not implicit, contracts matter in corporate governance. Questions about these assumptions prompt a search for what Zingales has called "new foundations". Although this article does not attempt to formulate these new foundations or to develop a new theory of the firm, it is apparent that some changes are needed in corporate governance and the theory of the firm – and, more to the point of this chapter, that these changes are related significantly to the development called the "new governance".

References

Alchian, A.A., and H. Demsetz. 1972. Production, information costs, and economic organization. *American Economic Review* 62: 777–795.

Bainbridge, S.M. 2008. *The new corporate governance in theory and practice*. New York, NY: Oxford University Press.

Blair, M.M. 1995. *Ownership and control: Rethinking corporate governance for the twenty-first century*. Washington, D.C.: Brookings Institution.

Blair, M.M., and L.A. Stout. 1999. A team production theory of corporate law. *Virginia Law Review* 85: 247–328.

Bottomley, S. 2007. *The constitutional corporation: Rethinking corporate governance*. Burlington, VT: Ashgate.

Cutler, A.C. 2003. *Private power and global authority: Transnational merchant law in the global political economy*. Cambridge: Cambridge University Press.

Easterbrook, F.H., and D.R. Fischel. 1991. *The economic structure of corporate law*. Cambridge, MA: Harvard University Press.

Fama, E.F., and M.C. Jensen. 1983. Separation of ownership and control. *Journal of Law and Economics* 26: 301–325.

Hall, R.B., and T.J. Biersteker, eds. 2002. *The emergence of private authority in global governance*. Cambridge: Cambridge University Press.

Hansmann, H. 1996. *The ownership of enterprise*. Cambridge, MA: Harvard University Press.

Jensen, M.C. 1993. The modern industrial revolution, exit, and the failure of internal control systems. *Journal of Finance* 48: 831–880.

Jensen, M.C., and W.H. Meckling. 1976. Theory of the firm: Managerial behavior, agency costs and ownership structure. *Journal of Financial Economics* 3: 305–360.

Kobrin, S.J. 2008. Globalization, transnational corporations and the future of global governance. In *Handbook of research on global corporate citizenship*, ed. A.G. Scherer and G. Palazzo. Northampton, MA: Edward Elgar.

Leana, C.R., and D.M. Rousseau. 2000. *Relational wealth: The advantages of stability in a changing economy*. New York, NY: Oxford University Press.

Mathews, J.T. 1997. Power shift. *Foreign Affairs*, January/February 1997, 50–66.

Matten, D., and A. Crane. 2005. Corporate citizenship: Toward an extended theoretical conceptualization. *Academy of Management Review* 30: 166–179.

Matten, D., A. Crane, and W. Chapple. 2003. Behind the mask: Revealing the true face of corporate citizenship. *Journal of Business Ethics* 45: 109–120.

Moon, J. 2002. The social responsibility of business and new governance. *Government and Opposition* 37: 385–408.

Moon, J., A. Crane, and D. Matten. 2005. Can corporations be citizens? Corporate citizenship as a metaphor for business participation in society. *Business Ethics Quarterly* 15: 429–453.

Palazzo, G., and A.G. Scherer. 2006. Corporate legitimacy as deliberation: A communicative framework. *Journal of Business Ethics* 66: 71–88.

Pattberg, P. 2005. The institutionalization of private governance: How business and nonprofit organizations agree on transnational rules. *Governance* 18: 589–610.

Post, J.E., L.E. Preston, and S. Sachs. 2002a. Managing the extended enterprise: The new stakeholder view. *California Management Review* 45: 6–28.

Post, J.E., L.E. Preston, and S. Sachs. 2002b. *Redefining the corporation: Stakeholder management and organizational wealth.* Stanford, CA: Stanford University Press.

Reinicke, W.H. 1998: *Global public policy: Governing without government?* Washington, D.C.: Brookings Institution.

Scherer, A.G., and G. Palazzo. 2007. Toward a political conception of corporate responsibility: Business and society seen from a Habermasian perspective. *Academy of Management Review* 32: 1096–1120.

Scherer, A.G., G. Palazzo, and D. Baumann. 2006. Global rules and private actors: Toward a new role of the transnational corporation in global governance. *Business Ethics Quarterly* 16: 505–532.

Shleifer, A., and R.W. Vishny. 1997. A survey of corporate governance. *Journal of Finance* 52: 737–783.

Steinmann, H., and A. Löhr. 1996. A republican concept of corporate ethics. In *Europe's challenges: Economic efficiency and social solidarity,* ed. S. Urban, 21–60. Wiesbaden: Gabler.

Van Oosterhout, J.H. 2005. Corporate citizenship: An idea whose time has not yet come. *Academy of Management Review* 30: 677–684.

Williamson, O.E. 1985. *The economic institutions of capitalism: Firms, markets, relational contracting.* New York, NY: Free Press.

Wolf, K.D. 2008. Emerging patterns of global governance: The new interplay between the state, business and civil society. In *Handbook of research on global corporate citizenship,* ed. A.G. Scherer and G. Palazzo, 225–248. Northampton, MA: Edward Elgar.

Zingales, L. 2000. In search of new foundations. *Journal of Finance* 55: 1623–1653.

List of Authors

JOHN R. BOATRIGHT is the Raymond C. Baumhart, S.J., Professor of Business Ethics and Professor of Management, Graduate School of Business, Loyola University of Chicago, Chicago, IL, USA.

ALEXANDER BRINK is Professor of Business Ethics, University of Bayreuth, Germany, and permanent Visiting Professor for Corporate Governance & Philosophy, Witten/Herdecke University, Germany.

THOMAS CLARKE is Professor of Management and Director of the UTS Research Centre for Corporate Governance, Sydney, NSW, Australia.

PAT DADE is Founding Director of Cultural Dynamics Strategy and Marketing Ltd, London, United Kingdom.

WIM DUBBINK is Associate Professor of Business Ethics, Department of Philosophy, Tilburg University, Tilburg, The Netherlands.

ANDREW J. FELO is Associate Professor of Accounting, School of Graduate Professional Studies at Great Valley, Pennsylvania State University, University Park, PA, USA.

BRUNO S. FREY is Professor of Behavioural Science, Warwick Business School, University of Warwick, United Kingdom, and Professor of Economics, University of Zurich, Zurich, Switzerland.

LES HIGGINS is Founding Director of Cultural Dynamics Strategy and Marketing Ltd, London, United Kingdom.

RONALD JEURISSEN is Professor of Business Ethics and Director of the European Institute for Business Ethics, Nyenrode Business University, Breukelen, The Netherlands.

JAMES KIRKBRIDE is Professor of International Business Law and Vice-Rector at London School of Business and Finance, London, United Kingdom.

KAI KÜHNE is Research Associate at the Institute for Labour Law and Industrial Relations in the European Community, University of Trier, Trier, Germany.

A. Brink (ed.), *Corporate Governance and Business Ethics*, Ethical Economy.   371
Studies in Economic Ethics and Philosophy 39, DOI 10.1007/978-94-007-1588-2,
© Springer Science+Business Media B.V. 2011

STEVE LETZA is Professor of Corporate Governance and Director of the European Centre for Corporate Governance, Liverpool John Moores University, Liverpool, United Kingdom.

SCOTT LICHTENSTEIN is Senior Lecturer, St James Business School, London, United Kingdom.

DIRK LINOWSKI is Director of the Institute for International Business Relations, Steinbeis University Berlin, Berlin, Germany.

CHRIS LOW is Head of the Division of Health and Wellbeing, Department of Health Sciences, University of Huddersfield, Huddersfield, United Kingdom.

ALEXEI M. MARCOUX is Associate Professor of Business Ethics, School of Business Administration, Loyola University Chicago, Chicago, IL, USA.

MARGIT OSTERLOH is Professor of Management Science, Warwick Business School, University of Warwick, Coventry, United Kingdom, and Professor of Management, University of Zurich, Zurich, Switzerland.

G.J. (DEON) ROSSOUW is CEO of the Ethics Institute of South Africa, Pretoria, South Africa, and Extraordinary Professor in Philosophy, University of Pretoria, Pretoria, South Africa.

DIETER SADOWSKI is Professor of Business Administration and Director of the Institute for Labour Law and Industrial Relations in the European Community, University of Trier, Trier, Germany.

ALEJO JOSÉ G. SISON is Professor of Philosophy, University of Navarre, Pamplona, Spain.

CLIVE SMALLMAN is Professor of Management and Head of School, School of Management, University of Western Sydney, Sydney, NSW, Australia.

ALOY SOPPE is Associate Professor of Financial Ethics, Erasmus School of Law, Erasmus University Rotterdam, Rotterdam, The Netherlands.

XIUPING SUN is Lecturer at Leeds Business School, Leeds Metropolitan University, Leeds, United Kingdom.

TILL TALAULICAR is Professor of Corporate Governance and Board Dynamics, Witten/Herdecke University, Witten, Germany.

JUNHUA TANG is Research Associate at the Chair of Microeconomics, University of Rostock, Rostock, Germany.

STEEN THOMSEN is Professor at the Department of International Economics and Management and Director of the Center for Corporate Governance, Copenhagen Business School, Copenhagen, Denmark.

BERT VAN DE VEN is Assistant Professor in the Department of Philosophy, Tilburg University, Tilburg, Netherlands.

JOSEF WIELAND is Professor of Business Administration & Economics with emphasis on Business Ethics and Director of the Konstanz Institute for Intercultural Management, Values and Communication, University of Applied Sciences Konstanz, Konstanz, Germany.

HOSSAM ZEITOUN is Doctoral Student and Assistant at the Department of Business Administration, University of Zurich, Zurich, Switzerland.